Software Engineering

Principles and Practice

SECOND EDITION

Hans van Vliet
Vrije Universiteit, Amsterdam

JOHN WILEY & SONS, LTD
Chichester ▪ New York ▪ Weinheim ▪ Brisbane ▪ Singapore ▪ Toronto

Baffins Lane, Chichester,
West Sussex PO19 1UD, England
National 01243 779777
International (+44) 1243 779777
e-mail (for orders and customer service enquiries):
cs-books@wiley.co.uk
Visit our Home Page on http://www.wiley.co.uk
or http://www.wiley.com

Reprinted August 2002

Other Wiley Editorial Offices

John Wiley & Sons, Inc., 605 Third Avenue,
New York, NY 10158-0012, USA

Weinheim • Brisbane • Singapore • Toronto

British Library Cataloguing in Publication Data

A catalogue record for this book is available from the British Library.
ISBN 0-471-97508-7

Typeset in 9/13pt Palatino.
Printed and bound in Great Britain by Biddles Ltd, Guildford and King's Lynn
This book is printed on acid-free paper responsibly manufactured from sustainable forestry, in which at least two trees are planted for each one used for paper production.

To

Marjan, Jasper and Marieke

Contents

Preface

Around 1990, my wife and I discussed whether or not we should move. We were getting restless after having lived in the same house for a long time. For lack of space, my study had been changed into a child's bedroom. I definitely needed a room of my own in order to finish the first edition of this book. My wife thought her kitchen too small.

The opportunity to buy a building lot in a new development plan arose. We gathered information, went to look for an architect, subscribed to the plan. Still, we were not sure whether we really wanted to leave our house. It was situated very nicely in a dead-end street, with a garden facing south and a playground in front. When asked, our children told us they did not want to move to a new neighborhood.

So, we asked an architect about the possibility of rebuilding our house. He produced a blueprint in which the altered house had a larger kitchen and four extra rooms. We were sold immediately. We told ourselves that this rebuilding would be cheaper as well, although the architect could not yet give us a reliable cost estimate.

After giving the rebuilding plan some more thought, we decided this was the way to go. My brother, who is employed in the building industry, warned us of the mess it would create. We thought we could handle it. We started the procedure to get the permissions, which takes at least half a year in The Netherlands – and costs money (this was not accounted for).

In August, a year later, we were finally ready to start. The rebuilding was estimated to take 60 working days at most. Unfortunately, the contract did not mention any fine should this period be exceeded. We agreed on a fixed price. Certain things, such as the new electrical wiring, a new central heating unit, and the cost of plumbing were not included. We hardly knew what those 'extras' would cost in the end. We did estimate them on the back of an envelope, and felt confident.

On September 15, the first pile was driven. Counting on good weather throughout the fall, this should have meant that all would be finished by Christmas. The building contractor, however, had other urgent obligations, and progress was rather slow in the beginning. About one week's work was done during the first month.

In October, part of the roof had to be removed. We could interrupt work until next spring – the safe way – or continue – rather tricky in a country as wet as ours. We prayed for some dry weeks and decided to go on. The contractor started to demolish part of our house. While doing so, some surprises showed up and an even larger part of the house had to be demolished. We were really lucky – it only rained for two days while our roof was open. Our bedrooms became rather wet and the kitchen was flooded. Sometime in November, the new roof was up and we could sleep quietly again.

By the end of November, we were getting nervous. There was still a lot of work to be done but several times the workmen did not show up. In the meantime, we had made arrangements for our new kitchen to be installed the week before Christmas. Before this, a door had to be cut in an existing brick wall. The old central heating unit was placed right behind that wall and had to be removed first. The new central heating unit, unfortunately, was not available yet (fall is the peak season for central heating units).

Work continued as far as possible. A new wall was erected, after which we could enter our (old) kitchen only from the outside. For a while, we even lived with no kitchen at all. To make a long story short, the contractor made it, but only barely. The new kitchen was installed. Upstairs, however, much work remained. The project was finally finished by the end of January, only six weeks late.

During the rebuilding, life had been rather provisional. My computer was stored away in the attic. The children had virtually no space to play indoors. Dust was everywhere. These circumstances can be dealt with for a while, but we became frantic towards the end. Though the work seemed to be finished by the end of January, a lot still remained to be done: rooms had to be painted and decorated, and all that had been packed needed to be unpacked again. It took several more months before life took its normal course again.

Several months later, some of the new wooden planks on the back façade started to crack. They had expanded during the summer heat; either the tongue was too wide or the groove too narrow. This, and various other minor problems were, eventually, rectified.

On the financial side: various tiny expenses not accounted for added up to a pretty sum. I am still not sure whether we chose the cheapest option, but I am absolutely sure that knocking down a house and rebuilding it while you still try to live in it is a nightmare. In that sense, my brother was more than right.

After the house rebuilding project and work on the first edition of this book was finished, I turned my attention to tidying up our garden. I designed a garden with various borders, terraces, a summer house and a pond. And I carried out all the work. I made one big mistake on this second project, which only manifested itself a couple of years later when I wanted to repaint the back façade. In order to do so, I had to put the legs of the ladder in the pond. So I did some rework and moved the pond.

This story is fairly typical of a software development project. Software too is often delivered late, does not meet its specifications and is, moreover, faulty. Software projects also tend to underestimate the impact of non-technical factors. The growing awareness of this in the late 1960s gave rise to the expression 'the software crisis.' Though we have made quite some progress since the term 'software engineering' was first coined back in 1968, many people are of the opinion that the software crisis is still rampant.

The field of software engineering aims to find answers to the many problems that software development projects are likely to meet when constructing large software systems. Such systems are complex because of their sheer size, because they are developed in a team involving people from different disciplines, and because they will be regularly modified to meet changing requirements, both during development and after installation.

Software engineering is still a young field compared to other engineering disciplines. All disciplines have their problems, particularly when projects reach beyond the engineers' expertise. It seems as if software development projects stretch their engineers' expertise all of the time.

The subject is rapidly moving and there are more questions than answers. Yet, a number of principles and practices have evolved in the thirty-odd years the field has existed. To foster and maintain software engineering as a professional discipline, the IEEE Computer Society and ACM have started a joint project – SWEBOK – to identify and validate the software engineering body of knowledge. This project will run from 1998 to 2001. The outcome of this project will be essential to the formulation of licensing requirements for software engineers. The licensing and accreditation of software engineers has already started, and is likely to become an important topic in the forthcoming years [Bag99].

This book addresses all of the knowledge areas identified in the SWEBOK project[1]. Of course, the relative attention paid to individual topics and the way these topics are treated reflects my own view of the field. This view can be summarized as follows:

- What is theory today may become practice tomorrow. For that reason, I have not limited myself to a discussion of well-established practices. Rather, I also pay attention to promising methods and techniques which have not yet outgrown the research environment, or hardly so: software reusability, quantitative assessment of software quality, and formal specifications, to name but a few.

- We may learn a lot from our own history. I do not only discuss techniques that have proven their worth and are in wide use today. I also discuss developments that are by now considered dead-ends. Knowing *why* a certain technique is no longer used is often valuable. My discussion of cost estimation models in chapter 7 is a case in point.

- Everything changes. Requirements change while development is still under way. People enter and leave the project team. The functionality of a toolset changes before the systems developed with it are replaced. And so on. Change is a recurring theme in this book.

- Human and social aspects are central. Most chapters of this book carry titles that sound fairly technical. Within these same chapters, though, I regularly touch upon human and social aspects of the trade. For example, requirements elicitation is by no means a purely technical issue, and the design of a system is heavily influenced by the prior experiences, both positive and negative, of the designer.

People actively involved in software development and maintenance — programmers, analysts, project managers — and students of computer science and software engineering alike must be aware of the problems incurred by large-scale software development, and the solutions proposed.

I firmly believe that none of the solutions proposed is a silver bullet: CASE, object-oriented software development, software reuse, architectural design, formal

[1]The Stone Man version of the SWEBOK Guide lists the following knowledge areas: software requirements analysis, software design, software construction, software testing, software maintenance, software configuration management, software quality analysis, software engineering management, software engineering infrastructure, and software engineering process. The software construction area covers both coding and unit testing; of these, only unit testing is covered in this book.

For more information on the SWEBOK project, see `http://www.swebok.org`.

specifications, process models; they each contribute their mite. The fundamental problems will, however, remain. Software systems are extremely complex artifacts. Their successful realization requires experience and talent from their designers. If applied in a thoughtful, conscientious manner, the methods and techniques discussed in this book may help you to become a professional software engineer.

Learning about Software Engineering

Most chapters of this book can be read and studied independently. In a classroom setting, the instructor has a large degree of freedom in choosing topics from this book, and the order in which to treat them. It is recommended that a first course in software engineering at least deals with the topics discussed in chapters 1–3 and 9–14 (in this order). Additional material can be chosen at will from the other chapters or be used as material for a secondary course. Two obvious clusters of material for a secondary course are chapters 4–8 and 15–19; see also figure 0.1.

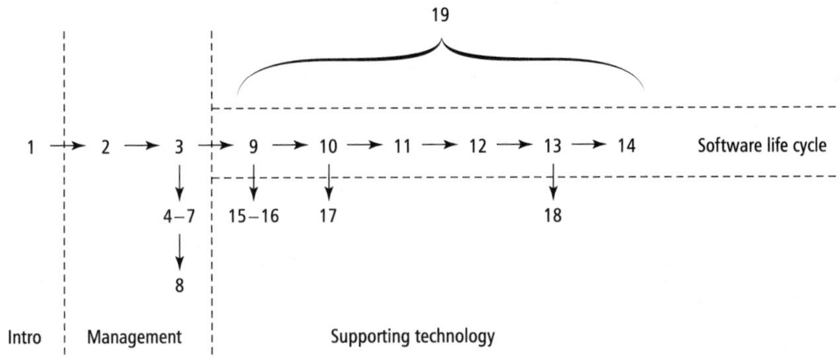

Figure 0.1 How the book is organized

A recurring problem in teaching software engineering is when and how to address project management issues. Computer science students often have difficulty in appreciating the importance of issues such as team organization and cost estimation. Software professionals know from the trenches that these non-technical issues are at least as important as the technical ones. Students of computer science or software engineering are more likely to understand the importance of management issues near the end of the course, possibly after they have been involved in some sort of practical work. However, a short treatment of the issues raised in chapters 2 and 3 should be given near the beginning of the course.

Much of what is said in this book sounds obvious. In fact it is. As one speaker at a software engineering education conference said: 'You cannot teach it, you can only preach it.' So this book is one long sermon on how to practice software development. Just as you cannot become a good hand at carpentry from reading a textbook on the subject, you cannot become a serious software engineer by merely reading and absorbing the material contained in this book. You need to practice it as well.

Doing practical work in a university setting is not easy. The many risks that real-life software development projects run cannot be realistically mimicked in a term project. Yet certain recurring problems in software development can be dealt with successfully. For example, small student teams may be asked to design, implement and test a nontrivial system, after which other teams get to maintain those systems.

Figure 0.2 The swimming equivalent of a correspondence course in software engineering (©*The Municipal Archives of Amsterdam. Reproduced with permission*)

Figure 0.2 depicts how schoolchildren in Amsterdam learned to swim around 1900. My father grew up in the countryside and learned it the hard way. His father simply tied a rope around his middle, threw him into the river that ran in front of the house, and shouted: 'Swim.' Nowadays, Dutch schoolchildren by and large all get their first swimming certificate before entering primary school. Their swimming lessons start off in a very gentle way, in a toddler pool, next to mamma and with lots of material to keep them floating. Gradually, the amount of floating material is reduced and the pool gets deeper. They do not get scared and usually enjoy the swimming lesson.

A similar range of possibilities is possible in a software engineering course. The dry swimming equivalent is not to be recommended. Doing it the hard way by involving the student in a real project has its problems too. The student may, figuratively speaking, drown in the day-to-day practical intricacies of the project. Some sort of intermediate scheme involving 'real-life' aspects in a protected setting, or a sequence of educational experiences with an increasing amount of realism, seems most appropriate. Issues of software engineering education are addressed in the yearly *Conference on Software Engineering Education*. See also [Sof97c] for a state-of-the-art overview.

In addition to this practical work, the exercises at the end of each chapter provide further learning material. Exercises that are simply numbered ask relatively simple questions about the chapter just read. Exercises marked with a ♡ or ♠ require the reader to reflect seriously on major issues or study additional sources to deepen his or her understanding.[2] Exercises marked with a ♡ may require one hour to answer. Exercises marked ♠ may require more than a day. The simple exercises give but a superficial knowledge of the field. Deep knowledge of software engineering will only be developed if you cut your teeth on a number of the marked exercises. Answers to these exercises and further teaching material may be obtained from `http://www.wiley.co.uk/vanvliet`.

What's changed?

Software engineering is a rapidly evolving field. Preparing this second edition therefore necessitated changes in each and every chapter. But some chapters changed more than others. The major changes are as follows:

- I considerably extended the chapter on requirements engineering (9), especially in the area of requirements elicitation.
- I expanded sections of the chapter on software design into new chapters on software architecture (10) and object-oriented analysis and design (12).
- I replaced the chapter on software psychology by a chapter that focuses completely on user interface design (16).
- I dropped the chapter on programming languages.

[2]Rather than writing 'his or her' all the time, I will use male pronouns throughout this text for brevity.

Furthermore, the order of the chapters has been changed a bit to allow for a clustering into coherent parts.

Acknowledgements

The present text is really a fourth edition. The first two editions appeared in Dutch only. I have used this material many times in courses, both for university students and software professionals. These people have, either consciously or unconsciously, helped to shape the text as it stands. I have received many useful suggestions from Hans de Bruin, Frank Niessink, Jacco van Ossenbruggen, Bastiaan Schönhage, Victor van Swede and Martijn van Welie. Special thanks go to Gerrit van der Veer, who co-authored chapter 16. Michael Lindvall, Magnus Runesson, Kristian Sandahl and Anders Subotic from the University of Linköping in Sweden used part of the manuscript in a study-circle in scientific editing. Their remarks have been very helpful, and sometimes made me blush. Finally, I have received very useful feedback from the following reviewers: G. Edmunds (University of Southampton), Ralph F. Grove (Indiana University of Pennsylvania), Richard L. Upchurch (University of Massachusetts Dartmouth), Laurie Williams (University of Utah), Benjamin Pierce (University of Pennsylvania) and Mario Winter (FernUniversität Hagen, Germany).

Shena Deuchars of Mitcham Editorial Services did a great job as copy-editor. Many people from John Wiley & Sons have contributed to this book. Dawn Booth handled all the production work. Sandra Heath designed the cover. Katrina Arens dealt with a host of chores. Special thanks go to Gaynor, second name 'Patience', Redvers-Mutton for her support and indefatigable optimism.

The drawings that go with the chapter headings were made by Tobias Baanders. They are inspired by the artwork of Jan Snoeck that adorns the Centre of Mathematics and Computer Science in Amsterdam. The litho on the front cover is called 'Waterfall' (M.C. Escher, 1961). It is appropriate in name and message alike.

Finally I thank Marjan, Jasper and Marieke for their patience and support. The schedule overrun of this project has been worse than that of many a software development project.

Hans van Vliet
Amsterdam, August 1999

1 Introduction

LEARNING OBJECTIVES

- To understand the notion of software engineering and why it is important
- To appreciate the technical (engineering), managerial, and psychological aspects of software engineering
- To understand the similarities and differences between software engineering and other engineering disciplines
- To know the major phases in a software development project, and have a rough idea of the distribution of cost over these phases
- To appreciate ethical dimensions in software engineering
- To be aware of the time frame and extent to which new developments impact software engineering practice

Computer science is still a young field. The first computers were built in the mid 1940s, since when the field has developed tremendously.

Applications from the early years of computerization can be characterized as follows: the programs were quite small, certainly when compared to those that are currently being constructed; they were written by one person; they were written and used by experts in the application area concerned. The problems to be solved were mostly of a technical nature, and the emphasis was on expressing known algorithms efficiently in some programming language. Input typically consisted of numerical data, read from such media as punched tape or punched cards. The output, also numeric, was printed on paper. Programs were run off-line. If the program contained errors, the programmer studied an octal or hexadecimal dump of memory. Sometimes, the execution of the program would be followed by binary reading machine registers at the console.

Present-day applications are rather different in many respects. Present-day programs are often very large and are being developed by teams that collaborate over periods spanning several years. The programmers are not the future users of the system they develop and they have no expert knowledge of the application area in question. The problems that are being tackled increasingly concern everyday life: automatic bank tellers, airline reservation, salary administration, electronic commerce, etc. Putting a man on the moon was not conceivable without computers.

In the 1960s, people started to realize that programming techniques had lagged behind the developments in software both in size and complexity. To many people, programming was still an *art* and had never become a *craft*. An additional problem was that many programmers had not been formally educated in the field. They had learned by doing. On the organizational side, attempted solutions to problems often involved adding more and more programmers to the project, the so-called 'million-monkey' approach.

As a result, software was often delivered too late, programs did not behave as the user expected, programs were rarely adaptable to changed circumstances, and many errors were detected only after the software had been delivered to the customer. This became known as the 'software crisis'.

This type of problem really became manifest in the 1960s. Under the auspices of NATO, two conferences were devoted to the topic in 1968 and 1969 [NR68], [BR69]. Here, the term 'software engineering' was coined in a somewhat provocative sense. Shouldn't it be possible to build software in the way one builds bridges and houses, starting from a theoretical basis and using sound and proven design and construction techniques, as in other engineering fields?

Software serves some organizational purpose. The reasons for embarking on a software development project vary. Sometimes, a solution to a problem is not feasible without the aid of computers, such as weather forecasting, or automated bank telling.

Sometimes, software can be used as a vehicle for new technologies, such as typesetting, the production of chips, or manned space trips. In yet other cases software may increase user service (library automation) or simply save money (automated stock control).

In many cases, the expected economic gain will be a major driving force. It may not, however, always be easy to prove that automation saves money (just think of office automation) because apart from direct cost savings, the economic gain may also manifest itself in such things as a more flexible production or a faster or better user service.

In [Boe81], the total expenditure on software in the US was estimated to be $40 billion in 1980. This is approximately 2% of the GNP. In 1985, the total expenditure had risen to $70 billion in the US and $140 billion worldwide. In 1997, the US market was $120 billion and it is expected to rise to $230 billion by 2002.

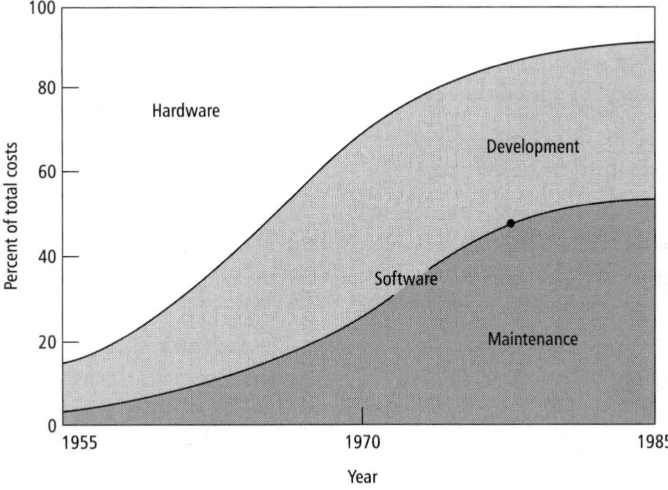

Figure 1.1 Relative distribution of hardware/software costs. (*Source: B.W. Boehm, Software Engineering*, IEEE Transactions on Computers, *©1976 IEEE Reproduced with permission*)

So the *cost* of software is of crucial importance. This concerns not only the cost of developing the software, but also the cost of keeping the software operational once it has been delivered to the customer. In the course of time, hardware costs have decreased dramatically. Hardware costs now typically comprise less than 20% of total expenditure (figure 1.1). The remaining 80% comprise all non-hardware costs: the cost of programmers, analysts, management, user training, secretarial help, etc.

An aspect closely linked with cost is *productivity*. In the 1980s, the quest for data processing personnel increased by 12% per year, while the population of people working in data processing and the productivity of those people each grew by approximately 4% per year [Boe87a]. This situation has not fundamentally changed [Jon99]. The net effect is a growing gap between demand and supply. The present state of affairs is even worse because of the Y2K and Euro efforts. The result is both a backlog with respect to the maintenance of existing software and a slowing down in the development of new applications. Eventually, the combined effect may have repercussions on the competitive edge of an organization.

The issues of cost and productivity of software development deserve our serious attention. However, this is not the complete story. Society is increasingly dependent on software. The quality of the systems we develop increasingly determines the quality of our existence. Consider as an example the following message from a Dutch newspaper on June 6, 1980, under the heading 'Americans saw the Russians coming':

> For a short period last Tuesday the United States brought their atomic bombers and nuclear missiles to an increased state of alarm when, because of a computer error, a false alarm indicated that the Soviet Union had started a missile attack.

Efforts to repair the error were apparently in vain, for on June 9, 1980, the same newspaper reported:

> For the second time within a few days, a deranged computer reported that the Soviet Union had started a nuclear attack against the United States. Last Saturday, the DoD affirmed the false message, which resulted in the engines of the planes of the strategic air force being started.

It is not always the world that is in danger. On a smaller scale, errors in software may have very unfortunate consequences, such as transaction errors in bank traffic; reminders to finally pay that bill of $0.00; a stock control system that issues orders too late and thus lays off complete divisions of a factory.

The latter example indicates that errors in a software system may have serious financial consequences for the organization using it. One example of such a financial loss is the large US airline company that lost $50M because of an error in their seat reservation system. The system erroneously reported that cheap seats were sold out, while in fact there were plenty available. The problem was detected only after quarterly results lagged considerably behind those of both their own previous periods and those of their competitors.

Errors in automated systems may even have fatal effects. One computer science weekly magazine contained the following message in April 1983:

> The court in Düsseldorf has discharged a woman (54), who was on trial for murdering her daughter. An erroneous message from a computerized system made the insurance company inform her that she was seriously ill. She was said to suffer from an incurable form of syphilis.

> Moreover, she was said to have infected both her children. In panic, she strangled her 15 year old daughter and tried to kill her 13 year old son and herself. The boy escaped, and with some help he enlisted prevented the woman from dying of an overdose. The judge blamed the computer error and considered the woman not responsible for her actions.

With increasing application of computers, the number of potential risks also increases. Baber compares the state of the art in the software engineering field with that in the fictitious land of Ret Up Moc where, around 2500 BC, great progress was being made at a few distinguished institutes in the area of designing buildings [Bab82]. The demand for engineers that were educated in this new way of designing buildings grew fast. The few experts at the engineering schools were snatched away by industry. Older practicing engineers had to be re-educated. Somebody therefore developed three-week crash courses and a designer kit that contained, amongst others, a designers' handbook, ruler, and sample forms and designs.

With these aids, many managed to draw up plans for new buildings. However, most designers did not really understand the underlying theory and 30% of the buildings collapsed before delivery. To tackle the danger to the workmen, elaborate test plans were developed. At certain critical moments during the construction process, everyone had to leave the work floor and large amounts of sand and rubble were dumped in and on the building under construction. If the building did not collapse under this, the rubble was removed and construction could continue. Upon delivery, a similar final test was performed. The owner received a contract in which the builder disclaimed in advance any responsibility for possible defects.

Besides this very instructive parable, Baber's book contains many anecdotes about computer projects that failed or nearly failed. The bimonthly *ACM Software Engineering Notes* contains a column 'Risks to the public in computer systems', which reports on large and small catastrophes caused by automation. Parnas' essays on the SDI program also point to the dangers of large-scale hazardous software development [Par85].

This all marks the enormous importance of the field of software engineering. Better methods and techniques for software development may result in large financial savings, in more effective methods of software development, in systems that better fit user needs, in more reliable software systems, and thus in a more reliable environment in which those systems function. Quality and productivity are the two central themes in the field of software engineering.

On the positive side, it is imperative to point to the enormous progress that has been made since the 1960s. Software is ubiquitous and scores of trustworthy systems have been built. These range from small spreadsheet applications to typesetting systems, banking systems, Web browsers and the Space Shuttle software. The techniques and methods discussed in this book have contributed their mite to the success of these and many other software development projects.

1.1 WHAT IS SOFTWARE ENGINEERING?

In various texts on this topic, one encounters a definition of the term software engineering. An early definition was given at the first NATO conference [NR68]:

> Software engineering is the establishment and use of sound engineering principles in order to obtain economically software that is reliable and works efficiently on real machines.

The definition given in the *IEEE Standard Glossary of Software Engineering Terminology* [IEE90a] is as follows:

> Software engineering is the application of a systematic, disciplined, quantifiable approach to the development, operation, and maintenance of software; that is, the application of engineering to software.

These and other definitions of the term software engineering use rather different words. However, the essential characteristics of the field are always, explicitly or implicitly, present:

- *Software engineering concerns the construction of large programs.*
  [DK76] make a distinction between **programming-in-the-large** and **programming-in-the-small**. The borderline between large and small obviously is not sharp: a program of 100 lines is small, a program of 50 000 lines of code certainly is not. Programming-in-the-small generally refers to programs written by one person in a relatively short period of time. Programming-in-the-large, then, refers to multi-person jobs that span, say, more than half a year. For example:

  - The NASA Space Shuttle software contains 40M lines of object code (this is 30 times as much as the software for the Saturn V project from the 1960s) [Boe81];

  - The IBM OS360 operating system took 5000 man years of development effort [Bro95].

  Traditional programming techniques and tools are primarily aimed at supporting programming-in-the-small. This not only holds for programming languages, but also for the tools (like flowcharts) and methods (like structured programming). These cannot be directly transferred to the development of large programs.

  In fact, the term program – in the sense of a self-contained piece of software that can be invoked by a user or some other system component – is not adequate here. Present-day software development projects result in systems containing a large number of (interrelated) programs.

- *The central theme is mastering complexity.*
  In general, the problems are such that they cannot be surveyed in their entirety. One is forced to split the problem into parts such that each individual part can be grasped, while the communication between the parts remains simple. The total complexity does not decrease in this way, but it does become manageable. In a stereo system there are components such as an amplifier, a receiver, and a tuner, and communication via a thin wire. In software, we strive for a similar separation of concerns. In a program for library automation, components such as user interaction, search processes and data storage could for instance be distinguished, with clearly given facilities for data exchange between those components. Note that the complexity of many a piece of software is not so much caused by the intrinsic complexity of the problem (as in the case of compiler optimization algorithms or numerical algorithms to solve partial differential equations), but rather by the vast number of details that must be dealt with.

- *Software evolves.*
  Most software models a part of reality, such as processing requests in a library or tracking money transfers in a bank. This reality evolves. If software is not to become obsolete fairly quickly, it has to evolve with the reality that is being modeled. This means that costs are incurred after delivery of the software system and that we have to bear this evolution in mind during development.

- *The efficiency with which software is developed is of crucial importance.*
  Total cost and development time of software projects is high. This also holds for the maintenance of software. The quest for new applications surpasses the workforce resource. The gap between supply and demand is growing. Important themes within the field of software engineering concern better and more efficient methods and tools for the development and maintenance of software.

- *Regular cooperation between people is an integral part of programming-in-the-large.*
  Since the problems are large, many people have to work concurrently at solving those problems. There must be clear arrangements for the distribution of work, methods of communication, responsibilities, and so on. Arrangements alone are not sufficient, though; one also has to stick to those arrangements. In order to enforce them, standards or procedures may be employed. Those procedures and standards can often be supported by tools. Discipline is one of the keys to the successful completion of a software development project.

- *The software has to support its users effectively.*
  Software is developed in order to support users at work. The functionality offered should fit users' tasks. Users that are not satisfied with the system will try

to circumvent it or, at best, voice new requirements immediately. It is not sufficient to build the system in the right way, we also have to build the right system. Effective user support means that we must carefully study users at work, in order to determine the proper functional requirements, and we must address usability and other quality aspects as well, such as reliability, responsiveness, and user-friendliness. It also means that software development entails more than delivering software. User manuals and training material may have to be written, and attention must be given to developing the environment in which the new system is going to be installed. For example, a new automated library system will affect working procedures within the library.

- *Software engineering is a field in which members of one culture create artifacts on behalf of members of another culture.*
  This aspect is closely linked to the previous two items. Software engineers are expert in one or more areas such as programming in Java, software architecture, testing, or the Unified Modeling Language. They are generally not experts in library management, avionics, or banking. Yet they have to develop systems for such domains. The thin spread of application domain knowledge is a common source of problems in software development projects.

  Not only do software engineers lack factual knowledge of the domain for which they develop software, they lack knowledge of its culture as well. For example, a software developer may discover the 'official' set of work practices of a certain user community from interviews, written policies, and the like; these work practices are then built into the software. A crucial question with respect to system acceptance and success, however, is whether that community actually follows those work practices. For an outside observer, this question is much more difficult to answer.

The above list shows that software engineering has many facets. Software engineering certainly is *not* the same as programming, although programming is an important ingredient of software engineering. Mathematical aspects play a role since we are concerned with the correctness of software. Sound engineering practices are needed to get useful products. Psychological aspects play a role in the communication between human and machine, and between humans. Finally, the development process needs to be controlled, which is a management issue.

The term 'software engineering' hints at possible resemblances between the construction of programs and the construction of houses or bridges. These kinds of resemblances do exist. In both cases we work from a set of desired functions, using scientific and engineering techniques in a creative way. Techniques that have been applied successfully in the construction of physical artifacts are also helpful when applied to the construction of software systems: development of the product in a number of phases, a careful planning of these phases, continuous audit of the whole process, construction from a clear and complete design, etc.

Even in a mature engineering discipline, say bridge design, accidents do happen. Bridges collapse once in a while. Most problems in bridge design occur when designers extrapolate beyond their models and expertise. A famous example is the Tacoma Narrows Bridge failure in 1940. The designers of that bridge extrapolated beyond their experience to create more flexible stiffening girders for suspension bridges. They did not think about aerodynamics and the response of the bridge to wind. As a result, that bridge collapsed shortly after it was finished. This type of extrapolation seems to be the rule rather than the exception in software development. We regularly embark on software development projects that go far beyond our expertise.

There are additional reasons for considering the construction of software as something quite different from the construction of physical products. The cost of constructing software is incurred during development and not during production. Copying software is almost free. Software is logical in nature rather than physical. Physical products wear out in time and therefore have to be maintained. Software does not wear out. The need to maintain software is caused by errors detected late or by changing requirements of the user. Software reliability is determined by the manifestation of errors already present, not by physical factors such as wear and tear. We may even argue that software wears out *because* it is being maintained.

Two characteristics that make software development projects extra difficult to manage are visibility and continuity. It is much more difficult to see progress in software construction than it is to notice progress in building a bridge. One often hears the phrase that a program 'is almost finished'. One equally often underestimates the time needed to finish up the last bits and pieces.

This '90% complete' syndrome is very pervasive in software development. Not knowing how to measure real progress, we often use a surrogate measure, the rate of expenditure of resources. For example, a project that has a budget of 100 person-days is perceived as being 50% complete after 50 person-days are expended. Strictly speaking, we then confuse speed with progress. Because of the imprecise measurement of progress and the customary underestimation of total effort, problems accumulate as time elapses.

Physical systems are often continuous in the sense that small changes in the specification lead to small changes in the product. This is not true with software. Small changes in the specification of software may lead to considerable changes in the software itself. In a similar way, small errors in software may have considerable effects. The Mariner space rocket to Venus for example got lost because of a typing error in a FORTRAN program.

We may likewise draw a comparison between software engineering and computer science. Computer science emerged as a separate discipline in the 1960s. It split from mathematics and has been heavily influenced by mathematics. Topics studied in computer science, such as algorithm complexity, formal languages, and the semantics of programming languages, have a strong mathematical flavor. PhD theses in computer science invariably contain theorems with accompanying proofs.

As the field of software engineering emerges from computer science, it has a similar inclination to focus on clean aspects of software development that can be formalized, in both teaching and research. We tend to assume that requirements can be fully stated before the project starts, concentrate on systems built from scratch, and ignore the reality of trading off quality aspects against the available budget. Not to mention the trenches of software maintenance. According to [Gib91], much of what the academic (computer science) community does in universities can be viewed, like mathematics, as naive paper exercises that ignore reality.

Software engineering and computer science do have a considerable overlap. The practice of software engineering however also has to deal with such matters as the management of huge development projects, human factors (regarding both the development team and the prospective users of the system) and cost estimation and control. Software engineers must *engineer* software. In their effort to set up an elaborate educational program in software engineering, the Software Engineering Institute (SEI) pays ample attention to these issues. This and other initiatives are aimed at making software engineering less of an aspiration and more of a profession [Gib89].

Software engineering has many things in common both with other fields of engineering and with computer science. It also has a face of its own in many ways.

1.2 PHASES IN THE DEVELOPMENT OF SOFTWARE

When building a house, the builder does not start with piling up bricks. Rather, the requirements and possibilities of the client are analyzed first, taking into account such factors as family structure, hobbies, finances and the like. The architect takes these factors into consideration when designing a house. Only after the design has been agreed upon is the actual construction started.

It is expedient to act in the same way when constructing software. First, the problem to be solved is analyzed and the requirements are described in a very precise way. Then a design is made based on these requirements. Finally, the construction process, i.e. the actual programming of the solution, is started. There are a distinguishable number of phases in the development of software. The phases as discussed in this book are depicted in figure 1.2.

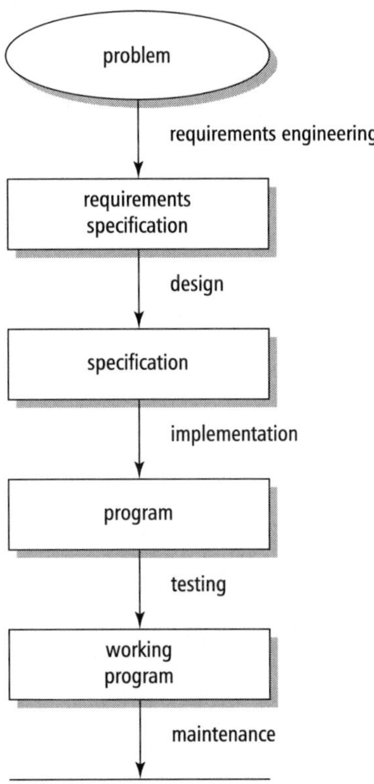

Figure 1.2 A simple view of software development

The **process model** depicted in figure 1.2 is rather simple. In reality, things will usually be more complex. For instance, the design phase is often split into a global, architectural design phase and a detailed design phase, and often various test phases are distinguished. The basic components, however, remain as given in figure 1.2. These phases have to be passed through in each project. Depending on the kind of project and the working environment, a more detailed scheme may be needed.

In figure 1.2, the phases have been depicted sequentially. For a given project these activities are not necessarily separated as strictly as indicated here. They may and usually will overlap. It is, for instance, quite possible to start implementation of one part of the system while some of the other parts have not been fully designed yet. As we will see in section 1.3, there is no strict linear progression from requirements engineering to design, from design to implementation, etc. Backtracking to earlier phases occurs, because of errors discovered or changing requirements.

Below, a short description is given of each of the basic components from figure 1.2. Various alternative process models will be discussed in chapter 3. These alternative models result from justifiable criticism of the simple-minded model depicted in figure 1.2. The sole aim of our simple model is to provide an adequate structuring of topics to be addressed. The maintenance phase is further discussed in section 1.3. All components of our process model will be treated much more elaborately in later chapters.

Requirements engineering. The goal of the requirements engineering phase is to get a complete description of the problem to be solved and the requirements posed by and on the environment in which the system is going to function. Requirements posed by the environment may include hardware and supporting software or the number of prospective users of the system to be developed. Alternatively, analysis of the requirements may lead to certain constraints imposed on hardware yet to be acquired or to the organization in which the system is to function. A description of the problem to be solved includes such things as:

- the functions of the software to be developed;
- possible future extensions to the system;
- the amount, and kind, of documentation required;
- response time and other performance requirements of the system.

Part of requirements engineering is a **feasibility study**. The purpose of the feasibility study is to assess whether there is a solution to the problem which is both economically and technically feasible.

The more careful we are during the requirements engineering phase, the larger is the chance that the ultimate system will meet expectations. To this end, the various people (among others, the customer, prospective users, designers, and programmers) involved have to collaborate intensively. These people often have widely different backgrounds, which does not ease communication.

The document in which the result of this activity is laid down is called the **requirements specification**.

Design. During the design phase, a model of the whole system is developed which, when encoded in some programming language, solves the problem for the user. To this end, the problem is decomposed into manageable pieces called **modules or components**; the functions of these modules and the **interfaces** between them are specified in a very precise way. The design phase is crucial. Requirements engineering and design are sometimes seen as an annoying introduction to programming, which is often seen as the real work. This attitude has a very negative influence on the quality of the resulting software.

Early design decisions have a major impact on the quality of the final system. These early design decisions may be captured in a global description of the system, i.e. its **architecture**. The architecture may next be evaluated, serve as a template for the development of a family of similar systems, or be used as a skeleton for the development of reusable components. As such, the architectural description of a system is an important milestone document in present-day software development projects.

During the design phase we try to separate the *what* from the *how*. We concentrate on the problem and should not let ourselves be distracted by implementation concerns. Modern specification methods adhere to this principle. They offer possibilities to formulate the operations of a module mathematically, by expressing their domain, range, and effect. These specification methods do not yield algorithms.

The result of the design phase, the (**technical**) **specification**, serves as a starting point for the implementation phase. If the specification is formal in nature, it can also be used to derive correctness proofs.

Implementation. During the implementation phase, we concentrate on the individual modules. Our starting point is the module's specification. It is often necessary to introduce an extra 'design' phase, the step from module specification to executable code often being too large. In such cases, we may take advantage of some high-level, programming-language-like notation, such as a **pseudocode**. (A pseudocode is a kind of programming language. Its syntax and semantics are in general less strict, so that algorithms can be formulated at a higher, more abstract, level.)

It is important to note that the first goal of a programmer should be the development of a well-documented, reliable, easy to read, flexible, correct, program. The goal is *not* to produce a very efficient program full of tricks. We will come back to the many dimensions of software quality in chapter 6.

During the design phase, a global structure is imposed through the introduction of modules and their interfaces. In the more classic programming languages, much of this structure tends to get lost in the transition from design to code. More recent programming languages offer possibilities to retain this structure in the final code through the concept of modules or classes.

The result of the implementation phase is an executable program.

Testing. Actually, it is wrong to say that testing is a phase following implementation. This suggests that you need not bother about testing until implementation is finished. This is not true. It is even fair to say that this is one of the biggest mistakes you can make.

Attention has to be paid to testing even during the requirements engineering phase. During the subsequent phases, testing is continued and refined. The earlier that errors are detected, the cheaper it is to correct them.

Testing at phase boundaries comes in two flavors. We have to test that the transition between subsequent phases is correct (this is known as **verification**). We also have to check that we are still on the right track as regards fulfilling user requirements (**validation**). The result of adding verification and validation activities to the linear model of figure 1.2 yields the so-called **waterfall model** of software development (see also chapter 3).

Maintenance. After delivery of the software, there are often errors that have still gone undetected. Obviously, these errors must be repaired. In addition, the actual use of the system can lead to requests for changes and enhancements. All these types of changes are denoted by the rather unfortunate term maintenance. Maintenance thus concerns all activities needed to keep the system operational after it has been delivered to the user.

An activity spanning all phases is **project management**. Like other projects, software development projects must be managed properly in order to ensure that the product is delivered on time and within budget. The visibility and continuity characteristics of software development, as well as the fact that many software development projects are undertaken with insufficient prior experience, seriously impede project control. The many examples of software development projects that fail to meet their schedule provide ample evidence of the fact that we have by no means satisfactorily dealt with this issue yet. Chapters 2–8 deal with major aspects of software project management, such as project planning, team organization, quality issues, cost and schedule estimation.

An important activity not identified separately is **documentation**. A number of key ingredients of the documentation of a software project will be elaborated upon in the chapters to follow. Key components of system documentation include the project plan, quality plan, requirements specification, architecture description, design documentation and test plan. For larger projects, a considerable amount of effort will have to be spent on properly documenting the project. The documentation effort must start early on in the project. In practice, documentation is often seen as a balancing item. Since many projects are pressed for time, the documentation tends to get the worst of it. However, it is important to realize that software which is not sufficiently documented is bound to incur high costs later on. Since the program will undergo changes after delivery, because of errors that went undetected or changing user requirements, the documentation is of crucial importance during maintenance.

A particularly noteworthy element of documentation is the user documentation. Software development should be task-oriented in the sense that the software to be delivered should support users in their task environment. Likewise, the user documentation should be task-oriented. User manuals should not just describe the features of a system, they should help people to get things done [Ret91]. We cannot simply rely on the structure of the interface to organize the user documentation (just as a programming language reference manual is not an appropriate source for learning how to program).

Figure 1.3 depicts the relative effort spent on the various activities up to delivery of the system. From this data a very clear trend emerges, the so-called 40–20–40 rule: only 20% of the effort is spent on actually programming (coding) the system, while the preceding phases (requirements engineering and design) and testing each consume about 40% of the total effort.

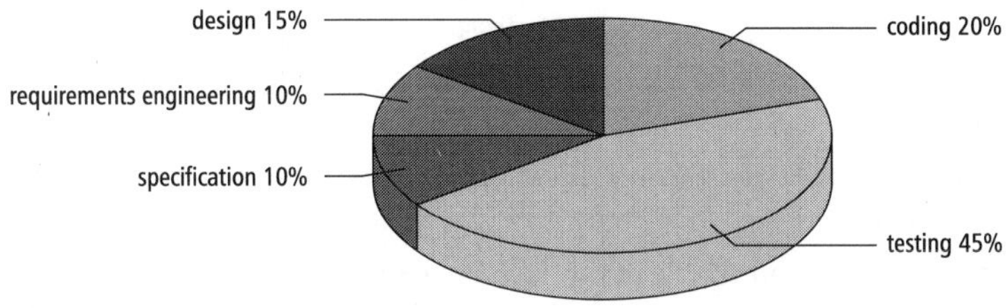

Figure 1.3 Relative effort for the various activities

Depending on specific boundary conditions, properties of the system to be constructed, and the like, variations to this rule can be found. For the majority of projects, however, this rule of thumb is quite workable.

This does not imply that the 40–20–40 rule is the one to be strived for. Errors made during requirements engineering are the ones that are most costly to repair (see also the chapter on testing). It is far better to put more energy into the requirements engineering phase, than to try to remove errors during the time-consuming testing phase or, worse still, during maintenance. According to [Boe87b], successful projects follow a 60–15–25 distribution: 60% requirements engineering and design, 15% implementation and 25% testing. The message is clear: the longer you postpone coding, the earlier you are finished.

Figure 1.3 does not show the extent of the maintenance effort. When we consider the total cost of a software system over its lifetime, it turns out that, on average, maintenance alone consumes 50–75% of these costs; see also figure 1.1. Thus, maintenance alone consumes more than the various development phases taken together.

1.3 MAINTENANCE OR EVOLUTION

The only thing we maintain is user satisfaction
[Leh80]

Once software has been delivered, it usually still contains errors which, upon discovery, must be repaired. Note that this type of maintenance is not caused by wearing. Rather, it concerns repair of hidden defects. This type of repair is comparable to that encountered after a newly-built house is first occupied.

The story becomes quite different if we start talking about changes or enhancements to the system. Repainting our office or repairing a leak in the roof of our house is called maintenance. Adding a wing to our office is seldom called maintenance.

This is more than a trifling game with words. Over the total lifetime of a software system, more money is spent on maintaining that system than on initial development. If all these expenses merely concerned the repair of errors made during one of the development phases, our business would be doing very badly indeed. Fortunately, this is not the case.

We distinguish four kinds of maintenance activities:

- **corrective** maintenance – the repair of actual errors;

- **adaptive** maintenance – adapting the software to changes in the environment, such as new hardware or the next release of an operating or database system;

- **perfective** maintenance – adapting the software to new or changed user requirements, such as extra functions to be provided by the system. Perfective maintenance also includes work to increase the system's performance or to enhance its user interface;

- **preventive** maintenance – increasing the system's future maintainability. Updating documentation, adding comments, or improving the modular structure of a system are examples of preventive maintenance activities.

Only the first category may rightfully be termed maintenance. This category, however, accounts only for about a quarter of the total maintenance effort. Approximately another quarter of the maintenance effort concerns adapting software to environmental changes, while half of the maintenance cost is spent on changes to accommodate changing user requirements, i.e. enhancements to the system (see figure 1.4).

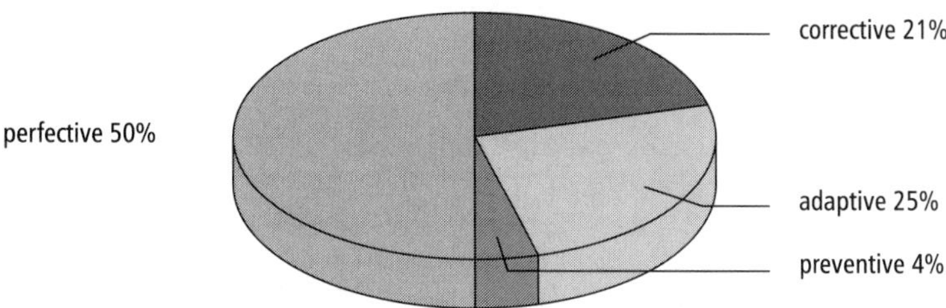

Figure 1.4 Distribution of maintenance activities

Changes in both the system's environment and user requirements are inevitable. Software models part of reality, and reality changes, whether we like it or not. So the software has to change too. It *has* to evolve. A large percentage of what we are used to calling maintenance is actually evolution. Maintenance because of new user requirements occurs in both high and low quality systems. A successful system calls for new, unforeseen functionality, because of its use by many satisfied users. A less successful system has to be adapted in order to satisfy its customers.

The result is that the software development process becomes cyclic, hence the phrase **software life cycle**. Backtracking to previous phases, alluded to above, does not only occur during maintenance. During other phases, also, we will from time to time iterate earlier phases. During design, it may be discovered that the requirements specification is not complete or contains conflicting requirements. During testing, errors introduced in the implementation or design phase may crop up. In these and similar cases an iteration of earlier phases is needed. We will come back to this cyclic nature of the software development process in chapter 3, when we discuss alternative models of the software development process.

1.4 FROM THE TRENCHES

And such is the way of all superstition, whether in astrology, dreams, omens, divine judgments or the like; wherein men, having a delight in such vanities, mark the events when they are fulfilled, but when they fail, though this happens much oftener, neglect and pass them by. But with far more subtlety does this mischief insinuate itself into philosophy and the sciences; in which the first conclusion colours and brings into conformity with itself all that come after, though far sounder and better. Besides, independently of that delight and vanity which I have described, it is the peculiar and perpetual error of the human intellect to be more moved and excited by affirmatives than by negatives; whereas it ought properly to hold itself indifferently disposed towards both alike. Indeed in the

> *establishment of any true axiom, the negative instance is the more forcible of the two.*
> Sir Francis Bacon, The New Organon, Aphorisms XLVI (1611)

> *Historical case studies contain a wealth of wisdom about the nature of design and the engineering method.*
> [Pet94]

In his wonderful book *Design Paradigms, Case Histories of Error and Judgment in Engineering*, Henri Petroski tells us about some of the greatest engineering successes and, especially, failures of all time. Some such failure stories about our profession have appeared as well. Three of them are discussed in this section.

These stories are interesting because they teach us that software engineering has many facets. Failures in software development projects often are not one-dimensional. They are not *only* caused by a technical slip in some routine. They are not *only* caused by bad management. They are not *only* the result of human communication problems. It is often a combination of many smaller slips, which accumulate over time, and eventually result in a major failure. To paraphrase a famous saying of Fred Brooks about projects getting late:

> 'How does a project really get into trouble?'
> 'One slip at a time.'

Each of the stories discussed below shows such a cumulative effect. Successes in software development will not come about if we just employ the brightest programmers. Or apply the newest design philosophy. Or have the most extensive user consultation. Or even hire the best manager. You have to do all of that. And even more.

1.4.1 Ariane 5, Flight 501

The maiden flight of the Ariane 5 launcher took place on June 4, 1996. After about 40 seconds, at an altitude of less than 4 kilometers, the launcher broke up and exploded. This $500M loss was ultimately caused by an overflow in the conversion from a 64-bit floating point number to a 16-bit signed integer. From a software engineering point of view, the Ariane 5 story is interesting because the failure can be attributed to different causes, at different levels of understanding: inadequate testing, wrong type of reuse, or a wrong design philosophy.

The altitude of the launcher and its movements in space are measured by an Inertial Reference System (SRI – Système de Référence Inertielle). There are two SRIs operating in parallel. Their hardware and software is identical. Most of the hardware and software for the SRI was retained from the Ariane 4. The fatal conversion took place in a piece of software in the SRI which is only meaningful before lift-off. Though this part of the software serves no purpose after the rocket has been launched, it keeps running for an additional number of seconds. This requirement was stated more than 10 years earlier for a somewhat peculiar reason. It allows for a quick restart of the countdown, in the case that it is interrupted close to lift-off. This requirement does not apply to the Ariane 5, but the software was left unchanged – after all, it worked. Since the Ariane 5 is much faster than the Ariane 4, the rocket reaches a much higher horizontal velocity within this short period after lift-off, resulting in the above-mentioned overflow. Because of this overflow, the first SRI ceased to function. The second SRI was then activated, but since the hardware and software of both SRIs are identical, the second SRI failed as well. As a consequence, wrong data were transmitted from the SRI to the on-board computer. On the basis of these wrong data, full nozzle deflections were commanded. These caused a very high aerodynamic load which led to the separation of the boosters from the main rocket. And this in turn triggered the self-destruction of the launcher.

There are several levels at which the Ariane 5 failure can be understood and explained:

- It was a software failure, which could have been revealed with more extensive testing. This is true: the committee investigating the event managed to expose the failure using extensive simulations.

- The failure was caused by reusing a flawed component. This is true as well but, because of physical characteristics of the Ariane 4, this flaw had never become apparent. There had been many successful Ariane 4 flights, using essentially the same SRI subsystem. Apparently, reuse is not compositional: the successful use of a component in one environment is no guarantee for successful reuse of that component in another environment.

- The failure was caused by a flaw in the design. The Ariane software follows a typical hardware design philosophy: if a component breaks down, the cause is assumed to be random and it is handled by shutting down that part and invoking a backup component. In the case of a software failure, which is not random, an identical backup is of little use. For the software part, a different line might have been followed. For instance, the component could be asked to give its best estimate of the required information.

1.4.2 Therac-25

The Therac-25 is a computer-controlled radiation machine. It has three modes:

- field-light mode. This position merely facilitates the correct positioning of the patient.

- electron mode. In electron therapy, the computer controls the (variable) beam energy and current, and magnets spread the beam to a safe concentration.

- photon (X-ray) mode. In photon mode, the beam energy is fixed. A 'beam flattener' is put between the accelerator and the patient to produce a uniform treatment field. A very high current (some 100 times higher than in electron mode) is required on one side of the beam flattener to produce a reasonable treatment dose at the other side.

The machine has a turntable which rotates the necessary equipment into position. The basic hazardous situation is obvious from the above: a photon beam is issued by the accelerator, while the beam flattener is not in position. The patient is then treated with a dose which is far too high. This happened several times. As a consequence, several patients have died and others have been seriously injured.

One of the malfunctions of the Therac-25 has become known as 'Malfunction 54'. A patient was set up for treatment. The operator keyed in the necessary data on the console in an adjacent room. While doing so, he made a mistake: he typed 'x' (for X-ray mode) instead of 'e' (for electron mode). He corrected his mistake by moving the cursor up to the appropriate field, typing in the correct code and pressing the return key a number of times until the cursor was on the command line again. He then pressed 'B' (beam on). The machine stopped and issued the message 'Malfunction 54'. This particular error message indicates a wrong dose, either too high or too low. The console indicated a substantial underdose. The operator knew that the machine often had quirks, and that these could usually be solved by simply pressing 'P' (proceed). So he did. The same error message appeared again. Normally, the operator would have audio and video contact with the patient in the treatment room. Not this time, though: the audio was broken and the video had been turned off. It was later estimated that the patient had received 16 000–25 000 rad on a very small surface, instead of the intended dose of 180 rad. The patient became seriously ill and died five months later.

The cause of this hazardous event was traced back to the software operating the radiation machine. After the operator has finished data entry, the physical set up of the machine may begin. The bending of the magnets takes about eight seconds. After the magnets are put into position, it again checks if anything has changed. If the operator manages to make changes **and** return the cursor to the command line position within the eight seconds it takes to set the magnets, part of these changes will result in changes in internal system parameters, but the system nevertheless 'thinks' that nothing has happened and simply continues. With the consequences as described above.

Accidents like this get reported to the Federal Drugs Administration (FDA). The FDA requested the manufacturer to take appropriate measures. The 'fix' suggested was as follows:

> Effective immediately, and until further notice, the key used for moving the cursor back through the prescription sequence (i.e. cursor 'UP' in-

> scribed with an upward pointing arrow) must not be used for editing or any other purpose.
>
> To avoid accidental use of this key, the key cap must be removed and the switch contacts fixed in the open position with electrical tape or other insulating material. ...
>
> Disabling this key means that if any prescription data entered is incorrect then an 'R' reset command must be used and the whole prescription reentered.

The FDA did not buy this remedy. In particular, they judged the tone of the notification not commensurate with the urgency for doing so. The discussion between the FDA and the manufacturer continued for quite some time before an adequate response was given to this and other failures of the Therac-25.

The Therac-25 machine and its software evolved from earlier models that were less sophisticated. In earlier versions of the software, for example, it was not possible to move up and down the screen to change individual fields. Operators noticed that different treatments often required almost the same data, which had to be keyed in all over again. To enhance usability, the feature to move the cursor around and change individual fields was added. Apparently, user friendliness may conflict with safety.

In earlier models also, the correct position of the turntable and other equipment was ensured by simple electromechanical interlocks. These interlocks are a common mechanism to ensure safety. For instance, they are used in lifts to make sure that the doors cannot be opened if the lift is in between floors. In the Therac-25, these mechanical safety devices were replaced by software. The software was thus made into a single point of failure. This overconfidence in software contributed to the Therac-25 accidents, together with inadequate software engineering practices and an inadequate reaction of management to incidents.

1.4.3 The London Ambulance Service

The London Ambulance Service (LAS) handles the ambulance traffic in Greater London. It covers an area of over 600 square miles and carries over 5000 patients per day in 750 vehicles. The LAS receives over 2000 phone calls per day, including more than 1300 emergency calls. The system we discuss here is a computer-aided dispatch (CAD) system. Such a CAD system has the following functionality:

- it handles call taking, accepts and verifies incident details including the location of the incident;
- it determines which ambulance to send;
- it handles the mobilization of the ambulance and communicates the details of the incident to the ambulance;

- it takes care of ambulance resource management, in particular the positioning of vehicles to minimize response times.

A fully-fledged CAD system is quite complex. In panic, someone might call and say that an accident has happened in front of Foyle's, assuming that everyone knows where this bookshop is located. An extensive gazetteer component including a public telephone identification helps in solving this type of problem. The CAD system also contains a radio system, mobile terminals in the ambulances, and an automatic vehicle location system.

The CAD project of the London Ambulance Service was started in the autumn of 1990. The delivery was scheduled for January 1992. At that time, however, the software was still far from complete. Over the first nine months of 1992, the system was installed piecemeal across a number of different LAS divisions, but it was never stable. On 26 and 27 October 1992, there were serious problems with the system and it was decided to revert to a semi-manual mode of operation. On 4 November 1992, the system crashed. The Regional Health Authority established an Inquiry Team to investigate the failures and the history that led to them. They came up with an 80-page report, which reads like a suspense novel. Below, we highlight some of the issues raised in this report.

The envisaged CAD system would be a major undertaking. No other emergency service had attempted to go as far. The plan was to move from a wholly manual process – in which forms were filled in and transported from one employee to the next via a conveyor belt – to complete automation, in one shot. The scheme was very ambitious. The participants seem not to have fully realized the risks they were taking.

Way before the project actually started, a management consultant firm had already been asked for advice. They suggested that a packaged solution would cost £1.5M and take 19 months. Their report also stated that if a package solution could not be found, the estimates should be significantly increased. Eventually, a non-package solution was chosen, but only the numbers from this report were remembered, or so it seems.

The advertisement resulted in replies from 35 companies. The specification and timetable were next discussed with these companies. The proposed timetable was 11 months (this is not a typo). Though many suppliers raised concerns about the timetable, they were told that it was non-negotiable. Eventually, 17 suppliers provided full proposals. The lowest tender, at approximately £1M, was selected. This tender was about £700 000 cheaper than the next lowest bid. No one seems to have questioned this huge difference. The proposal selected superficially suggests that the company had experience in designing systems for emergency services. This was not a lie: they had developed administrative systems for such services. The LAS system also was far larger than anything they had previously handled.

The proposed system would impact quite significantly on the way ambulance crews carried out their jobs. It would therefore be paramount to have their full co-operation. If the crews did not press the right buttons at the right time and in the right order, chaos could result. Yet, there was very little user involvement during the requirements engineering process.

The intended CAD system would operate in an absolutely objective and impartial way and would always mobilize the optimum resource to any incident. This would overcome many of the then present working practices which management considered outmoded and not in the interest of LAS. For instance, the new system would allocate the nearest available resource regardless of the originating station. The following scenario may result:

- John's crew has to go to an accident a few miles east of their home base.
- Once there, they are directed to a hospital a few miles further east to deliver the patient.
- Another call comes in and John happens to be nearest. He is ordered to travel yet a few miles further east.
- And so on.

In this way, crews may have to operate further and further away from their home base, and in unfamiliar territory. They lose time, because they take wrong turns, or may even have to stop to ask for directions. They also have further to travel to reach their home station at the end of a shift. Crews didn't like this aspect of the new system.

The new system also took away the flexibility local emergency stations had in deciding which resource to allocate. In the new scheme, resource management was fully centralized and handled by the system. So, suppose John runs down to where the ambulances are parked and the computer has ordered him to take car number 5. John is in a hurry and maybe he cannot quickly spot car number 5, or maybe it is parked behind some other cars. So John thinks about this patient waiting for him and decides to take car number 4 instead. This means trouble.

The people responsible for those requirements were misguided or naive in believing that computer systems in themselves can bring about such changes in human practices. Computers are there to help people do their job, not vice versa. Operational straitjackets are doomed to fail.

The eventual crash on 4 November 1992 was caused by a minor programming error. Some three weeks earlier, a programmer had been working on part of the system and forgot to remove a small piece of program text. The code in itself did no harm. However, it did allocate a small amount of memory every time a vehicle mobilization was generated by the system. This memory was not deallocated. After three weeks, all memory was used up and the system crashed.

The LAS project as a whole did not fail because of this programmer mistake. That was just the last straw. The project schedule was far too tight. Management of both the London Ambulance Service and the contractor had little or no experience with software development projects of this size and complexity. They were far too optimistic in their assessment of risks. They assumed that all the people who would interact with the system, would do so in exactly the right way, all of the time. They assumed the hardware parts of the system would work exactly as specified. Management decided on the functionality of the system, with hardly any consultation with the people that would be its primary users. Any project with such characteristics is doomed to fail. From the very first day.

1.5 SOFTWARE ENGINEERING ETHICS

Suppose you are testing part of a big software system. You find quite a few errors and you're certainly not ready to deliver. However, your manager is pressing you. The schedule has already slipped by quite a few weeks. Your manager in turn is pressed by his boss. The customer is eagerly awaiting delivery of the system. Your manager suggests that you should deliver the system as is, continue testing, and replace the system by a better version within the next month. How would you react to this scheme? Would you simply give in? Argue with your manager? Go to his boss? Go to the customer?

The development of complex software systems involves many people: software developers, testers, technical managers, general managers, customers, etc. Within this temporary organization, the relationship between individuals is often asymmetrical: one person participating in the relationship has more knowledge about something than the other. For example, a software developer has more knowledge about the system under construction than his manager. Such an asymmetric relationship asks for trust: if the developer says that development of some component is on schedule, his manager cannot but believe this message. At least for a while. Such reliance provides opportunities for unethical behavior, such as embezzlement. This is the more so if there also is a power relationship between these individuals.

It is not surprising then that people within the software engineering community have been discussing a software engineering code of ethics. Two large organizations of professionals in our field, the IEEE Computer Society and ACM, have jointly developed such a code. This code contains eight principles, listed in figure 1.5.

	Keyword	Principle
1	Public	Software engineers shall act consistently with the public interest
2	Client and employer	Software engineers shall act in a manner that is in the best interests of their client and employer and that is consistent with the public interest
3	Product	Software engineers shall ensure that their products and related modifications meet the highest professional standards possible
4	Judgment	Software engineers shall maintain integrity and independence in their professional judgment
5	Management	Software engineering managers and leaders shall subscribe to and promote an ethical approach to the management of software development and maintenance
6	Profession	Software engineers shall advance the integrity and reputation of the profession consistent with the public interest
7	Colleagues	Software engineers shall be fair to and supportive of their colleagues
8	Self	Software engineers shall participate in lifelong learning regarding the practice of their profession and promote an ethical approach to the practice of the profession

Figure 1.5 Software engineering code of ethics

Each of these principles is further refined into a set of clauses. Some of these clauses are statements of aspiration: for example, a software engineer should strive to fully understand the specifications of the software on which he works. Aspirations direct professional behavior. They require significant ethical judgment. Other clauses express obligations of professionals in general: for example, a software engineer should, like any other professional, provide service only in areas of his competence. A third type of clause is directed at specific professional behavior within software engineering: for example, a software engineer should ensure realistic estimates of the cost and schedule of any project on which he works.

There are a number of clauses which bear upon the situation of the tester mentioned above:

- Approve software only if you have a well-founded belief that it is safe, meets specifications, passes appropriate tests, and does not diminish quality of life or privacy or harm the environment (clause 1.03[1]).

- Ensure adequate testing, debugging, and review of software and related documents on which you work (clause 3.10).

- As a manager, do not ask a software engineer to do anything inconsistent with this code of ethics (clause 5.11).

[1]Clause 1.03 denotes clause no 3 of principle no. 1 (Public).

- Be accurate in stating the characteristics of software on which you work, avoiding not only false claims but also claims that might be supposed to be speculative, vacuous, deceptive, misleading, or doubtful (clause 6.07).

The code is not a simple algorithm to discriminate between acceptable and unacceptable behavior. Rather, the principles stated should influence you, as a software engineer, to consider who is affected by your work. The software you develop affects the public. The health, safety and welfare of the public is the primary concern of this code of ethics. Adhering to this, or a similar, code of ethics is not something to merely consider on a Friday afternoon. It should become a way of life.

1.6 QUO VADIS?

A lot of progress has been made over the past 30 years. For each of the major phases, numerous techniques and tools have been developed. A number of these have found widespread use. In their assessment of design and coding practices for example, DeMarco and Lister found that a number of widely acclaimed techniques (such as the use of small units, strong module binding and structured programming) are indeed applied in practice and pay off [DL89]. However, the short sketches in the preceding section (and the more elaborate discussion in the following chapters) show that a lot of research is still needed to make software engineering into a truly mature engineering discipline.

It takes some time before technology developed in research laboratories gets applied in a routine way. This holds for physical products such as the transistor, but also for methods, techniques, and tools in the area of software technology. The first version of the UNIX operating system goes right back to 1971. Only since the late 1980s, has interest in UNIX spread widely. In the early 1960s, studies of the cost of software were first made. In the 1980s there was a growing interest in quantitative models for estimating software costs (see also the later chapter on cost estimation). Dijkstra's article on programming as a human activity appeared in 1965. In the late 1970s the first introductory textbooks on structured programming were published. The term software engineering was introduced in 1968. In the 1980s large national and international programs were initiated to foster the transition of this new technology. The above list can be extended with many other examples [RR85]. This maturation process generally takes at least 10 to 15 years.

In a seminal article entitled 'No silver bullet: essence and accidents of software engineering', Brooks discusses a number of potentially fruitful approaches to dramatically increase software productivity [Bro87]. He distinguishes two types of problem which hamper software construction: essential and accidental difficulties. Essential difficulties have to do with the essence of software, such as the high complexity of present-day systems. Accidental difficulties are just there because we have not adequately dealt with them yet. For example, hardware which is too slow or has insufficient memory constitutes an accidental difficulty. Accidental difficulties can be dealt with. Unfortunately, most of these have been dealt with already. What keeps us at work is the essence of software.

As a consequence, there is no single new technique which will bring us an order of magnitude improvement in software productivity. Quite a large number of developments are under way, though, each of which contributes its mite. According to Brooks, these developments will together lead to a significant productivity improvement. He comments on a number of these widely acclaimed developments.

Brooks advocates object-oriented program construction. Encapsulation and inheritance each remove an accidental difficulty. But the essence remains, so we should not expect miracles from these techniques. He does not expect spectacular improvements from artificial intelligence, graphical programming techniques or program verification either. Programming environments and other tools may yet make some useful contributions, but a lot of work has to be gone through in order to get a marginal return of investment. He expects by far the highest result from rapid prototyping, incremental development, the identification and development of great designers, and exploitation of the mass market to avoid constructing what can be bought.

While technology improvements do offer considerable potential, they are not enough. In many organizations, the software process is sufficiently confused and incoherent that non-technological factors impede the effective application of technology [Hum89]. Thus, managerial, organizational, psychological and other non-technological issues deserve our attention as well.

There is no silver bullet. But we need not be afraid of the werewolf either. By a careful study of the many innovations and an investigation of their true merits, a lot of improvements in both quality and productivity can be achieved. The remainder of this text is devoted to a critical assessment of these technological and non-technological developments.

To close this chapter is a list of important periodicals that contain material which is relevant to the field of software engineering:

- *Transactions on Software Engineering* (IEEE), a bimonthly periodical in which research results are reported;

- *Software* (IEEE), a bimonthly journal which is somewhat more general in scope;

- *Software Engineering Notes*, a bimonthly newsletter from the ACM Special Interest Group on Software Engineering;

- *Transactions on Software Engineering and Methodology* (ACM), a quarterly journal which reports research results;

- *The Journal of Systems and Software* (Elsevier), a monthly journal covering both research papers and reports of practical experiences;

- *Proceedings of the International Conference on Software Engineering* (ACM/IEEE), proceedings of the most important international conference in the field, organized every year;

- *Proceedings of the International Conference on Software Maintenance* (IEEE), organized yearly;

- *Software Maintenance: Research and Practice* (Wiley), quarterly journal devoted to topics in software maintenance.

1.7 SUMMARY

Software engineering is concerned with the problems that have to do with the construction of *large* programs. When developing such programs, a phased approach is followed. First, the problem is analyzed, and then the system is designed, implemented and tested. This practice has a lot in common with the engineering of physical products. Hence the term software engineering. Software engineering, however, also differs from the engineering of physical products in some essential ways.

Software models part of the real world surrounding us, like banking or the reservation of airline seats. This world around us changes over time. So the corresponding software has to change too. It has to evolve together with the changing reality. Much of what we call software maintenance, actually is concerned with ensuring that the software keeps pace with the real world being modeled.

We thus get a process model in which we iterate earlier phases from time to time. We speak about the software life cycle.

The most important problems that we try to tackle in the field of software engineering are the quality of the software being delivered and the productivity of the people working in the field. On both a national and international scale, interest in this field is growing. Large research efforts are being undertaken and the topic is slowly penetrating university curricula.

In most computer science curricula, software engineering does not have a very prominent place. In most cases, a one or two semester course is offered in which some kind of practical project work is included. A number of full MSc programs in software engineering exist. [Gib91] speculates that there will be more than 100 such degree programs by 2000.

1.8 FURTHER READING

For a more elaborate discussion of the differences and similarities between software engineering and a mature engineering discipline, viz. bridge design, see [SG86]. [Lev92] compares software engineering with the development of high-pressure steam engines.

The four kinds of maintenance activities stem from [LS80].

The Ariane failure is described in [JM97]. I found the report of the Inquiry Team at `http://www.cnes.fr/ARCHIVES/news/rapport_501.html`. An elaborate discussion of the Therac-25 accidents can be found in [LT93]. The Inquiry into the London Ambulance Service is described in [PWB93]. [Neu95] is a book wholly devoted to computer-related risks. [Flo96] is a collection of stories about information systems that failed, including the LAS system. [Pet94] is a wonderful book on failures in engineering. [Sof99] is a special issue with stories about successful IT projects.

The ACM/IEEE Software Engineering code of ethics is discussed in [GMR97]. The text of the code can also be found at `http://computer.org/tab/seprof/code.htm`. [Eps97] is a collection of (fictional) stories addressing the interaction between ethics and software engineering. [Oz94] discusses ethical questions of a real-life project.

Exercises

1. Define the term software engineering.

2. What are the essential characteristics of software engineering?

3. What are the major phases in a software development project?

4. What is the difference between verification and validation?

5. Define four kinds of maintenance activity.

6. Why is the documentation of a software project important?

7. Explain the 40–20–40 rule of thumb in software engineering.

8. What is the difference between software development and software maintenance?

9. ♡ Do you think the linear model of software development is appropriate? You may wish to reconsider this issue after having read the remainder of this text.

10. ♡ Discuss the major differences between software engineering and some other engineering discipline, such as bridge design or house building. Would you consider state-of-the-art software engineering as a true engineering discipline?

11. ♠ Quality and productivity are major issues in software engineering. It is often advocated that automated tools (CASE tools) will dramatically improve both quality and productivity. Study a commercial CASE tool and assess the extent to which it improves the software development process and its outcome.

12. ♡ Medical doctors have their Hippocratic oath. Could a similar ethical commitment by software engineers be instrumental in increasing the quality of software systems?

13. ♠ Suppose you are involved in an office automation project in the printing industry. The system to be developed is meant to support the work of journal editors. The management objective for this project is to save labor cost; the editors' objective is to increase the quality of their work. Discuss possible ramifications of these opposing objectives on the project. You may come back to this question after having read chapter 9 or [HK89].

14. ♠ Study both the technical and user documentation of a system at your disposal. Are you satisfied with them? Discuss their possible shortcomings and give remedies to improve their quality.

15. ♠ Take a piece of software you wrote more than a year ago. Is it documented adequately? Does it have a user manual? Is the design rationale reflected in the technical documentation? Can you build an understanding of the system from its documentation that is sufficient for making non-trivial changes to it? Repeat these questions for a system written by one of your colleagues.

16. ♠ Try to gather quantitative data from your organization that reveals how much effort is spent on various kinds of maintenance activity. Are these data available at all? If so, is the pattern like that sketched in section 1.3? If not, can you explain the differences?

17. ♠ A 1999 Computer Society survey lists the following candidate fundamental principles of software engineering:

    A. Apply and use quantitative measurements in decision-making.

    B. Build with and for reuse.

    C. Control complexity with multiple perspectives and multiple levels of abstraction.

    D. Define software artifacts rigorously.

E. Establish a software process that provides flexibility.
F. Implement a disciplined approach and improve it continuously.
G. Invest in the understanding of the problem.
H. Manage quality throughout the life cycle as formally as possible.
I. Minimize software components interaction.
J. Produce software in a stepwise fashion.
K. Set quality objectives for each deliverable product.
L. Since change is inherent to software, plan for it and manage it.
M. Since tradeoffs are inherent to software engineering, make them explicit and document them.
N. To improve design, study previous solutions to similar problems.
O. Uncertainty is unavoidable in software engineering. Identify and manage it.

For each of these principles, indicate whether you (strongly) agree or (strongly) disagree, and why. You may wish to re-appraise these principles after having studied the rest of this book.

Part I

Software Management

Contents

Software development projects often involve several people for a prolonged period of time. Large projects may even range over several years and involve hundreds of people. Such projects must be carefully planned and controlled. The main aspects that deserve the continuous attention of project managers are introduced in chapter 2, and further dealt with in chapters 3–7: progress, information, people, quality, cost and schedule.

To be able to assess progress during software development, one opts for a phased approach with a number of well-defined milestone events. The linear ordering of activities which underlies the most popular software development model, the waterfall model, renders it an impossible idealization of reality though. It assumes software development proceeds in an orderly, sequential manner. Real projects proceed in far less rational ways. The waterfall model of software development is not feasible, much like Escher's Waterfall, reproduced on the front cover, is unfeasible. Chapter 3 discusses various alternative models of the development process.

Many documents are produced during the lifetime of a project. Worse still, many changes to these documents must be accommodated. Careful procedures are needed to manage and control their consistency, a topic known as configuration management, which is dealt with in chapter 4.

Finding the right organizational framework and the right mix of skills for a development team is a difficult matter. Little well-founded theory is available for this. Yet, many stories of successful and less successful projects discern some of the intricacies of project team issues. Chapter 5 sketches the major issues involved.

Software quality is becoming an increasingly important topic. With the increasing penetration of automation in everyday life, more and more people are coming into contact with software systems, and the quality of those systems is becoming a major concern. Quality cannot be added as an afterthought. It has to be built in from the very beginning. Chapter 6 discusses the many dimensions of quality of both the software product and the software process.

Software development takes time and money, and this is looked at in chapter 7. When commissioning a building project, you expect a reliable estimate of the cost and development time up front. Getting reliable cost and schedule estimates for software development projects is still largely a dream. Software development cost is notoriously difficult to estimate reliably at an early stage. Since progress is difficult to 'see' – just when is a piece of software 50% complete? – schedule slippages often go undetected for quite a while, and schedule overruns are the rule, rather than the exception.

The management part ends with chapter 8 in which I try to reconcile the various approaches sketched in chapters 3–7. A taxonomy of software development projects is given, together with recommended management practices for dealing with such projects. Chapter 8 also deals with risk management and some well-known techniques for project planning and control.

2 Introduction to Software Engineering Management

LEARNING OBJECTIVES

- To be aware of the contents of a project plan
- To understand the major dimensions along which a software development project is controlled

Many software development projects get into trouble at the end: software is delivered too late, budgets are overrun, customers are dissatisfied. Often, the underlying problems are of a technical nature. Equally often, however, the problems can be traced back to the organization or management of the project.

Some characteristic reasons people give when software is delivered too late, are exemplified by the following [TPW81]:

- the programmers did not tell the truth about the actual status of their code;
- management grossly underestimated the time needed to complete the project;
- management did not allow sufficient time to carefully plan the project;
- the real status of the project was never made clear;
- the programmers' productivity turned out to be considerably lower than expected;
- the customer did not know what he wanted.

Apparently, it is not easy to complete successfully a software development project. This book mainly deals with technical aspects of software development: design, specification, implementation and testing of software systems. As we learn to control these aspects better, we will also learn to satisfy our customer's demands better. The organizational and managerial aspects of software development projects are at least as important as the technical aspects, though.

Before we embark on a discussion of these organizational and managerial aspects, let us first pay some attention to the boundaries of a software development project as they are drawn in this book.

A software development project is usually not started in complete isolation. There are other projects within the organization that this particular project needs to be tuned to, priorities between projects have to be decided upon, etc. The term **information planning** is often used to refer to this meta-project planning process.

Information planning results in a set of boundary conditions for each project, much like the zoning regulations set the conditions for a building project. Establishing a company-wide information plan is a problem on its own, and will not be addressed here. (We will, however, pay ample attention to some issues which generally surpass the boundaries of individual software development projects, such as configuration control and quality assurance.)

Also in a more technical sense, software is not generally developed in isolation. In most cases, software is not written from scratch. It must interface with existing software, extend existing software, use existing subroutine libraries, build upon an existing framework, and so on.

In some sense, the notion of a 'software development project' is a misnomer. We do not just develop software, we develop systems. Broadly speaking, a system transforms inputs into outputs. Software is an important ingredient of the systems we develop, but it is by no means the only ingredient. The technical and user documentation, the hardware, the procedures that govern the use of the system, and even the people using the software, may be considered as part of that same system.

Consider for example a system for library automation. The system will contain various software components, such as a database component to store information on books and customers and an interaction component to process user requests. As well as the development of these components, attention should be paid to matters like:

- techniques to identify books electronically, such as a barcode scheme;
- the selection and acquisition of special hardware both for scanning those identifications and for producing identifications for new books;
- setting up a scheme to provide all books with the new identification code;
- instruction of library employees to handle the new types of equipment (training material and courses, operating procedures, and the like);
- production of user-friendly documentation for the library customers.

Whenever the notion 'software development project' is used in the following, it should be understood in this wider sense. This is graphically illustrated in figure 2.1.

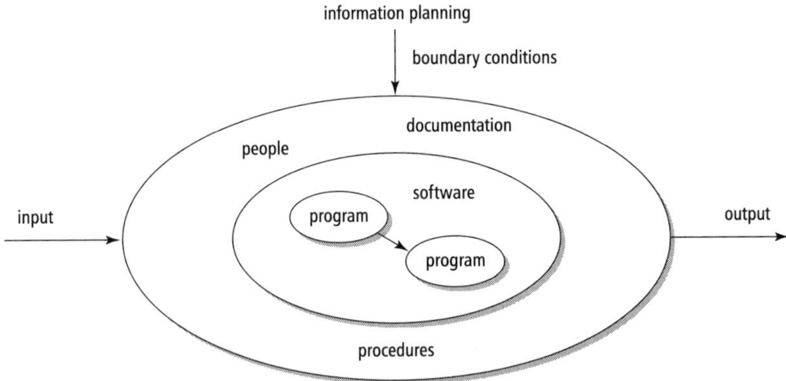

Figure 2.1 The systems view of a software development project

Thus, our systems encompass a number of components. In a narrow sense, the software component itself may also consist of a number of interacting components.

These latter components correspond to programs as we know them from introductory computer science textbooks. In general, a software development project results in a set of programs which collectively provide us with the desired functionality.

Given a project's boundary conditions, a software development project may get started. Planning the project is the very first step to be undertaken. Part of this planning process is to identify the project characteristics and their impact on the development process. The result of the planning phase is laid down in a document, the **project plan**, which aims to provide a clear picture of the project to both the customers and the development team. The contents of the project plan are discussed in section 2.1.

During the execution of the project, a number of elements have to be managed: time, information, organization, quality, and money (see section 2.2). Each of these elements is further elaborated upon in a separate chapter.

2.1 PLANNING A SOFTWARE DEVELOPMENT PROJECT

Before we embark on a software development project, it has to be carefully planned. This entails, amongst other things, an assessment of project properties that may affect the development process. A number of properties, however, will not be sufficiently well understood until the requirements engineering phase has ended. Like many other aspects of a software development project, planning is not a one-shot activity. Rather, it is highly dynamic in nature. The project plan can serve as a guide during the project.

The major constituents of a project plan are:

1. **Introduction** In the introduction to the project plan, the background and history of the project are given, together with its aims, the project deliverables, the names of the persons responsible, and a summary of the project.

2. **Process model** In chapter 1, we introduced a simple life cycle model in order to discuss the various activities to be dealt with in a software development project. There exist many variations of this process model, some of which are discussed in chapter 3. For each project, one has to decide upon the exact process model to be followed: which activities are being undertaken, which milestones can be identified, how do we ascertain whether those milestones are reached, and which are the critical paths.

   Different types of projects have different characteristics, and so call for different process models.

3. **Organization of the project** The relationship of the project to other entities and the organization of the project itself are dealt with under this heading. The

project will have a relationship with the user organization, the parent organization, and possibly with other organizations.

The prospective users will from time to time be involved in the project. The project plan has to state which information, services, resources and facilities are to be provided by the users and when these are to be provided.

Within the project team, various roles can be identified: project manager, tester, programmer, analyst, etc. One has to clearly delineate these roles and identify the responsibilities of each of them. If there are gaps in the knowledge required to fulfill any of these roles, the training and education needed to fill these gaps have to be identified. Different forms of team organization are discussed in chapter 5.

4. **Standards, guidelines, procedures** Software projects are big projects. Usually, a lot of people are involved. A strong working discipline is therefore needed, in which each person involved follows the standards, guidelines and procedures agreed upon. Besides being stated on paper, many of these can be supported or enforced by tools. Of extreme importance are clear agreements about documentation: when is documentation to be delivered, how is the quality of the documentation to be assessed, how does one ensure that the documentation is kept up-to-date?

   To a large extent, these standards and procedures will be described in separate documents, such as the Configuration Control Plan or the Quality Assurance Plan.

5. **Management activities** Management activities are guided by goals and priorities set for the project. For example, management will have to submit regular reports on the status and progress of the project. It will also have to follow certain priorities in balancing requirements, schedule and cost.

6. **Risks** Potential risks have to be identified as early as possible. There will always be risks: hardware may not be delivered on time, qualified personnel may not be available when required, critical information may be lacking when it is needed, and so on. It is rather naive to suppose that a software development project runs smoothly. Even in well-established fields like construction, there is always something that goes wrong. One should diagnose the risks of a software project early on, and provide measures to deal with them; see also chapter 8.

   The more uncertain various aspects of the project are, the larger the risks.

7. **Staffing** At different points in time, the project will require different amounts of personnel, with different skills. The start, duration, amount and expertise of personnel categories are listed under this heading.

8. **Methods and techniques** Under this heading, the methods and techniques to be used during requirements engineering, design, implementation and testing are given. Typically, the way version and configuration control for software components is dealt with is described here too. A large proportion of the technical documentation will be produced during these phases. One thus has to state how this documentation will be taken care of.

   The necessary test environment and test equipment is described. During testing, considerable pressure will normally be put on the test equipment. Therefore, this activity has to be planned carefully. After unit testing, the various components are integrated in some order. The order in which components are integrated and tested has to be stated explicitly. Also, the procedures to be followed during acceptance testing, i.e. the testing under user supervision, have to be given. Testing will be discussed in chapter 13.

9. **Quality assurance** Which organization and procedures will be used to assure that the software being developed meets the quality requirements stated? The many aspects of a Quality Assurance Plan may also be dealt with in a separate document. The topic of quality assurance is discussed in chapter 6.

10. **Work packages** Larger projects must be broken down into activities, manageable pieces that can be allocated to individual team members. Each of these activities has to be identified in the project plan. The hierarchical decomposition of the project is depicted in a work breakdown structure (see also section 8.4).

11. **Resources** During the project, many resources are needed. The hardware, CPU-cycles and tools needed to support the project are listed under this entry. One should also indicate the personnel needed for the various process phases.

12. **Budget and schedule** The total budget for the project has to be allocated to the various activities as indicated in the work breakdown structure. The activities also have to be scheduled in time, e.g. using a PERT chart (see section 8.4). The way in which resources and other expenditures are tracked is also indicated under this heading. The topic of cost and time estimation will be dealt with extensively in chapter 7.

13. **Changes** It has been stated before that changes are inevitable. One has to ensure that these changes are dealt with in an orderly way. One thus needs clear procedures on how proposed changes will be handled. Each proposed change

must be registered and reviewed. When a change request has been approved, its impact (cost) has to be estimated. Finally, the change has to be incorporated into the project. Changes that are entered via the back door lead to badly structured code, insufficient documentation and cost and time overruns. Since changes lead to different versions of both documentation and code, the procedures to be followed in dealing with such changes are often handled in the context of a Configuration Management Plan.

14. **Delivery** The procedures to be followed in handing over the system to the customer must be stated.

The project plan aims to provide a clear picture of the project to both the customers and the project team. If the objectives are not clear, they will not be achieved.

Despite careful planning, surprises will still crop up during the project. However, careful planning early on leads to fewer surprises and makes one less vulnerable to these surprises. The project plan addresses a number of questions which anticipate possible future events. It gives orderly procedures for dealing with those events, so that justifiable decisions can be reached.

2.2 CONTROLLING A SOFTWARE DEVELOPMENT PROJECT

After a project plan has been drawn up and approved, the execution of the project may start. During the project, control has to be exerted along the following dimensions:

- time,
- information,
- organization,
- quality,
- money.

Progress of a software development project (the **time** aspect) is hard to measure. Before the proposed system has been finished, there is only a (large) pile of paper. Utterances such as '90% of the code has been written' should be taken with a pinch of salt. A much too rosy picture of the actual state of affairs is usually given. The phased approach introduced in chapter 1, and its variants, aim at providing the manager with an instrument to measure and control progress. The time needed to build a system is obviously related to the size of the system, and thus to the total manpower required. Larger systems require more time to develop, although we may try to shorten development time by allocating more personnel. Part of the control problem for software development projects is to trade off time against people. Adding more people to shorten development time does not come for free. The more people that are involved, the more time will be needed for coordination and communication. After a certain point, adding more people actually lengthens the development time. Part of the time control problem is phrased in Brooks' Law: 'Adding people to a late project only makes it later.' We will come back to this issue in the chapter on cost estimation.

The **information** that has to be managed, above all, is the documentation. Besides technical and user documentation, this also entails documentation on the project itself. Documentation concerning the project includes such things as: the current state of affairs, changes that have been agreed upon, and decisions that have been made. This type of documentation can best be handled in the context of configuration management.

All members of the development team must understand their role in the team and what is expected of them. It is very important that these expectations are clear to all people involved. Unspoken and unclear expectations lead to situations in which individual team members set their own goals, either consciously or unconsciously. These **organizational** aspects deserve the continuous attention of the project manager. Secondly, the organization of a team and the coordination of the people involved will, at least partly, depend upon characteristics of the project and its environment. This dependence has to be recognized and taken into account when setting up a project team.

The **quality** aspect is gaining in importance. Customers are no longer satisfied with the purely technical solutions offered by computer specialists. They want systems that fit their real needs. The quality requirements for software and its development often conflict with one another. During a project we will have to assess whether or not the quality requirements are being met. This quality assessment has to occur on a regular basis, so that timely actions can be undertaken. Quality is not an add-on feature, it has to be built in.

Controlling expenses (the **money** aspect) largely means controlling labor costs. Though the cost of hardware and tools cannot be ignored, these can usually be estimated fairly precisely early in the project. Moreover, these are usually much less of an issue than personnel costs.

Estimating the cost of software thus means that we must estimate the manpower required to build the software. The manpower needed is very much dependent on the size of the software, for instance measured as the amount of code to be delivered. Many other factors, though, influence this cost or, alternatively, the productivity with which the software can be produced. A well-balanced team with experienced people will be much more productive than a newly-formed team with inexperienced people. Extremely strict quality constraints, such as very high reliability or a very fast response time, may also severely reduce productivity.

A number of models have been proposed that try to quantify the effect of those different cost drivers on the manpower required (see chapter 7).

Software development is a very labor-intensive process. One of our hopes is that better tools and the increased use of those tools will lead to a significant increase in productivity and, consequently, a significant decrease in the cost involved in developing software. A second way, at least in principle, to increase productivity dramatically, is reuse of existing software. Both these topics will be discussed in chapters to follow. As these trends continue, software development starts to become a capital-intensive activity, rather than a labor-intensive one [Weg84].

Continuous assessment of the project with respect to these control aspects is of the utmost importance and will from time to time lead to adjustments in time, cost, organization, information, or quality, or some combination thereof. Project management is a very dynamic activity.

In order to be able to adequately control a project, we need quantitative data which is collected while the project is being executed. For instance, data about errors discovered during unit testing may help us in estimating further test effort needed. Data about the time and effort spent up to a specific point will guide us in re-estimating the schedule and cost. To measure is to know.

These data are also valuable in a post-mortem evaluation of the project. In a post-mortem evaluation we assess the present project in order to improve our performance on projects yet to come: what have we done wrong, what have we learned, what needs to be done differently on the next project?

Unfortunately, in practice very little hard data is ever gathered, let alone retained for later use. Most software development organizations have little insight into what they are doing. They tend to operate in a somewhat chaotic way, especially when facing a crisis. By identifying key factors that affect the controllability of the software development process, we may find ways to improve on it. This topic is further treated in chapter 6, where we discuss the Software Capability Maturity Model.

2.3 SUMMARY

This chapter provides an introduction to the management of software engineering projects.

Before we embark on a software development project, it has to be carefully planned. This planning process results in a document, the project plan, which provides a clear picture of the project to both the customers and the project team.

Once the project plan has been drawn up and the project has started, its execution must be controlled. We identified five entities that require our continuous attention for project control:

- Time: How do we assess progress towards the project's goals? Usually, some phased approach is followed which aims to provide management with a means to measure and control progress.
- Information: How do we handle the vast number of documents that are produced in the course of a project? In particular, maintaining the integrity of the set of documents and handling all change requests require careful procedures.
- Organization: How do we organize the project team and coordinate the activities of team members?
- Quality: How do we define and assess quality requirements for both the development process and the resulting product?
- Money: How do we estimate the cost of a project? These costs are to a large extent determined by the size of the software.

Each of these controlling aspects is further elaborated upon in a separate chapter (chapters 3–7). The various dimensions of project control will then be reconciled in chapter 8.

Exercises

1. In what sense is the phrase 'software development project' a misnomer?
2. What are the major constituents of a project plan?
3. List five dimensions along which a software development project has to be controlled.
4. How may software development become a capital-intensive activity, rather than a labor-intensive one?
5. ♠ Consider a software development project you have been involved in. Did the project have a project plan? Did the project plan address the issues listed in section 2.1? If some of these issues were not addressed, do you think it would have helped the project if they had been?
6. ♡ Do you think quantitative project data are important? In what way can they contribute to project planning?

7. ♠ Consider once again a software development project you have been involved in. To what extent were any environmental issues such as user training and working procedures adequately dealt with in the project?

8. ♡ A program written for personal use imposes rather less stringent requirements than a product that is also to be used by other people. According to [Bro95], the latter may require three times as much effort. Discuss possible reasons for this considerable increase in cost.

3 The Software Life Cycle Revisited

LEARNING OBJECTIVES

- To be aware of a number of generic models to structure the software development process
- To appreciate the pros and cons of these models
- To understand the similarities between software maintenance and software evolution
- To recognize that it is profitable to extend the scope of software management beyond an individual development project
- To be aware of process modeling as a way to describe software development processes explicitly

In chapter 1, we introduced a simple model of the software life cycle. We distinguished several consecutive phases: requirements engineering, design, implementation, testing, maintenance. It was stated that, in practice, one often uses more sophisticated process models. In this chapter we continue this discussion. We will introduce various alternative models to structure the software development process.

Software development projects are often very large projects. A number of people work on such a project for a long time and therefore the whole process needs to be controlled: progress needs to be monitored, people and resources need to be allocated at the right point in time, etc. Earlier on, it was pointed out that progress of a software development project is particularly difficult to measure.

In order to control progress we use a phased development in which a number of clearly identifiable milestones are established between the start and finish of the project. We use a similar mechanism when constructing a house: foundations are laid, the first floor is reached, the house is weatherproofed, and so on. Often, the payment of installments is coupled to reaching those milestones.

In general, the milestones identified in a software development project correspond to the points in time at which certain documents become available:

- after requirements engineering, there is a requirements specification;
- after the design phase there is a (technical) specification of the system;
- after implementation there is a set of programs;
- after testing has been completed there is a test report.

Traditional models for the phased development of software are, to a large extent, 'document-driven'. The pile of paper that is produced in the course of the project guides the development process. This way of viewing the development process does not in general fit reality sufficiently well. In real projects, explicit feedback to earlier phases occurs after errors have been detected, prototyping techniques are applied, and software evolution entails rather more than is phrased in the term 'maintenance'. In the next section we discuss the waterfall model, a well-known variation of the process model introduced in chapter 1. In sections 3.2–3.6 we will discuss several other models that try to dispose of some or all of the drawbacks of the document-driven approach mentioned above.

Evolutionary models take into account that much of what is called maintenance is really evolution. It would then seem natural to explicitly bear this anticipated evolution in mind from the very start. This is usually not the case. Most often, the initial development of a software system is strictly separated from the subsequent maintenance phase. The major goal of a software development project then boils down to delivering a first version of the system to the user. This may result in excessive maintenance costs to make the system fit the real user needs. In section 3.7 it is argued that, in order to be able to properly assess costs and benefits, total life cycle cost rather than just development cost should be our primary focus. Going one step further, we may argue that management should concentrate on product families rather than individual products, thereby granting an incentive both to the building of reusable parts and the reuse of (parts of) existing products when developing new ones.

From all the possible life cycle models we have to choose a particular one for any given project. This involves defining the individual steps and phases, their possible interaction, their deliverables, etc. By using an explicit process modeling language, which may be supported by tools, we may increase our understanding of the software process, we are provided with a handle to improve our control of software development, and we are given a baseline for process improvement. This type of process modeling is discussed in section 3.8.

3.1 THE WATERFALL MODEL

The waterfall model is essentially a slight variation of the model introduced in chapter 1. The waterfall model is generally attributed to Royce [Roy70]. However, a clearly phased approach to the development of software, including iteration and feedback, could already be found in publications from the early 1960s.

The waterfall model particularly expresses the interaction between subsequent phases. Testing software is not an activity which strictly follows the implementation phase. In **each** phase of the software development process, we have to compare the results obtained against those that are required. In all phases, quality has to be assessed and controlled.

In figure 3.1, V & V stands for Verification and Validation. Verification asks if the system meets its requirements (are we building the system right) and thus tries to assess the correctness of the transition to the next phase. Validation asks if the system meets the user's requirements (are we building the right system).

Both the model introduced in chapter 1 and the waterfall model place considerable emphasis on a careful analysis before the system is actually built. We want to prevent putting much energy into constructing a system which later turns out not to satisfy the user's requirements.

We therefore try to identify and tie down the user's requirements as early as possible. These requirements are documented in the requirements specification. On the basis of this document we may verify in subsequent phases whether or not these requirements are being met. Since it is difficult in practice, if not impossible, to completely specify the user's requirements, a regular test should also be carried out with the prospective user. These tests are termed validation. Through these validation

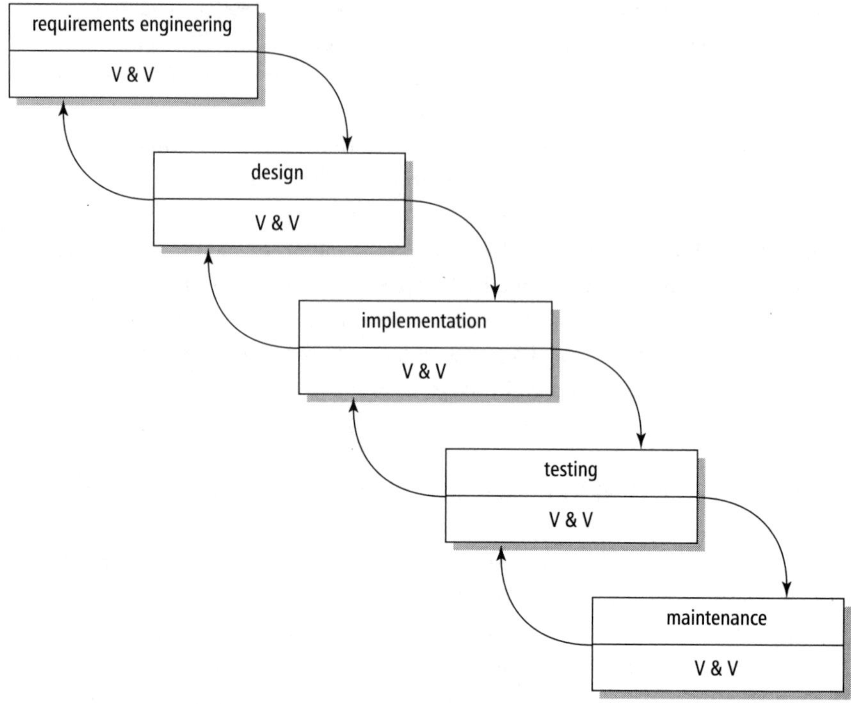

Figure 3.1 The waterfall model

steps we may prevent the system under development diverging from the, possibly incompletely specified, user requirements.

One reason for this type of approach is the fact that, in the past, insufficient tools were available to synthesize software. Design, implementation and testing of software are labor-intensive and time-consuming tasks. With the increasing availability of tools, for example to prototype software or execute specifications, considerable savings on these tasks come within reach. The development of software may then follow a more exploratory road. Potential solutions can be tried out and may be rejected.

McCracken and Jackson compare the waterfall model with a shop where the customer is obliged to give an order upon entering [MJ81]. There is no opportunity to look around, compare prices, change one's mind, or decide upon a different menu for today's dinner. Some things can be ordered by mail, but not all.

The waterfall model of software development, like Escher's waterfall, is unrealistic.

There is ample quantitative evidence that the classical document-driven model has many shortcomings. In many a software development project, the strict sequencing of phases advocated by the waterfall model is not actually obeyed. Figure 3.2 shows the average breakdown of activities across life cycle phases for a number of projects. In this figure, the label 'coding' refers to a phase which encompasses both implementation and unit testing.

Activity	Phase			
	Design	Coding	Integration testing	Acceptance testing
Integration testing	4.7	43.4	26.1	25.8
Coding	6.9	70.3	15.9	6.9
Design	49.2	34.1	10.3	6.4

Figure 3.2 Breakdown of activities across life cycle phases, after [Zel88]

So, for example, only 50% of the design effort was found to occur during the actual design phase, while one-third of the design effort occurs during the coding period. Even worse, over 16% of the design effort takes place after the system is supposed to be finished.

The software design behavior of individual designers may be characterized as an **opportunistic process** [GC88]. Designers move back and forth across levels of abstraction ranging from application domain issues to coding issues. Milestone dates seem to be somewhat arbitrary, and a significant part of the activities crosses phase boundaries.

3.2 PROTOTYPING

It became clear in the preceding section that it is often difficult to get and maintain a sufficiently accurate perception of the requirements of the prospective user. This is not surprising, though. It is in general not sufficient to take the *existing* situation as the one and only starting point for setting up software requirements. An important reason for embarking on a software development project is that one is not pleased with the present situation. What is wanted instead of the present situation is often not easy to determine. This holds even more in cases where we are concerned with a new application and the customer does not know the full possibilities of automation. In such cases, the development of one or more prototypes may help.

Analogies with the development of other products are appealing here. When developing a new car or chip, one will also build one or more prototypes. These prototypes are tested intensively before a real production line is set up. For the development of the push-button telephone, about 2000 prototypes were tested, with variations in form, size and positioning of the buttons, size and weight of the mouthpiece, etc.

It is possible to follow a similar road with software development. In this context a prototype can be described as a working model of (possibly parts of) a software system, which emphasizes certain aspects. There is, however, one big difference between the development of software and the development of physical products such as cars, chips or telephones: in developing physical products, the highest costs are generally incurred during production, when multiple copies of the product are being produced. In software development, making multiple copies of the product is almost free. If we were to follow the hardware approach to prototyping in software development, and produce a prototype with the same functionality as the final product, we would in fact develop an operational system, with correspondingly high costs. It does not then seem plausible to start all over again and develop the 'real' system in a different way.

Using the definition given above and with the aim of developing a software prototype relatively cheaply, it is important that certain aspects are emphasized. This can be achieved through, for example:

- the use of very high-level languages, in which an executable version can be created quickly. This executable but probably rather inefficient version can be used to test the usability of the proposed system;

- the development of a system with less functionality, in particular as regards quality attributes such as speed and robustness.

One of the main difficulties for users is to express their requirements precisely. It is natural to try to clarify these through prototyping. This can be achieved by developing the user interface quickly. The prospective user may then work with a system that contains the interaction component but not, or to a much lesser extent, the software that actually processes the input. In this way, the user may get a good impression of what the future system will provide him with, **before** large investments are made to realize the system. Prototyping thus becomes a tool for requirements engineering. This is illustrated graphically in figure 3.3.

This figure shows that the various phases are gone through in two ways. The left-hand side of the figure is concerned with the prototyping stages. The iteration corresponds to the user-validation process, whereby new or changed requirements trigger the next cycle. The right-hand side concerns the actual production of the operational system. The difference between the two branches is that, by using different

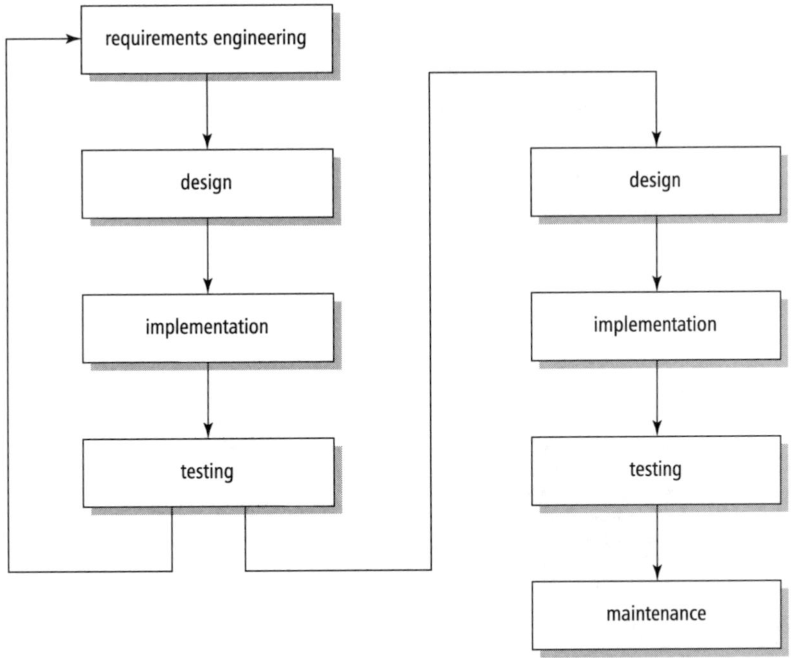

Figure 3.3 Prototyping as a tool for requirements engineering

techniques and tools, the left-hand side can be traversed much more quickly and against much lower costs.

In figure 3.3, the prototyping phases and the later production phases have been clearly separated. This is appropriate, since we will use different techniques during the actual production phase, put much more emphasis on documentation, and so on. It is even feasible not to carry over the software product from the prototyping phases to the actual production phase, but to explicitly throw it away after the prototyping phases have come to an end. This is known as *throwaway prototyping*. It is not necessary to do so, though. The prototype may evolve to the final product. The user starts by formulating the raw requirements, on the basis of which a first version of the system is produced. The user starts to work with this system, which leads to new, or changed, requirements. The next version is then developed. After a number of such iterations, the user is satisfied and the last version developed is the product to be delivered. This is known as *evolutionary prototyping*. In practice, evolutionary prototyping is used much more often than throwaway prototyping. Discarding a (partly) working system is a hurdle which is not easily taken.

Both throwaway and evolutionary prototyping entail advantages and disadvantages. Figure 3.4 summarizes the pattern of pros and cons that emerges in case studies that describe experiences of applying a prototyping approach. Note that some properties can be influenced in both a positive and a negative way. Depending on circumstances, either or both may occur in an actual project. For example, the maintenance cost may go down because user needs are better satisfied. On the other hand, the maintenance cost may go up because development has been done in a quick and dirty way.

Advantages

- The resulting system is easier to use
- User needs are better accommodated
- The resulting system has fewer features
- Problems are detected earlier
- The design is of higher quality
- The resulting system is easier to maintain
- The development incurs less effort

Disadvantages

- The resulting system has more features
- The performance of the resulting system is worse
- The design is of lesser quality
- The resulting system is harder to maintain
- The prototyping approach requires more experienced team members

Figure 3.4 Pros and cons of prototyping

Users as well as developers are generally more positive about systems developed using a prototyping approach. This positive attitude concerns both the development process and the resulting product. Users feel more involved in the development process and have fewer conflicts with the designers. The extensive user involvement results in systems which better satisfy user needs.

Since users need not express all their requirements up front in a prototyping approach, there is less tendency to ask for bells and whistles. As a consequence, the end result is a leaner system whose functionality closer matches the real user requirements. If users are shown a working system at an early stage and are given the opportunity to try it out, chances are that problems are detected at an early stage as well. This prevents a waste of manpower which would otherwise be needed to redo part of the work. If users are in a position to influence and modify the design, the system features will better reflect their requirements and the system will be easier to use.

The use of special-purpose prototyping tools or languages makes it easy to add features. Since the time interval between successive versions of the prototype is small, users may think that it is easy to realize new features and may specify additional requirements. Both these effects may result in systems having more, rather than fewer, features.

Prototyping involves iterative design steps and, because of the repeated attention to the design, its quality may increase. Since it is known a priori that the design will evolve during subsequent prototyping steps, greater attention will be given to quality factors such as flexibility and modularity and, as a result, design quality may improve as well. In throwaway prototyping, the quality of the final design is often higher because of the learning experience of the prototyping steps. Also, this final design step is hardly, if at all, patched up because of rework actions. Because of these aspects, the resulting systems are often found to be easier to maintain as well.

On the other hand, prototyping generally does not enforce strict design and development standards. If we are concerned with a short development time, certain necessary activities will receive less attention. The chances are that documentation is sacrificed for speed. Because of additions resulting from frequent rework steps, the design quality of an evolutionary prototype may deteriorate. For that reason too, the resulting systems are less maintainable. Especially in evolutionary prototypes, the robustness of the system will often be less than is customary with a more traditional approach. In these systems, performance tends to be worse because attention is focused on functionality and performance measures are either not taken at all or at a point in time at which they have become too difficult to realize.

It is generally felt that prototyping projects require an experienced team. Prototyping involves making far-reaching design decisions, especially during early iterations. In each iteration, user requests have to be weighed, both mutually and against the ease and cost of their realization. Inexperienced team members are more likely to make poor choices, thereby seriously threatening the success of a prototyping effort.

From this discussion, we may gather the following recommendations for the use of prototyping techniques:

- prototyping is particularly useful in situations where the user requirements are unclear or ambiguous. Prototyping seems a good way to clarify those requirements;

- prototyping is also particularly useful for systems with a considerable emphasis on the user interface and which show a high degree of user interaction;

- users and designers must be well aware of the prototyping approach and its pitfalls. Users should realize that changing software is not all that easy. Users should also realize that a prototype is a prototype and not a production-quality system. Designers should be aware of the characteristics of prototyping projects and not become frustrated by frequent changes in user requirements;

- prototyping must also be planned and controlled. We must impose limits on the number of iterations. We must establish explicit procedures for documenting and testing prototypes. The positive aspects of the traditional approach, which make the process manageable and controllable, should also be applied in this case.

By taking appropriate counter-measures, the potential disadvantages of prototyping can be guarded against. Prototyping is then a viable alternative process model for many a software development project.

3.3 INCREMENTAL DEVELOPMENT

In the preceding section, we discussed a way of using prototypes for which the final system is the last of a series of prototypes. Under careful management control in order to ensure convergence, the next version is planned to accommodate new or changed user requirements. There is another way to work towards the final system in a number of iterations.

We proceed incrementally. The functionality of the system is produced and delivered to the customer in small increments. Starting from the existing situation we proceed towards the desired situation in a number of (small) steps. In each of these steps, the phased approach that we know from the waterfall model, is employed.

Developing software this way avoids the 'Big Bang' effect, i.e. for a long time nothing happens and then, suddenly, there is a completely new situation. Instead of building software, the software grows. With this incremental approach, the user is closely involved in planning the next step. Redirecting the project becomes easier since we may incorporate changed circumstances more quickly.

Incremental development can also be used to fight the 'overfunctionality' syndrome. Since users find it difficult to formulate their real needs, they tend to demand too much. Lacking the necessary knowledge of the malleability of software and its development process, they may be inclined to think that everything can be achieved. As a consequence, essential features appear next to bells and whistles in the list of requirements. Analysts are not able to distinguish one from the other, nor are they able to accurately estimate the effort required to implement individual features. Chances then are that much effort is spent on realizing features that are not really needed. As a result, many of today's systems offer a rich functionality, yet are at the same time ill-suited for the task at hand. For one thing, these systems are difficult to use simply because of the complexity incurred by their rich functionality.

With the incremental approach, attention is first focused on the essential features. Additional functionality is only included if and when it is needed. Systems thus developed tend to be leaner and yet provide sufficient support to their users.

Incremental development is strongly advocated in [Gil88]. It is doubtful whether the time increment advocated by Gilb, up to a maximum of a few weeks, is always reasonable. But the advantages of incremental development are considerable even with different time increments. Surprises that lurk within the traditional approach and that pose considerable difficulties on the management side of software development projects can be greatly diminished when software is developed and delivered incrementally.

3.4 RAPID APPLICATION DEVELOPMENT

Rapid Application Development (RAD) has a lot in common with other iterative development process models. It emphasizes user involvement, prototyping, reuse, the use of automated tools, and small development teams. In addition to that, it employs the notion of a *time box*, a fixed time frame within which activities are done. In most development models, a set of requirements is fixed and then the project attempts to fulfill these requirements within some estimated period of time. Within RAD, the time frame is decided upon first and then the project tries to realize the requested functionality within that time frame. If it turns out that not all of the functionality can be realized within the time frame, some of the functionality is sacrificed. The agreed deadline however is immovable.

The RAD life cycle consists of four phases:

- requirements planning,
- user design,
- construction,
- cutover.

The requirements planning and user design phases have much in common and may be combined for smaller projects. Together, they typically take less than two months. The main techniques used in these phases are known as Joint Requirements Planning (JRP) and Joint Application Design (JAD). Both these techniques make heavy use of workshops in which the developers and the prospective users work *together* (hence the adjective *Joint*).

The goal of the JRP workshop is to get the requirements right the first time. For that reason, it is imperative that the key players, i.e. the end users of the system, be present. During the JRP workshop too, requirements are prioritized, since it is likely that not all of them will be implemented in the first version of the system. This requirement prioritization is known as *triage*. Triage usually means a process used on the battlefield and in emergency rooms to sort injured people into groups based on their need for or likely benefit from immediate medical treatment. In RAD, the triage process is used to make sure that the most important requirements are addressed first.

It is customary to have two JAD workshops during the design phase. Again, the end users play an essential role in these workshops. The first JAD workshop yields an initial design of the system. The developers then construct a prototype, to be experimented with by the users. This prototype is evaluated during the second JAD workshop, improvements are decided upon, and the design is finalized.

The system is constructed by a so-called SWAT team, a highly skilled team of about four people. SWAT stands for Skilled With Advanced Tools (see also chapter 5). The SWAT team becomes involved after the first JAD workshop. The team typically does its job in less than two months. In order to be able to do so, heavy use is made of tools and existing components are reused whenever feasible. Within the time allotted (the time box), the SWAT team constructs a series of evolutionary prototypes. Developers and users work closely together during this process. Each prototype is reviewed by the users and the review sessions result in requests for enhanced or changed functionality. The agreed upon time frame is *not* exceeded. If necessary, some of the functionality is sacrificed instead.

For a SWAT team to operate successfully, and deliver a good result in a very short time span, it has to feel a definite 'ownership' of the problem to be addressed. In such a situation, it is not very helpful if time estimates and deadlines are fixed by some manager. Instead, the SWAT team itself estimates the time, the SWAT team decides upon the number and length of the time boxes, and the SWAT team decides which functionality to implement in each iteration.

During the cutover phase, the final testing of the system takes place, users are trained, and the system is installed.

There are many variations on the RAD process model described above. For example, it is possible to have explicit time boxes for the construction of each of the intermediate prototypes as well. It is also possible to have JRP or JAD sessions after each prototyping cycle. The main ingredients, however, remain: prototyping, considerable user involvement, SWAT teams, and time boxes.

JRP and JAD have much in common with a design method known as Participatory Design (PD), or the Scandinavian school of software development. Both emphasize end-user involvement. They differ, however, in their goals. User involvement in JRP and JAD is primarily intended to speed up the process of producing the right system. User involvement in PD is motivated by a strong interest in the social context of the work environment.

3.5 INTERMEZZO: MAINTENANCE OR EVOLUTION

Old payroll programs never die;
they just get fat around the middle
Robert Granholm (Datamation, 1971)

In chapter 1, it was pointed out that a considerable maintenance effort is inevitable. Each maintenance task, whether it concerns repairing an error or adapting a system to new user requirements, in principle entails all aspects of the initial development cycle. During maintenance, we also have to analyze the problem and conceive a design which is subsequently implemented and tested.

The first big difference is that these changes are being made to an existing product. However, during initial development we often do not start from scratch either. If an existing organization decides to automate its order administration, the system may have to interface with already existing systems for, say, stock administration and bookkeeping. Thus, maintenance activities differ in degrees from initial development, rather than fundamentally. This relative difference is even more apparent when the system is prototyped or developed incrementally.

The second main difference, time pressure, has a much larger impact. Time pressure is most strongly felt when repairing errors, for then it is quite possible that certain parts of the organization have to shut down because the software is not operational. In such cases, we have to work against time to identify and repair the errors. Often one patches the code and skips a thorough analysis and design step. The structure of the system tends to suffer from such patches. The system's entropy increases, which hampers later maintenance activities. Worse still, the system's documentation may not be updated. Software and the corresponding documentation then grow apart, which will again hamper future maintenance activities. A more elaborate discussion of maintenance issues is given in chapter 14.

Lehman and Belady [LB85] have extensively studied the dynamics of software systems that need to be maintained and grow in size. Based on those quantitative studies, they formulated the following laws of software evolution (explained below):

1. **Law of continuing change** A system that is being used undergoes continuous change, until it is judged more cost-effective to restructure the system or replace it by a completely new version.

2. **Law of increasing complexity** A program that is changed becomes less and less structured (the entropy increases) and thus becomes more complex. One has to invest extra effort in order to avoid increasing complexity.

3. **Law of program evolution** The growth rate of global system attributes may seem locally stochastic, but is in fact self-regulating with statistically determinable trends.

4. **Law of invariant work rate** The global progress in software development projects is statistically invariant.

5. **Law of incremental growth limit** A system develops a characteristic growth increment. When this increment is exceeded, problems concerning quality and usage will result.

In an early publication, Lehman compares the growth of software systems with that of cities and bureaucracies [Leh74]. He makes a distinction between progressive and anti-regressive activities in software development. Lehman considers this model also applicable to socio-economic systems. In a city, for instance, progressive activities contribute to an increase in the living standard or quality of life. Anti-regressive activities, such as garbage collection, serve to maintain the status quo. If insufficient attention is paid to those anti-regressive activities, decline will set in. Anti-regressive activities often are not interesting, politically speaking. It is an investment in the future, which had better be left to others. (The same phenomenon can be observed in the growth of the chemical industry and the resulting pollution problems.)

According to Lehman, the same kinds of activity occur within a software development project. Generating new code and changing existing code are progressive activities. These are interesting, challenging and rewarding activities. They provide the user with new or better functionality. Writing documentation, improving the structure of the code, and maintaining good communication between the people involved are anti-regressive activities. Neglecting these activities may not be harmful in the short term, but it certainly will be in the long term. For each system, we have to look for a proper balance between both kinds of activity.

The working of the third law (the law of program evolution) can be illustrated by means of figure 3.5 which depicts the growth pattern of system attributes over time. System attributes include the length (measured in lines of code), the number of modules, the number of user-callable functions, etc. The time axis may denote the release number, the number of months the system is operational, or the like. (The actual data studied by Lehman concern the relation between the number of modules and the release number of the OS360 operating system.)

The relation depicted in figure 3.5 is almost linear. The ripples in the figure are very regular as well. Periods of more than linear growth alternate with periods of less than linear growth. Lehman explains the more than linear growth by pointing at the pressure from users to get more functionality as fast as possible. The developers or maintainers tend to bend under this pressure. As a consequence, one uses tricks and shortcuts in the code, documentation lags behind, errors are introduced and the system is insufficiently tested. After a while, more attention is paid to anti-regressive activities: code needs to be restructured and documentation brought up to date before further growth is possible. The two kinds of activity stabilize over time.

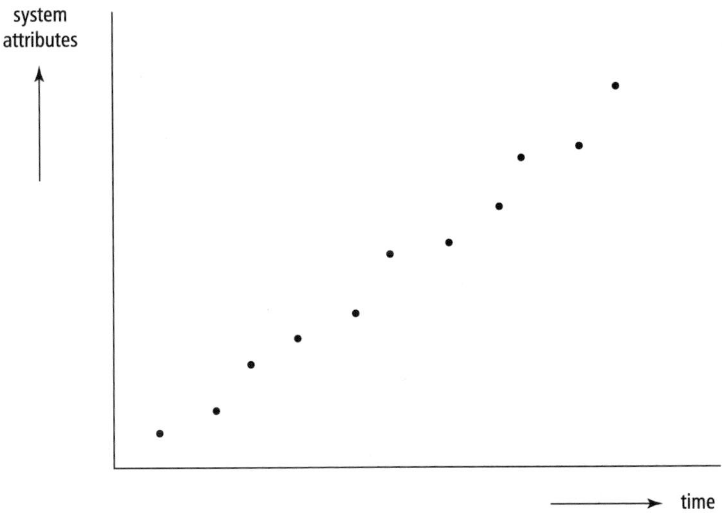

Figure 3.5 Growth of system attributes over time

The fourth law (the law of invariant work rate) seems rather surprising at first sight. Lehman and Belady found that such things as manpower and other resources do not correlate at all to the speed with which systems grow or change. Apparently, large systems are in some sort of saturated state. More people can be kept at work but, in the long run, they have no perceived impact on the evolution of the system.

More than average growth in some version of a system was, in Lehman and Belady's observations, almost always followed by a less than average growth in the next version (as expressed in the fifth law – the law of incremental growth limit). In one of the systems they investigated, a substantially higher growth inevitably led to problems: lower reliability, higher costs, etc. Here too, a self-regulating feedback was observed.

From the preceding discussion, it follows that we have to be alert during maintenance. We have to preserve quality at each and every step. We may try to preclude the dangers sketched above by explicitly engaging ourselves in the various development phases during maintenance. The cyclic process followed during initial development then occurs during maintenance too. As with prototyping, the time needed to go through the complete cycle will in general be much shorter than during initial development. This way of looking at maintenance closely resembles the evolutionary view of software development. Realizing the first version of a software system is only the first step. True enough, this first step is more costly than most steps that follow, but it is not fundamentally different. In chapter 1 we already noticed that such an approach may also have positive effects on the social and organizational environment in which software development takes place.

The waterfall model gives us a *static* view of the system to be developed. Reality is different. In developing software, and in particular during maintenance, we are concerned with an evolving system. As remarked before: software is not built, it grows.

3.6 THE SPIRAL MODEL

In the preceding sections we noticed that it is helpful to view software development as a cyclic process. Each cycle includes the same phases: requirements engineering, design, implementation and testing. Some of those cycles serve to get a firmer grasp of user requirements (prototyping), other cycles serve to adapt an existing operational system (maintenance).

If we look somewhat more closely at the main cycle of a software development effort, we notice that phases are not always executed strictly sequentially. It may be that the whole cycle is first traversed in order to build part of the system and, once this part is finished, the same cycle is gone through for other parts of the system. With the incremental approach, this is the intention from the beginning.

During the development of a software system, a number of problems have to be solved. In solving a problem, the most difficult parts are often tackled first, or the parts that have the highest risks with respect to a successful completion of the project.

Following this line of thought, Boehm suggests a spiral model of the software development process, in which each convolution of the spiral gives rise to the following activities [Boe88]:

- identify the sub-problem which has the highest associated risk;

- find a solution for that problem.

The various process models discussed before can be coupled with Boehm's spiral model in a natural way (see figure 3.6):

- If obtaining the proper set of user requirements is seen as the area with highest risk, follow the spiral a few times around to solve this sub-problem (i.e., prototype).

- If, starting from a precise requirements specification, the main question is to obtain a robust and well-documented system, follow the spiral once, using the traditional process model with its phases and corresponding milestones as intermediate steps.

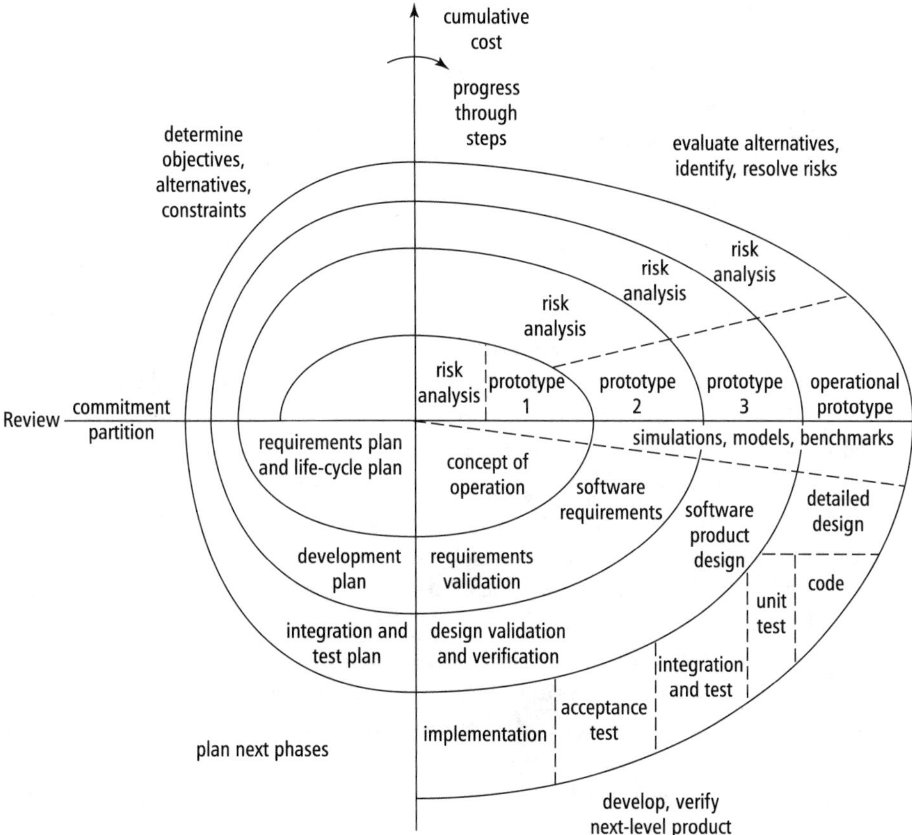

Figure 3.6 The spiral model (*Source: B.W. Boehm, A spiral model of software development and enhancement*, IEEE Computer **21**, *5 (1988) ©1988 IEEE*)

- If developing software incrementally, track the spiral a number of times, once for each increment.
- During maintenance, the reported errors or changing requirements are triggers to track the spiral.

Viewed this way, the spiral model subsumes the other process models discussed so far.

3.7 TOWARDS A SOFTWARE FACTORY

Most software development organizations exhibit a fairly strict separation between initial development and subsequent maintenance of a product. A software development project ends as soon as the product is delivered to the clients. The subsequent evolution of the product is left to the maintenance department. As a consequence, the major goal of the development team is to get the product accepted.

In its worst form, quality, documentation, and even functionality may get sacrificed in order to deliver something to the user. Many necessary activities get deferred to the maintenance phase. Even in a more optimistic scenario, there is no real incentive for the development team to produce a system that can be easily maintained and adapted to changing requirements. That is simply not what they are being paid for.

To jump off this bandwagon, assessment of a software product and its development should not be limited to the initial development phases. It should instead extend over its total life cycle. We should be concerned with *product* management rather than project management. Product management assesses the user-based quality aspects ('fitness-for-use'), costs and benefits of a product from its inception to the very end of its life. In particular, the effort required to produce the initial system is not the only criterion that counts.

Going a step further, we may consider managing the development of a family of (similar) products. When similar products are developed, we may hope to reuse elements from earlier products during the development of new products. Such is not the habit in software development though. In many an organization there is no incentive to reuse elements (code, design, or any other artifact) from another system since, again, that is not what we are being paid for. Similarly, there is no incentive to produce reusable elements, since the present project is all that counts.

As an alternative, we may conceive of the notion of a software factory.[1] The assets of a software factory are made up of the combined knowledge of its workers and its set of semi-products. When a new product is required, it is (mostly) built out of existing semi-products. The goal of the software factory is to optimize its ability to deliver products. It does so by increasing the combined knowledge of its workers and its set of semi-products.

Applied to the development of software products, the software factory paradigm emphasizes the development of reusable elements, ranging from individual routines to (domain-specific) software architectures and frameworks that serve as fill-in-the-blanks skeleton systems. To make this a conceivable notion, we need

[1] The notion of a software factory is used here to emphasize one factory-like concept: reusability across products. The label is also often associated with Japanese efforts to improve software development productivity through standardization, division of labor, mechanization and automation, and the production of interchangeable (i.e. reusable) parts.

to extend management responsibility to cover a family of products rather than an individual product.

Building reusable elements requires extra effort which is not paid back until those elements are indeed reused. It not only requires different cost-estimating procedures and development paradigms, but also a different attitude amongst developers. One way to engender this is to reward people both for producing reusable elements and for reusing elements produced by someone else.

A more elaborate discussion of software reusability is given in chapter 17. Software architectures and frameworks are discussed in chapter 10. At the technical level, the shift from individual projects to product families is supported by the paradigm of object-oriented software development (see chapter 12).

3.8 PROCESS MODELING

Without a repeatable process, the only repeatable results you are likely to produce are errors.
[MSG96]

In the 1980s, Osterweil launched the idea of describing software development processes as programs. These **process programs** are written in a **process programming language**. Like other programming languages, process programming languages have a rigorously defined syntax and semantics. As a simple example, consider the Pascal-like description of a review process in figure 3.7.[2] It describes the consecutive steps of a review process. The process has two inputs: the document to be reviewed and some number which serves as a threshold. The routine returns a boolean indicating whether or not another review is to be scheduled.

```
function review (document, threshold): boolean;
begin prepare-review;
    hold-review (document, no-of-problems);
    make-report;
    return no-of-problems < threshold
end review;
```

Figure 3.7 A process program for the review process

[2]In a review, a document (such as piece of code or a design) is first studied individually by a couple of reviewers. The problems found are then discussed by the reviewers and the author of the document (see section 13.4.2).

In figure 3.7, the review process is described in terms of the successive activities to be performed: first, the review is prepared, then the meeting is held, and finally a report is made. We may also describe the process in terms of the states it can be in. After the preparation activities (distribution of the document amongst participants, scheduling of a meeting, and the like), the document is ready to be reviewed. After the meeting has been held, a report can be written. And after the report has been written, further steps can be taken. Figure 3.8 describes the review process in terms of states and transitions between states. The box labeled review process describes the review process proper. The inputs and outputs of the process are indicated by arrows leading into and out of the box. This figure uses the UML notation for state diagrams (a variant of the state transition diagram); see section 12.2.2.

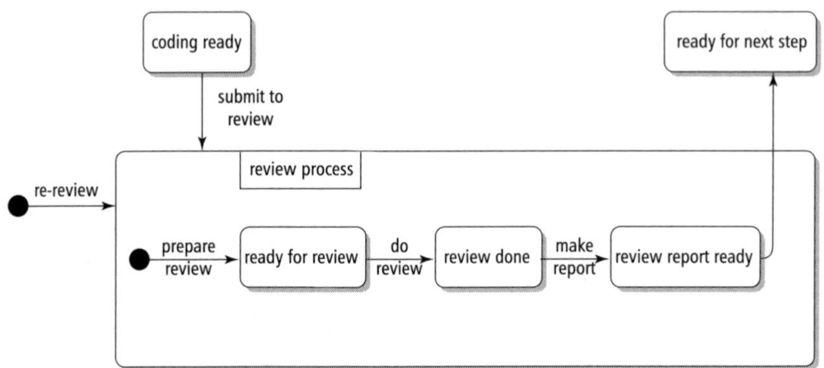

Figure 3.8 State transition diagram of the review process

Petri nets provide yet another formalism to describe process models. Figure 3.9 gives a Petri net view of the review process. A Petri net is a directed graph with two types of node: places and transitions. A place is depicted as a circle. It denotes a (partial) state of the system. A place is either marked or unmarked. In figure 3.9, the place code ready is marked, but review scheduled is not. A transition is depicted by a straight line. A transition receives input from one or more places, and delivers output to one or more places. These inputs and outputs are denoted by arrows leading to and from a transition. A transition denotes an activity which can be performed (in Petri net terminology, 'fired') if all of its input places are marked. Places can thus be thought of as preconditions for activities. In figure 3.9, the review meeting cannot be held, since it has not been scheduled yet. Once it has been scheduled, the corresponding place is marked and the transition can be fired. The markings are then removed from all of the input places and all of the output places are marked instead.

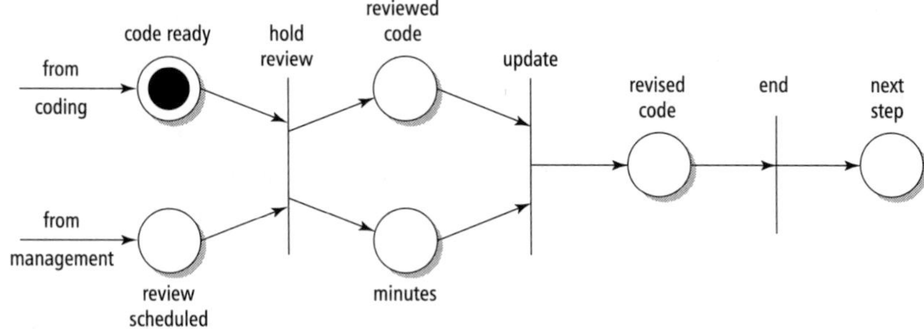

Figure 3.9 Petri net view of the review process

Petri nets are an attractive modeling technique for processes, since they allow a certain amount of nondeterminism and parallellism. For example, the process in figure 3.9 does not specify the order in which coding and scheduling activities are to be performed. They may go on in parallel; synchronization takes place when both are finished.

A precise description of the software process, be it in a programming-language notation, a graphical notation, or otherwise, serves three main purposes:

- It facilitates understanding and communication. In a software development project, people have to work together. They thus need to have a shared view of the processes to be carried out and the roles they are to play in those processes. Either model of the review process given above can be used for this purpose.

- It supports process management and improvement. A precise description of activities to be performed can be used by project management to assign tasks and to keep track of who is doing what. If the software development process is to be improved, you first have to know what the current process is, i.e. it has to be modeled.

- It may serve as a basis for automated support. This automated support may guide or enforce the order in which tasks are being carried out. For instance, a reviewer may automatically be sent a message indicating that a certain piece of code is ready for review as soon as its author releases that code. The automated support may also be used to monitor and track progress, collect process information and metrics, and so on.

The description of the review process in figure 3.7 is very deterministic. It can be completely automated and executed without human intervention. In general, the work that is being modeled will be carried out by both humans and machines. The neutral term **enactment** is used to denote the execution of the process by either humans or machines. Support for process enactment is often combined with support for configuration management (see section 4.1).

Though the precise modeling of the software process has definite advantages, the resulting process formality, or even rigidity, holds certain dangers and limitations as well:

- Many aspects of the software development process are heuristic or creative in nature and do not lend themselves to an algorithmic description. For example, the actual debugging or design processes will be quite difficult to capture in a process model.

- A process model is a model and, thus, a simplification of reality. For example, the above models of the review process do not specify what to do if the minutes of the meeting are not delivered or the review is not held because the author of the code is on sick-leave, and so on.

- Process models often focus on the transformation of artifacts, such as code, a requirements specification, or a test plan. The progression of stages through which the artifact evolves then gets confused with the organization of the processes through which people actually develop those artifacts. This argument was used earlier when we criticized the waterfall model. It is supported by the studies of Zelkowitz and Guindon reported in section 3.1. Parnas uses similar arguments when he criticizes the view that the software design process is a rational one [PC87].

- Processes that do not directly transform artifacts tend to be ignored (for example, learning the application domain, handling requirements that fluctuate or conflict, and dealing with breakdowns in communication or coordination [CKI88].

- Processes are treated as discrete rather than continuous in time (i.e. each project invokes a separate process). This view inhibits the transfer of knowledge between projects, as was discussed in the previous section.

Process modeling receives a lot of attention in the research literature. It is indicative of the need for more formal approaches to the description of the software process. The current trend in process modeling research is aimed at providing developers with computer guidance and assistance, rather than trying to fully automate the process. Such precise descriptions provide a basis for a range of support functions, ranging from the enactment of design steps to agenda management.

3.9 SUMMARY

In this chapter we have addressed the software life cycle again. There are quite a few arguments against the strict sequential ordering of phases as discussed in chapter 1. The traditional approach is, to a large extent, document-driven. On the way from start to finish a number of milestones are identified. Reaching those milestones is determined by the availability of certain documents. These documents then play a key role in controlling the development process.

Several other development techniques, such as prototyping, incremental development, Rapid Application Development, software evolution, as well as daily practice, hardly fit this model. A more differentiated view of the software development process is needed. An interesting integrating model is offered by Boehm's spiral model.

In most organizations, a fairly strict separation is found between software development and software maintenance. In section 3.7 we argued that software management should be concerned with the complete life cycle of a product. Going a step further, we may give an incentive to the development of reusable elements by extending the scope of management responsibility to cover a range of products. The current interest in software architectures and frameworks is indicative of this trend.

Finally, we introduced the notion of process modeling, which is aimed at describing the software development process in a precise and unambiguous way. Such descriptions are not intended to fully replace human activities, but rather to support them.

3.10 FURTHER READING

The waterfall model is generally attributed to Royce [Roy70] and became well known through [Boe76]. However, a clearly phased approach to the development of software, including iteration and feedback, can already be found in earlier publications: [Ben83] and [Hos61].

Advantages and disadvantages of prototyping, based on an analysis of 22 published case studies and 17 first-hand accounts, are given in [GB94]. [VC97] address the different views held by analysts and managers of the pros and cons of prototyping.

For a very elaborate discussion of RAD, see [Mar91]. Participatory Design is described in [FMR+89]. [CAC93a] is a special issue on Participatory Design. It contains articles describing experiences with Participatory Design, as well as a comparison of RAD and Participatory Design.

A factory-like view of software development was suggested at the very first conference on Software Engineering [McI68]. The term 'software factory' is also often associated with Japanese efforts to improve software development productivity [Cus89].

[Ost87] launched the idea of describing software development processes as programs. Critical appraisals of this view are given in [Leh87], [CKSI87] and [Cur89]. The current trends in software process modeling are described in [FW96].

Exercises

1. Describe the waterfall model of software development.

2. Describe the Rapid Application Development (RAD) approach to software development.

3. Discuss the main differences between prototyping and incremental development.

4. Discuss the main differences between incremental development and RAD.

5. Discuss the law of continuing change.

6. How does the spiral model subsume prototyping, incremental development, and the waterfall model?

7. What is a software factory?

8. What is the main purpose of having an explicit description of the software development process in a process model?

9. What is process enactment?

10. ♠ Suppose you are involved in a large project concerning the development of a patient planning system for a hospital. You may opt for one of two strategies. The first strategy is to start with a thorough analysis of user requirements, after which the system is built according to these requirements. The second strategy starts with a less complete requirements analysis phase, after which a pilot version is developed. This pilot version is installed in a few small departments. Further development of the system is guided by the experience gained in working with the pilot version. Discuss the pros and cons of both strategies. Which strategy do you favor?

11. Discuss the relative merits of throwaway prototyping as a means to elicit the 'true' user requirements and prototyping as an evolutionary development method.

12. In what ways may the notion of a software factory impact the structure of the software development process?

13. ♡ Software maintenance increases system entropy. Discuss possible ways to counteract this effect.

14. ♡ One of the reasons for using document-driven approaches in software development projects is that the documents provide some measure of project progress. Do you think this measure is adequate? Can you think of better ways to measure progress?

15. ♡ Discuss the differences between RAD and Participatory Design (see also [CWG93]).

16. ♠ Describe the requirements engineering process depicted in figure 9.1 in a notation like a programming language. Be as precise as possible. Discuss the advantages and limitations of the resulting process description.

17. ♠ Describe the requirements engineering process depicted in figure 9.1 in a state transition diagram. Discuss the advantages and limitations of the resulting process description.

4 Configuration Management

LEARNING OBJECTIVES

- To understand the main tasks and responsibilities of software configuration management
- To be aware of the contents of a configuration management plan
- To appreciate the interplay between the role of configuration management in software development and the capabilities of supporting tools

Careful procedures are needed to manage the vast number of elements (source code modules, documentation, change requests, etc.) that are created and updated over the lifetime of a large software system. This is called **configuration management**.

In the course of a software development project, quite a few documents are produced. These documents are also changed from time to time. Errors have to be corrected, change requests have to be taken care of, etc. Thus, at each point in time during a project, different versions of the same document may exist in parallel.

Often too, a software system itself is not monolithic. Software systems exist in different versions or configurations. Different versions come about when changes are implemented after the system has been delivered to the customer. From time to time, the customer is then confronted with a new release. Different versions of components of a system may also exist during development. For instance, if a change request has been approved, a programmer may be implementing that change by rewriting one or more components. Another programmer, however, may still be using the previous version of those same components.

Different configurations also come about if a set of components may be assembled into a system in more than one way. Take, for example, the system called ACK, the Amsterdam Compiler Kit [TvSKS83]. ACK consists of a set of programs to develop compilers for ALGOL-like languages. Important components of ACK are:

- front ends for languages such as Pascal, C, or Modula-2. A front end for language X will translate programs in that language into the universal intermediate code EM;
- different EM-optimizers;
- back ends, which translate EM-code to assembler-code for a variety of real machines.

A compiler is then obtained by selecting a front end for a specific language, a back end for a specific machine and, optionally, one or more optimizers. Each compiler is a configuration, a certain combination of elements from the ACK system.

The key tasks of configuration management are discussed in section 4.1. A Configuration Management Plan lays down the procedures that describe how to approach configuration management. The contents of this document are discussed in section 4.2. Configuration management is often supported by tools. The discussion of those tools is largely postponed until chapter 19.

4.1 TASKS AND RESPONSIBILITIES

Configuration management is concerned with the management of all artifacts produced in the course of a software development project. Though configuration management also plays a role during the operational phase of a system, when different combinations of components can be assembled into one system and new releases of a system are generated, the discussion below centers around the role of configuration management during system development.

We will for the moment assume that, at any point in time, there is one official version of the complete set of documents related to the project. This is called the **baseline**. A baseline is 'a specification or product that has been formally reviewed and agreed upon, that thereafter serves as the basis for further development, and that can be changed only through formal change control procedures' [IEE90a]. Thus, the baseline is the shared project database, containing all approved items. The baseline may or may not be stored in a real database and supported by tools to assist in retrieving and updating its elements. The items contained in the baseline are the **configuration items**. A configuration item is 'an aggregation of hardware, software, or both, that is designated for configuration management and treated as a single entity in the configuration management process' [IEE90a]. Possible configuration items are:

- source code modules,
- object code modules,
- the requirements specification,
- the design documentation,
- the test plan,
- test cases,
- test results,
- the user manual.

At some point in time, the baseline will contain a requirements specification. As time goes on, elements will be added: design documents, code modules, test reports, etc. A major task of configuration management is to maintain the integrity of this set of artifacts.

This is especially important if changes are to be incorporated. Suppose that, during testing, a major flaw in some module is discovered. We then have to retrace our steps and correct not only that code module but also the corresponding design documents, and possibly even the requirements specification. This may affect work being done by other people still using the old version. Worse still, someone else may wish to make changes to the very same module at the same time. Configuration management takes care of controlling the release and change of these items throughout the software life cycle.

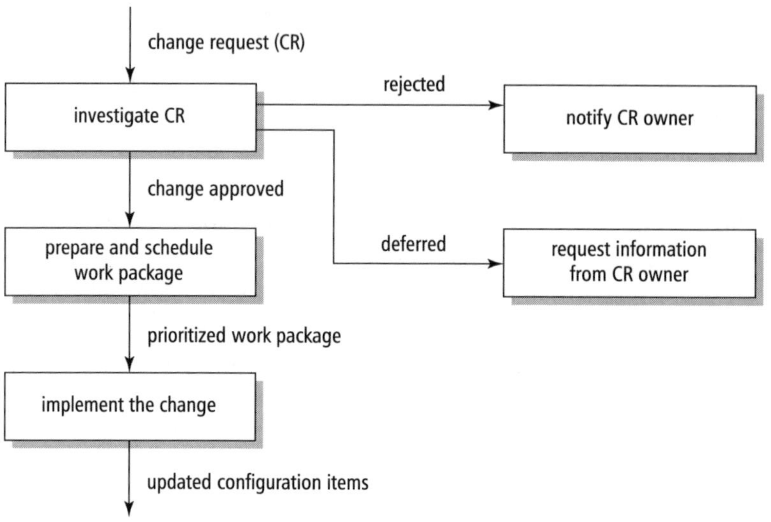

Figure 4.1 Workflow of a change request

The way to go about this is to have one shared library or database that contains all approved items, the so-called baseline. Adding an item to this database, or changing an item, is subject to a formal approval scheme. For larger projects, this is the responsibility of a separate body, the Configuration (or Change) Control Board (CCB). The CCB ensures that any change to the baseline is properly authorized and executed. The CCB is staffed with people from the various parties involved in the project, such as development, testing, and quality assurance.

Any proposed change to the baseline is called a change request. A change request may concern an error found in some code module, a discrepancy found between a design document and its implementation, an enhancement caused by changed user requirements, etc. A change request is handled as follows (see also figure 4.1):

- The proposed change is submitted to the CCB. To be able to assess the proposed change, the CCB needs information as to how the change affects both the product and the development process. This includes information about the estimated amount of new or changed code, additional test requirements, the relationship to other changes, potential costs, complexity of the change, the severity of the defect (if it concerns one), resources needed, etc. Usually, a special change request form is provided to specify the information needed by the CCB.

- The CCB assesses the change request. The change request may be approved, rejected, or deferred if further information is required. If the request is approved, it eventually results in a work package which has to be scheduled.

- The CCB makes sure that all configuration items affected will eventually be updated accordingly. Configuration management provides a means to establish the status of all items and, thereby, of the whole project.

Thus, configuration management is not only about keeping track of all the different versions of elements of a system; it also encompasses workflow management tasks. The process depicted in the state transition diagram in figure 4.1, for example, describes what goes on in the life cycle of a change request. The process model thus defined exemplifies how the workflow of change requests can be managed.

In a similar vein, the state transition diagram in figure 4.2 shows the workflow of developer tasks during the development of a system component. It shows the possible states of a system component and the transitions in between. For example, after a component has been coded, it is unit tested. If bugs are found during unit testing, further coding is necessary. Otherwise, the component enters the review stage. If the review reveals problems, the coding stage is re-entered. Otherwise, the component is submitted to the CCB for formal approval. Finally, if unit testing does not reveal any errors, the review stage is skipped.

If components are kept under configuration control, configuration management can be used to manage the workflow of development tasks as well. Changes in the status of a component then trigger subsequent activities, as indicated in the development workflow model.

We have to take care that the workflow schemes do not unnecessarily curtail the day-to-day working of the people involved in the project. New items should not be added to the baseline until they have been thoroughly reviewed and tested. Items from the shared database may be used freely by the participants. If an item has to be changed, the person responsible for implementing the change gets a copy of that item and the item is temporarily locked, so that others can not simultaneously update the same item. The person implementing the change is free to tinker with the copy. After the change has been thoroughly tested, it is submitted back to the CCB. Once the CCB has approved it, the revised item is included in the database, the change itself is documented with the item, and the item is unlocked again. A sequence of documented changes thus provides a revision history of that item.

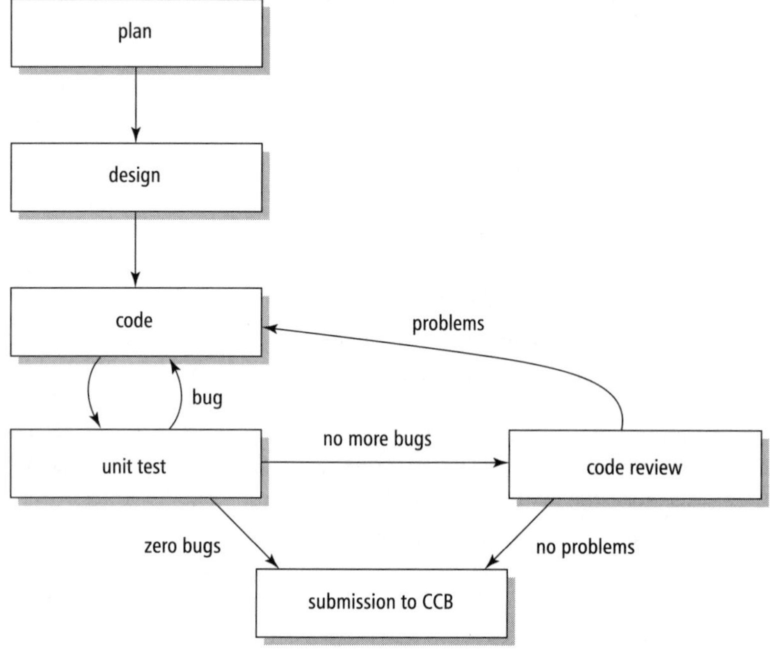

Figure 4.2 State transition diagram of development activities

When an item is changed, the old version is kept as well. The old version still has to be used by others until they have adapted to the change. Also, we may wish to go back to the old version if another change is requested. We thus have different versions of one and the same item, and must be able to distinguish them. This can be done through some numbering scheme, where each new version gets identified by the next higher number. We then get, for a component X, versions X.0, X.1, X.2, and so on.

In a more sophisticated environment, we may even create different branches of revisions. Figure 4.3 gives an example of such a forked development. In the example, module X.2.1. is, say, the result of fixing a bug in module X.2. Module X.3 may concern an enhancement to X.2. It should be noted that merging those parallel development paths again can be difficult. Also, the numbering schemes soon tend to become incomprehensible.

Configuration management is generally supported by powerful tools. These tools lock and unlock elements, provide for automatic numbering of revisions, and, by default, provide users with the latest version of an item. Rather than keeping

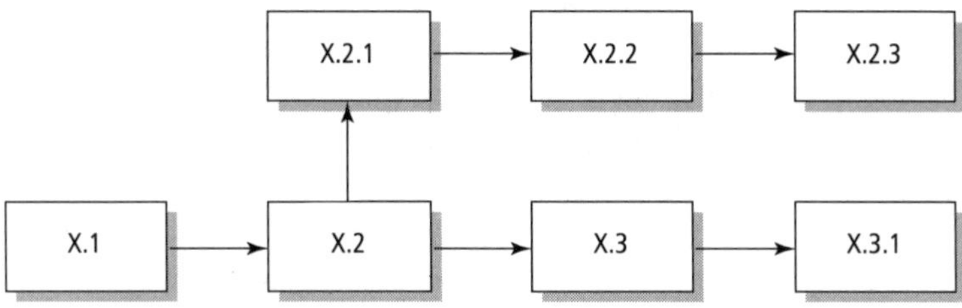

Figure 4.3 Parallel development paths

a copy of each version, such tools only keep track of what has changed from the previous version (the so-called **deltas**). If an item is changed, the tools prompt the user and ask him to document the change. In this way, the history of an item is recorded.

Many configuration-management tools employ the above **version-oriented** model of configurations. A physical change in a component then results in a new version, and different versions are thus characterized by their difference (i.e. delta). There is a trend to use logical changes, rather than physical ones, as a basic unit of work in configuration management. This so-called **change-oriented** model gives a more intuitive way of working and may prevent a lot of user errors when configuring a system. Rather than identifying a configuration by some arcane sequence of numbers, it is now identified by some baseline plus a set of changes. The set of changes may be empty. We thus specify

baseline X plus 'fix table size problem'

rather than

{X.3.1, Y.2.7, Z.1.4, ... }.

Configuration-management tools also offer help in assembling an executable version of the system. One writes a 'program' that identifies the various components of the required system and their mutual dependencies. The system in question is then generated by executing this 'program': the components are retrieved automatically from the database containing the source code modules, and all modules are translated and linked together into an executable system. If the system is smart enough, only those modules that have been changed are translated anew.

Such tools are a crucial element in environments where large software systems are being developed. Tools for configuration and version management will be discussed more extensively in chapter 19.

4.2 CONFIGURATION MANAGEMENT PLAN

The procedures for configuration management are laid down in a document, the Configuration Management Plan. For the contents of this plan, we will follow the corresponding IEEE Standard [IEE90b]. This document describes methods to identify configuration items, to control change requests, and to document the implementation of those change requests. A sample table of contents of the Configuration Management Plan is given in figure 4.4. The main constituents of this plan are:

Management This section describes how the project is being organized. Particular attention is paid to responsibilities which directly affect configuration management: how are change requests being handled, how are development phases closed, how is the status of the system maintained, how are interfaces between components identified? Also, the relationship with other functional organizations, such as software development and quality assurance, is delineated.

Activities This section describes how a configuration will be identified and controlled and how its status will be accounted and reported. A configuration is identified by a baseline: a description of the constituents of that configuration. Such a configuration must be formally approved by the parties involved.

1. *Introduction*
   a. Purpose
   b. Scope
   c. Definitions and acronyms
   d. References
2. *SCM management*
   a. Organization
   b. SCM responsibilities
   c. Applicable policies, directives and procedures
3. *SCM activities*
   a. Configuration identification
   b. Configuration control
   c. Configuration status accounting
   d. Configuration audits and reviews
   e. Interface control
   f. Subcontractor / vendor control
4. *SCM schedules*
5. *SCM resources*
6. *SCM plan maintenance*

Figure 4.4 Sample structure of a software configuration management (SCM) plan (*Source:* IEEE Standard for Software Configuration Management Plans, *IEEE Std 828-1990. ©1990 IEEE Reproduced with permission*)

Clear and precise procedures are needed with respect to the processing of change requests if a software development project is to be controlled. A Configuration Control Board (CCB) usually has the responsibility to evaluate and approve or reject proposed changes. The authority, responsibility, and membership of the CCB have to be stated. Since software components are usually incorporated in a library, procedures for controlling this library have to be established as well.

In order to be able to control a software development project, data have to be collected and processed. Information that is normally required includes: the present status of components, versions and change requests, as well as reports of approved changes and their implementation.

Changes to configuration items may affect items outside the scope of the plan, such as hardware items. These external items have to be identified and their interfaces controlled. In a similar vein, interfaces to items developed outside the project have to be identified and controlled.

4.3 SUMMARY

Configuration management is concerned with the management of all artifacts produced in the course of a software development project. It entails the following major activities:

- Configuration items must be identified and defined. A configuration item is a collection of elements that is treated as one unit for the purpose of configuration management. Examples of possible configuration items are the requirements specification, a software module, a test report, and the user documentation.

- The release and change of these items throughout the software life cycle must be controlled. This means that orderly procedures must be established as to whom is authorized to change or release configuration items.

- The status of configuration items and change requests must be recorded and reported. For example, the status of a change request may be: proposed, approved, rejected, or incorporated.

For larger projects, a Configuration Control Board is usually established. The CCB is responsible for evaluating all change requests and maintaining the integrity of the complete set of documents that relate to a project. Its tasks and the further procedures for configuration management are laid down in a separate document, the Configuration Management Plan.

The history and development of configuration management is closely tied to the history and development of configuration-management tools. In the early days, these tools emphasized the logging of physical file changes. There was little support for process aspects. Present-day configuration-management systems address process aspects as well (workflow management) and increasingly adopt a change-oriented rather than a version-oriented view of configurations. More and more, configuration-management tools function as document-management tools in that they support co-operation among a group of people working together on a collection of shared objects.

4.4 FURTHER READING

A readable introduction to the topic of configuration management is given in [Bab86]. Other sources are [BHS80] (very complete, but somewhat outdated) and [BM95]. Current research is reported in annual workshops [Som96] and [Con97]. [Web96] describes the emerging change-oriented configuration management technology.

Father references on technical aspects of configuration management are given in a later chapter, when tools for configuration and version control are discussed.

Exercises

1. What are the main tasks of configuration management?

2. Describe the role of the Configuration Control Board.

3. What is a configuration item?

4. What is a baseline?

5. Explain the difference between version-oriented and change-oriented configuration management.

6. Discuss the main contents of a configuration management plan.

7. ♡ Discuss differences and similarities between configuration management during development and maintenance.

8. ♡ Discuss possible differences between configuration management in a traditional waterfall development model and the evolutionary development models (see also [BD91].

9. ♡ Configuration management at the implementation level is often supported by tools. Can you think of ways in which such tools can also support the control of other artifacts (design documents, test reports, etc.)?

10. ♠ Devise a configuration management scheme for a small project (say, less than one person-year) and a large project (say, more than ten person-years). Give a rationale for the possible differences between those schemes.

11. ♠ To what extent could configuration-management tools support the gathering of quantitative project data? To what extent could such tools support project control?

5 People Management and Team Organization

LEARNING OBJECTIVES

- To be aware of the importance of people issues in software development
- To know of different ways to organize work
- To know of major types of management styles
- To appreciate different ways to organize a software development team

People are the organization's most important asset
[Hum97a]

In most organizations that develop software, programmers, analysts and other professionals work together in a team. An adequate team structure will depend on many factors, such as the number of people involved, their experience and involvement in the project, the kind of project, individual differences and style. These factors also influence the way projects are to be managed. In this chapter, we will discuss various aspects of people management, as well as some of the more common team organizations for software development projects.

The work to be done within the framework of a project, be it a software development project, building a house, or the design of a new car, involves a number of tasks. A critical part of management responsibility is to coordinate the tasks of all participants.

This coordination can be carried out in a number of ways. There are both external and internal influences on the coordination mechanism. Internal influences originate from characteristics of the project. External influences originate from the project's organizational environment. If these influences ask for conflicting coordination mechanisms, conflicts between the project and the environment are lurking around the corner.

Consider as an example a highly innovative software development project, to be carried out within a government agency. The characteristics of the project may ask for a flexible, informal type of coordination mechanism, where the commitment of specialized individuals, rather than a strict adherence to formal procedures, is a critical success factor. On the other hand, the environment may be geared towards a bureaucracy with centralized control, which tries to impose formal procedures onto project management. These two mechanisms do not work harmoniously. As a consequence, management may get crushed between those opposing forces.

Section 5.1 further elaborates the various internal and external factors that affect the way projects are managed, and emphasizes the need to pay ample attention to the human element in project management.

Software development involves teamwork. The members of the team have to coordinate their work, communicate their decisions, etc. For a small project, the team will consist of up to a few individuals. As the size of the project increases, so will the team. Large teams are difficult to manage, though. Coordinating the work of a large team is difficult. Communication between team members tends to increase exponentially with the size of the team (see also chapter 7). Therefore, large teams are usually split into smaller teams in a way that confines most of the coordination and communication within the sub-team.

Section 5.2 discusses several ways to organize a software development team. Of these, the hierarchical and matrix organizations can be found in other types of business too, while the chief programmer, SWAT and open structured team are rather specific to software development.

5.1 PEOPLE MANAGEMENT

A team is made up of individuals, each of whom has personal goals. It is the task of project management to cast a team out of these individuals, whereby the individual goals are reconciled into one goal for the project as a whole.

Though the individual goals of people may differ, it is important to identify project goals at an early stage, and unambiguously communicate these to the project members. Project members ought to know what is expected of them. If there is any uncertainty in this respect, team members will determine their own goals: one programmer may decide that efficiency has highest priority, another may choose efficient use of memory, while yet a third will decide that writing a lot of code is what counts. Such widely diverging goals may lead to severe problems.

Once project goals are established and the project is under way, performance of project members with respect to the project goals is to be monitored and assessed. This can be difficult, since much of what is being done is invisible and progress is hard to measure.

Ideally, we would like to have an indication of the functionality delivered and define productivity as the amount of functionality delivered per unit of time. Productivity is mostly defined as the number of lines of code delivered per man-month. Everyone will agree that this measure is not optimal, but nothing better has been found. One of the big dangers of using this measure is that people tend to produce as much code as possible. This has a very detrimental effect. The most important cost driver in software development projects is the amount of code to be delivered (see also the chapter on cost estimation). Writing less code is cheaper, therefore, and reuse of existing code is one way to save time and money. It should therefore be strongly advocated. Using the amount of code delivered per man-month as a productivity indicator offers no incentive for software reuse.

Another aspect of people assessment occurs in group processes like peer reviews, inspections and walkthroughs. These techniques are used during verification and validation activities, to discover errors or assess the quality of the code or documentation. In order to make these processes effective it is necessary to clearly separate the documents to be assessed from their authors. Weinberg used the term egoless programming in this context [Wei71]. An assessment of the product of someone's work should not imply an assessment of that person.

One of the major problems in software development is the coordination of activities of team members. As development projects grow bigger and become more complex, coordination problems quickly accumulate. To counteract these problems, management formalizes communication, for example by having formal project meetings, strictly monitored inspections, and an official configuration control board. However, informal and interpersonal communication is known to be a primary way in which information flows into and through a development organization. It is unwise to rule out this type of communication altogether.[1] Informal, interpersonal communication is most easily accomplished if people are physically at close quarters. Even worse, people are inclined to trade the ease with which information can be obtained against its quality. They will easily accept their neighbor's advice, even if they know that much better advice can be found on the next floor. To counteract this tendency, it is wise to bring together diverse stakeholders in controlled ways, for example by having domain experts in the design team, by having users involved in the testing of software, or through participatory design approaches.

Team management entails a great many aspects, not the least important of which concern the care for the human element. Successes among software development projects can often be traced to a strong focus on cultural and sociological concerns, such as efforts to create a blame-free culture, or the solicitation of commitment and partnership. This chapter touches upon only a few aspects thereof. [Bro95], [DL87] and [Met87] give many insightful observations regarding the human element of software project management.

In the remainder of this section we will confine ourselves to two rather general taxonomies for coordination mechanisms and management styles.

5.1.1 Coordination Mechanisms

In his classic text *Structures in Fives: Designing Effective Organizations*, Mintzberg distinguishes between five typical organizational configurations. These configurations reflect typical, ideal environments. Each of these configurations is associated with a specific coordination mechanism: a preferred mechanism for coordinating the tasks to be carried out within that configuration type. Mintzberg's configurations and associated coordination mechanisms are as follows:

- **Simple structure** In a simple structure there may be one or a few managers, and a core of people who do the work. The corresponding coordination mechanism

[1]One shining example hereof is the following anecdote from [Wei71]. The manager of a university computing center got complaints about students and programmers chatting and laughing at the department's coffee machine. Being a real manager, and concerned about productivity, he removed the coffee machine to some remote spot. Quickly thereafter, the load on the computing center consultants increased considerably. The crowd near the coffee machine was in fact an effective, informal communication channel, through which the majority of problems were solved.

is called *direct supervision*. This configuration is often found in new, relatively small organizations. There is little specialization, training and formalization. Coordination lies with separate people, who are responsible for the work of others.

- **Machine bureaucracy** When the content of the work is completely specified, it becomes possible to execute and assess tasks on the basis of precise instructions. Mass-production and assembly lines are typical examples of this configuration type. There is little training and much specialization and formalization. The coordination is achieved through *standardization of work processes*.

- **Divisionalized form** In this type of configuration, each division (or project) is granted considerable autonomy as to how the stated goals are to be reached. The operating details are left to the division itself. Coordination is achieved through *standardization of work outputs*. Control is executed by regularly measuring the performance of the division. This coordination mechanism is possible only when the end result is specified precisely.

- **Professional bureaucracy** If it is not possible to specify either the end result or the work contents, coordination can be achieved through *standardization of worker skills*. In a professional bureaucracy, skilled professionals are given considerable freedom as to how they carry out their job. Hospitals are typical examples of this type of configuration.

- **Adhocracy** In projects that are big or innovative in nature, work is divided amongst many specialists. We may not be able to tell exactly what each specialist should do, or how they should carry out the tasks allocated to them. The project's success depends on the ability of the group as a whole to reach a non-specified goal in a non-specified way. Coordination is achieved through *mutual adjustment*.

The coordination mechanisms distinguished by Mintzberg correspond to typical organizational configurations, like a hospital, or an assembly line factory. In his view, different organizations call for different coordination mechanisms. Organizations are not all alike. Following this line of thought, factors external to a software development project are likely to exert an influence on the coordination mechanisms for that project.

Note that most real organizations do not fit one single configuration type. Different parts of one organization may well be organized differently. Also, Mintzberg's configurations represent abstract ideals. In reality, organizations may tend towards one of these configurations, but carry aspects of others as well.

5.1.2 Management Styles

The development of a software system, the building of a house, and the planning of and participation in a family holiday are comparable in that each concerns a co-ordinated effort carried out by a group of people. Though these projects are likely to be dealt with in widely different ways, the basic assumptions that underlie their organizational structures and management styles have a lot in common.

These basic assumptions can be highlighted by distinguishing between two dimensions in managing people:

- **Relation directedness** This concerns attention to an individual and his relationship to other individuals within the organization.

- **Task directedness** This concerns attention to the results to be achieved and the way in which these results must be achieved.

Both relation and task directedness may be high or low. This leads to four basic combinations, as depicted in figure 5.1. Obviously, these combinations correspond to extreme orientations. For each dimension, there is a whole spectrum of possibilities.

		Task directedness: low	Task directedness: high
Relation directedness	low	separation style	commitment style
	high	relation style	integration style

Figure 5.1 Four basic management styles, cf [Red70]

The style that is most appropriate for a given situation depends on the type of work to be done:

- **Separation style** This management style is usually most effective for routine work. Efficiency is the central theme. Management acts like a bureaucrat and applies rules and procedures. Work is coordinated hierarchically. Decision-making is top-down, formal, and based on authority. A major advantage of this style is that it results in a stable project organization. On the other hand, real innovations are difficult to accomplish. This style closely corresponds to Mintzberg's coordination through standardization of work processes.

- **Relation style** This style is usually most effective in situations where people have to be motivated, coordinated and trained. The tasks to be performed are bound to individuals. The work is not of a routine character, but innovative, complex, and specialized. Decision-making is a group process; it involves negotiation and consensus building. An obvious weak spot of this style is that it may result in endless chaotic meetings. The manager's ability to moderate efficient decision-making is a key success factor. This style best fits Mintzberg's mutual adjustment coordination mechanism.

- **Commitment style** This is most effective if work is done under pressure. For this style to be effective, the manager has to know how to achieve goals without arousing resentment. Decision making is not done in meetings. Rather, decisions are implied by the shared vision of the team as to the goals of the project. A potential weak spot of this style is that, once this vision has been agreed upon, the team is not responsive to changes in its environment, but blindly stumbles on along the road mapped out. This style best fits Mintzberg's professional bureaucracy.

- **Integration style** This fits situations where the result is uncertain. The work is explorative in nature and the various tasks are highly interdependent. It is the manager's task to stimulate and motivate. Decision-making is informal, bottom-up. This style promotes creativity, and individuals are challenged to get the best out of themselves. A possible weak spot of this style is that the goals of individual team members become disconnected to those of the project, and that they start to compete with one another. Again, Mintzberg's coordination through mutual adjustment fits this situation well.

Each of the coordination mechanisms and management styles identified may be used within software development projects. It is only reasonable to expect that projects with widely different characteristics ask for different mechanisms. For an experienced team asked to develop a well-specified application in a familiar domain, coordination may be achieved through standardization of work processes. For a complex and innovative application, this mechanism is not likely to work, though.

In chapter 8, we will identify various types of software development project and indicate which type of coordination mechanism and management style best fits those projects. It should be noted that the coordination mechanisms suggested in chapter 8 stem from internal factors, i.e. characteristics of the project on hand. As noted before, the project's environment will also exert influence on its organization.

Notice that we looked from the manager to the team and its members in the above discussion. Alternatively, we may look at the relation and task *maturity* of individual team members. Relation maturity concerns the attitude of employees towards their job and management. Task maturity is concerned with technical competence. It is important that the manager aligns his dealings with team members with their respective relation and task maturity. For example, a fresh graduate may have high task maturity and low relation maturity, and so his introduction into a skilled team may warrant some careful guidance.

5.2 TEAM ORGANIZATION

Within a team, different roles can be distinguished. There are managers, testers, designers, programmers, and so on. Depending on the size of the project, more than one role may be carried out by one person, or different people may play the same role. The responsibilities and tasks of each of these roles have to be precisely defined in the project plan.

People cooperate within a team in order to achieve an optimal result. Yet it is advisable to strictly separate certain roles. It is a good idea to create a test team that is independent of the development team. Similarly, quality assurance should, in principle, be conducted by people not directly involved in the development process.

Large teams are difficult to manage and are therefore often split up into smaller teams. By clearly defining the tasks and responsibilities of the various sub-teams, communication can be largely confined to communication between members of the same sub-team. Quantifying the cost of interpersonal communication yields insights into effects of team size on productivity and helps to structure large development teams effectively. Some simple formulas for doing so are derived in chapter 7.

In the following subsections we discuss several organizational forms for software development teams.

5.2.1 Hierarchical Organization

In an environment which is completely dedicated to the production of software, we often encounter hierarchical team structures. Depending on the size of the organization or project, different levels of management can be distinguished.

Figure 5.2 gives an example of a hierarchical organization. The rectangles denote the various sub-teams in which the actual work is done. Circled nodes denote managers. In this example, two levels of management can be distinguished. At the lower level, different teams are responsible for different parts of the project. The managers at this level have a primary responsibility in coordinating the work within their respective teams. At the higher level, the work of the different teams is coordinated.

This type of hierarchical organization often reflects the global structure of the system to be developed. If the system has three major subsystems, there may be three teams, one for each subsystem, as indicated in figure 5.2. As indicated in this figure, there may also be functional units associated with specific project-wide responsibilities, such as quality assurance and testing.

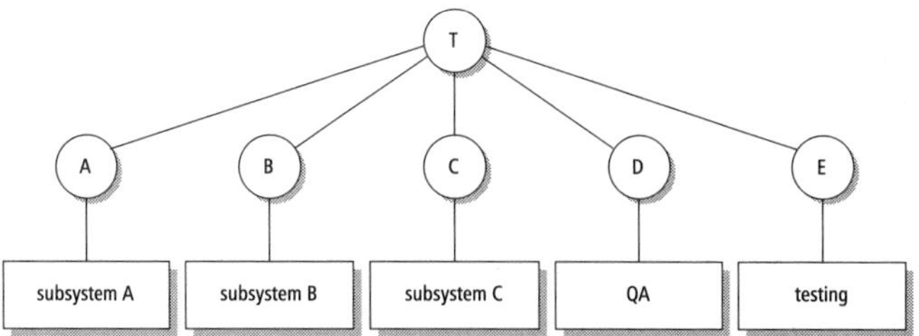

Figure 5.2 A hierarchical team organization

It is not possible to associate the hierarchical organization with only one of the coordination mechanisms introduced above. For each unit identified, any one of the coordination mechanisms mentioned earlier is possible. Also, one need not necessarily apply the same mechanism in each node of the hierarchy. Having different coordination mechanisms within one and the same project is not without problems, though.

Based on an analysis of the characteristics of various subsystems, the respective managers may wish to choose a management style and coordination mechanism that best fits those characteristics. If one or more of the subsystems is highly innovative in nature, their management may opt for a mutual adjustment type of coordination. The higher levels within the hierarchy will usually tend towards a coordination mechanism based on some form of standardization, by imposing rules and procedures as in a machine bureaucracy, or measuring output as in a divisionalized configuration. In such cases, internal and external powers may well clash at one or more of the intermediate levels.

Another critical point in any hierarchical organization is the distance between the top and the bottom of the hierarchical pyramid. The 'real' work is generally done at the lower levels of this pyramid. The people at these lower levels generally possess the real knowledge of the application. The higher one rises in the hierarchy, the less specific the knowledge becomes (this is the main reason why management at these higher levels tends towards coordination through standardization). Yet, most decisions are taken at a fairly high level. In many cases, signals from the lower level somehow get subsumed at one of the intermediate levels.

If information seeps through the various levels in the hierarchy, it tends to become more and more rose-colored. The following scenario is not entirely fictitious:

- bottom: we have severe troubles in implementing module X;

- level 1: there are some problems with module X;

- level 2: progress is steady, I do not foresee any real problems;
- top: everything proceeds according to our plan.

These kinds of distortion are difficult to circumvent altogether. They are, however, reinforced by the fact that the organizational line along which progress is reported is also the line along which the performance of team members is measured and evaluated. Everyone is favored by a positive evaluation and is thus inclined to color the reports accordingly. If data on a project's progress is being collected and processed by people not directly involved in the assessment of team members, you have a much higher chance that the information collected is of sufficient reliability.

An equally problematic aspect of hierarchical organizations lies in the fact that one is judged, both socially and financially, according to the *level* at which one stands within the organization. It is thus natural to aspire to higher and higher levels within the hierarchy. It is, however, not at all clear that this is desirable. The Peter Principle says: in a hierarchical organization each employee in general rises until reaching a level at which he is incompetent. A good programmer need not be a good manager. Good programming requires certain skills. To be a good manager, different skills are needed. In the long run, it seems wiser to maintain people at a level at which they perform well, and reward them accordingly.

5.2.2 Matrix Organization

In an environment where software is a mere byproduct, we often encounter some sort of matrix organization. People from different departments are then allocated to a software development project, possibly part-time. In this type of organization it is sometimes difficult to control progress. An employee has to satisfy several bosses and may have the tendency to play off one boss against another.

We may also use a matrix organization in an environment completely dedicated to software development. The basic unit, then, is a small, specialized group. There may be more than one unit with the same specialization. Possible specializations are, for instance, graphics programming, databases, user interfaces, quality control. The units are organized according to their specialty. Projects, on the other hand, may involve units with different specialties. Individuals are thus organized along two axes, one representing the various specialist groups and one representing the projects to which they are assigned. This type of matrix organization is depicted in figure 5.3.

In such a situation, the project manager is responsible for the successful completion of the project. The manager in charge of one or more units with the same specialty has a longer-term mission, such as maintaining or enlarging the knowledge and expertise of the members of his team. Phrased in terms of the basic management dimensions discussed earlier, the project manager is likely to emphasize task

	real-time programming	graphics	databases	QA	testing
project C	X			X	X
project B	X		X	X	X
project A		X	X	X	X

Figure 5.3 A matrix organization

directedness, while the unit manager will emphasize relation directedness. Such an organization can be very effective, provided there is sufficient mutual trust and the willingness to cooperate and pursue the project's goals.

5.2.3 Chief Programmer Team

A team organization known as the chief programmer team was proposed by Harlan Mills around 1970. The kernel of such a team consists of three people. The chief programmer is team leader. He takes care of the design and implements key parts of the system. The chief programmer has an assistant who can stand in for the chief programmer, if needed. Thirdly, a librarian takes care of the administration and documentation. Besides these three people, an additional (small) number of experts may be added to the chief programmer team.

In this type of organization, fairly high demands are made upon the chief programmer. The chief programmer has to be very competent in the technical area, but he also has to have sufficient management capabilities. In other words, are there enough chief programmers? Also, questions of competence may arise. The chief programmer plays a very central role. He takes all the decisions. The other team members may well challenge some of his qualities.

The early notion of a chief programmer team seems somewhat elitist. It resembles a surgeon team in its emphasis on highly specialized tasks and charismatic leadership. The benefits of a team consisting of a small group of peers over huge development teams struggling to produce ever larger software systems may be regained in a modified form of the chief programmer team though.

In this modified form, peer group aspects prevail. The development team then consists of a small group of people collectively responsible for the task at hand. In particular, jobs are not structured around life cycle stages. There are no analysts, designers, or programmers, though the role of tester may be assigned to a specific person. Different levels of expertise may occur within the group. The most experienced persons act as chief programmer and deputy chief programmer, respectively. At the other end of the scale, one or two trainees can be assimilated and get the necessary on-the-job training. A trainee may well act as the team's librarian.

5.2.4 SWAT Team

In projects with an evolutionary or iterative process model such as RAD, a project organization known as the SWAT team is sometimes used. SWAT stands for Skilled With Advanced Tools. We may view the SWAT team as a software development version of a project team in which both task and relation directedness are high.

A SWAT team is relatively small. It typically has four or five members. Preferably, the team occupies one room. Communication channels are kept very short. The team does not have lengthy formal meetings with formal minutes. Rather, it uses workshops and brainstorming sessions of which little more than a snapshot of a white-board drawing is retained.

A SWAT team typically builds incremental versions of a software system. In order to do so effectively, it employs reusable components, very high-level languages, and powerful software generators. The work of team members is supported and coordinated through groupware or workflow management software.

As in the chief programmer team, the leader of a SWAT team is like a foreman in the building industry: he is both a manager and a co-worker. The members of a SWAT team are generalists. They may have certain specialties, but they must also be able to do a variety of tasks, such as participate in a workshop with customers, build a prototype, and test a piece of software.

Team motivation is very important in a SWAT team. A SWAT team often adopts a catchy name, motto or logo. This label then expresses their vision. Individuals derive pride and self-esteem from their membership of a SWAT team.

5.2.5 Open Structured Team

Software development involves complex problem solving, and an open management style, with much attention for the relation dimension, is well-suited for this type of work. However, software development projects also need a fair amount of sound, predictable behavior in order to get the project done, on time, and within budget.

For example, in a pure relation-style project structure, it may be difficult to come to a decision. If there is no consensus proposal on a certain issue, one may resort to majority voting. The outvoted minority then loses its sense of ownership, one of the important success factors of this management style. If the minority does not put up with the result, the team may even break apart.

The open structured team tries to combine an open management style, paying ample attention to the relations between members of the team, with some clear structure imposed on the way the team acts. An open structured team has a technical leader who is externally responsible and resolves issues for which no consensus can be reached. In this respect, the technical leader resembles the chief programmer. Other functional roles, such as a moderator or recorder for meetings, rotate amongst members of the team. Finally, an open structured team keeps a structural external record of all of its proceedings (its products, processes, deferred decisions, rejected options, and so on).

The open structured team thus tries to combine the best of two worlds: a strong focus on the individual specialist and his commitment to the project's goals, as well as centralized coordination activities to ensure that the project achieves its goals in a timely and effective manner.

5.2.6 General Principles for Organizing a Team

No matter how we try to organize a team, the key point is that it ought to be a *team*. From many tests regarding productivity in software development projects, it turns out again and again that factors concerning team capabilities have a far greater influence than anything else. Factors such as morale, group norms and management style play a more important role than such things as the use of high-level languages, product complexity, and the like (see, for instance, [Law81]).

Some general principles for team organization are given in [HC72]. In particular, these general principles also apply to the organization of software development projects:

- **Use fewer, and better, people** Highest productivity is achieved by a relatively small group of people. This holds for novelists, soccer players and bricklayers. There is no reason to believe that it does not equally apply to programmers and other people working in the software field. Also, large groups require more communication, which has a negative effect on productivity and leads to more errors.

- **Try to fit tasks to the capabilities and motivation of the people available** In other words: take care that the Peter Principle does not apply in your situation. In many organizations, excellent programmers can be promoted only into managerial positions. It is far better to also offer career possibilities in the more technical areas of software development and maintenance.

- **In the long run, an organization is better off if it helps people to get the most out of themselves** So you should not pursue either of the following:

  - The reverse Peter Principle: people rise within an organization to a level at which they become indispensable. For instance, a programmer may become the only expert in a certain system. If he does not get a chance to work on anything else, it is not unlikely that this person, for want of a more interesting and challenging task, will leave your organization. At that point, you are in real trouble.

- The Paul Principle: people rise in an organization to a level at which their expertise becomes obsolete within five years. Given the speed with which new developments enter the market place in software engineering, and computer science in general, it is very important that people get the opportunity to grow and stay abreast of new developments.

- **It is wise to select people such that a well-balanced and harmonious team results** In general, this means that it is not sufficient only to have a few top experts. A soccer team needs regular players as well as stars. Selecting the proper mix of people is a complicated task. There are various good texts available that specifically address this question (for example, [Wei71], [Met87]).

- **Someone who does not fit the team should be removed** If it turns out that a team does not function as a coherent unit, we are often inclined to wait a little while, see how things develop, and hope for better times to come. In the long run, this is detrimental.

5.3 SUMMARY

Software is written by humans. Their productivity is partly determined by such factors as the programming language used, machine speed, and available tools. The organizational environment in which one is operating is equally important, though. Good team management distinguishes itself from bad team management above all by the degree to which attention is paid to these human factors. The human element in software project management was discussed in section 5.1, together with well-known taxonomies of coordination mechanisms and management styles.

There are different ways to organize software developers in a team. These organizational forms and some of their caveats were discussed in section 5.2. Hierarchical and matrix organizations are not specific to software development, while the chief programmer, SWAT and open structured teams originated in the software field. Each of the latter somehow tries to reconcile the two types of management typically required in software development projects: an individualistic, personal approach where one tries to get the best out of team members, and a hierarchical, top-down management style to get things done in time and within budget.

5.4 FURTHER READING

A still very relevant source of information on psychological factors related to software development is [Wei71]. [Bro95], [DL87] and [Met87] also contain a number of valuable observations. Coordination problems in software development are discussed in [KS95]. [Sof96a] and [CAC93b] are special journal issues on managing software projects.

[Min83] is the classic text on the organization of management. The basic management styles discussed in section 5.1.2 are based on [Red70] and [Con93].

The chief programmer team is described in [Bak72]. Its modified form is described in [MB87]. SWAT is discussed in [Mar91]. The open structured team is described in [Con93].

Exercises

1. Explain Mintzberg's classification of organizational configurations and their associated coordination mechanisms.

2. Discuss Reddin's basic management styles.

3. What are the critical issues in a hierarchical team organization?

4. Highlight the differences between a chief programmer team, a SWAT team and an open structured team.

5. Which of Reddin's management styles fits in best with a SWAT team?

6. What is the Peter Principle? Where does it crop up in software development?

7. ♡ Consider a software development project you have been involved in. Which style of coordination mechanism or management style best fits this project? Do you consider the management to have been adequate, or does the discussion in section 5.1 point to possible improvements?

8. ♡ From a management point of view, discuss possible pros and cons of having a technical wizard on your development team.

9. ♠ Write an essay on the role of people issues in software development. To do so, you may consult some of the books that focus on people issues in software development, such as [Bro95], [Met87], [Wei71] or [DL87].

10. ♠ Discuss the pros and cons of an organization in which the primary departmentalization is vertical (i.e. by specialty, such as databases, human-computer

interfaces, or graphics programming) as opposed to one in which the primary departmentalization is horizontal (for example, design, implementation, and testing).

11. ♡ Discuss the pros and cons of letting people rotate between projects from different application domains as opposed to letting them become true experts in one particular application domain.

6 On Managing Software Quality

LEARNING OBJECTIVES

- To appreciate the need for sound measurements in determining software quality
- To critically assess various taxonomies of quality attributes
- To be able to contrast different views on software quality
- To be aware of international standards pertaining to software quality
- To know about the Software Capability Maturity Model
- To understand how an organization may set up its own measurement program

In their landmark book *In Search of Excellence*, Peters and Waterman identify a number of key factors that set the very successful companies of the world apart from the less successful ones. One of those key factors is the commitment to quality of the very successful companies. Apparently, quality pays off.

Long-term profitability is not the only reason why attention to quality is important in software development. Because of the sheer complexity of software products and the often frequent changes that have to be incorporated during the development of software, continuous attention to, and assessment of, the quality of the product under development is needed if we ever want to realize satisfactory products. This need is aggravated by the increasing penetration of software technology into everyday life. Low-quality products will leave customers dissatisfied, will make users neglect the systems that are supposed to support their work, and may even cost lives.

One frightening example of what may happen if software contains bugs, has become known as 'Malfunction 54'. The Therac-25, a computerized radiation machine, was blamed in incidents that caused the death of two people and serious injuries to others. The deadly mystery was eventually traced back to a software bug, named 'Malfunction 54' after the message displayed at the console; see also section 1.4.2. Commitment to quality in software development not only pays off, it is a sheer necessity.

This commitment calls for careful development processes. This attention to the development process is based on the premise that the quality of a product is largely based on the quality of the process that leads to that product, and that this process can indeed be defined, managed, measured, and improved.

Besides the product–process dichotomy, a conformance–improvement dichotomy can be distinguished as well. If we impose certain quality requirements on the product or process, we may devise techniques and procedures to ensure or test that the product or process does indeed *conform to* these objectives. Alternatively, schemes may be aimed at *improving* the quality of the product or process.

Figure 6.1 gives examples of these four different approaches to quality. Most of software engineering is concerned with improving the quality of the products we develop, and the label 'best practices' in this figure refers to all of the goodies mentioned elsewhere in this book. The other three approaches are discussed in this chapter.

Before we embark on a discussion of the different approaches to quality, we will first elaborate on the notion of software quality itself, and how to measure it. When talking about the height of people, the phrase 'Jasper is 7 ft' conveys more information than 'Jasper is tall'. Likewise, we would like to express all kinds of quality attributes in numbers. We would prefer a statement of the form 'The availability of the system is 99%' to a mere 'The availability of the system is high'. Some of the caveats of the measurement issues involved are discussed in section 6.1. In section 6.2, we will discuss various taxonomies of quality attributes, including ISO 9126. This is by no

	Conformance	Improvement
Product	ISO 9126	'best practices'
Process	ISO 9001 SQA	CMM SPICE Bootstrap

Figure 6.1 Different approaches to quality

means the final word on software quality, but it is a good reference point to start from. This discussion also allows us to further illustrate some of the problems with measuring quality in quantitative terms.

'Software quality' is a rather elusive notion. Different people will have different perspectives on the quality of a software system. A system tester may view quality as 'compliance to requirements', whereas a user may view it as 'fitness for use'. Both viewpoints are valid, but they need not coincide. As a matter of fact, they probably won't. Part of the confusion about what the quality of a system entails and how it should be assessed, is caused by mixing up these different perspectives. Rather than differentiating between various perspectives on quality, Total Quality Management (TQM) advocates an eclectic view: quality is the pursuit of excellence in everything. Section 6.3 elaborates on the different perspectives on quality.

ISO, the International Standards Organization, has established several standards that pertain to the management of quality. The one most applicable to our field, the development and maintenance of software, is ISO 9001. This standard will be discussed in section 6.4.

ISO 9001 states general requirements for a quality system. They have to be augmented by more specific procedures, aimed specifically at quality assurance and control for software development. The IEEE Standard for Quality Assurance Plans is meant to provide such procedures. It is discussed in section 6.5.

Software quality assurance procedures provide the means to review and audit the software development process and its products. Quality assurance by itself does not guarantee quality products. Quality assurance merely sees to it that work is done the way it is supposed to be done.

The Capability Maturity Model (CMM)[1] is the best known attempt at directions on how to improve the development process. It uses a five-point scale to rate

[1]Capability Maturity Model and CMM are registered trademarks in the U.S. Patent and Trademark Office.

organizations and indicates key areas of focus in order to progress to a higher maturity level. SPICE and Bootstrap are similar approaches to process improvement. CMM is discussed in section 6.6.

Quality actions within software development organizations are aimed at finding opportunities to improve the development process. These improvements require an understanding of the development process, which can be obtained only through carefully collecting and interpreting data that pertain to quality aspects of the process and its products. Some hints on how to start such a quality improvement program are given in section 6.8.

6.1 ON MEASURES AND NUMBERS

> *When you can measure what you are speaking about, and express it in numbers, you know something about it; but when you cannot measure it, when you cannot express it in numbers, your knowledge is of a meagre and unsatisfactory kind; it may be the beginning of knowledge, but you have scarcely in your thoughts advanced to the stage of science.*
> [Lord Kelvin, 1900]

> *It is the mark of an instructed mind to rest satisfied with the degree of precision which the nature of a subject admits, and not to seek exactness when only an approximation of the truth is possible.*
> [Aristotle, 330 BC]

Suppose we want to express some quality attribute, say the complexity of a program text, in a single numeric value. Larger values are meant to denote more complex programs. If such a mapping C from programs to numbers can be found, we may next compare the values of $C(P_1)$ and $C(P_2)$ to decide whether program P_1 is more complex than program P_2. Since more complex programs will be more difficult to comprehend and maintain, this type of information is very useful, e.g. for planning maintenance effort.

What then should this mapping be? Consider the program texts in figure 6.2. Most people will concur that text (a) looks less complex than text (b). Is this caused by:

- its length,
- the number of gotos,
- the number of if-statements,
- a combination of these attributes,
- something else?

(a)

```
procedure bubble
     (var a: array [1..n] of integer; n: integer);
var i, j, temp: integer;
begin
     for i:= 2 to n do
          j:= i;
          while j > 1 and a[j] < a[j-1] do
               temp:= a[j];
               a[j]:= a[j-1];
               a[j-1]:= temp;
               j:= j-1;
          enddo
     enddo
end;
```

(b)

```
procedure bubble
     (var a: array [1..n] of integer; n: integer);
var i, j, temp: integer;
begin
     for i:= 2 to n do
          if a[i] ≥ a[i-1] then goto next endif;
          j:= i;
     loop: if j ≤ 1 then goto next endif;
          if a[j] ≥ a[j-1] then goto next endif;
          temp:= a[j];
          a[j]:= a[j-1];
          a[j-1]:= temp;
          j:= j-1;
          goto loop;
     next: skip;
     enddo
end;
```

Figure 6.2 Two versions of a sort routine (a) structured, (b) unstructured

Suppose we decide that the number of if-statements is what counts. The result of the mapping then is 0 for text (a) and 3 for text (b), and this agrees with our intuition. However, if we take the sum of the number of if-statements, gotos, and loops, the result also agrees with our intuition. Which of these mappings is the one sought for? Is either of them 'valid' to begin with? What does 'valid' mean in this context?

A number of relevant aspects of measurement, such as attributes, units and scale types can be introduced and related to one another using the measurement framework depicted in figure 6.3. This framework also allows us to indicate how metrics can be used to describe and predict properties of products and processes, and how to validate these predictions.

The model in figure 6.3 has seven constituents:

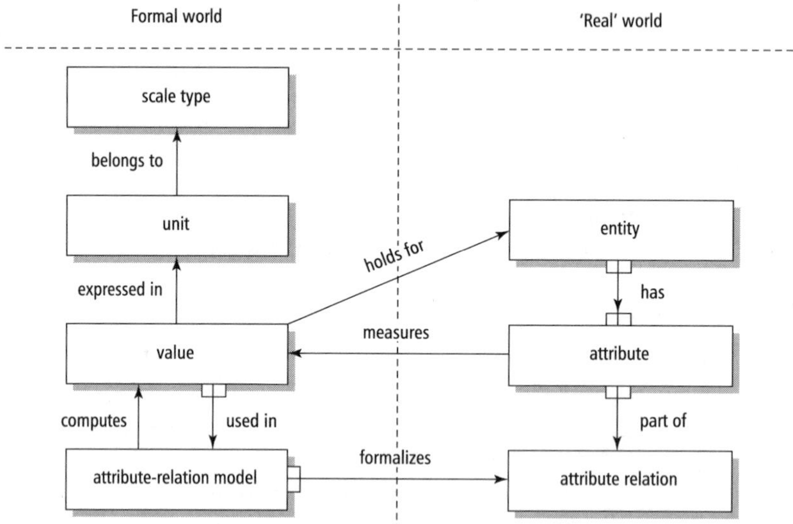

Figure 6.3 A measurement framework (*Source: B. Kitchenham, S. Lawrence Pfleeger & N. Fenton, Towards a Framework for Software Measurement Validation*, IEEE Transactions on Software Engineering **21**, *12 (1995) ©1995 IEEE*)

- **Entity** An entity is an object in the 'real' world of which we want to know or predict certain properties. Entities need not denote material objects; projects and software are entities too.

- **Attribute** Entities have certain properties which we call attributes. Different entities may have the same attribute: both people and cars have a weight. And of course a single entity can have more than one attribute. The forks that adorn the arrow labeled 'has' in figure 6.3 indicate that this relationship is *n-to-m*.

- **Attribute relation** Different attributes of one or more entities can be related. For example, the attributes 'length' and 'weight' of an entity 'snake' are related.

Similarly, the number of man-months spent on a project is related to the cost of that project. Also, an attribute of one entity can be related to an attribute of another entity. For example, the experience of a programmer may be related to the cost of a development project he is working on.

- **Value** The former three constituents of the model reside in the 'real' world. We want to formally characterize these objects by *measuring* attributes, i.e. assigning values to them.
- **Unit** Obviously, this value is expressed in a certain unit, such as meters, seconds or lines of code.
- **Scale types** This unit in turn belongs to a certain scale type. Some common scale types are:
  - **Nominal** Attributes are merely classified: the color of my hair is gray, white or black.
  - **Ordinal** There is a (linear) ordering in the possible values of an attribute: one type of material is harder than another, one program is more complex than another.
  - **Interval** The same as ordinal, but the 'distance' between successive values of an attribute is the same, as in a calendar, or the temperature measured in degrees Fahrenheit.
  - **Ratio** The same as interval, with the additional requirement that there exists a value 0, as in the age of a software system, or the temperature measured in degrees Kelvin.
  - **Absolute** In this case we simply count the number of occurrences, as in the number of errors detected in a program.

  Note that we can sometimes measure an attribute in different units, where these units lie on different scales. For example, we can measure temperature on an ordinal scale: it either freezes, or it doesn't. We can also measure it on an interval scale: in degrees Fahrenheit or Celsius. Or we can measure it on a ratio scale: in degrees Kelvin.
- **Attribute-relation model** If there exists a relation between different attributes of, possibly different, entities in the 'real' world, we may express that relation in a formal model: the attribute-relation model. This model computes (predicts) the value of an attribute in which we are interested from the values of one or more other attributes from the model. The fork at the arrow labeled 'formalizes' in figure 6.3 indicates that we can have more than one model for the same attribute relation.

Measurement is a mapping from the empirical, 'real' world to the formal, relational world. A **measure** is the number or symbol assigned to an attribute of an entity by this mapping. The value assigned obviously has a certain unit, e.g. lines of code. The unit in turn belongs to a certain scale, such as the ratio scale for lines of code, or the ordinal scale for the severity of a failure.

In mathematics, the term **metric** has a very specific meaning: it describes how far apart two points are. In our field, the term is often used in a somewhat sloppy way. Sometimes it denotes a measure, sometimes the unit of a measure. We will use the term to denote the combination of:

- an attribute of an entity,
- the function which assigns a value to that attribute,
- the unit in which this value is expressed, and
- its scale type.

For each scale type, certain operations are allowed, while others are not. In particular, we can not compute the average for an ordinal scale, but only its median (middle value). Suppose we classify a system as either 'very complex', 'complex', 'average', 'simple' or 'very simple'. The assignment of numbers to these values is rather arbitrary. The only prerequisite is that a system that is classified as, say, 'very complex' is assigned a larger value than a system classified as, say, 'complex'. If we call this mapping W, the only requirement thus is: W(very complex) $>$ W(complex) $> \ldots >$ W(very simple).

Very complex	Complex	Average	Simple	Very simple
5	4	3	2	1
100	10	5	2	1

Figure 6.4 Example mappings for an ordinal scale

Figure 6.4 gives an example of two valid assignments of values to this attribute. Suppose we have a system with three components, which are characterized as 'very complex', 'average' and 'simple', respectively. By assigning the values from the first row, the average would be 3, so the whole system would be classified to be of average complexity. Using the values from the second row, the average would be 35, something between 'complex' and 'very complex'. The problem is caused by the fact that, with an ordinal scale, we do not know whether successive values are *equidistant*. When computing an average, we tacitly assume they are.

We often can not measure the value of an attribute *directly*. For example, the speed of a car can be determined from the values of two other attributes: a distance and the time it takes the car to travel that distance. The speed is then measured *indirectly*, by taking the quotient of two direct measures. In this case, the attribute-relation model formalizes the relation between the distance traveled, time, and speed.

We may distinguish between *internal* and *external* attributes. Internal attributes of an entity can be measured purely in terms of that entity itself. Modularity, size, defects encountered, and cost are typical examples of internal attributes. External attributes of an entity are those which can be measured only with respect to how that entity relates to its environment. Maintainability and usability are examples of external attributes. Most quality factors we discuss in this chapter are external attributes. External attributes can be measured only *indirectly*, since they involve the measurement of other attributes.

Empirical relations between objects in the real world should be preserved in the numerical relation system that we use. If we observe that car A drives faster than car B, then we would rather like our function S which maps the speed observed to some number to be such that $S(A) > S(B)$. This is called the **representation condition**. If a measure satisfies the representation condition, it is said to be a **valid measure**.

The representation condition can sometimes be checked by a careful assessment of the attribute-relation model. For example, we earlier proposed to measure the complexity of a program text by counting the number of if-statements. For this (indirect) measure to be valid we have to ascertain that:

- any two programs with the same number of if-statements are equally complex, and

- if program A has more if-statements than program B, then A is more complex than B.

Since neither of these statements is true in the real world, this complexity measure is not valid.

The validity of more complex indirect measures is usually ascertained through statistical means. Most of the cost estimation models discussed in chapter 7, for example, are validated in this way.

Finally, the scale type of indirect measures merits some attention. If different measures are combined into a new measure, the scale type of the combined measure is the 'weakest' of the scale types of its constituents. Many cost estimation formulas contain factors whose scale type is ordinal, such as the instability of the requirements or the experience of the design team. Strictly speaking, different values that result from applying such a cost estimation formula should then be interpreted as indicating that certain projects require more effort than others. The intention though is to interpret them on a ratio scale, i.e. actual effort in man-months. From a measurement-theory point of view, this is not allowed.

6.2 A TAXONOMY OF QUALITY ATTRIBUTES

Some of the first elaborate studies on the notion of 'software quality' appeared in the late 1970s [MRW77, BBK$^+$78]. In these studies, a number of aspects of software systems are investigated that somehow relate to the notion of software quality. In the ensuing years, a large number of people have tried to tackle this very same problem. Many taxonomies of quality factors have been published. The fundamental problems have not been solved satisfactorily, though. The various factors that relate to software quality are hard to define. It is even harder to measure them quantitatively. On the other hand, real quality can often be identified surprisingly easily.

In the *IEEE Glossary of Software Engineering Terminology*, quality is defined as 'the degree to which a system, component, or process meets customer or user needs or expectations'. Applied to software, then, quality should be measured primarily against the degree to which user requirements are met: correctness, reliability, usability, and the like. Software lasts a long time and is adapted from time to time in order to accommodate changed circumstances. It is important to the user that this is possible within reasonable costs. The customer is therefore also interested in quality factors which relate to the structure of the system rather than its use: maintainability, testability, portability, etc.

We will start our discussion of quality attributes with McCall's taxonomy. McCall distinguishes between two levels of quality attributes. Higher-level quality attributes, known as **quality factors**, are external attributes and can, therefore, be measured only indirectly. McCall introduced a second level of quality attributes, termed **quality criteria**. Quality criteria can be measured either subjectively or objectively. By combining the ratings for the individual quality criteria that affect a given quality factor, we obtain a measure for the extent to which that quality factor is being satisfied. Users and managers tend to be interested in the higher-level, external quality attributes.

For example, we can not directly measure the reliability of a software system. We may however directly measure the number of defects encountered so far. This direct measure can be used to obtain insight into the reliability of the system. This involves a theory of how the number of defects encountered relates to reliability, which can be ascertained on good grounds. For most other aspects of quality though, the relation between the attributes that can be measured directly and the external attributes we are interested in is less obvious, to say the least.

Table 6.1 lists the quality factors and their definitions, as they are used by McCall *et al.* These quality factors can be broadly categorized into three classes. The first class contains those factors that pertain to the use of the software after it has become operational.

Correctness: The extent to which a program satisfies its specifications and fulfills the user's mission objectives.

Reliability: The extent to which a program can be expected to perform its intended function with required precision.

Efficiency: The amount of computing resources and code required by a program to perform a function.

Integrity: The extent to which access to software or data by unauthorized persons can be controlled.

Usability: The effort required to learn, operate, prepare input, and interpret output of a program.

Maintainability: The effort required to locate and fix an error in an operational program.

Testability: The effort required to test a program to ensure that it performs its intended function.

Flexibility: The effort required to modify an operational program.

Portability: The effort required to transfer a program from one hardware and/or software environment to another.

Reusability: The extent to which a program (or parts thereof) can be reused in other applications.

Interoperability: The effort required to couple one system with another.

Table 6.1 Quality factors (*Source: J.A. McCall, P.K. Richards & G.F. Walters,* Factors in Software Quality, *RADC-TR-77-369, US Department of Commerce, 1977*)

The second class pertains to the maintainability of the system. The third class contains factors that reflect the ease with which a transition to a new environment can be made. These three categories are depicted in figure 6.5.

Table 6.2 lists the (lower-level) quality criteria and their definitions. Finally, figure 6.6 indicates the relation between quality factors and quality criteria. Thus, column 1 of this table indicates that the factor Correctness is considered to be a function of the criteria Traceability, Consistency and Completeness. The definitions of the

Product operation:	
Correctness	Does it do what I want?
Reliability	Does it do it accurately all of the time?
Efficiency	Will it run on my hardware as well as it can?
Integrity	Is it secure?
Usability	Can I run it?
Product revision:	
Maintainability	Can I fix it?
Testability	Can I test it?
Flexibility	Can I change it?
Product transition:	
Portability	Will I be able to use it on another machine?
Reusability	Will I be able to reuse some of the software?
Interoperability	Will I be able to interface it with another system?

Figure 6.5 Three categories of software quality factors (*Source: J.A. McCall, P.K. Richards & G.F. Walters,* Factors in Software Quality, *RADC-TR-77-369, US Department of Commerce, 1977*)

various terms as they are given in tables 6.1 and 6.2 should be borne in mind while interpreting figure 6.6.

Figure 6.6 does not tell us yet what the exact relation is between quality factors and quality criteria. One possibility is to look for linear equations of the form

$$F_a = m_1c_1 + m_2c_2 + \ldots + m_nc_n$$

Here, F_a denotes the degree to which factor a is being met. m_i is a constant denoting the relative importance of criterion i, and c_i is the degree to which criterion i is being met. The constants m_i are to be determined by trial and error. This formula is one example of how to combine direct measurements into an indirect measurement by means of an attribute-relation model. There is as yet no accepted means to determine this relation more precisely.

Formulas such as the one given above presuppose that it is possible to measure quality quantitatively. This is not all that easy, though. For lack of sound quality indicators, we often fall back onto the use of procedures or standards. These procedures and standards are our 'best guesses'. We suspect that following certain procedures or adhering to certain standards yields a higher-quality product. In retrospect, the degree to which these procedures and standards are being followed, can be checked and used as quality indicators.

We will make a distinction between quality criteria which are based on objectively measurable properties and criteria which are based on subjective scores. Most of the quality criteria mentioned above can really only be assessed subjectively.

Access audit: The ease with which software and data can be checked for compliance with standards or other requirements.

Access control: The provisions for control and protection of the software and data.

Accuracy: The precision of computations and output.

Communication commonality: The degree to which standard protocols and interfaces are used.

Completeness: The degree to which a full implementation of the required functionality has been achieved.

Communicativeness: The ease with which inputs and outputs can be assimilated.

Conciseness: The compactness of the source code, in terms of lines of code.

Consistency: The use of uniform design and implementation techniques and notations throughout a project.

Data commonality: The use of standard data representations.

Error tolerance: The degree to which continuity of operation is ensured under adverse conditions.

Execution efficiency: The run-time efficiency of the software.

Expandability: The degree to which storage requirements or software functions can be expanded.

Generality: The breadth of the potential application of software components.

Hardware independence: The degree to which the software is dependent on the underlying hardware.

Instrumentation: The degree to which the software provides for measurements of its use or identification of errors.

Modularity: The provision of highly independent modules.

Operability: The ease of operation of the software.

Self-documentation: The provision of in-line documentation that explains the implementation of components.

Simplicity: The ease with which the software can be understood (this usually implies the avoidance of practices which increase the complexity of the software).

Software system independence: The degree to which the software is independent of its software environment — non-standard language constructs, operating system, libraries, database management system, and the like.

Storage efficiency: The run-time storage requirements of the software.

Traceability: The ability to link software components to requirements.

Training: The ease with which new users can use the system.

Table 6.2 Quality criteria (*Source: J.A. McCall, P.K. Richards & G.F. Walters,* Factors in Software Quality, *RADC-TR-77-369, US Department of Commerce, 1977*)

A subjective assessment of some criteria can be obtained by giving a rating on a scale from, say, 0 (extremely bad) to 10 (extremely good). Such a subjective metric is difficult to use, though. Different people assessing the same criterion are likely to give different ratings. This renders a proper quality assessment almost impossible.

We may do somewhat better by further decomposing a criterion into objectively measurable properties of the system. For example, rather than directly assessing consistency, we may take into consideration a number of properties that ascribe to consistency, such as the use of standard design representations, calling sequence conventions, error handling conventions, naming conventions, and so on. For each of these, procedures can be established, and we may simply count the percentage of modules that violate these rules. In the next step, we may combine the numbers thus obtained back into one number again. We must realize, however, that this indirect measure is still subjective. Though the properties we measure are objective, their combination into one criterion is still open to a subjective interpretation. Yet, this approach is the one to be preferred, since different people will now assess a given system identically.

Another example of the indirect introduction of subjectivity occurs when we try to capture the notion of complexity (this criterion is not contained in McCall's taxonomy). McCabe defined the notion of complexity in terms of the number of elementary decisions in a program (see chapter 11). Though this number is clearly an objective measure, its interpretation as a complexity metric is still subjective.

Subjectivity may thus enter the picture in two ways: Directly, because we can only measure the corresponding criterion subjectively, or indirectly via an interpretation of properties that can be measured objectively.

There are very few quality factors or criteria for which sufficiently sound numerical measures exist. The best, and in our view the only, example is software reliability, when software reliability is defined as we did in footnote a) to table 6.1. Using solid statistical theory, we may predict the occurrence of future failures (i.e. reliability) based on data about past failures. (We will come back to this topic in the chapter on software reliability.)

McCall's taxonomy of quality factors and quality criteria may rightfully be criticized. For some factors, such as reliability for instance, better definitions can be given. Similarly, one may dispute the list of quality criteria given in table 6.2. The most notable case in point is the omission of complexity. We all know that complex programs are hard to understand, error-prone, and difficult to adapt. We all know that it is a good programming practice to strive for clear, easy to understand, simple program structures. Thus, complexity bears on quality.

In the *IEEE Glossary*, complexity is defined as 'the degree to which a system or component has a design or implementation that is difficult to understand and verify'. Various authors have added complexity to their taxonomy of quality criteria.

	Correctness	Reliability	Efficiency	Integrity	Usability	Maintainability	Testability	Flexibility	Portability	Reusability	Interoperability
Access audit				X							
Access control				X							
Accuracy		X									
Communication commonality											X
Completeness	X										
Communicativeness					X						
Conciseness						X					
Consistency	X	X				X					
Data commonality											X
Error tolerance		X									
Execution efficiency			X								
Expandability								X			
Generality								X		X	
Hardware independence									X	X	
Instrumentation							X				
Modularity						X	X	X	X	X	X
Operability					X						
Self-documentation						X	X	X	X	X	
Simplicity		X				X	X				
Software system independence									X	X	
Storage efficiency			X								
Traceability	X										
Training					X						

Figure 6.6 Relation between quality factors and quality criteria (*Source: J.A. McCall, P.K. Richards & G.F. Walters,* Factors in Software Quality, *RADC-TR-77-369, US Department of Commerce, 1977*)

Complexity metrics are mostly used at the source code level, where they are used to assess the complexity of individual program components, such as modules and procedures. Some of the well-known complexity metrics are dealt with in the chapter on design.

Other, more fundamental, criticisms to schemes like the one discussed above, are:

- The quality factors are not independent, but overlap. Some factors will impact one another in a positive sense, while others will do so negatively. An example from the first category is reliability versus correctness. Efficiency, on the other hand, will in general have a negative impact on most other quality factors. This means that we will have to make trade-offs between quality factors. If high requirements are decided upon for one factor, we may have to relax others. Important trade-offs between quality factors are given in figure 6.7. A + in this figure indicates that factors reinforce one another; a – indicates conflicting goals.

- There is little relation between the quality factors identified and life cycle activities. Most quality factors can only be assessed after the fact. What we should do is to cross-reference quality factors to software engineering techniques. For instance, though there are techniques and tools in existence to achieve reliable software, we can not at present measure *progress* towards achieving reliable software.

	Correctness	Reliability	Efficiency	Integrity	Usability	Maintainability	Testability	Flexibility	Portability	Reusability	Interoperability
Correctness											
Reliability	+										
Efficiency											
Integrity			−								
Usability	+	+	−	+							
Maintainability	+	+	−		+						
Testability	+	+	−		+	+					
Flexibility	+	+	−	−	+	+	+				
Portability			−			+	+				
Reusability		−	−	−		+	+	+	+		
Interoperability			−	−					+		

Figure 6.7 Trade-offs between McCall's quality factors

In a recent ISO standard, ISO 9126, yet another effort has been made to define a set of quality characteristics (see figure 6.8). Their definitions are given in tables 6.3 and 6.4. Whereas the quality factors and criteria as defined by McCall and others are heavily interrelated (see figure 6.6), the ISO scheme is hierarchical: each sub-characteristic is related to exactly one characteristic.

The ISO quality characteristics strictly refer to a software *product*. Their definitions do not capture *process* quality issues. For example, security can partly be handled by provisions in the software and partly by proper procedures. Only the former is covered by the sub-characteristic 'security' of the ISO scheme. Furthermore, the sub-characteristics concern quality aspects that are *visible* to the user. Reusability, for example, is not included in the ISO scheme. In a sense, the earlier taxonomies reflect a product view, whereas ISO 9126 reflects a user view on quality (see also section 6.3).

ISO 9126 not only contains definitions of quality characteristics and sub-characteristics, but also gives a number of possible metrics for each sub-characteristic. The universal applicability of these metrics is somewhat doubtful, though. For example, there is no straightforward relation between the number of examples and illustrations per command and the ease of learning of a software product, as is suggested by this standard (i.e. quite a few of the metrics proposed violate the representation

Characteristic	Subcharacteristics
Functionality	Suitability Accuracy Interoperability Security
Reliability	Maturity Fault tolerance Recoverability
Usability	Understandability Learnability Operability Attractiveness
Efficiency	Time behavior Resource utilization
Maintainability	Analyzability Changeability Stability Testability
Portability	Adaptability Installability Co-existence Replaceability

Figure 6.8 ISO 9126 quality characteristics and sub-characteristics

condition). As far as the independence of quality characteristics is concerned, ISO standard 9126 is a definite step forward, however.

In order to be able to control software quality, we have to know what it is. From the above discussion it follows that this can not be done in a fully satisfactory way as yet. We may however make a start. Within a given organization, quality characteristics and sub-characteristics may be defined. We may define the various sub-characteristics and describe the measurable properties and subjective scores on which they are based. We may also indicate how these sub-characteristics contribute, in our view, to the various quality characteristics.

As the next step, we may determine to what extent the different quality characteristics must be fulfilled for a given project. In this way, the notion of software quality is precisely defined. We may then also determine whether or not the quality objectives are being met.

Quality requirements that can not be quantified can not be controlled.

Functionality: The capability of the software to provide functions which meet stated and implied needs when the software is used under specified conditions.

Reliability: The capability of the software to maintain the level of performance of the system when used under specified conditions.

Usability: The capability of the software to be understood, learned, used and liked by the user, when used under specified conditions.

Efficiency: The capability of the software to provide the required performance, relative to the amount of resources used, under stated conditions.

Maintainability: The capability of the software to be modified. Modifications may include corrections, improvements or adaptation of the software to changes in environment, and in requirements and functional specifications.

Portability: The capability of software to be transferred from one environment to another.

Table 6.3 Quality characteristics of ISO 9126 (*Source:* ISO Standard 9126: *Software Quality Characteristics and Metrics. Reproduced by permission of ISO*)

Suitability: The capability of the software to provide an adequate set of functions for specified tasks and user objectives.

Accuracy: The capability of the software to provide the right or agreed results or effects.

Interoperability: The capability of the software to interact with one or more specified systems.

Security: The capability of the software to prevent unintended access and resist deliberate attacks intended to gain unauthorized access to confidential information, or to make unauthorized modifications to information or to the program so as to provide the attacker with some advantage or so as to deny service to legitimate users.

Maturity: The capability of the software to avoid failure as a result of faults in the software.

Fault tolerance: The capability of the software to maintain a specified level of performance in cases of software faults or of infringement of its specified interface.

Recoverability: The capability of the software to re-establish its level of performance and recover the data directly affected in the case of a failure.

Table 6.4: continued overleaf

Understandability: The capability of the software product to enable the user to understand whether the software is suitable, and how it can be used for particular tasks and conditions of use.
Learnability: The capability of the software product to enable the user to learn its application.
Operability: The capability of the software product to enable the user to operate and control it.
Attractiveness: The capability of the software product to be liked by the user.

Time behavior: The capability of the software to provide appropriate response and processing times and throughput rates when performing its function, under stated conditions.
Resource utilization: The capability of the software to use appropriate resources in an appropriate time when the software performs its function under stated condition.

Analysability: The capability of the software product to be diagnosed for deficiencies or causes of failures in the software, or for the parts to be modified to be identified.
Changeability: The capability of the software product to enable a specified modification to be implemented.
Stability: The capability of the software to minimize unexpected effects from modifications of the software.
Testability: The capability of the software product to enable modified software to be validated.

Adaptability: The capability of the software to be modified for different specified environments without applying actions or means other than those provided for this purpose for the software considered.
Installability: The capability of the software to be installed in a specified environment.
Co-existence: The capability of the software to co-exist with other independent software in a common environment sharing common resources.
Replaceability: The capability of the software to be used in place of other specified software in the environment of that software.

Table 6.4: Quality sub-characteristics of ISO 9126 (*Source:* ISO Standard 9126: *Software Quality Characteristics and Metrics. Reproduced by permission of ISO*)

6.3 PERSPECTIVES ON QUALITY

> *What I (and everybody else) mean by the word quality cannot be broken down into subjects and predicates [...] If quality exists in an object, then you must explain why scientific instruments are unable to detect it [...] On the other hand, if quality is subjective, existing only [in the eye of] the observer, then this Quality is just a fancy name for whatever you'd like [...] Quality is not objective. It doesn't reside in the material world [...] Quality is not subjective. It doesn't reside merely in the mind.*
> [Robert Pirsig, *Zen and the Art of Motorcycle Maintenance*, 1974]

Users will judge the quality of a software system by the degree to which it helps them accomplish tasks and by the sheer joy they have in using it. The manager of those users is likely to judge the quality of the same system by its benefits. These benefits can be expressed in cost savings or in a better and faster service to clients.

During testing, the prevailing quality dimensions will be the number of defects found and removed, or the reliability measured, or the conformance to specifications. To the maintenance programmer, quality will be related to the system's complexity, its technical documentation, and the like.

These different viewpoints are all valid. They are also difficult to reconcile. Garvin distinguishes five definitions of software quality:

- Transcendent definition
- User-based definition
- Product-based definition
- Manufacturing-based definition
- Value-based definition.

Transcendent quality concerns innate excellence. It is the type of quality assessment we usually apply to novels. We may consider *Zen and the Art of Motorcycle Maintenance* an excellent book, we may try to give words to our admiration but these words are usually inadequate. The practiced reader gradually develops a good feeling for this type of quality. Likewise, the software engineering expert may have developed a good feeling for the transcendent qualities of software systems.

The user-based definition of quality concerns 'fitness for use' and relates to the degree in which a system addresses the user's needs. It is a subjective notion. Since different users may have different needs, they may assess a system's quality rather differently. The incidental user of a simple word-processing package may be quite happy with its functionality and possibilities while a computer scientist may be rather disappointed. The reverse situation may befall a complex system like LaTeX.

In the product-based definition, quality relates to attributes of the software. Differences in quality are caused by differences in the values of those attributes. Most of the research into software quality concerns this type of quality. It also underlies the various taxonomies of quality attributes discussed above.

The manufacturing-based definition concerns conformance to specifications. It is the type of quality definition used during system testing, whereas the user-based definition is prevalent during acceptance testing.

Finally, the value-based definition deals with costs and profits. It concerns balancing time and cost on the one hand, and profit on the other hand. We may distinguish various kinds of benefit, not all of which can be phrased easily in monetary terms:

- **Increased efficiency** Benefits are attributed to cost avoidance or reduction, and their measures are economic.

- **Increased effectiveness** This is primarily reflected through better information for decision making. It can be measured in economic terms or through key performance indicators, such as a reduced time to market.

- **Added value** Benefits enhance the strategic position of the organization, e.g. through an increased market share. The contribution of the information technology component often can not be isolated.

- **Marketable product** The system itself may be marketable, or a marketable product may be identified as a by-product of system development.

- **Corporate IT infrastructure** Communication networks, database environments and the like provide little benefit by themselves, but serve as a foundation for other systems.

Software developers tend to concentrate on the product-based and manufacturing-based definitions of quality. The resulting quality requirements can be expressed in quantifiable terms, such as the number of defects found per man-month, or the number of decisions per module. The quality attributes discussed in the previous section fall into these categories. Such quality requirements however can not be directly mapped onto the, rather subjective, quality viewpoints of the users, such as 'fitness for use'. Nevertheless, users and software developers will have to come to an agreement on the quality requirements to be met.

One way to try to bridge this gap is to define a common language between users and software developers in which quality requirements can be expressed. An example is given in [Gil88], where all quality attributes are quantified in user terms. Figure 6.9 gives one example of how a quality attribute can be expressed in

Attribute:	friendliness
Scale:	days on the job for employees to learn tasks supplied by new system
Test:	90% successful completion of assigned tasks in employee test for the system, within twice the average time of an experienced user
Worst:	1 to 7 days
Plan:	less than 1 day (to passing of test)
Best:	less than 2 hours

Figure 6.9 A quality attribute definition that can be used by both users and developers

user terms, and yet provides sufficient means to software developers to determine whether or not the requirement is met.

Developers tend to have a mechanistic, product-oriented view on quality, whereby quality is associated with features of the product. In this view, quality is defined by looking from the program to the user (user friendliness, acceptability, etc.). To assess the quality of systems used in organizations, we have to adopt a process-oriented view on quality as well, where quality is defined by looking from the user to the program. This leads to notions like 'adequacy' and 'relevance'. For example, a helpdesk staffed with skilled people may contribute considerably to the quality of a system as perceived by its users, but this quality attribute generally does not follow from a product-based view on quality.

A very eclectic view on quality is taken in Total Quality Management (TQM). In TQM, quality applies to each and every aspect of the organization, and it is pursued by each and every employee of that organization. TQM has three cornerstones:

1. **Customer value strategy** Quality is a combination of benefits derived from a product and sacrifices required of the customer. The right balance between these benefits and sacrifices has to be sought. The key stakeholder in this balancing act is the customer, rather than the customer's boss. The attitude is not 'We know what is best for the customer', but 'Let's first determine what the customer needs'.

2. **Organizational systems** Systems encompass more than software and hardware. Other materials, humans, work practices, belong to the system as well. Moreover, systems cross unit or department boundaries. In the TQM-view, systems eliminate complexity rather than people. In TQM, culture is not dominated by power struggles. Rather, the organization takes advantage of the employees' pride in craftsmanship. Human resources are regarded as a critical resource rather than a mere cost factor.

3. **Continuous improvement** A 'traditional' environment is reactive: improvement is triggered in case of a problem or the development of a new product. In TQM, quality is pursued proactively. Errors are not viewed as personal failures which require punishment, but as opportunities for learning. Performance is not evaluated in retrospect as either good or bad, but variation in performance is analyzed statistically to understand causes of poor performance. Authority is not imposed by position and rules, but is earned by communicating a vision.

TQM thus stresses improvement rather than conformance. CMM (see section 6.6) builds on TQM, and many of the requirements engineering techniques discussed in chapter 9 owe a tribute to TQM as well.

6.4 THE QUALITY SYSTEM

ISO, the International Organization for Standardization, has developed ISO 9000, a series of standards for quality management systems. The series consists of five parts: ISO 9000-1, ISO 9001–9003, and ISO 9004-1. ISO 9000-1 gives guidelines for the selection and use of the series of standards on quality systems. ISO 9001-9003 discuss three different models for quality systems. The one most suited to software development is ISO 9001, 'Quality systems - Model for quality assurance in design, development, production, installation and servicing'.[2] ISO 9004-1 contains guidelines for the individual elements of the various standards.

Below, we will highlight the main constituents of ISO 9001. It should be emphasized that the requirements specified in this standard are complementary, and not alternative, to the technical requirements of the product.

ISO 9001 describes its scope as: 'This International Standard specifies quality system requirements for use when a contract between two parties requires the demonstration of a supplier's capability to design and supply products. The requirements specified in this International Standard are aimed primarily at preventing nonconformity at all stages from design to servicing.' The field of application is defined as: 'contractual situations when:

a) the contract specifically requires design effort and the product requirements are stated principally in performance terms or they need to be established;

b) confidence in product conformance can be attained by adequate demonstration of certain supplier's capabilities in design, development, production, installation and servicing'.

[2]ISO 9002 describes a model that applies only to production, installation and servicing; ISO 9003 describes a model applicable to final inspection and test.

Thus, clause a) indicates that the model still applies if the requirements are not completely specified in advance. This is very useful for software development, since requirements are usually not stable. Clause b) specifies that we must be reasonably sure in advance that the supplier possesses sufficient capabilities to reach the goals set forth.

1. Management responsibility
2. Quality system
3. Contract review
4. Design control
5. Document and data control
6. Purchasing
7. Control of customer-supplied product
8. Product identification and traceability
9. Process control
10. Inspection and testing
11. Control of inspection, measuring and test equipment
12. Inspection and test status
13. Control of nonconforming product
14. Corrective and preventive action
15. Handling, storage, packaging, preservation, and delivery
16. Control of quality records
17. Internal quality audits
18. Training
19. Servicing
20. Statistical techniques

Figure 6.10 Ingredients of ISO 9001

The topics to be addressed in a quality system along the lines of ISO 9001 are listed in figure 6.10. Appendix A further elaborates upon these ingredients. As can be inferred from figure 6.10, a quality system needs to address a large number of issues. Though ISO 9001 is not specifically aimed at software products (one might even claim that the standard suggests application to quality control for physical products) it is entirely possible to apply this standard to software quality control as well.

Many organizations try, or have already tried, to obtain ISO 9000 registration. The time and cost this takes depends on how much the current process deviates from the ISO standards. If the current quality system is not already close to conforming, then ISO registration may take at least one year. ISO registration is granted when a third-party accredited body assesses the quality system and concludes that it does conform to the ISO standard. Reregistration is required every three years and surveillance audits are required every six months. ISO registration thus is a fairly drastic and costly affair, after which you certainly cannot lean back, but have to keep the organization alert.

Since software development projects have some rather peculiar characteristics (frequent changes in requirements during the development process, the rather invisible nature of the product during its development), there is a need for quality assurance procedures which are tailored towards software development. This is the topic of the next section.

6.5 SOFTWARE QUALITY ASSURANCE

The purpose of Software Quality Assurance (SQA) is to make sure that work gets done the way it is supposed to be done. More specifically, the goals of SQA [Hum89] are:

- to improve software quality by appropriately monitoring the software and its development process;
- to ensure full compliance with the established standards and procedures for the software and the development process;
- to ensure that any inadequacies in the product, the process, or the standards are brought to management's attention so these inadequacies can be fixed.

Note that the SQA people themselves are not responsible for producing quality products. Their job is to review and audit, and to provide the project and management with the results of these reviews and audits.

There are potential conflicts of interest between the SQA organization and the development organization. The development organization may be facing deadlines and may want to ship a product, while the SQA people have revealed serious quality problems and wish to defer shipment. In such cases, the opinion of the SQA organization should prevail. For SQA to be effective, certain prerequisites must be fulfilled:

- It is essential that top management commitment is secured, so that suggestions made by the SQA organization can be enforced. If this is not the case, SQA soon becomes a costly padding and a mere nuisance to the development organization;
- The SQA organization should be independent from the development organization. Its reporting line should also be independent;
- The SQA organization should be staffed with technically competent and judicious people. They need to cooperate with the development organization. If the two organizations operate as adversaries, SQA won't be effective. We must realize that, in the long run, the aims of the SQA organization and the development organization are the same: the production of high-quality products.

The review and audit activities and the standards and procedures that must be followed are described in the Software Quality Assurance Plan.

IEEE standard 730 offers a framework for the contents of a Quality Assurance Plan for software development [IEE89]. Figure 6.11 lists the entries of such a document. Appendix B contains a fuller description of its various constituents. IEEE standard 730 applies to the development and maintenance of critical software. For non-critical software, a subset of the requirements may be used.

IEEE standard 983 [IEE86b] is a useful complement to standard 730. IEEE Standard 983 offers further guidelines as to the contents of a quality assurance plan, the implementation of a quality assurance plan, and its evaluation and modification.

1. Purpose
2. Reference documents
3. Management
4. Documentation
5. Standards, practices, conventions, and metrics
6. Reviews and audits
7. Test
8. Problem reporting and corrective action
9. Tools, techniques, and methodologies
10. Code control
11. Media control
12. Supplier control
13. Records collection, maintenance, and retention
14. Training
15. Risk management

Figure 6.11 Main ingredients of IEEE Std 730

The Software Quality Assurance Plan describes how the quality of the software is to be assessed. As noted before, some quality factors, such as reliability, can be determined objectively. Most factors at present can be determined only subjectively. Most often then, we will try to assess the quality by reading documents, by inspections, by walkthroughs and by peer reviews. In a number of cases, we may profitably employ tools during quality assurance, in particular, for static and dynamic analysis of program code. The actual techniques to be applied here will be discussed in the chapter on testing.

6.6 THE CAPABILITY MATURITY MODEL (CMM)

Consider the following course of events in a hypothetical software development project. Some organization is to develop a distributed library automation system. A centralized computer hosts both the software and the database. A number of local libraries are connected to the central machine through telephone lines. The organization has some experience with library automation, albeit only with stand-alone systems.

In the course of the project, a number of problems manifest themselves. At first they seem to be disconnected and they do not alarm management. It turns out that the requirements analysis has not been all that thorough. Local requirements turn out to differ on some minor points. Though the first such deviations can be handled quite easily, keeping track of all change requests becomes a real problem after a while. When part of the system has been realized, the team starts to test the connections with the host machine. The telephone lines turns out not to be reliable enough, and special provisions are needed to prevent loss of data. Early back-of-the-envelope calculations as regards the speed of algorithms have been inadequate and some major algorithms will have to be redesigned.

The project gets into a crisis eventually. Management has no proper means to handle the situation. It tries to cut back on both functionality and quality in a somewhat haphazard way. In the end, a rather unsatisfactory system is delivered two months late. During the subsequent maintenance phase, a number of problems are solved, but the system never becomes a real success.

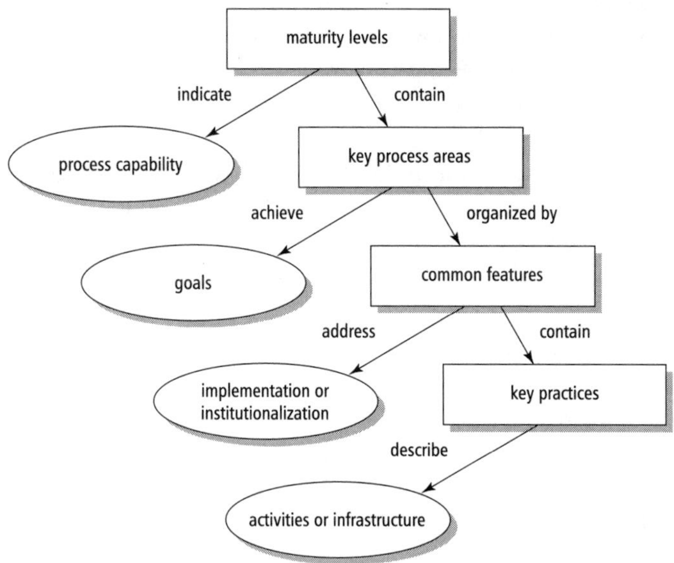

Figure 6.12 Global structure of the Capability Maturity Model (*Source: M.C. Paulk et al.*, The Capability Maturity Model, ©*Addison-Wesley, 1994. Reproduced with permission*)

Though the above description is hypothetical, it is not all that unrealistic. Many an organization has insufficient control over its software development process. If a project gets into trouble, it is usually discovered quite late and the organization has no other means but to react in a somewhat chaotic way. More often than not, speed is confused with progress.

An important step in trying to address these problems is to realize that the software development process can indeed be controlled, measured, and improved. In order to gauge the process of improving the software development process, Watts Humphrey developed a software maturity framework which has evolved into the *Capability Maturity Model* (CMM). This framework owes tribute to Total Quality Management (TQM), which in turn is based on principles of statistical quality control as formulated by Walter Shewart in the 1930s and further developed by W. Edwards Deming and Joseph Juran in the 1980s. The version described here is CMM version 1.1. CMM was developed at the Software Engineering Institute (SEI) of Carnegie Mellon University.

In CMM, the software process is characterized into one of five **maturity levels**, evolutionary levels toward achieving a mature software process. To achieve a certain maturity level, a number of **key process areas** must be in place. These key process areas indicate important issues that have to be addressed in order to reach that level. Taken together, the key process areas of a level achieve the set of goals for that level. Each key process area contains a number of **key practices**, i.e. activities and infrastructure that help in the implementation and institutionalization of that key process area. For convenience, the key practices are organized in five sections called **common features** (see figure 6.12).

Figure 6.13 lists the maturity levels and associated key process areas. Figure 6.14 lists the common features and gives example key practices for the Level 2 key process area Software Configuration Management.

CMM's maturity levels can be characterized as follows:

- **Initial** At the initial process level, the organization operates without formalized procedures, project plans, or cost estimates. Tools are not adequately integrated. Many problems are overlooked or forgotten, and maintenance poses real problems. Software development at this level can be characterized as being ad-hoc. Performance can be improved by instituting basic project management controls:

  - **Requirements management** involves establishing and maintaining an agreement with the customer on the requirements of the software system. Since requirements inevitably change, controlling and documenting these requirements is important.

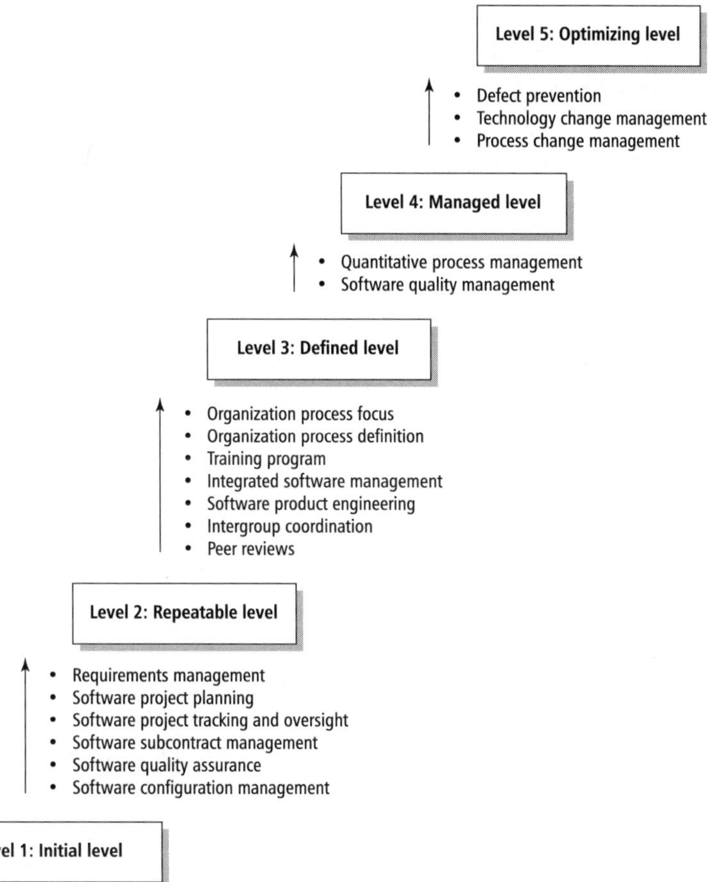

Figure 6.13 Maturity levels and associated key process areas (*Source: M.C. Paulk et al.*, The Capability Maturity Model, ©*Addison-Wesley Longman 1995. Reproduced with permission*)

- **Software project planning** involves making plans for executing and managing the project. To be able to do any planning, an approved statement of work to be done is required. From this statement of work, estimates for the size of the project, resources needed, and schedule are determined, and risks to the project are identified. The results are documented in the project plan. This plan is used to manage the project; it is updated when necessary.

Commitment to perform: establish organizational policies.
- The project follows a written policy for implementing SCM.

Ability to perform: ensure that the necessary resources, structure and training are available.
- A board having the authority for managing the software baselines exists or is established.

Activities performed: plan, do, check, act.
- A configuration management library system is established as a repository for the software baseline.

Measurement and analysis
- Measurements are made and used to determine the status of SCM activities.

Verifying implementation: review, audit, SQA activities.
- The SCM activities are reviewed with the project manager on both a periodic and event-driven basis.

Figure 6.14 Common features and example key practices for the Level 2 key process area Software Configuration Management (SCM)

- **Software project tracking and oversight** is concerned with the visibility of actual progress. Intermediate results have to be reviewed and tracked with respect to the project plan. When necessary, the project plan has to be realigned with reality.
- **Software subcontract management**. Where applicable, work done by subcontractors has to be managed: plans for their part of the work have to be made, and progress of their part of the job has to be monitored.
- **Software quality assurance** involves reviewing and auditing products and procedures to validate that they comply with agreed upon standards and procedures.
- **Software configuration management** is concerned with establishing and maintaining the integrity of all work items during the entire project life cycle. This involves identification of configuration items and baselines, and procedures to control changes to them.

- **Repeatable** The main difference between the initial process level and the repeatable process level is that the repeatable level provides control over the way plans and commitments are established. Through prior experience in doing similar work, the organization has achieved control over costs, schedules, and change requests, and earlier successes can be repeated. The introduction of new tools, the development of a new type of product, and major organizational changes however still represent major risks at this level. The key process areas needed to advance to the next level are aimed at standardizing the software process *across* the projects of the organization:
  - **Organization process focus** involves the establishment and funding of a separate group responsible for the organization's process activities. This

group assesses the software process on a regular basis, maintains information on the software process and its results in a database, and assists in the careful introduction of new tools and techniques. In this way, improvement of the organization's process capabilities is made a responsibility of the organization as a whole, rather than the individual project manager.

- **Organization process definition**. The organization develops and maintains a standard software process. Each project uses a tailored version of this standard process.
- **Training program**. The purpose of the training program is to develop the necessary skills and knowledge of individuals to perform their roles. Training needs are identified at the level of the organization, project and individual. The fulfillment of these needs is addressed as well.
- **Integrated software management** involves developing a project-specific software process from the organization's standard process, as well as the actual management of the project using the tailored process. Since the software processes of different projects have a common ancestor, projects may now share data and lessons learned.
- **Software product engineering** concerns the building and maintenance of the software using the process defined by the Integrated Software Management key process area. Major activities are the development, maintenance and documentation of the requirements, design and code, the planning and execution of tests, and maintenance of the consistency across work products, all according to the project's process.
- **Intergroup coordination** is concerned with the interaction between the software engineering group and other groups, such as quality assurance, end users or their representatives, and contract management, to identify, track and resolve issues. Its purpose is to better satisfy customer needs.
- **Peer reviews**, like walkthroughs and inspections, are practices in which peers try to identify errors and areas where changes are needed. Peer reviews are aimed at removing defects early and efficiently.

• **Defined** At the defined process level, a standard process for the development and maintenance of software is in place. The organization has achieved a solid foundation, and may now start to examine that process and decide how to improve its process. Major steps to advance to the next level are:

- **Quantitative process management**, which involves the setting of performance goals, measuring process performance, analyzing these measurements, and making the appropriate adjustments to the process in order to bring it in line with the defined limits. There is, therefore, an organization-wide measurement program and the results of it are used to continuously improve the process. An example process measure is the number of lines of code reviewed per hour.

  - **Software quality management** is aimed at defining measurable goals for the quality of the *product* (as opposed to the process). These quality goals are monitored and revised throughout the software life cycle.

- **Managed** At the managed process level, quantitative data is gathered and analyzed on a routine basis. Everything is under control, and attention may therefore shift from being reactive – what happens to the present project? – to being proactive – what can we do to improve future projects? The focus shifts to opportunities for continuous improvement:

  - **Defect prevention** is concerned with identifying common causes of defects, and preventing them from recurring.
  - **Technology management** is concerned with the identification of new technologies, and their orderly transition into the organization.
  - **Process change management** is concerned with the continuous improvement of the process in order to improve the quality of the products, the productivity of the software development organization, and reduction of the time needed to develop products.

- **Optimizing** At the final, optimizing, level, a stable base has been reached from which further improvements can be made. The step to the optimizing process level is a paradigm shift. Whereas attention at the other levels is focused on ways to improve the product, emphasis at the optimizing level has shifted from the product to the process. The data gathered can now be used to improve the software development process itself.

In 1989, Humphrey investigated the state of software engineering practice with respect to the CMM [HKK89]. Although this study concerned the DoD software community, there is little reason to expect that the situation was much rosier in another environment. According to his findings, software engineering practice at that time was largely at the initial level. There were a few organizations operating at the repeatable level, and a few projects operating at the defined level. No organization or project operated at the managed or optimizing levels.

In the ensuing years, a lot has happened. Many organizations have initiated a software process improvement program (SPI) to achieve a higher maturity level. Most of these improvement programs concern a move to the repeatable or defined level. The number of organizations at these levels has significantly increased since

1989. There are still very few organizations or projects at the managed or optimizing level.

Reports from practical experience show that it takes about two years per level to move from the initial to the defined level (there are not enough data points for the higher levels). The cost ranges from $500 to $2000 per employee per year. The benefits, however, seem to easily outweigh the cost. Several companies have reported a return on investment of at least 5 to 1: every dollar invested in a process improvement program resulted in cost savings of at least $5.

To address the needs of small companies and small project teams, the Software Engineering Institute developed the Personal Software Process (PSP), a self-improvement process designed to help individuals to improve the way they work. Like the CMM, the PSP distinguishes between several maturity levels. The first step in PSP is to establish some basic measurements, such as development time and defects found, using simple forms to collect these data. At the next level, these data are used to estimate time and quality. At still higher levels, the personal data are used to *improve* the individual's performance.

The basic principles of the CMM and the PSP are thus very similar: know thy process, measure thy performance, and base thy improvement actions on an analysis of the data gathered. The PSP does not yet have an assessment instrument to determine the maturity level.

BOOTSTRAP and SPICE are two other CMM-like maturity models. BOOTSTRAP uses a separate maturity rating for each of its practices. One of the interesting features of BOOTSTRAP is that all assessment results are collected in a database, thus allowing an organization to position itself by comparing its scores with those of similar organizations.

SPICE is an international initiative and has become an international standard (ISO/IEC 15504). SPICE stands for Software Process Improvement and Capability dEtermination. SPICE distinguishes different process categories, such as the management process, customer–supplier process and engineering process. The capability (maturity) level is determined for each process category and each process. Like BOOTSTRAP, SPICE thus results in a maturity profile. The SPICE methodology places heavy emphasis on the way process assessments are performed.

6.7 SOME CRITICAL NOTES

Software development organizations exist to develop software rather than processes.
[Fay97]

The massive attention of organizations to obtaining CMM or ISO 9000 certification holds the danger that focus shifts from developing software to developing processes. A certified organization, however, does not guarantee the quality of the software developed under it. A mature development process is not a silver bullet. A framed certificate definitely is not.

The SEI's Capability Maturity Model seems most appropriate for the really big companies. It is doubtful whether small companies can afford the time and money required by a process improvement program as advocated by CMM. It is also doubtful whether they can afford to implement some of the key process areas, such as setting up an organization process group. Though the Personal Software Process may alleviate part of this criticism, at present the PSP does not have the same status as the CMM.

CMM's maturity levels constitute a rather crude five-point scale. If the assessment of a level 2 organization reveals that it fails the level 3 criteria on just one tiny issue, the verdict is rather harsh: the organization simply remains at level 2. This may not improve morale after two years of hard labor and significant investment. For one thing, this implication of maturity assessments places high demands on their reliability.

The rather crude assessment of organizations on a five-point scale may have other far-reaching consequences. The US Department of Defense will require level 3 certification to qualify for contracts. Will this imply that level 1 and level 2 organizations are necessarily performing below standard? If level 3 certification is all that matters, is it worthwhile to aim for level 4 or 5?

CMM's levels are like an instrument panel of an airplane with one gauge, which moreover can display only a few discrete values and thus provides the pilot with very little information. One may also envisage a software maturity 'instrument panel' with many gauges, each of which shows a lot of detail. BOOTSTRAP and SPICE are frameworks that result in a maturity profile rather than a single score.

6.8 GETTING STARTED

In the preceding sections we discussed various ways to review the quality of a software product and the associated development process. The development organization itself should actively pursue the production of quality products, by setting quality goals, assessing its own performance and taking actions to improve the development process.

This requires an understanding of possible inadequacies in the development process and possible causes thereof. Such an understanding is to be obtained through the collection of data on both the process and the resulting products, and a proper interpretation of those numbers. It is rather easy to collect massive amounts of data and apply various kinds of curve-fitting techniques to them. In order to be able to properly interpret the trends observed, they should be backed by sound hypotheses.

An, admittedly ridiculous, example is given in figure 6.15. The numbers in this table indicate that black cows produce more milk than white cows. A rather naive interpretation is that productivity can be improved significantly by repainting all the white cows.

Color	Average production
White	10
Black	40

Figure 6.15 Hypothetical relation between the color of cows and the average milk production

Though the example itself is ridiculous, its counterpart in software engineering is not all that far-fetched. Many studies, for example, have tried to determine a relation between numbers indicating the complexity of software components and the quality of those components. Quite a few of those studies found a positive correlation between such complexity figures and, say, the number of defects found during testing. A straightforward interpretation of those findings then is to impose some upperbound on the complexity allowed for each component. However, there may be good reasons for certain components having a high complexity. For instance, [RAC90] studied complexity metrics of a large number of modules from the MINIX operating system. Some of these, such as a module that handles escape character sequences from the keyboard, were considered justifiably complex. Experts judged a further decomposition of these modules not justified. Putting a mere upperbound on the allowed value of certain complexity metrics is too simple an approach.

An organization has to discover its opportunities for process improvements. The preferred way to do so is to follow a stepwise, evolutionary approach in which the following steps can be identified:

1. Formulate hypotheses

2. Carefully select appropriate metrics

3. Collect data

4. Interpret those data

5. Initiate actions for improvement

These steps are repeated, so that the effect of the actions is validated, and further hypotheses are formulated. By following this approach, the quest for quality will permeate your organization, which will subsequently reap the benefits.

One example of this approach is discussed in [vG91]. He describes an empirical study of reasons for delay in software development. The study covered six development projects from one department. Attention was focused on the collection of data relating to time and effort, viz. differences between plan and reality. A one-page data collection form was used for this purpose (see figure 6.16).

	Planned	Actual	Difference	Reason
Effort	–	–	–	–
Starting date	–	–	–	–
Ending date	–	–	–	–
Duration	–	–	–	–

Figure 6.16 Time sheet for each activity

Some thirty reasons for delay were identified. These were classified into six categories after a discussion with the project leaders, and finalized after a pilot study. The reasons for delay were found to be specific to the environment.

A total of 160 activities were studied from mid 1988 to mid 1989. About 50% of the activities overran their plan by more than 10%. Comparison of planned and actual figures showed that the relative differences increased towards the end of the projects. It was found that one prime reason for the difference between plan and reality was 'more time spent on other work than planned'. The results were interpreted during a meeting with the project leaders and the department manager. The discussion confirmed and quantified some existing impressions. For some, the discussion provided new information. It showed that maintenance actions constantly interrupted development work. The meeting included a discussion on possible actions for improvement. It was decided to schedule maintenance as far as possible in 'maintenance weeks' and include those in quarterly plans. Another analysis study was started to gain further insights into maintenance activities.

This study provides a number of useful insights, some of which reinforce statements made earlier:

- The 'closed loop' principle states that information systems should be designed such that those who provide input to the system are also main users of its output. Application of this principle results in feedback to the supplier of data, who is thereby forced to provide accurate input. It also prevents users from asking more than they need. In the above example, the data was both collected and analyzed by the project leaders. The outcome was reported back to those same project leaders and used as a starting point for further actions.

- Local data collection should be for local use. Data collected may vary considerably between departments. Data is best used to gain insight in the performance of the department where the data is collected. Use in another department makes little sense.

- The focus should be on continuous improvement. The data collection effort was aimed at locating perceived deficiencies in the software development process. It revealed causes for these deficiencies and provided an opportunity for improvement. The question is not one of 'who is right and who is wrong', but rather 'how can we prevent this from happening again in future projects'.

- The study did not involve massive data collection. Simple data sheets were used, together with unambiguous definitions of the meaning of the various metrics. The approach is incremental, whereby the study gives an opportunity for small improvements, and shows the way for the next study.

6.9 SUMMARY

In this chapter, we paid ample attention to the notion of quality. Software quality does not come for free. It has to be actively pursued. The use of a well-defined model of the software development process and good analysis, design and implementation techniques are a prerequisite. However, quality must also be controlled and managed. To be able to do so, it has to be defined rigorously. This is not without problems, as we have seen in sections 6.2 and 6.3. There exist numerous taxonomies of quality attributes. For each of these attributes, we need a precise definition, together with a metric that can be used to state quality goals, and to check that these quality goals are indeed being satisfied. Most quality attributes relate to aspects that are primarily of interest to the software developers. These engineer-oriented quality views are difficult to reconcile with the user-oriented 'fitness for use' aspects.

For most quality attributes, the relation between what is actually measured (module structure, defects encountered, etc.) and the attribute we are interested in is insufficiently supported by a sound hypothesis. For example, though programs with a large number of decisions are often complex, counterexamples exist which show that the number of decisions (essentially McCabe's cyclomatic complexity) is not a good measure of program complexity. The issue of software metrics and the associated problems is further dealt with in chapter 11.

Major standards for quality systems have been defined by ISO and IEEE. These standards give detailed guidelines as regards the management of quality. The importance of careful software quality assurance procedures is increasingly being recognized.

Quality assurance by itself does not guarantee quality products. It has to be supplemented by a quality program within the development organization. Section 6.8 advocates an evolutionary approach to establishing a quality program. Such an approach allows us to gradually build up expertise in the use of quantitative data to find opportunities for process improvements.

We finally sketched the software maturity framework developed by the Software Engineering Institute. This framework offers a means to assess the state of software engineering practice, as well as a number of steps to improve the software development process. The SEI's Capability Maturity Model results in a rather coarse assessment on a single, five-point scale. Similar initiatives, like BOOTSTRAP and SPICE, yield a finer-grained maturity profile.

One of the major contributions of CMM and similar initiatives is their focus on *continuous improvement*. This line of thought has subsequently been successfully applied to other areas, resulting in, amongst others, a People-CMM, a Formal specifications-CMM, and a Measurement-CMM.

6.10 FURTHER READING

[FP96] provides a very thorough overview of the field of software metrics. The measurement framework discussed in section 6.1 is based on [KPF95]. [Sof97b], [Com94] and [JSS95a] are special journal issues on software metrics. Many of the articles in these issues deal with the application of metrics in quality programs.

One of the first major publications on the topic of measurement programs is [GC87]. Success factors for measurement programs can be found in [HF97]. [Pfl95] elaborates on the relation between metrics programs and maturity levels. [NvV98b] give a CMM-like framework for the measurement capability of software organizations.

The best known taxonomies of software quality attributes are given in [MRW77] and [BBK+78]. The ISO quality attributes are described in [ISO97]. Critical discussions of these schemes are given in [KP96] and [FP96].

Garvin's quality definitions are given in [Gar84]. Different kinds of benefit in a value-based definition of quality are discussed in [Sim96]. For an elaborate discussion of Total Quality Management, see [BYAR94] or [Ish85].

The Capability Maturity Model is based on the seminal work of Watts Humphrey [Hum88, Hum89]. For a full description of the Capability Maturity Model version 1.1, see [PWCe94]. Its evolution is discussed in [Pau95]. Practical experiences with software process improvement programs are discussed in [WR94], [Be95], [RAvG96], [Das94], [DS97] and [FO99]. A survey of benefits and costs of software process improvement programs is given in [HZG+97]. The Space Shuttle Onboard Software project is an example of a project rated at CMM Level 5; it is described in [SBR95] and [BCK+94].

The Personal Software Process (PSP) is described in [Hum95], [Hum96] and [Hum97a]. BOOTSTRAP is described in [KSK+94] and SPICE in [EEDM97] and [Rou95].

Criticisms of CMM-like approaches are found in [Fay97], [FL97] and [Oul96]. [EEM95b] and [EEBS96] discuss the reliability of process assessments.

Process improvement is the topic of several special journal issues; see [CAC97b], [Sof94a]. The journal *Software Process: Improvement and Practice* is wholly devoted to this topic.

Exercises

1. Define the following terms: measurement, measure, metric.

2. What is the difference between an internal and an external attribute?

3. Define the term *representation condition*. Why is it important that a measure satisfies the representation condition?

4. What is the main difference between an ordinal scale and an interval scale? And between an interval scale and a ratio scale?

5. What are the main differences between the user-based and product-based definitions of quality?

6. Which are the three categories of software quality factors distinguished by McCall?

7. Discuss the transcendent view of software quality.

8. Which of Garvin's definitions of quality is mostly used by the software developer? And which one is mostly used by the user?

9. Which quality viewpoint is stressed by ISO 9126?

10. Discuss the cornerstones of Total Quality Management.

11. What is the purpose of Software Quality Assurance?

12. Why should the Software Quality Assurance organization be independent of the development organization?

13. Why should project members get feedback on the use of quality data they submit to the Quality Assurance Group?

14. Describe the maturity levels of the Capability Maturity Model.

15. What is the major difference between level 2 and level 3 of the Capability Maturity Model?

16. Why is it important to quantify quality requirements?

17. ♠ Consider a software development project you have been involved in. How was quality handled in this project? Were quality requirements defined at an early stage? Were these requirements defined such that they could be tested at a later stage?

18. ♡ Define measurable properties of a software product that make up the quality criteria Modularity and Operability. Do these properties constitute an objective measure of these criteria? If not, in what ways is subjectivity introduced?

19. ♡ The quality factor Reusability influences several other quality factors, both positively and negatively, as indicated in figure 6.7. Can you think of arguments that explain these influences?

20. ♡ Give a possible staffing for an SQA group, both for a small development organization (less than 25 people) and a large development organization (more than 100 people).

21. ♠ Draw up a Quality Assurance Plan for a project you have been involved in.

22. ♠ One quality requirement often stated is that the system should be 'user-friendly'. Discuss possible differences between the developer's point of view and the user's point of view in defining this notion. Think of alternative ways to define system usability in measurable terms.

23. ♠ Using the classification of the Capability Maturity Model, determine the maturity level that best fits your organization. Which steps would you propose

to advance the organization to a higher maturity level? Are any actions being pursued to get from the current level to a more mature one?

24. ♠ Write a critical essay on software maturity assessment, as exemplified by the Capability Maturity Model. The further reading section provides ample pointers to the literature on this topic.

25. ♡ In 1988 and 1998, two surveys were conducted to assess the state of the art in software cost estimation in The Netherlands. One of the questions concerned the various stakeholders involved in developing a cost estimate. The resulting percentages were as follows:

	1988	1998
Management	48.9	75.8
Staff department	22.8	37.4
Development team	22.6	23.6
Project manager	36.7	42.3
Customer	15.4	15.9
Other	8.9	8.2
Average # of parties involved	1.55	2.03

It was concluded that the situation had improved. In 1998, the average number of parties involved had increased and this was felt to be a good sign. For each individual category, the percentage had gone up as well.

Can you think of a possibly negative conclusion from this same set of data, i.e. that the situation has become *worse* since 1988?

7
Cost Estimation

LEARNING OBJECTIVES

- To appreciate the use of quantitative, objective approaches to software cost estimation
- To be aware of the history of software cost estimation and the lessons to be learned from those early efforts
- To understand well-known techniques for estimating software cost and effort
- To understand techniques for relating effort to development time

When commissioning a house construction, decorating the bathroom, or laying-out a garden, we expect a precise estimate of the costs to be incurred before the operation is started. A gardener is capable of giving a rough indication of the cost on the basis of, say, the area of land, the desired size of the terrace or grass area, whether or not a pond is required, and similar information. The estimate can be made more precise in further dialog, before the first bit of earth is turned. If you expect a similar accuracy as regards the cost estimate for a software development project, you are in for a surprise.

Estimating the cost of a software development project is a rather unexplored field, in which one all too often relies on mere guesstimates. There are exceptions to this procedure, fortunately. There now exist a number of algorithmic models that allow us to estimate total cost and development time of a software development project, based on estimates for a limited number of relevant cost drivers. Some of the important algorithmic cost estimation models will be discussed in section 7.3.

In most cost estimation models, a simple relation between cost and effort is assumed. The effort may be measured in man-months, for instance, and each man-month is taken to incur a fixed amount, say, of $5000. The total estimated cost is then obtained by simply multiplying the estimated number of man-months by this constant factor. In this chapter, we will freely use the terms cost and effort as if they are synonymous.

The notion of total cost is usually taken to indicate the cost of the initial software development effort, i.e. the cost of the requirements engineering, design, implementation and testing phases. Thus, maintenance costs are not taken into account. Unless explicitly stated otherwise, this notion of cost will also be used by us. In the same vein, development time will be taken to mean: the time between the start of the requirements engineering phase and the point in time when the software is delivered to the customer. Lastly, the notion of cost as it is used here, does not include possible hardware costs either. It concerns only personnel costs involved in software development.

Research in the area of cost estimation is far from crystallized. Different models use different measures and cost drivers, so that mutual comparisons are very difficult. Suppose some model uses an equation of the form:

$$E = 2.7 KLOC^{1.05}$$

This equation shows a certain relation between effort needed (E) and the size of the product ($KLOC$ = Kilo Lines Of Code = Lines Of Code/1000). The effort measure could be the number of man-months needed. Several questions come to mind immediately: What is a line of code? Do we count machine code, or the source code in some high-level language? Do we count comment lines, or blank lines that increase readability? Do we take into account holidays, sick-leave, and the like, in our notion of the man-month, or does it concern a net measure? Different interpretations of these notions may lead to widely different results. Unfortunately, different models do use different definitions of these notions. Sometimes, it is not even known which definitions were used in the derivation of the model.

To determine the equations of an algorithmic cost estimation model, we may follow several approaches. Firstly, we may base our equations on the results of experiments. In such an experiment, we in general vary one parameter, while the other parameters are kept constant. In this way, we may try to determine the influence of the parameter that is being varied. As a typical example, we may consider the question of whether or not comments help to build up our understanding of a program. Under careful control of the circumstances, we may pose a number of questions about one and the same program text to two groups of programmers. The first group gets program text without comments, the second group gets the same program text, with comments. We may check our hypothesis using the results of the two groups. The, probably realistic, assumption in this experiment is that a better and faster understanding of the program text has a positive effect on the maintainability of that program.

This type of laboratory experiment is often performed at universities, where students play the role of programmers. It is not self-evident that the results thus obtained will also hold in industrial settings. In practice, there may be a rather complicated interaction between different relevant factors. Also, the subjects need not be representative. Finally, the generalization from laboratory experiments that are (of necessity) limited in size to big software development projects with which professionals are confronted is not possible. The general opinion is that results thus obtained have limited validity, and certainly need further testing.

A second way to arrive at algorithmic cost estimation models is based on an analysis of real project data, in combination with some theoretical underpinning. An organization may collect data about a number of software systems that have been developed. These data may concern the time spent on the various phases that are being distinguished, the qualifications of the personnel involved, the points in time at which errors occurred, both during testing and after installation, the complexity, reliability and other relevant project factors, the size of the resulting code, etc. Based on a sound hypothesis of the relations between the various entities involved and a (statistical) analysis of these data we may derive equations that numerically characterize these relations. An example of such a relation is the one given above, which relates E to $KLOC$. The usability and reliability of such equations is obviously very much dependent upon the reliability of the data on which they are based. Also, the hypothesis that underlies the form of the equation must be sound.

The findings obtained in this way reflect an average, a best possible approximation based on available data. We therefore have to be very careful in applying the results obtained. If the software to be developed in the course of a new project cannot be compared with earlier products because of the degree of innovation involved, one is in for a big surprise. For example, estimating the cost of the Space Shuttle project cannot be done through a simple extrapolation from earlier projects. We may hope, however, that the average software development project has a higher predictability as regards effort needed and the corresponding cost.

The way in which we obtain quantitative relations implies further constraints on the use of these models. The model used is based on an analysis of data from earlier projects. Application of the model to new projects is possible only insofar as those new projects resemble old projects, i.e. the projects on whose data the model is based. If we have collected data on projects of a certain kind and within a particular organization, a model based on these data cannot be used without amendment for different projects in a possibly different organization. A model based on data about administrative projects in a government environment has little predictive value for the development of real-time software in the aerospace industry. This is one of the reasons why the models of, for example, [WF77] and [Boe81] (see section 7.3 for more detailed discussions of these models) yield such different results for one and the same problem description.

The lesson to be learned is that blind application of the formulae from existing models will not solve your cost estimation problem. Each model needs tuning to the environment in which it is going to be used. This implies the need to continuously collect your own project data, and to apply statistical techniques to calibrate model parameters.

Other reasons for the discrepancies between existing models are:

- Most models give a relation between man-months needed and size (in lines of code). As remarked before, widely different definitions of these notions are used.

- The notion 'effort' does not always mean the same thing. Sometimes, one only counts the activities starting from the design, i.e. after the requirements specification has been fixed. Sometimes also, one includes maintenance effort.

Despite these discrepancies, the various cost estimation models do have a number of characteristics in common. These common characteristics reflect important factors that bear on development cost and effort. The increased understanding of software costs allows us to identify strategies for improving software productivity, the most important of which are:

- Writing less code. System size is one of the main determinants of effort and cost. Techniques that try to reduce size, such as software reuse and the use of high-level languages, can obtain significant savings.

- Getting the best from people. Individual and team capabilities have a large impact on productivity. The best people are usually a bargain. Better incentives, better work environments, training programs and the like provide further productivity improvement opportunities.

- Avoiding rework. Studies have shown that a considerable effort is spent redoing earlier work. The application of prototyping or evolutionary development process models and the use of modern programming practices (information hiding) can yield considerable savings.

- Developing and using integrated project support environments. Tools can help us eliminate steps or make steps more efficient.

A distinction is often made between **programming-in-the-small** and **programming-in-the-large**. Programming-in-the-small refers to small projects in which a single programmer exerts himself in a concentrated effort during a limited period of time. On the other hand, programming-in-the-large refers to projects in which a team of programmers is involved for a considerable period of time. Obviously, these are two extreme orientations, with many possible intermediate forms.

A number of studies have been done in which the main focus was to estimate the effort needed for a limited programming task. Some of the first experiments in this area were done by Halstead, who developed a rather elaborate model that has become known as *software science*. This model is discussed more extensively in chapter 11. At the core of this model lies the observation that counting lines of code can be problematic, even if we have a very accurate definition of 'line of code'. Some lines are more complicated than others. According to Halstead, it is better to start from the number of syntactic units, as they are recognized by a compiler. Halstead makes a distinction between *operators* and *operands*. Operators denote some action. Examples of operators are the standard operators ($+$, $-$, $\times$, etc), but also the semicolon that denotes composition of instructions, and constructs like **if-then-else** and **while-do**. Operands denote data: variables and constants. According to Halstead, counting the number of operators and operands in a program yields a better size measure than simply counting the number of lines.

The four basic entities in Halstead's model are, for a given program:

n_1 = the number of unique (i.e. different) operators
n_2 = the number of unique (i.e. different) operands
N_1 = the total number of occurrences of operators
N_2 = the total number of occurrences of operands

For the length of a program, Halstead gives the following equation:

$$N = N_1 + N_2$$

In this way, we obtain a refinement of the simple lines of code measure LOC. Both LOC and N (and also McCabe's complexity metric, also discussed in chapter 11) turn out to correlate well with programming effort. It is therefore interesting to look for possibilities of estimating entities like LOC or N at an early stage. The value of N is highly dependent on the values of n_1 and n_2. Not surprisingly, the value for n_1 is rather constant for many programs in a given high-level language. This constant depends on the language chosen. For, given a particular programming language, the maximum number of unique operators is fixed: they are all listed in the syntax of the language. Most non-trivial programs will use a large percentage of these operators at least once. A further hypothesis could be that n_2 is mainly determined by the number of variables ($VARS$) that occur in the program. Based on these assumptions, several studies investigated empirical relations of the form:

$$LOC = \alpha + \beta \times VARS$$

Each program would thus contain about α lines of code, plus an additional β lines for each variable occurring in that program. Not surprisingly, the accuracy of predictions obtained this way generally increases as the environment gets more homogeneous. In one study, a much more accurate prediction was found if variables were weighted by the number of subprograms in which they were used. Since an estimate of $VARS$ can be obtained relatively early if a top-down design method is used in combination with a strongly-typed language like Pascal, such a model offers a good starting point for an early cost estimate.

Generalization of these results to really big programs is not straightforward. In large programs, factors like the complexity of the interfaces between components and the necessary communication between the people involved play a role which cannot be neglected. At this macro level, the relations found will in general be more complicated. In the next sections, we will further discuss various models for estimating software cost at the macro level. In particular, we will discuss and compare some of the well-known algorithmic models in section 7.3.

Given an estimate of the size of a project, we will next be interested in the development time needed. With a naive view, we may conjecture that a project with an estimated effort of 100 man-months can be done in 1 year with a team of 8.5 people, but equally well in one month with a team of 100 people. This view is too naive. A project of a certain size corresponds to a certain nominal physical time period. If we try to shorten this nominal development time too much, we get into the 'impossible region' and the chance of failure sharply increases. This phenomenon will be further discussed in section 7.4.

7.1 HOW NOT TO ESTIMATE COST

Cost estimates are often colored in a political way, i.e. arguments other than the purely technical may (partly) determine the outcome. Typical lines of reasoning that reflect those non-technical arguments are:

- We were given 12 months to do the job, so it will take 12 months. This might be seen as a variation of Parkinson's Law: work fills the time available.

- We know that our competitor put in a bid of $1M, so we need to schedule a bid of $0.9M. This is sometimes referred to as 'price to win'.

- We want to show our product at the trade show next year, so the software needs to be written and tested within the next nine months, though we realize that this is rather tight. This could be termed the 'budget' method of cost estimation.

- Actually, the project needs one year, but I can't sell that to my boss. We know that ten months is acceptable, so we will settle for ten months.

Politically-colored estimates can have disastrous effects, as has been shown all too often during the short history of our field. Political arguments almost always play a role if estimates are being given by people directly involved in the project, such as the project manager, or someone reporting to the project manager. Very soon, then, estimates will influence, or be influenced by, the future assessment of those persons.

Many of the models to be discussed in the following sections are based on data about past projects. The arguments stated above may also influence this data collection process. A seemingly objective model may thus turn out to be useless, since the data on which the model is based are unreliable. A careful data collection procedure is therefore needed. In large organizations, one may set up a separate unit whose only task is to gather data and deliver accountable cost estimates. This unit has to treat the data supplied in a proprietary way.

Besides the reliability of the available data and the uncertainty of what exactly has been measured, one of the main problems is the sheer *lack* of quantitative data about past projects. There simply is not enough data available. Though the importance of such a database is now widely recognized we still do not routinely collect data on current projects. It seems as if we cannot spare the time to collect data; we have to write software. [DeM82] makes a comparison with the medieval barber who also acted as a physician. He could have made the same objection: 'We cannot afford the time to take our patient's temperature, since we have to cut his hair.'

For lack of hard data, the cost of a software development project is often estimated through a comparison with earlier projects. If the estimator is very experienced, reasonable cost estimates may result. However, the learning effect of earlier experiences may lead to estimates that are too pessimistic in this case. We may expect that experience gained with a certain type of application will lead to a higher productivity for subsequent projects. Similar applications thus give rise to lower costs.

[McC68] describes a situation in which a team was asked to develop a FORTRAN compiler for three different machines. The effort needed (in man-months) for these three projects is given in figure 7.1.

Compiler	Number of man-months needed
1	72
2	36
3	14

Figure 7.1 Learning effect in writing a FORTRAN compiler

On the other hand, peculiar circumstances and particular characteristics of a specific project tend to get insufficient attention if cost is estimated through comparison with earlier projects. For example, a simple change of scale (automation of a local library with 25 000 volumes as opposed to a university library with over 1 000 000 volumes), slightly harsher performance requirements, a compressed schedule (which incurs a larger team and thus increases overhead because of communication) may have a significant impact on the effort required in terms of man-months.

Careless application of the comparison method of cost estimation leads to estimates like: the cost of this project is equal to the cost of the previous project.

We may also involve more than one expert in the estimation process. In doing so, each expert gives an estimate based on his own experience and expertise. Factors that are hard to quantify, such as personality characteristics and peculiar project characteristics, may thus be taken into account. Here too, the quality of the estimate cannot exceed the quality of the experts.

If a group of people has to come up with a collective verdict, we will often find that some group members have a far higher impact on the outcome than others. Some members may not press their opinion or may become impressed by the volubility of their companions. This may well have a negative impact on the end result. In order to anticipate this undesirable effect, we may employ the Delphi-method if more than one expert is consulted. In the Delphi-method, each expert delivers his opinion on paper. A moderator collects the estimates thus obtained and redistributes them among the experts. In this process, the names of the experts and their estimates are decoupled. Each of the experts then delivers a new estimate, based on the information received from the moderator. This process is continued until a consensus is reached.

Another method that aims to get a more reliable estimate is to have the expert produce more than one estimate. We all have the tendency to conceive an optimistic estimate as being realistic. (Have you ever heard of a software system that got delivered ahead of time?) To obviate this tendency, we may employ a technique in which the expert is asked for three estimates: an optimistic estimate a, a realistic estimate m, and a pessimistic estimate b. Using a beta-distribution, the expected effort then is $E = (a + 4m + b)/6$. Though this estimate will probably be better than the one simply based on the average of a and b, it seems justified to warn against too much optimism. Software has the tendency to grow, and projects have the tendency to far exceed the estimated effort.

7.2 EARLY ALGORITHMIC MODELS

The message from the preceding section is clear. To be able to get really reliable estimates, we need to extensively record historical data. These historical data can be used to produce estimates for new projects. In doing so, we will predict the expected cost on account of *measurable* properties of the project at hand. Just as the cost of laying out a garden might be a weighted combination of a number of relevant attributes (size of the garden, size of the grass area, yes/no for a pond), so we would like to estimate the cost of a software development project. In this section, we will discuss some early efforts to get at algorithmic models to estimate software cost.

[Nel66] gives a linear model for estimating the effort needed for a software development project. Linear models have the form

$$E = a_0 + \sum_{i=1}^{n} a_i x_i$$

Here, the $a_i, i = 0, \ldots, n$ are constants, and $x_i, i = 1, \ldots, n$ denote factors that impact the effort needed, i.e. cost. A large number of factors may influence productivity, and hence the effort required. By carefully analyzing data on past projects, and different combinations of factors, we may try to get a model with a small number of factors only. Nelson, for instance, suggests a model that takes into account 14 factors:

$$\begin{aligned} E = & -33.63 + 9.15x_1 + 10.73x_2 + 0.51x_3 + 0.46x_4 + 0.40x_5 + 7.28x_6 \\ & -21.45x_7 + 13.5x_8 + 12.35x_9 + 58.82x_{10} + 30.61x_{11} + 29.55x_{12} \\ & +0.54x_{13} - 25.20x_{14} \end{aligned}$$

In this equation, E denotes the estimate of the number of man-months needed. The meaning of the factors x_i and their possible values are given in figure 7.2.

Several observations can be made about this model. In developing software for defense applications, in which the software will often be embedded in target machines that differ from the host machine (an example might be flight-control software for missiles), factors like x_{12} and x_{14} will undoubtedly have a significant impact

Factor	Description	Possible values
x_1	Instability requirements specification	0–2
x_2	Instability design	0–3
x_3	Percentage of math instructions	percentage
x_4	Percentage of I/O instructions	percentage
x_5	Number of subprograms	number
x_6	Use of high-level language	0(yes) / 1(no)
x_7	Business application	0(yes) / 1(no)
x_8	Stand-alone program	0(yes) / 1(no)
x_9	First program on this machine	1(yes) / 0(no)
x_{10}	Concurrent development of hardware	1(yes) / 0(no)
x_{11}	Use of random-access device	1(yes) / 0(no)
x_{12}	Different host and target machine	1(yes) / 0(no)
x_{13}	Number of trips	number
x_{14}	Development by defense organization	0(yes) / 1(no)

Figure 7.2 Factors from the model of [Nel66]

on cost. This will probably not be the case in a completely different environment. This shows again that the database with project data that underlies the model will have a significant impact on the factors that break the surface. Less likely in this model is the penalty for using an assembly language rather than some high-level language (x_6): about 7 man-months, regardless of the size of the project. Similarly, the negative constant a_0 and the two other factors that count negative strike as somewhat unlikely.

From a strict measurement theory point of view, Nelson's formula is not meaningful. The scale type of factor x_1, for example, is ordinal, which means that only a linear ordering is imposed on possible values of x_1. Thus, larger values of x_1 mean a higher instability of the requirements specification. The scale type of x_1 does not allow expressions like 'requirements specification A is twice as unstable as requirements specification B'. If different measures are combined into a new measure, the scale type of the combined measure is the 'weakest' of the scale types of its constituents. In the case of Nelson's formula, the scale type of E would be ordinal too. We may then interpret different values of E as indicating that certain projects require more effort than others. The intention though is to interpret E as a ratio scale, i.e., actual effort in man-months. Strictly speaking, this is not allowed. The same objection can be raised against many other models discussed in this chapter.

In general, linear models don't work all that well. Though there is a large number of factors that impact productivity, it is very unlikely that they do so independently and linearly.

It is well to draw your attention at this point to the would-be accuracy of this type of formula. In Nelson's formula, the various constants are given with a precision of two decimals. Simply applying this formula would yield a point-estimate, such as the cost of this project is 97.32 man-months. We have to watch for the pitfall stated by the slogan 'there are three kinds of lie: ordinary lies, big lies, and statistics'. Nelson's formula is the result of a statistical analysis of real project data and has to be interpreted as such. This means that an estimate A obtained using this formula should be interpreted as: the probability that this project costs B man-months, where $(1-\alpha)A \leq B \leq (1+\alpha)A$, is greater than or equal to β, with suitable values for α and β (such as, for example, $\alpha = 0.2$ and $\beta = 0.9$). If the average height of men is 7 ft, this means that there is a fairly high chance that a randomly selected man has a height which is between 6 and 8 ft. The probability that he is exactly 7 ft high is very small. There also is a probability that his height is less than 6 ft or more than 8 ft.

Cost estimates obtained through this kind of model thus yield cost intervals and a certain non-zero probability remains that the real cost will lie outside this interval. The usability of those estimates then is strongly determined by the size of the interval and the probability that the real cost will indeed fall within that interval. Especially for large-scale development efforts, it is good practice to use the upper value of the cost interval rather than the point estimate that results from simply applying the formula. These remarks also hold for the algorithmic models to be discussed in section 7.3.

One way in which an expert could arrive at a cost estimate is through a bottom-up process. For each module, a separate cost estimate can be obtained and the total cost is then taken to be the sum of the module costs, with some correction applied because of the integration of all the modules.

Wolverton describes a model in which a simple cost matrix is used as a starting point to determine module costs. In this matrix, a limited number of different types of modules is distinguished, together with a number of complexity levels. Figure 7.3 contains such a (hypothetical) cost matrix. The matrix elements reflect the cost (in dollars) per line of code.

Given a cost matrix C, a module of type i, complexity j and size S_k, will incur an estimated module cost $M_k = S_k \times C_{ij}$.

This type of model also has its problems. Besides the difficulty of assessing module integration costs, the user has to subjectively assess the complexity class of each module, which yields a fair dose of uncertainty altogether. Other factors which may reasonably be expected to impact productivity as well, such as programming experience and hardware characteristics, are not taken into account. Extending the cost matrix in order to accommodate these factors only increases the subjectivity of the method.

	complexity				
	low		⟷		high
module type	1	2	3	4	5
1. Data management	11	13	15	18	22
2. Memory management	25	26	27	29	32
3. Algorithm	6	8	14	27	51
4. User interface	13	16	19	23	29
5. Control	20	25	30	35	40

Figure 7.3 A hypothetical cost matrix

7.3 LATER ALGORITHMIC MODELS

In the introduction to this chapter, we noticed that programming effort is strongly correlated with program size. There exist various (non-linear) models which express this correlation. A general form is

$$E = (a + bKLOC^c)f(x_1, \dots, x_n)$$

Here, $KLOC$ again denotes the size of the software (lines of code/1000), while E denotes the effort in man-months. a, b and c are constants, and $f(x_1, \dots, x_n)$ is a correction which depends on the values of the entities $x_1, \dots, x_n$. In general, the base formula

$$E = a + bKLOC^c$$

is obtained through a regression analysis of available project data. Thus, the primary cost driver is software size, measured in lines of code. This nominal cost estimate is tuned by correcting it for a number of factors that influence productivity (so-called cost drivers). For instance, if one of the factors used is 'experience of the programming team', this could incur a correction to the nominal cost estimate of 1.50, 1.20, 1.00, 0.80 and 0.60 for a very low, low, average, high and very high level of expertise, respectively.

Figure 7.4 contains some of the well-known base formulae for the relation between software size and effort. For reasons mentioned before, it is difficult to compare these models. It is interesting to note, though, that the value of c fluctuates around the value 1 in most models.

This phenomenon is well known from the theory of economics. In a so-called economy of scale, one assumes that it is cheaper to produce large quantities of the same product. The fixed costs are then distributed over a larger number of units,

Origin	Base formula	See section
Halstead	$E = 0.7\,KLOC^{1.50}$	11.1.4
Boehm	$E = 2.4\,KLOC^{1.05}$	7.3.2
Walston–Felix	$E = 5.2\,KLOC^{0.91}$	7.3.1

Figure 7.4 Some base formulae for the relation between size and effort

which decreases the cost per unit. We thus realize an increasing return on investment. In the opposite case, we find a diseconomy of scale: after a certain point the production of additional units incurs extra costs.

In the case of software, the lines of code are the product. If we assume that producing a lot of code will cost less per line of code, formulae like those of Walston–Felix ($c < 1$) result. This may occur, for example, because the cost of expensive tools like program generators, programming environments and test tools can be distributed over a larger number of lines of code. Alternatively, we may reason that large software projects will be more expensive, relatively speaking. There will be a larger overhead because of the increased need for communication and management control, because of the problems and interfaces getting more complex, and so on. Thus, each additional line of code requires more effort. In such cases, we obtain formulae like those of Boehm and Halstead ($c > 1$).

There is no really convincing argument for either type of relation, though the latter ($c > 1$) may seem more plausible. Certainly for large projects, the effort required does seem to increase more than linearly with size.

It is clear that the value of the exponent c strongly influences the computed value E, certainly for large values of $KLOC$. Figure 7.5 gives the values for E, as they are computed for the earlier-mentioned models and some values for $KLOC$. The reader will notice large differences between the models. For small programs, Halstead's model yields the lowest cost estimates. For projects in the order of one million lines of code, this same model yields a cost estimate which is an order of magnitude higher than that of Walston–Felix. [Moh81] compares 13 different quantitative cost estimation models. For one fictitious project, the estimated cost ranges from \$362 500 to \$2 776 667. Other studies show similar results.

However, we should not immediately conclude that these models are useless. It is much more likely that there are big differences in the characteristics between the sets of projects on which the various models are based. Recall that the actual numbers used in those models result from an analysis of real project data. If these data reflect widely different project types or development environments, so will the models. We cannot simply copy those formulae. Each environment has its own specific character-

$KLOC$	$E = 0.7 KLOC^{1.50}$	$E = 2.4 KLOC^{1.05}$	$E = 5.2 KLOC^{0.91}$
1	0.7	2.4	5.2
10	22.1	26.9	42.3
50	247.5	145.9	182.8
100	700.0	302.1	343.6
1000	22135.9	3390.1	2792.6

Figure 7.5 E versus $KLOC$ for various base models

istics and tuning the model parameters to the specific environment (a process called calibration) is necessary.

The most important problem with this type of model is to get a *reliable* estimate of the software size early on. How should we estimate the number of pages in a novel not yet written? Even if we know the number of characters, the number of locations and the time interval in which the story takes place, we should not expect a realistic size estimate up front. The further advanced we are with the project, the more accurate our size estimate will get. If the design is more or less finished, we may (possibly) form a reasonable impression of the size of the resulting software. Only if the system has been delivered, do we know the exact number.

The customer, however, needs a reliable cost estimate early on. In such a case, lines of code is a measure which is too inexact to act as a base for a cost estimate. We therefore have to look for an alternative. In sections 7.3.4 and 7.3.5 we will discuss two models based on quantities which are known at an earlier stage.

We may also switch to another model during the execution of a project, since we may expect to get more reliable data as the project is making progress. We then get a cascade of increasingly detailed cost estimation models. COCOMO 2 is an example of this; see section 7.3.6.

7.3.1 Walston–Felix

The base equation of Walston and Felix' model [WF77] is

$$E = 5.2 KLOC^{0.91}$$

Some 60 projects from IBM were used in the derivation of this model. These projects differed widely in size and the software was written in a variety of programming languages. It therefore comes as no surprise that the model, applied to a subset of these 60 projects, yields unsatisfactory results.

In an effort to explain these wide-ranging results, Walston and Felix identified 29 variables that clearly influenced productivity. For each of these variables, three levels were distinguished: high, average and low. For a number of projects (51) Walston and Felix determined the level of each of these 29 variables, together with the productivity obtained (in terms of lines of code per man-month) in those projects. These results are given in figure 7.6 for some of the most important variables. Thus, the average productivity turned out to be 500 lines of code per man-month for projects with a user interface of low complexity. With a user interface of average or high complexity, the productivity is 295 and 124 lines of code per man-month, respectively. The last column contains the productivity change PC, the absolute value of the difference between the high and low scores.

Variable	Value of variable Average productivity (LOC)			| high – low | (PC)
Complexity of user interface	<normal 500	normal 295	>normal 124	376
User participation during requirements specification	none 491	some 267	much 205	286
User-originated changes in design	few 297	–	many 196	101
User-experience with application area	none 318	some 340	much 206	112
Qualification, experience of personnel	low 132	average 257	high 410	278
Percentage programmers participating in design	<25% 153	25–50% 242	>50% 391	238
Previous experience with operational computer	minimal 146	average 270	extensive 312	166
Previous experience with programming languages	minimal 122	average 225	extensive 385	263
Previous experience with application of similar or greater size and complexity	minimal 146	average 221	extensive 410	264
Ratio of average team size to duration (people/month)	<0.5 305	0.5–0.9 310	>0.9 171	134

Figure 7.6 Some productivity intervals (*Source: C.E. Walston and C.P. Felix, A method for programming measurement and estimation,* ©IBM Systems Journal, *1977*)

According to Walston and Felix, a productivity index I can now be determined for a new project, as follows:

$$I = \sum_{i=1}^{29} W_i X_i$$

The weights W_i are defined by

$$W_i = 0.5 \log(PC_i)$$

Here, PC_i is the productivity change of factor i. For the first factor from figure 7.6 (complexity of the user interface), the following holds: $PC_1 = 376$, so $W_1 = 1.29$. The variables X_i can take on values $+1$, 0 and -1, where the corresponding factor scores as low, average or high (and thus results in a high, average or low productivity, respectively). The productivity index obtained can be translated into an expected productivity (lines of code produced per man-month). Details of the latter are not given in [WF77].

The number of factors considered in this model is rather high (29 factors out of 51 projects). Also it is not clear to what extent the various factors influence each other. Finally, the number of alternatives per factor is only three, and does not seem to offer enough choice in practical situations.

Nevertheless, the approach taken by Walston and Felix and their list of cost drivers have played a very important role in directing later research in this area.

7.3.2 COCOMO

COCOMO (COnstructive COst MOdel) is one of the algorithmic cost estimation models best documented. In its simplest form, called Basic COCOMO, the formula that relates effort to software size, reads

$$E = bKLOC^c$$

Here, b and c are constants that depend on the kind of project that is being executed. COCOMO distinguishes three classes of project:

- **Organic** A relatively small team develops software in a known environment. The people involved generally have a lot of experience with similar projects in their organization. They are thus able to contribute at an early stage, since there is no initial overhead. Projects of this type will seldom be very large projects.

- **Embedded** The product will be embedded in an environment which is very inflexible and poses severe constraints. An example of this type of project might be air traffic control, or an embedded weapon system.

- **Semidetached** This is an intermediate form. The team may show a mixture of experienced and inexperienced people, the project may be fairly large, though not excessively large, etc.

For the various classes, the parameters of Basic COCOMO take on the following values:

organic:	$b = 2.4$, $c = 1.05$
semidetached:	$b = 3.0$, $c = 1.12$
embedded:	$b = 3.6$, $c = 1.20$

Figure 7.7 gives the estimated effort for projects of each of those three modes, for different values of $KLOC$ (though an 'organic' project of one million lines is not very realistic). Amongst others, we may read from this figure that the constant c soon starts to have a major impact on the estimate obtained.

KLOC		Effort in man-months	
	organic ($E = 2.4 KLOC^{1.05}$)	semidetached ($E = 3.0 KLOC^{1.12}$)	embedded ($E = 3.6 KLOC^{1.20}$)
1	2.4	3.0	3.6
10	26.9	39.6	57.1
50	145.9	239.4	392.9
100	302.1	521.3	904.2
1000	3390.0	6872.0	14333.0

Figure 7.7 Size versus effort in Basic COCOMO

Basic COCOMO yields a simple, and hence a crude, cost estimate based on a simple classification of projects into three classes. In his book *Software Engineering Economics*, Boehm also discusses two other, more complicated, models, termed Intermediate COCOMO and Detailed COCOMO, respectively. Both these models take into account 15 cost drivers – attributes that affect productivity, and hence costs.

All these cost drivers yield a multiplicative correction factor to the nominal estimate of the effort. (Both these models also use values for b which slightly differ from that of Basic COCOMO.) Suppose we found a nominal effort estimate of 40 man-months for a certain project. If the complexity of the resulting software is low, then the model tells us to correct this estimate by a factor of 0.85. A better estimate then would be 34 man-months. On the other hand, if the complexity is high, we get an estimate of $1.15 \times 40 = 46$ man-months.

The nominal value of each cost driver in Intermediate COCOMO is 1.00 (see also figure 7.14. So we may say that Basic COCOMO is based on nominal values for each of the cost drivers.

On top of this set of cost drivers, the detailed model adds a further level of refinement. First of all, this model is phase-sensitive, the idea being that not all cost drivers influence each phase of the development cycle in the same way. So, rather than having one table with effort multipliers as in Intermediate COCOMO, Detailed COCOMO uses a set of such tables. These tables show, for each cost driver, a separate effort multiplier for each major development phase. Furthermore, Detailed COCOMO uses a hierarchy for the product to be developed, in which some cost drivers have an impact on the estimate at the module level, while others have an impact at the (sub)system level.

The COCOMO formulae are based on a combination of expert judgment, an analysis of available project data, other models, etc. The basic model does not yield very accurate results for the projects on which the model has been based. The intermediate version yields good results and, if one extra cost driver (volatility of the requirements specification) is added, it even yields very good results. Further validation of the COCOMO models using other project data is not straightforward, since the necessary information to determine the ratings of the various cost drivers is in general not available. So we are left with the possibility of only testing the basic model. Here, we obtain fairly large discrepancies between the effort estimated and the actual effort needed.

A major advantage of COCOMO is that we know all its details. A major update of the COCOMO model, better reflecting current and future software practices, is discussed in section 7.3.6.

7.3.3 Putnam

Norden studied the distribution of manpower over time in a number of software development projects in the 1960s. He found that this distribution often had a very characteristic shape which is well-approximated by a Rayleigh distribution. Based upon this finding, Putnam developed a cost estimation model in which the manpower required (MR) at time t is given by

$$MR(t) = 2Kate^{-at^2}$$

a is a speed-up factor which determines the initial slope of the curve, while K denotes the total manpower required, including the maintenance phase. K equals the volume of the area delineated by the Rayleigh curve (see figure 7.8).

The shape of this curve can be explained theoretically as follows. Suppose a project consists of a number of problems for which a solution must be found. Let $W(t)$ be the fraction of problems for which a solution has been found at time t. Let $p(t)$ be the problem-solving capacity at time t. Progress at time t then is proportional to the product of the available problem-solving capacity and the fraction of problems yet unsolved. If the total amount of work to be done is set to 1, this yields:

$$\frac{dW}{dt} = p(t)(1 - W(t))$$

After integration, we get

$$W(t) = 1 - \exp(-\int^{t} p(\alpha)d\alpha)$$

If we next assume that the problem-solving capacity is well approximated by an equation of the form $p(t) = at$, i.e. the problem-solving capacity shows a linear increase

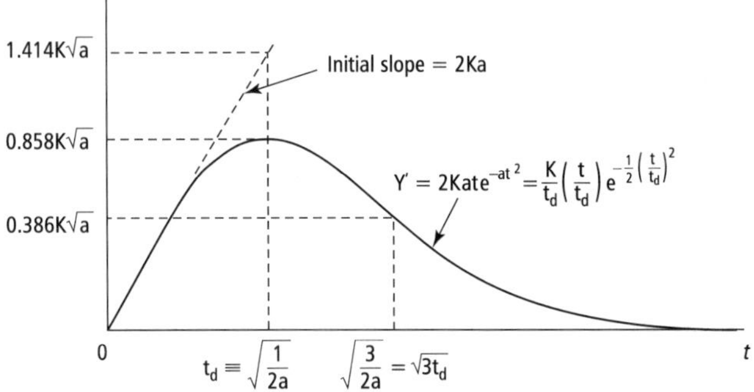

Figure 7.8 The Rayleigh-curve for software schedules (*Source: M.L. Shooman,* Tutorial on software cost models, *IEEE Catalog nr TH0067-9 (1979), ©1979 IEEE Reproduced with permission)*

over time, the progress is given by a Rayleigh distribution:

$$\frac{\mathrm{d}W}{\mathrm{d}t} = ate^{-(at^2)/2}$$

Integration of the equation for $MR(t)$ that was given earlier yields the cumulative effort I:

$$I(t) = K(1 - e^{-at^2})$$

In particular, we get $I(\infty) = K$. If we denote the point in time at which the Rayleigh-curve assumes its maximum value by T, then $a = 1/(2T^2)$. This point T will be close to the point in time at which the software is being delivered to the customer. The volume of the area delineated by the Rayleigh curve between points 0 and T then is a good approximation of the initial development effort. For this, we get

$$E = I(T) = 0.3945K$$

This result is remarkably close to the often-used rule of thumb: 40% of the total effort is spent on the actual development, while 60% is spent on maintenance.

Various studies indicate that Putnam's model is well suited to estimating the cost of very large software development projects (projects that involve more than 15 man-years). The model seems to be less suitable for small projects.

A serious objection to Putnam's model, in our opinion, concerns the relation it assumes between effort and development time if the schedule is compressed relative to the nominal schedule estimate: $E = c/T^4$. Compressing a project's schedule in this model entails an extraordinary large penalty (see also section 7.4).

7.3.4 DeMarco

Models like COCOMO are based on an early estimate of the amount of code to be delivered. Such an estimate is difficult, if not impossible, to obtain at an early stage. DeMarco proposed a model that would allow us to estimate cost at the requirements engineering stage of software development.

DeMarco uses dataflow diagrams to model a system. These dataflow diagrams depict the various data transformations. Together, they provide a network of functions to be performed. We may distinguish different levels in this network, levels that differ in the degree of abstraction with which we view the system being modeled.

DeMarco's cost estimation model is based on the number of functional primitives (FP) in the human–computer interface of the system. Functional primitives are those primitives that occur at the lowest level of the network depicted by the dataflow diagrams. Obviously, some primitives are 'bigger' or more complex than others, so that we need some correction in order to arrive at a more uniform metric.

With respect to size, such a correction can be achieved as follows: At the component level, the function network depicts the system as a sequence of interrelated primitive operations. Each of these operations involves some input and output elements. DeMarco estimates the relative size of a transformation (its information content) through a function of the number of elements TC involved in that transformation. Analogous to [Hal77], this results in

$$Size(FP) = k \times TC_{FP} \times \log_2(TC_{FP})$$

for some constant k.

The complexity is next taken care of by applying some multiplicative corrective factor. To this end, each primitive function is classified using a taxonomy of function classes. The following list shows some of the classes from DeMarco's taxonomy, with the multiplicative factors in parentheses:

- functions that compose or decompose data (0.6)
- functions that update information (0.5)
- functions that analyze data and take subsequent actions (1.0)
- functions that evaluate input from the human–computer interface (0.8)
- functions that check for internal consistency (1.0)
- functions for text manipulation (1.0)
- functions that synchronize the interaction with the user (1.5)
- functions that generate output (1.0)

- functions that do simple calculations (0.7)
- functions that do complex calculations (2.0)

So, rather than using the raw functional primitive metric FP, DeMarco uses an adjusted value FP' which involves a correction to accommodate differences in both size and complexity:

$$FP' = \sum_i \alpha_i \times TC_i \times \log_2 TC_i$$

Here, i goes through the set of functional primitives, while α_i denotes the correction factor associated with the class to which the i-th primitive belongs.

Finally, we are left to decide on a relation between FP' and effort needed (E), such as, for example

$$E = aFP'^b$$

where a and b are again determined using data from past projects. DeMarco has not further elaborated this line of thought. He does point at the necessity to gather project data yourself and derive an organization-specific model from your own set of data.

The structure of this cost estimation model looks like that of some of the models we discussed before. The basic unit, however, is a functional primitive, rather than a line of code. This is attractive, since we may hope to be able to identify and count functional primitives at a relatively early stage. This is not the case if we stick to lines of code.

7.3.5 Function Point Analysis

Like DeMarco's model, function point analysis (FPA) is a method of estimating costs in which the problems associated with determining the expected amount of code are circumvented. FPA is based on counting the number of different data structures that are used. In the FPA method, it is assumed that the number of different data structures is a good size indicator. FPA is particularly suitable for projects aimed at realizing business applications for, in these applications, the structure of the data plays a very dominant role. The method is less suited to projects in which the structure of the data plays a less prominent role, and the emphasis is on algorithms (such as compilers and most real-time software).

The following five entities play a central role in the FPA-model:

- Number of input types (I). The input types refer only to user input that results in changes in data structures. It does not concern user input which is solely concerned with controlling the program's execution. Each input type that has a different format, or is treated differently, is counted. So, though the records of a master file and those of a mutation file may have the same format, they are still counted separately.

- Number of output types (O). For the output types, the same counting scheme is used.

- Number of inquiry types (E). Inquiry types concern input that controls the execution of the program and does not change internal data structures. Examples of inquiry types are: menu selection and query criteria.

- Number of logical internal files (L). This concerns internal data generated by the system, and used and maintained by the system, such as, for example, an index file.

- Number of interfaces (F). This concerns data that is output to another application, or is shared with some other application.

By trial and error, weights have been associated with each of these entities. The number of (unadjusted) function points, UFP, is a weighted sum of these five entities:

$$UFP = 4I + 5O + 4E + 10L + 7F$$

With FPA too, a further refinement is possible, by applying corrections to reflect differences in complexity of the data types. In that case, the constants used in the above formula depend on the estimated complexity of the data type in question. Figure 7.9 gives the counting rules when three levels of complexity are distinguished. So, rather than having each input type count as four function points, we may count three, four or six function points, based on an assessment of the complexity of each input type.

Each input type has a number of data element types (attributes), and refers to zero or more other file types. The complexity of an input type increases as the number of its data element types or referenced file types increases. For input types, the mapping of these numbers to complexity levels is given in figure 7.10. For the other file types, these tables have the same format, with slightly different numbers along the axes.

As in other cost estimation models, the unadjusted function point measure is adjusted by taking into account a number of application characteristics that influence development effort. Figure 7.11 contains the 14 characteristics used in the FPA model. The degree of influence of each of these characteristics is valued on a six-point scale, ranging from zero (no influence, not present) to five (strong influence). The total degree of influence DI is the sum of the scores for all characteristics. This number is then converted to a technical complexity factor (TCF) using the formula

$$TCF = 0.65 + 0.01DI$$

Type	Complexity level		
	Simple	Average	Complex
Input (I)	3	4	6
Output (O)	4	5	7
Inquiry (E)	3	4	6
Logical internal (L)	7	10	15
Interfaces (F)	5	7	10

Figure 7.9 Counting rules for (unadjusted) function points

# of file types	# of data elements		
	1 – 4	5 – 15	> 15
0 or 1	simple	simple	average
2 – 3	simple	average	complex
> 3	average	complex	complex

Figure 7.10 Complexity levels for input types

The (adjusted) function point measure FP is now obtained through

$$FP = UFP \times TCF$$

Finally, there is a direct mapping from (adjusted) function points to lines of code. For instance, in [Alb79] one function point corresponds to 65 lines of PL/I, or to 100 lines of COBOL, on average.

In FPA, it is not simple to decide exactly when two data types should be counted as separate. Also, the difference between, for example, input types, inquiry types, and interfaces remains somewhat vague. The International Function Point User Group (IFPUG) has published extensive guidelines on how to classify and count the various entities involved. This should overcome many of the difficulties that analysts have in counting function points in a uniform way.

Further problems with FPA have to do with its use of ordinal scales and the way complexity is handled. FPA distinguishes three levels of component complexity only. A component with 100 elements thus gets at most twice the number of function points of a component with one element. Recently, it has been suggested that a model which uses the raw complexity data, i.e. the number of data elements and file types referenced, might work as well as, or even better than, a model which uses an

Data communications
Distributed functions
Performance
Heavily used configuration
Transaction rate
Online data entry
End-user efficiency
Online update
Complex processing
Reusability
Installation ease
Operational ease
Multiple sites
Facilitate change

Figure 7.11 Application characteristics in FPA

ordinal derivative thereof. In a sense, complexity is counted twice: both through the complexity level of the component and through one of the application characteristics. Yet it is felt that highly complex systems are not adequately dealt with, since FPA is predominantly concerned with counting externally visible inputs and outputs.

In applying the FPA cost estimation method, it still remains necessary to calibrate the various entities to your own environment. This holds the more for the corrections that reflect different application characteristics, and the transition from function points to lines of code.

7.3.6 COCOMO 2: Variations on a Theme

COCOMO 2 is a revision of the 1981 COCOMO model, tuned to the life cycle practices of the 1990s and 2000s. It reflects our cumulative experience with and knowledge of cost estimation. By comparing its constituents with those of previous cost estimation models, it also offers us a means to learn about significant changes in our trade over the past decades.

COCOMO 2 provides three increasingly detailed cost estimation models. These models can be used for different types of projects, as well as during different stages of a single project:

- the **Application Composition** model, mainly intended for prototyping efforts, for instance to resolve user interface issues. (Its name suggests heavy use of existing components, presumably in the context of a powerful CASE environment.)

- the **Early Design** model, aimed at the architectural design stage

- the **Post-Architecture** model for the actual development stage of a software product

The Post-Architecture model can be considered an update of the original COCOMO model; the Early Design model is an FPA-like model; and the Application Composition model is based on counting system components of a large granularity, such as screens and reports.

The Application Composition model is based on counting Object Points. Object Points have nothing to do with objects as in object-oriented development. In this context, objects are screens, reports, and 3GL modules.

The roots of this type of model can be traced back to several variations on FPA-type size measures. Function points as used in FPA are intended to be a user-oriented measure of system function. The user functions measured are the inputs, outputs, inquiries, etc. We may conjecture that these user-functions are technology-dependent, and that FPA primarily reflects the batch-oriented world of the 1970s.

Present-day administrative systems are perhaps better characterized by their number of menus or screens. This line of thought has been pursued in various studies. [BKK91] compared Object Points with Function Points for a sample of software projects, and found that Object Points did almost as well as Function Points. Object Points, however, are easier to determine, and at an earlier point in time.

Total effort is estimated in the Application Composition model as follows:

1. Estimate the number of screens, reports, and 3GL components in the application.

2. Determine the complexity level of each screen and report (simple, medium or difficult). 3GL components are assumed to be always difficult. The complexity of a screen depends on the number of views and tables it contains. The complexity of a report depends on the number of sections and tables it contains. A classification table similar to those in FPA (see figure 7.12 for an example) is used to determine these complexity levels.

3. Use the numbers given in figure 7.13 to determine the relative effort (in Object Points) to implement the object.

4. The sum of the Object Points for the individual objects yields the number of Object Points for the whole system.

5. Estimate the reuse percentage, resulting in the number of New Object Points (NOP) as follows: $NOP = ObjectPoints \times (100 - \%Reuse)/100$.

6. Determine a productivity rate $PROD = NOP/man\text{-}month$. This productivity rate depends on the experience and capability of both the developers and the

maturity of the CASE environment they use. It varies from 4 (very low) to 50 (very high).

7. Estimate the number of man-months needed for the project: $E = NOP/PROD$.

# of views	# and source of data tables total < 4 (< 2 on server < 3 on client)	total < 8 (2 – 3 on server 3 – 5 on client)	total ≥ 8 (> 3 on server > 5 on client)
< 3	simple	simple	medium
3 – 7	simple	medium	difficult
> 8	medium	difficult	difficult

Figure 7.12 Complexity levels for screens

Object type	Complexity simple	medium	difficult
Screen	1	2	3
Report	2	5	8
3GL component			10

Figure 7.13 Counting Object Points

The Early Design model uses unadjusted function points (UFPs) as its basic size measure. These unadjusted function points are counted in the same way they are counted in FPA. Next, the unadjusted function points are converted to Source Lines Of Code (SLOC), using a ratio SLOC/UFP which depends on the programming language used. In a typical environment, each UFP may correspond to, say, 91 lines of Pascal, 128 lines of C, 29 lines of C++, or 320 lines of assembly language. Obviously, these numbers are environment-specific.

The Early Design model does not use the FPA scheme to account for application characteristics. Instead, it uses a set of seven cost drivers, which are a combination of the full set of cost drivers of the Post-Architecture model. The intermediate, reduced set of cost drivers is:

- product reliability and complexity, which is a combination of the required software reliability, database size, product complexity and documentation needs cost drivers
- required reuse, which is equivalent to its Post-Architecture counterpart
- platform difficulty, which combines execution time, main storage constraints, and platform volatility
- personnel experience, which combines application, platform, and tool experience
- personnel capability, which combines analyst and programmer capability and personnel continuity.
- facilities, which is a combination of the use of software tools and multi-site development
- schedule, which again equals its Post-Architecture counterpart

These cost drivers are rated on a seven-point scale, ranging from extra low to extra high. The values assigned are similar to those in figure 7.14. Thus, the nominal values are always 1.00, and the values become larger or smaller as the cost driver is estimated to deviate further from the nominal rating. After the unadjusted function points have been converted to Kilo Source Lines Of Code ($KSLOC$), the cumulative effect of the cost drivers is accounted for by the formula

$$E = KSLOC \times \prod_i \mathit{cost\ driver}_i$$

Finally, the Post-Architecture model is the most detailed model. Its basic effort equation is very similar to that of the original COCOMO model:

$$E = a \times KSLOC^b \times \prod_i \mathit{cost\ driver}_i$$

It differs from the original COCOMO model in its set of cost drivers, the use of lines of code as its base measure, and the range of values of the exponent b.

The differences between the COCOMO and COCOMO 2 set of cost drivers reflect major changes in the field. The set of COCOMO 2 cost drivers and the associated effort multipliers are given in figure 7.14. The values of the effort multipliers in this figure are the result of calibration on a certain set of projects. The changes are as follows:

- Four new cost drivers have been introduced: required reusability, documentation needs, personnel continuity, and multi-site development. They reflect the growing influence of the corresponding aspects on development cost.

- Two cost drivers have been dropped: computer turnaround time and use of modern programming practices. Nowadays, developers use workstations and (batch-processing) turnaround time is no longer an issue. Modern programming practices have evolved into the broader notion of mature software engineering practices, which are dealt with in the exponent b of the COCOMO 2 effort equation.

- The productivity influence, i.e. the ratio between the highest and lowest value, of some cost drivers has been increased (analyst capability, platform experience, language and tools experience) or decreased (programmer capability).

In COCOMO 2, the user may use both $KSLOC$ and UFP as a base measure. It is also possible to use UFP for part of the system. The UFP counts are converted to $KSLOC$ counts as in the Early Design model, after which the effort equation applies.

Rather than having three 'modes', with slightly different values for the exponent b in the effort equation, COCOMO 2 has a much more elaborate scaling model. This model uses five scale factors W_i, each of which is rated on a six-point scale from very low (5) to extra high (0). The exponent b for the effort equation is then determined by the formula:

$$b = 1.01 + 0.01 \times \sum_i W_i$$

So, b can take on values in the range 1.01 to 1.26, thus giving a more flexible rating scheme than that used in the original COCOMO model.

The scale factors used in COCOMO 2 are:

- precedentedness, indicating the novelty of the project to the development organization. Aspects like the experience with similar systems, the need for innovative architectures and algorithms, and the concurrent development of hardware and software are reflected in this factor.

- development flexibility, reflecting the need for conformance with pre-established and external interface requirements, and a possible premium on early completion.

- architecture/risk resolution, which reflects the percentage of significant risks that have been eliminated. In many cases, this percentage will be correlated with the percentage of significant module interfaces specified, i.e. architectural choices made.

- team cohesion, accounting for possible difficulties in stakeholder interactions. This factor reflects aspects like the consistency of stakeholder objectives and cultures, and the experience of the stakeholders in acting as a team.

- process maturity, reflecting the maturity of the project organization according to the Capability Maturity Model (see section 6.6).

Only the first two of these factors were, in a crude form, accounted for in the original COCOMO model.

Cost drivers	Rating					
	Very low	Low	Nominal	High	Very high	Extra high
Product factors						
Reliability required	0.75	0.88	1.00	1.15	1.39	
Database size		0.93	1.00	1.09	1.19	
Product complexity	0.75	0.88	1.00	1.15	1.30	1.66
Required reusability		0.91	1.00	1.14	1.29	1.49
Documentation needs	0.89	0.95	1.00	1.06	1.13	
Platform factors						
Execution time constraints			1.00	1.11	1.31	1.67
Main storage constraints			1.00	1.06	1.21	1.57
Platform volatility		0.87	1.00	1.15	1.30	
Personnel factors						
Analyst capability	1.50	1.22	1.00	0.83	0.67	
Programmer capability	1.37	1.16	1.00	0.87	0.74	
Application experience	1.22	1.10	1.00	0.89	0.81	
Platform experience	1.24	1.10	1.00	0.92	0.84	
Language and tool experience	1.25	1.12	1.00	0.88	0.81	
Personnel continuity	1.24	1.10	1.00	0.92	0.84	
Project factors						
Use of software tools	1.24	1.12	1.00	0.86	0.72	
Multi-site development	1.25	1.10	1.00	0.92	0.84	0.78
Required development schedule	1.29	1.10	1.00	1.00	1.00	

Figure 7.14 Cost drivers and associated effort multipliers in COCOMO 2 (*Source: B.W. Boehm et al.,* COCOMO II Model Definition Manual, *University of Southern California, 1997. Reproduced with permission*)

The original COCOMO model allows us to handle reuse in the following way. The three main development phases, design, coding and integration, are estimated to take 40%, 30% and 30% of the average effort, respectively. Reuse can be catered for by separately considering the fractions of the system that require redesign (DM), recoding (CM) and re-integration (IM). An adjustment factor AAF is then given by the formula

$$AAF = 0.4DM + 0.3CM + 0.3IM$$

An adjusted value $AKLOC$, given by

$$AKLOC = KLOC \times AAF/100$$

is next used in the COCOMO formulae, instead of the unadjusted value $KLOC$. In this way a lower cost estimate is obtained if part of the system is reused.

By treating reuse this way, it is assumed that developing reusable components does not require any extra effort. You may simply reap the benefits when part of a system can be reused from an earlier effort. This assumption does not seem to be very realistic. Reuse does not come for free (see also chapter 17).

COCOMO 2 uses a more elaborate scheme to handle reuse effects. This scheme reflects two additional factors that impact the cost of reuse: the quality of the code being reused and the amount of effort needed to test the applicability of the component to be reused.

If the software to be reused is strongly modular, strongly matches the application in which it is to be reused, and the code is well-organized and properly documented, then the extra effort needed to reuse this code is relatively low, and estimated to be 10%. This penalty may be as high as 50% if the software exhibits low coupling and cohesion, is poorly documented, and so on. This extra effort is denoted by the software understanding increment SU.

The degree of assessment and assimilation (AA) denotes the effort needed to determine whether a component is appropriate for the present application. It ranges from 0% (no extra effort required) to 8% (extensive test, evaluation and documentation required).

Both these percentages are added to the adjustment factor AAF, yielding the equivalent kilo number of new lines of code, $EKLOC$:

$$EKLOC = KLOC \times (AAF + SU + AA)/100$$

7.4 DISTRIBUTION OF MANPOWER OVER TIME

Having obtained an estimate of the total number of man-months needed for a given project, we are still left with the question of how many calendar months it will take. For a project estimated at 20 man-months, the kind of schedules you might think of, include:

- 20 people work on the project for 1 month;
- 4 people work on the project for 5 months;
- 1 person works on the project for 20 months.

These are not realistic schedules. We noticed earlier that the manpower needed is not evenly distributed over the time period of the project. From the shape of the Rayleigh curve we find that we need a slowly increasing manpower during the development stages of the project.

Cost estimation models generally provide us with an estimate of the development time (schedule) T as well. Contrary to the effort equations, the various models show a remarkable consistency when it comes to estimating the development time, as is shown in figure 7.15.

Walston–Felix	$T = 2.5E^{0.35}$
COCOMO (organic)	$T = 2.5E^{0.38}$
COCOMO 2 (nominal schedule)	$T = 3.0E^{0.33+0.2\times(b-1.01)}$
Putnam	$T = 2.4E^{1/3}$

Figure 7.15 Relation between development time and effort

The values T thus computed represent nominal development times. It is worthwhile studying ways to shorten these nominal schedules. Obviously, shortening the development time means an increase in the number of people involved in the project.

In terms of the Rayleigh curve model, shortening the development time amounts to an increase of the value a, the speed-up factor which determines the initial slope of the curve. The peak of the Rayleigh curve then shifts to the left and at the same time it shifts up. We thus get a faster increase of manpower required at the start of the project and a higher maximum workforce.

Such a shift does not go unpunished. Different studies show that individual productivity decreases as team size grows. There are two major causes of this phenomenon:

- As the team gets larger, the communication overhead increases, since more time will be needed for consultation with other team members, tuning of tasks, and the like.

- If manpower is added to a team during the execution of a project, the total team productivity decreases at first. New team members are not productive right from the start. At the same time, they require time from the other team members during their learning process. Taken together, this causes a decrease in total productivity.

The combination of these two observations leads to the phenomenon that has become known as Brooks' Law: Adding manpower to a late project only makes it later.

By analyzing a large amount of project data, Conte *et al.* found the following relation between average productivity L (measured in lines of code per man-month) and average team size P [CDS86]:

$$L = 777P^{-0.5}$$

In other words, individual productivity decreases exponentially with team size.

A theoretical underpinning hereof can be given on account of Brooks' observation regarding the number of communication links between the people involved in a project. This number is determined by the size and structure of the team. If, in a team of size P, each member has to coordinate his activities with those of all other members, the number of communication links will be $P(P-1)/2$. If each member needs to communicate with one other member only, this number will be $P-1$. Less communication than that seems unreasonable, since we would then have essentially independent teams. (If we draw team members as nodes of a graph and communication links as edges, we expect the graph to be connected.)

The number of communication links thus varies from roughly P to roughly $P^2/2$. In a true hierarchical organization, this leads to P^α communication paths, with $1 < \alpha < 2$.

For an individual team member, the number of communication links varies from 1 to $P-1$. If the maximum individual productivity is L and each communication link results in a productivity loss l, the average productivity will be

$$L_\gamma = L - l(P-1)^\gamma$$

where γ, with $0 < \gamma \leq 1$, is a measure of the number of communication links. (We assume that there is at least one person who communicates with more than one other person, so $\gamma > 0$.) For a team of size P, this leads to a total productivity

$$L_{tot} = P \times L_\gamma = P(L - l(P-1)^\gamma)$$

For a given set of values for L, l and γ, this is a function which, for increasing values of P, goes from 0 to some maximum and then decreases again. There thus is a certain optimum team size P_{opt} that leads to a maximum team productivity. The team productivity for different values of the P is given in figure 7.16. Here, we assume that individual productivity is 500 LOC/man-month ($L = 500$), and the productivity loss is 10% per communication link ($l = 50$). With full interaction between team members ($\gamma = 1$) this results in an optimum team size of 5.5 persons.

Everything takes time. We can not shorten a software development project indefinitely by exchanging time against people. Boehm sets the limit at 75% of the nominal development time, on empirical grounds. A system that has to be delivered too fast, gets into the 'impossible region'. The chance of success becomes almost nil if the schedule is pressed too far. See also figure 7.17.

Team size	Individual productivity	Total productivity
1	500	500
2	450	900
3	400	1200
4	350	1400
5	300	1500
5.5	275	1512
6	250	1500
7	200	1400
8	150	1200

Figure 7.16 Impact of team size on productivity

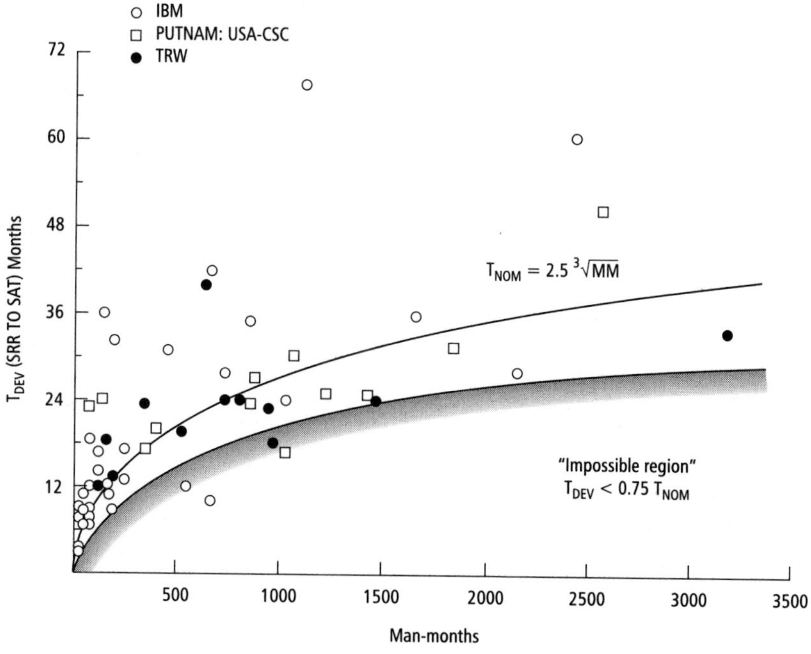

Figure 7.17 The impossible region (*Source: B.W. Boehm,* Software Engineering Economics, *fig. 27-8/page 471, ©1981, Reprinted by permission of Prentice-Hall, Inc., Englewood Cliffs, NJ*)

In any case, a shorter development time will induce higher costs. We may use the following rule of thumb: compressing the development time by X% results in a cost increase of X% relative to the nominal cost estimate [Boe84a].

7.5 SUMMARY

The discussion about which cost estimation model is best has not finished yet. The various models discussed yield widely different results. [Rub85], for instance, gives estimates for one and the same (hypothetical) project, using different cost estimation models. Some of his results are given in figure 7.18 (ESTIMACS is a model based on function points, see [Rub83]). The results are symptomatic of many studies in this area. Major reasons for these discrepancies have been hinted at in this chapter. Both differences in definitions of the entities involved and differences in environmental characteristics add to the phenomenon observed.

	Putnam	COCOMO	ESTIMACS
Effort	200 man-months	363 man-months	17100 hours
Schedule	17 months	23 months	16 months
Peak team size	17	22	15

Figure 7.18 Different estimates for one project

It remains to be seen whether we will ever get one, general, cost estimation model. The number of parameters that impact productivity simply seems to be too large. Yet, each organization may develop a model which is well suited for projects to be undertaken within that organization. An organization may, and should, build a database with data on its own projects. Starting with a model like COCOMO 2, the different parameters, i.e. applicable cost drivers and values for the associated effort multipliers, may then be determined. In the course of time, the model will become more closely tuned to the organizational environment, resulting in better and better estimates.

Though we advocate the use of algorithmic cost estimation models, a word of caution should be made. Present-day models of this kind are not all that good yet. At best, they yield estimates which are at most 25% off, 75% of the time, *for projects used to derive the model.*

Even when a much better performance is realized, some problems remain when using the type of cost estimation model obtained in this way:

- Even though a model like COCOMO 2 looks objective, a fair amount of subjectivity is introduced through the need to assign values to the various levels of a number of cost drivers. Based on an analysis of historical project data, [Jon86] lists 20 factors which certainly influence productivity, and another 25 for which it is probable. The set of COCOMO 2 cost drivers already allows for a variation of 1:800. A much smaller number of relevant cost drivers would reduce a model's vulnerability to the subjective assessment of project characteristics.

- The models are based on data from *old* projects and reflect the technology of those projects. In some cases, the project data are even fairly old. The impact of more recent developments, such as prototyping, the use of fourth-generation languages, and object-oriented programming, as well as changes in the kind of applications, such as a shift from batch-oriented systems to highly interactive, direct-manipulation type systems, cannot easily be taken into account, since we do not have sufficient data on projects which use those techniques.

- Almost all models take into account attributes that impact the initial development of software. Attributes which specifically relate to maintenance activities are seldom taken into account. Also, factors like the amount of documentation required, the number of business trips (in case development is not localized at one spot) are often lacking. Yet, these factors may have a significant impact on the effort needed.

Algorithmic models usually result from applying statistical techniques like regression analysis to a given set of project data. For a new project, the parameters of the model have to be determined, and the model yields an estimate and, in some cases, a confidence interval. Alternatively, we may search the set of project data for a project which most resembles the project at hand, and use its realized effort as an estimate for the cost of the new project. This is a form of case-based reasoning (CBR) as known from AI. The application of CBR to cost estimation is also known as analogy-based estimation. Results with this cost estimation technique suggest that it is a viable alternative to algorithmic models.

A problem of a rather different nature is the following: In the introduction to this chapter we compared software cost estimation with cost estimation for laying out a garden. When laying out a garden, we often follow a rather different line of thought, namely: given a budget of, say, \$10 000, what possibilities are there? What happens if we trade off a pond against something else?

Something similar is also possible with software. Given a budget of \$100 000 for library automation, what possibilities are there? Which user interface can we expect, what will the transaction speed be, how reliable will the system be? To be able to answer this type of question, we need to be able to analyze the sensitivity of an estimate to varying values of relevant attributes. Given the uncertainty about which attributes are relevant to start with, this trade-off problem is still largely unsolved.

While executing a task, people have to make a number of decisions. These decisions are strongly influenced by requirements set or proposed. The cost estimate is one such requirement which will have an impact on the end result. We may imagine a hypothetical case in which model A estimates the cost at 300 man-months. Now suppose the project actually takes 400 man-months. If model B would have estimated the project at 450 man-months, is model B better than model A? It is quite possible that, starting from the estimate given by model B, the eventual cost would have been 600 man-months. The project's behavior is also influenced by the cost estimate. Choices made during the execution of a project are influenced by cost estimates derived earlier on.

Finally, estimating the cost of a software development project is a highly dynamic activity. Not only may we switch from one model to another during the course of a project, estimates will also be adjusted on the basis of experiences gained. Switching to another model during the execution of a project is possible, since we may expect to get more reliable data while the project is making progress. We may, for instance, imagine the use of a cascade of cost estimation models, such as ESTIMACS – DeMarco – COCOMO, or the series of increasingly detailed COCOMO 2 models.

We cannot, and should not, rely on a one-shot statistical cost estimate. Controlling a software development project implies a regular check of progress, a regular check of estimates made, re-establishing priorities and weighing stakes, as the project is going on.

7.6 FURTHER READING

General information on cost estimation models can be found in [CDS86], [Boe81], [FP96], [Fai92] and [Gil86]. [Jon86], [Boe87a] and [BP88] are sources of information on productivity and productivity improvement. [CDS86] contains a wealth of information on the application of statistical techniques in relation to software cost estimation. Comparisons between the effort estimated and the actual effort needed can be found in [CDS86], [KT84] and [KT85]. [Bro95] provides many insights into the relation between total effort and project schedule.

Early size prediction for programming-in-the-small is studied in [Wan84] and [Lok96]. [CSM79] discuss the correlation between size measures like LOC and Halstead's N with effort.

Early cost estimation models are described in [Nel66] and [Wol74].

The Walston–Felix model is described in [WF77]. For DeMarco's model, see [DeM82]. The model of Putnam and Norden is described in [Nor70], [Put78].

[Boe81] is the definitive source on the original COCOMO model. COCOMO 2 is described in [BCH+95] and [Boe97].

Function point analysis (FPA) is developed by Albrecht [Alb79, AG83]. Critical appraisals of FPA can be found in [Sym88], [Kem93], [KP92], [AR92] and [AR96]. A detailed discussion of function points, its counting process and some case studies, is provided by [GH96].

Results of the application of analogy-based estimation are given in [SSK96] and [SS97].

The relation between project behavior and its cost estimate is discussed in [AHM86] and [AHSR93].

Exercises

1. How may Halstead's model be used to estimate software cost?
2. In which ways may political arguments influence cost estimates?
3. What does the Walton–Felix model look like?
4. How may the Rayleigh-curve be related to software cost estimation?
5. Give a sketch of Function Point Analysis (FPA).
6. Give a sketch of COCOMO 2.
7. Discuss the major differences between COCOMO 2 and FPA.
8. Give a rationale for Brooks' Law.
9. In which sense does Function Point Analysis (FPA) reflect the batch-oriented world of the 1970s?
10. How may early cost estimates influence the way in which a project is executed?
11. Why is it difficult to compare different cost estimation models?
12. Suppose you are involved in a project which is estimated to take 100 man-months. How would you estimate the nominal calendar time required for this project? Suppose the project is to be finished within six calendar months. Do you think such a schedule compression is feasible?
13. Why should software cost models be recalibrated from time to time?
14. ♠ How would you calibrate the COCOMO 2 model to fit software development in your organization?

15. ♡ Suppose you are managing a project which is getting behind schedule. Possible actions include: renegotiating the time schedule, adding people to the project, and renegotiating quality requirements. In which ways can these actions shorten the time schedule? Can you think of other ways to finish the project on time?

16. ♡ Suppose you have a LOC-based cost estimation model available whose parameters are based on projects from your own organization that used COBOL as the implementation language. Can you use this model to estimate the cost of a project whose implementation language is Pascal? What if the model is based on projects that used C?

17. ♡ Can you give an intuitive rationale for the values of the COCOMO 2 cost drivers (figure 7.14) that relate to project attributes?

8
Project Planning and Control

LEARNING OBJECTIVES

- To appreciate looking at project control from a system point of view
- To be aware of typical project situations, and ways in which projects can be successfully dealt with in such situations
- To understand how risks can be prevented from becoming problems
- To know techniques for the day-to-day planning and control of software development projects

Software development projects differ widely. These differences are reflected in the ways in which these projects are organized and managed. For some projects, the budget is fixed and the goal of the project is to maximize the quality of the end product. For others, quality constraints are fixed in advance, and the goal is to produce effectively a system that meets those quality constraints. If the developing organization has considerable experience with the application domain and the requirements are fixed and stable, a tightly structured approach may yield a satisfactory solution. In applications with fuzzy requirements and little previous experience in the development team, a much more exploratory approach may be desirable.

It is important to identify those project characteristics early on, because they will influence the way a project is organized, planned and controlled. In section 8.1, we will discuss project control from a systems point of view. This allows us to identify the major dimensions along which software development projects differ. These dimensions lead to a taxonomy of software development projects, which will be discussed in section 8.2. For each of the project categories distinguished, we will indicate how best to control the various entities identified in previous chapters. This type of assessment is to be done at the project planning stage.

This assessment links global risk categories to preferred control situations. Daily practice, however, is more complex. An actual project faces many risks, each of which has to be handled in turn. Even risks for which we hoped to have found an adequate solution, may turn into problems later on. Risk factors therefore have to be monitored, and contingency plans have to be developed. The early identification of risks and the development and carrying out of strategies to mitigate these risks is known as **risk management**. Risk management is discussed in section 8.3.

Software development projects consist of a number of interrelated tasks. Some of these will have to be handled sequentially (a module cannot be tested until it has been implemented), while others may be handled in parallel (different modules can be implemented concurrently). The dependencies between tasks can be depicted in a network from which a project schedule can be derived. These and similar tools for the micro-level planning and control of software development projects are discussed in section 8.4.

8.1 A SYSTEMS VIEW OF PROJECT CONTROL

In the preceding chapters, we discussed several entities that need to be controlled. During the execution of a software development project, each of these entities needs to be monitored and assessed. From time to time, adjustments will have to be made. To be able to do so, we must know which entities can be varied, how they can be varied, and what the effect of adjustments is.

To this end, we will consider project control from a systems point of view. We now consider the software development project itself as a system. Project control may then be described in terms of:

- the system to be controlled, i.e. the software development project;
- the entity that controls the system, i.e. the project manager, his organization and the decision rules he uses;
- information which is used to guide the decision process. This information may come from two sources. It may either come from the system being controlled (such as a notice of technical problems with a certain component) or it may have a source outside the system (such as a request to shorten development time).

The variables that play a role in controlling a system may be categorized into three classes: irregular variables, goal variables, and control variables.

Irregular variables are those variables that are input to the system being controlled. Irregular variables cannot be varied by the entity that controls the system. Their values are determined by the system's environment. Examples of irregular variables are the computer experience of the user or the project staffing level.

An important precondition for effective control is knowledge of the project's goals. In developing software, various conflicting goals can be distinguished. One possible goal is to *minimize development time*. Since time is often pressing, this goal is not unusual. Another goal might be to *maximize efficiency*, i.e. development should be done as cheaply as possible. Optimal use of resources (mostly manpower) is then needed. Yet a third possible goal is to *maximize quality*. Each of these goals is possible, but they can be achieved only if it is known which goals are being pursued. These goals collectively make up the set of goal variables.

Finally, the decision process is guided by the set of control variables. Control variables are entities which can be manipulated by the project manager in order to achieve the goals set forth. Examples of possible control variables are the tools to be used, project organization, efficiency of the resulting software.

It is not possible to make a rigid separation between the various sets of variables. It depends on the situation at hand whether a particular variable should be taken as an irregular variable, goal variable, or control variable. If the requirements are stable and fixed, one may for instance try to control the project by employing adequate personnel and using a proper set of tools. For another project, manpower may be fixed and one may try to control the project by extending the delivery date, relaxing quality constraints, etc.

However, in order to be able to control a project, the different sets of variables must be known. It must be known where control is, and is not, possible. This is only one prerequisite, though. In systems theory, the following conditions for effective control of a system are used:

- the controlling entity must know the goals of the system;
- the controlling entity must have sufficient control variety;
- the controlling entity must have information on the state, input and output of the system;
- the controlling entity must have a conceptual control model. It must know how and to what extent the different variables depend on and influence each other.

When all these conditions are met, control can be rational, in which case there is no uncertainty, since the controlling entity is completely informed about every relevant aspect. The control problem can then be structured and formalized. Daily practice of software development is different, though. There is insufficient room for control or the effect of control actions is not known. Control then becomes much more intuitive or primitive. It is based on intuition, experience, and rules of thumb.

The degree to which a software development project can be controlled increases as the control variety increases. This control variety is determined by the number of control variables and the degree to which they can be varied. As noticed before, the control variety is project dependent.

Controlling software development means that we must be able to measure both the project and the product. Measuring a project means that we must be able to assess progress. Measuring a product means that we must be able to determine the degree to which quality and functional requirements are being met.

Controlling software development projects implies that effective control actions are possible. Corrective actions may be required if progress is not sufficient or the software does not comply with its requirements. Effective control means that we know what the effect of control actions is. If progress is insufficient and we decide to allocate extra manpower, we must understand the impact of this extra manpower on the time schedule. If the quality of a certain component is less than required and we decide to allocate extra test time, we must know how much test time is required in order to achieve the desired quality.

In practice, controlling a software development project is not a rational process. The ideal systems theory situation is not met. There are a number of uncertainties which make managing such projects a challenging activity. Below, we will discuss a few idealized situations, based on the uncertainty of various relevant aspects.

8.2 A TAXONOMY OF SOFTWARE DEVELOPMENT PROJECTS

In the preceding section, we identified several conditions that need to be satisfied in order to be able to control projects rationally. Since these conditions are often not met, we will have to rely on a different control mechanism in most cases. The control mechanism best suited to any given situation obviously depends on relevant characteristics of the project at hand.

Based on an analysis of software development project characteristics that are important for project control, we will distinguish several project situations, and indicate how projects can successfully be controlled in these situations. This discussion is based on [Hee89].

We will group project characteristics into three classes: product characteristics, process characteristics, and resource characteristics. From the point of view of project control, we are interested in the degree of *certainty* of those characteristics. For example, if we have clear and stable user requirements, product certainty is high. If part of the problem is to identify user requirements, or the user requirements frequently change during the development project, product certainty is low.

If product certainty is high, control can be quite rational, insofar as it depends on product characteristics. Since we know what the product is supposed to accomplish, we may check compliance with the requirements and execute corrective actions if needed. If product certainty is low, this is not feasible. We either do not know what we are aiming at, or the target is constantly moving. It is only reasonable to expect that control will be different in those cases.

For the present discussion, we are interested only in project characteristics that may differ between projects. Characteristics common to most or all of software development projects, such as the fact that they involve teamwork, will not lead to different control paradigms.

We will furthermore combine the characteristics from each of the three categories identified above, into one metric, the certainty of the corresponding category. This leaves us with three dimensions along which software development projects may differ:

- **Product certainty** Product certainty is largely determined by two factors: whether or not user requirements are clearly specified, as regards both functionality and quality, and the volatility of those user requirements. Other product characteristics are felt to have a lesser impact on our understanding of what the end-product should accomplish.

- **Process certainty** The degree of (development) process certainty is determined by such factors as: the possibility of redirecting the development process, the degree to which the process can be measured and the knowledge we have about the effect of control actions, and the degree to which new, unknown tools are being used.

- **Resource certainty** The major determinant here is the availability of the appropriate qualified personnel.

If we allow each of these certainty factors to take one of two values (high and low), we get eight control situations, although some of them are not very realistic. If we have little or no certainty about the software to be developed, we can hardly expect to be certain about the process to be followed and the resources needed to accomplish our goals. Similarly, if we do not know how to carry out the development process, we also do not know which resources are needed.

This leaves us with four archetypal situations, as depicted in figure 8.1. Below, we will discuss each of these control situations in turn. In doing so, we will pay attention to the following aspects of those control situations:

- the kind of control problem;
- the primary goals to be set in controlling the project;
- the coordination mechanism to be used;
- the development strategy, or process model, to be applied;
- the way and degree to which cost can be estimated.

	Realization	Allocation	Design	Exploration
Product certainty	high	high	high	low
Process certainty	high	high	low	low
Resource certainty	high	low	low	low

Figure 8.1 Four archetypal control situations

- **Realization problem** If the requirements are known and stable, it is known how the software is to be developed, there is sufficient control variety, the effect of control actions is known, and sufficient resources are available, we find ourselves in an ideal situation, a situation not often encountered in our field. The main emphasis will be on realization: how can we, given the requirements, achieve our goal in the most effective way? As for the development strategy, we may use some linear process model. Feedback to earlier phases, as in the waterfall model, is needed only for verification and validation activities.

To coordinate activities in a project of this type, we may use direct supervision. Work output can be standardized, since the end result is known. Similarly, the work processes and worker skills can be fixed in advance. There will thus be little need for control variety as far as these variables are concerned.

Management can be done effectively through a separation style. The work to be done is fixed through rules and procedures. Management can allocate tasks and check their proper execution.

As for cost estimation, we may successfully use one of the more formalized cost models, provided that the model has been calibrated for the current environment. A cost estimation thus obtained can be used to guard the project's progress and yields a target to be achieved.

- **Allocation problem** This situation differs from the previous one in that there is uncertainty as regards the resources. The major problem then becomes one of the availability of personnel. Controlling a project of this kind tends to become one of controlling capacity. The crucial questions become: How do we get the project staffed? How do we achieve the desired end-product with limited means?

  According to Mintzberg, one has to try to standardize the process as far as possible in this case. This makes it easier to move personnel between tasks. Guidelines and procedures may be used to describe how the various tasks have to be carried out.

  As regards the development strategy, we may again opt for the waterfall model. We may either contract out the work to be done, or try to acquire the right type and amount of qualified personnel.

  As for cost estimation, we may again use some cost estimation model. Since there is uncertainty as regards resources, there is a need for sensitivity analyses in order to gain insight into such questions as: What will happen to the total cost and development time if we allocate three designers of level A rather than four designers of level B?

- **Design problem** If the requirements are fixed and stable, but we do not know how to carry out the process, nor which resources to employ, the problem is one of design. Note that the adjective *design* refers to the design of the project, not the design of the software. We have to answer such questions as: which milestones are to be identified, which documents must be delivered and when, what personnel must be allocated, how will responsibilities be assigned?

  In this situation, we have insufficient knowledge of the effect of allocating extra personnel, other tools, different methods and techniques. The main problem then becomes one of controlling the development process.

In Mintzberg's classification, this can best be pursued through standardization of work outputs. Since the output is fixed, control should be done through the process and the resources. The effect of such control actions is not sufficiently known, however.

In order to make a project of this kind manageable, one needs overcapacity. As far as the process is concerned, this necessitates margins in development time and budget. Keeping extra personnel is not feasible, in general.

In these situations, we will need frequently to measure progress towards the project's goals in order to allow for timely adjustments. Therefore, we may want to go from a linear development model to an incremental one. This preference will increase as the uncertainty increases.

Cost estimation will have to rely on data from past projects. We will usually not have enough data to use one of the more formalized cost estimation models. In this situation too, we will need sensitivity analyses. This need will be more pressing than in the previous situation, since the uncertainty is greater. The project manager will be interested in the sensitivity of cost estimates to certain cost drivers. He might be interested in such questions as: what will happen to the development schedule if two extra analysts are assigned to this project or: what will the effect be on the total cost if we shorten the development time by x days? By viewing cost estimation in this way, the manager will gain insight to, and increase his feeling for, possible solution strategies.

- **Exploration problem** If the product certainty, process certainty and resource certainty are all low, we get the most difficult control situation.

  Because of these uncertainties, the work will be exploratory in nature. This situation does not fit a coordination mechanism based on standardization. In a situation as complex and uncertain as this one, coordination can best be achieved through mutual adjustment. The structure is one of adhocracy. Experts from various disciplines work together to achieve some as yet unspecified goal.

  A critical success factor in these cases is the commitment of all people involved. Work cannot be split up into neat tasks. Flexibility in work patterns and work contents is important. Adherence to a strict budget cannot be enforced upon the team from above. The team members must commit themselves to the project. Management has to place emphasis on their relations with the team members.

  Controlling a project of this kind is a difficult and challenging activity. To make a project of this kind manageable, our goal will be to maximize output, given the resources available to the project. This maximization may concern the quality of the product, or its functionality, or both.

Since requirements are not precisely known, some form of prototyping is appropriate as a process model. The larger the uncertainty, the more often we will have to check whether we are still on the right track. Thus, some development strategy involving many small steps is to be used. Cost estimation using some formalized model clearly is not feasible in these circumstances. The use of such models presupposes that we know enough of the project at hand to be able to compare it with previous projects. Such is not the case, though.

We may rely on expert judgments to achieve a rough cost estimate. Such a cost estimate, however, cannot and should not be used as a fixed anchor point as to when the project should be finished and how much it may cost. There are simply too many uncertainties involved. Rather, it provides us with some guidance as to the magnitude of the project. Based on this estimate, effort and time can be allocated for the project, for instance to produce a certain number of prototypes, a feasibility study, or a pilot implementation of part of the product. The hope is that in time the uncertainties will diminish sufficiently so that the project shifts to one of the other situations.

The four control situations discussed above are once more depicted in figure 8.2, together with a short characterization of the various control aspects discussed above.

By taking these aspects into account during the planning stage of a software development project, we can tailor the project's management to the situation at hand. In doing so, we recognize that software development projects are not all alike. Neglecting those project-specific characteristics is likely to result in project failures, failures that have often been reported upon in the literature, but equally often remain hidden from the public at large.

8.3 RISK MANAGEMENT

Risk management is project management for adults
Tim Lister

In the previous section, we identified global risk categories and tied them to preferred control situations. In this section, the emphasis is on individual risks and their management *during* project execution. In some sense too, the discussion below takes a more realistic point of view, in that we also consider adverse situations such as unrealistically tight schedules and design gold plating.

Potential risks of a project must be identified as early as possible. It is rather naive to suppose that a software project will run smoothly from start to finish. It

Problem type	Realization	Allocation	Design	Exploration
Product certainty Process certainty Resource certainty	high high high	high high low	high low low	low low low
Primary goal in control	Optimize resource usage Efficiency and schedule	Acquisition, training of personnel	Control of the process	Maximize result Lower risks
Coordination, management style	Standardization of product, process, and resources Hierarchy, separation style	Standardization of product and process	Standardization of process	Mutual adjustment Commitment Relation style
Development strategy	Waterfall	Waterfall	Incremental	Incremental Prototyping
Cost estimation	Models Guard process	Models Sensitivity analysis	Database with project data Sensitivity analysis	Expert estimate Risk analysis Provide guidance

Figure 8.2 Four control situations (*Source: F.J. Heemstra,* How much does software cost, *©Kluwer Bedrijfswetenschappen, 1989, Reproduced with permission*)

won't. We should identify the risks of a software project early on and provide measures to deal with them. Doing so is not a sign of unwarranted pessimism. Rather, it is a sign of wisdom.

In software development, we tend to ignore risks. We assume an optimistic scenario under all circumstances and we do not reserve funds for dealing with risks. We rely on heroics when chaos sets in. If risks are identified at all, their severity is often underestimated, especially by observers higher in the hierarchy. A designer may have noticed that a certain subsystem poses serious performance problems. His manager assumes that the problem can be solved. His manager's manager assumes the problem *has* been solved.

A risk is a possible future negative event that may affect the success of an effort. So, a risk is not a problem, yet. It may become one, though, and risk management is concerned with *preventing* risks from becoming problems. Some common examples of risks and ways to deal with them, are:

- Requirements may be unstable, immature, unrealistic, or excessive. If we merely list the requirements and start to realize the system in a linear development mode, it is likely that a lot of rework will be needed. This results in schedule and budget overruns, since this rework was not planned. If the requirements volatility is identified as a major risk, an evolutionary development strategy can be chosen. This situation fits the exploration-problem category as identified in the previous section.

- If there is little or no user involvement during the early development stages, a real danger is that the system will not meet user needs. If this is identified as a risk, it can be mitigated, e.g. by having users participate in design reviews.

- If the project involves different or complex domains, the spread of application knowledge within the project team may be an issue. Recognizing this risk may result in timely attention and resources for a training program for team members.

At the project planning stage, risks are identified and handled. A risk management strategy involves the following steps:

1. Identify the risk factors. There are many possible risk factors. Each organization may develop its own checklist of such factors. The top ten risk factors from [Boe89] are listed in figure 8.3.

2. Determine the risk exposure. For each risk, we have to determine the probability p that it will actually occur and the effect E (e.g. in dollars or loss of man months) that it will have on the project. The risk exposure then equals $p \times E$.

3. Develop strategies to mitigate the risks. Usually, this will only be done for the N risks that have the highest risk exposure, or for those risks whose exposure exceeds some threshold α.

   There are three general strategies to mitigate risks: avoidance, transfer, and acceptance. We may avoid risks by taking precautions so that they will not occur: buy more memory, assign more people, provide for a training program for team members, and the like. We may transfer risks by looking for another solution, such as a prototyping approach to handle unstable requirements. Finally, we may accept risks. In the latter case, we have to provide for a contingency plan, to be invoked when the risk does become a problem.

4. Handle risks. Risk factors must be monitored. For some risks, the avoidance or transfer actions may succeed, and those risks will never become a problem. We may be less lucky for those risks that we decided up front not to handle. Also, some of our actions may turn out to be less successful, and risks that we hoped to have handled adequately may become a problem after all. Finally, project characteristics will change over time, and so will the risks. Risk management

Risk	Description
Personnel shortfall	May manifest itself in a variety of ways, such as inexperience with the domain, tools or development techniques to be used, personnel turnover, loss of critical team members, or the mere size of the team.
Unrealistic schedule/budget	Estimates may be unrealistic with respect to the requirements.
Wrong functionality	May have a variety of causes, such as an imperfect understanding of the customer needs, the complexity of communication with the client, insufficient domain knowledge of the developers and designers.
Wrong user interface	In certain situations, the user-friendliness of the interface is critical to its success.
Gold plating	Developers may wish to develop 'nice' features not asked for by the customer.
Requirements volatility	If many requirements change during development, the amount of rework increases.
Bad external components	The quality or fuctionality of externally supplied components may be below what is required for this project.
Bad external tasks	Subcontractors may deliver inadequate products, or the skills obtained from outside the team may be inadequate.
Real-time shortfalls	The real-time performance of (parts of) the system may be inadequate.
Capability shortfalls	An unstable environment or new or untried technology pose a risk to the development schedule.

Figure 8.3 Top ten risk factors

thus is a cyclic process, and occasionally risks must be handled by re-assessing the project, invoking a contingency plan, or even a transfer to crisis mode.

When you return to figure 8.3 after having studied the remainder of this book, you will note that many of the risk factors listed are extensively addressed in various chapters. These risk factors surface as cost drivers in cost estimation models, the quest for user involvement in requirements engineering and design, the attention for process models like prototyping and Rapid Application Development, and so on.

As Tom Gilb says: 'If you don't actively attack the risks, they will actively attack you' [Gil88, p. 72].

8.4 TECHNIQUES FOR PROJECT PLANNING AND CONTROL

A project consists of a series of activities. We may graphically depict the project and its constituent activities by a **work breakdown structure** (WBS). The WBS reflects the decomposition of a project into subtasks down to a level needed for effective planning and control. Figure 8.4 contains a very simple example of a work breakdown structure for a software development project. The activities depicted at the leaves of the work breakdown structure correspond to unit tasks, while the higher-level nodes constitute composite tasks. We will assume that each activity has a well-defined beginning and end that is indicated by a milestone, a scheduled event for which some person is held accountable and which is used to measure and control progress. The end of an activity is often a deliverable, such as a design document, while the start of an activity is often triggered by the end of some other activity.

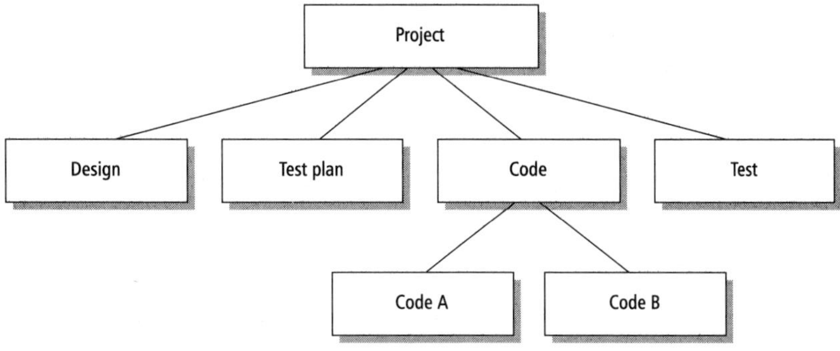

Figure 8.4 Simple work breakdown structure for a software development project

Activities usually consume resources, such as people or computer time, and always have a certain duration. Activities must often be executed in a specific order. For example, we can not test a module before it is coded. This type of relation between tasks can be expressed as constraints. Usually, the constraints concern temporal relations between activities. Such constraints are also called precedence relations. Project planning involves the scheduling of all activities such that the constraints are satisfied and resource limits are not exceeded. Several techniques are available to support this scheduling task.

The activities from the simple WBS of a software development project, together with their duration and temporal constraints, are given in figure 8.5. Note that figure 8.5 contains more information on temporal relations than is given in the WBS. Though the left-to-right reading of the WBS suggests a certain time ordering, it does not give the precise precedence relations between activities.

The set of activities and their constraints can also be depicted in a network. For our example, this network is given in figure 8.6. The nodes in the network denote activities. This type of network is therefore known as an 'activity-on-node' network. Each node also carries a weight, the duration of the corresponding activity. An arrow from node A to node B indicates that activity A has to be finished before activity B can start.

These network diagrams are often termed **PERT charts**. PERT is an acronym for Program Evaluation and Review Technique. PERT charts were developed and

Activity	Duration	Constraints
Design	10	–
Test plan	5	Design finished
Code A	10	Design finished
Code B	5	Design finished
Test	10	Code finished, Test plan finished

Figure 8.5 Activities, their duration and temporal constraints

first used successfully in the management of the Polaris missile program in the 1950s. While the original PERT technique was concerned solely with the time span of activities and their interrelations, subsequent developments have led to a variety of techniques that accommodate an increasing number of project factors.

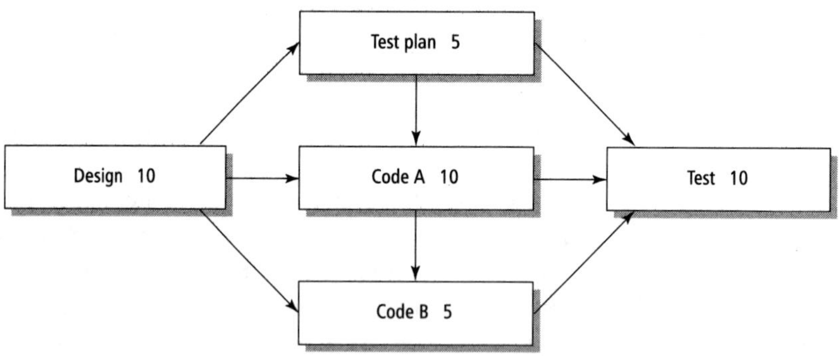

Figure 8.6 Example of a PERT chart

From the PERT chart we may compute the earliest possible point in time at which the project can be completed. Let us assume that the network has a unique start node B and end node E. If there is more than one node with in-degree 0 (i.e. having no predecessors in the network), a new start node B is created with outgoing edges to all nodes having in-degree 0. This new node B gets a zero weight (duration). A similar procedure is followed to create the end node E if there is more than one node having out-degree 0.

We next label each node i in the network with an ordered pair of numbers (S_i, F_i). S_i and F_i denote the earliest possible time at which activity i can start and finish, respectively. The algorithm for doing so involves a breadth-first search of the network (cf. [Boe81]):

1. The start node B is labeled (0, D_B), where D_B is the duration of activity B;

2. For all unlabeled nodes whose predecessors are all labeled nodes, the earliest possible starting time is the latest finishing time of all the predecessor nodes:

$$S_N = \max_{i \in P(N)} F_i$$

where $P(N)$ is the set of predecessor nodes of N.

The corresponding finishing time is $F_N = S_N + D_N$, where D_N is the duration of activity N.

Node N is labeled as (S_N, F_N).

3. Repeat Step 2 until all nodes have been labeled.

The earliest possible finishing time of the whole project now equals F_E, E being the end node of the network.

We may subsequently compute the latest point in time at which activity L should finish: for each node N,

$$L_N = \min_{i \in Q(N)} S_i$$

where $Q(N)$ is the set of successor nodes of N.

The results of this computation can be graphically presented in a **Gantt chart** (these charts are named after their inventor). In a Gantt chart, the time span of each activity is depicted by the length of a segment drawn on an adjacent calendar. The Gantt chart of our software development example is given in figure 8.7. The gray areas show slack (or float) times of activities. It indicates that the corresponding activity may consume more than its estimated time, or start later than the earliest possible starting time, without affecting the total duration of the project. For each activity N, the corresponding segment in the Gantt chart starts at time S_N and ends at L_N.

Activities without slack time are on a **critical path**. If activities on a critical path are delayed, the total project gets delayed as well. Note that there always is at least one sequence of activities that constitutes a critical path.

In an 'activity-on-node' network, the activities are depicted as nodes, while the arrows denote precedence relations between activities. Alternatively, we may depict a set of interrelated activities in an 'activity-on-arrow' network. In an activity-on-arrow network, the arrows denote activities, while the nodes represent the completion of milestone events. Figure 8.8 depicts the example as an activity-on-arrow network. The latter representation is intuitively appealing, especially if the length of an arrow reflects the duration of the corresponding activity. Note that this type of network may have to contain dummy activities which are not needed in the activity-on-node network. These dummy activities represent synchronization of interrelated activities. In

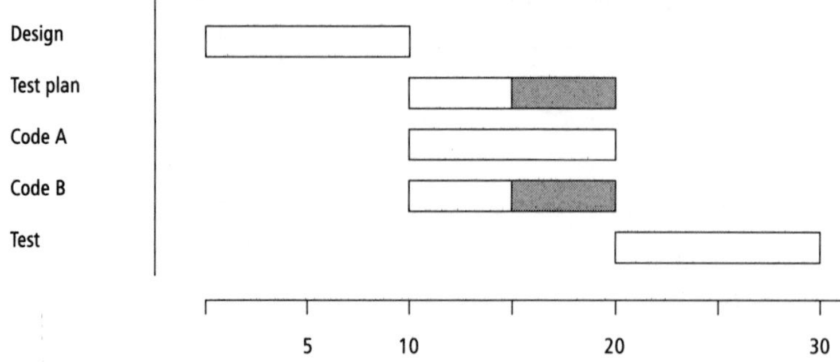

Figure 8.7 Example of a Gantt chart

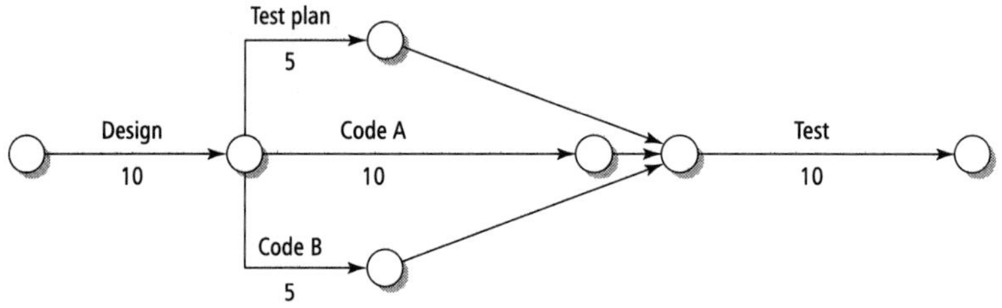

Figure 8.8 An activity-on-arrow network

our example, dummy activities (arrows) are needed to make sure that the activity *test* is not started until the activities *test plan*, *code A* and *code B* have all been completed.

The PERT technique has evolved considerably since its inception 35 years ago. For example, as well as expressing a constraint that activity B may start only after an activity A has ended, we may also specify that activity B may only start after activity A has started. We may also extend the technique so that it handles resource constraints. For instance, if we have only one programmer available, the Gantt chart of figure 8.7 would not work, since it assumes that coding of modules A and B is done in parallel. The PERT technique may even be extended further to allow for sensitivity analysis. By allowing so-called 'what-if' questions ('what if we allocate three designers rather than four', 'what if coding module A takes two months rather than one') we get a feeling for the sensitivity of a schedule to certain variations in resource levels, schedule overruns, and the like.

Critical Path Method – CPM – is, as the name suggests, a technique very similar to PERT and developed at around the same time.

In our discussion, we presented a Gantt chart as a graphical visualization of a schedule that results from network analysis. Actually, we may use a Gantt chart as a scheduling mechanism in its own right. We may simply list all activities and indicate their earliest starting time and latest ending time on the calendar. Gantt charts by themselves, however, do not carry information on dependencies between activities. This makes it hard to adjust schedules, for instance when a certain activity slips. As far as planning goes, we therefore prefer the use of Gantt charts as a means to visualize the result of network analysis.

Using the information contained in the Gantt chart and knowledge of personnel resources required for each activity, we may establish a personnel plan indicating how many people are required in each unit of time. Since people costs are a major part of project expenditures, this personnel plan provides a direct means to plan project expenditures.

When the project is under way, its control is based on monitoring the project's progress and expenditures. Time spent per activity per project member can be recorded on time cards. These time cards are the basis for determining cumulative effort and expenditure. These cumulative data can be compared with the planned levels of effort and expenditure. In order to properly judge whether the project is still on track, management needs progress information as well. The most common way to provide this is via milestone reports: activities cannot be considered completed until a proper report has been produced and accepted.

The Gantt chart provides a very direct means to compare actual project status with the project schedule. Schedule slippage shows itself immediately. Slippage of activities on a critical path then necessitates prompt management action: renegotiation of the schedule, the project's deliverables, or both. Note that schedule slippage is a sneaky affair; projects get behind one day at a time. Note also that project schedules should at any point in time reflect the true project. An accepted change necessitates reconsideration of the schedule.

8.5 SUMMARY

In this chapter we looked at project control from a systems point of view and gained insight into how different kinds of projects can be managed and controlled. We identified four archetypal situations, which demand different process models, coordination mechanisms and management styles.

Real projects face many risks, and it is a wise project manager who pays attention to them early on. A risk is a possible future negative event that may affect success. It is not a problem yet, but it may become one. Risk management is concerned with *preventing* risks from becoming problems. It involves the following steps:

1. Identify the risk factors.
2. Determine the risk exposure, i.e. the probability that a risk will happen, multiplied by its cost.
3. Develop strategies to mitigate risks, especially those with a high risk exposure. Risks may be avoided (e.g. by hiring more people), transferred (e.g. by choosing a different development strategy), or accepted.
4. Handle the risks: monitor risk factors and take action when needed.

In section 8.4, we focused on the planning and control of activities within a project. By depicting the set of activities and their temporal relations in a graph, techniques like PERT offer simple yet powerful means to schedule and control these activities (see, for example, [Boe81]).

8.6 FURTHER READING

Some general software project management sources are: [Boe81], [Gil88], [Bro95] and [Hum97b].

[Boe89] gives a good overview of software risk management. Risk management experiences are reported on in [Sof97a].

Exercises

1. List the conditions for effective systems control.
2. Is the waterfall approach suitable for a realization-type problem? If so, why?
3. Is the waterfall approach suitable for an exploration-type problem? If so, why?
4. What is risk management?
5. How can risks be mitigated?
6. Rephrase the cost drivers of the COCOMO cost estimation model as risk factors.
7. What is a work breakdown structure?
8. What is a PERT chart?
9. What is a Gantt chart?

10. ♠ Classify a project you have been involved in with respect to product certainty, process certainty, and resource certainty. Which of the archetypal situations sketched in section 8.2 best fits this project? In what ways did actual project control differ from that suggested for the situation identified? Can you explain possible differences?

11. ♡ Consider the patient planning system mentioned in exercise 3.10. Suppose the project team consists of several analysts and two members from the hospital staff. The analysts have a lot of experience in the design of planning systems, though not for hospitals. As a manager of this team, which coordination mechanism and management style would you opt for?

12. ♡ Discuss the pros and cons of a hierarchical as well as a matrix team organization for the patient planning project.

13. ♠ Consider a project you have been involved in. Identify the major irregular, control, and goal variables for this project. In what ways did the control variables influence project control?

14. ♡ Suppose one of your team members is dissatisfied with his situation. He has been involved in similar projects for several years now. You have assigned him these jobs because he was performing so well. Discuss possible actions to prevent this employee from leaving the organization.

15. ♡ Suppose you are the manager of a project that is getting seriously behind schedule. Your team is having severe problems with testing a particular subsystem. Your client is pressing you to deliver the system on time. How would you handle this situation? How would you handle the situation if you were a member of the team and your manager was not paying serious attention to your signals?

Part II

The Software Life Cycle

Contents

When designing a garden, you begin by formulating your requirements – how large should the grass-area be, should you leave a corner to raise potatoes, where should the sand-bin be put, do not the requirements interfere with future maintenance work on the house (!), etc. After that, a design is drawn up which is carefully documented in a blueprint. Only then will the gardener cut the first sod. A similar approach is followed when developing software. In a number of phases – requirements engineering, design, implementation, testing – the software system will take shape. After the software is delivered to the client it must be maintained. Reiteration of phases occurs because changes have to be incorporated and errors must be corrected. The result is a highly cyclical process, the so-called software life cycle.

The various phases of the initial development cycle are the topics of chapters 9–13, and chapter 14 is devoted to software maintenance.

Chapter 9 covers requirements engineering, the first major phase in a software development project. The most challenging and difficult aspect of requirements engineering is to get a complete description of the problem to be solved. Part of this chapter is devoted to discussing a number of techniques for eliciting requirements from the user. These requirements must be communicated to stakeholders with widely different interests. Users want a description in which their expert language is used. Software designers are better served with a more formal description. Chapter 9 discusses a number of techniques for specifying requirements.

Requirements engineering is followed by design. During the design phase, the problem is decomposed into components. The main result of the design phase is a description of these components and their interfaces. Often, the design phase is split into a global, architectural design phase followed by a detailed design phase. Chapter 10 deals with the architectural aspects of design. Chapter 11 is concerned with design methods, design quality, and the documentation of a design. Chapter 12 deals with one specific approach to analysis and design: object-oriented analysis and design.

Chapter 13 is concerned with software testing. The bulk of this chapter is devoted to discussing and comparing a number of techniques for testing individual components (units) of a software system.

Chapter 14 covers software maintenance, i.e. everything that is done to a system after its initial development. Software maintenance entails more than the correction of errors. Users request additional requirements, the hardware or software platform on which the system runs may be changed, supporting software may be replaced, etc. Maintenance concerns all activities needed to keep the system operational after it has been delivered.

9 Requirements Engineering

LEARNING OBJECTIVES

- To understand that requirements engineering is a cyclical process involving three types of activity: elicitation, specification, and validation
- To appreciate the role of social and cognitive issues in requirements engineering
- To be able to distinguish a number of requirements elicitation techniques
- To be aware of the contents of a requirements specification document
- To know various techniques and notations for specifying requirements
- To be aware of different perspectives and aspects that may be distinguished in modeling requirements

The hardest single part of building a system is deciding what to build
[Bro87]

The requirements engineering phase is the first major step towards the solution of a data processing problem. During this phase, the user's requirements with respect to the future system are carefully identified and documented. These requirements concern both the functions to be provided and a number of additional requirements, such as those regarding performance, reliability, user documentation, user training, cost, and so on. During the requirements engineering phase we do not yet address the question of *how* to achieve these user requirements in terms of system components and their interaction. This is postponed until the design phase.

A requirement is 'a condition or capability needed by a user to solve a problem or achieve an objective' [IEE90a]. The 'user' alluded to in this definition may be an end user of the system, a person behind the screen. However, it may also denote several classes of indirect users, such as people who do not themselves turn the knobs but rather use the information that the system delivers. It may also denote the client (customer) who pays the bill. During requirements engineering, different types of user may be the source of different types of requirements. Hopefully, the end users will be the main source of information regarding the functional, task-related requirements. Other requirements, e.g. those that relate to security issues, may well be phrased by other stakeholders. We will use the term 'user' to denote both direct (end-) users and other stakeholders involved in the requirements engineering process.

The result of the requirements engineering phase is documented in the **requirements specification**. The requirements specification reflects the mutual understanding of the problem to be solved between the analyst and the client. It is the basis for a contract, be it formal or informal, between the client of the system and the development organization. Eventually, the system delivered will be assessed by testing its compliance with the requirements specification.

The requirements specification serves as a starting point for the next phase, the design phase. In the design phase the architecture of the system is devised in terms of system components and interfaces between those components. The design phase results in a specification as well: a precise description – preferably in some formal language – of the design architecture, its components, and its interfaces.

The notion 'specification' thus has several meanings. To prevent confusion, we will always use the prefix 'requirements' if it denotes the result of the requirements engineering phase.

To make matters worse, the phase in which the user's requirements are analyzed and documented is also sometimes called specification. We feel this to be somewhat of a misnomer and will not use the term as such.

We use the term **requirements engineering** rather than the narrower notion of **requirements analysis** to emphasize that it is an iterative and co-operative process of analyzing a problem, documenting the resulting observations, and checking the accuracy of the understanding gained. Requirements engineering not only involves technical concerns of how to represent the requirements. Social and cognitive aspects play a dominant role as well.

Requirements engineering and design generally cannot be strictly separated in time. In some cases, the requirements specification is very formal and can be viewed as a high-level design specification of the system to be built. Often, a preliminary design is done after an initial set of requirements has been determined. Based on the result of this design effort, the requirements specification may be changed and refined. This type of iteration also occurs when prototyping techniques are being used. Well-known techniques such as SADT and data flow diagrams are used to structure and document both requirements specifications and designs.

It is only for ease of presentation that the requirements engineering and design phases are strictly separated and treated consecutively in this book.

During requirements engineering, a number of quite different matters are being addressed. Let us look at an example and consider the (hypothetical) case of a university's library automating its operation. We will start with the library containing a number of cabinets. These cabinets hold a huge number of cards, one per book. Each card contains the names of the authors, the book title, ISBN, publication year, and other useful data. The cards are ordered alphabetically by the name of the first author of each book.

This ordering system in fact presents major problems as it only works well if we know the first author's name. If we only know the title, or if we are interested in books on a certain topic, the author catalog is of little or no help.

By duplicating each card a number of times, and putting them in different catalogs – say, one ordered by author's names, one by title, one by topic, etc – this problem can be overcome. But, the process is error-prone and takes a lot of effort.

A software solution seems obvious. If we store the data for each book once in a database, we may subsequently sort the entries in many different ways. Appropriate tools can enable the user to search the database interactively. By placing a number of terminals in the library, service can be greatly enhanced.

During the requirements engineering phase, a number of user requirements will be raised. Some of those requirements will concern updating the database, that is adding, deleting and changing records. Others will concern functions to be provided to ordinary members of the library, such as:

- Give a list of all books written by X;

- Give a list of all books whose title contains Y;

- Give a list of all books on topic Z;
- Give a list of all books that arrived after date D.

It is expedient to try somehow to group user requirements into a few categories, ranging from 'essential requirements' to 'nice features'. As noted in chapter 3, users tend to have difficulties in articulating their real needs. Chances are, then, that much effort is spent on realizing features which later turn out to be mere bells and whistles. By using a layered scheme in both the formulation of user requirements and their subsequent realization, some of the problems that beset present-day software development projects can be circumvented. In our library system example, for instance, the requirement 'Give a list of all books that arrived after date D' could be classified as a nice feature. Service is not seriously degraded if this function is not provided, since we may temporarily place the acquisitions on a dedicated shelf.

It is also possible to try to predict a number of future requirements, which will not be implemented in the present project. It is, however, sensible to pay attention to these matters at an early stage, so that they can be accommodated during the design of the system. Possible future requirements of our library system could include such things as:

- Storing information about books that have been ordered but have not been received;
- Storing information about library members, such as their name and address, and the dates on which books are lent to them, which can then be used to generate a reminder notice for books not returned on time.

The above functions concern the use of the software by library members and library personnel. There are other stakeholders as well, though. For example, library management may wish to use the system to get information on member profiles in order to improve the title acquisition process.

Besides these requirements, which directly relate to the functions of the software to be delivered, a number of other matters should be addressed during the requirements engineering phase. For our library example, as a minimum, the following points have to be addressed:

- On which machine will the system be implemented, and which operating system will be used? If the data is to be stored in some DBMS, which (type of) DBMS is to be used? What type of terminal is to be used and how many terminals will be supported?
- Which classes of users can be distinguished? In our example, both library personnel and library members will have to be served. What kind of knowledge

do these users have? Will certain functions of the system be restricted to certain classes of user? Normal library members will probably not be allowed to update the database or print the contents of the database.

- What is the size of the database and how is it expected to grow in the course of time? These factors influence both storage capacity needed and algorithms to be used. For a database containing several thousands of books, some not very efficient searching algorithm might suffice. For the Library of Congress, the situation is quite different, though.

- What response time should the system offer? A search request for a certain book will have to be answered fairly quickly. If the user has to wait too long for an answer, he will become dissatisfied and search the shelves directly. Related questions concern the interaction between response time and the expected number of question sessions per unit of time.

- How much will a system of this kind cost? In our library example, we should not only pay attention to the direct costs incurred by the software development effort. The cost of converting the information contained in the present file cabinets to a suitable database format should not be neglected. These, less visible, indirect costs may well outweigh the direct cost of designing and implementing the new system.

This relatively simple example already shows that it is not sufficient to merely list the functional requirements of the new system. The system's envisioned environment and its interaction with that environment should be analyzed as well.

In our example, this concerns the library itself, to start with. The consequences of introducing a system like this one can be much greater than it seems at first sight. Working procedures may change, necessitating retraining of personnel, changes in personnel functions and the overall organizational structure. Some members of staff may even become redundant. Checking whether membership fees have been paid might involve interfacing with the financial system, owned by another department.

In general, the setting up of an automated system may have more than just technical repercussions. Often, not enough attention is paid to these other repercussions. The lack of success of many software development projects can be traced back to a neglect of non-technical aspects.

Before the actual design and implementation starts, the feasibility of a software development project should be assessed. First, the technical feasibility: can the hardware and software envisaged deliver the performance asked for; is the environment capable of timely delivery of the necessary data for the system? If all books have to be re-labeled because the new system uses a different classification scheme, this could easily require more time than the design, implementation and testing of the new software.

Part of the feasibility study is an economic feasibility study. Do the gains outweigh the cost? The cost of a software development effort is largely determined by the time, in man-months, needed to develop the software. At the requirements engineering phase, only global attributes are known, so that a first cost estimation will be global. As time goes by and the project progresses, the estimates will, hopefully, become more accurate. In chapter 7, we discussed the problems associated with estimating costs, and the various models that have been developed for this purpose.

The gains of a software development project are often difficult to express in dollars. For a stock control system, we may directly translate the benefits (less average stock and a higher availability of stock items) into money savings. The increased user service expected from our library automation project is, however, much more difficult to quantify.

In defining requirements engineering as a process to identify, document and validate user requirements, we tacitly assumed that a user is available to participate in this process. Much software developed today however is *market-driven* rather than *customer-driven*. For example, rather than developing a system for one specific library, we could develop a 'generic' library application. Requirements for this generic library application are created by exploring the library domain, while trade-offs between requirements are based on market considerations, product fit, and the like. We may decide that our system need not address the concerns of the Library of Congress (too small a market), while it should definitely interface with accounting system Y, since that system is widely used in university departments, and this is perceived to be an important market for our library application.

Unfortunately, most requirements engineering techniques offer little support for market-driven software development.

Following [LK95], we distinguish three processes in requirements engineering:

- **Requirements elicitation** In general, the requirements analyst is not an expert in the domain being modeled. Through interaction with domain specialists, such as professional librarians, he has to build himself a sufficiently rich model of that domain. Thus, requirements elicitation is about *understanding* the problem. The fact that different disciplines are involved in this process complicates matters. In many cases, the analyst is not a mere outside observer of the domain to be modeled, simply eliciting facts from domain specialists. He may have to take a stand in a power struggle or decide between conflicting requirements, thereby actively participating in the construction of the domain of interest. Differences between market-driven and customer-driven development are particularly relevant during this stage. Section 9.1 discusses various issues related to, and a number of techniques used in, requirements elicitation.

- **Requirements specification** Once the problem is understood, it has to be *described*. In section 9.2, we give guidelines for the contents of a requirements specification document. This document describes the product to be delivered, not the process of how it is developed. Project requirements are described in the project plan, discussed in chapter 2. Quite a number of techniques exist for specifying requirements, ranging from very informal (natural language) to very formal (mathematical). Throughout this book, a number of such modeling techniques are discussed: formal specification techniques in chapter 15, object-oriented techniques in chapter 12, and techniques for specifying quality requirements in chapter 6. The design techniques discussed in chapter 11 are often also used for specifying requirements. Section 9.3 is confined to a discussion of some of the basic techniques for modeling requirements.

- **Requirements validation and verification** Once the problem is described, the different parties involved have to *agree upon* its nature. We have to ascertain that the correct requirements are stated (validation) and that these requirements are stated correctly (verification). Some verification and validation techniques that can be applied at this early stage are sketched in section 9.5.

Obviously, these processes involve iteration and feedback. The major interactions are shown in figure 9.1.

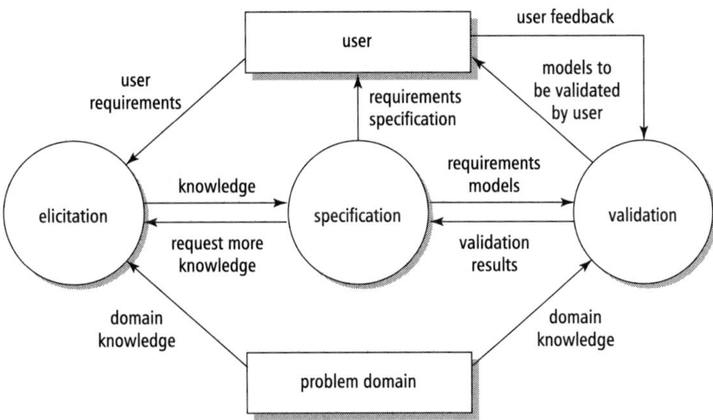

Figure 9.1 A framework for the requirements engineering process (*Source: P. Loucopoulos & V. Karakostas,* Systems Requirements Engineering, *1995. Reproduced with permission of The McGraw-Hill Companies*)

The emphasis in our discussion of requirements engineering will be on modeling the external behavior of the system, i.e. all those parts and aspects of the system that *end users* consider important. Other views or perspectives are relevant as well, for instance, a model which highlights the way the system supports the business. Furthermore, a number of *aspects* of the system are often considered and modeled separately, e.g. a data and function aspect. Section 9.4 discusses a general framework for information systems modeling, which puts our discussion of requirements engineering in a wider perspective.

9.1 REQUIREMENTS ELICITATION

In chapter 1, the first part of the software life cycle was depicted as shown in figure 9.2. The fact that the text 'requirements specification' is placed in a rectangle suggests, not unjustly, that it concerns something very concrete and explicit. The 'problem' is less well defined, less clear, even fuzzy in many cases. The primary goal of the requirements engineering phase is to elicit the contours and constituents of this fuzzy problem. This process is also known as **conceptual modeling**.

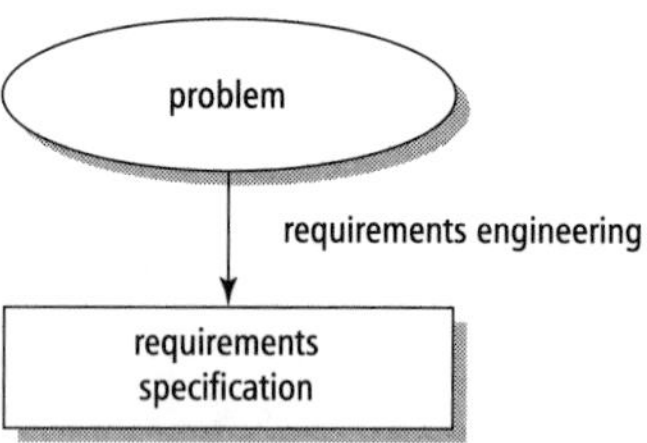

Figure 9.2 The first part of the software life cycle

During requirements engineering we are modeling part of reality. The part of reality in which we are interested is referred to as the **universe of discourse** (UoD). Example UoDs are a library system, a factory automation system, an assembly line, an elevator system.

The model constructed during the requirements engineering phase is an **explicit conceptual model** of the UoD. The adjective 'explicit' indicates that the model must be able to be communicated to the relevant people (such as analysts and users). To this end it should contain all relevant information from the UoD. One of the persistent problems of requirements analysis and, for that matter, analysis in general, is to account for all of the relevant influences and leave out irrelevant details.

In our library example we could easily have overlooked the fact that in a number of cases the author's name as it appears on the cover of a book is not the 'canonical' author's name. This phenomenon occurs in particular with authors from countries that use non-Latin scripts. The transcription of the Russian name 4EXOB reads 'Chekhov' in English and 'Tsjechow' in Dutch. In such cases, librarians want to include the author's name twice: once the name is spelled as it appears on the book, and once the name is spelled as it is used in the various search processes. An answer to a question like 'which books by Chekhov does our library possess?' should also inform us about the non-English titles.

Subtle mismatches between the analyst's notion of terms and concepts and their proper meaning within the domain being modeled can have profound effects. Such mismatches can most easily occur in domains we already 'know', such as a library. An illuminating discussion of potential problems in (formally) specifying requirements of a library system can be found in [Win88]. Problems noted include:

- A library employee may also be a member of the library, so the two sets of system users are not disjoint;
- There is a difference between a book (identified by its ISBN) and the (physical) copies of a book owned by the library. We have carefully made this distinction in the formal specification of a number of library functions in section 15.2.1;
- It is not sufficient to simply denote the status of a book by a boolean value present/not present (i.e. lent out). For instance, a book or, more properly, a copy of a book, may be lost, stolen, or in repair.

People involved in a UoD have an **implicit conceptual model** of that UoD. An implicit conceptual model consists of the background knowledge shared by people in the UoD. The fact that this knowledge is shared gives rise to 'of course' statements by people from within the UoD, because this knowledge is taken for granted. ('Of course, a copy of a book is not the same as a book.') Part of the implicit conceptual model is not verbalized. It contains tacit knowledge, knowledge that is skillfully applied and functions in the background. Finally, an implicit conceptual model contains habits, customs, prejudices and even inconsistencies.

During conceptual modeling, an implicit conceptual model is turned into an explicit one. In doing so, the analyst is confronted with two types of problem: analysis problems and negotiation problems. Analysis problems arise from the fact that part of the implicit conceptual model is not verbalized, that the implicit conceptual model evolves with time, that the user and analyst talk a different language, and that the implicit conceptual model cannot be completely codified. Negotiation problems arise because people in the UoD may counteract the analysis process, because the implicit conceptual models of people in the UoD may differ, or because of opposing interests of people involved (such as library personnel versus their managers). Both types of problems are discussed below.

The problem to be addressed by the automated system arises from the user, a human. This person must be able to describe this problem in both a correct and complete way. It must be communicated to a person who in general has a rather different background. The analyst often lacks a sufficiently profound knowledge of the application domain in which the problem originated. He has to learn the language of the application domain and become acquainted with its terminology, concepts and procedures. Especially in large projects, the application knowledge tends to be thinly spread amongst the specialists involved, which easily leads to integration and coordination difficulties.

In our earlier example, it is the librarian who has to express his wishes. It is possible that the inclusion of two author names ('Tsjechow' and 'Chekhov') is seen as an obvious detail which need not be brought forward explicitly. The analyst at the other side of the table may still get the impression that he has a complete picture of the system. This type of omission may have severe consequences.

> A number of years back a large automated air defense system was being developed in the US. During one of the final tests of this system, an alarm signal was issued. One of the computers detected an unknown missile. It turned out to be the moon. This possibility had not been thought of.

Eliciting correct and complete information is an important prerequisite for success. This turns out to be rather problematic in practice. Asking the prospective user what is wanted does not generally work. More often than not we get a rather incomplete and inaccurate picture of the situation. Important reasons for this are the human limitations for processing information, selecting information, and solving problems. These limited human capabilities are yet aggravated by such factors as:

- the complexity and variation in requirements that can be imposed upon software;

- the differences in background between the client, or user, and the software specialist.

In research on human information processing one often uses a model in which human memory consists of two components: a short-term memory in which information is being processed, and a long-term memory in which the permanent knowledge is stored. Short-term memory has a limited capacity: one often says that it has about seven slots. Long-term memory on the other hand has a very large capacity.

So, information is processed in a relatively small part of human memory. Long-term memory is thus accessed in an indirect way. In addition, humans also employ external memories when information is being processed: a blackboard, a piece of paper, etc.

If a person being interviewed during requirements engineering only uses his short-term memory, the limitations thereof may have an impact on the results. This may easily occur if no use is being made of external memories. Things can be forgotten, simply because our short-term memory has limited capacity.

Humans are also inclined to be prejudiced about selecting and using information. We are, in particular, inclined to let recent events prevail. In making up a requirements specification, this leads to requirements bearing on the present situation, presently available information, recent events, etc.

Humans are not very capable of rational thinking. They will simplify things and use a model which does not really fit reality. Other limitations that influence our model of reality are determined by such factors as education, prejudice, practice, etc. This same kind of simplification occurs when software requirements are drawn up. And the result will be limited by the same factors.

We cannot always expect the user to be able to precisely state his requirements at an early stage. One reason for investigating the opportunities of automation is often because of a certain dissatisfaction with the present situation. One is not satisfied with the present situation and has the impression that automation will help. Whether this is true or not – many data processing problems are organizational problems – simply automating the present situation is not always the solution. Something different is wanted, though it is not clear what. Only when insight into the possibilities of automation is gained, will real requirements show themselves. This is one of the reasons for the sheer size of the maintenance problem. About half of the maintenance effort concerns adapting software to (new) requirements of the user. To counteract this trend, software development process models that acknowledge this learning process, such as prototyping and incremental development, are to be preferred over those that don't, i.e. the waterfall model and its variants.

Through a careful analysis, we may hope to build a sound perspective of user requirements and anticipate future changes. However, no matter how much time is spent in a dialog with the prospective users, future changes remain hard to foresee. We may even go one step further and stipulate that requirements will *never* be complete. In this respect, specifying requirements has much in common with weather-forecasting: there is a limit to how far the future can be predicted.

In a situation where the goal of a software development project is to improve an existing 'system', be it a manual process or a (partly) automated one, it is generally helpful to explicitly distinguish two modeling steps. In the first step, the current situation is modeled. Based on an analysis of the strengths and weaknesses of the current situation, the situation-to-be is next modeled. Business Process Redesign, in particular, stresses the distinction between these two modeling steps.

For the requirements engineering phase to be successful we need methods and techniques that try to bypass the difficulties sketched above. The degree to which powerful techniques are required depends on the experience of the people involved in the requirements engineering phase (both users and analysts) and the expertise of the analyst with the application domain. Section 9.1.1 discusses a number of techniques for requirements elicitation.

Most requirements engineering methods, and software development methods in general, are Taylorian in nature. Around the turn of this century, Taylor introduced the notion of 'scientific management', in which tasks are recursively decomposed into simpler tasks and each task has one 'best way' to accomplish it. By careful observations and experiments this one best way can be found and formalized into procedures and rules. Scientific management has been successfully applied in many a factory operation. The equivalent in requirements engineering is to interview domain experts and observe end users at work in order to obtain the 'real' user requirements. After this, the experts go to work and implement these requirements. During the latter process there is no further need to interact with the user community. This view of software development is a functional, and rational, one. Its underlying assumption is that there is one objective truth, which merely needs to be discovered during the analysis process.

Though this view has its merits in drawing up requirements in purely *technical* realms, many UoDs of interest involve people as well – people whose model of the world is incomplete, subjective, irrational, and may conflict with the world view of others. In such cases, the analyst is not a passive outside observer of the UoD. Rather, he actively participates in the *shaping* of the UoD.

It is increasingly being recognized that the Taylorian, functional, approach is not the only, and need not be the most appropriate, approach to the requirements engineering process.

Analysts have a set of assumptions about the nature of the subject of study. Such a set of assumptions is commonly called a 'paradigm'. In our field, these assumptions concern the way in which analysts acquire knowledge (epistemological assumptions) and their view of the social and technical world (ontological assumptions).

The assumptions about knowledge result in an objectivist–subjectivist dimension. If the analyst takes the objectivist point of view, he applies models and methods derived from the natural sciences to arrive at the one and only truth. In the subjectivist position, his principal concern is to understand how the individual creates, modifies and interprets the world he or she is in.

The assumptions about the world result in an order–conflict dimension. The order point of view emphasizes order, stability, integration, and consensus. On the other hand, the conflict view stresses change, conflict, and disintegration.

These two dimensions and their associated extreme positions yield four paradigms for requirements engineering and, more generally, information systems development:

Functionalism (objective–order). In the functionalist paradigm, the developer is the system expert who searches for measurable cause–effect relationships. An empirical organizational reality is believed to exist, independent of the observer. Systems are developed to support rational organizational operation. Their effectiveness and efficiency can be tested objectively, by tests similar to those used in other engineering disciplines.

Social-relativism (subjective–order). In this paradigm, the analyst operates as a facilitator. Reality is not something immutable 'out there', but is constructed in the human mind. The analyst is a change agent. He seeks to facilitate the learning of all people involved.

Radical-structuralism (objective–conflict). In the radical paradigm the key assumption is that system development intervenes in the conflict between two or more social classes for power, prestige, and resources. Systems are often developed to support the interests of the owners, at the expense of the interests of labor. In order to redress the power balance, this paradigm suggests that the analyst should act as a labor partisan. System requirements should evolve from a cooperation between labor and the analyst. This approach is thought to lead to systems that enhance craftsmanship and working conditions.

Neohumanism (subjective–conflict). The central theme in this paradigm is emancipation. Systems are developed to remove distorting influences and other barriers to rational discourse. The system developer acts as a social therapist in an attempt to draw together, in an open discussion, a diverse group of individuals, including customers, labor, and various levels of management.

The order position takes a unitary view on society, while the conflict position takes a pluralistic stand. We may distinguish yet two other approaches to requirements engineering, based on the idea that pluralism need not necessarily result in conflicts, but may also be handled in a co-operative way. This results in two additional approaches:

Democratic The democratic approach assumes that differences between groups can be managed, for example through negotiation. Through workshops and other types of meetings, the politics of requirements engineering can be handled. Joint Application Development is an example of such an approach.

Network Here, the organization is seen as a network of co-operating people who also have their individual aims and goals. Rather than building large, centralized systems, people can be accommodated with small, networked systems, together with the ability to customize these to fit their own specialized needs.

Admittedly, these paradigms reflect extreme orientations. In practice, some mixture of assumptions will usually guide the requirements engineering process. Yet it is fair to say that the majority of system development techniques emphasizes the functionalist view.

In the subjectivist–objectivist dimension, it is important to realize that a good deal of subjectivism may be involved in the shaping of the UoD. If we have to develop a system to, say, control a copying machine, we may safely take a functional stand. We may expect such a machine to operate purely rationally. In the analysis process, we list the functions of the machine, its internal signals, conditions, and so on, in order to get a satisfactory picture of the system to be developed. Once these requirements are identified, they can be frozen and some waterfall-like process model can be employed to realize the system.

If, however, our task is to develop a system to support people in doing their job, such as some office automation system, a purely functional view of the world may easily lead to ill-conceived systems. In such cases, end-user participation in the shaping of the UoD is of paramount importance. Through an open dialog with the people concerned, we may encourage the prospective users to influence the system to be developed. Part of the analyst's job in this case is to reconcile the views of the participants in the analysis process. Continuous feedback during the actual construction phases with possibilities for redirection may further enhance the chance of success. It is the future users who are going to work with the system. It is of no avail to confront them with a system that does not satisfy their needs.

A dissatisfied user will try to neglect the system or, at best, express additional requirements immediately. The net result is that the envisaged gain in efficiency or effectiveness is not reaped.

An illuminating and well-documented example of possible effects of following a fairly radical paradigm is given in [PWB93]; see also section 1.4.3. The system concerns the Computer Aided Despatch System for the London Ambulance Service. Though the system would significantly impact the way ambulance crews carried out their jobs, there was little consultation with them. Some of the consequences of this approach were the following [PWB93, pp 40–41]:

- The system allocated the nearest available resource regardless of originating station, so crews often had to operate further and further from their home base. This resulted in them operating in unfamiliar territory with further to go to reach their home station at the end of a shift.

- The new system took away the flexibility crews previously had for the station to decide on which resource to allocate. This inevitably led to problems when a different resource was used to the one that was allocated.

- The lack of voice contact made the whole process more impersonal and exacerbated the 'them and us' situation.

If the conceptual models of the participants differ, we may either look for a compromise, or opt for one of the views expressed. It is impossible to give general guidelines on how to handle such cases. Looking for a compromise can be a tedious affair and may lead to a system that no one is really happy with. Opting for one particular view of the world will make one party happy, but may result in others completely neglecting the system developed. Worse yet, they may decide to develop a competing system.

9.1.1 Requirements Elicitation Techniques

Figure 9.1 lists two main sources of information for the requirements elicitation process: the users and the (application) domain. This model really presupposes that there exists something 'out there' to start with, and from which requirements can be elicited. In market-driven software development though, this is often not the case, and requirements elicitation in such projects is more like requirements invention or problem-formulation, guided by marketing and sales considerations.

Figure 9.3 lists a number of elicitation techniques, which are elaborated upon below. The figure also tells us that the user is the major source of information in some techniques, while the domain is predominant in others. Furthermore, the figure indicates whether each technique is particularly useful to model the current, as opposed to the anticipated future, situation.

You should generally vacuum a rug in two directions rather than one; likewise, you should use multiple requirements elicitation techniques.

Technique	Main info source		Strong on	
	Domain	User	Current	Future
Interview		X	X	
Delphi technique		X	X	
Brainstorming session		X		X
Task analysis		X	X	
Scenario (use-case) analysis		X	X	X
Ethnography	X		X	
Form analysis	X		X	
Analysis of natural language descriptions	X		X	
Synthesis of reqs from an existing system	X		X	
Domain analysis	X		X	
Use of reference models	X		X	
Business Process Redesign (BPR)	X		X	X
Prototyping		X		X

Figure 9.3 A sample of requirements elicitation techniques

Asking We may simply ask the users what they expect from the system. A presupposition then is that the user is able to bypass his own limitations and prejudices. Asking may take the form of an interview, a brainstorm, or a questionnaire. In an open-ended interview, the user freely talks about his tasks. This is the easiest form of requirements elicitation, but it suffers from all of the drawbacks mentioned before.

In a structured interview, the analyst tries to overcome these by leading the user, for example through closed or probing questions.

In discussion sessions with a group of users, we often find that some users are far more articulate than others, and thus have a greater influence on the outcome. The consensus thus reached need not be well-balanced. To overcome this problem, a Delphi technique may be employed. The Delphi technique is an iterative technique in which information is exchanged in a written form until a consensus is reached. For example, participants may write down their requirements, sorted in order of importance. The sets of requirements thus obtained are distributed to all participants, who reflect on them to obtain a revised set of requirements. This procedure is repeated several times until sufficient consensus is reached.

Task analysis Employees working in some domain perform a number of tasks, such as handling requests to borrow a book, cataloging new books, ordering books, etc. Higher-level tasks may be decomposed into subtasks. For example, the task 'handle request to borrow a book' may lead to the following subtasks:

- check member identification,
- check for limit on the number of books that may be borrowed,
- register book as being borrowed by the library member,
- issue a slip indicating the due back date.

Task analysis is a technique to obtain a hierarchy of tasks and subtasks to be carried out by people working in the domain. Any of the other techniques discussed may be used to get the necessary information to draw this hierarchy. There are no clear-cut rules as to when to stop decomposing tasks. A major heuristic is that at some point users tend to 'refuse' to decompose tasks any further. For instance, when being asked how the member identification is checked, the library employee may say 'Well, I simply check his id.' At this point, further decomposition is meaningless.

Task analysis is often applied at the stage when (details about) the human–computer interaction component are being decided upon. This underestimates its potency as a general requirements elicitation technique. It also gives the (wrong) impression that users are only concerned with the 'look and feel' of the interface.

Scenario-based analysis Instead of looking for generic plans as in interviews or task analysis, the analyst may study **instances** of tasks. A scenario is a story which tells us how a specific task instance is executed. The scenario can be real or artificial. An example of a real scenario is that the analyst observes how a library employee handles an actual user request. We may ask the library employee to verbalize what he is doing and make an audio or video recording thereof. This **think aloud** method is a fairly unobtrusive technique to study people at work. It is often used to assess prototypes or existing information systems.

Alternatively, we may construct artificial scenarios and discuss these with the user. As a first shot, we may for example draw up the following scenario for returning a book:

1. The due back date for the book is checked. If the book is overdue, the member is asked to pay the appropriate fine.

2. The book is recorded as again being eligible for checking-out.

3. The book is put back in its proper place.

When this scenario is discussed with the library employee, a number of related issues may crop up, either through probing questions from the analyst, or because the user contrasts the scenario with daily practice. Example questions that could be raised include such things as:

- What happens when the person returning the book is not a registered member of the library?

- What happens when the book returned is damaged?

- What happens if the member returning this book has other books that are overdue or an outstanding reservation for another book?

In essence, this type of story-telling provides the user with an artificial mock-up version of the software eventually to be delivered. It serves as a paper-based prototype to gain a better understanding of the requirements. Scenario-based analysis is often used in object-oriented analysis and design methods. It is then called **use-case analysis**; see section 12.2.5.

Scenario-based analysis is often done in a somewhat haphazard way. In that case, there is no way of telling whether enough scenarios have been drawn up and a sufficiently accurate and complete picture of the requirements is obtained. Current research in this area is aimed at finding methods to analyze, generate and validate scenarios in a systematic way.

Ethnography A major disadvantage of eliciting requirements through, for example, interviews is that the analyst imposes his view of how the world is ordered onto the user. Such methods may fail if the analyst and user do not share a category system. The analyst may, for example, ask the following:

'If a member wants to borrow a book while he or she still has an outstanding fine, will you:

a) Refuse the request, or

b) Handle the request anyway.'

This binary choice need not map actual practice. The library employee may, for example, grant the request provided part of the outstanding fine is settled or if he knows the member to be trustworthy.

Thinking aloud protocols are based on the idea that users have well-defined goals and subgoals, and that they traverse such goal trees in a neat top-down manner. People however often do not have preconceived plans, but rather proceed in somewhat opportunistic ways.

A disadvantage of task analysis is that it considers individual tasks of individual persons, without taking into account the social and organizational environment in which these tasks are executed.

Ethnographic methods are claimed not to have such shortcomings. In ethnography, groups of people are studied in their natural settings. It is well-known from sociology, where for example Polynesian tribes are studied by living with them for an extended period of time. Likewise, user requirements can be studied by participating in their daily work for a period of time, for example by becoming a library employee. The analyst becomes an apprentice, recognizing that the future users of the system are the real experts in their work.

Form analysis A lot of information about the domain being modeled can often be found in various forms being used. For example, to request some conference proceedings from another library, the user might have to fill in a form such as given in figure 9.4.

Proceedings Request Form	
Member name	....
Member address	....
	....
Title	....
Series no	....
Editor	....
Place	....
Publisher	....
Year	....
Signature	....

Figure 9.4 A sample form

Forms provide us with information about the data objects of the domain, their properties, and their interrelations. They are particularly useful as an input to modeling the data aspect of the system; see also section 9.3.1.

Library users often have incomplete knowledge of the information sources they are interested in. For example, someone might be looking for the proceedings of the *International Conference on Software Engineering* that took place in Berlin. Only if the various entries from the above form are used as entities in the underlying data model, can such a query be answered easily. In this case, the form directly points at a useful requirement which might otherwise go unnoticed.

Natural language descriptions Like forms, natural language descriptions provide a lot of useful information about the domain to be modeled. The operating instructions for library employees might for instance contain a paragraph like the one given in figure 9.5. This text gives us such information as:

- There are (at least) two accounts that orders can be charged to;
- There is a list of staff members authorized to sign off such requests;
- There is the possibility of ordering multiple copies of titles, such as this book on *Software Engineering*, on behalf of students.

Title acquisition

Before a request to acquire a title can be complied with, form B has to be filled in completely. A request cannot be handled if not signed by an authorized staff member or the account to be charged ('Student' or 'Staff') is not indicated. A request is not to be granted if the title requested is already present in the title catalog, unless it is marked 'Stolen' or 'Lost', or the account is 'Student'.

Figure 9.5 A sample instruction for library employees

Often, natural language descriptions (and forms) provide the analyst with background information to be used in conjunction with other elicitation techniques such as interviews. Natural language descriptions in particular tend to assume a lot of tacit knowledge by the reader. For example, if form B contains an ISBN, this saves the library employee some work, but the request will probably still be handled if this information is not provided. A practical problem with natural language descriptions is that they are often not kept up-to-date. Like software documentation, their validity tends to deteriorate with time.

Natural language descriptions are often taken as a starting point in object-oriented analysis techniques. This is further discussed in chapter 12.

Derivation from an existing system Starting from an existing system, for instance a similar system in some other organization or a description in a text book, we may formulate the requirements of the new system. Obviously, we have to be careful and take the peculiar circumstances of the present situation into account.

Rather than looking at one particular system, we may also study a number of systems in some application domain. This meta-requirements analysis process is known as **domain analysis**. Its goal generally is to identify reusable components, concepts, structures, and the like. It is dangerous to look for reusable requirements in immature domains. Requirements may then be reused simply because they are available, not because they fit the situation at hand. They become 'dead wood'. In the context of requirements analysis, domain analysis can be viewed as a technique for deriving a 'reference' model for systems within a given domain. Such a reference model provides a skeleton (architecture) that can be augmented and adapted to fit the specific situation at hand.

Domain analysis and requirements reuse are further discussed in chapter 17, in the context of software reuse.

Business Process Redesign (BPR). In many software development projects, the people involved jump to conclusions rather quickly: automation is the answer. Even worse, their conclusion might be that automating the current situation is the answer. In Business Process Redesign (or Business Process Reengineering), a rather different strategy is followed. It is an organizational activity to radically redesign business processes to achieve competitive breakthroughs in, e.g. quality, cost, or user satisfaction. In BPR, we depart completely from the existing ways of doing things. In BPR, the following steps are distinguished:

1. Identify processes for innovation. Two major approaches for doing so are the exhaustive and high-impact approach. In the exhaustive approach, an attempt is made to identify all processes, which are then prioritized for their redesign urgency. The high-impact approach attempts to identify the most important processes only, or the ones that conflict with the business vision.

2. Identify change levers. In this step, opportunities facilitating process improvement are identified. Three types of lever can be recognized: organizational enablers (such as empowering teams), human resource enablers (such as task enrichment) and information technology enablers.

3. Develop process visions. For redesign to be successful, the organization needs to know which goals it wants to reach. This is described in the process vision. The main components of a process vision are: process objectives (measurable targets of the future performance of the system), process attributes (qualitative and descriptive properties of the future process), critical success factors and constraints (organizational, cultural, and technological).

4. Understand the existing process. This includes documenting the existing process, measuring it, and identifying problematic aspects. It allows us to assess the health of the existing process, and brings problems to the surface.

5. Design and prototype the new process. This is the final step. Prototyping makes it possible to try out new structures, thereby reducing the risk of failure.

BPR is not really a requirements elicitation technique proper. It is mentioned here because it emphasizes an essential issue to be addressed during the requirements engineering phase. Business processes should not be driven by information technology. Rather, information technology should enable them. Though a complete BPR effort is not necessary or feasible in many situations, rethinking the existing processes and procedures is a step which is all too often thoughtlessly skipped in software development projects.

As an example, consider our library automation project once again. Careful inspection of the current situation might reveal that things aren't all that bad. However, the impression is that the number of requests that could not be granted has steadily risen in the past years. This is perceived to be the main cause of the increasing number of dissatisfied users. Since service to its customers has high priority, one of the objectives is to decrease the number of requests that cannot be satisfied by 50% within two years. For this to be possible, the library should be allowed to spend the available budget at its own discretion, rather than being triggered by signals from researchers only (this sounds radical, doesn't it). It is therefore decided to augment the existing automated system with modules to keep track of both successful and unsuccessful requests. Based on the insights gained from this measurement process during a period of three months, a decision will be taken as to how large a percentage of the annual budget will be reallocated.

Prototyping Given the fact that it is difficult, if not impossible, to build the right system from the start, we may decide to use prototypes. Starting from a first set of requirements, a prototype of the system is constructed. This prototype is used for experiments, which lead to new requirements and more insight into the possible uses of the system. In one or more ensuing steps, a more definite set of requirements is developed. Prototyping is discussed in section 3.2.

Of these requirements elicitation techniques, asking is the least certain strategy, while prototyping is the least uncertain. Besides the experience of both users and analysts, the uncertainty of the process is also influenced by the stability of the environment, the complexity of the product to be developed and the familiarity with the problem area in question. We may try to estimate the impact of those factors on the vulnerability of the resulting requirements specification, and then decide on a certain primary method for requirements elicitation based on this estimate.

For a well-understood problem, with very experienced analysts, interviewing the prospective users may suffice. However, if it concerns an advanced and ill-understood problem from within a rapidly changing environment and the analysts have little or no experience in the domain in question, it seems wise to first construct one or more prototypes.

It is generally wise to have multiple customer–developer links in a software development project, and during requirements engineering in particular. [KC95] studied the relation between project success and the number and type of such customer–developer links. The authors observed a strong correlation between the number of links and project success: more links implied more successful projects. The relative contribution to project success diminishes as the number of links grows; there is no need to have more than, say, half a dozen links. A further interesting observation from this study is that links with *direct* users have more impact on project success than links with *indirect* users such as user representatives or sales people. Finally, it was noted that customer-driven development projects tend to use and prefer different types of link to market-driven development projects. For example, the favorite link for custom development – facilitated teams – was not used by package developers, while the favorite link for package developers – support lines – was seldom used for custom projects.

We should be very careful in our assessment of which requirements elicitation technique to choose. It is all too common to be too optimistic about our ability to properly assess software requirements.

As an example, consider the following anecdote from a Dutch newspaper. A firm in the business of farm automation had developed a system in which microchips were put in cows' ears. Subsequently, each individual cow could be tracked: food and water supply was regulated and adjusted, the amount and quality of the milk automatically recorded and analyzed, etc. Quite naturally, this same technique was next successfully applied to pigs. Thereafter, it was tried on goats. A million-dollar, fully automated goat farm was built. But alas, things did not work out that well for goats. Contrary to cows and pigs, goats eat everything, including their companions' chips.

9.2 THE REQUIREMENTS SPECIFICATION DOCUMENT

The end-product of the requirements engineering phase is a requirements specification. The requirements specification is an a posteriori reconstruction of the results of this analysis phase. Its purpose is to communicate these results to others. It serves as an anchor point against which subsequent steps can be justified.

The requirements specification is the starting point for the next phase: design. Consequently, a very precise, even mathematical description is preferable. On the other hand, the specification must also be understandable to the user. This often means a readable document, using natural language and pictures. In practice, one has to look for a compromise. Alternatively, the requirements specification may be presented in different, but consistent, forms to the different audiences involved.

Besides readability and understandability, various other requirements for this document can be stated [IEE93]:

- A requirements specification should be *correct*. There is no procedure to guarantee correctness. The requirements specification should be validated against other (superior) documents and the actual needs of the users to assess its correctness.

- A requirements specification should be *unambiguous*, both to those who create it and to those who use it. We must be able to uniquely interpret requirements. Because of its very nature, this is difficult to realize in a natural language.

- A requirements specification should be *complete*. All significant matters relating to functionality, performance, constraints, and the like, should be documented. The responses to both correct and incorrect input should be specified; phrases like 'to be determined' are particularly insidious. Unfortunately, it is not always feasible to complete the specification at an early stage. If certain requirements can only be made specific at a later stage, the requirements specification should at least document the ultimate point in time at which this should have happened.

- A requirements specification should be (internally) *consistent*, i.e. different parts of it should not be in conflict with each other. Conflicting requirements can be both logical and temporal. Using different terms for one and the same object may also lead to conflicts.

- Requirements should be ranked for *importance* or *stability*. Typically, some requirements are more important than others. In some cases, a simple ranking scheme like 'essential', 'worthwhile', and 'optional' will suffice; in other cases, a more sophisticated classification scheme may be needed. We may indicate the stability of requirements by indicating the likelihood, or the expected number, of changes. Through the explicit incorporation of this type of information in the requirements document, users are stimulated to give more consideration to each requirement. It also gives developers the opportunity to better direct their attention.

- A requirements specification should be *verifiable*. This means that there must be a finite process to determine whether or not the requirements have been met. Phrases like 'the system should be user-friendly' are not verifiable. Likewise, the use of quantities that cannot be measured, as in 'the system's response time should usually be less than two seconds', should be avoided. A requirement like 'for requests of type X, the system's response time is less than two seconds in 80% of cases, with a maximum machine load of Y', is verifiable.

- A requirements specification should be *modifiable*. Software models part of reality. Therefore it changes. The corresponding requirements specification has to evolve together with the reality being modeled. Thus, the document must be organized in such a way that changes can be accommodated readily (a looseleaf form, for example kept in machine-readable form). Redundancy must be prevented as much as possible, for otherwise there is the danger that changes lead to inconsistencies.

- A requirements specification should be *traceable*. The origin and rationale of each and every requirement must be traceable. A clear and consistent numbering scheme makes it possible that other documents can uniquely refer to parts of the requirements specification.

As a guideline for the contents of a requirements specification we will follow IEEE Standard 830. This standard does not give a rigid form for the requirements specification. In our opinion, the precise ordering and contents of the elements of this document also is less essential. The important point is to choose a structure which adheres to the above constraints. In IEEE Standard 830, a global structure such as depicted in figure 9.6, is used.

1. *Introduction*
    - 1.1 Purpose
    - 1.2 Scope
    - 1.3 Definitions, acronyms and abbreviations
    - 1.4 References
    - 1.5 Overview
2. *Overall description*
    - 2.1 Product perspective
    - 2.2 Product functions
    - 2.3 User characteristics
    - 2.4 Constraints
    - 2.5 Assumptions and dependencies
    - 2.6 Requirements subsets
3. *Specific requirements*

Figure 9.6 Global structure of the requirements specification (*Source: IEEE Recommended Practice for Software Requirements Specifications*, IEEE Std 830, 1993. *Reproduced by permission of IEEE*)

For any nontrivial system, the detailed requirements will constitute by far the largest part of the requirements document. It is therefore helpful to somehow categorize these detailed requirements. This can be done along different dimensions, such as:

- **Mode**. Systems may behave differently depending on the mode of operation, such as training or operational. For example, performance or interface requirements may differ between modes.

- **User class**. Different functionality may be offered to different classes of users, such as library members and library personnel.

- **Objects**. Requirements may be classified according to the objects (real-world entities) concerned. This classification scheme is a natural one when used in conjunction with an object-oriented analysis technique (see chapter 12).

- **Response**. Some systems are best described by placing together functions in support of the generation of a response, for example functions associated with catalog queries or library member status information.

- **Functional hierarchy**. When no other classification fits, some functional hierarchy, for example organized by common inputs, may be used.

As an example, figure 9.7 gives a refinement of the section on specific requirements along the dimension of user classes,

---

3. *Specific requirements*
   - 3.1 External interface requirements
     - 3.1.1 User interfaces
     - 3.1.2 Hardware interfaces
     - 3.1.3 Software interfaces
     - 3.1.4 Communications interfaces
   - 3.2 Functional requirements
     - 3.2.1 User class 1
       - 3.2.1.1 Functional requirement 1.1
       - 3.2.1.2 Functional requirement 1.2
       - ...
     - 3.2.2 User class 2
     - ...
   - 3.3 Performance requirements
   - 3.4 Design constraints
   - 3.5 Software system attributes
   - 3.6 Other requirements

Figure 9.7 Prototype outline of the section on Specific Requirements (*Source: IEEE Recommended Practice for Software Requirements Specifications*, IEEE Std 830-1993. *Reproduced by permission of IEEE*)

A further clarification of the various components is given in Appendix C. As an example, figure 9.8 contains (part of) a possible requirements specification for the library example mentioned earlier, following the IEEE guidelines.

1. *Introduction.*
   1.1 *Purpose.* This document states the requirements of an automated library system for a medium-sized library of a research institute. The requirements stated serve as a basis for the acceptance procedure of this system. The document is also intended as a starting point for the design phase.
   1.2 *Scope.* The intended product automates the library functions described in DOC1. Its purpose is to provide a more effective service to the library users, in particular through the online search facilities offered. More details of the performance requirements are given in section 3.3 of this document. Once this system is installed, the incorporation of new titles will go from an average of 15 minutes down to an average of 5 minutes.
   1.3 *Definitions, acronyms and abbreviations.* Library member: ..., Library personnel: ..., User: The term user may refer to both library members and library personnel, and is used to denote either class of users. Title catalog: ..., PICA: ..., etc.
   1.4 *References*. DOC1: ..., DOC2: ..., etc.
   1.5 *Overview.* Section 2 of this document gives a general overview of the system. Section 3 gives more specific requirements for functions offered. These functions are categorized according to the class of user they support: (external) members of the library and library personnel, respectively.

2. *Overall description.*
   2.1 *Product perspective*. The already installed database system X will be used to store the various catalogs as well as the library member administration. There are no interfaces to other systems. The system will be realized on the Y configuration. System Y has a maximum capacity of 32 terminals with full screen support, connected through a local network of type W. the maximum external storage capacity for the catalogs of the system is 1500 MB. Library personnel will use a barcode reader to enter member, book and journal identifications. The interface protocol to the barcode reader is described in DOC4.
   2.2 *Product functions.* The system provides two types of function:
      – Functions by which users may search the catalogs of books and journal articles. A list of these functions is given in DOC1. A more detailed description is given in section 3.2.1.
      – Functions by which library personnel may update the administration of borrowed titles and the system's catalogs; see section 3.2.2.

      The user of the system selects one of the functions offered through the main menu (section 3.2.1.1 and 3.2.2.1.)
   2.3 *User characteristics.* The library members are incidental users of this system and have little knowledge of automated systems of this kind. The system therefore has to be self-instructing. Specific requirements are formulated in sections 3.1.1 and 3.3. The library personnel will be trained in the use of the system; see section 3.1.1.
   2.4 *Constraints.* Library members may only search the catalogs of books and journal articles; they are not allowed to update a catalog or the user administration. The latter functionality is to be offered on dedicated terminals only.
   2.5 *Assumptions and dependencies ...*
   2.6 *Requirements subsets ...*

3. *Specific requirements.*
   3.1 *External interface requirements.*
      3.1.1 *User interfaces.* The screen formats for the different features are specified in Appendix A. Appendix B lists the mapping of commands to function keys. The user can get online help at any point by giving the appropriate command. Appendix C contains a list of typical usage scenarios. These usage scenarios will be used as acceptance criteria: 80% of the users must be able to go through them within ten minutes. An instruction session for library personnel should take at most two hours.
      3.1.2 *Hardware interfaces.* The user interface is screen-oriented. The system uses up to ten function keys.
      3.1.3 *Software interfaces.* The interface with database system X is described in DOC2.
      3.1.4 *Communications interfaces.* Not applicable.

3.2 *Functional requirements.*

Library member functions.

3.2.1.1 *Select member feature.* The user selects one of the options from the main menu. Subsequent actions are described in sections 3.2.1.2 and 3.2.1.3.
At any point, the user has the option to return to the main menu (see Appendix B).

3.2.1.2 *Search book catalog.* Given (part of) a book title or author name, the user may search the book catalog for titles that match the input given. The user is offered a screen with two fill-in-the-blank areas (one for the title and one for the author), one of which is to be filled in.
Input. The input may contain both upper and lower case letters. Special symbols allowed are listed in DOC1. Any other glyphs entered are discarded and are not shown on the screen. The input is considered complete when the processing command is issued.
Processing. All lower case letters are turned into upper case letters. The string thus obtained is used when querying the database. A database entry matches the title string given if the transformed input is a substring of the title field of the entry. The same holds for the author field if (part of) an author name is input.
Output. A list of titles that match the input is displayed. Up to four titles are shown on the screen. The user may traverse the list of titles found using the screen scrolling commands provided. A warning is issued if no title matches the input given.

3.2.1.3 *Search article catalog ...*

Library personnel functions.

3.2.2.1 *Select personnel feature.* On dedicated terminals, library personnel are offered an extended main menu, listing the options available to all users, as well as the options available to library personnel only. The latter are described in sections 3.2.2.2 and 3.2.2.3.

3.2.2.2 *Borrow title ...*

3.2.2.3 *Modify catalog ...*

3.3 *Performance requirements.* The system will initially support ten terminals. Its maximum capacity is 32 terminals. The present database holds 25 000 book titles and 500 journal subscriptions. The storage capacity needed for these data is 300 MB. On average 1000 books and 2000 journal issues enter the library per year. The average journal issue has six articles. This requires a storage capacity of 15 MB per year.
The system must be able to serve 20 users simultaneously. With this maximum load and a database size of 450 MB, user queries as listed in sections 3.2.1 and 3.2.2 must be answered within five seconds in 80% of the cases.

3.4 *Design constraints.*

3.4.1 *Standards compliance.* Title descriptions must be stored in PICA-format. This format is described in DOC3.

3.4.2 *Hardware limitations.* See section 2.1.

3.5 *Software system attributes.*

3.5.1 *Availability.* During normal office hours (9 am – 5 pm) the system must be available 95% of the time. A backup of the system is made every day at 5 pm.

3.5.2 *Security.* The functions described in section 3.2.2 are restricted to library employees and provided on dedicated terminals only ...

3.5.3 *Maintainabilty ...*

3.6 *Other requirements ...*

Figure 9.8 Partly worked-out requirements specification for the library example

The IEEE framework for the requirements specification is especially appropriate in classic models for the software development process: the waterfall model and its variants. When a prototyping technique is used to determine the user interface, the IEEE framework can be used to describe the outcome of that prototyping process. The framework assumes a model in which the result of the requirements engineering process is unambiguous and complete. Though it is stated that requirements should be ranked for importance, and requirements that may be delayed until future versions may be included as subsets, this does not imply that a layered view of the system can be readily derived from a requirements document drawn up this way.

A more fundamental problem with the IEEE framework is that it describes the end product only. Before this final stage is reached, the 'current' set of requirements is in a constant state of flux. The requirements engineering process involves a large number of decisions and negotiations. Information regarding the rationale behind decisions (such as why a certain feature is included or who is responsible for the inclusion of a certain feature) usually gets lost along the way. This severely hampers the traceability of requirements, both during the requirements engineering process and beyond.

As an example, consider the following issue which may crop up during the requirements engineering phase for our library system. The library system has to offer certain features to register and handle fines. An item not returned in time incurs a fine of, say, \$0.25 per day. John, one of the library employees involved in the specification process, takes the following position (denoted 'Pos A' in figure 9.9): members should be warned about outstanding fines at the earliest possible moment. His argument ('Arg A') is that service is degraded if a member cannot borrow an item because some other member has not returned that item on time. Mary, the library manager, takes a rather different position ('Pos B'): members should *not* be warned about outstanding fines until the due-back date has expired one month. Her argument ('Arg B') is that fines are a most welcome addition to the library budget, which is under severe pressure because of the continuing price increase of journal subscriptions.

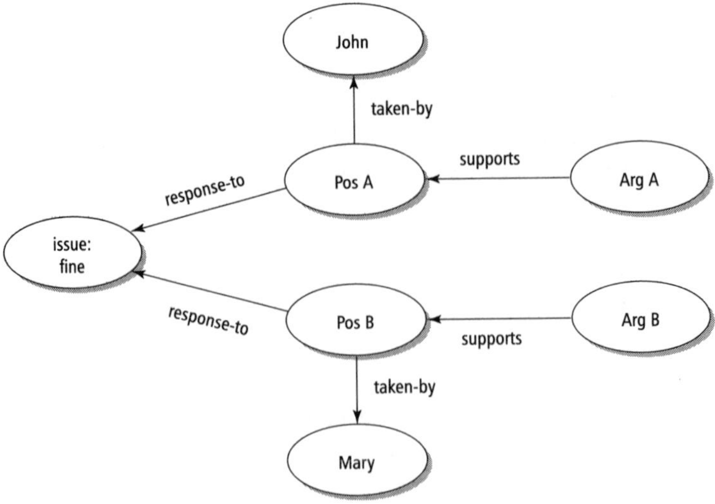

Figure 9.9 Network representation of conflicting requirements

This situation is graphically depicted in the network in figure 9.9. The network contains nodes of types 'issue', 'position' and 'argument', and directed links of type 'response-to', 'taken-by' and 'supports'. Capturing this type of information in a hypertext system seems a natural choice. A hypertext representation offers possibilities to store, trace and manipulate the very diverse types of information being gathered during the requirements engineering phase. An early system along these lines is gIBIS, a hypertext system designed to capture early design decisions.

CASE tools to support the (graphical) representation of requirements generally impose rather strict semantics. They cannot cope with incomplete or inconsistent information. By viewing requirements as office documents, some degree of informality is explicitly recognized. Hypertext or multimedia approaches to capturing requirements have recently been suggested as a means to help fill the gap between the early, difficult to formalize stage of requirements engineering and its more formalized end-product.

Irrespective of the format chosen for representing requirements, the success of a product strongly depends upon the degree to which the desired system is properly described during the requirements engineering phase. Small slips in the requirements specification may necessitate large changes in the final software. Software is not continuous, as we noted earlier.

The importance of a solid requirements specification cannot be stressed often enough. In some cases, up to 95% of the code of large systems has had to be rewritten in order to adhere to the ultimate user requirements.

9.3 REQUIREMENTS SPECIFICATION TECHNIQUES

The document that is produced during requirements engineering – the requirements specification – serves two groups of people. For the user, the requirements specification is a clear and precise description of the functionality that the system has to offer. For the designer, it is the starting point for the design. It is not easy to serve both groups with one and the same document.

The user is in general best served by a document which speaks his language, the language that is used within the application domain. In the example used before, this would result in using terms like 'title description' and 'catalog'.

The designer on the other hand, is best served with a language in which concepts from his world are used. In terms of the library example, he may prefer concepts like records (an instance of which might be termed 'title description') or files. In one sense, this boils down to a difference in language. However, this difference is of fundamental importance with respect to the later use of the system's description.

If the system is described in the user's language, the requirements specification is mostly phrased in some natural language. If we try to somewhat formalize this description, we may end up with a technique in which certain forms have to be filled in or certain drawing techniques have to be applied.

If, on the other hand, the expert language of the software engineer plays a central role, we often use some formal language. A requirements specification phrased in such a formal language may be checked using formal techniques, for instance with regard to consistency and completeness.

In practice, an outspoken prevalence for the user's expert language shows itself. We may then use existing concepts from the environment in which the system is going to be used. Admittedly, these concepts are not sharply defined, but in general there are no misconceptions between the experts in the application domain as regards the meaning of those concepts. A description in terms of those concepts can thus still be very *precise*. Since the first goal of the requirements specification is to get a *complete* description of the problem to be solved, the user's expert language then would be the best language for the requirements specification.

However, there are certain drawbacks attached to the use of natural language. [Mey85] gives an example which illustrates very well what may go wrong when natural language is used in a requirements specification. Meyer lists seven sins which may beset the analyst when using natural language:

- **Noise** This refers to the presence of text elements that do not contain information relevant to the problem. Variants hereof are redundancy and regret. Redundancy occurs when things are repeated. Since natural language is very flexible, related matters can easily be phrased in completely different ways. When this happens the cohesion between matters gets blurred. Regret occurs when statements are reversed or shaded. In the library example, for instance, we could have used the phrase 'a list of all books written by author D' several times and only then realize that this list may be empty, necessitating some special reaction from the system.

- **Silence** Silence occurs when aspects that are of importance for a proper solution of the problem, are not mentioned. An example of this was that the need for two variants on an author's name was not stated explicitly.

- **Over-specification** This occurs when elements of a requirements specification correspond to aspects of a possible solution, rather than to aspects of the problem. As an example, we could have specified that books be kept sorted by the first author's name. Over-specification limits the solution space for the designer.

- **Contradictions** If the description of one and the same aspect is given more than once, in different words, contradictions may occur. This risk is especially threatening when one tries to be too literary. A requirements specification is not meant to be a novel.

- **Ambiguity** Natural language allows for more than one meaning for one and the same phrase. Ambiguity can easily occur when terms are used that belong to the jargon of one or both parties. A 'book' may both denote a physical object and a more abstract entity of which several instantiations (copies) may exist.

- **Forward references** References to aspects of the problem that are only defined later on in the text. This especially occurs in large documents that lack a clear structure. Natural language in itself does not enforce a clear structure.

- **Wishful thinking** A description of aspects of the system such that a realistic solution will be hard to find.

A possible alternative given by Meyer is to first describe and analyze the problem using some formal notation and then translate it back into natural language. The natural language description thus obtained will in general represent a more precise notion of the problem. And it is readable to the user. Obviously, both these models must now be kept up-to-date.

Quite a number of techniques and accompanying notations have evolved to support the requirements engineering process. Most often, the representation generated is a set of semantic networks. Each such representation has various types of nodes and links between nodes, distinguished by visual clues such as their shape or natural language labels. Nodes typically represent things like processes, stores, objects, and attributes. Nodes are joined by arrows representing relationships such as data flow, control flow, abstraction, part-whole, or is-part-of.

Typical examples of such techniques and their representations are discussed in sections 9.3.1–9.3.3. Entity–Relationship Modeling (section 9.3.1) is the most widely-known technique to model the data aspect of an information system. Finite State Machines (section 9.3.2) can be viewed as a technique to model the functional aspect. They have a much wider applicability though, and constitute a basic underlying mechanism for many modeling techniques. Structured Analysis and Design Technique (SADT, section 9.3.3) is an elaborate graphical technique for modeling the functional aspect. Finally, section 9.3.4 touches upon the issue of how to specify non-functional requirements.

9.3.1 Entity–Relationship Modeling

In data-intensive systems, modeling the (structure of) the data is an important concern. Until the 1970s, data modeling techniques very much mixed up implementation concerns with concerns arising from the logical structure of the UoD. For example, the book catalog would be modeled as a 'table' containing 'tuples' ('records') with alphanumeric fields containing the title and author, and numeric fields containing the publication year and number of pages.

Entity–relationship modeling (ERM), as pioneered by Chen, is directed at modeling the logical, semantic structure of the UoD, rather than its realization in some database system. Entity relationship models are depicted in **entity–relationship diagrams** (ERDs). There are many variants of ERM, which differ in their graphical notations and extensions to Chen's original approach. The basic ingredients of ERM are given in figure 9.10.

entity	distinguishable object of some type
entity type	type of a set of entities
attribute value	piece of information (partially) describing an entity
attribute	type of a set of attribute values
relationship	association between two or more entities

Figure 9.10 ERM concepts and their meaning

An entity is a 'thing' that can be uniquely identified. Entities are usually depicted in an ERD as rectangles. Example entities are:

- tangible objects, such as copies of a book, identified by some number;
- intangible objects, such as books identified by their ISBN, or members of some organizational construct, such as library employees identified by their employee number.

Entities have properties known as attributes. For example, some library employee may have the name 'Jones'. Here, 'Jones' is the value of the attribute called 'name'. Attributes are usually depicted as circles or ellipses.

Both entities and attribute values have a **type**. As modelers, we tend to view a type as a set of properties shared by its instances. As implementors, we tend to view a type as a set of values with a number of associated operations. For the attribute 'number of books on loan', the set of values could be the set 0 .. 10 with operations such as increment and decrement. For the entity type 'book copy', candidate operations would be 'borrow', 'return', and so on.

Entities are linked through relationships. For example, the relationship 'borrow' involves the entities 'book copy' and 'library member'. Most often, a relationship is binary, i.e. it links two entities. A relationship is denoted by a diamond linked to the entities involved.

Entity–relationship models impose restrictions on the cardinality of relationships. In its simplest form, the relationships are 1–1, 1–N, or N–M. The relationship 'borrow' is 1–N: a copy of a book can be borrowed by one member only, while a member may have borrowed more than one book copy. In an ERD, these cardinality constraints are often indicated by small adornments of the arrows linking the entities.

An example entity–relationship diagram is given in figure 9.11. Cardinality constraints have been indicated by explicitly indicating the set of possibilities. Thus, this ERD states that a book copy can be borrowed by at most one member, and a member may borrow up to 10 book copies.

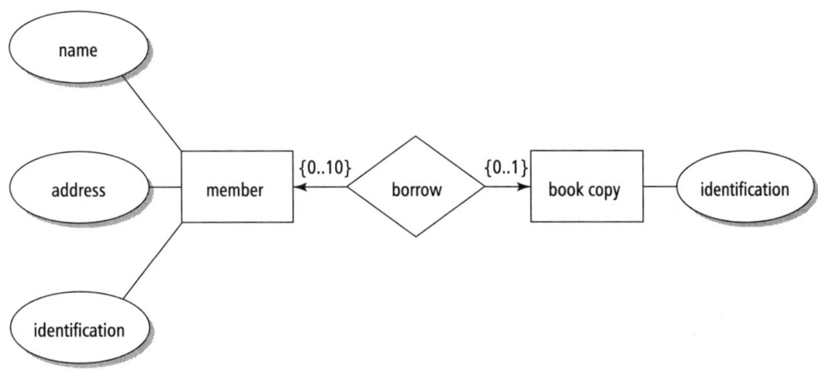

Figure 9.11 An entity--relationship diagram

An entity–relationship model can be obtained using any of the elicitation techniques discussed before. In particular, form analysis and analysis of natural language descriptions are often used. Since ERMs tell only part of the story, additional techniques have to be employed to model other aspects. Many Structured Analysis techniques, for example, incorporate ERM to model the data aspect.

Entity–relationship modeling is a natural outgrowth of database modeling. Originally, ERM was intended to model the logical structure of data, rather than the logical structure of the UoD. In heuristics on how to obtain a 'good' entity–relationship model, these roots are still visible. For example, some of these heuristics resemble normalization constraints from database theory. This may explain why some do not commend entity–relationship modeling as a requirements specification technique (see, e.g. [Dav93b]).

Present-day ERM has a lot in common with object-oriented analysis techniques. For example, subtype–supertype relations between entity types are included in many ERM-techniques. Conversely, the class diagram of object-oriented analysis (see section 12.2.1) includes many elements from ERM.

9.3.2 Finite State Machines

At any one point in time, our library is in one of a (vast) number of possible states. The state of the library can be expressed in terms of things like:

- the collection of titles available,
- the collection of titles ordered but not yet received,
- the collection of library members,
- the balance of the account from which acquisitions are paid.

Any action occurring in the library, be it the return of a book or the appointment of a new employee, transforms the current state s into a new state s'.

Requirements specification techniques which model a system in terms of states and transitions between states are called **state-based** modeling techniques. A simple yet powerful formalism for specifying states and state transitions is the **Finite State Machine** (FSM). An FSM consists of a finite number of states and a set of transitions from one state to another that occur on input signals from a finite set of possible stimuli. The initial state is a specially designated state from which the machine starts. Usually, one or more states are designated as final states. Pictorially, FSMs are represented as **state transition diagrams** (STD). In a state transition diagram, states are represented as bubbles with a label identifying the state, and transitions are indicated as labeled arcs from one state to another, where the label denotes the stimulus which triggers the transition. Figure 9.12 gives an FSM depicting the possible states of a book copy and the transitions between those states. The final state is the one labeled 'written off'. Any of the others could be designated as the initial state.

Figure 9.12 models only a tiny part of the library system. It does not describe the complete state of the system in any one bubble, nor does it depict all possible state transitions. Modeling a system in one large and monolithic STD is not to be recommended. Such a structure soon becomes unwieldy and difficult to understand. Though we could model the system in a series of FSMs, we would still have the problem of how to integrate these into one model.

A possible way out is to allow for a hierarchical decomposition of FSMs. This is the essence of a notation known as **statecharts**. In statecharts, groups of states can be viewed as a single entity at one level, to be refined at the next level of abstraction. Object-oriented analysis techniques usually employ some variant of the statechart; see also section 12.2.2. STATEMATE[1] is a set of tools supporting statecharts.

[1]STATEMATE is a registered trademark of i-Logic, Inc.

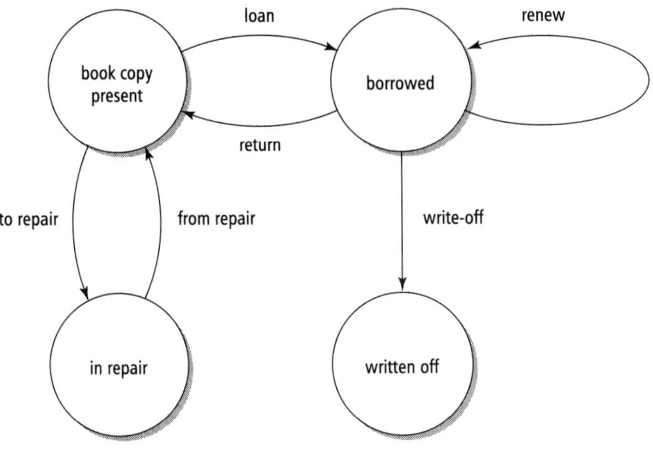

Figure 9.12 A state transition diagram

9.3.3 SADT

Structured Analysis (SA) is a graphical language developed by D.T. Ross in the 1970s. Structured Analysis and Design Technique (SADT)[2] is based on SA. SADT is both a graphics notation and an approach to system description. It includes guidelines on how to interview people, conduct reviews, and the like. The discussion below concentrates on the graphical aspects of SA(DT).

SA contains about 40 basic components, some of which are depicted in figure 9.13. Each of these basic components has a very specific semantics. We may now describe a system using a combination of natural language and the drawing techniques from SA.

This way of graphically depicting a system is very much like a blueprint used for buildings or radios. There is a clear philosophy behind SA. It is not a free-hand sketching technique. During requirements analysis, a clear description must be made of the actions to be performed by the system. This description is called the **functional architecture**. Based on this functional architecture, a **system architecture** is built during the subsequent design phase. This system architecture implements the functions of the functional architecture.

The functional architecture is both hierarchical and modular. This is depicted schematically in figure 9.14. At the highest level, the global architecture of the system is sketched. Each of the components is further detailed at the second level. The

[2]SADT is a trademark of SofTech.

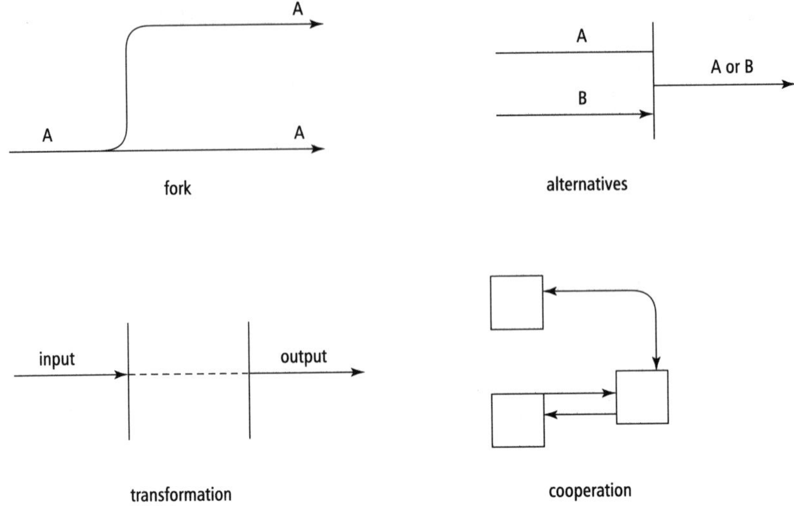

Figure 9.13 Some components of SA

component at the second level may in turn be further broken down, etc. In this way, a top-down hierarchical decomposition results.

A system may be described in SADT from different viewpoints. This is similar to the way in which one uses different drawings in house construction: one for the electrical wiring, another for the water supply, etc.

The most important viewpoints from which a system is described in SADT are activities and things, or, in our jargon, activities and data. These viewpoints are pairs; they represent the same system (or system component) but viewed from different perspectives. Below, we will concentrate on the activity viewpoint, which is the one most often used.

Let us return to our library example. A customer who wants to borrow a book, addresses himself to one of the employees, who in turn satisfies the request. This has been depicted in figure 9.15 in the notation of SA. The activity – handling the request – is placed within the box. The input to this activity, the customer's request, is depicted by the arrow that enters the box from the left. The output is depicted by an arrow that exits the box at the right. The arrow that enters the box from above denotes things that constrain the activity. In this case, a catalog constrains how the request is handled: a book can only be borrowed if it is available. Finally, the arrow entering the box from below denotes the mechanism by which the activity is handled. It represents, at least in part, *how* activities are realized. The mechanism arrow usually describes some physical aspects of an activity, such as storage places, people, or devices.

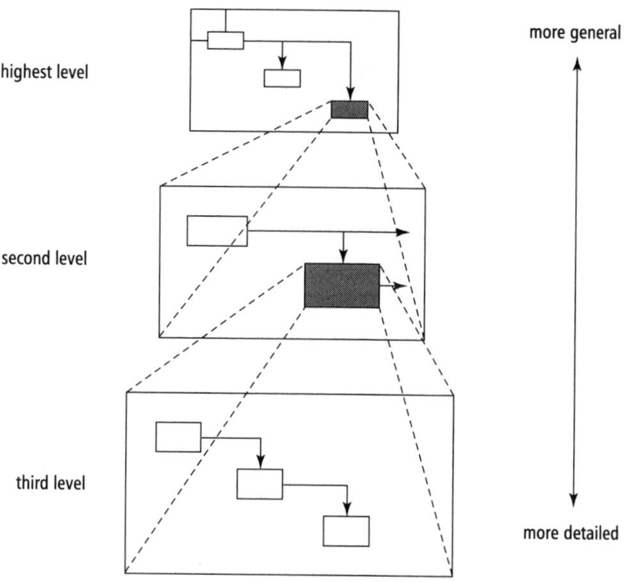

Figure 9.14 Hierarchical decomposition in SADT

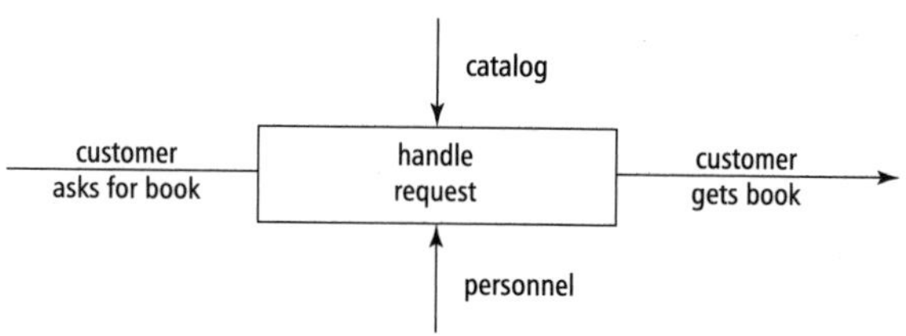

Figure 9.15 An activity

SADT diagrams are constraint diagrams. They describe both the input and output of an activity, and possible constraints that apply to the transformation. The arrows in the diagram depict the interfaces between activities and, especially at the higher levels, between the system and its environment.

In figure 9.16, a small part of the library automation project is worked out in more detail, again using the SADT-notation. Figure 9.16a depicts a top-level view of the system, a slightly modified version of figure 9.15. The customer enters a request at the terminal. Handling this request is constrained by the library's catalog and by passwords. The latter are used to distinguish between library personnel and

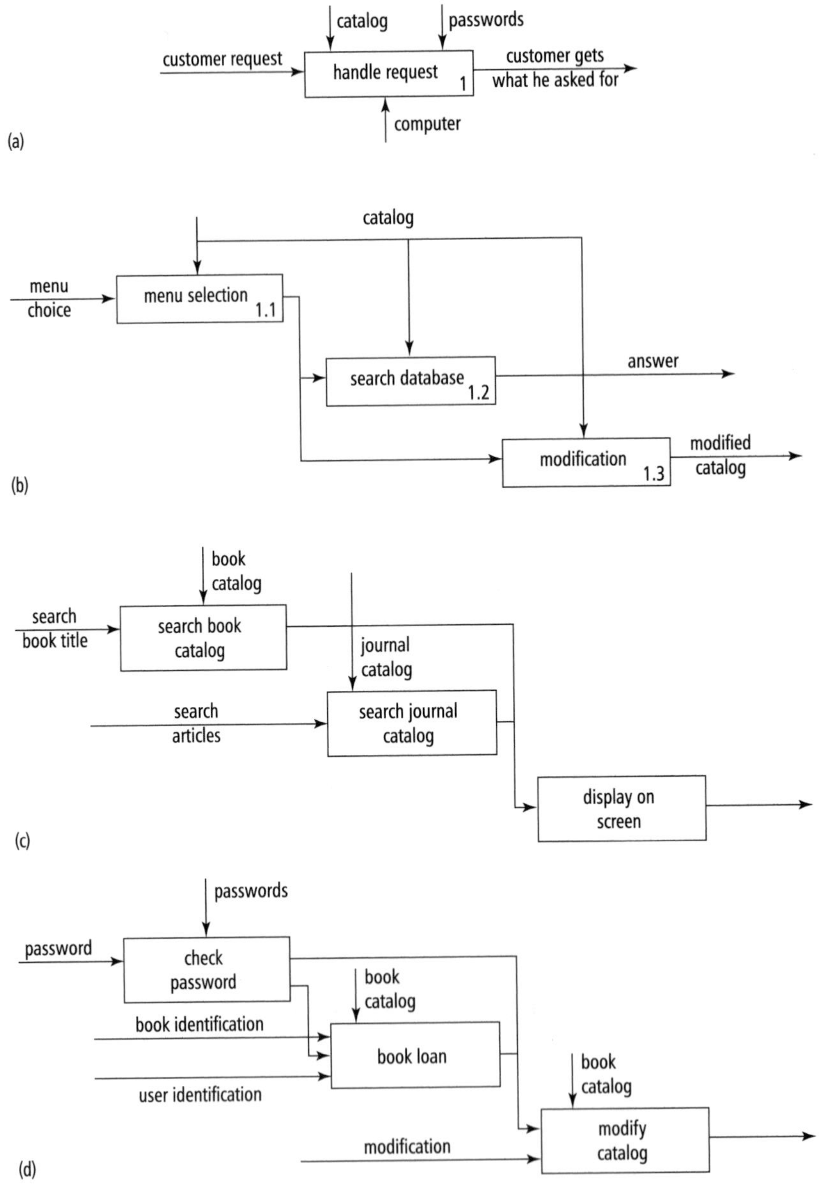

Figure 9.16 Library automation. (a) Level 0 (b) Level 1 (c) Level 2, refinement of element 1.2 (d) Level 2, refinement of element 1.3

members; members are not allowed to update the database. Decomposition of this top-level view results in the diagram in figure 9.16b. Handling a user request involves two steps. First, the user selects an option, and next the action corresponding to that selection is executed. Finally, figures 9.16c and 9.16d give further refinements of two such actions, the searching of a catalog and the modification of the database.

9.3.4 Specifying Non-Functional Requirements

The IEEE framework depicted in figure 9.7 lists four types of non-functional requirements: external interface requirements, performance requirements, design constraints and software system attributes. These non-functional requirements can be viewed as constraints placed upon the development process or the products to be delivered.

External interface requirements and design constraints are generally phrased in terms of (non-negotiable) obligations to be met. They are dictated at the start of the project and often concern matters which surpass an individual development project. Examples of such requirements include:

- hardware, software and communications interfaces to be complied with;
- user interfaces that have to obey company standards;
- report formats to be adhered to;
- process constraints such as ISO 9000 compliance or a prescribed development method;
- hardware limitations caused by the available infrastructure.

The remaining non-functional requirements are also known as quality requirements. Quality requirements are notoriously difficult to specify and verify. This topic is dealt with extensively in chapter 6. At this point, we merely wish to re-emphasize two essential issues: quality requirements should be expressed in objective, measurable terms and perfection incurs infinite cost.

Like all other requirements, quality requirements should be verifiable. Requirements such as 'the system should be flexible', 'the system should be user-friendly', or 'response times should be fast', can never be verified and should not therefore appear in the requirements specification. Other phraseology can be used such as 'for activities of type A the system should have a maximum response time of one second in 80% of the cases, while a maximum response time of three seconds is allowed in the remaining 20% of the cases'.

Conversely, extreme levels of quality requirements, such as zero defects or response times of less than 1 second in 100% of the cases, generally incur extremely high costs, or are not feasible at all. Given the fact that users find it difficult to express their true requirements, they may be inclined to ask for too much where quality requirements are concerned, just 'to be on the safe side'. To the analyst and developers, it is likewise difficult to assess the feasibility of those requirements. How can we be sure about response times before even one line of code has been written?

Consider the following example of what may and may not be technically feasible. Suppose we have an application in which two kinds of transactions may occur. Those transactions are characterized by their frequency, CPU-time needed and the number of physical I/O transports. The average I/O access time is also given. Using a statistical distribution describing the dynamics of these systems, one may then answer questions such as: 'how much capacity should the CPU have in order to achieve a response time of at most 2 seconds in X% of cases?' Some given configuration may satisfy the constraints for the case X = 80. A somewhat more stringent requirement (X = 90) may require doubling the CPU-capacity. An even more severe requirement (X = 95) might well not be achievable by the range of machines available.

At first sight, the differences between these requirements seem marginal. They turn out to have a tremendous effect, though. An early and careful analysis of the technical feasibility may yield surprising answers to a number of important questions. There are many examples of projects in which lots of money was spent on software development efforts which turned out to be not practically feasible [Bab82].

9.4 A MODELING FRAMEWORK

In software development, several groups of people are involved. They are each interested in different properties of the system, based on the role they play in the development. To make communication possible between these groups, the appropriate perspectives, or views, on the system must be modeled, and the appropriate language for doing so must be used. Different perspectives imply different abstraction levels, in the sense that irrelevant issues are omitted (abstracted) from a model presented to a given interest group. For example, an end user's interest is only in the system's behavior towards him, not in internal data formats. The latter is of great interest to a different interest group though, viz. the implementors.

Furthermore, various aspects of the system are often considered and modeled separately, e.g. a data and function aspect. During or after this modeling process, some integration must take place to ensure consistency between different aspect models.

Here, we may draw an analogy between information system development and house building. In house building too, different plans (i.e. models) are drawn up for different interest groups such as the owner and the constructor. For each interest group we usually have different plans for different aspects, such as a construction plan for the heating system and a construction plan for plumbing. Obviously, these different models should 'match' one another; e.g. the different tube systems should not get entangled.

Several frameworks to model information systems have been proposed. The dimensions used in these frameworks are usually based on the notions of abstraction levels or perspectives on the one hand and aspects on the other. The framework discussed below distinguishes four perspectives of an information system:

- **The business perspective** models the way the business is done in so far as this is relevant to system development. This view is particularly important for the customer who ordered the project in customer-driven development (or marketing people in market-driven development) and for the company's management, organizational staff, and information analysts.

- **The information perspective** models the information supply necessary to support the business. At this stage, system boundaries, i.e. decisions on what will be internal and external to the computerized system, need not be resolved yet. This view is relevant to the same groups of people as the business perspective and to various categories of system users.

- **The functionality perspective** models the external behavior of the system, that is all those parts and aspects of the information system that the users of the system consider important. Categories of users involved include both direct users (the ones behind the screen) and indirect users (those who use the information). Also, several types of information specialists will be interested in this model, e.g. information analysts, functional designers, and functional administrators such as data administrators and controllers.

- **The implementation perspective** describes the internal functioning of the system that must realize the needed functionality as described in the functionality view. This view has of course special interests for technical designers, system analysts, programmers, technical administrators and maintenance personnel.

Information systems are not a purpose on their own, but rather serve to support a business. It is therefore necessary to investigate the way that business is run, i.e. to have a business model that abstracts from information supply details. Neglecting this may result in systems that do not fit business needs. The information perspective concentrates on the way the information supply may support the business, abstracting away from functionality (precise system behavior). While doing so, rather diverse and possibly conflicting views, wishes and needs are charted, positions are taken on issues, priorities are determined, and compromises are agreed upon. Only if the benefits of the system and its relationship with the business processes are perfectly clear and there is an agreement on objectives, will a functional view alone suffice.

In companies where information supply is part of the primary process, as is the case in our library example, the business perspective tends to strongly resemble the information supply perspective. A clear view of the primary process, however, makes it possible to concentrate on the primary business processes, thereby improving the usefulness of the information system.

In our library, for example, the aim of the primary process might be phrased as:

- To efficiently relate user queries to information sources, and

- To optimize the cost-benefit ratio between these queries and the available stock.

Neglecting these aims may lead to a system which satisfactorily supports some secondary goals, such as having a good administration of library members and up-to-date catalogs, but which is less than satisfactory with respect to the primary aims.

Requirements engineering as discussed in this chapter is about modeling the business, information, and functionality perspective, with an emphasis on the latter. Modeling the implementation perspective falls within the realm of design.

Usually, development methods concentrate on one or a few aspects only. Types of development approaches for information systems are often named after the aspect that is seen as most important: 'data-oriented development', 'object-oriented development', 'real-time systems development', etc. Using an eclectic approach, in which many relevant aspects are considered and their importance determined, and only then are particular ones focused on, we may consider at least the following aspects:

- The **goals and constraints** aspect models the goals that are pursued in each perspective of the system and the constraints that must be respected. For example, a goal in the business perspective of our library could be 'improvement of library service by 20%'. In the functionality perspective, a goal could be 'registration of due dates'. Constraints concern quality, performance and resource requirements, e.g. 'reminder notices should be issued on the first working day after the expiration date'.

- The **function** of a system is to transform input into output. An example is a function 'compute fee' which transforms the input 'fee rules' and 'member data' into the output 'fee to pay'. We may view a function as a black box, thus emphasizing its purpose. We may also take a white-box view of a function and consider its inner workings as well. We then see *how* the input is transformed to some output. If the function aspect is modeled hierarchically, a black-box view at one level is refined into a white-box view at the next level.

- The **data** aspect models entities, entity types, attributes, relationships between entity types, and constraints on data.

- There are three fundamental types of **communication** interfaces: man–machine interfaces, machine–machine interfaces, and man–man interfaces.

- An information system is supposed to support people. The involvement of people in the system is an important but complex matter. Modeling this **organization** aspect includes both 'organizational structure' and 'quality of work life' issues.

- The hardware, systems software and infrastructure facilities, and other resources together constitute the **technical structure**, the means that allow the information system to work.

- Finally, the system components may be spread over various locations. Modeling the **distribution** aspect gives an understanding of the people, machines, information supply, data storage and data processing etc. at each location.

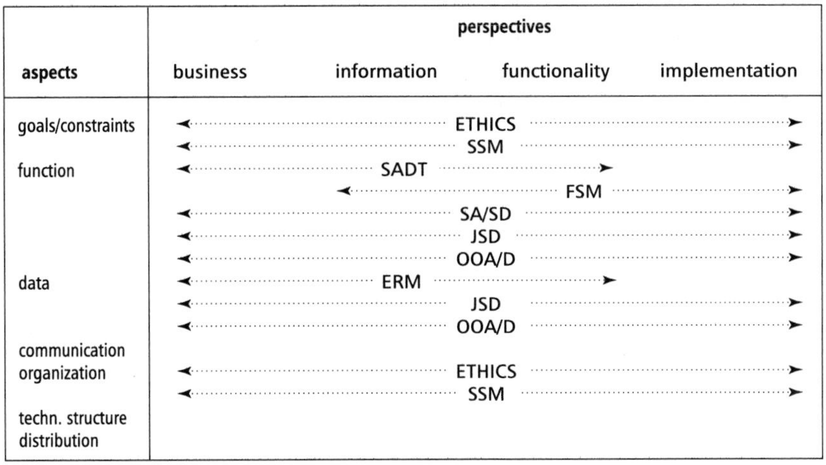

	perspectives			
aspects	business	information	functionality	implementation
goals/constraints	◄······	······ ETHICS	······	······►
	◄······	······ SSM	······	······►
function	◄······	SADT ······►		
		◄······	FSM ······	······►
	◄······	······ SA/SD	······	······►
	◄······	······ JSD	······	······►
	◄······	······ OOA/D	······	······►
data	◄······	ERM ······►		
	◄······	······ JSD	······	······►
	◄······	······ OOA/D	······	······►
communication				
organization	◄······	······ ETHICS	······	······►
	◄······	······ SSM	······	······►
techn. structure				
distribution				

Figure 9.17 Scope of modeling techniques

One should note that these seven aspects are not exhaustive. Aspects may be added when the need arises. Additional aspects are often derived from quality and performance requirements, such as security and reliability (for safety-critical systems). Also, composite aspects may be defined that combine several basic aspects. For example, in object-oriented approaches, the basic aspects 'data' and 'function' are replaced by one composite 'object' aspect. At a finer level of granularity, the basic aspects making up a composite aspect may still be modeled separately.

Figure 9.17 indicates the primary scope of a number of modeling techniques within the basic framework discussed above.[3] Many of these techniques are elaborated upon elsewhere in this book. It shows that different perspectives or levels of abstraction can be accommodated within most modeling techniques. It also shows that the data and function aspect receive by far the most attention.

9.5 VERIFICATION AND VALIDATION

In chapter 1, we argued that a careful study of the correctness of the decisions made at each stage is a critical success factor. This means that during requirements engineering we should already start verifying and validating the decisions laid down in the requirements specification.

The requirements specification should reflect the mutual understanding of the problem to be solved by the prospective users and the development organization: has everything been described, and has it been described properly. Validating the requirements thus means checking them for properties like correctness, completeness, ambiguity, and internal and external consistency. Of necessity, this involves user participation in the validation process. They are the owners of the problem and they are the only ones to decide whether the requirements specification adequately describes their problem.

If the requirements specification itself is expressed in a formal language, the syntax and semantics of that representation can be verified through formal means. However, the requirements specification can never be completely validated in a formal way, simply because the point of departure of requirements engineering is informal. Most of the testing techniques applied at this stage are therefore informal as well. They are meant to ascertain that the parties involved have the same, proper understanding of the problem. A major stumbling block to this stage is ensuring the user understands the contents of the requirements specification. The techniques applied at this stage often resolve to a translation of the requirements into a form palatable to user inspection: natural-language paraphrasing, the discussion of possible usage scenarios, prototyping, and animation.

Besides testing the requirements specification itself, we also generate at this stage the test plan to be used during system or acceptance testing. A test plan is a document prescribing the scope, approach, resources, and schedule of the testing

[3]OOA/D stands for Object-Oriented Analysis and Design. ETHICS [Mum83] and SSM (Soft Systems Methodology) [CS90] emphasize social, organizational, and human aspects of design.

activities. It identifies the items and features to be tested, the testing tasks to be performed, and the personnel responsible for these tasks. We may at this point develop such a plan for the system testing stage, i.e. the stage at which the development organization tests the complete system against its requirements. Acceptance testing is similar, but is performed under supervision of the user organization. Acceptance testing is meant to determine whether or not the users accept the system.

A more elaborate treatment of the various verification and validation techniques will be given in chapter 13.

9.6 SUMMARY

During requirements engineering we try to get a complete and clear description of the problem to be solved and the constraints that must be satisfied by any solution to that problem. During this phase, we do not only consider the functions to be delivered, but we also pay attention to requirements imposed by the environment. The requirements engineering phase results in a series of models concentrating on different aspects of the system (such as its functionality, user interface and communication structure) and different perspectives (audiences). The result of this process is documented in a requirements specification. A good framework for the contents of the requirements specification is given in [IEE93]. It should be kept in mind that this document contains an a posteriori reconstruction of an as yet ill-understood iterative process.

This iterative process involves three types of activity:

- requirements elicitation, which is about *understanding* the problem,
- requirements specification, which is about *describing* the problem, and
- requirements validation, which is about *agreeing upon* the problem.

During requirements engineering we are modeling part of reality. The part of reality we are interested in is referred to as the universe of discourse (UoD). The modeling process is termed conceptual modeling.

People involved in a UoD have an implicit conceptual model of that UoD. During conceptual modeling, an implicit model is turned into an explicit one. The explicit conceptual model is used to communicate with other people, such as users and designers, and to assess the validity of the system under development during all subsequent phases. During the modeling process, the analyst is confronted with two types of problem: analysis problems and negotiation problems. Analysis problems have to do with getting the requirements right. Negotiation problems arise because different people involved may have different views on the UoD to be modeled, opposing interests, and so on.

Existing approaches to requirements engineering are largely Taylorian in nature. They fit a functional view of software development in which the requirements engineering phase serves to elicit the 'real' user requirements. It is increasingly being recognized that the Taylorian approach need not be the most appropriate approach to requirements engineering. Many UoDs under consideration involve people whose world model is incomplete, irrational, or in conflict with the world view of others. In such cases, the analyst is not a passive outside observer of the UoD, but actively participates in shaping the UoD. The analyst gets involved in negotiation problems and has to choose the view of some party involved, or assist in obtaining some compromise.

The following description techniques are often used for the requirements specification:

- natural language,
- pictures, and
- formal language.

An advantage of using natural language is that the specification is very readable and understandable to the user and other non-professionals involved. Pictures may be put to advantage in bringing across the functional architecture of the system. A well-known example from this category is SADT. A formal language allows us to use tools in analyzing the requirements. Because of its precision, it is a good starting point for the design phase. We may also argue that both formal and informal notations be used, since they augment and complement each other. For each of the parties involved, a notation should be chosen that is appropriate to the task at hand.

A major drawback of most representations is that they model only the final product. They do not capture the decision process that led to the final set of requirements and they are not very well suited to handle changes to an evolving set of requirements. Current research in this area is aimed at investigating the suitability of hypertext technology and mechanisms for expressing multiple, possibly conflicting, views. These novel approaches tend to view requirements as documents, rather than expressions in some formal language.

9.7 FURTHER READING

There are several text books fully devoted to requirements engineering. [Dav93b] provides a fairly complete coverage of 'classic' requirements specification techniques. [Wie96] discusses a number of requirements specification techniques in quite some depth. The distinction between implicit and explicit conceptual models is made there too. [LK95] and [KS97b] have a stronger emphasis on the full requirements engineering process. The state of the practice in requirements engineering is discussed in [LPR93], [Pot93], [EEM95a], and reflected in this chapter.

[Poh93] emphasizes the role of social and cognitive issues in requirements engineering. The thin spread of application knowledge amongst the specialists involved is discussed in [CKI88]. Difficulties of requirements engineering for market-driven software development are addressed in [Pot93].

The objectivist–subjectivist and order–conflict dimensions and the resulting four paradigms for requirements engineering are discussed in [HK89]. The extension of this work is described in [BS93].

Task analysis is discussed in [Seb88]. Scenario-based requirements engineering techniques are discussed in [WPJH98] and [TrS98b]. [HSG$^+$94] describe a method to analyze, generate and validate scenarios in a systematic way. Business Process Redesign is described in [Kee91] and [TC93]. A framework for BPR is given in [Dav93a].

Research in requirements elicitation is aimed at developing techniques which overcome our limitations as humans in conveying information. An early overview of this type of problem is given in [Dav82]. A more recent survey and evaluation of elicitation techniques is given in [GL93]. Example experience reports are given in [SBRS94] and [SK97] (ethnographic approach) and [BH95a] (the analyst as an apprentice to the user).

gIBIS, a hypertext system designed to capture early design decisions, is described in [CB88]. Hypertext and multimedia approaches to capturing requirements are discussed in [WCS94] and [PTA94]. Mechanisms for expressing multiple, possibly conflicting, views are discussed in [NKF94], [EN95] and [vLDL98].

Entity–relationship modeling was pioneered by Chen [Che76]. Many texts on database modeling include an elaborate discussion of ERM; see for example [BCN92]. Statecharts are described in [Har88]. For a discussion of STATEMATE, see [HLN$^+$90].

Structured Analysis (SA) is a graphical language developed by D.T. Ross in the 1970s [RS77] and [Ros77]. SADT is based on SA. A very elaborate discussion of SADT is provided in [MM88].

Several frameworks to model information systems have been proposed; see e.g. [Zac87], [ZS92], [OHM$^+$88] and [vSvV93]. The discussion in section 9.4 is based on [vSvV93].

Exercises

1. What are the three major types of activity in requirements engineering?

2. What is requirements elicitation?

3. What is the difference between an implicit and an explicit conceptual model?
4. In what sense are most requirements engineering techniques Taylorian in nature?
5. Describe the requirements elicitation technique called task analysis.
6. Describe the requirements elicitation technique called scenario-based analysis.
7. In which circumstances is ethnography a viable requirements elicitation technique?
8. List and discuss the major quality requirements for a requirements document.
9. List and discuss major drawbacks of using natural language for specifying requirements.
10. Explain the following concepts from entity–relationship modeling: entity, entity type, attribute value, attribute, relationship.
11. Give a general description of SADT.
12. ♠ Draw up a requirements specification for a system whose development you have been involved with, following IEEE 830. Discuss the major differences between the original specification and the one you wrote.
13. ♡ What are major differences in the external environment of an office automation system and that of an embedded system, like an elevator control system. What impact will these differences have on the requirements elicitation techniques to be employed?
14. ♡ For an office information system, identify different types of stakeholders. Can you think of ways in which the requirements of these stakeholders might conflict?
15. ♡ Refine the framework in figure 9.1 such that it reflects the situation in which we have to explicitly model both the current and the new work situation.
16. ♡ Discuss pros and cons of the following descriptive means for a requirements specification: full natural language, constrained natural language, a pictorial language like SADT, and a formal language like VDM (see chapter 15).
17. ♡ Which of the descriptive means mentioned in the previous exercise would you favor for describing the requirements of an office automation system? And which one for an elevator control system?

18. ♠ Take the requirements specification document from a project you have been involved in and assess it with respect to the requirements for such a document as listed in section 9.2 (unambiguity, completeness, etc.).

19. ♡ How would you test the requirements stated in the document from the previous exercise? Are the requirements testable to start with?

20. ♠ How would you go about determining the requirements for a hypertext-like browsing system for a technical library. Both users and staff of the library only have experience with keyword-based retrieval systems.

21. ♡ As an analyst involved in the development of this hypertext browsing system, discuss possible stands in the subjectivist–objectivist and order–conflict dimensions. What are the arguments for and against these stands?

22. ♠ Write a requirements specification for a hypertext browsing system.

23. ♡ Study the following specification for a simple line formatter:

    The program's input is a stream of characters whose end is signaled with a special end-of-text character, ET. There is exactly one ET character in each input stream. Characters are classified as:

    - break characters – BL (blank) and NL (new line);
    - nonbreak characters – all others except ET;
    - the end-of-text indicator – ET.

    A *word* is a non-empty sequence of nonbreak characters. A *break* is a sequence of one or more break characters. Thus, the input can be viewed as a sequence of words separated by breaks, with possible leading and trailing breaks, and ending with ET.

    The program's output should be the same sequence of words as in the input, with the exception that an oversize word (i.e. a word containing more than MAXPOS characters, where MAXPOS is a positive integer) should cause an error exit from the program (i.e. a variable, Alarm, should have the value TRUE). Up to the point of an error, the program's output should have the following properties:

    1 A new line should start only between words and at the beginning of the output text, if any.
    2 A break in the input is reduced to a single break character in the output.
    3 As many words as possible should be placed on each line (i.e. between successive NL characters).

4 No line may contain more than MAXPOS characters (words and BLs).

Identify as many trouble spots as you can in this specification. Compare your findings with those in [Mey85].

24. ♡ What are the major uses of a requirements specification. In what ways do these different uses affect the style and contents of a requirements document?

10
Software Architecture

LEARNING OBJECTIVES

- To appreciate the role of software architecture in software development
- To be able to characterize some important software architectural styles
- To be able to distinguish different architectures for one and the same problem situation and recognize how these architectures can be used to evaluate early design decisions
- To understand the role of design patterns and be able to illustrate their properties

A good design is the key to a successful product. Almost 2000 years ago, the Roman architect Vitruvius recorded what makes a design good: durability (*firmitas*), utility (*utilitas*), and charm (*venustas*). These quality requirements still hold, for buildings as well as software systems. A well-designed system is easy to implement, is understandable and reliable, and allows for smooth evolution. Badly-designed systems may work at first, but they are hard to maintain, difficult to test, and unreliable.

During the design phase, the system is decomposed into a number of interacting components. The top-level decomposition of a system into major components together with a characterization of how these components interact, is called its **software architecture**. Viewed this way, software architecture is synonymous with global design. There is, however, more to software architecture than mere global design.

Software architecture serves three main purposes:

- It is a vehicle for communication among stakeholders. A software architecture is a global, often graphic, description that can be communicated with the customers, end users, designers, and so on. By developing scenarios of anticipated use, relevant quality aspects can be analyzed and discussed with various stakeholders.

- It captures early design decisions. In a software architecture, the global structure of the system has been decided upon, through the explicit assignment of functionality to components of the architecture. These early design decisions are important since their ramifications are felt in all subsequent phases. It is therefore paramount to assess their quality at the earliest possible moment. By evaluating the architecture, a first and global insight into important quality aspects can be obtained. The global structure decided upon at this stage also structures development: the work-breakdown structure may be based on the decomposition chosen at this stage, testing may be organized around this same decomposition, and so on.

- It is a transferable abstraction of a system. The architecture is a basis for reuse. Design decisions are often ordered, from essential to nice features. The essential decisions are captured in the architecture, while the nice features can be decided upon at a later stage. The software architecture thus provides a basis for a family of similar systems, a so-called **product line**. The global description captured in the architecture may also serve as a basis for training, e.g. to introduce new team members.

The traditional view holds that the requirements fully determine the structure of a system. Traditional design methods as discussed in chapter 11 work that way. Their aim is to systematically bridge the gap between the requirements and some blueprint of an operational system in which all of the requirements are met. It is increasingly being recognized that other forces influence the architecture (and, for that matter, the design) as well:

- Architecture is influenced by the development organization. In our library example, for example, the hardware and software for reading bar codes might be subcontracted to some organization having special expertise in that area. There will then be one or more system components with externally-dictated functionality and interfaces to deal with this part of the problem. If an organization deploys one or more systems with a certain architecture, (maintenance) expertise will be structured according to the decomposition chosen in that architecture and there will be a pressure to have future systems follow that same architecture.

- Architecture is influenced by the background and expertise of the architect. If an architect has positive experience with, say, a layered architecture, he is likely to use that same approach on his next project.

- Architecture is influenced by its technical and organizational environment. In financial applications, for instance, government rules may require a certain division of functionality between system components. In embedded systems, the functionality of hardware components may influence the functionality of and interaction between software components. Finally, the software engineering techniques prevalent in the development organization will exert influence on the architecture.

This mutual influencing between an architecture and its environment is a cyclical process. For example, an architecture yields certain units of work, corresponding to the components distinguished in the architecture. If the same components occur over and over again, expertise will be organized according to the functionality embedded in these components. The development organization may then become expert in certain areas. This expertise then becomes an asset which may affect the goals of the development organization. The organization may try to develop and market a series of similar products in which this expertise is exploited.

Traditional design is inward-looking: given a set of requirements, how can we derive a system that meets those requirements. Software architecture has an outward focus as well: it takes into account how the system fits into its environment.

Some years ago, software architecture was defined as:

> The architecture of a software system defines that system in terms of computational components and interactions among those components [SDK$^+$95].

A more recent definition is:

> The software architecture of a program or computing system is the structure or structures of the system, which comprise software components,

the externally visible properties of those components, and the relationships among them [BCK98].

The latter definition reflects, among others, the insight that there may be more than one structure that is of interest. In house construction, we also use different drawings: one for the electrical wiring, one for the water supply, etc. These drawings reflect different structures which are all part of the same overall architecture. We generally observe the architecture through one of these more specific views. The same holds for the software architecture. Typically, at least the following views are recognized:

- a **conceptual**, or **logical view**, which describes the system in terms of major design elements and their interactions;
- an **implementation view**, which gives a view of the system in terms of modules or packages and layers;
- a **process view** which describes the dynamic structure of the system in terms of tasks, processes, their communication, and the allocation of functionality to run-time elements. This view is only needed if the system has a significant degree of concurrency;
- a **deployment view**, which contains the allocation of tasks to physical nodes. This view is only needed if the system is distributed.

Often, these architectural views are augmented by a set of scenarios that exemplify important architectural aspects of the system envisaged. Some of these scenarios might correspond to situations that the system must be able to handle. Others might correspond to envisaged extensions of the system and be used to analyze the flexibility of the architecture.

In specific cases, additional architectural views may be helpful or needed. In systems for which the user interface is of critical importance, a separate user-interface view may be developed. In electronic commerce applications, a view highlighting security aspects may come in handy. And so on.

In the remainder of this chapter we will concentrate on the conceptual view. The conceptual view is the main result of the architectural design phase, and the main input to the detailed design phase.

Today's work in software architecture is broad in scope. Almost any topic in software engineering is being rethought in architectural terms. Example questions include: how to reengineer the architecture of a legacy system, how does software architecture influence the software development process, how to test a software architecture, etc. The discussion in this chapter is mainly focused on how to identify, name, and describe software architectures.

One interesting theory of problem-solving in the programming domain states that programmers solve such problems using **programming plans**, program fragments that correspond to stereotypical actions, and rules that describe programming conventions. For example, to compute the sum of a series of numbers, a programmer uses the 'running total loop plan'. In this plan, some counter is initialized to zero and incremented with the next value of a series in the body of a loop. Experts tend to recall program fragments that correspond to plan structures before they recall other elements of the program. This nicely maps onto the idea that knowledge is stored in human memory in meaningful units (chunks).

An expert programmer has at his disposal a much larger number of knowledge chunks than a novice programmer. This concerns both programming knowledge and knowledge about the application domain. Both during the search for a solution and during program comprehension, the programmer tries to link up with knowledge already present. As a corollary, part of our education as programmer or software engineer should consist of acquiring a set of useful knowledge chunks.

At the level of algorithms and abstract data types, such a body of knowledge has been accumulated over the years, and has been codified in text books and libraries of reusable components. As a result, abstractions, such as QuickSort, embodied in procedures and abstract data types, such as Stack and BinaryTree, have become part of our vocabulary and are routinely used in our daily work.

The concepts embodied in these abstractions are useful during the design, implementation and maintenance of software for the following reasons:

- They can be used in a variety of settings and can be given unique names. The names are used in communicating the concepts and serve as labels when retrieving and storing them in human memory. The label QuickSort rings the same bell for all people working in our field.

- We have notations and mechanisms to support their use and reuse, such as procedure calls and the module concept.

- We have organized related concepts into (semantic) networks that can be searched for an item that fits the problem at hand. For example, we know the time and space tradeoffs between QuickSort and BubbleSort, or between a standard binary search tree and an AVL-tree, and we know the grounds on which to make a choice.

A very active field of research these days is aimed at identifying and describing components at a higher level of abstraction, i.e. above the level of a module or abstract data type. These higher-level abstractions are known as **design patterns** and **software architectural styles** (or **architectural patterns**).

Part of today's work in software architecture is aimed at characterizing and classifying these software architectural styles, as well as developing appropriate notations and supporting tools. The ultimate goal is that the resulting abstractions become part of the vocabulary of software engineers, much like abstract data types are already part of that vocabulary.

Design patterns are collections of a few modules (or, in object-oriented circles, classes) which are often used in combination, and which together provide a useful abstraction. A design pattern is a recurring solution to a standard problem. The prototypical example of a pattern is the MVC (Model–View–Controller) pattern known from Smalltalk. We may view design patterns as micro-architectures.

Two further notions often used in this context are (**application**) **framework** and **idiom**. An application framework is a semi-finished system which needs to be instantiated to obtain a complete system. It describes the architecture of a family of similar systems. It is thus tied to a particular application domain. The best known examples are frameworks for building user interfaces. An idiom is a low-level pattern, specific to some programming language. For example, the *Counted Pointer* idiom [BMR$^+$96, pp 353–358] can be used to handle references to objects created dynamically in C++. It keeps a reference counter which is incremented or decremented when references to an object are added or removed. Memory occupied by an object is freed if no references to that object remain, i.e. when the counter becomes zero. Frameworks and idioms thus offer solutions that are more concrete and language-specific than the architectural styles and design patterns we will discuss.

The work in the area of software architecture and design patterns has been strongly influenced by the ideas of the architect Christopher Alexander, as formulated in his books *The Timeless Way of Building* and *A Pattern Language*. The term 'pattern' derives from Alexander's work, and the format used to describe software architectural styles and design patterns is shaped after the format Alexander used to describe his patterns, like 'alcove', 'office connection' or 'public outdoor room'.

In the next section, an elaborate example will be given. This example illustrates four possible architectures for a given problem. The example shows the advantages and disadvantages of these different architectures and illustrates the various trade-offs involved. Section 10.2 continues this discussion by giving an overview of the major issues involved in software architectural styles. Design patterns are discussed in section 10.3.

10.1 AN EXAMPLE: PRODUCING A KWIC-INDEX

If we are looking for a book on software engineering, we may consult the title catalog of our library. If we are lucky, this book would be found under 'S'. A book entitled 'Introduction to software engineering' would be harder to find, since it might be categorized under 'I'. This problem can be solved by referencing each title a number of times, once for each word in the title. Doing so by hand is a cumbersome and error-prone process. Automation of this process seems an obvious choice.

A program for doing so is part of many software packages used by libraries. The input consists of a number of lines, corresponding to the titles we want to include in our catalog. From each line, we generate n 'shifts', where n is the number of words in that line. If w_i is the i-th word from a line, then the first shift equals $w_1, \ldots, w_n$ (i.e. the original line). The second shift equals $w_2, \ldots, w_n, w_1$; the third shift is $w_3, \ldots, w_n, w_1, w_2$; and so on. A title

Software engineering should be a compulsory topic.

thus results in the following shifts:

Software engineering should be a compulsory topic.
engineering should be a compulsory topic. Software
should be a compulsory topic. Software engineering
be a compulsory topic. Software engineering should
a compulsory topic. Software engineering should be
compulsory topic. Software engineering should be a
topic. Software engineering should be a compulsory

These shifts are then, together with those of other lines, sorted in the standard lexicographic order. The output is a KWIC-index. KWIC stands for Key Word In Context. It is easy to search for titles in a KWIC-index once you know part of the title.

When designing software to solve a problem like this one, the first step is to decide on a top-level decomposition: what are the major components and how do they interact. We will discuss four possible decompositions for this problem.

The example is taken from a seminal paper by Parnas.[1] Parnas used the example to highlight the differences between designs using shared data and designs using information hiding when it comes to changing representations or algorithms. The decompositions given in sections 10.1.1 and 10.1.2 originate from this paper. The third decomposition employs both implicit invocation and abstract data types. A major advantage of implicit invocation is that it offers a good way to enhance the system's functionality. The fourth decomposition is inspired by the UNIX pipe-and-filter mechanism.[2]

Except for very large data collections, this example is fairly easy to solve. A solution in Pascal results in a program that numbers less than 400 lines. A real problem,

[1]Source: D.L. Parnas, On the criteria to be used in decomposing systems into modules, *Comm. of the ACM* **15**, 12 (1972), ACM, New York. Reproduced by permission of the Association for Computing Machinery, Inc.

[2]Originally, the various solutions to this problem were not conceived as instances of typical architectural styles. The credit for viewing them as such goes to [SG96].

such as crops up in practice, that underpins the need for a proper decomposition cannot be dealt with in the space available here. The purpose of the following exposition is to contrast different solutions to – architectures for – this problem and highlight the differences.

10.1.1 Main Program and Subroutines with Shared Data

A closer inspection of the problem formulation shows that the following tasks must be accomplished:

1. Read and store the input;
2. Determine all shifts;
3. Sort the shifts;
4. Write out the sorted shifts.

These tasks are allocated to different modules which will be called, in the appropriate order, from a control module.

As a next step, we have to decide on the internal representation of the data. The module that determines all shifts must know how the input is stored by the input module. These agreements on the internal representation of data are thus part of the design.

Following this line of thought we may distinguish the following modules in our first decomposition:

Module 1: Input This module reads the input. The input is stored in memory such that the lines are available for further processing by subsequent modules. The input is stored in a table called Store. Each table entry holds a fixed number of characters, say, ten.

Module 2: Shift The shift module is called after all input lines have been read and stored. It builds a table called Shifts which contains, for each shift, the index in Store of the first character of that shift.

Module 3: Sort This module uses the tables produced by modules 1 and 2. It produces a new table, Sorted. Sorted has the same structure as Shifts. The ordering of the entries in Sorted is such that the corresponding shifts are in lexicographic order. Thus, Sorted is a permutation of Shifts.

Module 4: Output The output module uses the tables from modules 1 and 3 to produce a neat output of the sorted shifts.

Module 5: Control The control module does little more than call the other modules in the appropriate order. It may also take care of error messages, memory organization and other bookkeeping duties.

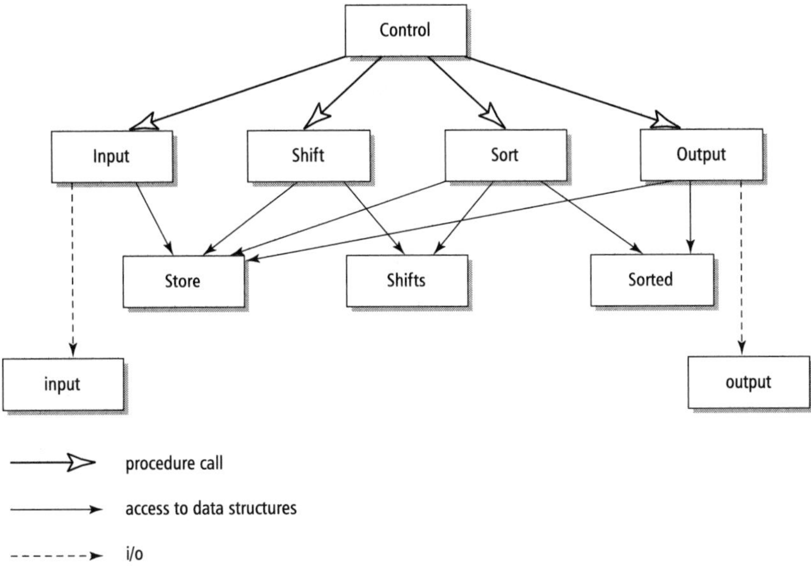

Figure 10.1 Main-program-with-subroutines solution of the KWIC-index program

The various components of this decomposition and their interactions are depicted in figure 10.1. The decomposition is strongly geared towards an ordering of the various actions to be performed with respect to time. The top-level module controls this ordering. The modules use shared storage for their data. These modules are generally implemented as subroutines.

A precise description of the interfaces between modules and the precise structure of the various tables has yet to be added to the description given above. However, even though it is incomplete, a lot can still be said about the decomposition. It is the kind of decomposition often used in practice. The system is decomposed into modules with well-defined interfaces. Each module has a well-defined task. The modules are limited in size. Each module is simple enough to be understood with relative ease.

Probably, quite a few programmers will arrive at such an architecture.

10.1.2 Abstract Data Types

In the first decomposition we observed that various modules need knowledge about the precise storage of data. As a consequence, decisions about data representations have to be made at an early stage. When the module Shift is being implemented, for instance, we must know how the data is stored by the input module. Decisions about data representations are in fact a mutual property of the modules that use those data.

We may also try to make such decisions locally rather than globally. In that case the user does not get direct access to the data structures, but is offered a procedural interface. The data can only be accessed through appropriate procedure calls.

This means that we only have to get an agreement on this procedural interface at the design stage. We must know which procedures to call, which parameters to provide and what results to expect. The way in which the procedures obtain those results is of no concern to the caller. The implementor of a module can make those decisions locally. These decisions do not interfere with the internal workings of other modules.

An obvious first candidate to which to apply this technique is the module that takes care of the input's storage. Viewed abstractly, the input of this program can be seen as a set of lines. The order in which these lines are stored is not relevant for the application. However, we do need a way to obtain information about lines stored. In order to get a simple mapping between lines stored and the subsequent retrieval of information about those lines, we stipulate that input lines are numbered from 1 onwards. This rank number will later be used to retrieve information. Furthermore, each line consists of an ordered number of words and each word consists of an ordered number of characters. In both cases the numbering starts at 1. We thus get the following.

Module 1: Store This module contains the following set of routines, callable by users of the module:

- InitStore initializes the module. This routine should be called before any of the other routines;
- PutChar(r, w, c, d) stores the characters. Character d is stored at position c of word w of line r;
- CloseStore finishes local administration. It is called after all input lines have been stored through successive calls of PutChar.

After CloseStore has been called, the user may retrieve the data stored through the following routines:

- Lines delivers the number of lines stored;
- Words(r) delivers the number of words in line r;
- Chars(r, w) delivers the number of characters in word w of line r;
- Char(r, w, c) delivers the character at position c of word w of line r.

In the above description of the module Store, we assume a sequential input of data, especially in PutChar. An implementation that accepts input in any order is conceivable, though not very realistic. This closely links up with the operation of the second module.

Module 2: Input The input module starts by initializing the module Store (through a call of InitStore). Next, the lines to be processed are read and stored through a series of calls of PutChar. Finally, CloseStore is called to close the administration kept by module 1. The input module does not provide services to any of the other modules.

As a next step, the shifts have to be determined. In the first decomposition, we decided on a particular way of doing so: a table which contains the start address of each shift. This is a design decision. We could also have taken a different decision, e.g. to explicitly construct the textual representation of each shift. The latter may be more advantageous if the input is not voluminous and the shifts are to be used a number of times.

Again, a more abstract view may help. Rather than making any assumptions about the exact representation of shifts, we may limit ourselves to agreements about the information that is needed and the way this information can be obtained. This again amounts to an agreement about a procedural interface. This interface shows a striking resemblance to that of module Store.

Module 3: Shift This module offers the following routines:

- InitShift initializes the module;
- ShiftLines yields the total number of shifts;
- ShiftWords(l) yields the number of words in shift l;
- ShiftChars(l, w) yields the number of characters in word w of shift l;
- ShiftChar(l, w, c) yields the c-th character of word w of shift l.

Whereas we spoke about lines in module Store, this module speaks about shifts. We still have to relate shifts to lines, though. This can be done as follows:

- if $i < j$, the shifts of line i precede those of line j;
- for each line, the first shift will be the original line, the second one will be the line shifted one word to the left, etc.

In this way we have ensured that, by calling ShiftCharacter with increasing values of l (counting from 1), all shifts will be obtained exactly once.

The last important step concerns sorting. Here again, we may hide decisions pertaining to representations and algorithms by presenting a different interface to the user of the sorting module:

Module 4: Sort The sorting module offers two functions to its users. The first one, InitSort, serves as an initialization routine. The second one, Ith, serves as an index. Ith(i) delivers the rank number of the shift that is i-th in the lexicographic ordering of all shifts. This rank number is to be used as a parameter to calls of routines from module Shift to obtain the textual representation of that shift.

Finally, we need output and control modules. These are very similar in function to those from the first decomposition. Figure 10.2 shows the general flavor of the architecture of the second decomposition.[3] For the modules Store and Shift, we did not include all routines and their calling patterns.

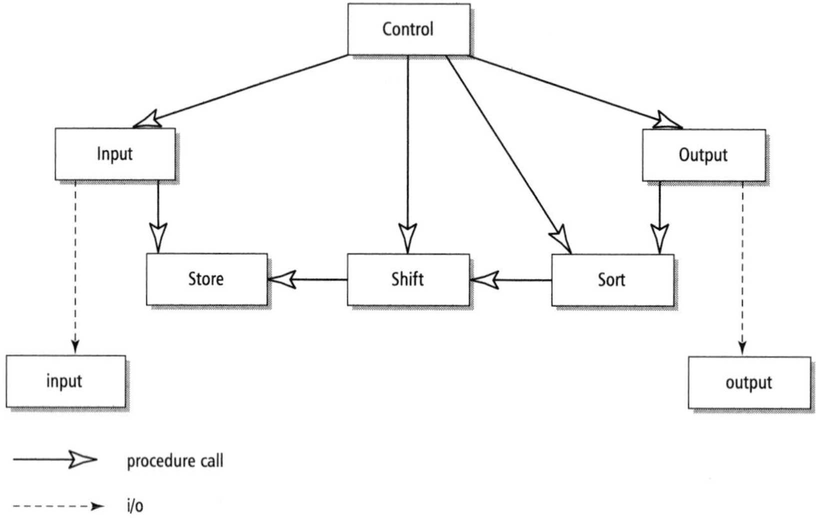

Figure 10.2 Abstract-data-type solution of the KWIC-index program

10.1.3 Implicit Invocation

A major advantage of abstract data types over shared data is that changes in data representations and algorithms can be accomplished relatively easily. Changes in functionality, however, may be much harder to realize.

For example, in practice, one will only generate shifts that start with a relevant word. Shifts starting with words such as 'a', 'be', 'the' or 'some' are not all that in-

[3]Though Store, Shift and Sort each use information hiding, only Store and Shift are abstract data types in a strict sense. The main secret of Store and Shift is the representation of certain data, whereas the main secret of Sort is of an algorithmic nature.

teresting. Starting from the abstract-data-type implementation discussed above, we may incorporate this functional enhancement through a filter between modules Output and Sort. This filter simply removes all (sorted) shifts that we are not interested in. If time is at a premium, however, this solution might not be acceptable. The running time of this system is dominated by the time it takes to sort the shifts and this solution wastes much time sorting records that are deleted later on. An alternative solution therefore is to change the Shift module such that only relevant shifts are generated.

Suppose we next wish to enhance the system's functionality even further by including a feature which allows us to generate only those shifts which start with any of a given set of keywords. Again, both solutions mentioned above are feasible. And again, the filter solution is inefficient. If we choose to tinker with the Shift module once more, it is likely that its original elegance gets lost.

Adding functionality in a scheme built around abstract data types cannot always be accommodated by adding new components, but may necessitate excessive changes in existing components.

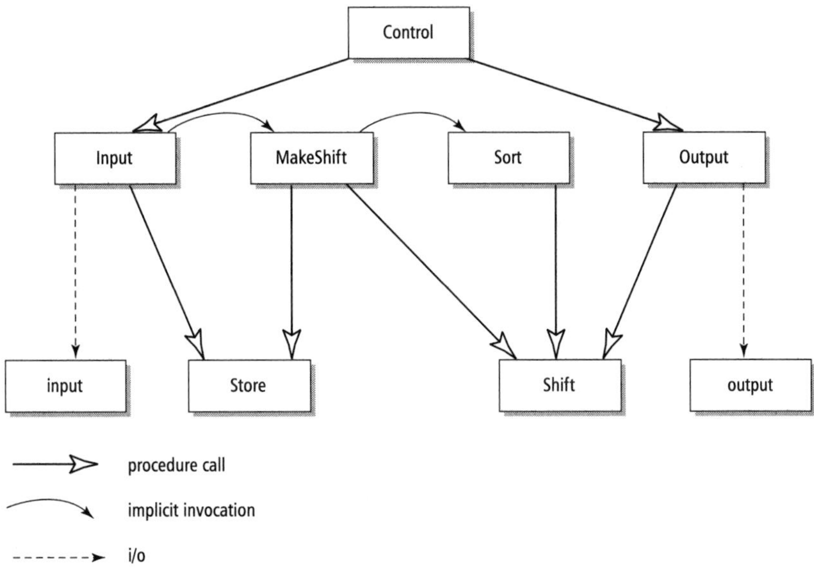

Figure 10.3 Implicit-invocation solution of the KWIC-index program

In such cases, an architecture based upon implicit invocation may help. This scheme also makes use of abstract data types to hide representations. However, in implicit invocation, the MakeShift module is not explicitly called (invoked). A so-called **event** is generated after the input is read and stored. Other modules in the system may express their interest in this event by associating a procedure with it; the procedures are automatically invoked each time the event is raised. In our case, the MakeShift module associates a procedure with this event. Likewise, MakeShift raises another event after it has done its work and Sort associates a procedure with that event. This is schematically depicted in figure 10.3.

The above scheme essentially mimics a batch process. First, all input is read and stored, then all shifts are generated, etc. It is relatively easy to turn it into a more interactive one. Rather than raising an event after *all* input has been read and stored, we may do so after *each* input line has been read and stored. The MakeShift module associates a procedure with this event and is invoked once for each input line. We may likewise raise an event after each shift is generated. If we associate a procedure that acts as a sieve with the latter event, the procedure can remove uninteresting shifts.

10.1.4 Pipes and Filters

Each of the aforementioned solutions to the KWIC-index problem involves a series of transformations, the major ones being from lines to shifts, and from shifts to sorted shifts. We could have devised separate programs for each transformation, ending up with a system exhibiting a batch-processing mode of operation.

Since each program in this scheme reads its input in the same order it is written by its predecessor, we need not explicitly create these intermediate files. Rather, we may use the pipe-and-filter mode of operation that is well-known from UNIX and directly feed the output of one transformation into the next one. In UNIX terms, this results in four filters and three pipes, as depicted in figure 10.4. The final program then is of the form

```
Input <input | Shift | Sort | Output >output
```

An important characteristic of this scheme is that any structure imposed on the data to be passed between adjacent filters has to be explicitly encoded in the datastream that connects these filters. This encoding scheme involves decisions which must be known to both filters. The data has to be unparsed by one filter while the next filter must parse its input in order to rebuild that structure.

In our case, the parsing and unparsing is relatively easy. The various datastreams are linear sequences of text lines, with little internal structure imposed on them. However, if more complex data structures are involved, the parsing and unparsing become more complex as well. For example, if some binary search tree has to be passed from filter A to filter B, it has to be linearized by A, e.g. into a postfix Polish expression. Next, B has to parse this expression to rebuild the tree.

Using pipes and filters, functional enhancements can often be accommodated with relative ease by plugging in another filter.

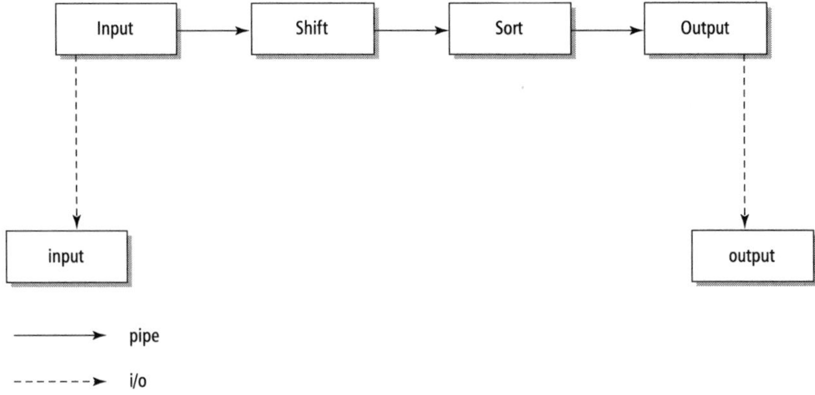

Figure 10.4 Pipes-and-filters solution of the KWIC-index program

The Achilles' heel of the pipes-and-filters scheme is error handling. Suppose module Input of the KWIC-index program detects an error. It is cumbersome to pass the resulting error message through intermediate filters to module Output because the intermediate filters have to disentangle their input. Instead, we may use a separate error channel, as in UNIX. Error messages however then get easily mixed up if filters run in parallel. Filters must also be able to resynchronize after an error has been detected and filters further downstream must be able to tolerate incomplete input. The uniform and proper handling of errors is a complicating factor in the use of pipes and filters.

10.1.5 Evaluation of the Architectures

All four schemes will work. The scheme using shared data is fairly conventional. The abstract-data-type scheme is in some sense more surprising. So is the implicit-invocation scheme, especially to those unfamiliar with the notion of event-driven control and language features to support it. Pipes and filters are very natural to those working in a UNIX-like environment.

Differences become apparent if we evaluate the architectures with respect to the following aspects:

- changes in data representation,
- changes in algorithms,
- changes in functionality,
- the degree to which modules can be implemented independently,

- comprehensibility,
- performance, and
- reuse.

Changes in data representation When conceiving a solution to the KWIC-index problem, a number of questionable decisions regarding the internal representation of data are taken. Some of these may be subject to change. Examples are:

- If the input is very large, it may be impractical to store all input in main memory.
- If there are only few lines, it may not be worth the effort to store the input in units of ten characters. Other formats are also conceivable.
- If the input is small or memory is large, it may be more advantageous to construct and store the shifts once rather than to use a table from which the shifts can be deduced.

The difference between the various decompositions becomes clear if we consider the impact of changing the above decisions. If we do not store the input in memory or change the storage format, *each* module in the main-program-with-subroutines decomposition must change because knowledge about internal representations is shared by all modules. In the abstract-data-type and implicit-invocation schemes, this knowledge is kept by the module Store only. It is completely hidden from the other modules. The necessary changes thus remain restricted to that one module.

If the shifts are constructed and stored, the modules Shift, Sort and Output in the main-program-with-subroutines decomposition must change. We need only adapt module Shift in the abstract-data-type and implicit-invocation decompositions.

In the pipes-and-filters decomposition, internal representations used in one filter remain hidden to the other filters. However, if data structures have to be passed from one filter to the next, a decision as to the format of this intermediate datastream affects both filters. Some decisions, such as the one to use a table from which shifts can be deduced rather than storing the shifts themselves, have a cascading effect. They tend to work their way to filters further downstream.

Changes in algorithms An example of a decision of an algorithmic nature is to sort the shifts all at once, rather than using some partial sorting algorithm, or even searching for each element when it is needed. In a number of cases it may be worthwhile to spread the sorting time across the time taken to print the complete index.

This change affects more than one module in the main-program-with-subroutines decomposition (Sort and Output). The Sort module in the other decompositions has been designed so that it is not visible to the user when the sorting takes place.

In general, changes in algorithms are difficult to accomplish when using shared data, since these changes often affect the data representations as well and therefore affect other components that make use of the data. When using abstract data types or information hiding, the impact of algorithmic changes depends on whether the change can be confined to one specific component. If the secret that characterizes the component is of an algorithmic nature (as is the case for the sorting decision), changes that only affect that secret can be confined to that component as well. If the change crosses the boundaries of a component, it tends to be more difficult to accomplish.

Algorithmic changes fit well into a pipe-and-filter scheme. The datastreams between filters tend to have a rather simple structure (usually just streams of ASCII characters). The parsing and unparsing that occurs on either end tends to remove much of the internal structure that is only used locally in one of the filters.

Changes in functionality As discussed in section 10.1.3, changes in functionality may be difficult to accomplish in an abstract-data-type scheme. In such a scheme, the overall processing algorithm tends to be spread across many components and specific functionality is often hard to assign to individual components. The implicit-invocation and pipe-and-filter schemes are particularly attractive in this respect, since functional changes can often be accommodated in a purely additive way. In a shared-data scheme, such changes sometimes necessitate excessive tinkering with existing code.

Independent development In the main-program-with-subroutines decomposition, the interfaces between the various modules consist of fairly complex descriptions of formats and tables. These correspond to design decisions that are essential to the final structure of the system. Decisions about the organization of the data are part of the development of those modules and cannot be neglected during design. In a sense, these decisions are a common property of those modules. They are visible to, and used by, the implementors of those modules.

The interfaces in the abstract-data-type and implicit-invocation decomposition are much more abstract. They consist of function names and information about the number and type of their parameters. Such decisions are fairly easy to make and the independent development of modules can easily be started.

We may illustrate this by visualizing the implementation of the KWIC-index program by two people. In order to do so, we split the program into two parts of approximately the same size. As far as the main-program-with-subroutines decomposition is concerned, all types and variables defined in the control module must be known to both developers. In the abstract-data-type and implicit-invocation decomposition, these types and variables are declared locally, so the developers only have to agree on the way functions are to be called.

In a pipe-and-filter scheme, decisions on the format of datastreams are the mutual responsibility of the developers of adjacent filters. Since these formats tend to be fairly simple, they often have a limited impact on the implementation of either filter, so that independent development of filters is easy.

Comprehensibility In order to fully comprehend the Sort module of the main-program-with-subroutines decomposition, you also have to know something of the Input and Shift modules. Certain aspects of the table organization derive their meaning from specific choices made in other modules. As a consequence, the system can be comprehended only as a whole. This does not hold for the other decompositions.

In an implicit-invocation scheme, it may be difficult to know 'who is in control'. If an event is raised in one component, it is not known which component is going to respond to that event. If more than one procedure is associated with an event, it may be difficult or even impossible, to decide in which order these event handlers will be called. The overall processing of such a system may therefore be more difficult to grasp than is the case in schemes with a centralized control.

Performance In both a shared-data and an abstract-data-type scheme, performance is good. The implicit-invocation scheme may involve some overhead caused by the scheduling of events. A pipe-and-filter scheme involves parsing and unparsing of data structures to be passed from one filter to the next. As a consequence, performance tends to be poorer in the latter two schemes.

Reuse Because of the intertwining of data representations and algorithms, reuse is difficult to achieve in a shared-data scheme. The other schemes are more attractive in this respect.

Reuse, however, is not just a matter of being able to rip a piece of code from a larger whole. Though the simplicity of the interaction between a component and its users is an important factor, the reusability of a component is to a much larger extent determined by the question of whether the *abstraction* it embodies is useful in another context.

Table 10.1 summarizes the above discussion. The contents of this table should be interpreted with care. The advantages and disadvantages listed hold for *this* application. The relative merits of different architectural styles may be judged differently for another type of application. Also, the different categories of changes usually do not show up in isolation. For example, changes in functionality often incur changes in data representation as well.

10.2 ARCHITECTURAL STYLES

In the previous section, we sketched four possible decompositions, or architectures, for the KWIC-index problem. Each of these architectures reflects a certain architectural style, such as a main program with subroutines or a sequence of filters connected

	Shared data	Abstract data type	Implicit invocation	Pipe and filter
Changes in data representation	–	+	+	–
Changes in algorithm	–	o	o	+
Changes in functionality	o	–	+	+
Independent development	–	+	+	+
Comprehensibility	–	+	o	+
Performance	+	+	–	–
Reuse	–	+	+	+

Table 10.1 Evaluation of architectures for the KWIC-index problem

through pipes. The description of these architectures is rather informal. The graphical representation is sketchy too. It is a simple box and line drawing, where the boxes and lines denote widely different things. In this section, we will give a more precise characterization of a number of common architectural styles.

In software engineering, we often draw a parallel with other engineering disciplines, in particular civil engineering. This comparison is made to highlight both similarities, such as the virtues of a phased approach, and differences, such as the observation that software is logical rather than physical, which hampers the control of progress. The comparison with the field of architecture is often made to illustrate the role of different views, as expressed in the different types of blueprint produced. Each of these blueprints emphasizes a particular aspect.

The classical field of architecture provides some further interesting insights for software architecture. These insights concern:

- the notion of architectural style,
- the relationship between style and engineering, and
- the relationship between style and materials.

Architecture is a (formal) arrangement of architectural elements. An architectural style abstracts from the specifics of an architecture. The decomposition in section 10.1.1 resulted in a specific architecture with one main program and four subroutines, sharing three data stores. If we abstract from these specifics, we obtain its architectural style, in which we concentrate on the types of its elements and their interconnections.

Viewed in this way, an architectural style describes a certain codification of elements and their arrangement. Conversely, an architectural style *constrains* both the elements and their interrelationships. For example, the Tudor style *describes* how a certain type of house looks and also *prescribes* how its design should look. In a similar vein we may characterize a software architectural style such as, say, the pipes-and-filter style.

Different engineering principles apply to different architectural styles. This often goes hand in hand with the types of materials used. Cottage-style houses and high-rise apartment-buildings differ in the materials used and the engineering principles applied. A software design based on abstract data types (= material) emphasizes separation of concerns by encapsulating secrets (= engineering principle). A design based on pipes and filters emphasizes bundling of functionality in independent processes.

When selecting a certain architectural style with its corresponding engineering principles and materials, we are guided by the problem to be solved as well as the larger context in which the problem occurs. We cannot build a skyscraper from wooden posts. Environmental regulations may prohibit us erecting high-rise buildings in rural areas. And, the narrow frontages of many houses on the Amsterdam canals are partly due to the fact that local taxes were based on the number of street-facing windows. Similar problem- and context-specific elements guide us in the selection of a software architectural style.

These similarities between classical architecture and software architecture provide us with clues as to what constitutes a software architectural style and what its description should look like.

In their search for a characterization of what a software architectural style entails, researchers in this field have been very much influenced by the works of the architect Christopher Alexander. In his book *A Pattern Language*, Alexander presents 253 'patterns', ranging in scale from how a city should look down to rules for the construction of a porch.

Perhaps his most famous pattern is about the height of buildings:

> 'There is abundant evidence to show that high buildings make people crazy.
>
> ...
>
> High buildings have no genuine advantage, except in speculative gains to banks and land owners. They are not cheaper, they do not help create open space, they make life difficult for children, they are expensive to maintain, they wreck the open spaces near them, and they damage the light and air and view. But quite apart from this, empirical evidence shows that they can actually damage people's minds and feelings.
>
> ...
>
> In any urban area, no matter how dense, keep the majority of buildings four stories high or less. It is possible that certain buildings should exceed this limit, but they should never be buildings for human habitation.'

An Alexandrian pattern is not a cookbook, black-box recipe for architects, any more than a dictionary is a toolkit for a novelist. Rather, a pattern is a flexible generic scheme providing a solution to a problem in a given context. In a narrative form, its application looks like this:

> IF you find yourself in <context>, for example <examples>, with <problem>,
> THEN for some <reasons>, apply <pattern> to construct a solution leading to a <new context> and <other patterns>.

The above 'Four-Story Limit' pattern may for example be applied in a context where one has to design a suburb. The citation gives some of the reasons for applying this pattern. If it is followed, it will give rise to the application of other patterns, such as those for planning parking lots, the layout of roads, or the design of individual houses.[4]

[Sha96b] characterizes a number of well-known software architectural styles in a framework that resembles a popular way of describing design patterns. Both the characterization and the framework are shaped after Alexander's way of describing patterns. We will use this framework to describe the architectural styles discussed in 10.1 as well as a few others. The framework has the following entries:

- **Problem** A description of the type of problem this style addresses. Certain characteristics of the requirements will guide the designer in his choice of a particular style. For example, if the problem consists of a series of independent transformations, a pipes-and-filter type of architecture suggests itself.

- **Context** A designer will be constrained in the use of a style by certain characteristics of the environment. Or, to put it the other way round, a style imposes certain requirements on the environment. For example, the pipes-and-filter style usually relies on operating system support for data transfer between filters.

[4]Here, we may note another similarity between classical architecture and software architecture. In the 1950s and 1960s, housing was a major problem in Western Europe and beyond. There were far too few houses available, while those available were mostly of a bad quality (damp, no bathroom, too small). In the post-war economic boom, many suburbs were constructed, with lots of spacious apartments, each one a container made of steel and concrete. These new suburbs solved one problem – the housing of a large number of people – but at the same time created other problems which only showed themselves much later, e.g. lack of community feeling and social ties, high crime rates. As a result, massive renovation projects have started and many a high-rise apartment building has been demolished. In software development, we developed company-wide systems in the 1970s and 1980s, with an emphasis on performance, uniformity, and standardized ways of working. Many of these systems are unable to cope satisfactorily with today's requirements of flexibility and adaptability, and are therefore being renovated.

Type	Description
computational	The component performs a computation of some sort. Usually, the input and output to the component are fairly simple, e.g. procedure parameters. The component may have a local state, but this state disappears after the component has done its job. Example components of this type are (mathematical) functions and filters.
memory	A memory component maintains a collection of persistent, structured data, to be shared by a number of other components. Examples are a database, a file system, or a symbol table.
manager	A manager component contains a state and a number of associated operations. When invoked, these operations use or update the state, and this state is retained between successive invocations of the manager's operations. Abstract data types and servers are example components of this type.
controller	A controller governs the time sequence of other events. A top-level control module and a scheduler are examples hereof.

Figure 10.5 Some component types (*Source: M. Shaw & D. Garlan,* Software Architecture: Perspectives on an Emerging Discipline, *page 149, ©1996, Reprinted by permission of Prentice-Hall*)

- **Solution** A description of the solution chosen. The major elements of a software architecture are **components** and **connectors**. Components are the building blocks of a software architecture. They usually embody a computational element of some sort (like a procedure), but a component can also be a data store (such as a database). The connectors describe how components interact. Some typical types of component and connector are given in figures 10.5 and 10.6.

  The order of execution of components is governed by the **control structure**. The control structure captures how control is transferred during execution.

  The choice of components and connectors is not independent. Usually, a style is characterized by a combination of certain types of component and connector, as well as a certain control structure. The **system model** captures the intuition behind such a combination. It describes the general flavor of the system.

- **Variants** Architectural styles give a rather general description. Often, certain variants or specializations may be identified, which differ from the general style.

- **Examples** One should include references to real examples of a style. Architectural styles do not stem from theoretical investigations, but result from identifying and characterizing best practice.

Type	Description
procedure call	With this type of connector, there is a single thread of control between the caller and the called component. Control is transferred to the component being called, and this component remains in control until its work has ended. Only then is control transferred back to the calling component. The traditional procedure call and the remote procedure call are examples of this type of connector.
data flow	With a data flow connector, processes interact through a stream of data, as in pipes. The components themselves are independent. Once input data to a component is available, it may continue its work.
implicit invocation	With implicit invocation, a computation is invoked when a certain event occurs, rather than by explicit interaction (as in a procedure call). Components raising events do not know which component is going to react and invoked components do not know which component raised the event to which they are reacting.
message passing	Message passing occurs when we have independent processes that interact through explicit, discrete transfer of data, as in TCP/IP. Message passing can be synchronous (in which case the sending/receiving process is blocked until the message has been completely sent/received) or asynchronous (in which case the processes continue their work independently).
shared data	When using shared data connectors, components operate concurrently on the same data space, as in blackboard systems or multiuser databases. Usually, some blocking scheme prevents concurrent writes to the same data.
instantiation	With instantiation, one component (the instantiator) provides space for the state required by another component (the instantiated), as in abstract data types.

Figure 10.6 Some connector types (*Source: M. Shaw & D. Garlan,* Software Architecture: Perspectives on an Emerging Discipline, *page 149-150, ©1996. Reprinted by permission of Prentice-Hall*)

For the styles discussed in section 10.1, the characterizations are given in figures 10.7–10.10. Figures 10.11 and 10.12 contain descriptions of two other architectural styles: the repository and layered styles.

The repository style fits situations where the main issue is to manage a richly structured body of information. In our library example in chapter 9, the data concerns things like the stock of available books and the collection of members of the library. These data are persistent and it is important that they always reflect the true state of affairs. A natural approach to this problem is to devise database schemas for the various types of data in the application (books, journals, library clients, reservations, and so on) and store the data in one or more databases. The functionality of the system is incorporated in a number of, relatively independent, computational elements. The result is a repository architectural style.

Modern compilers are often structured in a similar way. Such a compiler maintains a central representation of the program to be translated. A rudimentary version of that representation results from the first, lexical, phase: a sequence of tokens rather than a sequence of character glyphs. Subsequent phases, such as syntax and semantic

Style: Main program with subroutines

Problem The system can be described as a hierarchy of procedure definitions. This style is a natural outcome of a functional decomposition of a system (see chapter 11). The top-level module acts as the main program. Its main task is to invoke the other modules in the right order. As a consequence, there is usually a single thread of control.

Context This style naturally fits in with programming languages that allow for nested definitions of procedures and modules.

Solution

System model Procedures and modules are defined in a hierarchy. Higher-level modules call lower-level modules. The hierarchy may be strict, in which case modules at level n can only call modules at level $n-1$, or it may be weak, in which case modules at level n may call modules at level $n-i$, with $i \geq 1$. Procedures are grouped into modules following such criteria as coupling and cohesion (see chapter 11).

Components (Groups of) procedures, which may have their own local data, and global data which may be viewed as residing in the main program.

Connectors Procedure call and shared access to global data.

Control structure There is a single, centralized thread of control; the main program pulls the strings.

Variants This style is usually applied to systems running on one CPU. Abstractly, the model is preserved in systems running on multiple CPUs and using the Remote Procedure Call (RPC) mechanism to invoke processes.

Examples [Par72]; see also section 10.1.1.

Figure 10.7 Main-program-with-subroutines architectural style (*Source: M. Shaw, Some Patterns for Software Architectures, **in** J.M. Vlissides et al.,* Pattern Languages of Program Design 2, *Reproduced by permission of M. Shaw*)

analysis, further enrich this structure into, for example, an abstract syntax tree. In the end, code is generated from this representation. Other tools, such as symbolic debuggers, pretty-printing programs, or static analysis tools, may also employ the internal representation built by the compiler. The resulting architectural style again is that of a repository: one memory component and a number of computational elements that act on that repository. Unlike the database variant, the order of invocation of the elements matters in the case of a compiler. Also, different computational elements enrich the internal representation, rather than merely update it.

The repository architectural style can also be found in certain AI applications. In computationally complex applications, such as speech recognition, an internal representation is built and acted upon by different computational elements. For example, one computational element may filter noise, another one builds up phonemes, etc. The internal representation in this type of system is called a **blackboard** and the architecture is sometimes referred to as a blackboard architecture. A major difference with traditional database systems is that the invocation of computational elements in a blackboard architecture is triggered by the current state of the blackboard, rather than by (external) inputs. Elements from a blackboard architecture enrich and refine the state representation until a solution to the problem is found.

Style: Abstract data type

Problem A central issue is to identify and protect related bodies of information. The style is especially suited for cases where the data representation is likely to change during the lifetime of the system. When the design matches the structure of the data in the problem domain, the resulting components encapsulate problem-domain entities and their operations.

Context Many design methods, most notably the object-oriented ones, provide heuristics to identify real-world objects. These objects are then encapsulated in components of the system. Object-oriented programming languages provide the class concept, which allows us to relate similar objects and reuse code through the inheritance mechanism.

Solution

System model Each component maintains its own local data. Components hide a secret, viz. the representation of their data.

Components The components of this style are managers, such as servers, objects, and abstract data types.

Connectors Operations are invoked through procedure calls (messages).

Control structure There is usually a single thread of control. Control is decentralized, however; a component may invoke any component whose services it requires.

Variants Methods or languages that are not object-oriented only allow us to hide data representations in modules. Object-oriented methods or languages differ as regards their facilities for relating similar objects (single or multiple inheritance) and their binding of messages to operations (compile time or runtime); see also chapter 12.

Examples [Par72]; see also section 10.1.2; [Boo94] gives a number of worked-out examples.

Figure 10.8 Abstract-data-type architectural style (*Source: M. Shaw, Some Patterns for Software Architectures, in J.M. Vlissides et al.,* Pattern Languages of Program Design 2, *Reproduced by permission of M. Shaw*)

Our final example of an architectural style is the layered architectural style. A prototypical instance hereof is the ISO Open System Interconnection Model for network communication. It has seven layers: physical, data, network, transport, session, presentation, and application. The bottom layer provides basic functionality. Higher layers use the functionality of lower layers. The different layers can be viewed as virtual machines whose 'instructions' become more powerful and abstract as we go from lower layers to higher layers.

In a layered scheme, by definition, lower levels cannot use the functionality offered by higher levels. The other way round, the situation is more varied. We may choose to allow layer n to use the functionality of each layer m, with $m < n$. We may also choose to limit the visibility of functionality offered by each layer, and for example restrict layer n to use only the functionality offered by layer $n-1$. A design issue in each case is how to assign functionality to the different layers of the architecture, i.e. how to characterize the virtual machine it embodies. If visibility is not restricted, some of the elegance of the layered architecture gets lost. This situation resembles that of programming languages containing low-level bit manipulation operations alongside while statements and procedure calls. If visibility is restricted,

Style: Implicit invocation

Problem We have a loosely-coupled collection of components, each of which carries out some task and may enable other operations. The major characteristic of this style is that it does not bind recipients of signals to their originators. It is especially useful for applications that need to be able to be reconfigured, by changing a service provider or by enabling and disabling operations.

Context This style usually requires an event handler that registers components' interests and notifies others. This can be achieved either through specialized operating system support or through specialized language features. Because of the intrinsically decentralized nature of systems designed this way, correctness arguments are difficult. For the same reason, building a mental model of such systems during program comprehension is difficult too.

Solution

System model Processes are independent and reactive. Processes are not invoked explicitly, but implicitly through the raising of an event.

Components Components are processes that signal events without knowing which component is going to react to them. Conversely, processes react to events raised somewhere in the system.

Connectors Components are connected through the automatic invocation of processes that have registered interest in certain events.

Control structure Control is decentralized. Individual components are not aware of the recipients of the signals.

Variants There are two major categories of systems exploiting implicit invocation. The first category comprises the so-called tool-integration frameworks as exemplified by many software development support environments. They consist of a number of 'toolies' running as separate processes. Events are handled by a separate dispatcher process which uses some underlying operating system such as UNIX sockets; see for example [Rei90]. The second category consists of languages with specialized notations and support for implicit invocation, such as the 'when-updated' features of some object-orientated languages; see for example [SHO90].

Examples [Garlan *et al*, 1992]; see also section 10.1.3; [SHO90].

Figure 10.9 Implicit-invocation architectural style (*Source: M. Shaw, Some Patterns for Software Architectures,* ***in*** *J.M. Vlissides et al.,* Pattern Languages of Program Design 2, *Reproduced by permission of M. Shaw*)

we may end up copying functionality to higher levels without increasing the level of abstraction.

[dLM95] gives an example of a layered architectural style for use in telecommunications. In this example, layers do not correspond to different levels of abstraction. Rather, the functionality of the system has been separated. Two main guidelines drive the assignment of functionality to layers in this architecture:

- hardware-dependent functionality should be placed in lower-level layers than application-dependent functionality.

- generic functionality should be placed in lower layers than specific functionality.

The resulting architecture has four layers:

Style: Pipes and filters

Problem A series of independent, sequential transformations on ordered data. Usually, the transformations are incremental. Often, the structure of the datastreams is very simple: a series of ASCII characters. If the data has a rich structure, this will imply quite some overhead for the parsing and unparsing of the data.

Context This style requires that the system can be decomposed into a series of computations, *filters*, that incrementally transform one or more input streams. It usually relies on operating system operations to transfer the data from one process to another (*pipes*). Error handling is difficult to deal with uniformly in a collection of filters.

Solution

System model The resulting systems are characterized by continuous data flow between components, where components incrementally transform datastreams.

Components The components are filters that perform local processing, i.e. they read part of their input data, transform the data, and produce part of their output. They have little internal state.

Connectors Datastreams (usually plain ASCII, as in UNIX).

Control structure Data flow between components. Each component usually has its own thread of control.

Variants Pure filters have little internal state and process their input locally. In the degenerate case they consume all of their input before producing any output. In that case, the result boils down to a batch-processing type of sytem.

Examples [DG90]; see also sections 10.1.4.

Figure 10.10 Pipes-and-filters architectural style (*Source: M. Shaw, Some Patterns for Software Architectures, **in** J.M. Vlissides et al.,* Pattern Languages of Program Design 2, *Reproduced by permission of M. Shaw*)

- *Operating system* This layer comprises the runtime system, database, memory management, and so on.
- *Equipment maintenance* This layer houses the control for peripheral devices and its interconnection structure. It deals with such things as data distribution and fault-handling of peripheral hardware. The bottom two layers together constitute the distributed operating infrastructure upon which applications run.
- *Logical-resource management* Logical resources come in two flavors. The first class contains abstractions from hardware objects. The second class consists of software-related logical objects, such as those for call-forwarding in telephony.
- *Service management* This layer contains the application functionality.

A similar line of thought can be followed in other domains. For instance, it is hard to predict how future household electronic equipment will be assembled into hardware boxes. Will the PC and the television be in the same box? Will the television and the video be combined or will they remain as separate boxes? No one seems to know. Since the half-life of many of these products is about six months, industry is forced to use a building-block approach, emphasizing reuse and the development of product families rather than products. A division of functionality into a hardware-related in-

Style: Repository

Problem The central issue is managing and maintaining a richly-structured body of information. The information must typically be manipulated in many different ways. The data is long-lived and its integrity is important.

Context This style often requires considerable support, in the form of a runtime system augmented with a database. Data definitions may have to be processed to generate support to maintain the correct structure of the data.

Solution

System model The major characteristic of this model is its centralized, richly structured body of information. The computational elements acting upon the repository are often independent.

Components There is one memory component and many computational processes.

Connectors Computational units interact with the memory component by direct access or procedure call.

Control structure The control structure varies. In traditional database systems, for example, control depends on the input to the database functions. In a modern compiler, control is fixed: processes are sequential and incremental. In blackboard systems, control depends on the state of the computation.

Variants Traditional database systems are characterized by their transaction-oriented nature. The computational processes are independent and triggered by incoming requests. Modern compilers, and software development support environments, are systems that increment the information contained in the repository. Blackboard systems have their origin in AI. They have been used for complex applications such as speech recognition, in which different computational elements each solve part of the problem and update the information on the blackboard.

Examples [BSS84] for software development environments; [Cor97] for blackboard architectures.

Figure 10.11 Repository architectural style (*Source: M. Shaw, Some Patterns for Software Architectures, **in** J.M. Vlissides et al.,* Pattern Languages of Program Design 2, *Reproduced by permission of M. Shaw*)

ner layer, a generic signal processing layer, and a user-oriented service layer suggests itself. The above architecture for telecommunications applications can be understood along the same lines.

In practice, we will usually encounter a mixture of architectural styles. For example, many software development environments can be characterized as a combination of the repository and layered architectural styles; see also chapter 19. The core of the system is a repository in which the various objects, ranging from program texts to work-breakdown structures, reside. Access to these objects as well as basic mechanisms for the execution and communication of tools are contained in a layer on top of this repository. The tools themselves are configured in one or more layers on top of these basic layers. Interaction between tools may yet follow another paradigm, such as implicit invocation.

Each of the above examples can be viewed as a **Domain-Specific Software Architecture** (DSSA). A DSSA comprises [HRPL+95]:

- a *reference architecture*, which describes a general computational framework for a significant domain of applications,

- a *component library*, which contains reusable chunks of domain expertise, and

---

Style: Layered

Problem We can identify distinct classes of services that can be arranged hierarchically. The system can be depicted as a series of concentric circles, where services in one layer depend on (call) services from inner layers. Quite often, such a system is split into three layers: one for basic services, one for general utilities, and one for application-specific utilities.

Context Each class of service has to be assigned to a specific layer. It may occasionally be difficult to properly identify the function of a layer succintly and, as a consequence, assign a given function to the most appropriate layer. This holds more if we restrict visibility to just one layer.

Solution

System model The resulting system consists of a hierarchy of layers. Usually, visibility of inner layers is restricted.

Components The components in each layer usually consist of collections of procedures.

Connectors Components generally interact through procedure calls. Because of the limited visibility, the interaction is limited.

Control structure The system has a single thread of control.

Variants A layer may be viewed as a virtual machine, offering a set of 'instructions' to the next layer. Viewed thus, the peripheral layers get more and more abstract. Layering may also result from a wish to separate functionality, e.g. into a user-interface layer and an application-logic layer. Variants of the layered scheme may differ as regards the visibility of components to outer layers. In the most constrained case, visibility is limited to the next layer up.

Examples [dLH95]; [HO96]; [BJNR98].

Figure 10.12 Layered architectural style (*Source: M. Shaw, Some Patterns for Software Architectures,* **in** *J.M. Vlissides et al.,* Pattern Languages of Program Design 2, *Reproduced by permission of M. Shaw*)

– an *application configuration method* for selecting and configuring components within the architecture to meet particular application requirements.

The reference architecture is a particular choice (combination) of architectural styles, without the semantic contents of its components. The component library adds the application-specific semantics, such as a lexical analyzer in a compiler, signal processing components in a telecommunications architecture, and components to add and remove objects from a database in an architecture for library automation. Such components can be identified through a process known as **domain analysis**; see also chapter 9. Finally, a specific application needs to be configured. In a compiler, for example, we have a choice as to whether or not to include certain optimization phases. Such a choice is usually done at design time. One may also conceive of situations in which components can be selectively enabled at run-time, depending on the specific task at hand. A DSSA that allows for easy instantiation to obtain actual implementations is also termed an application framework. A major driver for developments in DSSAs and frameworks lies in their reuse opportunities; see also chapter 17.

10.3 DESIGN PATTERNS

A design pattern is a recurring structure of communicating components that solves a general design problem within a particular context. A design pattern differs from an architectural style in that it does not address the structure of a complete system, but only that of a few (interacting) components. Design patterns may thus be termed micro-architectures. On the other hand, a design pattern encompasses more than a single component, procedure or module.

The archetypical example of a design pattern is the Model–View–Controller (MVC) pattern. Interactive systems consist of computational elements as well as elements to display data and handle user input. It is considered good design practice to separate the computational elements from those that handle I/O. This separation of concerns is achieved by the MVC pattern.

MVC involves three components: the Model, the View, and the Controller. The model component encapsulates the system's data as well as the operations on those data. The model component is independent of how the data is represented or how input is done. A view component displays the data that it obtains from the model component. There can be more than one view component. Finally, each view has an associated controller component. A controller handles input actions. Such an input action may cause the controller to send a request to the model, for example to update its data, or to its view, for example to scroll.

For any given situation, the above description has to be considerably refined and made more precise. For instance, a controller may or may not depend on the state of the model. If the controller does not depend on the state of the model, there is a one-way flow of information: the controller signals an input event and notifies the model. If the controller does depend on the state of the model, information flows in the other direction as well. The latter type of dependence can be observed in most word-processing systems for example, where menu entries are made active or inactive depending on the state of the model.

MVC was first used in the Smalltalk environment. Since then it has been applied in many applications. In various graphical user interface platforms, a variant has been applied in which the distinction between the view and the controller has been relaxed. This variant is called the Document–View pattern; see [Kru96].

Design patterns have a number of properties which explain what they offer, as well as why and how they do so:

- A pattern addresses a recurring design problem that arises in specific design situations and presents a solution to it. Many software systems include computational elements as well as user-interface elements. For reasons of flexibility, we may wish to separate these as much as possible. MVC offers a solution to precisely this recurring problem.

- A pattern must balance a set of opposing forces, i.e. characteristics of the problem that have to be dealt with in its solution. For example, in interactive applications we want to be able to present information in different ways, changes to the data must be reflected immediately in all views affected by these changes, and different 'look and feel' interfaces should not affect the application code. MVC seeks to balance all these forces.

- Patterns document existing, well-proven design experience. Patterns are not invented; they evolve with experience. They reflect best practices. MVC, for example, is used in various application frameworks as well as in scores of interactive systems.

- Patterns identify and specify abstractions above the level of single components. MVC has three, interacting components which *together* solve a given problem.

- Patterns provide a common vocabulary and understanding for design principles. By now, MVC has become a widely known label for a certain solution to a certain problem. We may use the term in conversation and writing much as we use terms like 'quicksort' or 'Gauss interpolation'. Patterns thus become part of our language for describing software designs.

- Patterns are a means of documentation. As with software architectures, patterns both describe and prescribe things. Descriptively, patterns offer a way to document your software, for example by simply using pattern names in its documentation. Prescriptively, pattern names give users hints as to how to extend and modify software without violating the pattern's vision. If your system employs MVC, computational aspects are strictly separated from representational aspects, and you know that this separation must be maintained during the system's evolution.

- Patterns support the construction of software with defined properties. On the one hand, MVC offers a skeleton for the construction of interactive systems. MVC however also addresses certain non-functional requirements, such as flexibility and changeability of user interfaces. These non-functional requirements often constitute the major problem directly addressed by the pattern.

When describing patterns it is customary to use a schema similar to that used for describing architectural styles. The main entries of such a schema therefore are:

- *context*: the situation giving rise to a design problem,

- *problem*: a recurring problem arising in that situation, and

- *solution*: a proven solution to that problem.

We will illustrate design patterns by sketching a possible application of two such patterns in a library automation system.

Suppose our library system involves a central database and a number of users, some of which are based at remote sites. We wish to optimize these remote accesses, for example by using a cache. However, we do not wish to clutter the application code with code that handles such optimizations. The *Proxy* pattern addresses this problem. In the Proxy pattern, a client does not directly address an original. Rather, the client addresses a proxy, a representative of that original. This proxy shields the non-application specific aspects, like the optimization through a cache in the above example. This Proxy pattern can be described as in figure 10.13.[5]

Context A client needs services from another component. Though direct access is possible, this may not be the best approach.

Problem We do not want to hard-code access to a component into a client. Sometimes, such direct access is inefficient; in other cases it may be unsafe. This inefficiency or insecurity is to be handled by additional control mechanisms, which should be kept separate from both the client and the component to which it needs access.

Solution The client communicates with a representative rather than the component itself. This representative, the *proxy*, also does any pre- and postprocessing that is needed.

Figure 10.13 The *Proxy* pattern

The Proxy pattern exists in many variants. The variant discussed above could be termed a *Cache Proxy*: emphasis is on sharing results from remote components. Other variants are: the *Remote Proxy* (which shields network access, inter-process communication, and so on), the *Protection Proxy* (protection from unauthorized access) and the *Firewall Proxy* (protection of local clients from the outside world). World Wide Web servers typically use a Firewall Proxy pattern to protect users from the outside world. Other example uses of the Proxy pattern can be found in frameworks for object-based client/server systems, such as the Common Object Request Broker Architecture (CORBA) and Microsoft's DCOM [Lew98].

Most users of the library system are incidental users for which we want a friendly interface, including powerful undo facilities. On the other hand, experienced library employees want a user interface with keyboard shortcuts for most commands. Furthermore, we want to be able to log user requests for later analysis, for example to find out which authors are much in demand. We want to separate these 'extras' from the actual application code. The *Command Processor* pattern addresses this issue. Ex-

[5]See [BMR+96, pp 263-275] for a more elaborate description.

ample uses of the Command Processor pattern can be found in user interface toolkits like ET++ and MacApp. Its characteristics are given in figure 10.14.[6]

Context User interfaces which must be flexible or provide functionality that goes beyond the direct handling of user functions. Examples are undo facilities or logging functions.

Problem We want a well-structured solution for mapping an interface to the internal functionality of a system. All 'extras' which have to do with the way user commands are input, additional commands such as undo and redo, and any non-application-specific processing of user commands, such as logging, should be kept separate from the interface to the internal functionality.

Solution A separate component, the *command processor*, takes care of all commands. The command processor component schedules the execution of commands, stores them for later undo, logs them for later analysis, and so on. The actual execution of the command is delegated to a supplier component within the application.

Figure 10.14 The *Command Processor* pattern

Applications typically involve a mixture of details that pertain to different realms, such as the application domain, the representation of data to the user, the access to a remote compute server, and so on. If these details are mixed up in the software, the result will be difficult to comprehend and maintain.

Expert designers have learned to separate such aspects so as to increase the maintainability, flexibility, adaptability (in short, the quality) of the systems they design. If needed, they introduce some intermediate abstract entity to bridge aspects of a solution they wish to keep separate. The Proxy and Command Processor patterns, as well as many other design patterns found in [GHJV95] and [BMR+96], offer elegant and flexible solutions to precisely these divide-and-conquer type design situations.

10.4 VERIFICATION AND VALIDATION

The software architecture captures early design decisions. Since these early decisions have a large impact, it is important to start testing even at this early stage.

Manual techniques, such as reviews and inspections, can obviously be applied at this stage. An interesting new development is the evaluation of a software architecture with respect to quality attributes such as maintainability, flexibility, and so on. This can be done by developing a set of scenarios and evaluating the extent to which the architecture meets the quality requirements for each of these scenarios (see also chapter 13).

The software architecture can be used to develop a *skeletal* version of the system. This skeletal version contains all of the architecture's components in a rudimen-

[6]see [BMR+96, pp 277–290] for a more elaborate description.

tary form. The skeletal system can be used as an environment for the incremental implementation of the system. It can also be used as an environment (test harness) for testing the system.

10.5 SUMMARY

Software architecture is concerned with the description of elements from which systems are built, the interaction among those elements, patterns that guide their composition, and constraints on those patterns. The field has been strongly influenced by the ideas of the architect Christopher Alexander.

Software architecture is a novel and still very immature branch of software engineering. It has hardly advanced beyond the stage of the mediaeval panel-work houses that adorn down-town areas in cities all over Europe. Some of our 'houses' will turn out to have been built on swampy grounds and disappear in the course of time. And some of them will hopefully stand the test of time.

Software architecture is an important notion, for more than one reason:

- The comparison with traditional architecture reveals commonalities which help us to get a better grip on the software design process and its products. Software architecture is not only concerned with the blueprint that is the outcome of the design process. The notion of an architectural style has merits of its own and the relationship between style on the one hand and engineering and materials on the other hand provide additional insights into what software design entails [PW92].

- The field may eventually yield a repertoire of concepts that software architects can use in their search for solutions. Expert designers in any field build on a vast collection of reusable concepts. These concepts are given unique names, which are used to communicate them, and serve as labels when retrieving and storing them in human memory. Software architecture is concerned with identifying, describing and categorizing components at a high level of abstraction. The resulting abstractions are to become part of the vocabulary of software engineers, much like abstract data types are already part of that vocabulary.

- Phrasing a software design in software architectural terms promotes consistency during development and maintenance. Phrasing the global design in terms of an architecture forces us to think about its general flavor, in terms of types of component and connector, as well as a certain control structure. By making this intuition explicit, it both *describes* and *prescribes* how the system should look and how it may evolve over time.

- A software architecture captures early design decisions. The architecture can be used to evaluate those decisions. It also provides a way to discuss those decisions and their ramifications with the various stakeholders.

- By considering software architectures for specific domains, we obtain generic solutions for recurring problems within that domain. Software architecture provides a handle for considering software designs for product families. It gives a framework for software reuse issues.

A design pattern is a recurring structure of communicating components that solves a general design problem within a particular context. A design pattern thus encompasses more than a single component. It involves some, usually 2–5, communicating components which *together* solve a problem. The problem that the pattern solves is a general, recurring one, which can be characterized by the context in which it arises. A design pattern differs from an architectural style in that it does not address the structure of a complete system, but only that of a few (interacting) components. Design patterns may thus be termed micro-architectures. Not surprisingly, the good things about design patterns are essentially those listed above for software architectures.

Design patterns describe best practices. They represent the collective experience of some of the most experienced and successful software designers. Their description, as found in textbooks, is the result of endless carving and smoothing. Some are the outcome of writers' workshops, a format commonly used to review literature, suggesting that we should review software literature with a profoundness like that used to review poetry (as a consequence, these writers' workshops are also known as workers' write shops).

The distinction between the notions software architecture and design pattern is by no means sharp. Some authors for example use the term 'architectural pattern' to denote the architectural styles we discussed in section 10.2. The notions application framework and idiom are generally used to denote a software architecture and design pattern, respectively, at a more concrete, implementation-specific level. But again, the distinction is not sharp.

10.6 FURTHER READING

Software architecture and design patterns have been strongly influenced by the works of the architect Christopher Alexander. It is certainly worthwhile to have a look at them [AIS77], [Ale79]. [Lea94] gives an introduction to his work for software engineers. [SG96] discusses the emerging field of software architecture, in particular software architectural styles. [BCK98] gives a broad overview of the field, including the various forces that influence software architecture and the purposes of a software architecture. It includes a number of case studies to illustrate these issues. The state of the art is reflected in [Don99]. A comparison between the classical field of architecture and software architecture is made in [PW92]. Different architectural views on the same system are the topic of [Kru95] and [SNH95].

The theory of programming plans stems from [Sol86].

The example in section 10.1 is taken from [Par72]. The implicit-invocation solution from section 10.1.3 was first given in [GKN92].

Many issues related to software architecture have not been touched upon in this chapter. These include efforts to classify software architectural styles along different dimensions [SC96], architecture description languages and supporting tools [SDK+95], the formal underpinnings of software architecture [AAG95], and the evaluation of software architectures [ABC+97]. The field is still too much in a state of flux for their treatment in a text book like this one.

Design patterns have their origin in the work of Cunningham and Beck, who developed patterns for user interfaces in Smalltalk, such as 'no more than three panes per window' [PW87b, p. 16]. MVC was first used in the Smalltalk environment [KP88]. Since that time, the topic has drawn a lot of attention, especially in object-oriented circles. A major collection of design patterns was published by the 'Gang of Four' in 1995 [GHJV95]. Another good collection of design patterns can be found in [BMR+96]. The latter text has a somewhat less object-oriented perspective than [GHJV95]. The use of patterns in modeling product families is addressed in [KM99].

Since 1994, there has been an annual conference on Pattern Languages of Programming [CS95b] and [VCK96]. [CAC96] contains a collection of articles on patterns, including one that details the organizational and sociological aspects of introducing patterns into a software development environment.

Exercises

1. Give a definition of the term 'software architecture'. Explain the different elements in this definition.

2. What is the difference between software architecture and top-level design?

3. What is the main purpose of a software architecture?

4. How may software architecture be used in the development of a line of software products?

5. What is the difference between the notions software architecture and design pattern?

6. What is the difference between the conceptual or logical view and the implementation view?

7. Describe in your own words the essence of the implicit-invocation architectural style.

8. In what sense does the abstract-data-type architectural style constrain the designer?

9. Why is error-handling difficult in the pipes-and-filter architectural style?

10. Why is language so important in software design?

11. Define the following component types: computational, memory, manager.

12. Define the following connector types: data flow, message passing, shared data.

13. In what sense may the layers in a layered architecture be viewed as virtual machines?

14. What are the properties of a design pattern?

15. ♠ To what extent may the development organization, background and expertise of the designer, and the technical environment have influenced the architecture of the World Wide Web? See also [BCK98, chapter 7].

16. ♡ What are the possible roles of software architecture and design patterns during software comprehension?

17. ♠ Write an essay on the influence of social and organizational issues on software architecture. See for example [Coc96].

18. ♡ The Document–View pattern relaxes the separation of view and controller in MVC. Describe the Document–View pattern in terms of the context in which it arises, the problem addressed, and its solution. Compare your solution with the Observer pattern in [GHJV95, p. 293].

19. ♡ How do design patterns impact the quality of a design?

11
Software Design

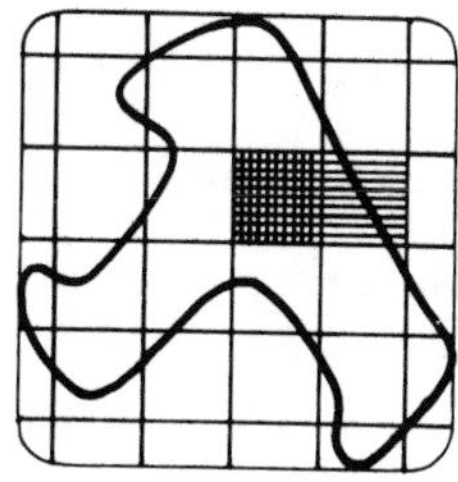

LEARNING OBJECTIVES

- To be able to discern desirable properties of a software design
- To understand different notions of complexity, at both the module and system level
- To be aware of some widely-known design methods
- To be aware of a global classification scheme for design methods
- To be aware of guidelines for the design documentation

During software development, we should adhere to a planned approach. If we want to travel from point A to point B, we will (probably) consult a map first. According to some criterion, we will then plan our travel scheme. The time-loss caused by the planning activity is bound to outweigh the misery that occurs if we do not plan our trip at all but just take the first turn left, hoping that this will bring us somewhat closer to our destination.

In designing a garden, we will also follow some plan. We will not start by planting a few bulbs in one corner, an apple tree in another, and a poplar next to the front door.

The above examples sound ridiculous. They are. Yet, many a software development project is undertaken in this way. Somewhat exaggeratedly, we may call it the 'programmer's approach' to software development. Far too much software is still being developed without a clear design phase. The reasons for this 'code first, design later' attitude are many:

- We do not want to, or are not allowed to, 'waste our time' on design activities.
- We have to, or want to, quickly show something to our customer.
- We are judged by the amount of code written per man-month.
- We are, or expect to be, pressed for time.

Such an approach grossly underestimates the complexity of software and its development. Just as with the furnishing of a house or the undertaking of a long trip, it is paramount to put thought into a plan, resulting in a blueprint that is then followed during actual construction. The outcome of this process (the blueprint) will be termed the **design** or, if the emphasis is on its notation, the (**technical**) **specification**. The process of making this blueprint is also called design. To a large extent, the quality of the design determines the quality of the resulting product. Errors made during the design phase often go undetected until the system is operational. At that time, they can be repaired only by incurring very high costs.

Design is a problem-solving activity and, as such, very much a matter of trial and error. In the presentation of a mathematical proof, subsequent steps dovetail well into each other and everything drops into place at the end. The actual discovery of the proof was probably quite different. The same holds for the design of software. We should not confuse the outcome of the design process with the process itself. The outcome of the design process is a 'rational reconstruction' of that process. (Note that we made precisely the same remark with respect to the outcome of the requirements engineering process.)

Software design is a 'wicked problem'. The term originated in research into the nature of design issues in social planning problems. Properties of wicked problems in this area are remarkably similar to properties of software design:

- There is no definite formulation of a wicked problem. The design process can hardly be separated from either the preceding requirements engineering phase or the subsequent documentation of the design in a specification. These activities will, in practice, overlap and influence each other. At the more global (architectural) stages of system design, the designer will interact with the user to assess fitness-for-use aspects of the design. This may lead to adaptations in the requirements specification. The more detailed stages of design often cannot be separated from the specification method used.

  One corollary of this is that the waterfall model does not fit the type of problem it is meant to address.

- Wicked problems have no stopping rule. There is no criterion that tells us when *the* solution has been reached. Though we do have a number of quality measures for software designs, there does not exist a single scale against which to measure the quality of a design. There probably never will be such a scale.

- Solutions to wicked problems are not true or false. At best, they are good or bad. The software design process is not analytic. It does not consist of a sequence of decisions each of which brings us somewhat closer to that one, optimal solution. Software design involves making a large number of trade-offs, such as those between speed and robustness. As a consequence, there is a number of *acceptable* solutions, rather than one best solution.

- Every wicked problem is a symptom of another problem. Resolving one problem may very well result in an entirely different problem elsewhere. For example, the choice of a particular dynamic data structure may solve the problem of an unknown input size and at the same time introduce an efficiency problem. A corollary of this is that small changes in requirements may have large consequences in the design or implementation. Elsewhere, we described this by saying that software is not continuous.

During design we may opt for a Taylorian, functionality-centered view and consider the design problem as a purely technical issue. Alternatively, we may realize that design involves user issues as well and therefore needs some form of user involvement. The role of the user during design need not be restricted to that of a guinea-pig in shaping the actual user interface. It may also involve much deeper issues.

Rather than approaching system design from the point of view that human weaknesses need to be compensated for, we may take a different stand and consider computerized systems as a means to support human strengths. Likewise, systems need not reflect the interests of system owners only. In a democratic world, systems can be designed so that all those involved benefit. This less technocratic attitude leads to extensive user involvement during all stages of system development.

Whereas traditional system development has a *production* view in which the technical aspects are optimized, the 'Scandinavian school' pays equal attention to the human system, and holds the view that technology must be compatible with organizational and social needs. The various possible modes of interaction between the designer or analyst on the one hand and the user on the other hand are also discussed in section 9.1. In this chapter, we concentrate on the technical issues of software design.

From the technical point of view, the design problem can be formulated as follows: how can we decompose a system into parts such that each part has a lower complexity than the system as a whole, while the parts together solve the user's problem. Since the complexity of the individual components should be reasonable, it is important that the interaction between components not be too complicated.

In chapter 10, we focused on a characterization of the *result* of the design process, the software architecture. In this chapter, we focus on the design *process*. There really is no universal design method. The design process is a creative one, and the quality and expertise of the designers are a critical determinant for its success. However, over the years a number of ideas and guidelines have emerged which may serve us in designing software.

The abstract data type solution to the KWIC-index example discussed in chapter 10 illustrates the single most important principle of software design: **information hiding**. It shows how to apply **abstraction** in software design. Abstraction means that we concentrate on the essential issues and ignore, abstract from, details that are irrelevant at this stage. Considering the complexity of the problems we are to solve, applying some sort of abstraction is a sheer necessity. It is simply impossible to take in all the details at once.

Section 11.1 discusses desirable design features that bear on quality issues, most notably maintainability and reusability. Five issues are identified that have a strong impact on the quality of a design: abstraction, modularity, information hiding, complexity, and system structure. Assessment of a design with respect to these issues allows us to get an impression of design quality, albeit not a very quantitative one yet.

A vast number of design methods exist, many of which are strongly tied to a certain notation. These methods give strategies and heuristics to guide the design process. Most methods use a graphical notation to depict the design. Though the details of those methods and notations differ widely, it is possible to provide broad characterizations in a few classes. The essential characteristics of those classes are elaborated upon in section 11.2.

In section 11.3, we discuss the various notations that may support the design process. This discussion is fairly brief, since a number of important notations are extensively dealt with in section 11.2, and chapters 9 (requirements engineering), 15 (specification) and 12 (object-oriented analysis and design).

During the design process too, quite a lot of documentation will be generated. This documentation serves various users, such as project managers, designers, testers, and programmers. Section 11.4 discusses IEEE Standard 1016. This standard contains useful guidelines for describing software designs. The standard identifies a number of roles and indicates, for each role, the type of design documentation needed.

Finally, section 11.5 discusses some verification and validation techniques that may fruitfully be applied at the design stage.

11.1 DESIGN CONSIDERATIONS

Up till now we have used the notion of 'module' in a rather intuitive way. It is not easy to give an accurate definition of that notion. Obviously, a module does not denote some random piece of software. We apply certain criteria when decomposing a system into modules.

At the programming language level, a module usually refers to an identifiable unit with respect to compilation. We will use a similar definition of the term 'module' with respect to design: a module is an identifiable unit in the design. In the decomposition from section 10.1.1, these units tended to be procedures. The modules from section 10.1.2 usually contain more than one procedure. The latter will often be the case.

There are, in principle, many ways to decompose a system into modules. Obviously, not every decomposition is equally desirable. In this section we are interested in desirable features of a decomposition, irrespective of the type of system or the design method used. These features can in some sense be used as a measure of the quality of the design. Designs that have those features are considered superior to those that do not have them.

The design features we are most interested in are those that facilitate maintenance and reuse: simplicity, a clear separation of concepts into different modules, and restricted visibility (i.e. locality) of information.[1] Systems that have those properties are easier to maintain since we may concentrate our attention on those parts that are directly affected by a change. These properties also bear on reusability, because the resulting modules tend to have a well-defined functionality that fits concepts from

[1]Obviously, an even more important feature of a design is that the corresponding system should perform the required tasks in the specified way. To this end, the design should be validated against the requirements.

the application domain. Such modules are likely candidates for inclusion in other systems that address problems from the same domain.

In the following subsections we discuss five interrelated issues that have a strong impact on the above features:

- abstraction,
- modularity,
- information hiding,
- complexity, and
- system structure.

11.1.1 Abstraction

Abstraction means that we concentrate on the essential features and ignore, *abstract from*, details that are not relevant at the level we are currently working. Consider, for example, a typical sorting module. From the outside we cannot (and need not be able to) discern exactly how the sorting process takes place. We need only know that the output is indeed sorted. At a later stage, when the details of the sorting module are decided upon, then we can rack our brains about the most suitable sorting algorithm.

The complexity of most software problems makes applying abstraction a sheer necessity. In the ensuing discussion, we distinguish two types of abstraction: *procedural abstraction* and *data abstraction*.

The notion of procedural abstraction is fairly traditional. A programming language offers if-constructs, loop-constructs, assignment statements, and the like. The transition from a problem to be solved to these primitive language constructs is a large one in many cases. To this end a problem is first decomposed into subproblems, each of which is handled in turn. These subproblems correspond to major tasks to be accomplished. They can be recognized by their description in which some verb plays a central role (for example: *read* the input, *sort* all shifts, *process* the next user request, *compute* the net salary). If needed, subproblems are further decomposed into even simpler subproblems. Eventually we get at subproblems for which a standard solution is available. This type of (top-down) decomposition is the essence of the main-program-with-subroutines architectural style. It is clearly recognizable in the decomposition discussed in section 10.1.1.

The result of this type of stepwise decomposition is a hierarchical structure. The top node of the structure denotes the problem to be solved. The next level shows its first decomposition into subproblems. The leaves denote primitive problems. This is schematically depicted in figure 11.1.

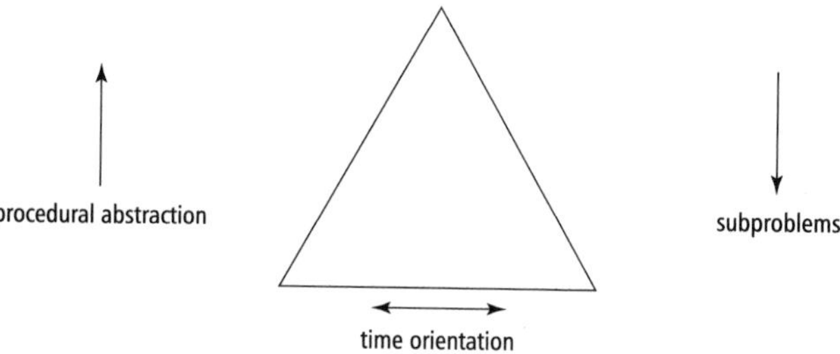

Figure 11.1 The idea of procedural abstraction

The procedure concept offers us a notation for the subproblems that result from this decomposition process. The application of this concept is known as procedural abstraction. With procedural abstraction, the name of a procedure is used to denote the corresponding sequence of actions. When that name is used in a program, we need not bother ourselves about the exact way in which its effect is realized. The important thing is that, after the call, certain prestated requirements are fulfilled.

This way of going about the process closely matches the way in which humans are inclined to solve problems. Humans too are inclined to the stepwise handling of problems. Procedural abstraction thus offers an important means of tackling software problems.

When designing software, we are inclined to decompose the problem so that the result has a strong time orientation. A problem is decomposed into subproblems that follow each other in time. In its simplest form, this approach results in input–process–output schemes: a program first has to read and store its data, next some process computes the required output from these data, and the result finally is output. As we noticed, application of this technique may result in programs that are difficult to adapt and hard to comprehend. Applying data abstraction results in a decomposition which shows this affliction to a far lesser degree.

Procedural abstraction is aimed at finding a hierarchy in the program's control structure: which steps have to be executed and in which order. Data abstraction is aimed at finding a hierarchy in the program's data. Programming languages offer primitive data structures for integers, real numbers, truth values, characters and possibly a few more. Using these building blocks we may construct more complicated data structures, such as stacks and binary trees. Such structures are of general use in application software. They occur at a fairly low level in the hierarchy of data structures. Application-oriented objects, such as 'paragraph' in text processing software or 'shift' in our KWIC-index example, are found at higher levels of the data structure hierarchy. This is schematically depicted in figure 11.2.

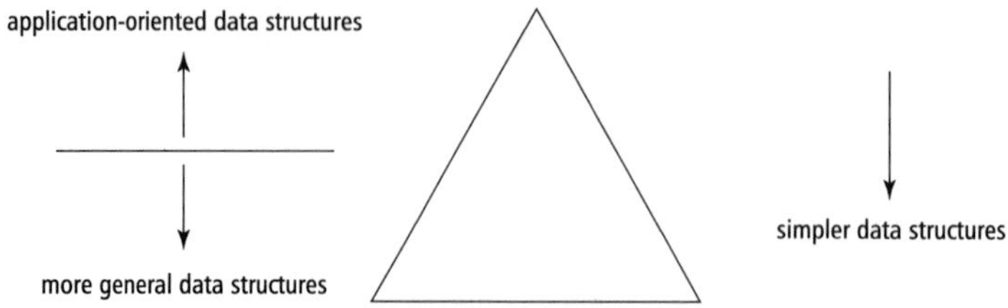

Figure 11.2 The idea of data abstraction

For the data, too, we wish to abstract from details that are not relevant at a certain level. In fact, we already do so when using the primitive data structures offered by our programming language. In using these, we abstract from details such as the internal representation of numbers and the way in which the addition of two numbers is realized. At the programming language level we may view the integers as a set of objects ($0, 1, -1, 2, -2, \ldots$) and a set of operations on these objects ($+, -, \times, /, \ldots$). These two sets together determine the data type integer. To be able to use this data type we need only name the set of objects and specify its operations.

We may proceed along the same lines for the data structures not directly supported by the programming language. A data type binary-tree is characterized by a set of objects (all conceivable binary trees) and a set of operations on those objects. When using binary trees, their representation and the implementation of the corresponding operations need not concern us. We need only ascertain the intended effect of the operations.

This technique was applied in section 10.1.2. Within the module Store, we have lines. The user of that module does not know how lines are represented. The user only has a number of operations on lines (Lines, Words, and the like) at his disposal.

Applying data abstraction during design is sometimes called **object-oriented design**, since the type of object and the associated operations are encapsulated in one module. The buzzword 'object-oriented' however also has a subtly different meaning. We will further elaborate upon this notion in chapter 12.

Languages such as Ada, Modula-2 and C++ offer a language construct (called **package**, **module**, and **struct**, respectively) that allows us to maintain a syntactic separation between the implementation and specification of data types. Note that it is also possible to apply data abstraction during design when the ultimate language does not offer the concept. However, it then becomes more cumbersome to move from design to code.

We noticed before that procedural abstraction fits in nicely with the way humans tend to tackle problems. To most people, data abstraction is a bit more complicated.

When searching for a solution to a software problem we will find that the solution needs certain data structures. At some point we will also have to choose a representation for these data structures. Rather than making those decisions at an early stage and imposing the result on all other components, you are better off if you create a separate subproblem and make only the procedural, implementation-independent, interfaces public. Data abstraction thus is a prime example of information hiding.

The development of these abstraction techniques went hand-in-hand with other developments, particularly those in the realm of programming languages. Procedures were originally introduced to avoid the repetition of instruction sequences. At a later stage we viewed the name of a procedure as an abstraction of the corresponding instruction sequence. Only then did the notion of procedural abstraction get its present connotation. In a similar vein, developments in the field of formal data type specifications and language notions for modules (starting with the **class** concept of SIMULA-67) strongly contributed to our present notion of data abstraction.

As a final note we remark that we may identify yet a third type of abstraction, **control abstraction**. In control abstraction we abstract from the precise order in which a sequence of events is to be handled. Though control abstraction is often implicit when procedural abstraction is used, it is sometimes convenient to be able to explicitly model this type of nondeterminacy, for instance when specifying concurrent systems. This topic falls outside the scope of this book.

11.1.2 Modularity

During design, the system is decomposed into a number of modules and the relationships between those modules are indicated. In another design of the same system, different modules may show up and there may be different relationships between the modules. We may try to compare those designs by considering both a typology for the individual modules and the type of connections between them. This leads us to two structural design criteria: **cohesion** and **coupling**.

Cohesion may be viewed as the glue that keeps the module together. It is a measure of the mutual affinity of the components of a module. In general we will wish to make the cohesion as strong as possible. In their classic text on *Structured Design*, Yourdon and Constantine identify the following seven levels of cohesion of increasing strength:

- **Coincidental cohesion** With coincidental cohesion, components are grouped into modules in a haphazard way. There is no significant relation between the components.

- **Logical cohesion** With logical cohesion, the components realize tasks that are logically related. One example is a module that contains all input routines.

These routines do not call one another and they do not pass information to each other. Their function is just very similar.

- **Temporal cohesion** A typical example of this type of cohesion is an initialization module. The various components of it are independent but they are activated at about the same point in time.

- **Procedural cohesion** A module exhibits procedural cohesion if it consists of a number of components that have to be executed in some given order. For instance, a module may have to first read some datum, then search a table, and finally print a result.

- **Communicational cohesion** This type of cohesion occurs if the components of a module operate on the same (external) data. For instance, a module may read some data from a disk, perform certain computations on those data, and print the result.

- **Sequential cohesion** Sequential cohesion occurs if the module consists of a sequence of components where the output of one component serves as input to the next component.

- **Functional cohesion** In a module exhibiting functional cohesion all components contribute to the one single function of that module. Such a module often transforms a single input datum into a single output datum. The well-known mathematical subroutines are a typical example of this. Less trivial examples are modules like 'execute the next edit command' and 'translate the program given'.

In a classic paper on structured design, Stevens *et al.* provide some simple heuristics that may be of help in establishing the degree of cohesion of a module [SMC74]. They suggest writing down a sentence that describes the function (purpose) of the module and examining that sentence. Properties to look for include the following:

- If the sentence is compound, has a connective (such as a comma or the word 'and'), or contains more than one verb, then that module is probably performing more than one function. It is likely to have sequential or communicational cohesion.

- If the sentence contains words that relate to time (such as 'first', 'next', 'after', 'then'), then the module probably has sequential or temporal cohesion.

- If the sentence contains words like 'initialize', the module probably has temporal cohesion.

The levels of cohesion identified above reflect the cohesion between the *functions* that a module provides. Abstract data types cannot easily be accommodated in this scheme. Macro and Buxton therefore propose adding an extra level, **data cohesion**, to identify modules that encapsulate an abstract data type [MB87]. Data cohesion is even stronger than functional cohesion.

It goes without saying that it is not always an easy task to obtain the strongest possible cohesion between the components of a module. Though functional cohesion may be attainable at the top levels and data cohesion at the bottom levels, we will often have to settle for less at the intermediate levels of the module hierarchy. The trade-offs to be made here are what makes design such a difficult, and yet challenging, activity.

The second structural criterion is **coupling**. Coupling is a measure of the strength of the intermodule connections. A high degree of coupling indicates a strong dependence between modules. A high degree of coupling between modules means that we can only fully comprehend this set of modules as a whole and may result in ripple effects when a module has to be changed, because such a change is likely to incur changes in the dependent modules as well. Loosely-coupled modules, on the other hand, are relatively independent and are easier to comprehend and adapt. Loose coupling therefore is a desirable feature of a design (and its subsequent realization). The following types of coupling can be identified (from tightest to loosest):

- **Content coupling** With content coupling, one module directly affects the working of another module. Content coupling occurs when a module changes another module's data or when control is passed from one module to the middle of another (as in a jump). This type of coupling can, and should, always be avoided.

- **Common coupling** With common coupling, two modules have shared data. The name originates from the use of COMMON blocks in FORTRAN. Its equivalent in block-structured languages is the use of global variables.

- **External coupling** With external coupling, modules communicate through an external medium, such as a file.

- **Control coupling** With control coupling, one module directs the execution of another module by passing the necessary control information. This is usually accomplished by means of flags that are set by one module and reacted upon by the dependent module.

- **Stamp coupling** Stamp coupling occurs when complete data structures are passed from one module to another. With stamp coupling, the precise format of the data structures is a common property of those modules.

- **Data coupling** With data coupling, only simple data is passed between modules.

The various types of coupling emerged in the 1970s and reflect the data type concepts of programming languages in use at that time. For example, programming languages of that time had simple scalar data types such as real and integer. They allowed arrays of scalar values and records were used to store values of different types. Modules were considered data-coupled if they passed scalars or arrays. They were considered stamp-coupled if they passed record data. When two modules are control-coupled, the assumption is that the control is passed through a scalar value.

Nowadays, programming languages have much more flexible means of passing information from one module to another, and this requires a more detailed set of coupling levels. For example, modules may pass control data through records (as opposed to scalars only). Modules may allow some modules access to their data and deny it to others. As a result, there are many levels of visibility between local and global. Finally, the coupling between modules need not be commutative. When module A passes a scalar value to B and B returns a value which is used to control the further execution of A, then A is data-coupled to B, while B is control-coupled to A.

As a result, people have extended and refined the definitions of cohesion and coupling levels. There have also been efforts to objectify these notions, by expressing coupling and cohesion in numbers; see also section 11.1.4.

Coupling and cohesion are dual characteristics. If the various modules exhibit strong internal cohesion, the intermodule coupling tends to be minimal, and vice versa.

Simple interfaces – weak coupling between modules and strong cohesion between a module's components – are of crucial importance for a variety of reasons:

- Communication between programmers becomes simpler. When different people are working on one and the same system, it helps if decisions can be made locally and do not interfere with the working of other modules.

- Correctness proofs become easier to derive.

- It is less likely that changes will propagate to other modules, which reduces maintenance costs.

- The reusability of modules is increased. The fewer assumptions that are made about a component's environment, the greater the chance of fitting another environment.

- The comprehensibility of modules is increased. Humans have limited memory capacity for information processing. Simple module interfaces allow for an understanding of a component independent of the context in which it is used.

- Empirical studies show that interfaces exhibiting weak coupling and strong cohesion are less error-prone than those that do not have these properties.

11.1.3 Information Hiding

The concept of information hiding originates from the seminal paper of Parnas that was discussed in section 10.1. The principle of information hiding is that each module has a secret which it hides to other modules. Its use as a guiding principle in design is aptly illustrated in the KWIC-index example. In the second decomposition, for example, module Store hides how lines are stored and module Sort hides how and when shifts are sorted.

Design involves a sequence of decisions, such as how to represent certain information, or in which order to accomplish tasks. For each such decision we should ask ourselves which other parts of the system need to know about the decision and how it should be hidden from parts that do not need to know.

Information hiding is closely related to the notions of abstraction, cohesion, and coupling. If a module hides some design decision, the user of that module may abstract from (ignore) the outcome of that decision. Since the outcome is hidden, it cannot possibly interfere with the use of that module. If a module hides some secret, that secret does not permeate the module's boundary, thereby decreasing the coupling between that module and its environment. Information hiding increases cohesion, since the module's secret is what binds the module's constituents together. Note that, in order to maximize its cohesion, a module should hide *one* secret only.

It depends on the programming language used whether the separation of concerns obtained during the design stage will be identifiable in the ultimate code. To some extent, this is of secondary concern. The design decomposition will be reflected, if only implicitly, in the code and should be explicitly recorded (for traceability purposes) in the technical documentation. It is of great importance for the later evolution of the system. A confirmation of the impact of such techniques as information hiding on the maintainability of software can be found in [Boe83].

11.1.4 Complexity

> *Like all good inventions, readability yardsticks can cause harm in misuse. They are handy statistical tools to measure complexity in prose. They are useful to determine whether writing is gauged to its audience. But they are not formulas for writing . . . Writing remains an art governed by many principles. By no means all factors that create interest and affect clarity can be measured objectively.*
> [Gun68]

In a very general sense, the complexity of a problem refers to the amount of resources required for its solution. We may try to determine complexity in this way by measuring, say, the time needed to solve a problem. This is a so-called *external* attribute: we are not looking at the entity itself (the problem), but at how it behaves.

In the present context, complexity refers to attributes of the software that affect the effort needed to construct or change a piece of software. These are *internal* attributes: they can be measured purely in terms of the software itself. For example, we need not execute the software to determine their values.

Both these notions are very different from the complexity of the computation performed (with respect to time or memory needed). The latter is a well-established field in which many results have been obtained. This is much less true for the type of complexity in which we are interested. Software complexity in this sense is still a rather elusive notion.

Serious efforts have been made to measure software complexity in quantitative terms. The resulting metrics are intended to be used as anchor points for the decomposition of a system, to assess the quality of a design or program, to guide reengineering efforts, etc. We then measure certain attributes of a software system, such as its length, the number of if-statements, or the information flow between modules, and try to relate the numbers thus obtained to the system's complexity. The type of software attributes considered can be broadly categorized into two classes:

- **intra-modular attributes** are attributes of individual modules, and

- **inter-modular attributes** are attributes of a system viewed as a collection of modules with dependencies.

In this subsection we are dealing with intra-modular attributes. Inter-modular attributes are discussed in the next subsection. We may distinguish two classes of complexity metrics:

- **Size-based** complexity metrics. The size of a piece of software, such as the number of lines of code, is fairly easy to measure. It also gives a fair indication of the effort needed to develop that piece of software (see also chapter 7). As a consequence, it could also be used as a complexity metric.

- **Structure-based** complexity metrics. The structure of a piece of software is a good indicator of its design quality, because a program that has a complicated control structure or uses complicated data structures is likely to be difficult to comprehend and maintain, and thus more complex.

The easiest way to measure software size is to count the number of lines of code. We may then impose limits on the number of lines of code per module. In [Wei71], for instance, the ideal size of a module is said to be 30 lines of code. In a variant hereof, limits are imposed on the number of components per module. Some people claim that a module should contain at most seven components as is prescribed for SADT, for instance. This number seven can be traced back to research in psychology, which suggests that human memory is hierarchically organized with a short-term memory of about seven slots, while there is a more permanent memory of almost unlimited capacity. If there are more than seven pieces of information, they cannot all be stored in short-term memory and information gets lost.

There are serious objections to the direct use of the number of lines of code as a complexity metric. Some programmers write more verbose programs than others. We should at least normalize the counting to counteract these effects and be able to compare different pieces of software. This can be achieved by using a prettyprinter, a piece of software that reproduces programs in a given language in a uniform way.

A second objection is that this technique makes it hard to compare programs written in different languages. If the same problem is solved in different languages, the results may differ considerably in length. For example, APL is more compact than COBOL.

Finally, some lines are more complex than others. An assignment like

```
a:= b
```

looks simpler than a loop

```
while p↑.next <> nil do p:= p↑.next
```

although they each occupy one line.

Halstead's method, also known as 'software science', uses a refinement of counting lines of code. This refinement is meant to overcome the problems associated with metrics based on a direct count of lines of code.

Halstead's method uses the number of operators and operands in a piece of software. The set of operators includes the arithmetic and Boolean operators, as well as separators (such as a semicolon between adjacent instructions) and (pairs of) reserved words. The set of operands contains the variables and constants used. Halstead then defines four basic entities:

- n_1 is the number of unique (i.e. different) operators in the program;
- n_2 is the number of unique (i.e. different) operands in the program;
- N_1 is the total number of occurrences of operators;
- N_2 is the total number of occurrences of operands.

Figure 11.3 contains a simple sorting program. Table 11.1 lists the operators and operands of this program together with their frequency. Note that there is no generally agreed definition of what exactly an operator or operand is. So the numbers given have no absolute meaning. This is part of the criticism of this theory.

```
procedure sort(var x: array; n: integer);
var i, j, save: integer;
begin
    for i:= 2 to n do
        for j:= 1 to i do
            if x[i] < x[j] then
            begin save:= x[i];
                x[i]:= x[j];
                x[j]:= save
            end
end;
```

Figure 11.3 A simple sorting routine

Using the primitive entities defined above, Halstead defines a number of derived entities, such as:

- Size of the vocabulary: $n = n_1 + n_2$.

- Program length: $N = N_1 + N_2$.

- Program volume: $V = N \log_2 n$.

  This is the minimal number of bits needed to store N elements from a set of cardinality n.

- Program level: $L = V^*/V$.

  Here V^* is the most compact representation of the algorithm in question. For the example in figure 11.3 this is sort(x, n);, so $n = N = 5$, and $V^* = 5 \log_2 5$. From the formula it follows that L is at most 1. Halstead postulates that the program level increases if the number of different operands increases, while it decreases if the number of different operators or the total number of operands increases. As an approximation of L, he therefore suggests: $\hat{L} = (2/n_1)(n_2/N_2)$.

- Programming effort: $E = V/L$.

  The effort needed increases with volume and decreases as the program level increases. E represents the number of mental discriminations (decisions) to be taken while implementing the problem solution.

- Estimated programming time in seconds: $\hat{T} = E/18$.

The constant 18 is determined empirically. Halstead explains this number by referring to [Str67], which discusses the speed with which human memory processes sensory input. This speed is said to be 5–20 units per second. In Halstead's theory, the number 18 is chosen. This number is also referred to as *Stroud's number*.

Operator	Number of occurrences
procedure	1
sort()	1
var	2
:	3
array	1
;	6
integer	2
,	2
begin ... **end**	2
for ... **do**	2
if ... **then**	1
:=	5
<	1
[ ]	6
$n_1 = 14$	$N_1 = 35$

Operand	Number of occurrences
x	7
n	2
i	6
j	5
save	3
2	1
1	1
$n_2 = 7$	$N_2 = 25$

Table 11.1 Counting the number of operators and operands in the sort routine

The above entities can only be determined after the program has been written. It is, however, possible to estimate a number of these entities. When doing so, the values for n_1 and n_2 are assumed to be known. This may be the case, for instance, after the detailed design step. Halstead then estimates program length as:

$$\hat{N} = n_1 \log_2 n_1 + n_2 \log_2 n_2$$

An explanation for this formula can be given as follows. There are $n_1 2^{n_1} \times n_2 2^{n_2}$ ways to combine the n given symbols such that operators and operands alternate. However, the program is organized and organization generally gives a logarithmic reduction in the number of possibilities. Doing so yields the above formula for $\hat{N}$.

Table 11.2 lists the values for a number of entities from Halstead's theory for the example program in figure 11.3.

Entity	Value
Size vocabulary	21
Program length	60
Estimated program length	73
Program volume	264
Level of abstraction	0.044
Estimated level of abstraction	0.040
Programming effort	6000
Estimated programming time	333s

Table 11.2 Values for 'software science' entities for the example program in figure 11.3

A number of empirical studies have addressed the predictive value of Halstead's formulae. These studies often give positive evidence of the validity of the theory.

The theory has also been heavily criticized. The underpinning of Halstead's formulas is not convincing. Results from cognitive psychology, like Stroud's number, are badly used, which weakens the theoretical foundation. Halstead concentrates on the coding phase and assumes that programmers are 100% devoted to a programming task for an uninterrupted period of time. Practice is likely to be quite different. Different people use quite different definitions of the notions of operator and operand, which may lead to widely different outcomes for the values of entities.

Yet, Halstead's work has been very influential. It was the first major body of work to point out the potential of software metrics for software development.

The second class of intra-modular complexity metrics concerns metrics based on the structure of the software. If we try to derive a complexity metric from the structure of a piece of software, we may focus on the control structure, the data structures, or a combination of these.

If we base the complexity metric on the use of data structures, we may for instance do so by considering the number of instructions between successive references to one and the same object. If this number is large, information about these variables must be retained for a long period of time when we try to comprehend that program text. Following this line of thought, complexity can be related to the average number of variables for which information must be kept by the reader.

The best-known complexity metric from the class of structure-based complexity metrics is McCabe's *cyclomatic complexity*. McCabe bases his complexity metric on a (directed) graph depicting the control flow of the program. He assumes that the graph of a single procedure or single main program has a unique start and end node, that each node is reachable from the start node, and that the end node can be reached from each node. In that case, the graph is connected. If the program consists of a main program and one or more procedures, then the control graph has a number of connected components, one for the main program and one for each of its procedures.

The cyclomatic complexity CV equals the number of predicates (decisions) plus 1 in the program that corresponds to this control graph. Its formula reads

$$CV = e - n + p + 1$$

where e, n and p denote the number of edges, nodes, and connected components in the control graph, respectively.

Figure 11.4 shows the control flow graph of the example program from figure 11.3. The numbers inside the nodes correspond to the line numbers from figure 11.3. The cyclomatic complexity of this graph is 13−11+1+1=4. The decisions in the program from figure 11.3 occur in lines 4, 5 and 6. In both for-loops the decision is to either exit the loop or iterate it. In the if-statement, the choice is between the then-part and the else-part.

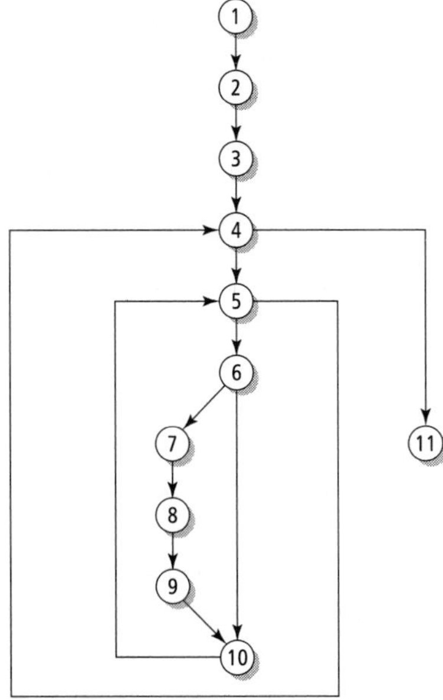

Figure 11.4 Control flow graph of the example program from figure 11.3

McCabe suggests imposing an upper limit of ten for the cyclomatic complexity of a program component. McCabe's complexity metric is also applied to testing. One criterion used during testing is to get a good coverage of the possible paths through the program. Applying McCabe's cyclomatic complexity leads to a structured testing strategy involving the execution of all linearly-independent paths (see also chapter 13).[2]

Complexity metrics like those of Halstead, McCabe and many others, all measure attributes which are in some sense related to the size of the task to be accomplished, be it the time in man-months, the number of lines of code, or something else. As such they may serve various purposes: determining the optimal size of a module, estimating the number of errors in a module, or estimating the cost of a piece of software.

All known complexity metrics suffer from some serious shortcomings, though:

- They are not very context-sensitive. For example, any program with five if-statements has the same cyclomatic complexity. Yet we may expect that different organizations of those if-statements (consecutive versus deeply nested, say) have their effect on the perceived complexity of those programs. In terms of measurement theory, this means that cyclomatic complexity does not fulfill the 'representation condition', which says that the empirical relations should be preserved in the numerical relation system. If we empirically observe that program A is more complex than program B, then any complexity metric F should be such that $F_A > F_B$.

- They measure only a few facets. Halstead's method does not take into account the control flow complexity, for instance.

We may formulate these shortcomings as follows: complexity metrics tell us something about the complexity of a program (i.e. a higher value of the metric is likely to induce a higher complexity), but a more complex program does not necessarily result in a higher value for a complexity metric. Complexity is made up of many specific attributes. It is unlikely that there will ever be one 'general' complexity metric.

We should thus be very careful in the use of these complexity metrics. Since they seem to measure along different dimensions of what is perceived as complexity, the use of multiple metrics is likely to yield better insights. But even then the results must be interpreted with care. [RAC90], for instance, evaluated various complexity metrics for a few systems, including the MINIX operating system. Of the 277 modules in MINIX, 34 have a cyclomatic complexity greater than ten. The highest value (58) was observed for a module that handles a number of ASCII escape character sequences from the keyboard. This module, and most others with a large cyclomatic

[2]The number of linearly-independent paths is related to the so-called cyclomatic number of a graph, which is why this is called the 'cyclomatic complexity'.

complexity, was considered 'justifiably complex'. An attempt to reduce the complexity by splitting those modules would increase the difficulty of understanding them while artificially reducing its complexity value. Complexity yardsticks too can cause harm in misuse.

Finally, we may note that various validations of both software science and cyclomatic complexity indicate that they are not substantially better indicators of coding effort, maintainability, or reliability than the length of a program (number of lines of code). The latter is much easier to determine, though.

The high correlation that is often observed between a size-related complexity metric and a control-related complexity metric such as McCabe's cyclomatic complexity should not come as a surprise. Large programs tend to have more if-statements than small programs. What counts, however, is the *density* with which those if-statements occur. This suggests a complexity metric of the form CV/LOC rather than CV.

11.1.5 System Structure

We may depict the outcome of the design process, a set of modules and their mutual dependencies, in a graph. The nodes of this graph correspond to modules and the edges denote relations between modules. We may think of many types of intermodule relations, such as:

- module A contains module B;
- module A follows module B;
- module A delivers data to module B;
- module A uses module B.

The type of dependencies we are interested in are those that determine the complexity of the relations between modules. The amount of knowledge that modules have of each other should be kept to a minimum. To be able to assess this, it is important to know, for each module, which other modules it *uses*, since that tells us which knowledge of each other they (potentially) use. In a proper design the information flow between modules is restricted to flow that comes about through procedure calls. The graph depicting the uses-relation is therefore often termed a **call graph**.

The call graph may have different shapes. In its most general form it is a directed graph (figure 11.5a).[3] If the graph is acyclic, i.e. it does not contain a path of

[3]We assume that the graph is connected, i.e. that there is a path between each pair of nodes if we ignore the direction of the arrows that link nodes. This assumption is reasonable, since

the form $M_1, M_2, \dots, M_n, M_1$, the uses-relation forms a hierarchy. We may then decompose the graph into a number of distinct layers such that a module at one layer uses only modules from lower layers (figure 11.5b). Going one step further, we get a scheme like the one in figure 11.5c, where modules from level i use only modules from level $i + 1$. Finally, if each module is used by only one other module, the graph reduces to a tree (figure 11.5d).

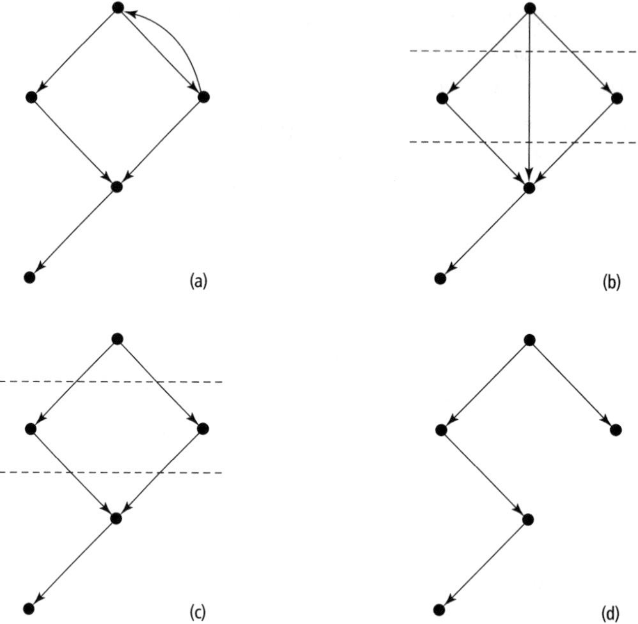

Figure 11.5 Module hierarchies. (a) directed graph, (b) directed acyclic graph, (c) layered graph, (d) tree

There are various aspects of the call graph that can be measured. Directly measurable attributes that relate to the 'shape' of the call graph include:

- its *size*, measured in terms of the number of nodes, the number of edges, or the sum of these;

- its *depth*, the length of the longest path from the root to some leaf node (in an acyclic directed graph);

otherwise the graph can be split into two or more disjoint graphs between which there is no information flow. These disjoint graphs then correspond to independent programs.

- its *width*, the maximum number of nodes at some level (in an acyclic directed graph).

We do not know of studies that try to quantitatively relate those measures to other complexity-related aspects such as debugging time, maintainability, etc. They may be used, though, as one of the parameters in a qualitative assessment of a design.

It is often stated that a good design should have a tree-like call graph. It is therefore worthwhile to consider the **tree impurity** of a call graph, i.e. the extent to which the graph deviates from a pure tree. Suppose we start with a connected (undirected) graph (like the ones in figure 11.5b-d, if we ignore the direction of the arrows). If the graph is not a tree, it has at least one cycle, i.e. a path from some node A via one or more other nodes back to A again. We may then remove one of the edges from this cycle, and the result will still be a connected graph. We may continue removing edges from cycles until the result is a tree. We did so in the transition from figure 11.5b to 11.5c to 11.5d. The final result is called the graph's **spanning tree**. The number of edges removed in this process is an indication of the graph's tree impurity.

In order to obtain a proper measure of tree impurity we proceed as follows. The complete graph K_n is the graph with n nodes and the maximum number of edges. This maximum number of edges is $n(n-1)/2$. A tree with n nodes has $(n-1)$ edges. Given a connected graph G with n nodes and e edges, we define its tree impurity $m(G)$ as the number of extra edges divided by the maximum number of extra edges:

$$m(G) = 2(e - n + 1)/(n - 1)(n - 2)$$

This measure of tree impurity fits our intuitive notion of that concept. The value of $m(G)$ lies between 0 and 1. It is 0 if G is a tree and 1 if it is a complete graph. If we add an edge to G, the value of $m(G)$ increases. Moreover, the 'penalty' of extra edges is proportional to the size of the spanning tree.

It is not always easy, or even meaningful, to strive for a neat hierarchical decomposition. We will often have to settle for a compromise. It may for instance be appropriate to decompose a system into a number of clusters, each of which contains a number of modules. The clusters may then be organized hierarchically, while the modules within a given cluster show a more complicated interaction pattern. Also, tree-like call graphs do not allow for reuse (if a module is reused within the same program, its node in the call graph has at least two ancestors).

The call graph allows us to assess the *structure* of a design. In deriving the measures above, each edge in the call graph is treated alike. Yet, the complexity of the information flow that is represented by the edges is likely to vary. As noted in the earlier discussion on coupling, we would like the intermodule connections to be 'thin'. Therefore, we would like a measure which does not merely count the edges, but which also considers the amount of information that flows through them.

The best known attempt to measure the total level of information flow between the modules of a system is due to Henry and Kafura [HK81]. Their measures were able to identify change-prone UNIX procedures and evaluate potential design changes. Shepperd studied the information flow measure extensively and proposed several refinements, thus obtaining a 'purer' metric [She90]. Using Shepperd's definitions, the information flow measure is based on the following notions of local and global data flow:

- A **local flow** from module A to module B exists if
  (a) A invokes B and passes it a parameter, or
  (b) B invokes A and A returns a value.
- A **global flow** from module A to module B exists if A updates some global data structure and B retrieves from that structure.

Using these notions of local and global data flow, Shepperd defines the 'complexity' of a module M as

$$complexity(M) = (\textit{fan-in}(M) \times \textit{fan-out}(M))^2$$

where

- *fan-in*(M) is the number of (local and global) flows whose sink is M, and
- *fan-out*(M) is the number of (local and global) flows whose source is M.

A weak point of the information flow metric is that all flows have equal weight. Passing one simple integer as parameter and invoking a complex global data structure contribute equally to this measure of complexity. The abstract data type architectural style easily results in modules with a high fan-in and fan-out. If the same system is built using global data structures, its information flow metric is likely to have a smaller value. Yet, the information flow both to and from the modules in the abstract data type style generally concern simple scalar values only, and are therefore considered simpler.

In a more qualitative sense, the information flow metric may indicate spots in the design that deserve our attention. If some module has a high fan-in, this may indicate that the module has little cohesion. Also, if we consider the information flow per level in a layered architecture, an excessive increase from one level to the next might indicate a missing level of abstraction.

During design, we (pre)tend to follow a top-down decomposition strategy. We may also take a completely different stand and try to *compose* a hierarchical system structure from a flat collection of system elements. Elements that are in some sense 'closest' to one another are grouped together. We then have to define some measure for the distance between elements and a mathematical technique known as cluster analysis can be used to do the actual grouping. Elements in the same group are more like other elements within the same group and less like elements in other groups. If the measure is based on the number of data types that elements have in common, this clustering results in abstract data types or, more generally, modules having high cohesion. If the measure is based on the number of data bindings between elements, the result is likely to have a low value for the information-flow metric.

The measure chosen, in a sense, determines how we define 'friendship' between elements. Close friends should be grouped in the same module while distant relatives may reside in different modules. The various qualitative and quantitative design criteria that we discussed above have different, but in essence very similar, definitions of friendship.

Though much work remains to be done, a judicious use of available design metrics is already a valuable tool in the design and quality assurance of software systems.

11.2 DESIGN METHODS

Having discussed the properties of a good system decomposition, we now come to a question which is at least as important: how do you get a good decomposition to start with?

There exist a vast number of design methods, a sample of which is given in table 11.3. These design methods generally consist of a set of guidelines, heuristics, and procedures on how to go about designing a system. They also offer a notation to express the result of the design process. Together these provide a *systematic* means for organizing and structuring the design process and its products.

For some methods, such as FSM or Petri nets, emphasis is on the notation, while the guidelines on how to tackle design are not very well developed. Methods like JSD, on the other hand, offer extensive prescriptive guidelines as well. Most notations are graphical and somewhat informal, but OBJ and Meta IV use a very formal mathematical language. Some methods concentrate on the design stage proper, while others are part of a wider methodology covering other life cycle phases as well. Examples of the latter are SSADM and JSD. Finally, some methods offer features that make them especially useful for the design of certain types of application, such as SA/WM (real-time systems) or Petri nets (concurrent systems).

In the following subsections we discuss three design methods often used:

- Functional decomposition, which is a rather general approach to system design. It is not tied to any specific method listed in table 11.3. Many different notations can be used to depict the resulting design, ranging from flowcharts or pseudocode to algebraic specifications.

- Data flow design, as exemplified by SA/SD.
- Design based on data structures, as is done in JSP, LCP and JSD.

Name	Description
Decision tables	Matrix representation of complex decision logic at the detailed design level.
E–R	Entity–Relationship Model. Family of graphical techniques for expressing data-relationships; see also chapter 9.
Flowcharts	Simple diagram technique to show control flow at the detailed design level. Exists in many flavors; see [Tri88] for an overview.
FSM	Finite State Machine. A way to describe a system as a set of states and possible transitions between those states; the resulting diagrams are called state transition diagrams; see also chapter 9.
JSD	Jackson System Development; see section 11.2.3. Successor to, and more elaborate than, JSP; has an object-oriented flavor.
JSP	Jackson Structured Programming. Data-structure-oriented method; see section 11.2.3.
LCP	Logical Construction of Programs, also known as the Warnier–Orr method; data-structure-oriented, similar to JSP.
Meta IV	Model-oriented specification language of VDM; highly mathematical [BJ82]; see chapter 15.
NoteCards	Example hypertext system. Hypertext systems make it possible to create and navigate through a complex organization of unstructured pieces of text [Con87].
OBJ	Algebraic specification method; highly mathematical [Gog86].
OOD	Object-oriented design; exists in many flavors; see chapter 12.
PDL	Program Design Language; example of a constrained natural language ('structured English') to describe designs at various levels of abstraction. Offers the control constructs generally found in programming languages. See [PK89] for an overview.

Table 11.3: cont'd overleaf

Name	Description
Petri nets	Graphical design representation, well-suited for concurrent systems. A system is described as a set of states and possible transitions between those states. States are associated with tokens and transitions are described by firing rules. In this way, concurrent activities can be synchronized [Pet81].
SA/SD	Structured Analysis/Structured Design. Data flow design technique; see also section 11.2.2.
SA/WM	Ward-Mellor extension to Structured Analysis so that real-time aspects can be described [WM85].
SADT	Structured Analysis and Design Technique. Graphical language emphasizing hierarchical relations; see also section 9.3.3.
SSADM	Structured Systems Analysis and Design Method. A highly prescriptive method for performing the analysis and design stages; UK standard [DCC92].
Statecharts	State transition diagrams, with extensions to allow for the expression of concurrency and different levels of abstraction [Har88].

Table 11.3: A sample of design methods

A fourth design method, object-oriented design, is discussed in chapter 12. Whereas the above three methods concentrate on identifying the *functions* of the system, object-oriented design focuses on the *data* on which the system is to operate. Object-oriented design has become very popular of late.

11.2.1 Functional Decomposition

In a functional decomposition the intended function is decomposed into a number of subfunctions that each solve part of the problem. These subfunctions themselves may be further decomposed into yet more primitive functions, and so on. Functional decomposition is a design philosophy rather than a design method. It denotes an overall approach to problem decomposition which underlies many a design method.

With functional decomposition we apply **divide-and-conquer** tactics. These tactics are analogous to, but not the same as, the technique of **stepwise refinement** as it is applied in programming-in-the-small. Using stepwise refinement, the refinements tend to be context-dependent. As an example, consider the following pseudo-code algorithm to insert an element into a sorted list:

```
procedure insert(a, n, x);
begin insert x at the end of the list;
    k:= n + 1;
    while element_k is not at its proper place
    do swap element_k and element_k − 1;
        k:= k-1
    enddo;
end insert;
```

The refinement of a pseudo-code instruction like element$_k$ is not at its proper place is done within the context of exactly the above routine, using knowledge of other parts of this routine. In the decomposition of a large system, it is precisely this type of dependency that we try to avoid. The previous section addressed this issue at great length.

During requirements engineering the base machine has been decided upon. This base machine need not be a 'real' machine. It can be a programming language or some other set of primitives that constitutes the bottom layer of the design. During this phase too, the functions to be provided to the user have been fixed. These are the two ends of a rope. During the design phase we try to get from one end of this rope to the other. If we start from the user function end and take successively more detailed design decisions, the process is called top-down design. The reverse is called bottom-up design.

Top-down design Starting from the main user functions at the top, we work down decomposing functions into subfunctions. Assuming we do not make any mistakes on the way down, we can be sure to construct the specified system. With top-down design, each step is characterized by the design decisions it embodies. To be able to apply a pure top-down technique, the system has to be fully described. This is hardly ever the case.

Bottom-up design Using bottom-up design, we start from a set of available base functions. From there we proceed towards the requirements specification through abstraction. This technique is potentially more flexible, especially since the lower layers of the design could be independent of the application and thus have wider applicability. This is especially important if the requirements have not been formulated very precisely yet, or if a family of systems has to be developed. A real danger of the bottom-up technique is that we may miss the target.

In its pure form, neither the top-down nor the bottom-up technique is likely to be used all that often. Both techniques are feasible only if the design process is a pure and rational one. And this is an idealization of reality. There are many reasons why the design process cannot be rational. Some of these have to do with the intangibles of design processes per se, some originate from accidents that happen to befall many a software project. Parnas lists the following reasons, amongst others [PC87]:

- Mostly, users do not know exactly what they want and they are not able to tell all they know.
- Even if the requirements are fully known, a lot of additional information is needed. This information is discovered only when the project is under way.
- Almost all projects are subject to change. Changes influence earlier decisions.
- People make errors.
- During design, people use the knowledge they already have, experiences from earlier projects, and the like.
- In many projects we do not start from scratch, but we build from existing software.

Design exhibits a 'yo-yo' character: something is devised, tried, rejected again, new ideas crop up, etc. Designers frequently go about in rather opportunistic ways. They frequently switch from high-level application domain issues to coding and detailed design matters, and use a variety of means to gather insight into the problem to be solved. At most, we may present the result of the design process as if it came about through a rational process.

A general problem with any form of functional decomposition is that it is often not immediately clear along which dimension the system is decomposed. If we decompose along the time-axis, the result is often a main program that controls the order in which a number of subordinate modules is called. In Yourdon's classification, the resulting cohesion type is temporal. If we decompose with respect to the grouping of data, we obtain the type of data cohesion exhibited in abstract data types. Both these functional decompositions can be viewed as an instance of some architectural style. Rather than worrying about which dimension to focus on during functional decomposition, you had better opt for a particular architectural style and let that style guide the decomposition.

At some intermediate level, the set of interrelated components comprises the software architecture as discussed in chapter 10. This software architecture is a product which serves various purposes: it can be used to discuss the design with different stakeholders; it can be used to evaluate the quality of the design; it can be the basis for the work breakdown structure; it can be used to guide the testing process, etc. If a software architecture is required, it necessitates a design approach in which, at quite an early stage, each and every component and connection is present. A bottom-up or top-down approach does not meet this requirement, since in both these approaches only part of the solution is available at intermediate points in time.

Parnas offers the following useful guidelines for a sound functional decomposition [Par78]:

1. Try to identify subsystems. Start with a *minimal* subset and define minimal extensions to this subset.

   The idea behind this guideline is that it is extremely difficult, if not impossible, to get a complete picture of the system during requirements engineering. People ask too much or they ask the wrong things. Starting from a minimal subsystem, we may add functionality incrementally, using the experience gained with the actual use of the system. The idea is very similar to that of incremental development, discussed in chapter 3.

2. Apply the information hiding principle.

3. Try to define extensions to the base machine step by step. This holds for both the minimal machine and its extensions. Such incremental extensions lead to the concept of a **virtual machine**. Each layer in the system hierarchy can be viewed as a machine. The primitive operations of this machine are implemented by the lower layers of the hierarchy. This machine view of the module hierarchy nicely maps onto a layered architectural style. It also adds a further dimension to the system structuring guidelines offered in section 11.1.5.

4. Apply the uses-relation and try to place the dependencies thus obtained in a hierarchical structure.

Obviously, the above guidelines are strongly interrelated. It has been said before that a strictly hierarchical tree structure of system components is often not feasible. A compromise that often is feasible is a layered system structure as depicted in figure 11.6.

The arrows between the various nodes in the graph indicate the uses-relation. Various levels can be distinguished in the structure depicted. Components at a given level only use components from the same, or lower, levels. The layers distinguished in this picture are not the same as those induced by the acyclicity of the graph (as discussed in section 11.1.5) but are rather the result of viewing a distinct set of modules as an abstract, virtual machine. Deciding how to group modules into layers in this way involves considering the semantics of those modules. Lower levels in this hierarchy bring us closer to the 'real' machine on which the system is going to be executed. Higher levels are more application-oriented. The choice of the number of levels in such an architecture is a, problem-dependent, design decision.

This work of Parnas heralds some of the notions that were later recognized as important guiding principles in the field of software architecture. The idea of a minimal subset to which extensions are defined is very similar to the notion of a

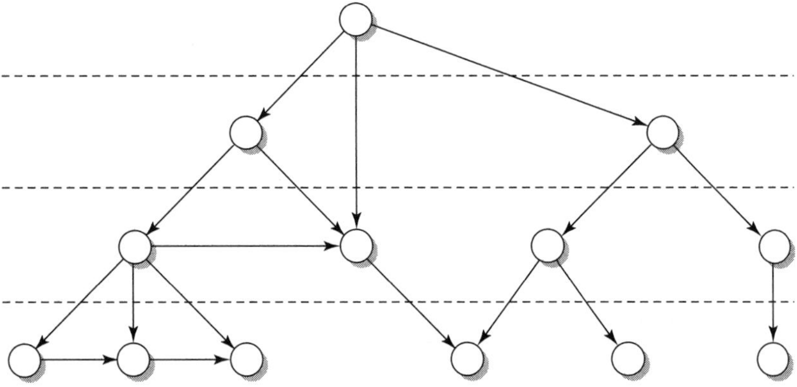

Figure 11.6 A layered system structure

product-line architecture: a basic architecture from which a family of similar systems can be derived. The layered approach is one of the basic architectural styles discussed in section 10.2.

11.2.2 Data Flow Design (SA/SD)

The data flow design method originated in the early 1970s with Yourdon and Constantine. In its simplest form, data flow design is but a functional decomposition with respect to the flow of data. A component (module) is a black box which transforms some input stream into some output stream. In data flow design, heavy use is made of graphical representations known as Data Flow Diagrams (DFD) and Structure Charts. Data flow design as we know it today is a two-step process. First, a logical design is derived in the form of a set of data flow diagrams. This step is referred to as *Structured Analysis* (SA). Next, the logical design is transformed into a program structure represented as a set of structure charts. The latter step is called *Structured Design* (SD). The combination is referred to as SA/SD.

Structured Analysis can be viewed as a proper requirements analysis method insofar it addresses the modeling of some Universe of Discourse. It should be noted that, as data flow diagrams are refined, the analyst performs an implicit (top-down) functional decomposition of the system as well. At the same time, the diagram refinements result in corresponding data refinements. The analysis process thus has design aspects as well.

Structured Design, being a strategy to map the information flow contained in data flow diagrams into a program structure, is a genuine component of the (detailed) design phase.

The main result of Structured Analysis is a series of data flow diagrams. Four types of data entity are distinguished in these diagrams:

External entities are the source or destination of a transaction. These entities are located outside the domain considered in the data flow diagram. External entities are indicated as squares.

Processes transform data. Processes are denoted by circles.

Data flows between processes, external entities and data stores. A data flow is indicated by an arrow. Data flows are paths along which data structures travel.

Data stores lie between two processes. This is indicated by the name of the data store between two parallel lines. Data stores are places where data structures are stored until needed.

We will illustrate the various process steps of SA/SD by analyzing and designing a simple library automation system. The system allows library clients to borrow and return books. It also reports to library management about how the library is used by its clients (for example, the average number of books on loan and authors much in demand).

At the highest level we draw a **context diagram**. A context diagram is a data flow diagram with one process, denoting 'the system'. Its main purpose is to depict the interaction of the system with the environment (the collection of external entities). For our simple library system this is done in figure 11.7. This diagram has yet to be supplemented by a description of the structure of both the input and output to the central process.

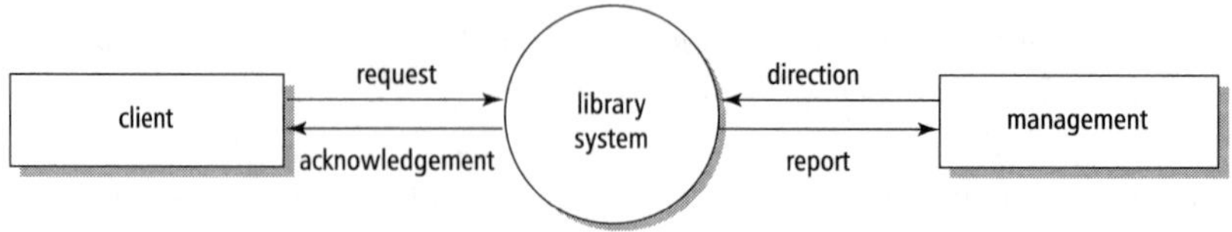

Figure 11.7 Context diagram for library automation

Next, this top-level diagram is further decomposed. For our example, this could lead to the data flow diagram of figure 11.8. In this diagram, we have expanded the central process node of the context diagram. A client request is first analyzed in a process labeled 'preliminary processing'. As a result, one of 'borrow title' or 'return

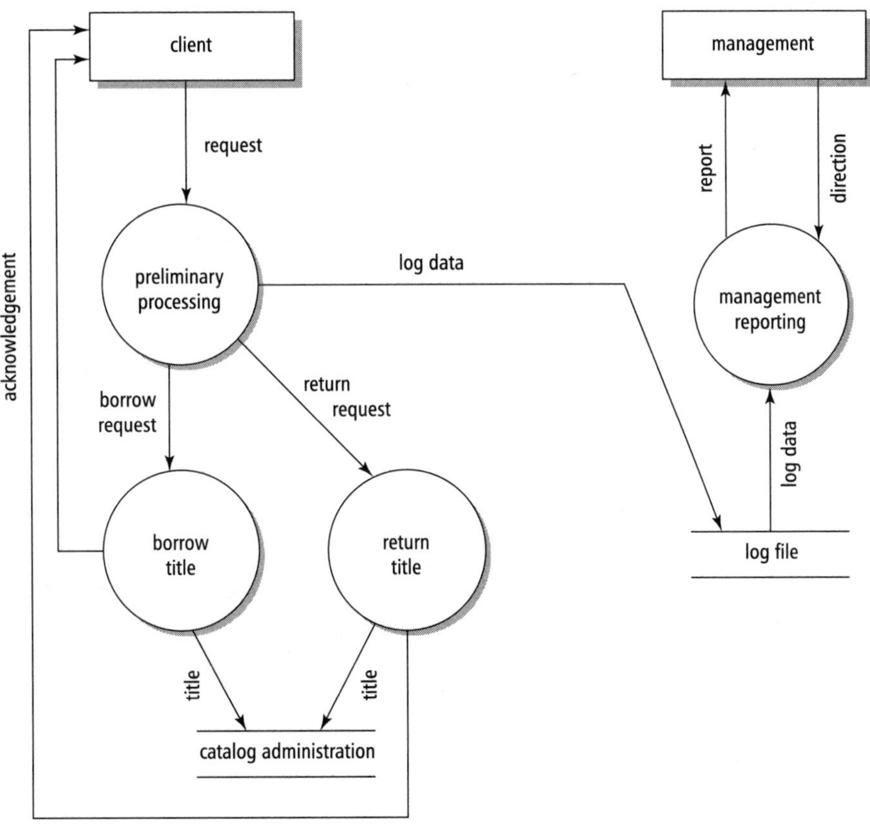

Figure 11.8 Data flow diagram for library automation

title' is activated. Both these processes update a data store labeled 'catalog administration'. Client requests are logged in a data store 'log file'. This data store is used to produce management reports.

For more complicated applications, various diagrams could be drawn, one for each subsystem identified. These subsystems in turn are further decomposed into diagrams at yet lower levels. We thus get a hierarchy of diagrams. As an example, a possible refinement of the 'preliminary processing' node is given in figure 11.9. In the lower level diagrams also, the external entities are usually omitted.

The top-down decomposition stops when a process becomes sufficiently straightforward and does not warrant further expansion. These primitive processes are described in *minispecs*. A minispec serves to communicate the algorithm of the process to relevant parties. It may use notations like structured natural language,

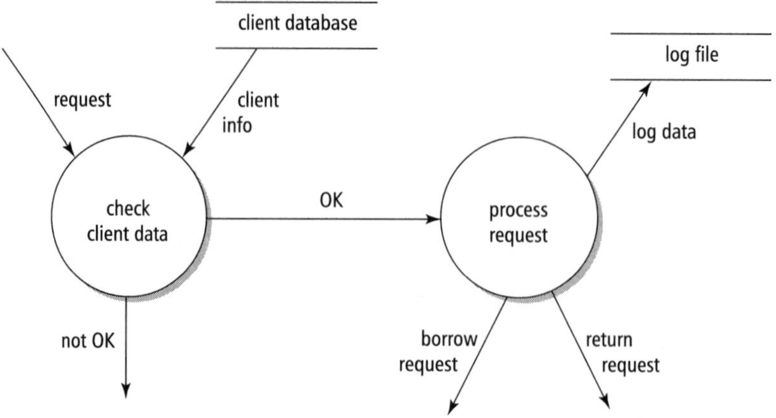

Figure 11.9 Data flow diagram for 'preliminary processing'

pseudocode, or decision tables. Example screen layouts can be added to illustrate how the input and output will look. An example minispec for the process labeled 'process request 'is given in figure 11.10.

Identification: Process request
Description:

1. Enter type of request
   1.1 If invalid, issue a warning and repeat step 1
   1.2 If step 1 has been repeated five times, terminate the transaction
2. Enter book identification
   2.1 If invalid, issue a warning and repeat step 2
   2.2 If step 2 has been repeated five times, terminate the transaction
3. Log the client identification, request type and book identification
4. ...

Figure 11.10 Example minispec for 'process request'

The contents of the data flows in a DFD are recorded in a data dictionary. Though this name suggests something grand, it is nothing more than a precise description of the structure of the data. This is often done in the form of regular expressions, like the example in figure 11.11. Nowadays, the static aspects of the data tend to be modeled in ER diagrams; see chapter 9.

The result of Structured Analysis is a logical model of the system. It consists of a set of DFDs, augmented by descriptions of its constituents in the form of minispecs,

borrow-request = client-id + book-id
return-request = client-id + book-id
log-data = client-id + [borrow | return] + book-id
book-id = author-name + title + (isbn) + [proc | series | other]

Conventions: [ ] means: include one of the enclosed options; + means: AND; () means: enclosed items are optional; options are separated by |

Figure 11.11 Example data dictionary entries

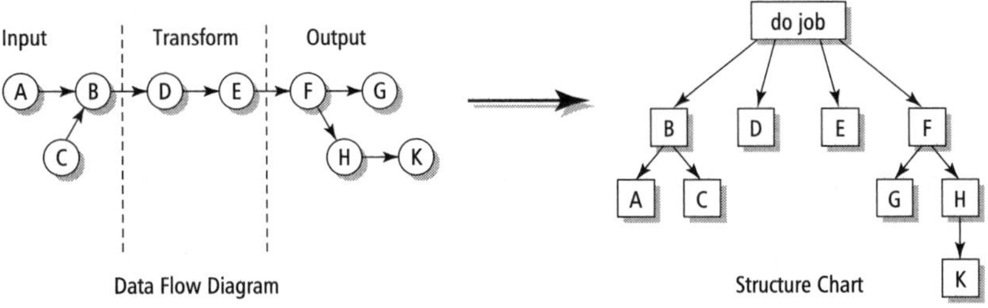

Figure 11.12 From data flow diagram to structure chart

formats of data stores, and so on. In the subsequent Structured Design step, the data flow diagrams are transformed into a collection of modules (subprograms) that call one another and pass data. The result of the Structured Design step is expressed in a hierarchical set of **structure charts**. There are no strict rules for this step. Text books on the data flow technique give guidelines, and sometimes even well-defined strategies, for how to get from a set of data flow diagrams to a hierarchical model for the implementation. These guidelines are strongly inspired by the various notions discussed in section 11.1, most notably cohesion and coupling.

The major heuristic involves the choice of the top-level structure chart. Many data-processing systems are essentially transform-centered. Input is read and possibly edited, a major transformation is done, and the result is output. One way to decide upon the central transformation is to trace the input through the data flow diagram until it can no longer be considered input. The same is done, in the other direction, for the output. The bubble in between acts as the *central transform*. If we view the bubbles in a DFD as beads, and the data flows as threads, we obtain the corresponding structure chart by picking the bead that corresponds to the central transformation and shaking the DFD.[4] The processes in the data flow diagram become the modules of the corresponding structure chart and the data flows become module calls. Note that the arrows in a structure chart denote module calls, whereas the arrows in a data flow diagram denote flows of data. These arrows often point in opposite directions; a flow of data from A to B is often realized through a call of B to A. Sometimes it is difficult to select one central transformation. In that case, a dummy root element is added and the resulting Input–Process–Output scheme is of the form depicted in figure 11.12.

Because of the transformation orientation of the structure chart, the relations between modules in the graph have a producer–consumer character. One module produces a stream of data which is then consumed by another module. The control flow is one whereby modules call subordinate modules so as to realize the required transformation. There is a potentially complex stream of information between modules, corresponding to the data flow that is passed between producer and consumer. The major contribution of Structured Design is found in the guidelines that aim to reduce the complexity of the interaction between modules. These guidelines concern the cohesion and coupling criteria discussed in section 11.1.

11.2.3 Design based on Data Structures

The best-known technique for design based on data structures originates with Michael Jackson. The technique is known as Jackson Structured Programming (JSP). Essentials of JSP have been carried over to Jackson System Development (JSD). JSP is a technique for programming-in-the-small and JSD is a technique for programming-in-the-large. We will discuss both techniques in turn.

The basic idea of JSP is that a good program reflects the structure of both the input and the output in all its facets. Given a correct model of these data structures, we may straightforwardly derive the corresponding program from the model. It is often postulated that the structure of the data is much less volatile than the transformations applied to the data. As a consequence, designs that take the data as their starting point should be 'better' too. This same argument is also used in the context of object-oriented analysis and design.

JSP distinguishes elementary and compound components. Elementary components are not further decomposed. There are three types of compound component: sequence, iteration and selection. Compound components are represented by diagrams (also called **Jackson diagrams** or **structure diagrams**) or some sort of pseudocode (called **structure text** or **schematic logic**). The base forms of both are

[4]We do the same when turning a free tree into an oriented tree. A free tree has no root. By selecting one node of the tree as the root, the parent–child relations are brought about.

given in figure 11.13. In the structure text, 'seq' denotes sequencing, 'itr' denotes iteration, 'sel' denotes selection, and 'alt' denotes alternatives.

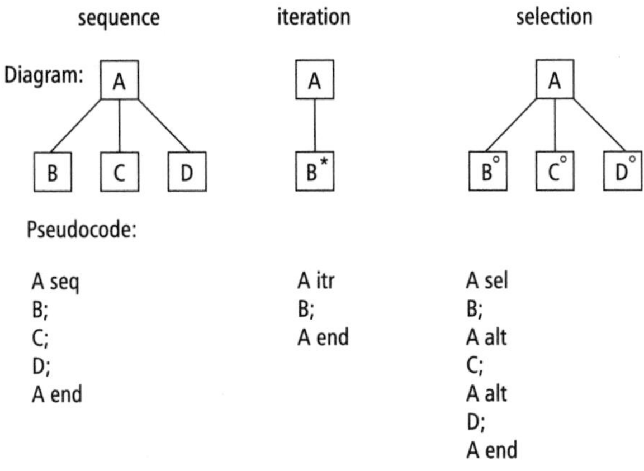

Figure 11.13 Compound components in Jackson's notation

Most modern programming languages have structures (loops, if-statements and sequential composition) for each of these diagrammatic notations or, for that matter, the corresponding pseudocode for the structure of data. The essence of Jackson's technique is that the structure diagrams of the input and output can be merged, thus yielding the global structure of the program.

To illustrate this line of thought, consider the following fragment from a library system. The system keeps track of which books from which authors are being borrowed (and returned). From this log, we want to produce a report which lists how often each title is borrowed. Using Jackson's notation, the input for this function could be as specified in figure 11.14.[5] A possible structure for the output is given in figure 11.15.

The program diagram to transform the log into a report is now obtained by merging the two diagrams; see figure 11.16. The structure of the resulting program can be derived straightforwardly from this diagram, and is of the form given in figure 11.17.

This merging of diagrams does not work for the lower levels of our problem: 'process mutation' and its subordinate nodes. The cause is something called a **structure clash**: the input and output data structures do not really match. The reason is that the input consists of a sequence of mutations. In the output, all mutations for

[5]For simplicity's sake, we have assumed that the input is already sorted by author.

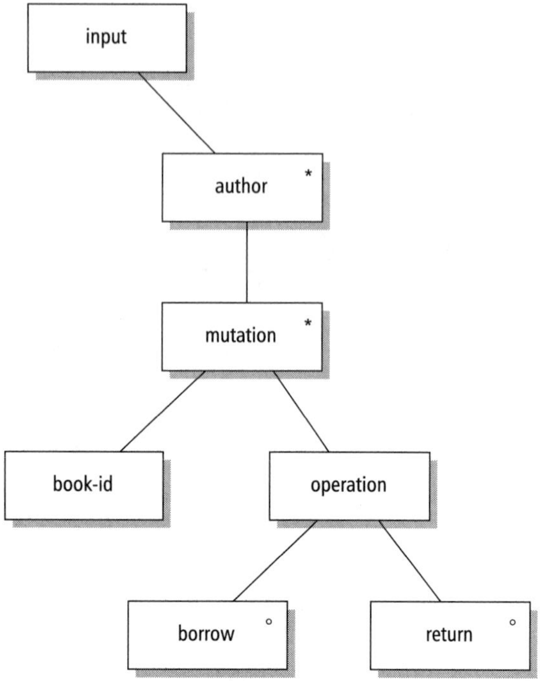

Figure 11.14 Log of books borrowed and returned, in JSP notation

one given book are taken together. So, the mutations have to be sorted first. We have to restructure the system, for instance as depicted in figure 11.18.

A clear disadvantage of the structure thus obtained is that there is now an intermediate file. Closer inspection shows that we do not really need this file. This is immediately clear if we depict the structure as in figure 11.19.

Here, we may *invert* component A1 and code it such that it serves as a replacement of component B2. Alternatively (and in this case more likely), we may invert B1 and substitute the result for component A2. In either case, the first-in-first-out type of intermediate file between the two components is removed by making one of the components a subordinate of the other.

This example shows the fundamental issues involved in the use of JSP:

1. Modeling input and output using structure diagrams,

2. Merging the diagrams to create the program structure, meanwhile

3. Resolving possible structure clashes, and finally

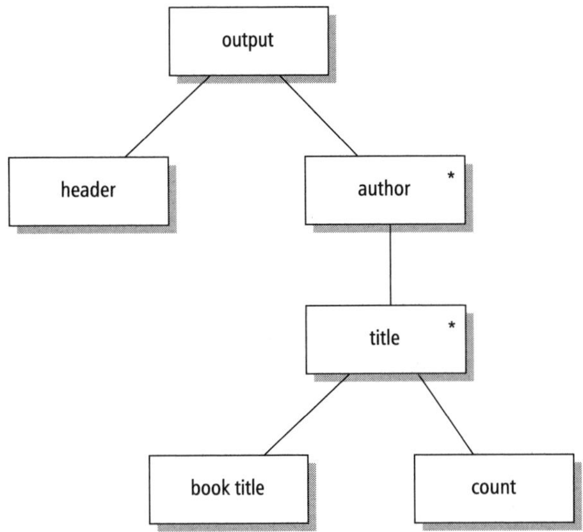

Figure 11.15 Report of books borrowed, in JSP notation

4. Optimizing the result through program inversion.

The hierarchy in the structure diagrams denotes a relation of the type 'consists of' between components of the data structures. The same type of relation occurs in the resulting modular structure of the system.

If we choose a linear notation for the structure diagrams, the result falls into the class of 'regular expressions'. Thus, the expressive power of these diagrams is that of a finite automaton. Some of the structure clashes crop up if the problem cannot be solved by a finite automaton.

Both in the functional decomposition and in the data flow design methods, the problem structure is mapped onto a functional structure. This functional structure is next mapped onto a program structure. In contrast, JSP maps the problem structure onto a data structure and the program structure is derived from this data structure. JSP is not much concerned with the question of how the mapping from problem structure to data structure is to be obtained.

Jackson System Development (JSD) tries to fill this gap. JSD distinguishes three stages in the software development process:

- A **modeling stage** in which a description is made of the real-world problem through the identification of entities and actions;

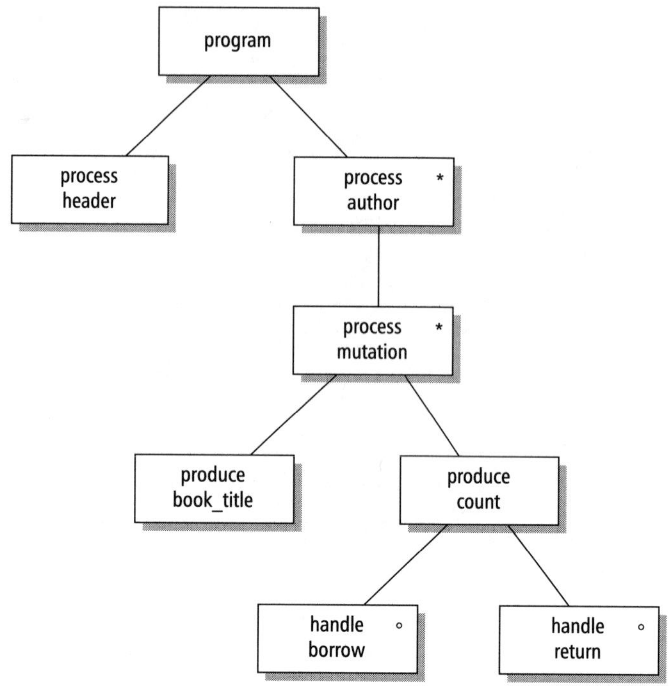

Figure 11.16 Result of merging the input and output diagrams

```
make header
until EOF loop
    process author:
        until end_of_author loop
            process_mutation:
                ...
        endloop
endloop.
```

Figure 11.17 Top-level structure of the program to produce a report

- A **network stage** in which the system is modeled as a network of communicating concurrent processes;
- An **implementation stage** in which the network of processes is transformed into a sequential design.

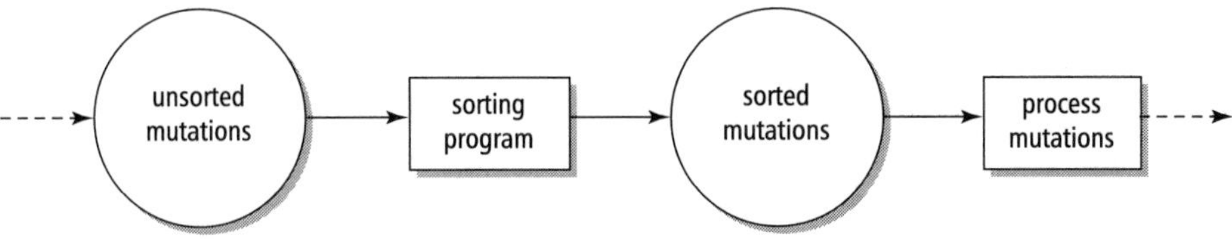

Figure 11.18 Restructuring of the system

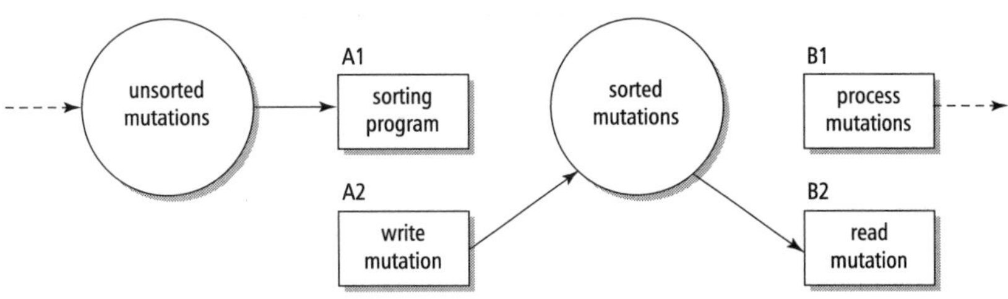

Figure 11.19 A different view of the system

The first step in JSD is to model the part of reality we are interested in, the Universe of Discourse (UoD). JSD models the UoD as a set of entities, objects in the real world that participate in a time-ordered sequence of actions. For each entity a process is created which models the life cycle of that entity. Actions are events that happen to an entity. For instance, in a library the life cycle of an entity Book could be as depicted in figure 11.20. The life cycle of a book starts when it is acquired. After that it may be borrowed and returned any number of times. The life cycle ends when the book is either archived or disposed of. The life cycle is depicted using **process structure diagrams** (PSDs). PSDs are hierarchical diagrams that resemble the structure diagrams of JSP, with its primitives to denote concatenation (ordering in time), repetition and selection. PSDs have a pseudocode equivalent called **structure text** which looks like the schematic logic of JSP.

Process structure diagrams are finite state diagrams. In traditional finite state diagrams, the bubbles (nodes) represent possible states of the entity being modeled while the arrows denote possible transitions between states. The opposite is true for PSDs. In a PSD, nodes denote state transitions and arrows denote states.

Following this line of thought, an entity Member can be described as in figure 11.21: members enter the library system, after which they may borrow and return books until they cease to be a member.

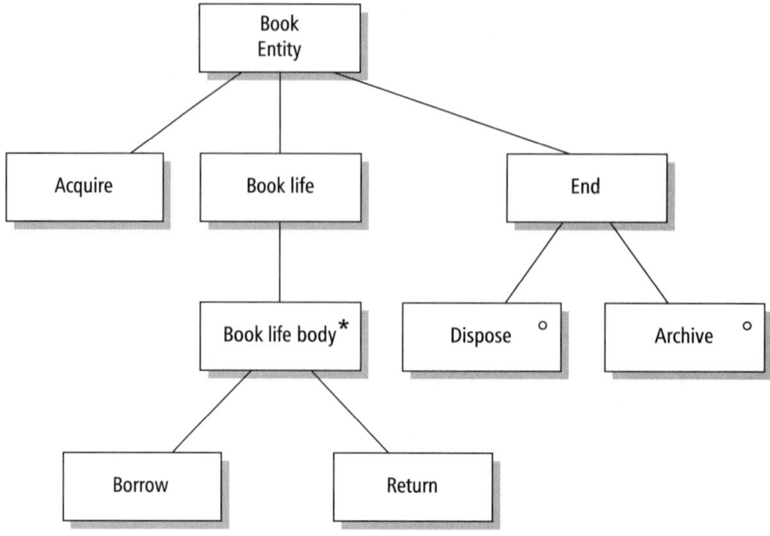

Figure 11.20 Process structure diagram for the entity Book

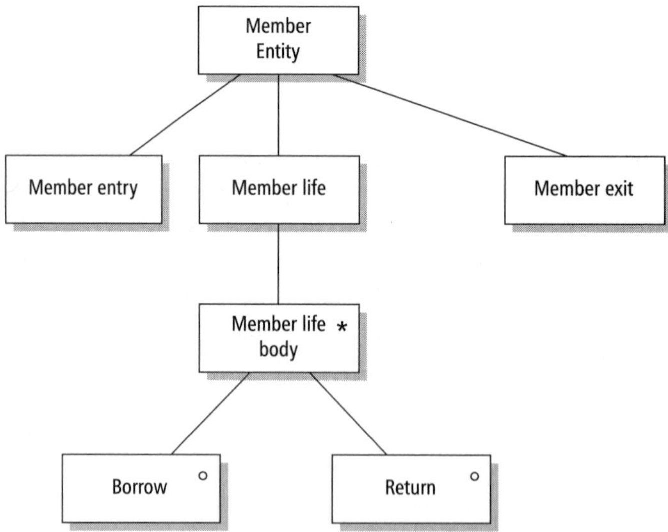

Figure 11.21 Process structure diagram for the entity Member

The modeling stage is concerned with identifying entities and the events (actions) that happen to them. These actions collectively constitute the life cycle of an entity. As with other design methods, there is no simple recipe to determine the set of entities and actions. The approach generally taken has a linguistic stance. From notes, documentation, interviews and the like, we may draw up a preliminary list of actions and entities. One heuristic is to look for real-world objects with which the system is to interact. Since a library is all about books, an entity Book immediately suggests itself. From statements like 'members borrow books' we may infer that an event Borrow occurs in the life cycle of both books and members. Once such a preliminary list is made up, further reflection should lead to a precisely demarcated life cycle of the entities identified.

Entities are made up of actions. These actions are atomic, i.e. they cannot be further decomposed into subactions. Actions respond to events in the real world. The action Acquire that is part of the life cycle of the entity Book is triggered when a real-world event, the actual acquisition of a book, takes place. In the process structure diagram, actions show up as leaf nodes.

Events are communicated to the system through data messages, called **attributes**. In a procedural sense these attributes constitute the parameters of the action. For the action Acquire we may have such attributes as ISBN, date-of-acquisition, title and authors.

Entities have attributes as well: local variables that keep information from the past and collectively determine its state. The entity Book for example may retain some or all of the information that was provided upon acquisition (ISBN, title, etc). Entities also have two special attributes. First, the *identifier attribute* uniquely identifies the entity. Second, each entity has an attribute that indicates its status. This attribute can be viewed as a pointer to some leaf node of the process structure diagram.

Each entity can be viewed as a separate, long-running, process. In the library example, each book and each member has its own life cycle. The processes though are not completely independent. During the network stage, the system is modeled as a network of interconnected processes. This network is depicted in a **system specification diagram** (SSD). JSD has two basic mechanisms for interprocess communication:

- An entity may inspect the *state vector* of another entity. This state vector describes the local state of an entity at some point in time.

- An entity may asynchronously pass information to another entity through a *datastream*.

Recall that the actions Borrow and Return occur in the life cycle of both Book and Member (see figures 11.20 and 11.21). Such common actions create a link between these entities. As a consequence, the life cycles of these entities will be synchronized with respect to these events.

If a member wants to borrow a book, certain information about that book is required. A Member entity may obtain that information by inspecting the state vector of the appropriate Book entity. This type of communication is indicated by the diamond in figure 11.22. In an implementation, state vector communication is usually handled through database access.

If our system is to log information on books being borrowed, we may model this by means of a datastream from an entity Book to an entity Log. A datastream is handled on a FIFO basis; it behaves like the UNIX filter. The notation for the datastream type of communication is given in figure 11.23.

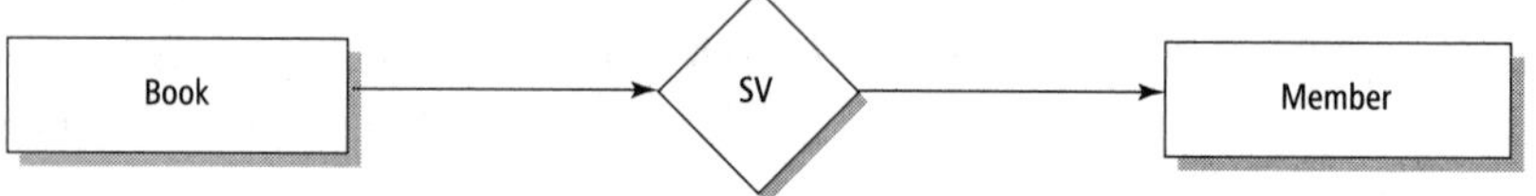

Figure 11.22 State vector communication (SV) between Member and Book

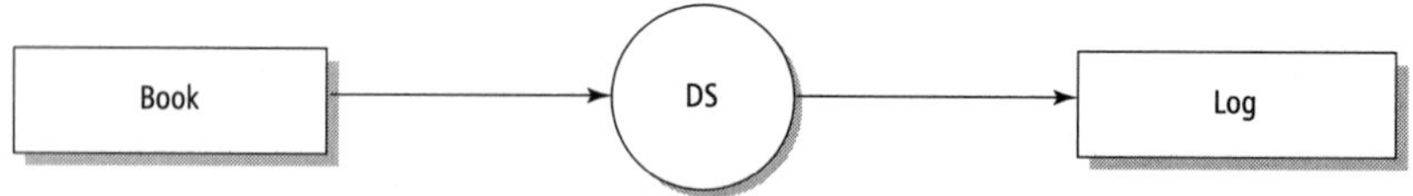

Figure 11.23 Datastream communication (DS) between Book and Log

The final stage of JSD is the implementation stage. In the implementation stage the concurrent model that is the result of the network stage is transformed into an executable system. One of the key concepts for this stage is program inversion: the communication between processes is replaced by a procedure call, so that one process becomes a subordinate of another process. This is very similar to the notion of program inversion as present in JSP.

11.2.4 How to Select a Design Method

It is not easy to compare the many design methods that exist. They all have their pros and cons. None of them gives us a straightforward recipe as to how to proceed from a list of requirements to a successfully implemented system. We always need some sort of magic in order to get a specific decomposition. The expertise and quality of the people involved have a major impact on the end result of the design process.

Problem solving is based on experience. It is estimated that an expert has over 50 000 chunks of domain-specific knowledge at his disposal. When solving a problem, we try to map the problem at hand onto the knowledge available. The greater this knowledge is, and the more accessible it is, the more successful this process will be.

The prescriptiveness of the design methods differs considerably. The various variants of functional decomposition and the object-oriented design methods rely heavily on the heuristic knowledge of the designers. Jackson's techniques seem to suffer less from this need. Especially if structure clashes do not occur, JSP provides a well-defined framework for how to tackle design. The prescriptive nature of JSP possibly explains to some extent its success, especially in the realm of administrative data-processing. JSD offers similar advantages. Its strict view of describing data structures as a list of events may lead to problems, however, if the data structures do not fit this model. JSP has a static view of the data. More importantly, it does not tell us *how* to organize the data. As such, this technique seems most suited for problems where the structure of the data has been fixed beforehand. JSD and object-oriented methods offer better support as regards the structuring of data. Though these methods give useful heuristics for the identification of objects, obtaining a well-balanced set of objects is still very much dependent on the skills of the designer.

The data flow technique has a more dynamic view of the data streams that are the base of the system to be constructed. We may often view the bubbles from a data flow diagram as clerks that perform certain transformations on incoming data to produce data for other clerks. The technique seems well-suited for circumstances where an existing manual system is to be replaced by a computerized one. A real danger, though, is that the existing system is just copied, while additional requirements are overlooked.

If we take into account that a substantial part of the cost of software is spent in *maintaining* that software, it is clear that such factors as flexibility, comprehensibility and modularity should play a crucial role when selecting a specific design technique. The ideas and guidelines of Parnas are particularly relevant in this respect. The object-oriented philosophy incorporates these ideas and is well-matched to current developments in programming languages, which allow for a smoother transition between the different development phases.

Quite a few attempts have been made to classify design methods along various dimensions, such as the products they deliver, the kind of representations used, or their level of formality. A simple but useful framework is proposed in [Blu94]. It has two dimensions: an orientation dimension and a model dimension.

In the orientation dimension, a distinction is made between problem-oriented techniques and product-oriented techniques. Problem-oriented techniques concentrate on producing a better understanding of the problem and its solution. Problem-oriented techniques are human-oriented. Their aim is to describe, communicate, and document decisions. Problem-oriented techniques usually have one foot in the requirements engineering domain. Conversely, product-oriented techniques focus on a correct transformation from a specification to an implementation. The second dimension relates to the products, i.e. models, that are the result of the design process. In this dimension, a distinction is made between conceptual models and formal models. Conceptual models are descriptive. They describe an external reality, the Universe of Discourse. Their appropriateness is established through validation. Formal models on the other hand are prescriptive. They prescribe the behavior of the system to be developed. Formal models can be verified.

	Problem-oriented	**Product-oriented**
Conceptual	I ER modeling Structured analysis	II Structured design
Formal	III JSD VDM	IV Functional decomposition JSP

Figure 11.24 Classification of design techniques

Using this framework, we may classify a number of techniques discussed in this book as in figure 11.24. The four quadrants of this matrix have the following characteristics:

I) **Understand the problem** These techniques are concerned with understanding the problem, and expressing a solution in a form that can be discussed with domain specialists (i.e. the users).

II) **Transform to implementation** Techniques in this category help to transform a collection of UoD-related concepts into an implementation structure.

III) **Represent properties** These techniques facilitate reasoning about the problem and its solution.

IV) **Create implementation units** This category contains techniques specifically aimed at creating implementation units such as modules.

The above arguments relate to characteristics of the problem to be solved. There are several other environmental factors that may impact the choice of a particular design technique and, as a consequence, the resulting design (similar arguments hold for the software architecture; see chapter 10):

- Familiarity with the problem domain. If the designers are well-acquainted with the type of problem to be solved, a top-down technique or a technique based on data structures may be very effective. If the design is experimental, one will go about it in a more cautious way, and a bottom-up design technique then seems more appropriate.

- Designer's experience. Designers that have a lot of experience with a given method will, in general, be more successful in applying that method. They are aware of the constraints and limitations of the method and will be able to successfully bypass the potential problems.

- Available tools. If tools are available to support a given design method, it is only natural to make use of them. In general, this also implies that the organization has chosen that design method.

- Overall development philosophy. Many design methods are embedded in a wider philosophy which also addresses other aspects of system development, ranging from ways to conduct interviews or reviews to full-scale models of the software life cycle. The organized and disciplined overall approach endorsed by such a development philosophy is an extra incentive for using the design method that goes with it.

11.3 NOTATIONS THAT SUPPORT THE DESIGN PROCESS

It is often said that a picture is worth a thousand words. In all sorts of designs, be they for houses, radios or other electronic appliances, extensive use is made of various drawing techniques. In many cases, the resulting drawings are the major outcome of the design process. It seems obvious to do the same when designing software.

There are a number of reasons why this is not as simple as it may at first appear:

- Software is far more subject to change. Incorporating those changes in the design takes a lot of effort and, if things have not been automated, reality and its pictorial counterpart will soon diverge.

- One of the major issues in software design is the hierarchical decomposition of the system. This seems to play a lesser role in other types of design, possibly because most radios and houses have a less complex structure than the average

5000-line program. Many drawing techniques do not impose very strict rules for this hierarchical decomposition.

- The outcome of the design is the major source of information for the programmer. The programmer is best served by a very precise description. Existing drawing techniques tend to be fairly simple and the pictures thus obtained have to be extensively decorated through natural language annotations. The text added often allows for multiple interpretations.

However, pictures may be a powerful tool in the design of software. This holds in particular for the global stages of design. In those stages there tends to be frequent interaction with the user. The user is often more at ease with pictures than with some formal description. Examples of this type of drawing technique are SADT and data flow diagrams.

We may envisage pictures to be generated automatically from a formal description. If this is done, these pictures at least have a sound semantics. As of now, quite a number of tools are available for applying this kind of drawing technique. Many of the shortcomings of these techniques are overcome by such tools.

Various types of symbology can be used to describe a design. Narrative text and formal languages represent extreme orientations along this dimension. A major advantage of formal languages is that they allow for formal checks. Narrative text tends to be unwieldy and ambiguous.

The low-level design is often documented in a constrained language, or pseudocode. A pseudocode generally supports the control structures offered by most high-level languages, such as **if–then–else** constructs, **while** or **repeat** constructs, and block structures like **begin–end**. They often provide for a number of useful data structures such as stacks, sequences, lists and sets, together with their usual operations. Apart from that, they impose hardly any strict rules as regards syntax or semantics and you may freely add new names and notations.

Software design languages based on an existing high-level programming language allow for a smooth transition from (detailed) design to code. The advantage of a special-purpose pseudocode language remains largely limited to the freedom in syntax and semantics. This seems marginal and need not be a real benefit. The use of low-level pseudocode hardly offers extra advantages over a high-level programming language. This shows the more from experiments that have demonstrated that the use of pseudocode hardly surpasses the level of a language like Pascal. One tends to repeat the story in pseudocode.

There is little evidence that one design notation is consistently better than another. An interesting experiment comparing different notations for the detailed design stage is described in [CSKB+89]. The notations were compared along two dimensions: spatial arrangement and symbology. Spatial arrangement concerns the visualization of control flow on the page. The symbology dimension includes narrative text, constrained language and ideograms. The authors conclude that for most tasks the constrained language is best. The spatial arrangement appeared to be important only when control flow information plays an essential role in the task at hand.

11.4 DESIGN DOCUMENTATION

A requirements specification is developed during requirements engineering. That document serves a number of purposes. It specifies the users' requirements and as such it often has legal meaning. It is also the starting point for the design and thus serves another class of user.

The same applies to the design documentation. The description of the design serves different users, who have different needs. A proper organization of the design documentation is therefore very important.

IEEE Standard 1016 discusses guidelines for the description of a design. This standard mainly addresses the kind of information needed and its organization. For the actual description of its constituent parts any of the notations discussed in section 11.3 can be used.

[BMP86] distinguishes between seven user roles for the design documentation:

1. The **project manager** needs information to plan, control and manage the project. He must be able to identify each system component and understand its purpose and function. He also needs information to make cost estimates and define work packages.

2. The **configuration manager** needs information to be able to assemble the various components into one system and to control changes.

3. The **designer** needs information about the function and use of each component and its interfaces to other components.

4. The **programmer** must know about algorithms to be used, data structures, and the kinds of interaction with other components.

5. The **unit tester** must have detailed information about components, such as algorithms used, required initialization, and data needed.

6. The **integration tester** must know about relations between components and the function and use of the components involved.

7. The **maintenance programmer** must have an overview of the relations between components. He must know how the user requirements are realized by the

various components. When changes are to be realized, he assumes the role of the designer.

In IEEE Standard 1016, the project documentation is described as an information model. The entities in this model are the components identified during the design stage. We used the term 'modules' for these entities. Each of these modules has a number of relevant attributes, such as its name, function, and dependencies. We may now construct a matrix in which it is indicated which attributes are needed for which user roles. This matrix is depicted in figure 11.25.

Attributes	User roles						
	1	2	3	4	5	6	7
Identification	X	X	X	X	X	X	X
Type	X	X				X	X
Purpose	X	X					X
Function	X		X			X	
Subordinates	X						
Dependencies		X				X	X
Interface			X	X	X	X	
Resources	X	X				X	X
Processing				X	X		
Data				X	X		

Figure 11.25 User roles and attributes (*Source: H.J. Barnard et al, A recommended practice for describing software designs: IEEE Standards Project 1016,* IEEE Transactions on Software Engineering SE-12, 2, *Copyright ©1986, IEEE*)

IEEE Standard 1016 distinguishes ten attributes. These attributes are minimally required in each project. The documentation about the design *process* is strongly related to the above design documentation. The design process documentation includes information pertaining to, among others, the design status, alternatives that have been rejected, and revisions that have been made. It is part of configuration control, as discussed in chapter 4. The attributes from IEEE Standard 1016 are:

- **Identification**: the component's name, for reference purposes. This name must be unique.

- **Type**: the kind of component, such as subsystem, procedure, module, file.

- **Purpose**: what is the specific purpose of the component. This entry will refer back to the requirements specification.

- **Function**: what does the component accomplish. For a number of components, this information will occur in the requirements specification.

- **Subordinates**: which components the present entity is composed of. It identifies a static is-composed-of relation between entities.
- **Dependencies**: a description of the relationships with other components. It concerns the uses-relation, see section 11.1.5, and includes more detailed information on the nature of the interaction (including common data structures, order of execution, parameter interfaces, and the like).
- **Interface**: a description of the interaction with other components. This concerns both the method of interaction (how to invoke an entity, how communication is achieved through parameters) and rules for the actual interaction (encompassing things like data formats, constraints on values and the meaning of values).
- **Resources**: the resources needed. Resources are entities external to the design, such as memory, printers, or a statistical library. This includes a discussion of how to solve possible race or deadlock situations.
- **Processing**: a description of algorithms used, way of initialization, and handling of exceptions. It is a refinement of the function attribute.
- **Data**: a description of the representation, use, format and meaning of internal data.

Figure 11.25 shows that different users have different needs as regards design documentation. A sound organization of this documentation is needed so that each user may quickly find the information he is looking for.

It is not necessarily advantageous to incorporate all attributes into one document: each user gets much more than the information needed to play his role. However, it is not necessarily advantageous to provide separate documentation for each user role: in that case, some items will occur three or four times, which is difficult to handle and complicates the maintenance of the documentation.

In IEEE 1016 the attributes have been grouped into four clusters. The decomposition is made such that most users need information from only one cluster, while these clusters contain a minimum amount of superfluous information for that user. This decomposition is given in table 11.4. It is interesting to note that each cluster has its own view on the design. Each such view gives a complete description, thereby concentrating on certain aspects of the design.

The **decomposition description** describes the decomposition of the system into modules. Using this description we may follow the hierarchical decomposition and as such describe the various abstraction levels.

The **dependencies description** gives the coupling between modules. It also sums up the resources needed. We may then derive how parameters are passed and which common data are used. This information is helpful when planning changes to the system and when isolating errors or problems in resource usage.

The **interface description** tells us how functions are to be used. This information constitutes a contract between different designers and between designers and programmers. Precise agreements about this are especially needed in multi-person projects.

The **detail description** gives internal details of each module. Programmers need these details. This information is also useful when composing module tests.

Design view	Description	Attributes	User roles
Decomposition	Decomposition of the system into modules	Identification, type, purpose, function, subcomponents	Project manager
Dependencies	Relations between modules and between resources	Identification, type, purpose, dependencies, resources	Configuration manager, maintenance programmer, integration tester
Interface	How to use modules	Identification, function, interfaces	Designer, integration tester
Detail	Internal details of modules	Identification, computation, data	Module tester, programmer

Table 11.4 Views on the design (*Source: H.J. Barnard et al, A recommended practice for describing software designs: IEEE Standards Project 1016,* IEEE Transactions on Software Engineering SE-12, 2, *Copyright ©1986, IEEE*)

11.5 VERIFICATION AND VALIDATION

Errors made at an early stage are difficult to repair and incur high costs if they are not discovered until a late stage of development. It is therefore necessary to pay extensive attention to testing and validation issues during the design stage.

The way in which the outcome of the design process can be subject to testing strongly depends upon the way in which the design is recorded. If some formal specification technique is used, the resulting specification can be tested formally. It may also be possible to do static tests, such as checks for consistency. Formal specifications may sometimes be executed, which offers additional ways to test the system. Such prototypes are especially suited to test the user interface. Users often have little idea of the possibilities to be expected and a specification-based prototype offers good opportunities for aligning users' requirements and designers' ideas.

Often, the design is stated in less formal ways, limiting the possibilities for testing to forms of reading and critiquing text, such as inspections and walkthroughs. However, such design reviews provide an extremely powerful means for assessing designs.

During the design process the system is decomposed into a number of modules. We may develop test cases based on this process. These test cases may be used during functional testing at a later stage. Conversely, the software architecture can be used to guide the testing process. A set of scenarios of typical or anticipated future usage can be used to test the quality of the software architecture.

A more comprehensive discussion of the various test techniques is given in chapter 13.

11.6 SUMMARY

Just like designing a house, designing software is an activity which demands creativity and a fair dose of craftsmanship. The quality of the designer is of paramount importance in this process. Mediocre designers will not deliver excellent designs.

The essence of the design process is that the system is decomposed into parts that each have less complexity than the whole. Some form of abstraction is always used in this process. We have identified several guiding principles for the decomposition of a system into modules. These principles result in desirable properties for the outcome of the design process, a set of modules with mutual dependencies:

- Modules should be internally cohesive, i.e. the constituents of a module should 'belong together' and 'be friends'. By identifying different levels of *cohesion*, a qualitative notion of module cohesion is obtained.

- The interfaces between modules should be as 'thin' as possible. Again, various levels of module *coupling* have been identified, allowing for an assessment of mutual dependencies between modules.

- Each module should hide one secret. *Information hiding* is a powerful design principle, whereby each module is characterized by a secret which it hides from its environment. Abstract data types are a prime example of the application of this principle.

- The structure of the system, depicted as a graph whose nodes and edges denote modules and dependencies between modules, respectively, should have a simple and regular shape. The most constrained form of this graph is a tree. In a less constrained form the graph is acyclic, in which case the set of modules can be split into a number of distinct layers of abstraction.

Abstraction is central to all of these features. In a properly-designed system we should be able to concentrate on the relevant issues and ignore the irrelevant ones. This is an essential prerequisite for comprehending a system, for implementing parts of it successfully without having to consider design decisions made elsewhere, and for implementing changes locally, thus allowing for a smooth evolution of the system.

The above features are highly interrelated and reinforce one another. Information hiding results in modules with high cohesion and low coupling. Cohesion and coupling are dual characteristics. A clear separation of concerns results in a neat design structure.

We have discussed several measures to quantify properties of a design. The most extensive research in this area concerns complexity metrics. These complexity metrics concern both attributes of individual modules (called intra-modular attributes) and attributes of a set of modules (called inter-module attributes). Journals like *IEEE Software* and *The Journal of Systems and Software* have in recent years devoted special issues to the application of metrics in the software development process. This is a sure sign of the growing importance of quantitative approaches to assessing both the process and its products (see also chapter 6).

A word of caution is needed, though. Software complexity is a very illusive notion, which cannot be captured in a few simple numbers. Different complexity metrics measure along different dimensions of what is perceived as complexity. Also, large values for any such metric do not necessarily imply a bad design. There may be good reasons to incorporate certain complex matters into one component.

A judicious and knowledgeable use of multiple design metrics is a powerful tool in the hands of the craftsman. Thoughtless application, however, will not help. To paraphrase Gunning, the inventor of the fog index (a popular readability measure for natural language prose): design metrics can cause harm in misuse.

There exist a great many design methods. They consist of a number of guidelines, heuristics and procedures on how to approach designing a system and notations to express the result of that process. Design methods differ considerably in their prescriptiveness, formality of notation, scope of application, and extent of incorporation in a more general development paradigm. Several tentative efforts have been made to compare design methods along different dimensions.

We discussed three design methods in this chapter that are in widespread use:

- functional decomposition,
- data flow design, and
- data structure design.

A fourth method, the object-oriented approach to system development, has become very popular of late. It will be discussed in chapter 12.

Finally, the design itself must also be documented. IEEE Standard 1016 may serve as a guideline for this documentation. It lists a number of attributes for each component of the design. These attributes may be clustered into four groups, each of which represents a certain view on the design.

Unfortunately, the design documentation typically describes only the design *result* and not the process that led to that particular result. Yet, information about choices made, alternatives rejected, and deliberations on the design decisions is a valuable additional source of information when a design is to be implemented, assessed, or changed.

11.7 FURTHER READING

[Bud93] is a good textbook on software design. I found the 'software as a wicked problem' analogy in that text. [BG81] and [FW83] are compilations of seminal articles on software design. For an interesting discussion on the 'Scandinavian' approach to system development, see [FMR+89] or [CAC93a].

The classic text on Structured Analysis and Design is [YC75]. Other names associated with the development of SA/SD are DeMarco [DeM79] and Gane and Sarson [GS79].

For a full exposition of JSP, the reader is referred to [Jac75] or [Kin88]. JSP is very similar to a method developed by J.-D. Warnier in France at about the same time [War74]. The latter is known as Logical Construction of Programs (LCP) or the Warnier–Orr method, after Ken Orr who was instrumental in the translation of Warnier's work. For a full exposition of JSD, see [Jac83], [Cam89] or [Sut88]. The graphical notations used in this chapter are those of [Sut88].

[FP96] present a rigorous approach to the topic of software metrics. The authors explain the essentials of measurement theory and illustrate these using a number of proposed metrics (including those for complexity, quality assessment, and cost estimation). Cohesion and coupling were introduced in [YC75]. Efforts to objectify these notions can be found in [OHK93], [Sel93] and [PCB92]. [SB91] and [AE92] describe empirical studies to validate the importance of weak coupling and strong cohesion.

Halstead's method, 'software science', is described in [Hal77] and [FL78]. Positive evidence of its validity is reported in [CSM79] and [Els76]. A good overview of the criticism of this method (as well as McCabe's cyclomatic complexity and Henri and Kafura's information flow metric) is given in [SI93]. McCabe's cyclomatic complexity is introduced in [McC76]. In most discussions of this metric, the wrong formula is used; see exercise 19 or [HS92]. Discussions in favor of using a (cyclomatic) complexity *density* metric can be found in [MTG92] and [HS95]. A very complete source on complexity metrics is [Zus90] which discusses just about every complexity metric ever proposed.

A fairly extensive comparison of design techniques is given in [Web88]. Dimensions considered by Webster include the application range, formality, expressiveness and tool support. Other such frameworks are proposed in [SO92], [KC93] and [Blu94].

Exercises

1. What is the difference between procedural abstraction and data abstraction?

2. List and explain Yourdon and Constantine's seven levels of cohesion.

3. Explain the notions cohesion and coupling.

4. In what sense are the various notions of coupling technology-dependent?

5. What is the essence of information hiding?

6. Give an outline of Halstead's software science.

7. Determine the cyclomatic complexity of the following program:

```
no_6:= true; sum:= 0;
for i to no_of_courses do
    if grade[i] < 7 then no_6:= false endif;
    sum:= sum + grade[i]
endfor;
average:= sum / no_of_courses;
if average ≥ 8 and no_6
    then print("with distinction")
endif;
```

8. Would the cyclomatic complexity be any different if the last if-statement were written as follows:

```
if average ≥ 8 then
    if no_6
        then print("with distinction")
    endif
endif;
```

Does this concur with your own ideas of a control complexity measure, i.e. does it fulfill the representation condition?

9. Give the formula and a rationale for the information flow complexity metric.

10. Is cyclomatic complexity a good indicator of system complexity?

11. Draw the call graphs for the first two decompositions from section 10.1 and determine their tree impurity. Do the numbers obtained agree with our intuitive idea about the 'quality' of the decompositions?

12. Compute Henri and Kafura's information flow metric for the first two decompositions from section 10.1. Do these numbers agree with our intuitive understanding?

13. What is functional decomposition?

14. Give a global sketch of the Data Flow Design method.

15. Explain what a structure clash is in JSP.

16. What is the main difference between problem-oriented and product-oriented design methods?

17. ♡ Assess the designs discussed in sections 10.1.1 and 10.1.2 with respect to: abstraction, modularity, information hiding, complexity, and system structure.

18. ♡ Assess the coupling and cohesion levels of the modules in the decompositions derived in sections 10.1.1 and 10.1.2.

19. ♡ Make it plausible that the formula for the cyclomatic complexity should read $CV = e - n + p + 1$ rather than $CV = e - n + 2p$. (Hint: consider the following program:

```
begin
    if A then B else C endif;
```

```
        call P;
        print("done")
    end;

    procedure P;
        begin
            if X then Y else Z endif
        end P;
```

Draw the flow graph for this program as well as for the program obtained by substituting the body of procedure P inline. Determine the cyclomatic complexity of both variants, using both formulae. See also [HS92].)

20. ♠ Write the design documentation for a project you have been involved in, following IEEE 1016.

21. ♠ Discuss the pros and cons of:

    - functional decomposition,
    - data flow design, and
    - design based on data structures

    for the design of each of:

    - a compiler,
    - a patient monitoring system, and
    - a stock control system.

22. ♠ Discuss the possible merits of those design techniques with respect to reusability.

23. ♠ Augment IEEE Standard 1016 such that it also describes the design rationale. Which user roles are in need of this type of information?

24. ♡ According to [FP96], any tree impurity metric m should have the following properties:

    a. $m(G) = 0$ if and only if G is a tree;

    b. $m(G_1) > m(G_2)$ if G_1 differs from G_2 only by the insertion of an extra arc;

    c. For $i = 1, 2$ let A_i denote the number of arcs in G_i and N_i the number of nodes in G_i. Then if $N_1 > N_2$ and $A_1 - N_1 + 1 = A_2 - N_2 + 1$, then $m(G_1) < m(G_2)$.

d. For all graphs G, $m(G) \leq m(K_N) = 1$ where N = number of nodes of G and K_N is the (undirected) complete graph of N nodes.

Give an intuitive rationale for these properties. Show that the tree impurity metric discussed in section 11.1.5 has these properties.

12
Object-Oriented Analysis and Design

LEARNING OBJECTIVES

- To know the terminology of object orientation
- To appreciate the various diagramming techniques used in object-oriented analysis and design
- To know about UML, the Unified Modeling Language
- To understand the general flavor of object-oriented analysis and design methods
- To be aware of some well-known object-oriented analysis and design methods
- To be aware of some object-oriented metrics

> *My guess is that object-oriented programming will be in the 1980s what structured programming was in the 1970s. Everyone will be in favor of it. Every manufacturer will promote his products as supporting it. Every manager will pay lip service to it. Every programmer will practice it (differently). And no one will know just what it is.*
> [Ren82]

> *My cat is object-oriented*
> [Kin89]

Every now and then some people claim to have found the ultimate solution to the software crisis. In the 1970s, structured programming was widely claimed to provide a definite answer to our problems. For a while, everything had to be structured: structured methods, structured design, structured testing, etc. Though many of these developments have considerably advanced the field of software engineering, our problems have not disappeared yet.

Something similar is currently happening with the adjective object-oriented. Today, objects are 'the right stuff'. We have object-oriented languages, object-oriented databases, object-oriented design methods, etc. But, as has been argued convincingly in [Bro87], there is no silver bullet. Software development will simply remain a difficult and painstaking process. At the same time, we must admit that the object-oriented viewpoint does have a number of advantages over other approaches. These advantages make it into an approach worth considering.

The concept of object orientation has its roots in the development of programming languages, most notably SIMULA-67 and Smalltalk. With respect to design (and requirements analysis), object orientation is best viewed by highlighting the differences with more traditional design methods such as functional decomposition and dataflow design. As noted in our discussion on JSD in chapter 11, these traditional techniques focus on identifying the *functions* that the system is to perform. In contrast, object-oriented methods focus on identifying and interrelating the *objects* that play a role in the system.

Section 12.1 introduces a number of relevant concepts, such as object, attribute, class, relationship. Partly because object-oriented methods have been developed from both a programming language perspective and from an analysis (modeling) perspective, and partly because the world of object orientation (OO) is still young and evolving, different terms are used to denote essentially the same concept. Worse still, one and the same term is sometimes used to denote different concepts.

There are quite a number of object-oriented analysis and design methods. In most of them, graphical notations play an important role. Though the details of these methods may differ considerably, their general flavor is quite similar. The first generation of object-oriented analysis and design methods was published around 1990.[1] As experience with applying these methods accumulated, they were extended and improved. The resulting second-generation approaches also frequently borrowed successful elements from one another.

Further unification processes are currently under way. Some of the major players in the field (Booch, Jacobson, and Rumbaugh) have joined forces and defined the Unified Modeling Language (UML). UML is meant as a unified notation for expressing a variety of models and can be used by a variety of object-oriented methods.

Section 12.2 discusses the main diagramming techniques used in object-oriented methods. Though the names of the diagrams and their graphical details may differ considerably, the overall flavor of the most important diagrams seems to be widely agreed upon. Section 12.2 uses the UML notational style to illustrate the different types of diagram.

Section 12.3 discusses the process of how to get from a problem statement to an assemblage of interacting objects. This section also touches upon the strong and weak spots of object-oriented analysis and design methods.

Design methods, whether object-oriented or otherwise, consist of notations to express the result of the design process as well as procedures, guidelines and heuristics on how to go about design. The latter concerns both the steps to be taken – the process model of the design method – and the design itself. For example, a design heuristic for object-oriented systems is that each method should send messages only to objects of a very limited set of classes. Efforts to quantify such heuristics have resulted in a number of metrics specifically aimed at object-oriented systems. The main object-oriented metrics are discussed in section 12.4.

12.1 ON OBJECTS AND RELATED STUFF

What matters is not how closely we model today's reality but how extensible and reusable our software is.
[Mey96]

The world around us is full of objects, animate and inanimate, concrete and abstract: trees and tables, cars and legal cases. According to some, object-oriented analysis and design is about modeling those real-world objects. By and large, this view has its origins in the Scandinavian school of programming language design (SIMULA-67) and software development. It may be termed the European view. According to others, object orientation is a way to improve programming productivity, by focusing on data abstraction and component reuse. Object-oriented analysis and design, then,

[1] Earlier publications mostly focused on object-oriented *programming*.

is about identifying reusable components and building their inheritance hierarchy. This latter view, which may be termed the American view, clearly shows itself in the above citation.

What then *is* an object? As might be expected, there are different views of what the notion of object entails. We may distinguish the following viewpoints:

- The modeling viewpoint: an object is a conceptual model of some part of a real or imaginary world. This is termed the European view. From this point of view, important characteristics are:

    - each object has an identity, which distinguishes it from all other objects;
    - objects have substance: properties that hold and can be discovered by investigating an object.

  From a practical point of view, object identity is an immutable tag, or an address, which uniquely identifies that object. Different objects occupy different regions of memory. Pragmatically also, objects may be regarded as implementations of abstract data types (ADTs). An object then consists of a mutable state, i.e. the set of variables of the ADT, and operations to modify or inspect the state. Typically, the only way to access an object is through these operations. These operations thus act as an interface to the object. An object then is a collection of three aspects:

  object = identity + variables + operations

  or

  object = identity + state + behavior

- The philosophical viewpoint: objects are existential abstractions, as opposed to universal abstractions. In some circles (notably Smalltalk), 'everything is an object'. In this view, objects act as a unifying notion underlying all computation. However, one may also argue that there are two rather distinct types of abstraction. Some kinds of entity have a natural beginning and end. They are created at some point in time, exist for a while, and are ultimately destroyed. The kinds of entities modeled as objects during object-oriented analysis and design typically belong to this class. Other kinds of entities, such as numbers, dates and colors, have 'eternal' existence. They are not instantiated; they cannot be changed; they 'live' forever. These entities are usually referred to as values.

- The software engineering viewpoint: objects are data abstractions, encapsulating data as well as operations on those data. This viewpoint stresses locality of information and representation independence; see also sections 11.1.1

and 11.1.3. However, not all object-oriented languages enforce data abstraction, and objects need not always encapsulate an abstract data type. We might claim that data abstraction and objects are somewhat orthogonal, independent dimensions.

A language that merely allows us to encapsulate abstract data types in modules is often termed **object-based**. The adjective object-oriented then is reserved for languages that also support **inheritance**. Inheritance is discussed below.

- The implementation viewpoint: an object is a contiguous structure in memory. Technically, an object may be regarded as a record of data and code elements. An object may be composite or aggregate, in which case it possesses other objects. These sub-objects in turn may possess even 'smaller' sub-objects, etcetera. The lowest-level objects in this hierarchy are atomic objects, typically denoting things like integers, real numbers or Booleans.

  The implementation of this 'possessed-by' relation appears to be intricate. On the one hand, objects may be contained in other objects. In this representation, all references are dispensed with. There is no concept of sharing. This scheme is known as **value semantics**. Value semantics is inadequate for object-oriented systems, since such systems require sharable objects. The opposite scheme is **reference semantics**: data is represented as either an atomic object or as an aggregate of references to other objects. Pure reference semantics is inefficient in the case of primitive objects like integers or characters. A combination in which aggregate objects may contain other objects, refer to other objects, or do both at the same time, is commonly used as a storage scheme. The choice of a particular storage model is to some extent reflected in the high-level language semantics (for example, where it concerns copying or comparing objects).

- The formal viewpoint: an object is a state machine with a finite set of states and a finite set of state functions. These state functions map old states and inputs to new states and outputs.

  Formalization of the concepts and constructions of object-oriented languages is difficult. Mathematical formalisms tend to be value-based. Imperative concepts, such as state and sharing, that are central to object-oriented languages do not fit easily within such schemes.

During analysis, the conceptual viewpoint is usually stressed. Those who are of the opinion that object-oriented analysis and design smoothly shade off into one another tend to keep this view during design. Others however are of the opinion that analysis and design are different, irrespective of whether they are object-oriented or not. They are likely to stress other viewpoints during design. The definition of an object as given in [CY91] also reflects the tension between a problem-oriented and a solution-oriented viewpoint: an object is 'an *abstraction* of something in a problem domain, reflecting the capabilities of a system to keep information about it, interact with it, or both; an *encapsulation* of Attribute values and their exclusive Services.' We will come back to this dichotomy in section 12.3.

As noted above, objects are characterized by a set of attributes (properties). A table has legs, a table top, size, color, etc. The **attribute** concept originates with Entity–Relationship Modeling; see section 9.3.1. In ERM, attributes represent *intrinsic properties* of entities, properties whose value does not depend on other entities. Attributes denote identifying and descriptive properties, such as name or weight. *Relationships* on the other hand denote *mutual* properties, such as an employee being assigned to a project or a book being borrowed by a member. In the context of object-oriented modeling, the term attribute is sometimes used to denote any field in the underlying data structure. In that case, the object's identity is an attribute, the state denotes the set of 'structural' attributes, and the operations denote the 'behavioral' attributes. We will use the term attribute to denote a structural attribute. Collectively, this set of attributes of an object thus constitutes its state. It includes the intrinsic properties, usually represented as values, as well as the mutual properties, usually represented as references to other objects.

At the programming-language level, objects that have the same set of attributes are said to belong to the same *class*. Individual objects of a class are called *instances* of that class. So we may have a class Table, with instances MyTable and YourTable. These instances have the same attributes, with possibly different values.

An object not only encapsulates its *state*, but also its *behavior*, i.e. the way in which it acts upon other objects and is acted upon by other objects. The behavior of an object is described in terms of *services* provided by that object. These services are invoked by *sending messages* from the object that requests the service to the object that is acted upon.

In order for a collection of objects to operate together as intended, each of the objects must be able to rely on the proper operation of the objects with which it interacts. In a *client-server* view, one object, the client, requests some service from another object, the server. This mutual dependency may be viewed as a contract between the objects involved. The client will not ask more than what is stated in the contract, while the server promises to deliver what is stated in the contract. In this perspective, services are also referred to as *responsibilities*.

The major behavioral aspect of an object concerns state changes. The state of an object instance is not static, but changes over time: the object instance is created, updated, and eventually destroyed. Also, certain information may be requested from an object. This information may concern the state of the object instance, but it may also involve a computation of some sort.

For example, a customer of a library may have attributes like Name, Address, and BooksOnLoan. It must be possible to create an instance of the object type Customer. When doing so, suitable values for its attributes must be provided. Once the instance has been created, state changes are possible: books are loaned and returned, the customer changes address, etc. Finally, the instance is destroyed when the customer ceases to be a member. Information requested may concern such things as a list of books on loan or the number of books on loan. The former is part of the state that describes a particular customer and can be retrieved directly from that state. NumberOfBooksOnLoan is a service that requires a computation of some sort, for example counting the number of elements in BooksOnLoan.

We will generally not be concerned with individual objects. Our goal is to identify and relate the object types (i.e. classes). We will often use the term object to denote an object type. One of our major concerns during object-oriented analysis and design is to identify this set of objects, together with their attributes (state) and services (behavior).

Relations between objects can be expressed in a classification structure. The major types of relation depicted in such structures are listed in figure 12.1.

Relationship	Example
Specialization/Generalization, is-a	Table *is-a* Furniture
Whole-part, has	Table *has* TableTop
Member-of, has	Library *has* Member

Figure 12.1 Major types of relations between objects

If we have objects Table and Chair, we may also define a more general object Furniture. Table and Chair are said to be *specializations* of Furniture, while Furniture is a *generalization* of Table and Chair. These relations are also known as 'is-a' relations. The is-a relation is a well-known concept from Entity–Relationship Modeling.

The generalization/specialization relations can be expressed in a hierarchical structure like the one in figure 12.2. In its most general form the classification structure is a directed acyclic graph (DAG). Many classification structures can be depicted as a tree though, in which case each object is a direct descendant of exactly one other object. At the programming-language level, **single inheritance** corresponds to a tree structure, while **multiple inheritance** corresponds to a DAG.

Different objects may share some of their attributes. Both tables and chairs have a height, for instance. Rather than defining the full set of attributes for each object, we may define common attributes at a higher level in the object hierarchy and let descendants *inherit* those attributes. We may therefore define the attribute

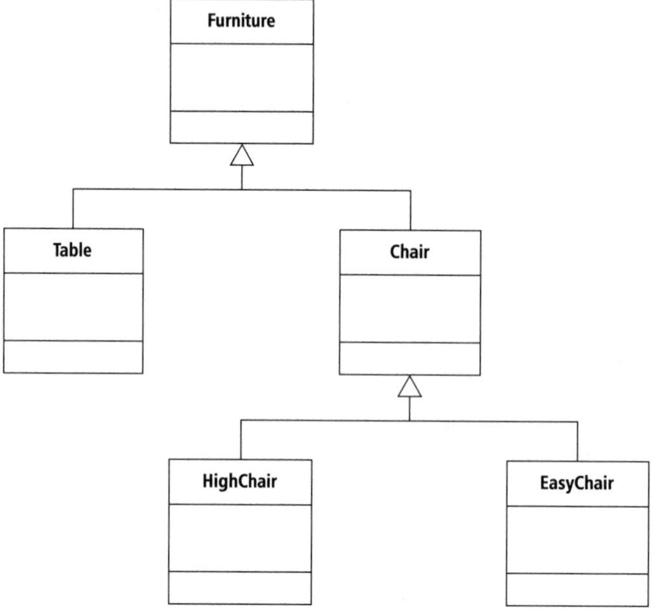

Figure 12.2 Object hierarchy

Height at the level of Furniture rather than at the level of each of its descendants. Obviously, this is just another way of looking at the object hierarchy. The fact that Chair and Table are both descendants of Furniture already suggests that they share certain properties, properties that are common to the various types of furniture. The fact that they are different descendants of Furniture also suggests that they each have unique properties.

Alternatively, we may view the object hierarchy as a *type hierarchy*. Chair and Table are *subtypes* of Furniture, just like Cardinal is a subtype of Integer. In this view, an object is a restriction of the objects of which it is a specialization. Each chair is a piece of furniture, but the reverse is not generally true.

By explicitly relating objects in the object hierarchy, a much tighter semantic binding between related objects is realized than is possible in more traditional design approaches. In a functional decomposition of our library automation problem for example, there is virtually no way to make the similarities between books and journals explicit in the design. In an object-oriented design, objects Book and Journal can be made descendants of a more general object Publication, and attributes like Publisher can be inherited from this more general type of object.

The is-a relation is one way to organize (object) types into a hierarchy. The part-of relation is another major organizational property of object types. A Table 'has' a

TableTop and Legs. A Publication 'has' a TitleDescription and a Publisher. This part-of relation *aggregates* components into a 'whole'. It describes how compound things are made up of simpler things. By definition, the compound is at a higher level of abstraction than its components.

An object like TableTop is made up of attributes, for example Color, Width and Length. At the next level, objects like TableTop and Legs are assembled into a higher-level object, viz. Table. At that level, we may introduce additional attributes, such as Size, so that Table may also be seen as an aggregate of the first kind. In general, a compound object consists of a number of (references to) other objects and a number of 'simple' attributes, i.e. values.

In the case of Table, the part-of relation is a real-world part-of relation. In the case of Publication, Publisher does not correspond to some part of the underlying real-world object. It merely is part of the *representation* of the object Publication. Sometimes, an explicit distinction is made between the real-world part-of relation and the representational part-of (or component-of) relation. Most object-oriented modeling methods do not make this distinction, though.

In many modeling methods, the part-of relation subsumes the *member-of* relation. The member-of relation is used to model the relationship between a set and its members. It is, however, sometimes useful to be able to distinguish between these organizational properties. For example, the part-of relation is generally considered to be transitive, whereas the member-of relation is not. If Book is a member of Library, and Library is a member of PublicInstitutions, we do not want to infer that Book is a member of PublicInstitutions.

12.2 OBJECT-ORIENTED ANALYSIS AND DESIGN NOTATIONS

Object-oriented analysis and design methods use a variety of graphical notations to depict the models developed. Notwithstanding this variety, the general flavor of these diagramming techniques seems to be widely agreed upon. In particular, there is an overwhelming agreement that at least the following types of diagram are required:

- a **class diagram** to depict the (static) decomposition of the system. A class diagram is a graph in which the nodes are objects (classes) and the edges are relationships between objects. By decorating the edges, many kinds of relationships can be modeled.

- a **state diagram** to model the dynamic behavior of single objects. Most object-oriented methods use some extension of finite state machines for this purpose. The nodes in a state diagram represent possible states of an object. The edges denote possible transitions between states.

- an **interaction diagram** to model the sequence of messages of which a typical interaction is composed. There are two types of interaction diagram: **sequence diagrams** emphasize the time ordering of events within an interaction and **collaboration diagrams** emphasize the objects and their relationships relevant to a particular interaction.

As will be elaborated upon in section 12.3, object-oriented methods by and large assume a relatively stable problem statement as a starting point. Object-oriented methods are not particularly strong on requirements elicitation. The idea of modeling and analyzing scenarios of system use was first proposed in [JCJO92]. These use cases can be modeled in various ways. The use case diagram provides an overview of a set of use cases. This diagram in itself is not a major innovation. Use cases, though, are a phenomenon that most object-oriented methods have now included in their repertoire. A collection of use cases can also be conceived as one possible view of the software architecture of a system.

Section 12.2.6 discusses yet another OO-related requirements elicitation tool: CRC cards. A CRC card simply is an index card with three fields: Class, Responsibility and Collaborators. It is a cheap, yet highly effective tool in the early phases of object-oriented software development.

In the following, we use the UML names for the various types of diagrams. Where needed, the corresponding diagram names in particular object-oriented methods will be indicated as well. The graphical conventions are also those of UML.

12.2.1 The Class Diagram

Class diagrams depict the static structure of a system. All object-oriented analysis and design methods provide some way to depict this static structure. This type of diagram comes under different names: it is called information model in OOA [SM92] and object model in OMT [RBP+91] and Fusion [CAB+94]. Class diagrams consist of elements, most often classes, and relationships between those elements. The elements are drawn as bubbles, rectangles, rounded rectangles, etc. The relationships are drawn as straight lines, a sequence of straight line segments, curved lines, etc., between elements.

The most common example of a class diagram is a diagram depicting the subclass–superclass hierarchy of objects. Figure 12.2 is an example of such a class diagram. The objects are denoted by rectangles that have three compartments. These compartments contain, from top to bottom:

- the name of the object,
- the list of attributes of the object, and
- the list of services of the object.

The hollow triangle indicates that the structure is a generalization/specialization structure (as opposed to a whole-part structure).

In our library example, we will have different kinds of publications. We might wish to model a general class Publication, with specializations like Book and Journal. A UML class diagram to denote this taxonomic relationship is given in figure 12.3. Generalization is shown as a solid path from the more specific element (such as Book) to the more general element (Publication), with a large hollow triangle at the end of the path. A group of generalization paths may be shown as a tree with a shared segment, as in figure 12.3. UML allows us to indicate semantic constraints between the subclasses in the diagram. The keyword disjoint in figure 12.3, for example, indicates that a descendant may not be descended from more than one of the subclasses: a Publication cannot be both a Book and a Journal. The opposite constraint, overlapping, can be used to denote that classes LibraryClients and LibraryPersonnel may have common descendants. The constraint incomplete indicates that the list of subclasses is known to be incomplete. It is a statement about the model itself, not about its graphical representation.

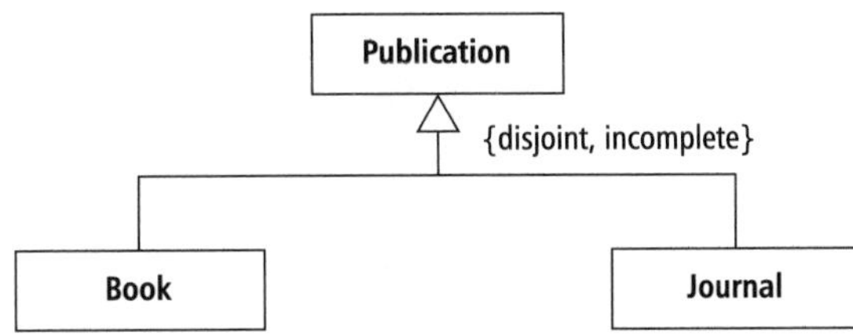

Figure 12.3 UML class diagram: generalization

The nodes in figure 12.3 contain just the names of the classes. UML allows for quite some variety in its notation. We may for instance depict a class as a rectangle with three compartments, as we did in figure 12.2. The second and third compartments then contain information about the attributes and operations, respectively. Figure 12.4 gives a possible representation for the class Book in which a number of analysis-level details have been added. We may even extend the notation further and add implementation-level details, such as whether attributes and operations are public or private. We may think of these different representations as different views of the same model element. We may envision tool support that allows the user to switch from one representation to another, suppressing or adding detail as the need arises.

Relationships in the sense of Entity–Relationship Modeling, i.e. mutual properties between two or more entities, can also be expressed in a class diagram. In

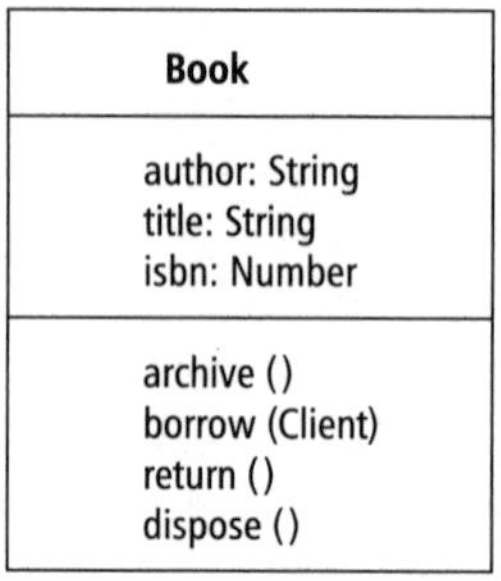

Book
author: String title: String isbn: Number
archive () borrow (Client) return () dispose ()

Figure 12.4 Analysis-level details in a UML class diagram

UML-terminology, such relationships are called **associations**.[2] A UML association connects two or more classes. This is shown by a sequence of solid line segments (a path) connecting those classes. This path may be adorned with a variety of glyphs and textual information to provide further specifics of the relationship. A simple relationship between a library and its clients is depicted in figure 12.5a. The (optional) name of the association is printed near the path. The solid triangle indicates the direction in which the name is to be read. The end of an association attached to a class is called an association role. These roles can be given names. Further adornments can be added to indicate properties of the role. In figure 12.5a we have added multiplicity information to the association roles: a client can be a member of one or more libraries, while a library may have zero or more clients.

An association such as Member-of also has class properties. For example, this association has attributes, e.g. MemberId, and operations, such as BecomeMember and CeaseToBeMember. Alternatively, we may say that class Membership has association properties. In UML, this model element is termed **association class**. It is shown as a class symbol attached by a dashed line to an association path, as in figure 12.5b.

The part-of relation (called **aggregation** in UML) can be depicted in different ways. One option is a solid filled diamond as an association role adornment, as in figure 12.6a. This option is known as **composition**. Composition is a strong notion of aggregation, in which the part object may belong to only one whole object. With composition, the parts are expected to live and die with the whole. Figure 12.6a shows a Book with parts title, author, and isbn. A book has one title and one ISBN, so these parts have multiplicity 1. We assume here that a book may have up to three

[2]UML associations are based on the association concept of OMT. OMT has a very rich notation to depict associations between classes.

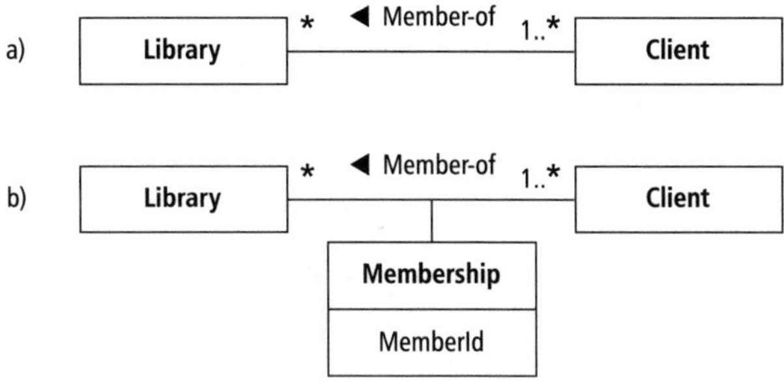

Figure 12.5 UML class diagram: (a) association and (b) association class

authors, so that part has multiplicity of 1..3. This part-of relationship is a relationship between a class and the classes of its attributes. An alternative notation for this part-of relation therefore consists of the top two compartments of the diagram for a class, as in figure 12.6b.

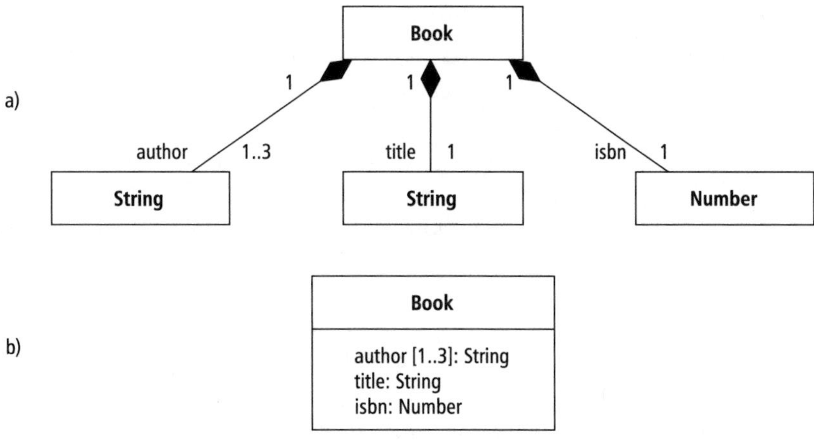

Figure 12.6 UML class diagram: composition as (a) association role adornment and (b) a simple class diagram

12.2.2 The State Diagram

A major class of services provided by an object relates to the object's life cycle: an object instance is created, updated zero or more times, and finally destroyed. State transition diagrams, which depict the possible states of an object and the transitions between those states, are a good help in modeling this life cycle.

Usually, the finite state machine model and its associated state transition diagram (see section 9.3.2) are extended in several ways when used in modeling the behavior of objects over time:

- In the classical finite state machine model, states do not have local variables. All necessary information is coded in the state. This easily leads to unwieldy models. For instance, suppose we want to model an object LibraryMember as follows: a person may become a member of the library, borrow up to 10 books, and cease to be a member of the library. This leads to a finite state machine with states like has-borrowed-0-books, has-borrowed-1-book, has-borrowed-2-books, ... , has-borrowed-10-books. If the number of books on loan could be modeled as a local variable, the number of states in the model would be reduced from 12 to 2.

  For this reason, the finite state machine is usually extended by adding local variables to the model. A state in this extended finite state machine then comprises both the explicit state represented by a node in the state transition diagram and the value of the model's variables.

  These local variables are not only used to decrease the number of states. State transitions may now also change the values of variables; the variables may be tested to determine the next state and transitions may be guarded by the value of the variables. In figure 12.7, the number of books on loan is kept in the local variable N. This variable is initialized to zero, updated when a book is borrowed or returned, and tested when a person terminates his membership.

- The components being modeled interact with the environment: there are input events and output actions. In all modeling methods that we know of, input events trigger transitions. When a person becomes a member of the library, this triggers the initial transition; when she borrows a book, it triggers a transition from a state, say, has-borrowed-7-books to a state has-borrowed-8-books. If the model has local variables, the latter state transition may result in a change in the value of such a local variable. In figure 12.7, the input events are denoted as strings that label state transitions (like Start and Borrow).

  Different modeling methods have different ways to handle output actions. Sometimes, output actions are associated with a transition (this is known as a Mealy machine), sometimes output actions are associated with a state (a Moore machine). In the latter case, the output action is carried out as soon as the state is entered. In a formal sense, Mealy machines and Moore machines have the same expressive power.

- Finite state diagrams may become unwieldy. Therefore, one may add some structure, through a hierarchy. Part of the model may be compressed into one state. If we are interested in the details of a state, we may 'zoom in' on that state.

Many modeling methods, including UML, depict the sequence of states that an object goes through in a variant of the **statechart**. Statecharts are extended finite state machines (i.e. they have local variables) in which output actions may be associated with both transitions and states and in which states can be arranged hierarchically. In UML, this type of diagram is called **state diagram**.

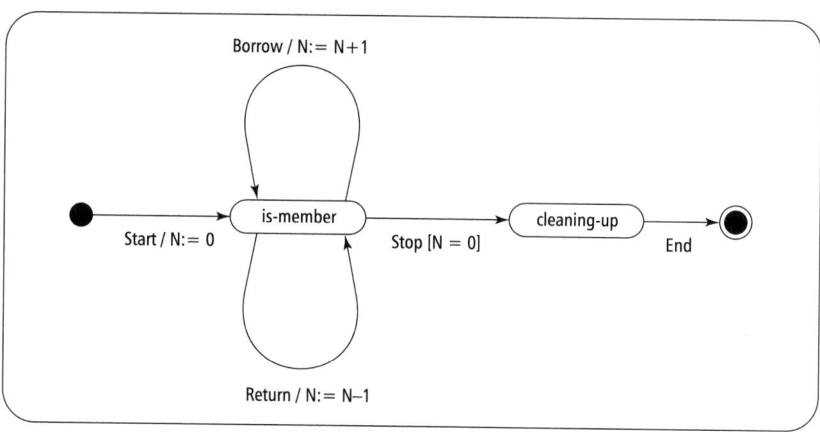

Figure 12.7 UML state diagram: object Member

As with class diagrams, UML has a rich notation for state diagrams. We will illustrate the major ingredients through a few examples; see also figures 12.7 and 12.8.

A state is some condition in the life of an object. It is shown as a rectangle with rounded corners. An initial (pseudo) state is shown as a small filled circle. This initial state is a mere notational device; an object can not be in such a state. It indicates the transition to the first 'real' state. A final (pseudo) state is shown as a small circle surrounding a small filled circle. This final state is also a notational device. A transition is shown as a solid arrow from one state to another. When a change of state occurs, that transition is said to 'fire'. A transition is labeled by a **transition string**. The transition string includes a description of the event which triggers the transaction, such as the borrowing of a book. The event may be guarded by a boolean expression. For example, the transition from state is-member to cleaning-up in figure 12.7 is guarded by the expression '$N = 0$'; it can only occur if the number of books on loan is zero. The transition string may include a procedural expression after the symbol '/'. This procedural expression is executed when the transition fires.

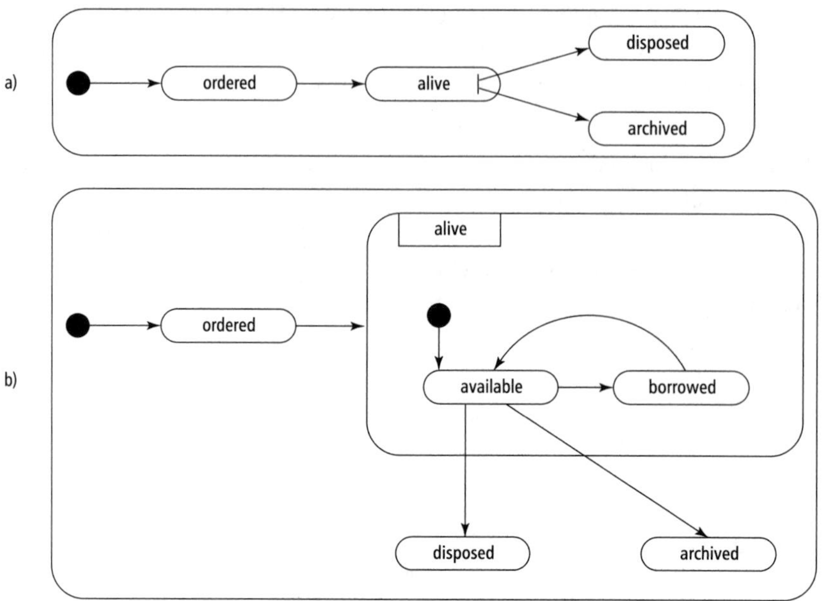

Figure 12.8 UML state diagram: object Book, (a) global view and (b) expanded view

Figure 12.8 gives an example of nested states. Figure 12.8a gives a global view of the life cycle of an object Book: a book is ordered, stays alive for a while, and is eventually either disposed of or archived. In figure 12.8b, state alive is expanded to show its finer structure. In this example, the state is refined into mutually exclusive disjoint substates: a book is *either* available *or* borrowed.[3] The transition from state ordered to state alive is drawn to the boundary of state alive. This is equivalent to a transition to the initial state within the graphics region of alive. The transition from the nested state available to states disposed and archived is made directly. To indicate this transition from a suppressed internal state of alive to disposed and archived in figure 12.8a, the transitions are not drawn from the boundary of alive, but from a so-called **stub**, shown as a small vertical line drawn inside its boundary.

[3]UML also allows you to refine a state into concurrent substates. For example, when a book is returned, several things have to be done. It has to be checked whether the book is returned within the fixed time. If not, some fine may be due. Possible outstanding reservations need to be checked as well and, if so, one of these reservations must be handled. These subprocesses can be handled concurrently. There can be a state returning book which, when refined, results in two or more concurrent, and-related substates. This is shown by tiling the graphics region of the state using dashed lines to separate subregions.

12.2.3 The Sequence Diagram

Objects communicate by sending messages. To carry out a certain task, a particular sequence of messages may have to be exchanged between two or more objects. The time ordering in which this sequence of messages has to occur may be depicted in a **sequence diagram**. This type of diagram is also known as an interaction diagram [JCJO92, Boo94] or an event trace diagram [RBP+91]. In the telecommunications domain, they are known as Message Sequence Charts and provide a standard notation for designing and specifying protocols. Some variant of the sequence diagram is used in many object-oriented analysis and design methods. This diagram is also used in the design pattern community, to graphically depict the interaction between two or more objects participating in a design pattern.

In a sequence diagram, the horizontal dimension shows the various objects that participate in the interaction. An object is shown as a vertical dashed line, its 'lifeline'. The period in which the object is active (within the particular sequence of messages depicted) is shown as a thin rectangle. If the distinction between active and inactive is not important, the entire lifeline may be shown as an activation, as in figure 12.9. The ordering in which the objects are shown carries no meaning.

The vertical dimension denotes the time sequencing of messages. Usually, only the *order* in which messages are displayed carries meaning. For real-time applications, the time axis may show actual numerical values.

Messages are shown as labeled arcs from one object to another. The vertical arrangement of messages indicates their order. The labels may also contain sequence numbers, which are particularly useful to indicate concurrency. A message may also be labeled with a guard, a boolean expression that states the condition which must hold for the message to be sent.

Figure 12.9 shows a possible sequence of interactions between a user, a catalog of available books, and an object which handles reservations. The user first sends a request to the catalog to look up a certain title. The catalog reacts by sending data about that title to the user. If the title is not available (this is indicated by a boolean expression, the guard, within square brackets), a request to reserve that title is sent to the object that handles reservations. Some time later, that title will become available again and reservations will be notified. The object reservations will then send a message to the catalog to hold that book and will notify the user that the title is now available. The ordering of those two messages is irrelevant, so they carry the same sequence number. The user may now borrow the title and the corresponding reservation will be removed.

Again, UML has a rich notational vocabulary for sequence diagrams. It is possible to distinguish asynchronous message-passing from synchronous message-passing, to indicate iteration, to show the creation and destruction of objects, and so

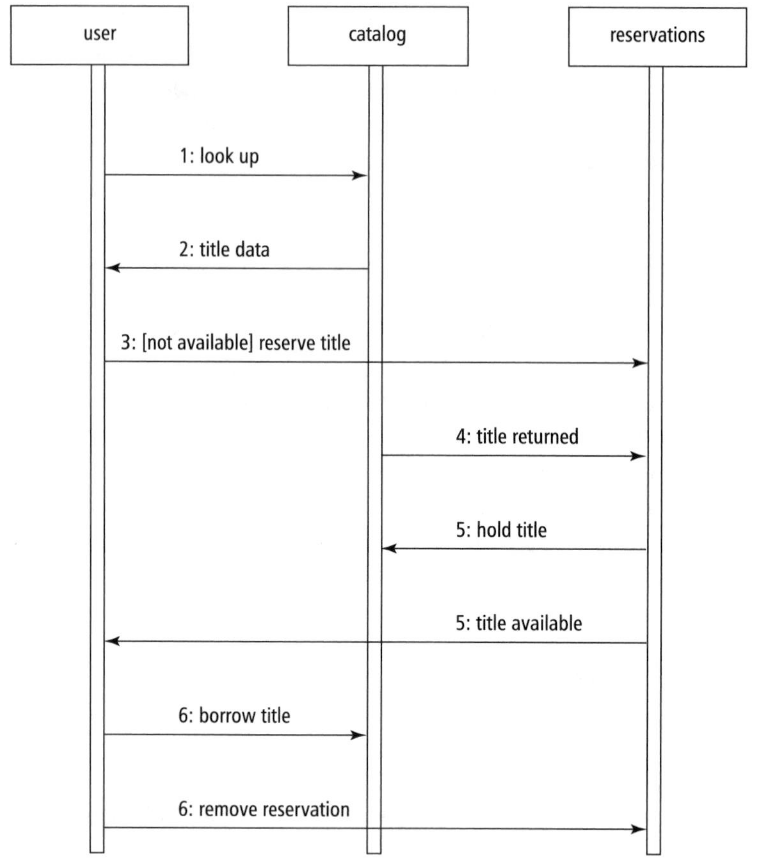

Figure 12.9 UML sequence diagram: reserving a title

on. The main purpose of the sequence diagram however remains the same: an easy-to-read overview of the passing of messages in a particular interaction sequence.

12.2.4 The Collaboration Diagram

The collaboration diagram is another way to show one possible scenario for the interaction between a number of related objects. A collaboration diagram is a directed graph where the nodes denote entities and the edges denote communication between those entities. This type of diagram is also known as an object diagram [Boo94] and an object interaction graph [CAB+94].

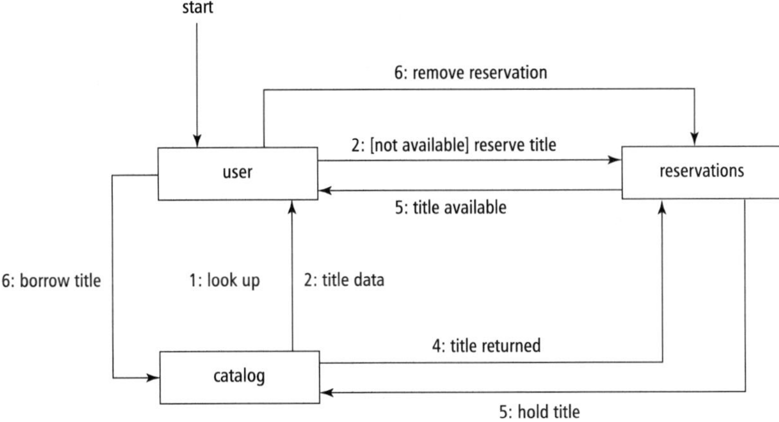

Figure 12.10 UML collaboration diagram: reserving a title

Figure 12.10 shows the same sequence of interactions as the scenario depicted in the sequence diagram in figure 12.9. Collaboration diagrams emphasize the objects and their relationships relevant to a particular interaction. To provide more detail about the interaction, relevant attributes may be shown inside the nodes (by adding another compartment as in a class diagram) and these attributes may be incorporated in the labels of the edges as well.

Sequence diagrams emphasize the ordering of messages. In a sequence diagram, sequence numbers are optional; in a collaboration diagram, they are mandatory since the ordering does not show itself graphically.

12.2.5 The Use Case Diagram

One possible requirements elicitation technique is scenario-based analysis; see also chapter 9. A scenario is a story which tells how a specific task instance is executed. Within the world of OO, **use case scenarios** have become popular. Use case scenarios are also used to depict and evaluate a software architecture; see chapters 10 and 13. They were first proposed in [JCJO92]. According to Jacobson, a use case scenario is 'a particular form or pattern or exemplar of usage, a scenario that begins with some user of the system initiating some transaction or sequence of interrelated events'.

A use case can be documented in various ways: as narrative text, formally using pre- and postconditions, for example, or graphically as in a state transition diagram. The **use case diagram** provides an overview of a set of use cases. Each use case is shown as an ellipse with the name of the use case. The use cases are enclosed by a rectangle denoting the system boundary. An actor that initiates or participates in a scenario is shown as a stick figure with the name of the actor below. Figure 12.11 shows part of the use case diagram for our library system. Borrowing a book involves two actors: a client and an employee of the library. Many other use cases will involve those two actors as well. The ordering of a new book needs approval of a supervisor, as does the remittance of a fine.

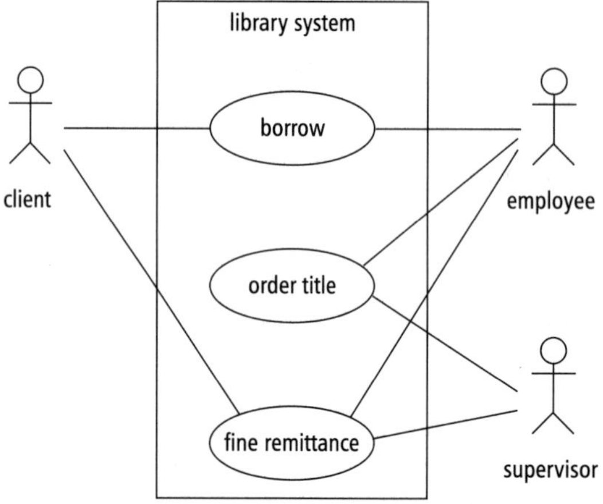

Figure 12.11 UML use case diagram

12.2.6 CRC Cards

CRC stands for Class – Responsibility – Collaborators. A CRC card is simply a 4″×6″ or 5″×7″ index card with three fields labeled Class, Responsibility and Collaborators. CRC cards were developed in response to a need to document collaborative design decisions. CRC cards are especially helpful in the early phases of software development, to help identify components, discuss design issues in multi-disciplinary teams, and specify components informally. CRC cards may be termed a low-tech tool, as opposed to the high-tech tools we commonly use. Yet they are highly useful. They are also fun to work with in our all-too-serious business meetings.

CRC cards are not only used in collaborative design sessions. Within the design pattern community, for instance, they are used to document the elements that participate in a pattern.

The word 'class' in CRC is a historical relic. CRC cards can be used to describe any design element. We will stick to the original terminology, however. The class name appears in the upper-left corner of the card. A bullet-list of responsibilities appears under the class name and a list of collaborators appears on the right part of the card.

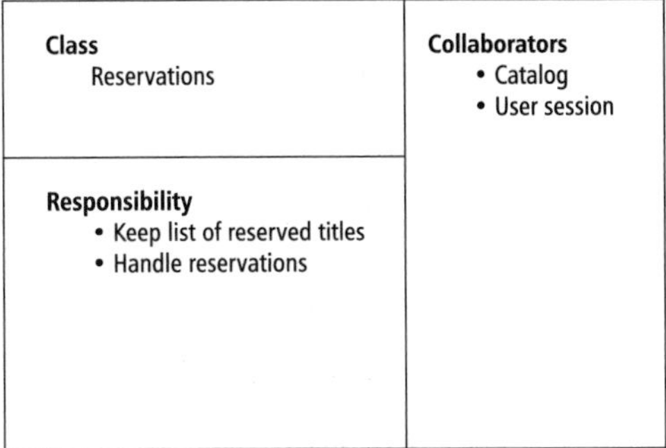

Figure 12.12 A CRC card

Figure 12.12 gives an example of a CRC card for a component Reservations in our library system. The main responsibilities of this component are to keep an up-to-date list of reservations and to handle reservations on a FIFO basis. Its collaborators are the catalog component and the user session component. The types of interaction with these components is shown in figure 12.10.

12.3 OBJECT-ORIENTED ANALYSIS AND DESIGN METHODS

The key concepts that play a role in the object-oriented approach to analysis and design have been mentioned already: objects, their attributes and services, and the relationships between objects. It follows quite naturally from the above that the object-oriented approach to systems analysis and design involves three major steps:

1. identify the objects;
2. determine their attributes and services;
3. determine the relationships between objects.

Obviously, these steps are highly interrelated and some form of iteration will be needed before the final design is obtained. The resulting picture of the system as a collection of objects and their interrelationships describes the **static** structure (decomposition) of the system. This static model is graphically depicted in some variant of the class diagram as described in section 12.2.1.

An object instance is created, updated zero or more times, and finally destroyed. Finite state diagrams depicting the possible states of an object and the transitions between those states are a good help in modeling this life cycle. We discussed one variant of this, the Process Structure Diagram (PSD) of JSD, in chapter 11. Object-oriented methods generally use some variant of the statechart to show this **dynamic** model of the behavior of system components; see section 12.2.2.

Components of the system communicate by sending messages. These messages are part of a task that the system has to perform. We may find out which messages are needed, and in which order they have to be exchanged, by considering typical usage scenarios. Scenario analysis is a requirements elicitation technique. In object-oriented circles, this technique is known as **use-case analysis**. The resulting model of the communication between system components is depicted in a sequence or collaboration diagram; see sections 12.2.3 and 12.2.4. These views are also part of the dynamic model.

The guidelines for finding objects and their attributes and services are mostly linguistic in nature, much like the ones mentioned in our discussion of JSD in chapter 11. Indeed, the modeling stage of JSD is object-oriented too. The guidelines presented below are loosely based on [CY91] and [RBP$^+$91]. Their general flavor is similar to that found in other object-oriented approaches. The global process models of some well-known object-oriented methods is discussed in sections 12.3.1–12.3.3.

The problem statement for a library automation system given in figure 12.13 will serve as an example to illustrate the major steps in object-oriented analysis and design. We will elaborate part of this problem in the text, and leave a number of detailed issues as exercises.

Problem statement

Design the software to support the operation of a public library. The system has a number of stations for customer transactions. These stations are operated by library employees. When a book is borrowed, the identification card of the client is read. Next, the station's bar code reader reads the book's code. When a book is returned, the identification card is not needed and only the book's code needs to be read.
Clients may search the library catalog from any of a number of PCs located in the library. When doing so, the user is first asked to indicate how the search is to be done: by author, by title, or by keyword.
...
Special functionality of the system concerns changing the contents of the catalog and the handling of fines. This functionality is restricted to library personnel. A password is required for these functions.
...

Figure 12.13 Problem statement for library automation

A major guiding principle for identifying objects is to look for important concepts from the application domain. Objects to be found in a library include Books, FileCabinets, Customers, etc. In an office environment, we may have Folders, Letters, Clerks, etc. These domain-specific entities are our prime candidates for objects.

They may be real-world objects, like books; roles played, like the customer of a library; organizational units, like a department; locations, like an office; or devices, like a printer. Potential objects can also be found by considering existing classification or assembly (whole-parts) structures. From interviews, documentation, and so on, a first inventory of objects can be made.

From the first paragraph of the problem description in figure 12.13, the following list of candidate objects can be deduced, by simply listing all the nouns:

software
library
system
station
customer
transaction
book
library employee
identification card
client
bar code reader
book's code

Some objects on this candidate list should be eliminated, though. Software, e.g., is an implementation construct which should not be included in the model at this point in time. A similar fate should befall terms like algorithm or linked list. At the detailed design stage, there may be reasons to introduce (or reintroduce) them as solution-oriented objects.

Vague terms should be replaced by more concrete terms or eliminated. System is a vague term in our candidate list. The stations and PCs will be connected to the same host computer, so we might as well use the notion computer instead of system.

Customer and client are synonymous terms in the problem statement. Only one of them is therefore retained. We must be careful in how we model client and library employee. One physical person may assume both roles. Whether it is useful to model these as distinct objects or as different roles of one object is difficult to decide at this point. We will treat them as separate objects for now, but keep in mind that this may change when the model gets refined.

The term transaction refers to an operation applied to objects, rather than an object in itself. It involves a sequence of actions such as handing an identification card and a book copy to the employee, inserting the identification card in the station, reading the book's bar code, and so on. Only if the transactions themselves have features which are important to the system, should they be modeled as objects. For instance, if the system has to produce profile information about client preferences, it is useful to have an object transaction.

The term book is a bit tricky in this context. A book in a library system may denote both a physical copy and an abstract key denoting a particular {author, title} combination. The former meaning is intended when we speak about the borrowing of a book, while the latter is intended where it concerns entries in the library catalog. Inexperienced designers may equate these interpretations and end up with the wrong system. We are interested (in this part of the system) in modeling book *copies*.

The last entry to be dropped from the list is book's code. This term describes an individual object rather than a class of objects. It should be restated as an attribute of an object, to wit book copy.

Figure 12.14 lists the relationships between objects that can be inferred from the problem statement. These relationships are directly copied from the problem statement, or they are part of the tacit knowledge we have of the domain.

From the problem statement:
employee operates station station has bar code reader bar code reader reads book copy bar code reader reads identification card
Tacit knowledge:
library owns computer library owns stations computer communicates with station library employs employee client is member of library client has identification card

Figure 12.14 Relationships inferred from the problem statement

The resulting objects and relationships are included in the initial class diagram of figure 12.15. We have only included the names of the relationships in this diagram. Further adornments, such as cardinality constraints and generalization/specialization information, may be included when the model gets refined.

We next identify the attributes of objects. Attributes describe an instance of an object. Collectively, the attributes constitute the state of the object. Attributes are identified by considering the characteristics that distinguish individual instances, yet are common properties of the instances of an object type. We thereby look for atomic attributes rather than composite ones. For our library customer, we would for example obtain attributes Name and Address rather than a composite attribute NameAndAddress. At this stage, we also try to prevent redundancies in the set of attributes. So rather than having attributes BooksOnLoan and NumberOfBooksOnLoan, we settle for the former only, since the latter can be computed from that attribute.

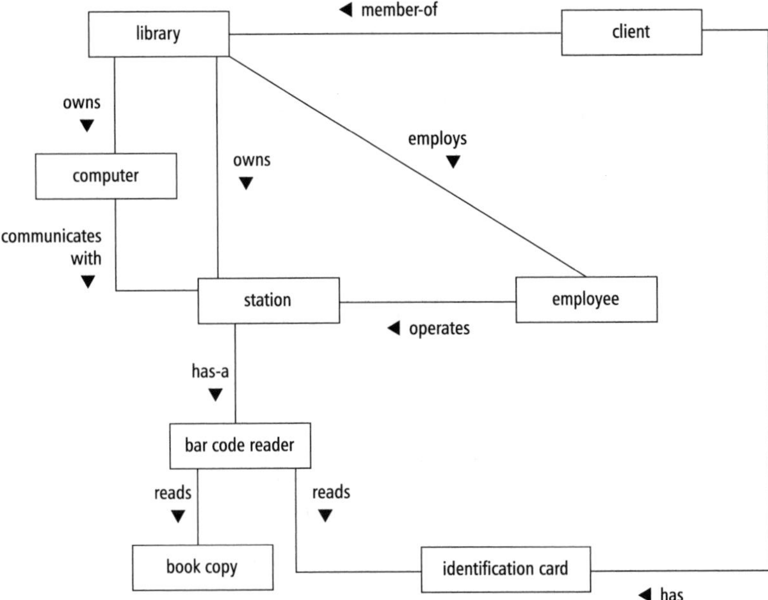

Figure 12.15 (Part of) the initial object model for a library system

The major services provided by an object are those that relate to its life cycle. For example, a copy of a book is acquired, is borrowed and returned zero or more times, and finally it goes out of circulation. A person becomes a member of the library and may borrow and return books, reserve titles, change address, pay fines, and so on, until he finally ceases to be a member.

These services concern the state of an object: they read and write the object's attributes. Services that provide information about the state of an object may or may not involve some type of computation. Note that it is always possible to optimize the actual implementation by keeping redundant information in the state as it is maintained by the object. For example, we may decide to include the number of books on loan in the state as implemented, rather than computing it when required. This need not concern us at this stage though. Whether services are actually implemented by computational means or by a simple lookup procedure is invisible to the object that requests the information.

Further insight into which services are required can be obtained by investigating usage scenarios. We may prepare typical dialogs between components of the system in both normal and exceptional situations. For example, we may consider the situation in which a client successfully borrows a book, one in which the client's identification card is no longer valid, one in which he still has to pay an outstanding fine, and so on. A sequence diagram for the normal situation of borrowing a book is shown in figure 12.16. A number of events take place when this interaction takes place. These events will be handled by operations of the objects involved.

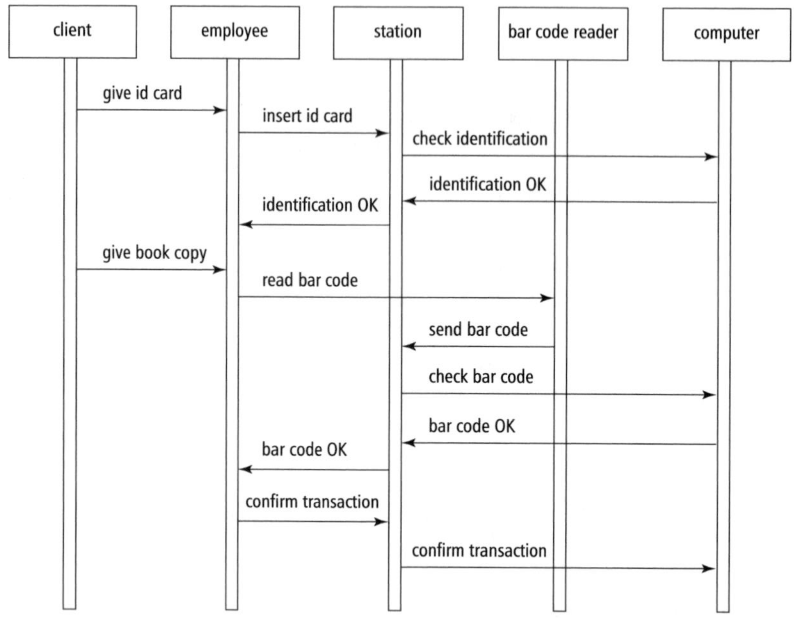

Figure 12.16 Sequence diagram for borrowing a book

Services are but one way through which objects may be related. The relations which give systems a truly object-oriented flavor are those which result from whole–part and generalization–specialization classifications.

Part of the classification of objects may result from the pre-existing real-world classifications that the system is to deal with. Further classification of objects into an object hierarchy involves a search for relations between objects. To start with, we may consider an object as a generalization of other possible objects. For instance, the object Book may be viewed as a generalization of objects Novel, Poetry and ReferenceBook. Whether these specializations are meaningful depends on the problem at hand. If the system does not need to distinguish between novels and poetry, we should not define separate objects for them. The distinction between novels and poetry on the one hand and reference books on the other is sensible, though, if novels and poetry can be borrowed, but reference books cannot.

In a similar way, we may consider similarities between objects, thus viewing them as specializations of a more general object. If our library system calls for objects Book and Journal that have a number of attributes in common, we may introduce a new object Publication as a generalization of these objects. The common attributes are lifted to the object Publication; Book and Journal then inherit these attributes. Note that generalizations should still reflect meaningful real-world entities. There is no point in introducing a generalization of Book and FileCabinet simply because they have a common attribute Location.

The object Publication introduced above is an *abstract object*. It is an object for which there are no instances. The library only contains instances of objects that are a specialization of Publication, such as Book and Journal. Its function in the object hierarchy is to relate these other objects and to provide an interface description to its users. The attributes and services defined at the level of Publication together constitute the common interface for all its descendants.

The generalization–specialization hierarchy also makes it possible to lift services to higher levels of the hierarchy. Doing so often gives rise to so-called **virtual functions**. Virtual functions are services of an object for which a (default) implementation is provided which can be redefined by specializations of that object. The notion of virtual functions greatly enhances reusability, since a variant of some object can now be obtained by constructing a specialization of that object in which some services are redefined.

Decisions as to which objects and attributes to include in a design, and how to relate them in the object hierarchy, are highly intertwined. For instance, if an object has one attribute only, it is generally better to include it as an attribute in other objects. Also, the instances of an object should have common attributes. If some attributes are only meaningful for a subset of all instances, then we really have a classification structure. If some books can be borrowed, but others cannot, this is an indication of a classification structure where the object Book has specializations such as Novel and ReferenceBook.

Note also that, over time, the set of attributes of and services provided by an object tends to evolve, while the object hierarchy remains relatively stable. If our library decides to offer an extra service to its customers, say borrowing records, we may simply adapt the set of attributes and extend the set of services for the object Customer.

Object-oriented design can be classified as a **middle-out** design method. The set of objects identified during the first modeling stages constitutes the middle level of the system. In order to implement these domain-specific entities, lower-level objects are used. These lower-level objects can often be taken from a class library. For the various object-oriented programming languages, quite extensive class libraries already exist. We may envisage a future in which collections of domain-specific classes will become available as well, in the form of 'domain libraries'. The higher levels of the design constitute the application-dependent interaction of the domain-specific entities.

12.3.1 The Booch Method

The global process model of the method described in [Boo94] is shown in figure 12.17. It consists of four steps, to be carried out in roughly the order specified. The process is iterative, so each of the steps may have to be done more than once. The first cycles are analysis-oriented, while later ones are design-oriented. The blurring of activities in this process model is intentional. Analysis and design activities are assumed to be under opportunistic control. It is therefore not deemed realistic to prescribe a purely rational order for the activities to be carried out.

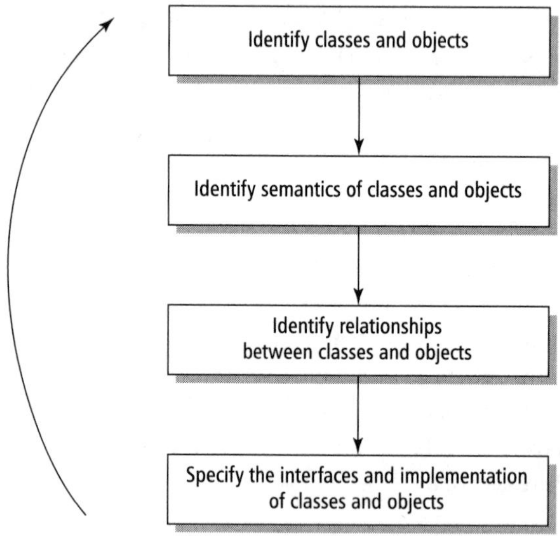

Figure 12.17 The process model of Booch (*Source: G. Booch,* Object-Oriented Analysis and Design with Applications, *©1994 Benjamin Cummings Publishing Company Inc., Reprinted by permission of Addison Wesley Longman*)

The first step is aimed at identifying classes and objects. The purpose of this step is to establish the boundaries of the problem and to obtain a first decomposition. During analysis, emphasis is on finding meaningful abstractions from the domain of application. During design, objects from the solution domain may be added. The major outcome of this step is a data dictionary containing a precise description of the abstractions identified.

The second step is concerned with determining the behavior and attributes of each abstraction, and the distribution of responsibilities over components of the system. Attributes and desired behavior are identified by analyzing typical usage scenarios. As this process proceeds, responsibilities may be reallocated to get a more balanced design, or be able to reuse (scavenge) existing designs. The outcome of this step is a reasonably complete set of responsibilities and operations for each abstraction. The results are documented in the data dictionary and, at a later stage, in interface specifications for each abstraction. The semantics of usage scenarios are captured in sequence and collaboration diagrams (termed **interaction diagram** and **object diagram**, respectively, in [Boo94]).

The third step is concerned with finding relationships between objects. During analysis, emphasis is on finding relationships between abstractions. During design, tactical decisions about inheritance, instantiation, and the like are made. The results are shown in class diagrams, collaboration diagrams, and so-called module diagrams which show the modular structure of a system.

Finally, the abstractions are refined up to a detailed level. A decision is made about the representation of each abstraction, algorithms are selected, and solution-oriented classes are added where needed.

The most notable characteristics of Booch's method are:

- A rich set of notations: it uses six types of diagram, each with a fairly elaborate vocabulary; as a result, many aspects of a system can be modeled.

- A poor process model: it is difficult to decide when to iterate, and what to do in a specific iteration.

12.3.2 The Object Modeling Technique (OMT)

The Object Modeling Technique consists of three phases: analysis, system design, and object design; see figure 12.18.

The analysis phase is concerned with understanding and modeling the application as well as the domain in which it operates. The output consists of three models:

- The object model describes the static, structural aspects of the system. The object model is obtained by identifying objects, their relationships and attributes. The result is documented in a class diagram (called an **object diagram** in OMT) and a data dictionary.

- The dynamic model describes the behavioral, control aspects of the system. This model is derived from scenarios for typical interaction. Events between objects are identified and shown in sequence diagrams and collaboration diagrams (called an **event trace** and an **event flow diagram**, respectively, in OMT).

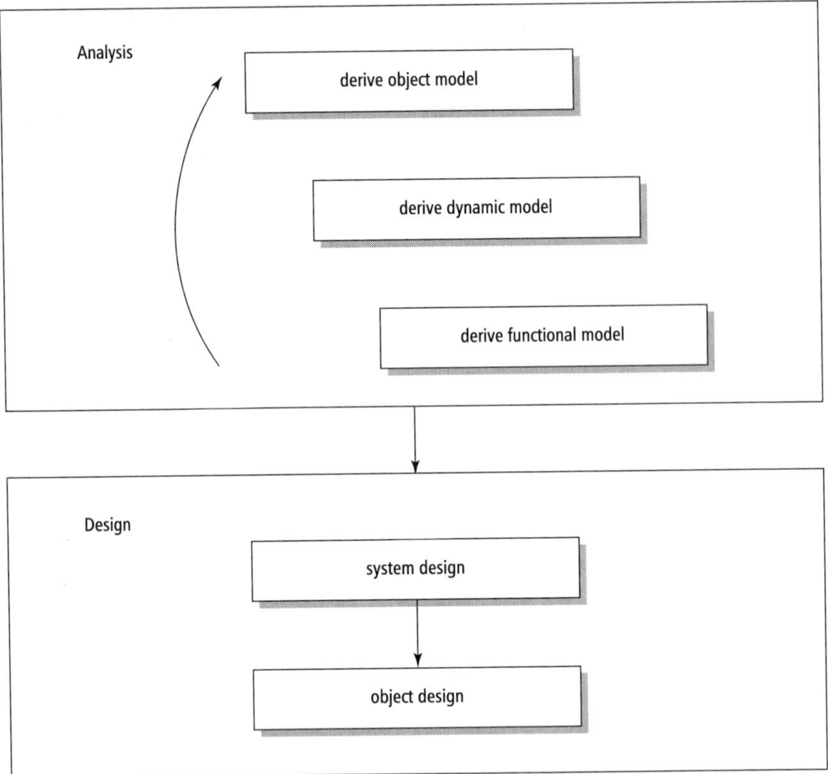

Figure 12.18 The process model of OMT

- The functional model describes the transformational, function aspects of the system. The functional model is shown in a data flow diagram.

The three models of the analysis phase are not developed in one sweep. Analysis is an iterative process. It is considered complete when all requirements are captured in the models.

The design phases of OMT do not introduce new models. System design is concerned with the architectural design of the system: the choice of architectural style, the decomposition of the system into subsystems, the allocation of processes to processors, and the like. Object design is concerned with the algorithmic aspects of individual components.

Like most object-oriented methods, OMT evolves. Since the publication of *Object-Oriented Modeling and Design* in 1991, a lot of experience with the method has been gained, and this has led to a number of changes and extensions to the method. The major changes are twofold. First, the diagrammatic conventions have evolved in the direction of the UML-notation as described in section 12.2. Secondly, the functional model has changed rather drastically. For most functions, a specification through pre- and postconditions is now sufficient. For complex functions, OMT now offers a kind of collaboration diagram as well as so-called object-oriented data flow diagrams.

The most notable characteristics of OMT are:

- A rich set of notations. OMT object diagrams, in particular, have a large vocabulary for expressing analysis and design information about objects and their relationships. This may be considered both a strength and a weakness.

- The analysis phase, which offers many heuristics for obtaining a collection of objects and their relationships.

OMT's design phase is not really concerned with global design issues. It is, rather, implementation-oriented. As a result, the step from analysis to design may be quite big. OMT's functional model seems to be the least successful part. Trying to reconcile an object-oriented view with a function-oriented view is difficult. Sometimes, the functional model simply is not produced.

12.3.3 Fusion

The Fusion method for object-oriented analysis and design has two major phases: analysis and design. Its global process model is shown in figure 12.19.

The analysis phase is aimed at determining the system's objects and their interactions. The static structure is shown in a class diagram (called an **object model** in Fusion), and documented in a data dictionary. The dynamics are shown in the interface model. The interface model consists of a life cycle model for each object, denoted by a regular expression (i.e., a flat representation of a state transition diagram) and a specification of the semantics of each operation in a pre- and postcondition style. The analysis process is assumed to be an iterative process. This iteration stops when the models are complete and consistent.

Fusion's design phase results in four models, which are essentially derived in the order indicated in figure 12.19. Object interaction graphs resemble collaboration graphs. They describe how objects interact at runtime: what objects are involved in a computation and how they are combined to realize a given specification. Visibility graphs describe how the communications between objects are realized. For each object, it is determined which other objects must be referenced and how. Different kinds of references are distinguished, taking into account aspects like the lifetime of the reference and whether references can be shared. Next, the object model, interac-

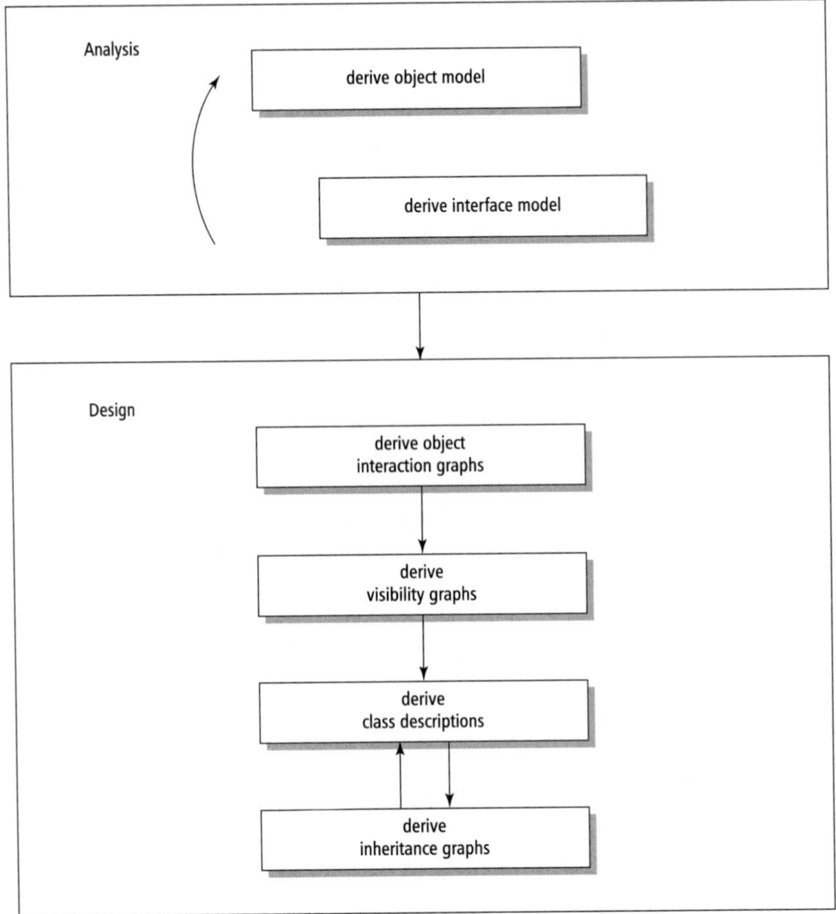

Figure 12.19 The process model of Fusion

tion graphs and visibility graphs are used to derive a description of each class. The operations and the initial set of attributes for each object are established at this stage. Finally, the inheritance relations are decided upon, and depicted in the inheritance graph, which is a class diagram. The class descriptions then are updated to reflect this inheritance structure.

The most notable characteristics of Fusion are:

- The attention paid to the design phase, which is greater than in the other methods discussed. Fusion defines four models for the design phase and gives detailed guidelines for the kind of things that have to be incorporated in these models.

- The version of the method as published in [CAB+94] hinges on the availability of a good requirements document. Recent extensions include the absorption of use cases to drive the analysis process.

- As a method, Fusion is very prescriptive. The contrast with the opportunistic approach of Booch is striking. Fusion's prescriptiveness might be considered both a strength and a weakness.

12.3.4 Object Orientation: Hype or the Answer?

> *Moving from OOA to OOD is a progressive expansion of the model.*
> [CY91, p. 178]
>
> *The transition from OOA to OOD is difficult.*
> [Dav95]
>
> *Strict modeling of the real world leads to a system that reflects today's reality but not necessarily tomorrow's. The abstractions that emerge during design are key to making a design flexible.*
> [GHJV95]

The above quotes hint at some important questions still left unanswered in our discussion of object-oriented methods:

- do object-oriented methods adequately capture the requirements engineering phase?

- do object-oriented methods adequately capture the design phase?

- do object-oriented methods adequately bridge the gap between these phases, if such a gap exists?

- are object-oriented methods really an improvement over more traditional methods?

The goal of requirements engineering is to model relevant aspects of the real world, the world in which the application has to operate. Requirements engineering activities concern both capturing knowledge of this world, and modeling it. The language and methods for doing so should be problem-oriented (domain-oriented). They should ease communication with users as well as validation of the requirements by users. Most object-oriented methods assume that the requirements have been established before the analysis starts. Of the three processes distinguished in chapter 9, elicitation, specification and validation, object-oriented methods by and large only cover the requirements *specification* subprocess. Though many object-oriented methods have incorporated use-case analysis, the purpose thereof primarily is to model the functional behavior of the system rather than to elicit user requirements.

A rather common view of OO proponents is that object-oriented analysis (OOA) and object-oriented design (OOD) are very much the same. OOD simply adds implementation-specific classes to the analysis model. This view, however, can be disputed. OOA should be problem-oriented; its goal is to increase our understanding of the problem. The purpose of design, whether object-oriented or otherwise, is to decide on the parts of a solution, their interaction, and the specification of each of these parts. This difference in scope places OOA and OOD at a different relative 'distance' from a problem and its solution, as shown in figure 12.20.

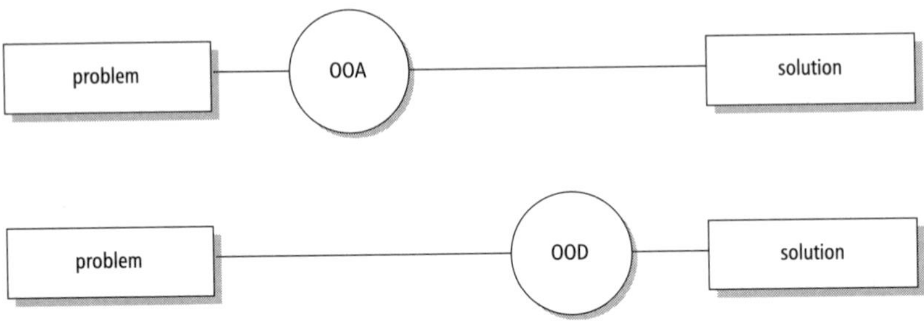

Figure 12.20 The 'distance' between OOA, OOD and a problem and its solution

There are good reasons to distinguish OOA-type activities and OOD-type activities, as is done in Fusion, for example. During design, attention is focused on specifying how to create and destroy objects, on identifying generalizations (abstract, if necessary) of objects in order to promote reuse or maintainability, and so on. An object Publication as a generalization of Book and Journal need not be considered during analysis, since it does not increase our understanding of the domain. On the other hand, an object like identification card may well disappear from the model during design.

Most software development organizations have accumulated a lot of experience in developing software following the traditional, function- or process-oriented style. The transition to an object-oriented style is a radical paradigm shift and is, therefore, difficult. Part of this difficulty is caused by the type of problems that besiege any major change. Management support is required, and sufficient budget has to be allocated, for example for training. People prefer not to change and may be entrenched in cultural norms. Problems easily accumulate if the first OO project is not a major success. On the other hand, expectations are high, miracles are expected, and the new technology is sometimes expected to solve a pre-existing problem, which it mostly doesn't because the root cause of that problem lies somewhere else.

Object-oriented approaches are still less mature than the more traditional paradigms. To give but a few examples: handling of real-time requirements in object-oriented methods is still difficult, measuring progress in OO projects is hard, we do not have good cost models for OO development, and scalability of OO systems as well as interoperability with other, non-OO types of system, is hard.

Both the personnel and technical reasons can be, and are, used to hold a brief for object orientation in the absence of hard evidence of increased productivity or quality. However, several experiments have been done to test the effectiveness of the OO paradigm, and the results seem to indicate some deeper problems too. For example, in one experiment it was tested how effective object-oriented models are as the main vehicle of communication between the typical customer and the developer [Moy96]. It was found that the traditional, functional models were easier to understand, provoked more questions and comments, gave a more holistic understanding of the business, and better helped to evaluate likely implementations. In another experiment it was tested whether novice analysts are able to develop requirements more easily with certain methods than with others, and whether they learn to use certain methods more readily than others [VC94]. And again, the results were negative for OO: novice analysts were better able to apply the process-oriented method, and significant learning only occurred for the process-oriented method. There may well be some truth in the observation that users do not think in objects; they think in tasks. From that point of view, use-case analysis may be seen as one way to introduce a functional view into an otherwise object-oriented approach.

12.4 OBJECT-ORIENTED METRICS

At the level of individual methods, we may assess quality characteristics of components by familiar metrics such as: length, cyclomatic complexity, and the like. At higher levels of abstraction, object-oriented systems consist of a collection of classes that interact by sending messages. Familiar inter-modular metrics which focus on the relationships between modules do not account for the specifics of object-oriented systems. In this section, we discuss a few metrics specifically aimed at characteristics of object-oriented systems. These metrics are listed in figure 12.21.

WMC is a measure for the size of a class. The assumption is that larger classes are in general less desirable. They take more time to develop and maintain, and they are likely to be less reusable. The formula is: WMC = $\sum_{i=1}^{n} c_i$, where c_i is the complexity of method i. For the complexity of an individual method we may choose

WMC	Weighted Methods per Class
DIT	Depth of class in Inheritance Tree
NOC	Number Of Children
CBO	Coupling Between Object classes
RFC	Response For a Class
LCOM	Lack of Cohesion of a Method

Figure 12.21 A suite of object-oriented metrics

its length, cyclomatic complexity, and so on. Most often, c_i is set at 1. In that case, we simply count the number of methods. Besides being simple, this has the advantage that the metric can be applied during design, once the class interface has been decided upon. Note that each entry in the class interface counts as one method, the principle being that each method which requires additional design effort should be counted. For example, different constructors for one and the same operation, as is customary in C++, count as different methods.

Classes in an object-oriented design are related through a subtype–supertype hierarchy. If the class hierarchy is deep and narrow, a proper understanding of a class may require knowledge of many of its superclasses. On the other hand, a wide and shallow inheritance structure occurs when classes are more loosely coupled. The latter situation may indicate that commonality between elements is not sufficiently exploited. DIT is the distance of a class to the root of its inheritance tree. Note that the value of DIT is somewhat language-dependent. In Smalltalk, for example, every class is a subclass of Object, and this increases the value of DIT. A widely accepted heuristic is to strive for a forest of classes, i.e. a collection of inheritance trees of medium height.

NOC counts the number of immediate descendants of a class. If a class has a large number of descendants, this may indicate an improper abstraction of the parent class. A large number of descendants also suggests that the class is to be used in a variety of settings, which will make it more error-prone. The idea thus is that higher values of NOC suggest a higher complexity of the class.

CBO is the main coupling metric for object-oriented systems. Two classes are coupled if a method of one class uses a method or state variable of the other class. The CBO is a count of the number of other classes with which it is coupled. As with the traditional coupling metric, high values of CBO suggest tight bindings with other components, and this is undesirable.

In the definition of CBO, all couplings are considered equal. However, if we look at the different ways in which classes may be coupled, it is reasonable to say that:

- access to state variables is worse than mere parameter passing;
- access to elements of a foreign class is worse than access to elements of a superclass;
- passing many complex parameters is worse than passing a few simple parameters;
- messages that conform to Demeter's Law[4] are better than those which don't.

If we view the methods as bubbles, and the couplings as connections between bubbles, CBO simply counts the number of connections for each bubble. In reality, we consider some types of couplings worse than others: some connections are 'thicker' than others, and some connections are to bubbles 'further away'. For the *representation condition* of measurement theory to hold, these empirical relations should be reflected in the numerical relation system.

RFC measures the 'immediate surroundings' of a class. Suppose a class C has a collection of methods M. Each method from M may in turn call other methods, from C or any other class. Let $\{R_i\}$ be the set of methods called from method M_i. Then the **response set** of this class is defined as: $\{M\} \cup_i \{R_i\}$, i.e. the set of messages that may potentially be executed if a message is sent to an object of class C. RFC is defined as the number of elements in the response set. Note that we only count method calls up to one level deep. Larger values of RFC means that the immediate surroundings of a class is larger in size. There is, then, a lot of communication with other methods or classes. This makes comprehension of a class more difficult and increases test time and complexity.

The final object-oriented metric to be discussed is the lack of cohesion of a method. The traditional levels of cohesion express the degree of mutual affinity of the components of a module. It is a measure of the glue that keeps the module together. If all methods of a class use the same state variables, these state variables serve as the glue which ties the methods together. If some methods use a subset of the state variables, while other methods use another subset of the state variables, the class lacks cohesion. This may indicate a flaw in the design, and it may be better to split it into two or more subclasses. LCOM is the number of disjoint sets of methods of a

[4]The Law of Demeter is a generally-accepted design heuristic for object-oriented systems. It says that the methods of a class should only depend on the top-level structure of their own class. More specifically, in the context of a class C with method M, M should only send messages to:

- the parameters of C, or
- the state variables of C, or
- C itself.

class. Any two methods in the same set share at least one local state variable. The preferred value for LCOM is 0.

There are obviously many more metrics that aim to address the specifics of object-oriented systems. Most of these have not been validated extensively, though. Several experiments have shown that the above set does have some merit. These metrics for example were able to predict fault-proneness of classes during design, and were found to have a strong relationship with maintenance effort.

12.5 SUMMARY

The roots of object orientation can be traced back to the programming language SIMULA-67, where the class concept was introduced for the first time. Some years later, in the early 1970s, the object-oriented programming language Smalltalk was developed at Xerox PARC. For the next 20 years, the OO-community, by and large, remained focused on object-oriented *programming*. Around 1990, the first generation of object-oriented *analysis and design* methods was published. In the ensuing years, these methods drew a lot of attention. As experience with them grew, they were extended and improved, which resulted in a second generation of these methods. These second-generation approaches also frequently borrowed successful elements from each other. Further unification efforts are currently under way. Some of the developers of successful first- and second-generation object-oriented methods have joined forces and defined the Unified Modeling Language (UML). UML is likely to become a unified notation for a variety of methods.

Notwithstanding the variety of methods that exist, the general flavor of their diagramming techniques as well as the guidelines on how to do object-oriented analysis and design are remarkably similar. There is an overwhelming agreement about the following types of diagram:

- a **class diagram** is used to show the static decomposition of the system.
- a **state diagram** is used to depict the dynamic behavior of objects.
- a **sequence** or **collaboration** diagram shows typical interactions consisting of an ordered sequence of messages.

Object-oriented analysis and design methods by and large assume a stable problem statement to start with. They are not particularly strong on requirements elicitation. **Use-case diagrams** and **CRC cards** are two well-known OO-related tools for eliciting requirements.

The object-oriented approach to analysis and design involves three major steps:

1. Identify the objects;

2. Determine their attributes and services;

3. Determine the relationships between objects.

These steps are highly interrelated and some form of iteration will generally occur. Some of the OO-methods assume that the first iterations of these steps are analysis-oriented, while later ones are design-oriented. They thus presume that the notations and mechanisms of object-oriented analysis and design are the same. In other methods, the distinction between analysis and design activities is drawn much sharper. As a result of these differences, the process models of the various methods may show quite some variation as well, even though the essential activities are the same.

The guidelines for finding objects and their attributes and services are mostly linguistic in nature. The heuristics for how to transform the result of analysis into a robust design are informal as well. Several attempts have been made to define metrics that specifically address the topology of an object-oriented system – a collection of interacting objects. For example, we may count the distance of an object to the root of its inheritance tree, or the number of methods in a class, and try to relate these to quality aspects such as maintainability. Experiments with these metrics have, as yet, been scarce and further validation is needed.

Proponents of object-oriented methods have claimed a number of advantages of the object-oriented approach over the more traditional, function-oriented, approaches to design:

- The object-oriented approach is more natural. It fits the way we view the world around us. The concepts that show up in the analysis model have a direct counterpart in the UoD being modeled, thus providing a direct link between the model and the world being modeled. This makes it easier for the client to comprehend the model and discuss it with the analyst.

- The object-oriented approach focuses on structuring the problem rather than any particular solution to it. This point is closely related to the previous one. In designs based on the functional paradigm the modules tend to correspond to parts of a solution to the problem. It may then not be easy to relate these modules to the original problem. The result of an object-oriented analysis and design is a hierarchy of objects with their associated attributes which still resembles the structure of the problem space.

- The object-oriented approach provides for a smoother transition from requirements analysis to design to code. In our discussion of the object-oriented approach it is often difficult to strictly separate UoD modeling aspects from design aspects. The object hierarchy that results from this process can be directly mapped onto the class hierarchy of the implementation (provided the implementation language is object-oriented too). The attributes of objects become encapsulated by services provided by the objects in the implementation.

- The object-oriented approach leads to more flexible systems that are easier to adapt and change. Because the real-world objects have a direct counterpart in the implementation, it becomes easy to link change requests to the corresponding program modules. Through the inheritance mechanism, changes can often be realized by adding another specialized object rather than through tinkering with the code. For example, if we wish to extend our system dealing with furniture by adding another type of chair, say armchair, we do so by defining a new object ArmChair, together with its own set of attributes, as another specialization of Chair.

- The object-oriented approach promotes reuse by focusing on the identification of real-world objects from the application domain. In contrast, more traditional approaches focus on identifying functions. In an evolving world, the objects tend to be stable, while the functions tend to change. For instance, in an office environment the functions performed are likely to change with time, but there will always be letters, folders, and so on. Thus, an object-oriented design is less susceptible to changes in the world being modeled.

- The inheritance mechanism adds to reusability. New objects can be created as specializations of existing objects, inheriting attributes from the existing objects. At the implementation level, this kind of reuse is accomplished through code sharing. The increasing availability of class libraries contributes to this type of code reuse.

- Objects in an object-oriented design encapsulate abstract data types. As such, an object-oriented design potentially has all the right properties (information hiding, abstraction, high cohesion, low coupling, etc).

The object-oriented approach, however, does not by definition result in a good design. It is a bit too naive to expect that the identification of domain-specific entities is all there is to good design. The following issues must be kept in mind:

- There are other objects besides the ones induced by domain concepts. Objects that have to do with system issues such as memory management or error recovery do not naturally evolve from the modeling of the UoD. Likewise, 'hypothetical' objects that capture implicit knowledge from the application domain may be difficult to identify.

- The separation of concerns that results from the encapsulation of both state and behavior into one component need not be the one that is most desirable.

For example, for many an object it might be necessary to be able to present some image of that object to the user. In a straightforward application of the object-oriented method, this would result in each object defining its own ways for doing so. This, however, is against good practices of system design, where we generally try to isolate the user interface from the computational parts. A clearly identifiable user interface component adds to consistency and flexibility.

- With objects too, we have to consider the uses relation. An object uses another object if it requests a service from that other object. It does so by sending a message. The bottom-up construction of a collection of objects may result in a rather loosely-coupled set, in which objects freely send messages to other objects. With a nod at the term spaghetti-code to denote overly complex control patterns in programs, this is known as the *ravioli* problem. If objects have a complicated usage pattern, it is difficult to view one object without having to consider many others as well.

All of these issues have to do with the design part of object-oriented analysis and design. Solution-oriented design aspects tend to be largely disregarded in these methods. Fusion is a noteworthy counter-example of this.

Next to problems that have to do with the design part of the process, there is the question of how to integrate object-oriented methods, tools and languages with those that already exist. We often tend to reinvent the wheel and do not build on previous results. Designers of object-oriented systems have often failed to incorporate features that have long proven to be useful. For example, object-oriented databases generally do not offer features like authorization and protection (let alone speed) at the same level as non-object-oriented databases.

12.6 FURTHER READING

The different views of the notion of object are discussed in [Tai93]. The various meanings of attribute and related notions such as aggregate, part and member are discussed in [MP96]. [Weg92] is a classic paper on the various dimensions of object-oriented modeling.

The notations used in section 12.2 are those of the Unified Modeling Language, version 1.0. [FS97] provides a good introduction to UML. UML is extensively discussed in three books by its creators: [BRJ98], [RJB98] and [JBR99]. Further information on UML can be found at URL `http://www.rational.com/uml/start/index.html`. Statecharts are discussed in [Har88]. CRC cards are described in [BC89].

A comparative discussion of a number of object-oriented methods is given in [Wie97]. The evolution of object-oriented methods is sketched in [Rum97]. Booch' method is discussed in [Boo94]. OMT is discussed in [RBP+91]. Extensions and modifications to this first-generation version can be found in [Rum95c, Rum95a, Rum95b]. Fusion is described in [CAB+94]. Updates to this 1994 version can be found in [Col96]. A number of applications of Fusion are given in [MLC96].

A critical discussion of the differences and similarities between object-oriented analysis and object-oriented design is given in [Dav95] and [HS93]. [Moy96] describes an experiment in which object-oriented methods and traditional methods are being compared. In [VC94], the ease of adoption of these types of methods by novice analysts is tested. Experiences with (the management of) object-oriented development projects is given in [Pit93], [Com96a], [CAC95], and [LMPR92].

Definitions of the object-oriented metrics introduced in section 12.4 can be found in [CK94]. A critical assessment of these metrics is given in [HM96] and [CS95a]. To meet some of this criticism, we have adopted the definition of LCOM, as suggested in [LH93]. Experiments to validate the Chidamber–Kemerer metrics suite are reported in [LH93], [BBM96], [SS98] and [HCN98].

Exercises

1. Define the following terms: object, state, attribute, message, and inheritance.

2. Explain the difference between the specialization–generalization relation and the whole–part relation.

3. Explain the difference between a class diagram and a state diagram.

4. Explain the difference between a sequence diagram and a collaboration diagram.

5. What are CRC cards and use-case scenarios used for in object-oriented analysis and design?

6. In what respects does a UML state diagram differ from a state transition diagram?

7. Discuss the general flavor of OMT.

8. Why is DIT – the depth of a class in the inheritance tree – a useful metric to consider when assessing the quality of an object-oriented system?

9. What does RFC – Response For a Class – measure?

10. How does the Law of Demeter relate to the maintainability of object-oriented systems?

11. Discuss the relative merits and drawbacks of deep and narrow versus wide and shallow inheritance trees.

12. What are the differences between object-oriented design and the simple application of the information hiding principle?

13. ♡ Extend the object model of figure 12.15 such that it also models user queries to the catalog.

14. ♡ Extend the model from the previous exercise such that it also includes the attributes and services of objects.

15. ♠ Write an essay on the differences and similarities of analysis and design activities in object-oriented analysis and design.

16. ♡ In what sense can the interface to a class be considered a contract? What are the repercussions of this for subtyping relations? (See [Mey92]).

17. ♠ Make an object-oriented design of the KWIC-index example from chapter 10. Discuss any major differences with the decompositions given in section 10.1.

18. ♡ Assess the design obtained in exercise 17 with respect to: abstraction, modularity, information hiding, complexity, and system structure.

19. ♡ Why would object-oriented design be more 'natural' than, say, data flow design? Assess the naturalness of the design obtained in exercise 17 above as opposed to the decompositions from section 10.1.

20. ♠ Discuss the assertion 'The view that object-oriented methods make change easy is far too simplistic'. Consult [LMPR92], who found that changes to object models were fairly localized, whereas changes to behavior models had more far-reaching consequences.

13 Software Testing

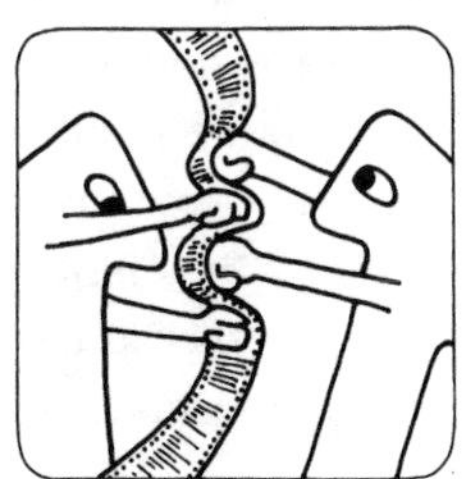

LEARNING OBJECTIVES

- To be aware of the major software testing techniques
- To see how different test objectives lead to the selection of different testing techniques
- To appreciate a classification of testing techniques, based on the objectives they try to reach
- To be able to compare testing techniques with respect to their theoretical power as well as practical value
- To understand the role and contents of testing activities in different life cycle phases
- To be aware of the contents and structure of the test documentation
- To be able to distinguish different test stages

Suppose you are asked to answer the kind of questions posed in [Bab82]:

- Would you trust a completely-automated nuclear power plant?
- Would you trust a completely-automated pilot whose software was written by yourself? What if it was written by one of your colleagues?
- Would you dare to write an expert system to diagnose cancer? What if you are personally held liable in a case where a patient dies because of a malfunction of the software?

You will (probably) have difficulties answering all these questions in the affirmative. Why? The hardware of an airplane probably is as complex as the software for an automatic pilot. Yet, most of us board an airplane without any second thoughts.

As our society's dependence on automation ever increases, the quality of the systems we deliver increasingly determines the quality of our existence. We cannot hide from this responsibility. The role of automation in critical applications and the threats these applications pose should make us ponder. *ACM Software Engineering Notes* runs a column 'Risks to the public in computer systems' in which we are told of numerous (near) accidents caused by software failures. The discussion on software reliability provoked by the Strategic Defense Initiative is a case in point [Par85, Mye86, Par87]. Discussions, such as those about the Therac-25 accidents or the maiden flight of the Ariane 5 (see section 1.4), should be compulsory reading for every software engineer.

Software engineering is still a very immature field. During software construction, many errors are still made. To locate and fix those errors through excessive testing is a laborious affair and mostly not all the errors are found. Good testing is at least as difficult as good design.

With the current state of the art we are not able to deliver fault-free software. Different studies indicate that 30–85 errors per 1000 lines of source code are made. During testing, quite a few of those errors are found and subsequently fixed. Yet, some errors do remain undetected. [Mye86] gives examples of extensively-tested software that still contains 0.5–3 errors per 1000 lines of code. A fault in the seat reservation system of a major airline company incurred a loss of $50M in one quarter. The computerized system reported that cheap seats were sold out while this was in fact not the case. As a consequence, clients were referred to other companies. The problems were not discovered until quarterly results were found to lag considerably behind those of their competitors.

As yet, scant theory on testing has been developed. Fortunately, however, there do exist a number of test methods and techniques that have proven to be effective in practice. A number of these will be discussed in this chapter.

Testing is often taken to mean executing a program to see whether it produces the correct output for a given input. This involves testing the end-product, the software itself. As a consequence, the testing activity often does not get the attention it deserves. By the time the software has been written, we are often pressed for time, which does not encourage thorough testing.

Postponing test activities for too long is one of the most severe mistakes often made in software development projects. This postponement makes testing a rather costly affair. Figure 13.1 shows the results of a study by Boehm about the cost of error correction relative to the phase in which the error is discovered. This picture shows that errors which are not discovered until after the software has become operational incur costs that are 10 to 90 times higher than those of errors that are discovered during the design phase.

The development methods and techniques that are applied in the pre-implementation phases are least developed, relatively. It is therefore not surprising that most of the errors are made in those early phases. An early study by Boehm showed that over 60% of the errors were introduced during the design phase, as opposed to 40% during implementation [Boe75]. Worse still, two-thirds of the errors introduced at the design phase were not discovered until after the software had become operational.

It is therefore incumbent on us to plan carefully our testing activities as early as possible. We should also start the actual testing activities at an early stage. If we do not start testing until after the implementation stage, we are really far too late. The requirements specification, design, and design specification may also be tested. The rigor hereof depends on the form in which these documents are expressed. This has already been hinted at in previous chapters. In section 13.2, we will again highlight the various verification and validation activities that may be applied at the different phases of the software life cycle. The planning and documentation of these activities is discussed in section 13.3.

Before we decide upon a certain approach to testing, we have to determine our test objectives. If the objective is to find as many errors as possible, we will opt for a strategy which is aimed at revealing errors. If the objective is to increase our confidence in the proper functioning of the software we may well opt for a completely different strategy. So the objective will have its impact on the test approach chosen, since the results have to be interpreted with respect to the objectives set forth. Different test objectives and the degree to which test approaches fit these objectives are the topic of section 13.1.

Testing software shows only the presence of errors, not their absence. As such, it yields a rather negative result: up to now, only n ($n \geq 0$) errors have been found. Only when the software is tested exhaustively are we certain about its functioning correctly. In practice this seldom happens. A simple program like

```
for i from 1 to 100 do
    print (if a[i] = true then 1 else 0 endif);
```

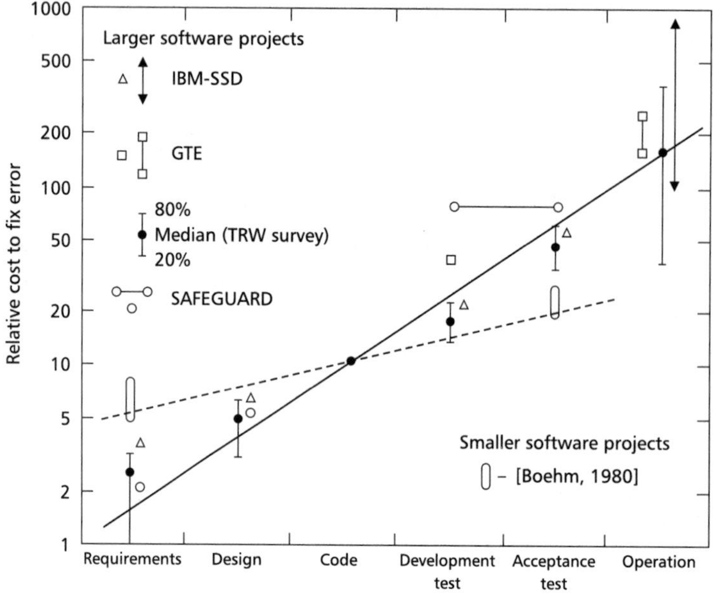

Figure 13.1 Relative cost of error correction (*Source: Barry B. Boehm,* Software Engineering Economics, *fig. 4.2, page 40, ©1981, Reprinted by permission of Prentice Hall, Inc. Englewood Cliffs, NJ*)

has 2^{100} different outcomes. Even on a very fast machine – say a machine which executes 10 million print instructions per second – exhaustively testing this program would take 3×10^{14} years.

An alternative to this brute force approach to testing is to prove the correctness of the software. Proving the correctness of software very soon becomes a tiresome activity, however. It furthermore applies only in circumstances where software requirements are stated formally. Whether these formal requirements are themselves correct has to be decided upon in a different way.

We are thus forced to make a choice. It is of paramount importance to choose a sufficiently small, yet adequate, set of test cases. Test techniques may be classified according to the criterion used to measure the adequacy of a set of test cases:

Coverage-based testing In coverage-based testing, testing requirements are specified in terms of the coverage of the product (program, requirements document, etc.) to be tested. For example, we may specify that all statements of the program should be executed at least once if we run the complete test set, or that all elementary requirements from the requirements specification should be exercised at least once.

Fault-based testing Fault-based techniques focus on detecting faults. The fault detecting ability of the test set then determines its adequacy. For example, we may artificially seed a number of faults in a program, and then require that a test set reveal at least, say, 95% of these artificial faults.

Error-based testing Error-based techniques focus on error-prone points, based on knowledge of the typical errors that people make. For example, off-by-1 errors are often made at boundary values such as 0 or the maximum number of elements in a list, and we may specifically aim our testing effort at these boundary points.

Alternatively, we may classify test techniques based on the source of information used to derive test cases:

Black-box testing, also called **functional** or **specification-based testing**. In black-box testing, test cases are derived from the specification of the software, i.e. we do not consider implementation details.

White-box testing, also called **structural** or **program-based testing**. This is a complementary approach, in which we *do* consider the internal logical structure of the software in the derivation of test cases.

We will use the first classification, and discuss different techniques for coverage-based, fault-based and error-based testing in sections 13.5–13.7. These techniques involve the actual execution of a program. Manual techniques which do not involve program execution, such as code reading and inspections, are discussed in section 13.4. In section 13.8 we assess some empirical and theoretical studies that aim to put these different test techniques in perspective.

The above techniques are applied mainly at the module level. This level of testing is often done concurrently with the implementation phase. It is also called **unit testing**. Besides the module level, we also have to test the integration of a set of modules into a system. Possibly also, the final system will be tested once more under direct supervision of the prospective user. In section 13.9 we will sketch these different test phases.

13.1 TEST OBJECTIVES

Until now, we have not been very precise in our use of the notion of an 'error'. In order to appreciate the following discussion, it is important to make a careful distinction between the notions *error*, *fault* and *failure*. An error is a human action that produces an incorrect result. The consequence of an error is software containing a fault. A fault thus is the manifestation of an error. If encountered, a fault may result in a failure.[1]

So, what we observe during testing are failures. These failures are caused by faults, which are in turn the result of human errors. A failure may be caused by more than one fault, and a fault may cause different failures. Similarly, the relation between errors and faults need not be 1–1.

One possible aim of testing is to find faults in the software. Tests are then intended to expose failures. It is not easy to give a precise, unique, definition of the notion of failure. A programmer may take the system's specification as reference point. In this view, a failure occurs if the software does not meet the specifications. The user, however, may consider the software erroneous if it does not match expectations. 'Failure' thus is a relative notion. If software fails, it does so with respect to something else (a specification, user manual, etc). While testing software, we must always be aware of what the software is being tested against.

In this respect a distinction is often made between 'verification' and 'validation'. The *IEEE Glossary* defines verification as the process of evaluating a system or component to determine whether the products of a given development phase satisfy the conditions imposed at the start of that phase. Verification thus tries to answer the question: Have we built the system right?

The term 'validation' is defined in the *IEEE Glossary* as the process of evaluating a system or component during or at the end of the development process to determine whether it satisfies specified requirements. Validation then boils down to the question: Have we built the right system?

Even with this subtle distinction in mind, the situation is not all that clear-cut. Generally, a program is considered correct if it consistently produces the right output. We may, though, easily conceive of situations where the programmer's intention is not properly reflected in the program but the errors simply do not manifest themselves. For example, some entry in a case statement may be wrong, but this fault never shows up because it happens to be subsumed by a previous entry. Is this program correct, or should it rather be classified as a program with a 'latent' fault? Even if it is considered correct within the context at hand, chances are that we get into trouble if the program is changed or parts of it are reused in a different environment.

As an example, consider the maiden flight of the Ariane 5. Within 40 seconds after take-off, at an altitude of 3700 meters, the launcher exploded. This was ulti-

[1]The *IEEE Glossary of Software Engineering Terminology* gives four definitions of the word 'error'. To distinguish between these definitions, the words 'error', 'fault', 'failure' and 'mistake' are used. The word 'error' in the *Glossary* is used to denote a measurement error, while 'mistake' is used to denote a human error. Though 'mistake' has the advantage of being less condemning, we follow the accepted software engineering literature in this respect. Our definitions of 'fault' and 'failure' are the same as those in the *Glossary*.

mately caused by an overflow in a conversion of a variable from a 64-bit floating point number to a 16-bit signed integer. The piece of software containing this error was reused from the Ariane 4 and had *never* caused a problem in any of the Ariane 4 flights. This is explained by the fact that the Ariane 5 builds up speed much faster than the Ariane 4, which in turn resulted in excessive values for the parameter in question; see also section 1.4.1.

With the above definitions of error and fault, such programs must be considered faulty, even if we cannot devise test cases that reveal the faults. This still leaves open the question of how to define errors. Since we cannot but guess what the programmer's real intentions were, this can only be decided upon by an oracle.

Given the fact that exhaustive testing is not feasible, the test process can be thought of as depicted in figure 13.2. The box labeled P denotes the object (program, design document, etc.) to be tested. The test strategy involves the selection of a subset of the input domain. For each element of this subset, P is used to 'compute' the corresponding output. The expected output is determined by an oracle, something outside the test activity. Finally, the two answers are compared.

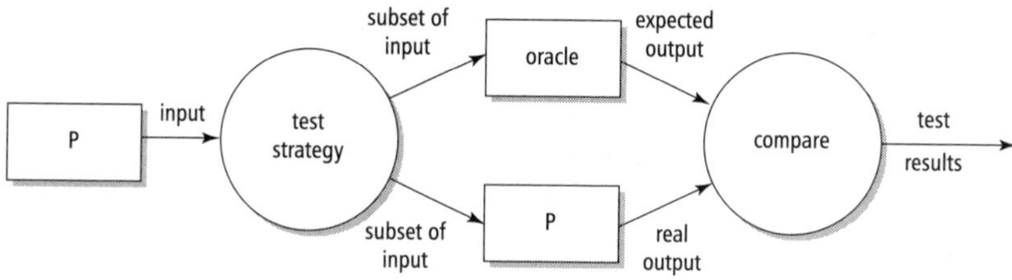

Figure 13.2 Global view of the test process

The most crucial step in this process is the selection of the subset of the input domain which will serve as the test set. This test set must be adequate with respect to some chosen test criterion. In section 13.1.1 we elaborate upon the notion of test adequacy.

Test techniques generally use some systematic means to derive test cases. These test cases are meant to provoke failures. Thus, the main objective is fault detection. Alternatively, our test objective could be to increase our confidence in failure-free behavior. These quite different test objectives, and their impact on the test selection problem, are the topic of section 13.1.2.

To test whether the objectives are reached, test cases are tried in order that faults manifest themselves. A quite different approach is to view testing as fault prevention. This leads us to another dimension of test objectives, which to a large extent parallels the evolution of testing strategies over the years. This evolution is discussed in section 13.1.3.

Finally, the picture so far considers each fault equally hazardous. In reality, there are different types of fault, and some faults are more harmful than others. All techniques to be discussed in this chapter can easily be generalized to cover multiple classes of faults, each with its own acceptance criteria.

Some faults are critical and we will have to exert ourselves in order to find those critical faults. Special techniques, such as fault tree analysis, have been developed to this end. Using fault tree analysis, we try to derive a contradiction by reasoning backwards from a given, undesirable, end situation. If such a contradiction can be derived, we have shown that that particular situation can never be reached.

13.1.1 Test Adequacy Criteria

Consider the program text in figure 13.3 and a test set S containing just one test case:

```
n = 2, A[1] = 10, A[2] = 5
```

If we execute the program using S, then all statements are executed at least once. If our criterion to judge the adequacy of a test set is that 100% of the statements are executed, then S is adequate. If our criterion is that 100% of the branches are executed, then S is not adequate, since the (empty) else-branch of the if-statement is not executed by S.

A **test adequacy criterion** thus specifies requirements for testing. It can be used in different ways: as stopping rule, as measurement, or as test case generator. If a test adequacy criterion is used as a stopping rule, it tells us when sufficient testing has been done. If statement coverage is the criterion, we may stop testing if all statements have been executed by the tests done so far. In this view, a test set is either good or bad; the criterion is either met, or it isn't. If we relax this requirement a bit and use, say, the percentage of statements executed as a test quality criterion, then the test adequacy criterion is used as a measurement. Formally, it is a mapping from the test set to the interval $[0, 1]$. Note that the stopping rule view is in fact a special case of the measurement view. Finally, the test adequacy criterion can be used in the test selection process. If a 100% statement coverage has not been achieved yet, an additional test case is selected that covers one or more statements yet untested. This generative view is used in many test tools.

Test adequacy criteria are closely linked to test techniques. For example, coverage-based test techniques keep track of which statements, branches, and so on, are executed, and this gives us an easy handle to determine whether a coverage-based adequacy criterion has been met or not. The same test technique, however, does not help us in assessing whether all error-prone points in a program have been tested.

In a sense, a given test adequacy criterion and the corresponding test technique are opposite sides of the same coin.

13.1.2 Fault Detection Versus Confidence Building

> *Failures are needles in the haystack of the input domain*
> [HT90]

Suppose we wish to test some module P which sorts an array A[1..n] of integers, $1 \leq n \leq 1000$. Since exhaustive testing is not feasible, we are looking for a strategy in which only a small number of tests are exercised. One possible set of test cases is the following:

Let n assume values 0, 1, 17 and 1000. For each of n = 17 and n = 1000, choose three values for the array A:

- A consists of randomly selected integers;
- A is sorted in ascending order;
- A is sorted in descending order.

In following this type of constructive approach, the input domain is partitioned into a finite, small number of subdomains. The underlying assumption is that these subdomains are **equivalence classes**, i.e. from a testing point of view each member from a given subdomain is as good as any other. For example, we have tacitly assumed that one random array of length 17 is as good a test as any other random array of length i with $1 < i < 1000$.

Suppose the actual sorting algorithm used is the one from figure 13.3. If the tests use positive integers only, the output will be correct. The output will not be correct if a test input happens to contain negative integers.

The test set using positive integers only does not reveal the fault because the inputs in the subdomains are not really interchangeable (instead of comparing the values of array entries, the algorithm compares their absolute values). Any form of testing which partitions the input domain works perfectly if the right subdomains are chosen. In practice however, we generally do not know where the needles are hidden, and the partition of the input domain is likely to be imperfect.

Both functional and structural testing schemes use a systematic means to determine subdomains. They often use peculiar inputs to test peculiar cases. Their intention is to provoke failure behavior. Their success hinges on the assumption that we can indeed identify subdomains with a high failure probability. Though this is a good strategy for fault detection, it does not necessarily inspire confidence.

The user of a system is interested in the probability of failure-free behavior. Following this line of thought, we are not so much interested in the faults themselves,

```
procedure selection-sort (A, n);
integer i, j, small, temp;
begin
    for i:= 1 to n-1 do
        small:= i;
        for j:= i+1 to n do
            if abs(A[j]) < abs(A[small]) then small:= j endif
        enddo;
        temp:= A[i]; A[i]:= A[small]; A[small]:= temp
    enddo
end selection-sort;
```

Figure 13.3 Erroneous selection sort procedure

but rather in their manifestations. A fault which frequently manifests itself will in general cause more damage than a fault which seldom shows up. This is precisely what we hinted at above when we discussed fault detection and confidence building as possible test objectives.

If failures are more important than faults, the goal pursued during the test phase may also change. In that case, we will not pursue the discovery of as many faults as possible but will strive for a high reliability. Random testing does not work all that well if we want to find as many faults as possible – hence the development of different test techniques. When pursuing a high reliability, however, it is possible to use random input.

In order to obtain confidence in the daily operation of a software system, we have to mimic that situation. This requires the execution of a large number of test cases that represent typical usage scenarios. Random testing does at least as good a job in this respect as any form of testing based on partitioning the input domain.

This approach has been applied in the Cleanroom development method. In this method, the development of individual modules is done by programmers who are not allowed to actually execute their code. The programmer must then convince himself of the correctness of his modules using manual techniques such as stepwise abstraction (see also section 13.4).

In the next step, these modules are integrated and tested by someone else. The input for this process is generated according to a distribution which follows the expected operational use of the system. During this integration phase, one tries to reach a certain required reliability level. Experiences with this approach are very promising.

The quantitative assessment of failure probability brings us into the area of software reliability. Chapter 18 is fully devoted to this topic.

13.1.3 From Fault Detection to Fault Prevention

In the early days of computing, programs were written and then debugged to make sure that they ran properly. Testing and debugging were largely synonymous terms. Both referred to an activity near the end of the development process when the software had been written, but still needed to be 'checked out'.

Today's situation is rather different. Testing activities occur in every phase of the development process. They are carefully planned and documented. The execution of software to compare actual behavior with expected behavior is only one aspect out of many.

[GH88] identifies four major testing models. These roughly parallel the historical development of test practices. The models and their primary goals are given in figure 13.4.

Model	Primary goal
Phase models	
Demonstration	Make sure that the software satisfies its specification
Destruction	Detect implementation faults
Life cycle models	
Evaluation	Detect requirements, design and implementation faults
Prevention	Prevent requirements, design and implementation faults

Figure 13.4 Major testing models (*Source: D. Gelperin & B. Hetzel, The growth of software testing,* Communications of the ACM **31**, *6 (1988) 687-695. Reproduced by permission of the Association for Computing Machinery, Inc.*)

The primary goal of the demonstration model is to make sure that the program runs and solves the problem. The strategy is like that of a constructive mathematical proof. If the software passes all tests from the test set, it is claimed to satisfy the requirements. The strategy gives no guidelines as to how to obtain such a test set. A poorly-chosen test set may mask poor software quality.

Most programmers will be familiar with the process of testing their own programs by carefully reading them or executing them with selected input data. If this is done very carefully, it can be beneficial. This method also holds some dangers, however. We may be inclined to consider this form of testing as a method to convince ourselves or someone else that the software does *not* contain errors. We will then, partly unconsciously, look for test cases which support this hypothesis. This type of demonstration-oriented approach to testing is not to be advocated.

Proper testing is a very destructive process. A program should be tested with the purpose of finding as many faults as possible. A test can only be considered successful if it leads to the discovery of at least one fault. (In a similar way, a visit to your physician is only successful if he finds a 'fault' and we will generally consider such a visit unsatisfactory if we are sent home with the message that nothing wrong could be found.)

In order to improve the chances of producing a high quality system, we should reverse the strategy and start looking for test cases that *do* reveal faults. This may be termed a proof by contradiction. The test set is then judged by its ability to detect faults.

Since we do not know whether any residual faults are left, it is difficult to decide when to stop testing in either of these models. In the demonstration-oriented model, the criteria most often used to determine this point in time seem to be the following:

- stop if the test budget has run out;

- stop if all test cases have been executed without any failures occurring.

The first criterion is pointless, since it does not tell us anything about the quality of the test effort. If there is no money at all, this criterion is most easily satisfied. The second criterion is pointless as well, since it does not tell us anything about the quality of the test cases.

The destruction-oriented model usually entails some systematic way of deriving test cases. We may then base our stop criterion on the test adequacy criterion that corresponds to the test technique used. An example of this might be: 'We stop testing if 100% of the branches are covered by the set of test cases, and all test cases yield an unsuccessful result.'

Both these models view testing as one phase in the software development process. As noted before, this is not a very good strategy. The life cycle testing models extend testing activities to earlier phases. In the evaluation-oriented model, the emphasis is on analysis and review techniques to detect faults in requirements and design documents. In the prevention model, emphasis is on the careful planning and design of test activities. For example, the early design of test cases may reveal that certain requirements cannot be tested and thus such an activity helps to prevent errors from being made in the first place.

We may observe a gradual shift of emphasis in test practice, from a demonstration-like approach to prevention-oriented methods. Though many organizations still concentrate their test effort late in the development life cycle, leading-edge organizations have shown that upstream testing activities can be most effective. Quantitative evidence hereof is provided in section 13.8.3.

Testing need not only result in software with fewer errors. Testing also results in valuable knowledge (error-prone constructs and so on) which can be fed back into the development process. In this view, testing is a learning process, which can be given its proper place in an improvement process.

13.2 TESTING AND THE SOFTWARE LIFE CYCLE

In the following subsections we will discuss the various verification and validation activities which can be performed during the requirements engineering, design, implementation and maintenance phases. In doing so, we will also indicate the techniques and tools that may be applied. These techniques and tools will be further discussed in subsequent sections. A summary is given in figure 13.5.

Phase	Activities
Requirements engineering	– determine test strategy – test requirements specification – generate functional test data
Design	– check consistency between design and requirements specification – evaluate the software architecture – test the design – generate structural and functional test data
Implementation	– check consistency between design and implementation – test implementation – generate structural and functional test data – execute tests
Maintenance	– repeat the above tests in accordance with the degree of redevelopment

Figure 13.5 Activities in the various phases of the software life cycle (Adapted from *W.R. Adrion, M.A. Branstad & J.C. Cherniavski, Validation, verification, and testing of computer software,* ACM Computing Surveys **14**, *2 (1982), Reproduced by permission of the Association for Computing Machinery, Inc.*)

13.2.1 Requirements Engineering

The verification and validation techniques applied during this phase are strongly dependent upon the way in which the requirements specification has been laid down. Something which should be done at the very least is to conduct a careful review or inspection in order to check whether all aspects of the system have been properly described. As we saw earlier, errors made at this stage are very costly to repair if they go unnoticed until late in the development process. Boehm gives four essential criteria for a requirements specification [Boe84b]:

- completeness;
- consistency;
- feasibility;
- testability.

Testing a requirements specification should primarily be aimed at testing these criteria.

The aim of testing the completeness criterion then is to determine whether all components are present and described completely. A requirements specification is incomplete if it contains such phrases as 'to be determined' or if it contains references to undefined elements. We should also watch for the omission of functions or products, such as back-up or restart procedures and test tools to be delivered to the customer.

A requirements specification is consistent if its components do not contradict each other and the specification does not conflict with external specifications. We thus need both internal and external consistency. Moreover, each element in the requirements specification must be traceable. It must, for instance, be possible to decide whether a natural language interface is really needed.

According to Boehm, feasibility has to do with more than functional and performance requirements. The benefits of a computerized system should outweigh the associated costs. This must be established at an early stage and necessitates timely attention to user requirements, maintainability, reliability, and so on. In some cases, the project's success is very sensitive to certain key factors, such as safety, speed, availability of certain types of personnel; these risks must be analyzed at an early stage.

Lastly, a requirements specification must be testable. In the end, we must be able to decide whether or not a system fulfills its requirements. So requirements must be specific, unambiguous, and quantitative.

Many of these points are raised by [Pos87]. According to Poston, the most likely errors in a requirements specification can be grouped into the following categories:

- missing information (functions, interfaces, performance, constraints, reliability, and so on);
- wrong information (not traceable, not testable, ambiguous, and so forth);
- extra information (bells and whistles).

Using a standard format for documenting the requirements specification, such as IEEE Standard 830 discussed in chapter 9, may help enormously in preventing these types of errors to occur in the first place.

Useful techniques for testing the degree to which criteria have been met, are mostly manual (reading documents, inspections, reviews). Scenarios for the expected use of the system can be devised with the prospective users of the system. In this way, a set of functional tests is generated.

At this stage also, a general test strategy for subsequent phases must be formulated. It should encompass the choice of particular test techniques; evaluation criteria; a test plan; a test scheme; and test documentation requirements. A test team may also be formed at this stage. These planning activities are dealt with in section 13.3.

13.2.2 Design

The criteria mentioned in the previous subsection (completeness, consistency, feasibility and testability) are also essential for the design. The most likely errors in design resemble the kind of errors one is inclined to make in a requirements specification: missing, wrong, and extraneous information. For the design too, a precise documentation standard is of great help in preventing these types of errors. IEEE Standard 1016, discussed in chapter 11, is one such standard.

During the design phase, we decompose the total system into subsystems, components and modules, starting from the requirements specification. We may then develop tests based on this decomposition process. Design is not a one-shot process. During the design process a number of successive refinements will be made, resulting in layers showing increasing detail. Following this design process, more detailed tests can be developed as the lower layers of the design are decided upon.

During the architectural design phase, a high-level conceptual model of the system is developed in terms of components and their interaction. By developing a number of scenarios of anticipated changes and assessing the degree to which the architecture supports these changes, quality aspects like maintainability and flexibility may be tested at an early stage.

During the design phase, we may also test the design itself. This includes tracing elements from the requirements specification to the corresponding elements in the design description, and vice versa. Well-known techniques for doing so are, amongst others, simulation, design walkthroughs, and design inspections.

At the requirements engineering phase, the possibilities for formally documenting the resulting specification are limited. Most requirements specifications make excessive use of natural language descriptions. For the design phase, there are ample opportunities to formally document the resulting specification. The more formally the design is specified, the more possibilities we have for applying verification techniques, as well as formal checks for consistency and completeness.

13.2.3 Implementation

During the implementation phase, we do the 'real' testing. One of the most effective techniques to find errors in a program text is to carefully read that text, or have it read. This technique has been successfully applied for a long time. Somewhat formalized variants are known as code-inspection and code-walkthrough. We may also apply the technique of stepwise abstraction. In stepwise abstraction, the function of the code is determined in a number of abstraction steps, starting from the code itself. The various manual test techniques will be discussed in section 13.4.

There are many tools to support the testing of code. We may distinguish between tools for static analysis and tools for dynamic analysis. Static analysis tools inspect the program code without executing it. They include tests like: have all variables been declared and given a value before they are used? Dynamic analysis tools are used in conjunction with the actual execution of the code, for example tools that keep track of which portions of the code have been covered by the tests so far.

We may try to prove the correctness of the code using formal verification techniques.

All of the above techniques are aimed at evaluating the quality of the source code as well as its compliance with design specifications and code documentation.

It is crucial to control the test information properly while testing the code. Tools may help us in doing so, for example test drivers, test stubs and test data generators. A test driver is a tool that generates the test environment for a component to be tested. A test stub does the opposite: it simulates the function of a component not yet available. In bottom-up testing, we will, in general, make much use of test drivers, while top-down testing implies the use of test stubs. The test strategy (top-down versus bottom-up) may be partly influenced by the design technique used. If the high level, architectural design is implemented as a skeletal system whose holes yet have to be filled in, that skeletal system can be used as a test driver.

Tools may also be profitable while executing the tests (test harnesses and test systems). A simple and yet effective tool is one which compares test results with expected results. The eye is a very unreliable medium. After a short time, all results look OK. An additional advantage of this type of tool support is that it helps to achieve a standard test format. This in turn helps with regression testing.

13.2.4 Maintenance

On average, more than 50% of total life-cycle costs is spent on maintenance. If we modify the software after a system has become operational (because an error is found late on, or because the system must be adapted to changed requirements), we will have to test the system anew. This is called regression testing. To have this proceed smoothly, the quality of the documentation and the possibilities for tool support, are crucial factors.

In a *retest-all* approach, all tests are rerun. Since this may consume a lot of time and effort, we may also opt for a *selective retest*, in which only some of the tests are rerun. A regression test selection technique is then used to decide which subset should be rerun. We would like this technique to include all tests in which the modified and original program produce different results, while omitting tests that produce the same results. Various strategies have been proposed for doing so; few of them have been implemented yet.

13.3 VERIFICATION AND VALIDATION PLANNING AND DOCUMENTATION

Like the other phases and activities of the software development process, the testing activities need to be carefully planned and documented. Since test activities start early in the development life cycle and span all subsequent phases, timely attention to the planning of these activities is of paramount importance. A precise description of the various activities, responsibilities and procedures must be drawn up at an early stage.

The planning of test activities is described in a document called the Software Verification and Validation Plan. We will base our discussion of its contents on the corresponding IEEE Standard 1012. Standard 1012 describes verification and validation activities for a waterfall-like life cycle in which the following phases are identified:

- Concept phase
- Requirements phase
- Design phase
- Implementation phase
- Test phase
- Installation and checkout phase

- Operation and maintenance phase

The first of these, the concept phase, is not discussed in the present text. Its aim is to describe and evaluate user needs. It produces documentation which contains, for example, a statement of user needs, results of feasibility studies, and policies relevant to the project. The verification and validation plan is also prepared during this phase. In our approach, these activities are included in the requirements engineering phase.

---

1. Purpose
2. Referenced documents
3. Definitions
4. Verification and validation overview
   4.1. Organization
   4.2. Master schedule
   4.3. Resources summary
   4.4. Responsibilities
   4.5. Tools, techniques and methodologies
5. Life-cycle verification and validation (V&V)
   5.1. Management of V&V
   5.2. Requirements phase V&V
   5.3. Design phase V&V
   5.4. Implementation phase V&V
   5.5. Test phase V&V
   5.5. Installation and checkout phase V&V
   5.7. Operation and maintenance phase V&V
6. Software verification and validation reporting
7. Verification and validation administrative procedures
   7.1. Anomaly reporting and resolution
   7.2. Task iteration policy
   7.3. Deviation policy
   7.4. Control procedures
   7.5. Standards, practices and conventions

Figure 13.6 Sample contents of the Verification and Validation Plan (*Source:* IEEE Standard for Software Verification and Validation Plans, *IEEE Std. 1012, 1986. Reproduced by permission of IEEE*)

The sections to be included in the Verification and Validation (V&V) Plan are listed in figure 13.6. The structure of this plan resembles that of other standards discussed earlier. The plan starts with an overview and gives detailed information on every aspect of the topic being covered. The various constituents of the Verification and Validation Plan are discussed in appendix D.

More detailed information on the many V&V tasks covered by this plan can be found in [IEE86a]. Following the organization proposed in this standard, the bulk of the test documentation can be structured along the lines identified in figure 13.7. The Test Plan is a document describing the scope, approach, resources, and schedule of intended test activities. It can be viewed as a further refinement of the Verification and Validation Plan and describes in detail the test items, features to be tested, testing tasks, who will do each task, and any risks that require contingency planning.

The Test Design documentation specifies, for each software feature or combination of such features, the details of the test approach and identifies the associated tests. The Test Case documentation specifies inputs, predicted outputs and execution conditions for each test item. The Test Procedure documentation specifies the sequence of actions for the execution of each test. Lastly, the Test Report documentation provides information on the results of testing tasks. It addresses the issues mentioned in section 6 of the Verification and Validation Plan. A detailed description of the contents of these various documents is given in the IEEE Standard for Software Documentation [IEE83].

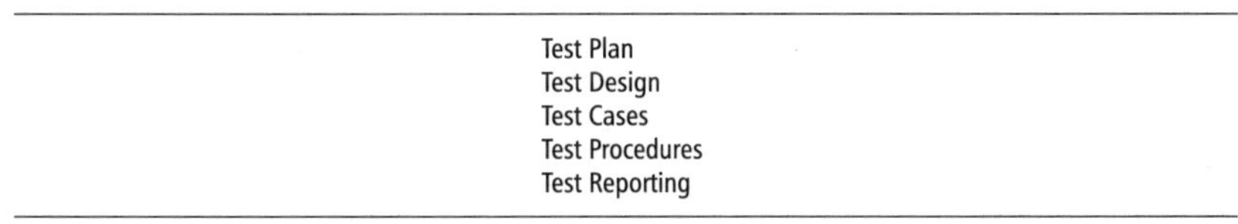

Test Plan
Test Design
Test Cases
Test Procedures
Test Reporting

Figure 13.7 Main constituents of test documentation, after [IEE83]

13.4 MANUAL TEST TECHNIQUES

A lot of research effort is spent on finding techniques and tools to support testing. Yet, a plethora of heuristic test techniques have been applied since the beginning of the programming era. These heuristic techniques, such as walkthroughs and inspections, often work quite well, although it is not always clear why.

Test techniques can be separated into **static** and **dynamic** analysis techniques. During dynamic analysis, the program is executed. With this form of testing, the program is given some input and the results of the execution are compared with the expected results. During static analysis, the software is generally not executed. Many static test techniques can also be applied to non-executable artifacts such as a design document or user manual. It should be noted, though, that the borderline between static and dynamic analysis is not very sharp.

A large part of the static analysis is nowadays done by the language compiler. For languages like Pascal and Ada, the compiler checks whether all variables have been declared, whether each function call has the proper number of actual parameters, and so on. These constraints are part of the language definition. We may also apply a more strict analysis of the program text, such as a check for initialization of variables, or a check on the use of non-standard, or error-prone, language constructs. In a number of cases, the call to a compiler is parameterized to indicate the checks one wants to be performed. Sometimes, separate tools are provided for these checks.

The techniques to be discussed in the following subsections are best classified as static techniques. The techniques for coverage-based, fault-based and error-based testing, to be discussed in sections 13.5–13.7, are mostly dynamic in nature.

13.4.1 Reading

We all read, and reread, and reread, our program texts. It is the most traditional test technique we know of. It is also a very successful technique to find faults in a program text (or a specification, or a design).

In general, it is better to have someone else read your texts. The author of a text knows all too well what the program (or any other type of document) ought to convey. For this reason, the author may be inclined to overlook things, suffering from some sort of trade blindness.

A second reason why reading by the author himself might be less fruitful, is that it is difficult to adopt a destructive attitude towards one's own work. Yet such an attitude is needed for successful testing.

A somewhat institutionalized form of reading each other's programs is known as **peer review**. This is a technique for anonymously assessing programs as regards quality, readability, usability, and so on.

Each person partaking in a peer review is asked to hand in two programs: a 'best' program and one of lesser quality. These programs are then randomly distributed amongst the participants. Each participant assesses four programs: two 'best' programs and two programs of lesser quality. After all results have been collected, each participant gets the (anonymous) evaluations of their programs, as well as the statistics of the whole test.

The primary goal of this test is to give the programmer insight into his own capabilities. The practice of peer reviews shows that programmers are quite capable of assessing the quality of their peers' software.

A necessary precondition for successfully reading someone else's code is a business-like attitude. Weinberg coined the term **egoless programming** for this [Wei71]. Many programmers view their code as something personal, like a diary. Derogatory remarks ('how could you be so stupid as to forget that initialization') can disastrously impair the effectiveness of such assessments. The opportunity for such an antisocial attitude to occur seems to be somewhat smaller with the more formalized manual techniques.

13.4.2 Walkthroughs and Inspections

Walkthroughs and inspections are both manual techniques that spring from the traditional desk-checking of program code. In both cases it concerns teamwork, whereby the product to be inspected is evaluated in a formal session, following precise procedures.

Inspections are sometimes called **Fagan inspections**, after their originator [Fag76, Fag86]. In an inspection, the code to be assessed is gone through statement by statement. The members of the inspection team (usually four) get the code, its specification, and the associated documents a few days before the session takes place.

Each member of the inspection team has a well-defined role. The *moderator* is responsible for the organization of inspection meetings. He chairs the meeting and ascertains that follow-up actions agreed upon during the meeting are indeed performed. The moderator must ensure that the meeting is conducted in a businesslike, constructive way and that the participants follow the correct procedures and act as a team. The team usually has two *inspectors* or *readers*, knowledgeable peers that paraphrase the code. Finally, the *code author* is a largely silent observer. He knows the code to be inspected all too well and is easily inclined to express what he intended rather than what is actually written down. He may, though, be consulted by the inspectors.

During the formal session, the inspectors paraphrase the code, usually a few lines at a time. They express the meaning of the text at a higher level of abstraction than what is actually written down. This gives rise to questions and discussions which may lead to the discovery of faults. At the same time, the code is analyzed using a checklist of faults that often occur. Examples of possible entries in this checklist are:

- wrongful use of data: variables not initialized, array index out of bounds, dangling pointers, etc.;

- faults in declarations: the use of undeclared variables or the declaration of the same name in nested blocks, etc.;

- faults in computations: division by zero, overflow (possible in intermediate results too), wrong use of variables of different types in the same expression, faults caused by an erroneous understanding of operator priorities, etc.;

- faults in relational expressions: using an incorrect operator ($>$ instead of $\geq$) or an erroneous understanding of priorities of Boolean operators, etc.;

- faults in control flow: infinite loops or a loop that gets executed $n+1$ or $n-1$ times rather than n times, etc.;

- faults in interfaces: an incorrect number of parameters, parameters of the wrong type, or an inconsistent use of global variables, etc.

The result of the session is a list of problems identified. These problems are not resolved during the formal session itself. This might easily lead to quick fixes and distract the team from its primary goal. After the meeting, the code author resolves all issues raised and the revised code is verified once again. Depending on the number of problems identified and their severity, this second inspection may be done by the moderator only or by the complete inspection team.

Since the goal of an inspection is to identify as many problems as possible in order to improve the quality of the software to be developed, it is important to maintain a constructive attitude towards the programmer whose code is being assessed.[2] The results of an inspection therefore are often marked confidential. These results should certainly *not* play a role in the formal assessment of the programmer in question.

In a walkthrough, the team is guided through the code using test data. These test data are mostly of a fairly simple kind. Otherwise, tracing the program logic soon becomes too complicated. The test data serves as a means to start a discussion, rather than as a serious test of the program. In each step of this process, the designer may be questioned regarding the rationale of the decisions. In many cases, a walkthrough boils down to some sort of manual simulation.

Both walkthroughs and inspections may profitably be applied at all stages of the software life cycle. The only precondition is that there is a clear, testable document. Both techniques not only serve to find faults. If properly applied, these techniques may help to promote team spirit and morale. At the technical level, the people involved may learn from each other and enrich their knowledge of algorithms, programming style, programming techniques, error-prone constructions, and so on. Thus, these techniques also serve as a vehicle for process improvement. Under the general umbrella of 'peer reviews', they are a CMM level 3 key process area (see section 6.6).

A potential danger of this type of review is that it remains too shallow. The people involved become overwhelmed with information, they may have insufficient knowledge of the problem domain, their responsibilities may not have been clearly delineated. As a result, the review process does not pay off sufficiently.

Parnas describes a type of review process in which the people involved have to play a more active role [PW87a]. Parnas distinguishes between different types of specialized design review. Each of these reviews concentrates on certain desirable properties of the design. As a consequence, the responsibilities of the people involved are clear. The reviewers have to answer a list of questions ('under which conditions

[2]One way of creating a non-threatening atmosphere is to always talk about 'problems' rather than 'faults'.

may this function be called', 'what is the effect of this function on the behavior of other functions', and the like). In this way, the reviewers are forced to study carefully the design information received. Problems with the questionnaire and documentation can be posed to the designers, and the completed questionnaires are discussed by the designers and reviewers. Experiments suggest that inspections with specialized review roles are more effective than inspections in which review roles are not specialized.

A very important component of Fagan inspections is the meeting in which the document is discussed. Since meetings may incur considerable costs or time-lags, one may try to do without them. Experiments suggest that the added value of group meetings, as far as the number of problems identified is concerned, is quite small.

13.4.3 Scenario-Based Evaluation

In various types of reviews, it is customary to develop a set of use cases, scenarios of typical interaction with the system, and have these use cases guide the testing process. The review then becomes a kind of manual simulation to test the system's functionality. Use cases may also serve to assess quality attributes such as flexibility and maintainability at the early, architectural design stage. Since the architecture reflects the earliest set of design decisions, being able to evaluate the design at that stage is bound to pay off.

Figure 13.8 shows the steps in one such evaluation method, Software Architecture Analysis Method (SAAM). This method is especially suited to assess the flexibility of an architecture.

1. Scenario development
2. Description of candidate architectures
3. Scenario classification
4. Scenario evaluation
5. Determination of scenario interaction
6. Overall evaluation

Figure 13.8 SAAM steps

In the first step, a collection of scenarios is developed. Next, candidate architectures for the system are decided upon. If there is only one such architecture, the process results in an evaluation of that architecture. If there is more than one candidate, the method allows us to make an informed choice.

Scenarios may describe both required and anticipated future behavior of the system. It is thus to be expected that not all scenarios are supported by the candidate architectures. In the third step, the scenarios are classified, for each candidate architecture, as either *direct* (i.e. fully supported) or *indirect* (not fully supported). In the fourth step, the architectural changes required for each indirect scenario are described, for instance by listing all affected components. Having done so, the interaction between different indirect scenarios is investigated. If semantically-different scenarios require a change in the same component, this may indicate an inappropriate separation of functionality in the design. It is a sign of high coupling, low cohesion, or both.

Finally, an overall evaluation is done. By assigning weights to scenarios and the possible changes required for realizing them, a ranking of candidate architectures or an assessment of an individual architecture is obtained. The evaluation of four different architectures for the KWIC-index example in chapter 10 may be considered such a scenario-based evaluation.

The application of this type of evaluation has additional benefits over the mere evaluation results. The construction of scenarios and their discussion with various stakeholders provides ample opportunity to raise a plethora of system-related issues. It thus promotes mutual understanding of the issues involved; it may point to alternative approaches and pinpoint weak spots or misunderstandings between stakeholders; it may also educate the stakeholders, and so on.

13.4.4 Correctness Proofs

The most complete static analysis technique is the proof of correctness. In a proof of correctness we try to prove that a program meets its specification. In order to be able to do so, the specification must be expressed formally. We mostly do this by expressing the specification in terms of two assertions which hold before and after the program's execution, respectively. Next, we prove that the program transforms one assertion (the precondition) into the other (the postcondition). This is generally denoted as

$$\{P\}\ S\ \{Q\}$$

Here, S is the program, P is the precondition, and Q is the postcondition. Termination of the program is usually proved separately. The above notation should thus be read as: if P holds before the execution of S, and S terminates, then Q holds after the execution of S.

Formally verifying the correctness of a not-too-trivial program is a very complex affair. Some sort of tool support is helpful, therefore. Tools in this area are often based on heuristics and proceed interactively.

Correctness proofs are very formal and, for that reason, they are often difficult for the average programmer to construct. The value of formal correctness proofs is sometimes disputed. We may state that the thrust in software is more important than some formal correctness criterion. Also, we cannot formally prove every desirable property of software. Whether we built the right system can only be decided upon through testing (validation).

On the other hand, it seems justified to state that a thorough knowledge of this type of formal technique will result in better software.

13.4.5 Stepwise Abstraction

In the top-down development of software components we often employ stepwise refinement. At a certain level of abstraction the function to be executed will then be denoted by a description of that function. At the next level, this description is decomposed into more basic units.

Stepwise abstraction is just the opposite. Starting from the instructions of the source code, the function of the component is built up in a number of steps. The function thus derived should comply with the function as described in the design or requirements specification.

Below, we will illustrate this technique with a small example. Consider the search routine of figure 13.9. We know, from the accompanying documentation, for instance, that the elements in array A are sorted when this routine is called.

We start the stepwise abstraction with the instructions at the innermost nesting level, the if-statement on lines 7–10. In these lines, x is being compared with A[mid]. Depending on the result of this comparison, one of high, low and found is given a new value. If we take into account the initializations on lines 4 and 6, the function of this if-statement can be summarized as

```
1  procedure binsearch
2      (A: array [1..n] of integer; x: integer): integer;
3  var low, high, mid: integer; found: boolean;
4  begin low:= 1; high:= n; found:= false;
5      while (low ≤ high) and not found do
6          mid:= (low + high) div 2;
7          if x < A[mid] then high:= mid - 1 else
8          if x > A[mid] then low:= mid + 1 else
9              found:= true
10         endif
11     enddo;
12     if found then return mid else return 0 endif
13 end binsearch;
```

Figure 13.9 A search routine

stop searching (found:= **true**) if x = A[mid], or
shorten the interval [low .. high] that might contain x, to an interval [low' .. high'], where high' - low' < high - low

Alternatively, this may be described as a postcondition to the if-statement:

(found = **true and** x = A[mid]) **or**
(found = **false and** x $\notin$ A[1 .. low' - 1] **and**
x $\notin$ A[high' + 1 .. n] **and** high' - low' < high - low)

Next, we consider the loop in lines 5–11, together with the initialization on line 4. As regards termination of the loop, we may observe the following. If 1 $\leq$ n upon calling the routine, then low $\leq$ high at the first execution of lines 5–11. From this, it follows that low $\leq$ mid $\leq$ high. If the element searched for is found, the loop stops and the position of that element is returned. Otherwise, either high gets assigned a smaller value, or low gets assigned a higher value. Thus, the interval [low .. high] gets smaller. At some point in time, the interval will have length of 1, i.e. low = high (assuming the element still is not found). Then, mid will be assigned that same value. If x still does not occur at position mid, either high will get the value low - 1, or low will get the value high + 1. In both cases, low > high, and the loop terminates. Together with the postcondition given earlier, it then follows that x does not occur in the array A. The function of the complete routine can then be described as:

result = 0 $\leftrightarrow$ x $\notin$ A[1 .. n]
1 $\leq$ result $\leq$ n $\leftrightarrow$ x = A[result]

So, stepwise abstraction is a bottom-up process to deduce the function of a piece of program text from that text.

13.5 COVERAGE-BASED TEST TECHNIQUES

Question: What do you do when you see a graph?
Answer: Cover it!
[Bei95]

In coverage-based test techniques, the adequacy of testing is expressed in terms of the coverage of the product to be tested, for example, the percentage of statements executed or the percentage of functional requirements tested.

Coverage-based testing is often based on the number of instructions, branches or paths visited during the execution of a program. It is helpful to base the discussion of this type of coverage-based testing on the notion of a control graph. In this control graph, nodes denote actions, while the (directed) edges connect actions with subsequent actions (in time). A path is a sequence of nodes connected by edges. The graph may contain cycles, i.e. paths $p_1, \ldots, p_n$ such that $p_1 = p_n$. These cycles correspond to loops in the program (or gotos). A cycle is called simple if its inner nodes are distinct and do not include p_1 (or p_n for that matter). Note that a sequence of actions (statements) that has the property that whenever the first action is executed, the other actions are executed in the given order may be collapsed into a single, compound, action. So when we draw the control graph for the program in figure 13.10, we may put the statements on lines 10–14 in different nodes, but we may also put them all in a single node.

In sections 13.5.1 and 13.5.2 we discuss a number of test techniques which are based on coverage of the control graph of the program. Section 13.5.3 illustrates how these coverage-based techniques can be applied at the requirements specification level.

13.5.1 Control-Flow Coverage

During the execution of a program, we will follow a certain path through its control graph. If some node has multiple outgoing edges, we choose one of those (which is also called a **branch**). In the ideal case, the tests collectively traverse all possible paths. This so-called **All-Paths coverage** is equivalent to exhaustively testing the program.

In general, this is not possible. A loop often results in an infinite number of possible paths. If we do not have loops, but only branch-instructions, the number of possible paths increases exponentially with the number of branching points. There may also be paths that are never executed (quite likely, the program contains a fault in that case). We therefore search for a criterion which expresses the degree to which the test data approximates the ideal covering.

Many such criteria can be devised. The most obvious is the criterion which counts the number of statements (nodes in the graph) executed. It is called the **All-Nodes coverage**, or **statement coverage**. This criterion is rather weak because it is relatively simple to construct examples in which 100% statement coverage is achieved, while the program is nevertheless incorrect.

Consider as an example the program given in figure 13.10. It is easy to see that one single test, with n = 2, a[1] = 5, a[2] = 3, will result in each statement being executed at least once. So, this one test achieves a 100% statement coverage. However, if we change, for example, the test a[i] ≥ a[i - 1] in line 6 to a[i] = a[i - 1], we still obtain a 100% statement coverage with this test. Although this test also yields the correct answer, the changed program is incorrect.

We get a stronger criterion if we require that at each branching node in the control graph, all possible branches are chosen at least once. This is known as **All-Edges coverage** or **branch coverage**. Here too, a 100% coverage is no guarantee of program correctness.

```
procedure bubble
    (var a: array [1..n] of integer; n: integer);
var i, j, temp: integer;
begin
    for i:= 2 to n do
        if a[i] ≥ a[i-1] then goto next endif;
        j:= i;
    loop: if j ≤ 1 then goto next endif;
        if a[j] ≥ a[j-1] then goto next endif;
        temp:= a[j];
        a[j]:= a[j-1];
        a[j-1]:= temp;
        j:= j-1;
        goto loop;
    next: skip;
    enddo
end;
```

Figure 13.10 A sort routine

Nodes that contain a condition, such as the boolean expression in an if-statement, can be a combination of elementary predicates connected by logical operators. A condition of the form

$$i > 0 \vee j > 0$$

requires at least two tests to guarantee that both branches are taken. For example,

$$i = 1, j = 1$$

and

$$i = 0, j = 1$$

will do. Other possible combinations of truth values of the atomic predicates ($i = 1$, $j = 0$ and $i = 0$, $j = 0$) need not be considered to achieve branch coverage. **Multiple condition coverage** requires that all possible combinations of elementary predicates in conditions be covered by the test set. This criterion is also known as **extended branch coverage**.

Finally, McCabe's cyclomatic complexity metric [McC76] has also been applied to testing. This criterion is also based on the control graph representation of a program.

A basis set is a maximal linearly-independent set of paths through a graph. The cyclomatic complexity (CV) equals this number of linearly-independent paths (see also section 11.1.4). Its formula is

$$CV(G) = V(G) + 1$$

Here, $V(G)$ is the graph's cyclomatic number:

$$V(G) = e - n + p,$$

where

e = the number of edges in the graph

n = the number of nodes

p = the number of components (a component is a maximal subgraph that is connected, i.e. a maximal subgraph for which each pair of nodes is connected by some path)

```
1   procedure insert(a, b, n, x);
2   begin bool found:= false;
3       for i:= 1 to n do
4           if a[i] = x
5           then found:= true; goto leave endif
6       enddo;
7   leave:
8       if found
9       then b[i]:= b[i] + 1
10      else n:= n + 1; a[n]:= x; b[n]:= 1 endif
11  end insert;
```

Figure 13.11 An insertion routine

As an example, consider the program text of figure 13.11. The corresponding control graph is given in figure 13.12. For this graph, $e = 13$, $n = 11$, and $p = 1$. So $V(G) = 3$ and $CV(G) = 4$. A possible set of linearly-independent paths for this graph is: $\{$1–2–3–4–5–6–7–8–9–11, 3–7, 4–6–3, 8–10–11$\}$.

A possible test strategy is to construct a test set such that all linearly-independent paths are covered. This adequacy criterion is known as the **cyclomatic-number criterion**.

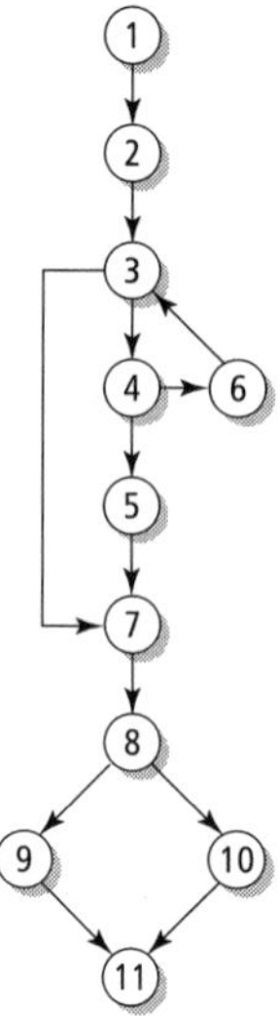

Figure 13.12 Control-flow graph of the insert routine from figure 13.11

13.5.2 Data Flow Coverage

Starting from the control graph of a program, we may also consider how variables are treated along the various paths. This is termed data flow analysis. With data flow analysis too, we may define test adequacy criteria and use these criteria to guide testing.

In data flow analysis, we consider the definitions and uses of variables along execution paths. A variable is *defined* in a certain statement if it is assigned a (new) value because of the execution of that statement. After that, the new value will be used in subsequent statements. A definition in statement X is *alive* in statement Y if there exists a path from X to Y in which that variable does not get assigned a new value at some intermediate node. In the example in figure 13.10, for instance, the definition of j at line 7 is still alive at line 13 but not at line 14. A path such as the one from line 7 to 13 is called **definition-clear** (with respect to j). Algorithms to determine such facts are commonly used in compilers in order to allocate variables optimally to machine registers.

We distinguish between two types of variable use: **P-uses** and **C-uses**. P-uses are predicate uses, like those in the conditional part of an if-statement. All other uses are C-uses. Examples of the latter are uses in computations or I/O statements.

A possible test strategy is to construct tests which traverse a definition-clear path between each definition of a variable to each (P- or C-) use of that definition and each successor of that use. (We have to include each successor of a use to force all branches following a P-use to be taken.) We are then sure that each possible use of a definition is being tested. This strategy is known as **All-Uses coverage**. A slightly stronger criterion requires that each definition-clear path is either cycle-free or a simple cycle. This is known as **All-DU-Paths** coverage. Several weaker dataflow criteria can be defined as well:

- **All-defs coverage** simply requires the test set to be such that each definition is used at least once.

- **All-C-uses/Some-P-uses coverage** requires definition-clear paths from each definition to each computational use. If a definition is used only in predicates, at least one definition-clear path to a predicate use must be exercised.

- **All-P-Uses/Some-C-uses coverage** requires definition-clear paths from each definition to each predicate use. If a definition is used only in computations, at least one definition-clear path to a computational use must be exercised.

- **All-P-Uses coverage** requires definition-clear paths from each definition to each predicate use.

13.5.3 Coverage-Based Testing of Requirements Specifications

Program code can be easily transformed into a graph model, thus allowing for all kinds of test adequacy criteria based on graphs. Requirements specifications, however, may also be transformed into a graph model. As a consequence, the various coverage-based adequacy criteria can be used in both black-box and white-box testing techniques.

Consider the example fragment of a requirements specification document for our library system in figure 13.13. We may rephrase these requirements a bit and present them in the form of elementary requirements and relations between them. The result can be depicted as a graph, where the nodes denote elementary requirements and the edges denote relations between elementary requirements; see figure 13.14. We may use this graph model to derive test cases and apply any of the control-flow coverage criteria to assess their adequacy.

Function `Order` allows the user to order new books. The user is shown a fill-in-the-blanks screen with fields like `Author`, `Title`, `Publisher`, `Price` and `Department`. The `Title`, `Price` and `Department` fields are mandatory. The `Department` field is used to check whether the department's budget is large enough to purchase this book. If so, the book is ordered and the department's budget is reduced accordingly.

Figure 13.13 A requirements specification fragment

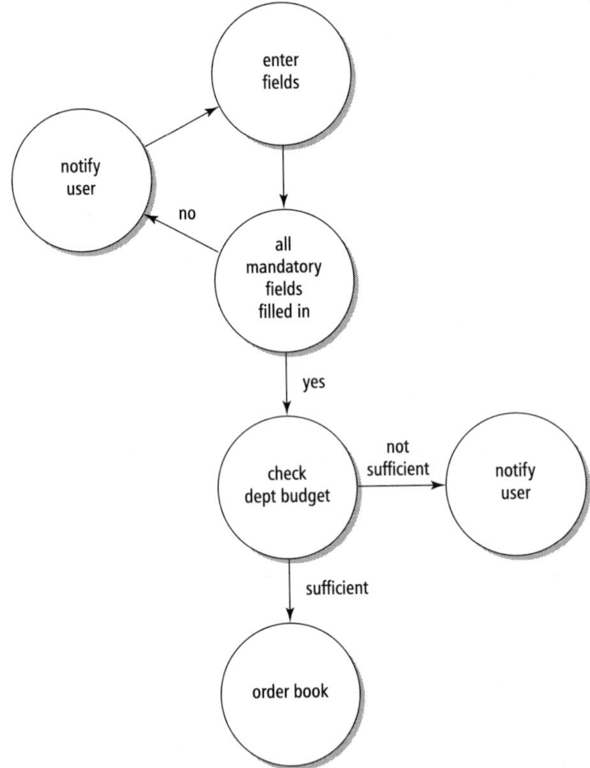

Figure 13.14 Graph model of requirements specification fragment

Generally speaking, a major problem in determining a set of test cases is to partition the program domain into a (small) number of equivalence classes. We try to do so in such a way that testing a representative element from a class suffices for the whole class. Using control-flow coverage criteria, for example, we assume that any test of some node or branch is as good as any other such test. In the above example, for instance, we assume that *any* execution of the node labeled 'check dept budget' will do.

The weak point in this procedure is the underlying assumption that the program behaves equivalently on all data from a given class. If such assumption is true, the partition is perfect and so is the test set. Such assumption will in general not hold however (see also section 13.1.2).

13.6 FAULT-BASED TEST TECHNIQUES

In coverage-based testing techniques, we consider the structure of the problem or its solution, and the assumption is that a more comprehensive covering is better. In fault-based testing strategies, we do not *directly* consider the artifact being tested when assessing the test adequacy. We only take into account the test set. Fault-based techniques are aimed at finding a test set with a high ability to detect faults.

We will discuss two fault-based testing techniques: fault seeding and mutation testing.

13.6.1 Fault Seeding

Text books on statistics often contain examples along the following lines: if we want to estimate the number of pikes in Lake Soft, we proceed as follows:

1. Catch a number of pikes, N, in Lake Seed;
2. Mark them and throw them into Lake Soft;
3. Catch a number of pikes, M, in Lake Soft.

Supposing that $M\prime$ out of the M pikes are found to be marked, the total number of pikes originally present in Lake Soft is then estimated as $(M - M\prime) \times N/M\prime$.

A somewhat unsophisticated technique is to try to estimate the number of faults in a program in a similar way. The easiest way to do this is to artificially seed a number of faults in the program. When the program is tested, we will discover both seeded faults and new ones. The total number of faults is then estimated from the ratio of those two numbers.

We must be aware of the fact that a number of assumptions underlie this method – amongst others, the assumption that both real and seeded faults have the same distribution.

There are various ways of determining which faults to seed in the program. A not very satisfactory technique is to construct them by hand. It is unlikely that we will be able to construct very realistic faults in this way. Faults thought up by one person have a fair chance of having been thought up already by the person that wrote the software.

Another technique is to have the program independently tested by two groups. The faults found by the first group can then be considered seeded faults for the second group. In using this technique, though, we must realize that there is a chance that both groups will detect (the same type of) simple faults. As a result, the picture might well get distorted.

A useful rule of thumb for this technique is the following: if we find many seeded faults and relatively few others, the result can be trusted. The opposite is not true. This phenomenon is more generally applicable: if, during testing of a certain component, many faults are found, it should not be taken as a positive sign. Quite the contrary, it is an indication that the component is probably of low quality. As Myers observed: 'The probability of the existence of more errors in a section of a program is proportional to the number of errors already found in that section.' [Mye79]. The same phenomenon has been observed in some experiments, where a strong linear relationship was found between the number of defects discovered during early phases of development and the number of defects discovered later.

13.6.2 Mutation Testing

Suppose we have some program P which produces the correct results for some tests T_1 and T_2. We next generate some variant $P\prime$ of P. $P\prime$ differs from P in just one place. For instance, a + is replaced by a −, or the value v_1 in a loop of the form

for var:= v_1 **to** v_2 **do**

is changed into $v_1 + 1$ or $v_1 - 1$. Next, $P\prime$ is tested using tests T_1 and T_2. Let us assume that T_1 produces the same result in both cases, whereas T_2 produces different results. Then T_1 is the more interesting test case, since it does not discriminate between two variants of a program, one of which is certainly wrong.

In **mutation testing**, a (large) number of variants of a program is generated. Each of those variants, or mutants, slightly differs from the original version. Usually, mutants are obtained by mechanically applying a set of simple transformations called mutation operators. Figure 13.15 lists a number of such mutation operators.

Replace a constant by another constant
Replace a variable by another variable
Replace a constant by a variable
Replace an arithmetic operator by another arithmetic operator
Replace a logical operator by another logical operator
Insert a unary operator
Delete a statement

Figure 13.15 A sample of mutation operators

Next, all these mutants are executed using a given test set. As soon as a test produces a different result for one of the mutants, that mutant is said to be dead. Mutants that produce the same results for all of the tests are said to be alive. As an example, consider the erroneous sort procedure in figure 13.3 and the correct variant thereof which compares array elements rather than their absolute values. Tests with an array which happens to contain positive numbers only will leave both variants alive. If a test set leaves us with many live mutants, then that test set is of low quality, since it is not able to discriminate between all kinds of variants of a given program.

If we assume that the number of mutants that is equivalent to the original program is 0 (normally, this number will certainly be very small), then the **mutation adequacy score** of a test set equals D/M, where D is the number of dead mutants and M is the total number of mutants.

There are two major variants of mutation testing: **strong mutation testing** and **weak mutation testing**. Suppose we have a program P with a component T. In strong mutation testing, we require that tests produce different results for program P and a mutant $P\prime$. In weak mutation testing, we only require that component T and its mutant $T\prime$ produce different results. At the level of P, this difference need not crop up. Weak mutation adequacy is often easier to establish. Consider a component T of the form

if x < 4.5 **then** ...

We may then compute a series of mutants of T, such as

if x > 4.5 **then** ...
if x = 4.5 **then** ...
if x > 4.6 **then** ...
if x < 4.4 **then** ...
...

Next, we have to devise a test set that produces different results for the original component T and at least one of its variants. This test set is then adequate for T.

Mutation testing is based on two assumptions: the *Competent Programmer Hypothesis* and the *Coupling Effect Hypothesis*. The Competent Programmer Hypothesis states that competent programmers write programs that are 'close' to being correct. So the program actually written may be incorrect, but it will differ from a correct version by relatively minor faults. If this hypothesis is true, we should be able to detect these faults by testing variants that differ slightly from the correct program, i.e. mutants. The second hypothesis states that tests that can reveal simple faults can also reveal complex faults. Experiments give some empirical evidence for these hypotheses.

13.7 ERROR-BASED TEST TECHNIQUES

Suppose our library system maintains a list of 'hot' books. Each newly-acquired book is automatically added to the list. After six months, it is removed again. Also, if a book is more than four months old and is being borrowed less than five times a month or is more than two months old and is being borrowed at most twice a month, it is removed from the list.

This rather complex requirement can be graphically depicted as in figure 13.16. It shows that the two-dimensional (age, average number of loans) domain can be partitioned into four subdomains. These subdomains directly relate to the requirements as stated above. The subdomains are separated by borders such as the line $age = 6$. For each border, it is indicated which of the adjacent subdomains is closed at that border by placing a hachure at that side of the border. A subdomain S is *closed* at a border if that border belongs to S; otherwise, it is *open* at that border.

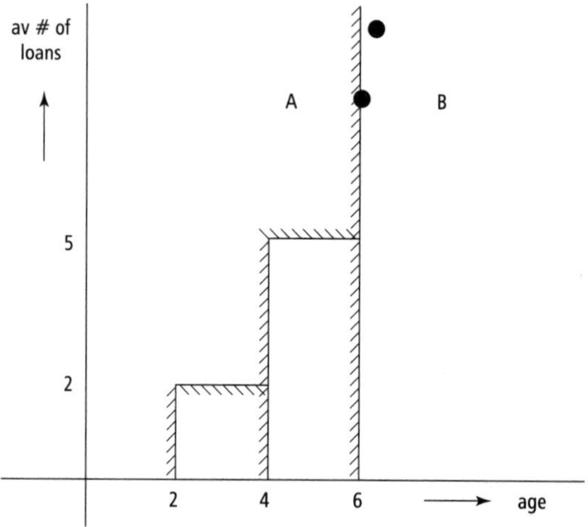

Figure 13.16 Partitioning of the input space

An obvious test technique for this requirement is to use an input from each of these subdomains. If the program follows the logic of the requirement, then test adequacy for that requirement equals path coverage for the corresponding program. However, in error-based testing, we focus on error prone points, and these are often found near the borders of subdomains.

One such test strategy concentrates on ON and OFF points. An ON point is a point on the border of a subdomain. If a subdomain is open with respect to some border, then an OFF point of a border is a point just inside that border. If a subdomain is closed with respect to some border, then an OFF point lies just outside that border. Two adjacent subdomains share the same ON point; they may share the same OFF point. In figure 13.16, the solid circle on the line $age = 6$ is an ON point of both A and B, while the circle just off this line is an OFF point of both these subdomains.

Suppose we have subdomains $D_i, i = 1, \ldots, n$. We may then construct a test set which contains N test cases for ON points of each border B of each subdomain D_i, and at least one test case for an OFF point of each border. The resulting test set is called $N \times 1$ **domain adequate**.

Above, we have illustrated this error-based technique in its black-box, specification-based form. The same technique can be applied to program text, though. If a program contains code of the form

```
if x > 6 then ...
elsif x > 4 and y < 5 then ...
elsif x > 2 and y ≤ 2 then ...
else ...
```

then we may identify the same four subdomains and use the same technique to test for boundary cases. In fact, this technique is just a systematic way to do what experienced programmers have done for a long time past: test for boundary values, such as 0, *nil*, lists with 0 or 1 element, and so on.

13.8 COMPARISON OF TEST TECHNIQUES

Most test techniques are heuristic in nature and lack a sound theoretical basis. Manual test techniques rely heavily on the qualities of the participants in the test process. But even the systematic approaches taken in functional and structural test techniques have a rather weak underpinning and are based on assumptions that are generally not true.

Experiments show that it is sometimes deceptively simple to make a system produce faults or even let it crash. [MFS90] describe one such experiment, in which they were able to crash or hang approximately 30% of the UNIX utilities on seven versions of the UNIX operating system. The utilities tested included commonly-used text editors and text formatters.

Similar results have been obtained in mutation analysis experiments. In one such experiment [KA85], 17 programs developed by different programmers from one and the same specification were used. These programs had all been thoroughly tested. Some of them had successfully withstood one million tests. For each of those programs, 24 mutants were created, each mutant containing one seeded fault. The programs thus obtained were each tested 25 000 times. The results can be summarized as follows:

- Some seeded faults were found quickly, some needed quite a few tests, and some remained undetected even after 25 000 tests. This pattern was found for each of the 17 programs;

- In some cases, the original program failed, while the modified program yielded the right result.

In the past, several attempts have been made to obtain more insights into the theoretical aspects of test techniques. An example is the research that is aimed at relating different test adequacy criteria. Test adequacy criteria serve as rules used to determine whether or not testing can be terminated. An important issue then is to decide whether one such criterion is 'better' than another. In section 13.8.1, we compare the strength of a number of test adequacy criteria discussed in previous sections. In section 13.8.2 we investigate a number of fundamental properties of test adequacy criteria. This type of research is aimed at gaining a deeper insight into properties of different test techniques.

Several experiments have been done to compare different test techniques. Real data from a number of projects are also available on the fault-detection capabilities of test techniques used in those projects. In section 13.8.3 we discuss several of these findings which may provide some practical insight into the virtues of a number of test techniques.

13.8.1 Comparison of Test Adequacy Criteria

A question that may be raised is whether, say, the All-Uses adequacy criterion is stronger or weaker than the All-Nodes or All-Edges adequacy criteria. We may define the notion 'stronger' as follows: criterion X is stronger than criterion Y if, for all programs P and all test sets T, X-adequacy implies Y-adequacy. In the testing literature this relation is known as 'subsume'. In this sense, the All-Edges criterion is stronger than (subsumes) the All-Nodes criterion. The All-Uses criterion, however, is not stronger than the All-Nodes criterion. This is caused by the fact that programs may contain statements which only refer to constants. For the program

```
if a < b
    then print(0)
    else print(1)
```

the All-Uses criterion will be satisfied by any non-empty test set, since this criterion does not require that each statement be executed. If we ignore references to constants, the All-Uses criterion is stronger than the All-Nodes criterion. With the same exception, the All-Uses criterion is also stronger than the All-Edges criterion.

A problem with any graph-based adequacy criterion is that it can only deal with paths that can be executed (feasible paths). Paths which cannot be executed are known as 'infeasible paths'. Infeasible paths result if parts of the graph are unreachable, as in

```
if true
    then x:= 1
    else x:= 2
```

The else-branch is never executed, yet most adequacy criteria require this branch to be taken. Paths that are infeasible also result from loops. If a loop is of the form

```
for i from 1 to 10 do
    body
```

there will be no feasible paths that traverse the resulting cycle in the graph any other than ten times.

There does not exist a simple linear scale along which the strength of all program-based adequacy criteria can be depicted. For the criteria discussed in sections 13.5–13.7, the subsume hierarchy is depicted in figure 13.17, as far as it is known. An arrow A $\rightarrow$ B indicates that A is stronger than (subsumes) B.

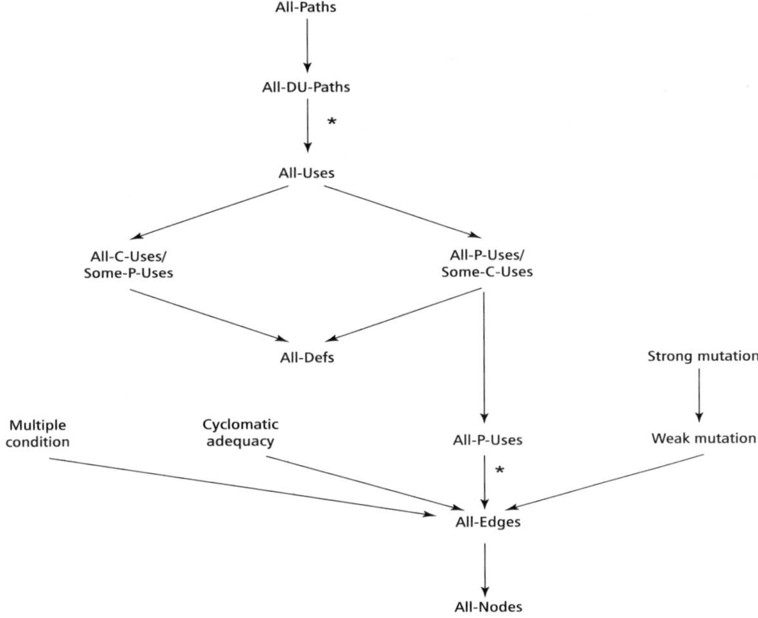

Figure 13.17 Subsume hierarchy for program-based adequacy criteria

In most cases, the subsume relation holds for both the feasible and infeasible versions of the criteria. Arrows adorned with an asterisk denote relations which hold only for the infeasible version.

The subsume relation compares the thoroughness of test techniques, not their ability to detect faults. Especially if an adequacy criterion is used in an a priori sense, i.e. if it is used to generate the next test case, the subsume relations of figure 13.17 do not necessarily imply better fault detection. However, if some other tool is used to generate test cases, and the criterion is only used a posteriori to decide when to stop testing, a stronger adequacy criterion implies better fault-detection ability as well.

The theoretical upper bounds for the number of test cases needed to satisfy most of the coverage-based adequacy criteria are quadratic or exponential. Empirical studies, however, show that, in practice, these criteria are usually linear in the number of conditional statements.

13.8.2 Properties of Test Adequacy Criteria

A major problem with any test technique is to decide when to stop testing. As noted, functional and structural test techniques provide only weak means for doing so. [Wey88] provides an interesting set of properties of test adequacy criteria. Although it is intuitively clear that any test adequacy criterion should satisfy all of the properties listed, it turns out that even some of the well-known test techniques such as All-Nodes coverage and All-Edges coverage fail to satisfy several of them.

The characteristics identified relate to program-based adequacy criteria, i.e. criteria that involve the program's structure. The first four criteria, however, are fairly general and should apply to any test adequacy criterion. The following 11 properties are identified in [Wey88]:[3]

- **Applicability property** For every program, there exists an adequate test set. Exhaustive testing obviously satisfies this criterion but, in general, we will look for a reasonably-sized test set. Both All-Nodes and All-Edges coverage criteria do not fulfill this property. If the program contains unexecutable code, there simply are no tests to cover those parts of the program.

- **Non-exhaustive applicability property** This property says that, even if exhaustive testing may be required in some cases, a criterion should certainly not require exhaustive testing in all circumstances.

- **Monotonicity property** This property states that once a program has been adequately tested, running some additional tests can do no harm. Obviously, the additional tests may reveal further faults, but this does not deem the original test set inadequate. It merely improves the quality of the test process.

[3]Reproduced by permission of the Association for Computing Machinery, Inc.

- **Inadequate empty set property** The empty test set is not an adequate test set for any program. A test adequacy criterion should measure how well the testing process has been conducted. If a program has not been tested at all, it certainly has not been adequately tested.

- **Antiextensionality property** This property states that semantic equivalence is not sufficient to imply that the programs are to be tested in the same way. For instance, routines BubbleSort and QuickSort are likely to require different test sets. This property is specific for program-based adequacy criteria, which depend on the implementation rather than the function being implemented. In a specification-based approach this property need not hold.

- **General multiple change property** Whereas the previous property states that semantic 'closeness' is not sufficient to imply that two programs can be tested in the same way, this property states that syntactic closeness is not sufficient either. Programs are said to be syntactically close if they have the same structure and the same dataflow characteristics. This is the case, for instance, when some of the relational or arithmetic operators in those programs differ. Though the shape of these programs is the same, testing them on the same data may well cause different paths through the flow graph being executed.

- **Antidecomposition property** This property states that if a component is adequately tested in one environment, this does not imply that it is adequately tested for some other environment. Put in other words: if some assembly of components is adequately tested, this does not imply that the individual components have been adequately tested as well. For example, a sorting routine may well be adequately tested in an environment where the size of the array is always less than ten. If we move that routine to an environment which requires much larger arrays to be sorted, it must be tested anew in that environment.

- **Anticomposition property** This property reflects just the opposite: even if components have been adequately tested in isolation, we still have to test their composition in order to ascertain that their interfaces and interactions work properly.

- **Renaming property** If two programs differ only in inessential ways, as is the case when different variable names are used, then an adequate test set for one of these programs also suffices for the other.

- **Complexity property** Intuitively, more complex programs require more testing. This property reflects this intuition by stating that for every program there exists other programs that require more testing.

- **Statement coverage property** One central property of program-based adequacy criteria is that they should at least cause every executable statement of the program to be executed.

As noted, the All-Nodes and All-Edges coverage metrics fail to satisfy the applicability criterion. This is rather unsatisfactory, since it implies that we may not be able to decide whether testing has been adequate. If a 50% coverage has been obtained using either of these criteria, we do not know whether additional tests will help. It may be that the other 50% of the statements or branches is not executed by any input.

Both the All-Nodes and All-edges criteria do not satisfy the antidecomposition and anticomposition criteria either. For example, if all statements of individual components are executed using some given test set, then this same test set is likely to satisfy that criterion on their composition. Further research along these lines is expected to deepen our insight into what test techniques may or may not accomplish.

13.8.3 Experimental Results

> *When one vacuums a rug in one direction only, one is likely to pick up less dirt than if the vacuuming occurs in two directions.*
> [CLS88, p. 386]

The most common techniques for module testing have been discussed in the previous sections. The effectiveness of those techniques is discussed in [BS87]. There, Basili and Selby describe an experiment in which both professional programmers and students participated. Three techniques were compared:

- stepwise abstraction;
- functional testing based on equivalence classes and boundary value analysis (see section 13.7);
- structural testing with 100% statement coverage.

Basili and Selby compared the effectiveness of these techniques as regards detecting faults, the associated costs, and the kinds of faults found. Some of the results of this experiment were:

- The professional programmers detected more faults with stepwise abstraction. Also, they did so faster than with the other techniques. They discovered more faults with functional testing as compared with structural testing. The speed with which they did so did not differ.
- In one group of students, the various test techniques yielded the same results as regards the number of faults found. In a second group, structural testing

turned out to be inferior to both other techniques. The speed with which faults were detected did not differ.

- The number of faults found, the speed of fault detection, and the total effort needed depended upon the kind of program being tested.

- More interface faults were found with stepwise abstraction.

- More faults in the control structure were found with functional testing.

Other experiments also indicate that there is no uniform 'best' test technique. Different test techniques tend to reveal different types of fault. The use of multiple test techniques certainly results in the discovery of *more* faults. It is difficult though to ascribe the discovery of faults to the use of a specific technique. It may well be that the mere fact that test techniques force us to pay systematic attention to the software is largely responsible for their success.

Several studies have reported on the fault detection capabilities of (Fagan) inspections. [Mye88] reports that about 85% of the major errors in the Space Shuttle software were found during early inspections. Inspections have been found to be superior to other manual techniques such as walkthroughs. Inspections were also found to have the additional benefit of improving both quality and productivity. There is some controversy about the added value of group meetings.

Finally, there is ample empirical evidence that early attention to fault detection and removal really pays off. Boehm's data presented in the introduction to this chapter can be augmented by other results, such as those of [CW89]. His data stem from a large real-time software project, consisting of about 700 000 lines of code developed by over 400 people. Some of his findings are reproduced in figure 13.18. For example, of the 676 design faults that could have been caught, 365 were caught during the design review (=54%). The overall design review efficiency was not much different from code review efficiency, while the testing phase was somewhat less efficient. The latter is not all that surprising, since the design and code reviews are likely to have removed many of the faults that were easy to detect. These results again suggest that the use of multiple techniques is preferable to the use of a single technique.

The results become much more skewed if we take into account the cost-effectiveness of the different test techniques. The cost-effectiveness metric used is the ratio of 'costs saved by the process' to 'costs consumed by the process'. The costs saved by the process are the costs that would have been spent if the process had not been performed and faults had to have been corrected later. The cost-effectiveness results found in this study are given in figure 13.19. These results indicate that, for every hour spent in design reviews and correcting design faults, more than eight hours of work are saved. The cost-effectiveness of the testing phase itself is remarkably low. This is not really surprising, since much time is wasted during the actual testing phase in performing tests that do not reveal any faults. These findings once more confirm the statement that early testing really pays off.

	% of design faults found	*% of coding faults found*	*Combined efficiency*
Design review	54	–	54
Code review	33	84	64
Testing	38	38	38

Figure 13.18 Fault-detection efficiency

Design review	*Code review*	*Testing*
8.44	1.38	0.17

Figure 13.19 Cost-effectiveness results found in [CW89]

13.9 DIFFERENT TEST STAGES

During the design phase, the system to be built has been decomposed into modules. Generally, these modules form some hierarchical structure. During testing, we will often let ourselves be led by this structure. We do not immediately start to test the system as a whole but start by testing the individual modules (called **module testing** or **unit testing**). Next, these modules are incrementally integrated into a system. Testing the composition of modules is called **integration testing**.

In doing this, we may take one of two approaches. In the first approach, we start by testing the low-level modules which are then integrated and coupled with modules at the next higher level. The subsystem thus obtained is tested next. Then gradually we move towards the highest-level modules. This is known as bottom-up testing. The alternative approach is top-down testing. In top-down testing, the top-level modules are tested first and are gradually integrated with lower-level modules.

In bottom-up testing, we often have to simulate the environment in which the module being tested is to be integrated. This environment is called a test driver. In top-down testing the opposite is true: we have to simulate lower-level modules, through so-called test stubs.

Both methods have advantages and disadvantages. For instance, in bottom-up testing it may be difficult to get a sound impression of the final system during the early stages of testing because whilst the top-level modules are not integrated, there is no system, only bits and pieces. With top-down testing, on the other hand, writing the stubs can be rather laborious. If the implementation strategy is one whereby a skeletal system is built first and then populated with components, this skeletal system can be used as a test driver and the test order then becomes much less of an issue.

In practice, it is often useful to combine both methods. It is not necessarily the case that some given design or implementation technique drives us in selecting a particular test technique. If the testing is to partly parallel the implementation, ordering constraints induced by the order of implementation have to be obeyed, though.

The program-based adequacy criteria make use of an underlying language model. Subtle differences in this underlying model may lead to subtle differences in the resulting flow graphs as used in coverage-based criteria, for instance. Roughly speaking, the results reported hold at the level of a procedure or subroutine in languages like FORTRAN, Pascal, and so on.

As a consequence, the corresponding test techniques apply at the level of individual methods in object-oriented programs. Testing larger components of OO programs, such as parameterized classes or classes that inherit part of their functionality from other classes, resembles regression testing as done during maintenance. We then have to decide how much retesting should be done if methods are redefined in a subclass, or a class is instantiated with another type as a parameter. Few results in this area have been obtained so far.

Other forms of testing exist besides module testing and integration testing. One possibility is to test the whole system against the user documentation and requirements specification after integration testing has finished. This is called the **system test**. A similar type of testing is often performed under supervision of the user organization and is then called **acceptance testing**. During acceptance testing, emphasis is on testing the usability of the system, rather than compliance of the code against some specification. Acceptance testing is a major criterion upon which the decision to accept or reject a system is based. In order to ensure a proper delivery of all necessary artifacts of a software development project, it is useful to let the future maintenance organization have a right of veto in the acceptance testing process.

If the system has to become operational in an environment different from the one in which it has been developed, a separate **installation test** is usually performed.

The test techniques discussed in the previous sections are often applied during module and integration testing. When testing the system as a whole, the tests often use random input, albeit that the input is chosen such that it is representative of the system's operational use. Such tests can also be used to quantitatively assess the system's reliability. Software reliability is the topic of chapter 18.

The use of random input as test data has proven to be successful in the Cleanroom development method. In several experiments, it was found that a select testing resulted in a high degree of statement and branch coverage. If a branch was not executed, it often concerned the treatment of an exceptional case.

13.10 SUMMARY

In this chapter we discussed a great number of test techniques. We emphasized the importance of early fault detection. It is important to pay attention to testing during the early stages of the software development process. Early testing activities are the ones that are most cost effective. Early testing activities provide opportunities to prevent errors from being made in the first place.

In practice, the various manual test techniques seem to be used most often. They turn out to be at least as successful as the various structural and functional techniques. Inspections in particular have been found to be a very cost-effective test technique. Next to the test techniques used, a major element in software fault detection and removal is the choice of personnel – some people are significantly better at finding and removing faults than others.

Since exhaustive testing is generally infeasible, we have to select an adequate set of test cases. Test techniques can be classified according to the criterion used to measure the adequacy of this test set. Three broad categories of test adequacy criteria can be distinguished:

- **Coverage-based testing**, in which testing requirements are specified in terms of the coverage of the product to be tested, for example, the percentage of statements executed.

- **Fault-based testing**, in which the focus is on detecting faults, for example, the percentage of seeded faults detected.

- **Error-based testing**, which focuses on testing error-prone points, such as 0, 1, or the upper bound of an array.

A test adequacy criterion can be used as stopping rule, as a measurement instrument, or as a generator of test cases. Test adequacy criteria and the corresponding test techniques can be viewed as two sides of the same coin. A coverage-based test technique makes it easy to measure coverage-based criteria, but does not help us in assessing whether all error-prone points have been tested.

Experimental evaluations show that there is no uniform best test technique. Different techniques tend to reveal different types of error. It is therefore wise to 'vacuum the carpet in more than one direction'.

An important line of research addresses the relative power of test adequacy criteria. A well-known measure to compare program-based test adequacy criteria is the subsume relation: criterion X subsumes Y if, for all programs P and all test sets T, X-adequacy implies Y-adequacy. Many of the well-known adequacy criteria have been related to one another in a subsume hierarchy.

As with any other life cycle activity, testing has to be carefully planned, controlled, and documented. Some of the IEEE Standards provide useful guidelines for doing this [IEE83, IEE86a].

13.11 FURTHER READING

Well-known textbooks on testing are [Mye79], [Bei90] and [Bei95]. For a further discussion of safety issues, see [Abb90] or [Lev91]. Fault-tree analysis is discussed in [Lev86]. [ZHM97] gives a very good overview of the types of test strategy discussed in sections 13.5–13.7 and the associated adequacy criteria. [RH96] gives a very good overview of regression test techniques. Testing object-oriented software is addressed in [CAC94]. An overview of testing tools is given in [Pos95].

The first attempts at developing some theory on testing date back to the 1970s [GG75], [How82], and [How85]. During the past ten years, much of that research has been directed towards finding and relating test adequacy criteria [Wey88], [CPRZ89], [Wey90], [FW93b], [FW93c], [PZ95], and [Zhu96]. Experimental evaluations of test adequacy criteria can be found in [FW93a], [Wey93], [OL94], [HOT97], and [FWH97]. Experiments that compare manual and functional or structural test techniques are reported upon in [BS87], [KL95], and [WRBM97].

The Cleanroom development method is described in [SBB87] and [MDL87]. Experiences with Cleanroom are discussed in [CDM86] and [TBS92]. Stepwise abstraction is described in [LMW79].

Inspections were introduced by Fagan in the 1970s [Fag76] and [Fag86]. [GG93] is a text book on inspections. There have been many experimental evaluations of inspections; see for instance [KM93], [Wel93], [GvS94], [PVB95], [PJ97], [PSTV97], [LSJ97] and [PSMV98].

The scenario-based software architecture analysis method (SAAM) is discussed in [BCK98]. A more general technique, in which tradeoffs between quality attributes are analyzed, is discussed in [KKB$^+$98].

The value of formal correctness proofs is disputed in [DLP79]. Heated debates in the literature show that this issue has by no means been resolved yet [Fet88].

Exercises

1. What is a test adequacy criterion? Which kinds of uses does it have?

2. Describe the following categories of test technique: coverage-based testing, fault-based testing, and error-based testing.

3. What assumptions underlie the mutation testing strategy?

4. What is the difference between black-box testing and white-box testing?

5. Define the following terms: error, fault, and failure.

6. What is a Fagan inspection?

7. Describe the role of scenario-based evaluation of a software architecture.

8. Define the following categories of control-flow coverage: All-Paths coverage, All-Edges coverage, All-Statements coverage.

9. Consider the following routine (in Modula-2):

```
procedure SiftDown(var A: array of integer; k, n: integer);
var parent, child, insert, Ak: integer;
begin
    parent:= k; child:= k + k;
    Ak:= A[k]; insert:= Ak;
    loop
        if child > n then exit end;
        if child < n then
            if A[child] > A[child+1] then child:= child+1 end
        end;
        if insert <= A[child]
            then exit
            else A[parent]:= A[child];
                parent:= child; child:= child + child
        end
    end;
    A[parent]:= Ak
end SiftDown;
```

(This operation performs the sift-down operation for heaps; if needed, you may consult any text on data structures to learn more about heaps.) The routine is tested using the following input:

n = 5, k = 2,
A[1] = 80, A[2] = 60, A[3] = 90, A[4] = 70, A[5] = 10.

Will the above test yield a 100% statement coverage? If not, provide one or more additional test cases that a 100% statement coverage is obtained from.

10. For the example routine from exercise 9, construct a test set that yields 100% branch coverage.

11. For the example routine from exercise 9, construct a test set that achieves All-Uses coverage.

12. Consider the following two program fragments:

Fragment 1:

```
found:= false; counter:= 1;
while (counter < n) and (not found)
do
    if table[counter] = element then found:= true end;
    counter:= counter + 1
end;
if found then writeln ("found") else writeln ("not found") end;
```

Fragment 2:

```
found:= false; counter:= 1;
while (counter < n) and (not found)
do
    found:= table[counter] = element;
    counter:= counter + 1
end;
if found then writeln ("found") else writeln ("not found") end;
```

Can the same test set be used if we wish to achieve a 100% branch coverage for both fragments?

13. What is mutation testing?

14. Which assumptions underlie mutation testing? What does that say about the strengths and weaknesses of this testing technique?

15. When is one testing technique stronger than another?

16. What is the difference between a system test and an acceptance test?

17. Contrast top-down and bottom-up integration testing.

18. ♠ Read [DLP79] and both [Fet88] and the reactions to it (cited in the bibliography entry for that article). Write a position paper on the role of correctness proofs in software development.

19. ♠ For a (medium-sized) system you have developed, write a Software Verification and Validation Plan (SVVP) following IEEE Standard 1012. Which of the issues addressed by this standard were not dealt with during the actual development? Could a more thorough SVVP have improved the development and testing process?

20. ♡ Consider the following sort routine:

```
procedure selectsort(var r: array [1 .. n] of integer);
var j, k, small: integer;
begin
    if n > 1 then
        for k:= 1 to n - 1 do
            small:= k;
            for j:= k + 1 to n do
                if r[j] < r[small] then small:= j end
            end;
            swap(r[k], r[small])
        end
    end
end selectsort;
```

Determine the function (by means of pre- and postconditions) of this routine using stepwise abstraction.

21. ♡ Generate ten mutants of the procedure in exercise 20. Next, test these mutants using the following set of test cases:

- an empty array;
- an array of length 1;
- a sorted array of length 10;
- an array of 10 elements that all have the same value;
- an array of length 10 with random elements.

Which of these mutants stay alive? What does this tell you about the quality of these tests?

22. ♡ Construct an example showing that the antidecomposition and anticomposition axioms from section 13.8.2 do not hold for the All-Nodes and All-Edges testing criteria. Why are these axioms important?

23. ♠ With one or two fellow students or colleagues, inspect a requirements or design document not produced by yourself. Is the documentation sufficient to do a proper inspection? Discuss the findings of the process with the author of the document. Repeat the process with a document of which you are the author.

24. ♡ Assess the strengths and weaknesses of:

    - functional or structural testing,
    - correctness proofs,
    - random testing, and
    - inspections

    for fault finding and confidence building, respectively.

25. ♡ One way of testing a high-level document such as a requirements specification is to devise and discuss possible usage scenarios with prospective users of the system to be developed. What additional merits can this technique have over other types of review?

26. ♡ How do you personally feel about a Cleanroom-like approach to software development?

14 Software Maintenance

LEARNING OBJECTIVES

- To know about well-known categories of maintenance task and data on their distribution
- To be able to discern major causes of maintenance problems
- To be aware of reverse engineering, its limitations, and tools to support it
- To appreciate different ways in which maintenance activities can be organized
- To understand major differences between development and maintenance and the consequences thereof

Like living organisms and most natural phenomena, software projects follow a life cycle that starts from emptiness, is followed by rapid growth during infancy, enters a long period of maturity, and then begins a cycle of decay that almost resembles senility.
[Jon89]

Software, unlike a child, does not grow smarter and more capable; unfortunately, it does seem to grow old and cranky.
[Lyo81]

Consider the 'Gemeenschappelijk Administratiekantoor' (GAK, or Joint Administration Office), a typical large organization that is heavily dependent upon automation for its daily operation. Some 100 Dutch organizations have commissioned GAK to implement social security acts and schemes, such as the Unemployment Benefits Act, the Sickness Benefits Act, and the Disablement Insurance Act. GAK also administers pensions and capital on behalf of pension funds and early retirement schemes. The annual cash flow runs into billions of Dutch guilders.

GAK has some 350 offices spread all over the country. It has a number of mainframes at a central site, as well as over 7000 terminals and 3000 printers connected through a country-wide network. The workload is over 40 000 transactions per hour. GAK has some 140 large application systems averaging 100 000 lines of code. Programs are written in a variety of languages, most notably COBOL, various 4GLs and JCL. The systems make use of huge databases implemented under IDMS, INGRES, and so on. Some of the basic information is shared by many systems. The structure of that information has a large impact on the overall application portfolio.

People involved in the maintenance of GAK's information systems dread election time. Changes in the political climate forecast changes in the regulations implemented by GAK's information systems. The workload may become excessive if these changes have to be realized within a short period of time, which is usually the case. There are more people involved in maintaining GAK's information systems, than there are people involved in developing new systems for GAK.

There are many organizations like GAK, organizations whose portfolio of information systems is vital for their day-to-day operation. At the same time, these information systems are ageing and it becomes increasingly difficult to keep them 'up and running'. An increasing percentage of the annual budget of these organizations is spent on keeping installed systems functioning properly.

It is estimated that there are more than 100 billion lines of code in production in the world. As much as 80% of it is unstructured, patched, and badly documented. It is a gargantuan task to keep these software systems operational: errors must be corrected, and systems must be adapted to changing environments and user needs. This is what software maintenance is about. Software maintenance is defined as [IEE90a]:

> The process of modifying a software system or component after delivery to correct faults, improve performance or other attributes, or adapt to a changed environment.

So software maintenance is, in particular, *not* limited to the correction of latent faults. Let us recall part of the discussion from chapter 1. Following [LS80], we distinguished four types of maintenance activity:[1]

- **Corrective maintenance** deals with the repair of faults found.
- **Adaptive maintenance** deals with adapting software to changes in the environment, such as new hardware or the next release of an operating system. Adaptive maintenance does not lead to changes in the system's functionality.
- **Perfective maintenance** mainly deals with accommodating new or changed user requirements. It concerns functional enhancements to the system. Perfective maintenance also includes activities to increase the system's performance or to enhance its user interface.
- **Preventive maintenance** concerns activities aimed at increasing the system's maintainability, such as updating documentation, adding comments, and improving the modular structure of the system.

Notice that 'real' maintenance activities – the correction of faults – accounts for about 25% of the total maintenance effort only. Half of the maintenance effort concerns changes to accommodate changing user needs, while the remaining 25% largely concerns adapting software to changes in the external environment (see figure 14.1).

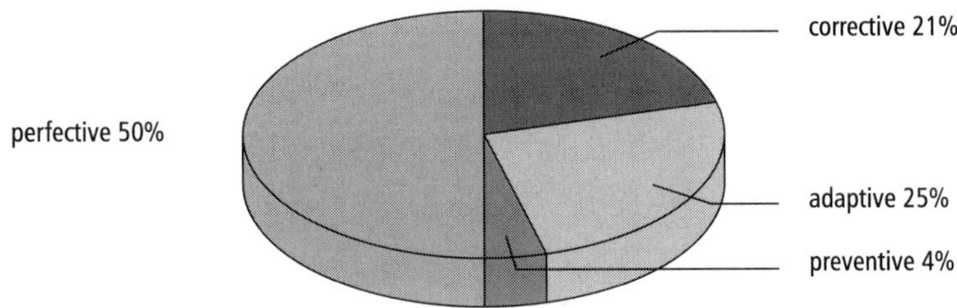

Figure 14.1 Distribution of maintenance activities

[1]The IEEE uses slightly different definitions. In particular, they combine Lientz and Swanson's adaptive and perfective categories, and call the combination adaptive maintenance. The reader should be aware of these different definitions of maintenance categories, especially when interpreting percentages spent on the different categories.

Recall also that the total cost of system maintenance is estimated to comprise at least 50% of total life cycle costs.

The above data are based on [LS80] and reflect the state of the practice in the 1970s. More recent studies have shown that the situation has not changed for the better. [NP90] raised the major maintenance issues once again and came to the disturbing conclusion that maintenance problems have remained pretty much the same, notwithstanding advances in structured development methodologies and techniques. Other studies give roughly the same results. The relative distribution of maintenance activities is about the same as it was 20 years ago. Systems though have become larger, maintenance staff has grown, there are more systems, and there is a definite trend to an increase in maintenance effort relative to development effort.

Changes in both the system's environment and user requirements are inevitable. Software models part of reality, and reality changes, whether we like it or not. So the software has to change too. It has to evolve. A large percentage of what we are used to calling maintenance, is actually evolution.

When looking for ways to reduce the maintenance problem, it is worth bearing in mind the classification of maintenance activities given above. Possible solutions to be considered include:

- Higher-quality code, better test procedures, better documentation and adherence to standards and conventions may help to save on corrective maintenance;

- By anticipating changes during requirements engineering and design and by taking them into account during realization, future perfective and adaptive maintenance can be realized more easily. In particular, the explicit evaluation of a software architecture with respect to ease of change is to be recommended. Through its inheritance and virtual typing capabilities, the object-oriented development paradigm in particular offers opportunities for isolating parts that are susceptible to changes from those that are less so;

- Finer tuning to user needs may lead to savings in perfective maintenance. This may, for example, be achieved through prototyping techniques or a more intensive user participation during the requirements engineering and design phase;

- Less maintenance is needed when less code is written. The sheer length of the source code is the main determinant of total cost, both during initial development and during maintenance. In particular, a 10% change in a module of 200 LOC is more expensive than a 20% change in a module of 100 LOC. The reuse of existing software in particular has a very direct impact on maintenance costs.

These possible actions are all concerned with initial software development. This is not surprising, since the key to better maintainable software is to be found there. All these issues have been discussed at great length in previous chapters.

Yet, maintenance problems will remain. Some of these problems are inherent – systems degrade when they are changed over and over again – while others are caused by simple facts of life: real development and maintenance activities are carried out in less than perfect ways. The major causes of the resulting maintenance problems are addressed in section 14.1.

This discussion of maintenance problems suggests two approaches to improve the situation. Section 14.2 discusses various ways to rediscover lost facts ('what does this routine accomplish', 'which design underlies a given system', and the like) and restructure existing software systems in order to improve their maintainability.

The second approach, discussed in section 14.3, entails a number of organizational and managerial actions to improve software maintenance.

14.1 MAJOR CAUSES OF MAINTENANCE PROBLEMS

The following story reveals many of the problems that befall a typical software maintenance organization. It is based on an anecdote once told by David Parnas and concerns the re-engineering of software for fighter planes.

The plane in question has two altimeters. The onboard software tries to read either meter and displays the result. The software for doing so is depicted in figure 14.2. The code is unstructured and does not contain any comments. With a little effort though its functioning can be discerned. A structured version of the same code is given in figure 14.3. What puzzles us is the meaning of the default value 3000. Why on earth does the system display the value 3000 (which, at first sight is not very peculiar) when both altimeters cannot be read?

```
IF not-read1 (V1) GOTO DEF1;
display (V1);
GOTO C;
DEF1: IF not-read2 (V2) GOTO DEF2;
display (V2);
GOTO C;
DEF2: display (3000);
C:
```

Figure 14.2 Unstructured code to read altimeters

The rationale for the default value could not be discerned from the (scarce or nonexistent) documentation. Eventually, the programmer who had written this code was traced. He said that, when writing this piece of code, he did not know what

```
if read-meter1 (V1) then display (V1) else
if read-meter2 (V2) then display (V2) else
    display (3000)
endif;
```

Figure 14.3 Structured code to read altimeters

to display in case both altimeters were unreadable. So he asked one of the fighter pilots what their average flying altitude was. The pilot made a back-of-the-envelope calculation and came up with the above value: the average flying altitude is 3000 feet. Hence this fragment.

The person reengineering the software rightfully thought that this was not the proper way to react to malfunctioning hardware. Fighter planes either fly at a very high altitude or very close to the ground. They don't fly in between. So he contacted the officials in charge and asked permission to display a clear warning message instead, such as a flashing 'PULL UP'.

The permission to change the value displayed was denied. Generations of fighter pilots were by now trained to react appropriately to the current default message. Their training manual even stated a warning phrase like 'If the altimeter reader displays the value 3000 for more than a second, PULL UP'.

This story can't be true. Or can it? It does illustrate some of the major causes of maintenance problems:

- unstructured code,
- maintenance programmers having insufficient knowledge of the system or application domain,
- documentation being absent, out of date, or at best insufficient.
- software maintenance has a bad image (this is not illustrated by the anecdote but is definitely a maintenance problem).

Unstructured code is used here as a generic term for systems that are badly designed or coded. It manifests itself in a variety of ways: the use of gotos, long procedures, poor and inconsistent naming, high module complexity, weak cohesion and strong coupling, unreachable code, deeply-nested if statements, and so on.

Even if systems were originally designed and built well, they may have become harder to maintain in the course of time. Much software that is to be maintained was developed in the pre-structured programming era. Parts of it may still be written in assembly language. It was designed and written for machines with limited processing and memory capacities. It may have been moved to different hardware or software platforms more than once without its basic structure having changed.

This is not the whole story either. The bad structure of many present-day systems at both the design and code level is not solely caused by their age. As a result of their studies of the dynamics of software systems, Lehman and Belady formulated a series of Laws of Software Evolution (see also chapter 3). The ones that bear most on software maintenance are:

Law of continuing change A system that is being used undergoes continuing change, until it is judged more cost-effective to restructure the system or replace it by a completely new version.

Law of increasing complexity A program that is changed, becomes less and less structured (the entropy increases) and thus becomes more complex. One has to invest extra effort in order to avoid increasing complexity.

Large software systems tend to stay in production for a long time. After being put into production, enhancements are inevitable. As a consequence of the implementation of these enhancements, the entropy of software systems increases over time. The initial structure degrades and complexity increases. This in turn complicates future changes to the system. Such software systems show signs of arthritis. Preventive maintenance may delay the onset of entropy but, usually, only a limited amount of preventive maintenance is carried out.

Eventually, systems cannot be properly maintained any more. In practice, it is often impossible to completely replace old systems by new ones. Developing completely new systems from scratch is either too expensive, or they will contain too many residual errors to start with, or it is impossible to re-articulate the original requirements. Usually, a combination of these factors applies. Increasing attention is therefore given to ways to 'rejuvenate' or 'recycle' existing software systems, ways to create structured versions of existing operational systems in order that they become easier to maintain.

At a low level this process can be supported by tools such as code restructurers and reformatters. To get higher-level abstractions generally requires human guidance and a sufficient understanding of the system.

This leads us to the second maintenance problem: the scant knowledge maintenance programmers have of the system or application domain. Note that the lack of application domain knowledge pertains to software development in general [CKI88]. The situation with respect to software maintenance is aggravated by the fact that there are usually scarce sources that can be used to build such an understanding. In many cases, the source code is the only reliable source. A major issue in software maintenance then is to gain a sufficient understanding of a system from its source code. The more spaghetti-like this code is, the less easy it becomes to disentangle it. An insufficient understanding results in changes that may have unforeseen ripple effects which in turn incurs further maintenance tasks.

Maintenance is also hampered if documentation is absent, insufficient, or out-of-date. Experienced programmers have learnt to distrust documentation: a disappointing observation in itself, albeit realistic. During initial development, documentation often comes off badly because of deadlines and other time constraints. Maintenance itself often occurs in a 'quick-fix' mode whereby the code is patched to accommodate changes. Technical documentation and other higher-level descriptions of the software then do not get updated. Maintenance programmers having to deal with these systems have become part historian, part detective, and part clairvoyant [Cor89].

Careful working procedures and management attention could prevent such a situation from occurring. But even then we are not sure that the right type of documentation will result. Two issues deserve our attention in this respect:

- A design rationale is often missing. Programmers and designers tend to document their final decisions, not the rationale for those decisions and the alternatives rejected. Maintenance programmers have to reconstruct this rationale and may easily make the wrong decisions.

- In trying to comprehend a piece of software, programmers often operate in an opportunistic mode. Based on their programming knowledge, in terms of programming plans and other stereotyped solutions to problems, they hypothesize a reasonable structure. Problems arise if the code does not meet these assumptions.

Finally, the noun 'maintenance' in itself has a negative connotation. Maintaining software is considered a second-rate job. Maintenance work is viewed as unchallenging and unrewarding. Preferably, new and inexperienced programmers are assigned to the maintenance group, possibly under the guidance of an experienced person. The more experienced people are to be found working on initial software development. In the structure of the organization, maintenance personnel ranks lower, both financially and organizationally, than programmers working on the development of new systems.

This tends to affect morale. Maintenance programmers are often not happy with their circumstances and try to change jobs as fast as possible. The high turnover of maintenance programmers precludes them from becoming sufficiently familiar with the software to be maintained which in turn hampers future maintenance.

It would be far better to have a more positive attitude towards maintenance. Maintaining software is a very difficult job. The job content of a maintenance programmer is more demanding than the job content of a development programmer. The programs are usually written by other people, people who can often not be consulted because they have left the firm or are entangled in the development of new systems. When making changes in an existing system, one is bound by the very structure of that system. There is generally a strong time pressure on maintenance personnel. Maintenance work requires more skills and knowledge than development does. It is simply more difficult [Cha87].

The maintenance group is of vital importance. It is they who keep things going. It is their job to ensure that the software keeps pace with the ever-changing reality. Compared to software development, software maintenance has more impact on the well-being of an organization.

14.2 REVERSE ENGINEERING AND RESTRUCTURING

> *What we're doing now with reverse engineering is Archeology. We're trying to gain an understanding of existing systems by examining ancient artifacts and piecing together the software equivalent of broken clay pots. Then we look to restructuring and reengineering to save the clay.*
> [Chi90]

It is fashionable in our trade to coin new terms once in a while and offer them as a panacea to the software crisis. One of the more recent magical terms is **reverse engineering**. It comes under different guises and means altogether different things to different people. In the discussion below we will use the terminology from [CCI90]. The different terms are illustrated in figure 14.4.

Chikofsky defines reverse engineering as 'the process of analyzing a subject system to

- identify the system's components and their interrelationships and
- create representations of the system in another form or at a higher level of abstraction.'

According to this definition, reverse engineering only concerns inspection of a system. Adaptations of a system and any form of restructuring, such as changing gotos into structured control constructs, do not fall within the strict definition of reverse engineering. Reverse engineering is akin to the reconstruction of a lost blueprint. Retiling the bathroom or the addition of a new bedroom is an altogether different affair. If this distinction is not carefully made, the meaning of the term reverse engineering dilutes too much and it reduces to a fancy synonym for maintenance.

The above definition still leaves open the question whether or not the resulting description is at a higher level of abstraction. To emphasize the distinction, Chikofsky uses the notions of **design recovery** and **redocumentation**, respectively.

Redocumentation concerns the derivation of a semantically-equivalent description at the same level of abstraction. Examples of redocumentation are the

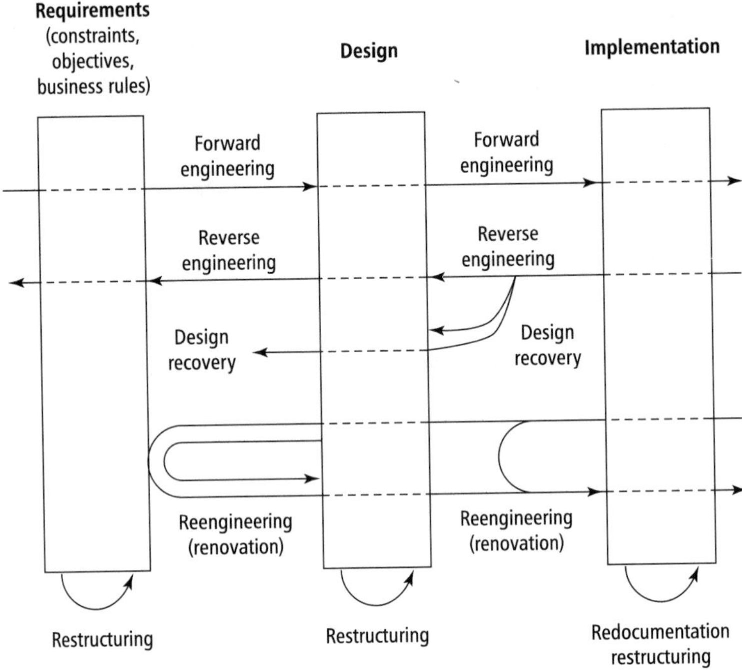

Figure 14.4 Reverse engineering and related notions (*Source: E.J. Chikofsky & J.H. Cross II, Reverse engineering and design recovery,* IEEE Software **7**, *1 (1990) pp 13–18, ©1990 IEEE)*

transformation of a badly-indented program into one having a neat lay-out or the construction of a set of flowcharts for a given program.

Design recovery concerns the derivation of a semantically-equivalent description at a higher level of abstraction. Some people limit the term reverse engineering to efforts that result in higher level descriptions and thus equate the term to what we have termed design recovery.

Note that a 100% functional equivalence is difficult to achieve in reverse engineering. The person carrying out the process (the reengineer) may encounter errors in the original system and may want to correct those. Such errors may be deeply hidden in the original system and become much more troublesome in the reverse engineered system. The programming language may be incompletely defined and its implementation may depend on certain machine characteristics. Data equivalence may be difficult to achieve because of typing issues, approximations, data conversions, etc. In practice, it seems sensible to solve this issue by agreeing on some acceptance test for the reengineered system, thereby relaxing the 100% functional equivalence requirement.

Obviously, reverse engineering is often done in circumstances where the target system is adapted as well. Two important subclasses are **restructuring** and **reengineering**.

Restructuring concerns the transformation of a system from one representation to another, at the same level of abstraction. The functionality of the system does not change. The transformation of spaghetti-code to structured code is a form of restructuring. The redesign of a system (possibly after a design recovery step) is another example of restructuring. A very specific form of restructuring is known as **revamping**. With revamping, only the user interface is modernized. For example, a legacy system may be given a Web-based user interface.

Restructuring is sometimes done in conjunction with efforts to convert existing software into reusable building blocks. Such reclamation efforts may well have higher (indirect) payoffs than the mere savings in maintenance expenditure for the particular system being restructured, especially if the effort concerns a family of similar systems. The latter is often done in combination with domain engineering and the development of a (reusable) architecture or framework; see also chapter 10.

With reengineering, also called **renovation**, real changes are made to the system. The reverse engineering step is followed by a traditional forward engineering step in which the required changes are incorporated.

Each of the above transformations starts from a given description of the system to be transformed. In most cases this will be the program code, which may or may not be adequately documented. However, it is also possible to, say, restructure an existing design or to reconstruct a requirements specification for a given design. For these transformations too, the term reverse engineering applies.

Both reverse engineering and restructuring can be done manually, but it is a rather tiresome affair. Quite a number of tools have been developed to support these processes. These tools are discussed in section 14.2.2. There are, however, some inherent limitations as to how much can be achieved automatically. These limitations are discussed in the next section.

14.2.1 Inherent Limitations

> *If you pass an unstructured, unmodular mess through one of these restructuring systems, you end up with at best, a structured, unmodular mess.*
> [Wen86]

Reverse engineering will mostly not be limited to redocumentation in a narrow sense. We will often be inclined to ask why certain things are being done the way they are done, what the meaning is of a certain code fragment, and the like. We must therefore investigate how programmers go about studying program text. The relevance of these issues shows from results of a study into maintenance activities [FH79]:

- maintenance programmers study the original program code about one and a half times as long as its documentation;
- maintenance programmers spend as much time reading the code as they do implementing a change.

Insights into the discovery process which takes place during maintenance activities will give us the necessary insight to put various developments regarding reverse engineering and restructuring into perspective.

In forward engineering activities we usually proceed from high-level abstractions to low-level implementations. Information gets lost in the successive steps involved in this process. If we want to reverse the route, this information must be reconstructed. The object we start with, a piece of source code in general, usually offers insufficient clues for a full reconstruction.

The programmer uses various sources of information in his discovery process. For example, if the design documentation is available, that documentation will reveal something about the structure of the system. A characteristic situation in practice is that the source code is the only reliable source of information. So this source code has to be studied in order to discover the underlying abstractions. The question is how the programmer goes about doing this.

Several theories have been developed to describe this comprehension process. Common to these theories is that expert programmers may draw on a vast number of knowledge chunks. These knowledge chunks are called in when software is developed.

Within the realm of programming, it is postulated that experts know of programming plans or beacons. A **programming plan** is a program fragment that corresponds to a stereotypical action. For example, to compute the sum of a series of numbers, a programmer uses the 'running total loop plan'. In this plan, some counter is initialized to zero and incremented with the next value of a series in the body of a loop. A **beacon** is a key feature that typically indicates the presence of a particular structure or operation. Beacons seem to be very diagnostic of program meaning.

For example, the kernel idea or central operation in a sorting program is a swap operation. If we are presented with a program that contains a swap operation, our immediate reaction would then be that it concerns some sorting program.

This type of program comprehension process occurs when studying existing software. Meaningful units are isolated from the 'flat' source text. Knowledge from human memory is called in during this process. The more knowledge the reader has about programming or the application domain, the more successful this process will be. The better the source code maps onto knowledge already available to the reader, the more effective this process will be.

During the comprehension process, the reader forms hypotheses and checks these hypotheses with the actual text. Well-structured programs and proper documentation ease this process. If application domain concepts map onto well-delineated program units then the program text will be more easily understood. If the structure of a program shows no relation with the structure of the application domain, or the reader cannot discern this structure, then understanding of the program text is seriously hampered.

As a side remark we note that there are two extreme strategies for studying program text:

- the as-needed strategy, and
- the systematic strategy.

In the as-needed strategy, program text is read from beginning to end like a piece of prose and hypotheses are formulated on the basis of local information. Inexperienced programmers in particular tend to fall back onto this strategy. In the systematic strategy, an overall understanding of the system is formed by a systematic top-down study of the program text. The systematic approach gives a better insight into causal relations between program components.

These causal relations play an important role when implementing changes. So-called delocalized plans, in which conceptually related pieces of code are located in program parts that are physically wide apart, may seriously hamper maintenance activities. If our understanding is based on local clues only, modifications may easily result in so-called ripple-effects, i.e. changes that are locally correct but lead to new problems at different, unforeseen places. Use of the as-needed strategy increases the probability of ripple effects.

During the comprehension process the programmer uses knowledge that has its origin outside the program text proper. To illustrate this phenomenon, consider the program text from figure 14.5.

The program fragment of figure 14.5 manipulates a boolean matrix A. Before this fragment is executed the matrix will have a certain value. The matrix is traversed in a rather complicated way (potentially, each element is visited n times) and once in

```
for i:= 1 to n do
    for j:= 1 to n do
        if A[j, i] then
            for k:= 1 to n do
                if A[i, k] then A[j, k]:= true endif
            enddo
        endif
    enddo
enddo
```

Figure 14.5 Warshall's algorithm to compute the transitive closure of a graph

a while an element of the array is set to true. But what does this fragment *mean*? What does it *do*?

An expert will 'recognize' Warshall's algorithm. Warshall's algorithm computes the transitive closure of a relation (graph). The notions 'transitive closure', 'relation' and 'graph' have a precise meaning within a certain knowledge domain. If you don't know the meaning of these notions, you haven't made any progress in understanding the algorithm either.

At yet another level of abstraction the meaning of this fragment could be described as follows. Suppose we start with a collection of cities. The relation A states, for each pair of cities i and j, whether there is a direct rail connection between cities i and j. The code fragment of figure 14.5 computes whether there is a connection at all (either direct or indirect) between each pair of cities.

Warshall's algorithm has many applications. If you know the algorithm, you will recognize the fragment reproduced in figure 14.5. If you don't know the algorithm, you will not discover the meaning of this fragment either.

As a second example, consider the code fragment of figure 14.6, adapted from [Big89]. The fragment will not mean much to you. Procedure and variable names are meaningless. A meaningful interpretation of this fragment is next to impossible.

The same code fragment is given in figure 14.7, though with meaningful names. From that version you may grasp that the routine has something to do with window management. The border of the current window is depicted in a lighter shade while the border of another window gets highlighted. The cursor is positioned in the now highlighted window and the process of that window is restarted. If we add a few comments to the routine, its text becomes fairly easy to interpret. Meaningful names and comments together provide for an informal semantics of this code which suffice for a proper understanding.

```
procedure A(var x: w);
    begin b(y, n1);
        b(x, n2);
        m(w[x]);
        y:= x;
        r(p[x])
    end;
```

Figure 14.6 An incomprehensible code fragment

```
procedure change_window(var nw: window);
    begin border(current_window, no_highlight);
        border(nw, highlight);
        move_cursor(w[nw]);
        current_window:= nw;
        resume(process[nw])
    end;
```

Figure 14.7 Code fragment with meaningful names

Common to these two examples as well as the altimeter anecdote from section 14.1 is that we need *outside* information for a proper interpretation of the code fragments. The outside information concerns concepts from a certain knowledge domain or a design rationale that was only present in the head of the programmer.

The window management example is illustrative for yet another reason. Tools manipulate sequences of symbols. In principle, tools do not have knowledge of the (external) meaning of the symbols being manipulated. In particular, a reverse engineering and restructuring tool has no knowledge of 'windows', 'cursor' and the like. These notions derive their meaning from the application domain, not from the program text itself. From the tool point of view, the texts of figures 14.6 and 14.7 are equally meaningful.

The above observations have repercussions for the degree to which tools can support the reverse engineering and restructuring process. Such tools cannot turn a badly-designed system into a good one. They cannot infer knowledge from a source text which is not already contained in that text without calling in external knowledge as an aid. In particular, completely automatic design recovery is not feasible.

14.2.2 Tools

During the reverse engineering process, the programmer builds an understanding of what the software is trying to accomplish and why things are done the way they are done. Several classes of tools may support the task of program understanding:

- Tools to ease perceptual processes involved in program understanding (reformatters). Tools may for example produce a neat lay-out in which nested instructions are indented and blank lines are put between successive procedures. More advanced tools print procedure names in a larger font or generate page headers which contain the name of the component, its version number, creation date, and the like.

- Tools to gain insight into the static structure of programs. For example, tools that generate tables of contents and cross-reference listings help to trace the use of program elements. Browsers provide powerful interactive capabilities for inspecting the static structure of programs. Hypertext systems provide mechanisms to extend the traditional flat organization of text by their capabilities for linking non-sequential chunks of information. If system-related information is kept in a hypertext form, this opens up new possibilities for interactive, dynamic inspection of that information. Code analyzers may be used to identify potential trouble spots by computing software complexity metrics, highlighting 'dead code', or indicating questionable coding practices. Finally, tools may generate a graphical image of a program text in the form of a flowchart, a control graph or a calling hierarchy.

- Tools to gain insight into the dynamic behavior of programs. Next to traditional text-oriented debugging systems there are systems which provide graphical capabilities to monitor program execution, e.g. to animate data structures.

Note that these tools provide support for maintenance tasks in general (alongside tools such as test coverage monitors, which keep track of program paths executed by a given set of test data, and source comparators, which identify changes between program versions). With respect to reverse engineering, the above tools may be classified as redocumentation tools. By far the majority of present-day reverse engineering tools fall into this category.

Tools which result in a description at a higher level of abstraction (design recovery tools) have some inherent limitations, as argued in the previous section. Tools for design recovery need a model of the application domain in which the concepts from that domain are modeled in an explicit way, together with their mutual dependencies and interrelations. Completely automatic design recovery is not feasible for the foreseeable future. Concepts from an application domain usually carry an informal semantics. Tools for design recovery may, in a dialog with the human user, search for patterns, make suggestions, indicate relations between components, etc. Such a tool may be termed a 'maintenance apprentice'.

A number of tools exist for restructuring program code. Such tools for example transform a program containing gotos into a semantically-equivalent program containing only structured control instructions.

The history of restructuring tools goes all the way back to the late 1960s. In 1966, Böhm and Jacopini published a seminal paper in which it was shown that gotos are not necessary for creating programs [BJ66]. The roots of restructuring tools like Recoder [Bus85] can be traced to the constructive proof given in Böhm and Jacopini's paper. Recoder structures the control flow of Cobol programs. There is a wide choice of such Cobol restructuring tools.

Restructuring tools can be very valuable – a well-structured program is usually easier to read and understand. A study reported in [GS89] provides evidence that structural differences do affect maintenance performance. Specifically, it was found that eliminating gotos and redundancy appears to decrease both the time required to perform maintenance and the frequency of ripple effects.

Yet, the merit of restructuring tools is limited. They will not transform a flawed design into a good one. The improved versions of the system used in Gibson's experiment were constructed manually. The improvements incorporated may well go beyond what can be achieved automatically.

14.3 ORGANIZATIONAL AND MANAGERIAL ISSUES

The duties of maintenance management are not different from those of other organizational functions, and software development in particular. In chapter 2 we identified five entities that require continuous attention of management:

- time, i.e. progress towards goals;
- information, in particular the integrity of the complete set of documents, including change requests;
- organization of the team, including coordination of activities;
- quality of the product and process;
- money, i.e. cost of the project.

In this section we address these issues from a maintenance perspective. We pay particular attention to issues that pose specific problems and challenges to maintenance. These issues are: the organization of maintenance activities, major differences between development and maintenance, the control of maintenance tasks, and quality assessment.

14.3.1 Organization of Maintenance Activities

The primary question to be addressed here is whether or not software maintenance should be assigned to a separate organizational unit. The following discussion is largely based on an insightful study of different forms of systems staff departmentalization presented in [SB90]. The authors of this article explore the strengths and weaknesses of three alternative bases for staff departmentalization. The three organizational forms with their focal strengths and weaknesses are listed in figure 14.8. We will sketch the W- and A-Type organizations and discuss the L-type organization with its pros and cons more elaborately.

W-Type	Departmentalization by work type (analysis versus programming) *Focal strength*: development and specialization of programming knowledge and skills *Focal weakness*: costs of coordination between systems analysts and programmers
A-Type	Departmentalization by application domain (application group A versus application group B) *Focal strength*: development and specialization of application knowledge *Focal weakness*: costs of coordination and integration among application groups
L-Type	Departmentalization by life-cycle phase (development versus maintenance) *Focal strength*: development and specialization of service orientation and maintenance skills *Focal weakness*: costs of coordination between development and maintenance units

Figure 14.8 Trade-offs between alternative organizational forms (*Source: E.B. Swanson & C.M. Beath, Departmentalization in software development and maintenance,* Communications of the ACM **33**, *6 (1990) pp 658-667. Reproduced by permission of the Association for Computing Machinery, Inc.*)

Traditionally, departmentalization in software development tended to be according to work type (a W-Type scheme). In such a scheme, people analyze user needs, or design systems, or implement them, or test them, etc. Even though they cooperate in a team, each team member has quite separate responsibilities and roles.

In a W-Type scheme, work assignments may originate from both development and maintenance projects. For example, a designer may be involved in the design of a (sub)system in the context of some development project or in the design of a change to an existing system. Likewise, a programmer may implement an algorithm for a new system or realize changes in an operational program.

Note that the development of new systems does not occur in a vacuum. Designers of new systems will reuse existing designs and must take into account constraints imposed by existing systems. Programmers involved in development projects have to deal with interfaces to existing software, existing databases, etc. In the W-Type scheme, the distinction between development and maintenance work is primarily a distinction between different *origins* of the work assignment.

A second form of departmentalization is one according to application areas, the A-Type scheme. Nowadays, computerized applications have extended to almost all corners of the enterprise. Systems have become more diversified. Application domain expertise has become increasingly important for successful implementation of information systems. Deep knowledge of an application domain is a valuable but scarce resource. Nurturing of this expertise amongst staff is one way to increase quality and productivity in both development and maintenance. In larger organizations, we may therefore find units with particular expertise in certain application domains, like financial systems, office automation, or real-time process control.

Finally, we may departmentalize according to life-cycle phases, as is done in the L-Type scheme. In particular, we may distinguish between development and maintenance. With an increasing portfolio of systems to be maintained and the increasing business need of keeping the growing base of information systems working satisfactorily, the division of development and maintenance into separate organizational units is found more often.

Separating development and maintenance has both advantages and disadvantages. The major advantages are:

- Clear accountability: we may clearly separate the cost and effort involved in maintenance activities from investments in new developments. If personnel are involved in both types of work, they have some freedom in charging their time. It is then more difficult to measure and predict the 'real' cost of software maintenance.

- Intermittent demands of maintenance make it difficult to predict and control progress of new system development. If people do both maintenance work and development, some control can be exercised by specifically allocating certain periods of time as maintenance periods. For instance, the first week of each calendar month may be set aside for maintenance. But even then, maintenance problems are rather unpredictable and some need immediate attention. Many a schedule slippage is due to the maintenance drain.

- A separation of maintenance and development facilitates and motivates the maintenance organization to conduct a meaningful acceptance test before the system is taken into production. If such an acceptance test is not conducted explicitly, maintenance may be confronted with low-quality software or systems which still need a 'finishing touch' which the development team has left undone for lack of time.

- By specializing on maintenance tasks, a higher quality of user service can be realized. By their very nature, development groups are focused on system delivery, whereas maintenance people are service-oriented and find pride in satisfying user requests. We will further elaborate upon this issue in section 14.3.2.

- By concentrating on the systems to be maintained, a higher level of productivity is achieved. Maintenance work requires specific skills of which a more optimal use can be made in a separate organization. If people are involved in both development and maintenance, more staff have to be allocated to maintenance and the familiarity with any particular system is spread more thinly.

On the other hand, the strict separation of development and maintenance has certain disadvantages as well:

- Demotivation of personnel because of status differences, with consequential degradation of quality and productivity. Managerial attitudes and traditional career paths are the main causes for these motivational problems. Conversely, proper managerial attention to maintenance work goes a large way towards alleviating the morale problem. For example, an organization may decide to hire new people into development only and explicitly consider a transfer to maintenance as a promotion. (Most organizations do exactly the opposite.)

- Loss of knowledge about the system (with respect to both its design and the application domain knowledge incorporated) when the system is transferred from development to maintenance. Various strategies can mitigate against this loss. For example, a future maintainer of a system may spend some time with the development team, a developer may stay with maintenance until the maintainers have become sufficiently acquainted with the system, or a designer may instruct the maintainers about the design of a system.

- Coordination costs between development and maintenance, especially when the new system replaces an existing one.

- Increased cost of system acceptance by the maintenance organization. If the system is explicitly carried over from development, certain quality and documentation criteria must be met. Within an A-type organization these requirements can often be relaxed a bit, or their fulfillment is postponed. It is by no means clear though that this really incurs an increase in cost. In the long run it may well be cheaper to only accept systems which pass a proper maintenance acceptance test.

- Possible duplication of communication channels to the user organization.

Based on an analysis of existing departmentalizations and the resulting list of strengths and weaknesses, Swanson and Beath express a slight preference for having development and maintenance as separate organizational units. We concur with that. Careful procedures could be devised that overcome some or all of the disadvantages listed. We should stress that personnel demotivation is a real issue in many organizations. It deserves serious management attention.

Combinations of departmentalization types are also possible. In particular, combinations of A-type and L-type departmentalizations are quite common. So, within the maintenance organization, smaller groups may specialize in some application domain, i.e. a specific collection of information systems. This may be termed the L-A-scheme. Conversely, in an A-L-scheme a small maintenance unit is found within a group that specializes in a certain application area. The L-A-scheme is more likely to exhibit the advantages of the L-scheme than the A-L-scheme does.

Too much specialization is a lurking danger though. A system should never become someone's private property. A variation of the reverse Peter principle applies here: people rise within an organization to a level at which they become indispensable. Job rotation is one way to avoid people from becoming too much entrenched in the peculiarities of a system. There is a trade-off though, since such a step also means that in-depth knowledge of a system is sacrificed.

14.3.2 Software Maintenance from a Service Perspective

> *Software maintenance organizations need to realize that they are in the customer service business.*
> [Pig96]

Software development results in a product, a piece of software. Software maintenance can be seen as providing a service. There are notable differences between products and services, which mean that the quality of products and services is judged differently. As a consequence, the quality of software development and software maintenance is also judged differently and maintenance organizations should pay attention to service-specific quality aspects.

Apparently, this is not widely recognized yet. Within the software maintenance domain, the focus is still on product aspects. The final phases of software development supposedly concern the delivery of an operations manual, installing the software, handling change requests and fixing bugs. In practice, the role of an IT department is much broader during the deployment stage, as is illustrated by the ubiquitous help desk.

This is confirmed by [SBA97] who report on a survey to find those aspects of software quality that customers consider most important. The main insight to be gained from their study is the strong emphasis customers place on service quality. The top five factors found in their study are: service responsiveness, service capacity, product reliability, service efficiency, and product functionality. They also quote an interesting result from a quality study in the telecommunications domain. To the question 'Would you recommend others to buy from this company?', a 100% yes was obtained from the category of users that had complained and got a satisfactory result. For the category that had not complained, this percentage was 87%. Apparently, it is more important to get a satisfactory service than to have no problems at all.

The main differences between products and services are as follows:

- Services are **intangible**, products are tangible. This is considered the most basic difference between products and services. Services – being benefits or activities – cannot be seen, felt, tasted, or touched, unlike products. Consequently, services cannot be counted, stored, patented, readily displayed, or communicated, and pricing is more difficult.

- Because services are created by activities, and activities are performed by humans, services tend to be more **heterogeneous** than products. Customer satisfaction depends on employee actions during the service delivery. Service quality depends on factors which are difficult to control, such as the ability of customers to articulate their needs, the ability and willingness of personnel to satisfy those needs, the presence or absence of other customers, and the level of demand for the service. These complicating factors make it hard to know whether the service was delivered according to plan or specification.

- Services are produced and consumed **simultaneously**, whereas production and consumption of products can be separated. For example, a car can be produced first, sold a few months later, and then be consumed over a period of several years. For services, production and consumption has to take place in parallel. The production of the service creates the set of benefits, whose consumption cannot be postponed. For example, a restaurant service – preparing a meal and serving the customer – by and large has to be produced while the customer is receiving the service. As a consequence, customers participate in and affect the transaction, customers may affect each other, employees affect the service outcome, and centralization and mass production are difficult.

- Services are **perishable**, products are not. Services cannot be saved or stored. They cannot be returned or resold, and it is difficult to synchronize supply and demand.

The difference between products and services is not clear-cut. Often, services are augmented with physical products to make them more tangible. For example, luggage tags may be provided with a travel insurance. In the same way, products are augmented with add-on services, such as a guarantee, to improve the quality perception of the buyer. In the service marketing literature, a product–service continuum is used to indicate that there is no clear boundary between products and services. This product–service continuum has pure products at one end, pure services at the other, and product–service mixtures in between. Figure 14.9 shows some example products and services along this continuum.

As this figure shows, products and services can be intertwined. In the case of fast-food, both the product, the food, and the service, quick delivery, are essential to

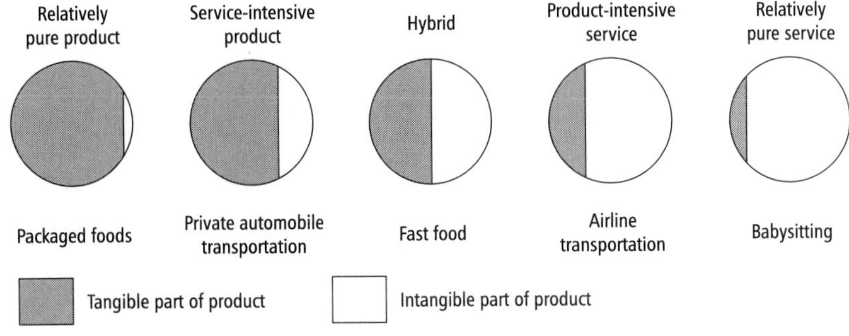

Figure 14.9 The product--service continuum (*Source: L.L. Berry & A. Parasuraman,* Marketing Services: Competing Through Quality, *1991, ©The Free Press*)

the customer. The quality of such a product–service mix is judged on both product and service aspects: does the food taste good and is it served quickly.

Let us return to the software engineering domain. A major difference between software development and software maintenance is the fact that software development results in a *product*, whereas software maintenance results in a *service* being delivered to the customer. Software maintenance has more service-like aspects than software development, because the value of software maintenance lies in activities that result in benefits for the customers, such as corrected faults and new features. Contrast this with software development, where the development activities themselves do not provide benefits to the customer. It is the resulting software system that provides those benefits.

As noted, the difference between products and services is not clear-cut. Consequently, this goes for software development and software maintenance as well. Figure 14.10 shows the product–service continuum with examples from the software engineering domain.

Service marketeers often use the gap model to illustrate how differences between perceived service delivery and expected service may come about. This gap model is depicted in figure 14.11. Service quality is improved if those gaps are closed. The difference between the perceived quality and the expected quality (gap 5) is caused by four other gaps. These four gaps, and suggested solutions for bridging them, are:

Gap 1 The expected service as perceived by the service provider differs from the service as expected by the customer. In the field of software maintenance, this difference is often caused by an insufficient relationship focus of the service provider. For example, a maintenance department may aim to satisfy certain

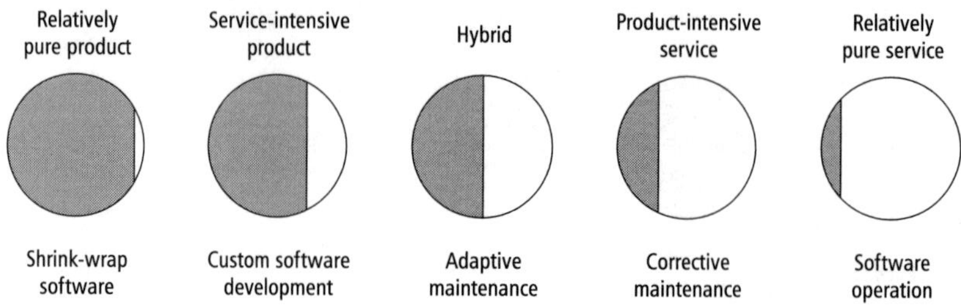

Figure 14.10 The product--service continuum for software development and maintenance

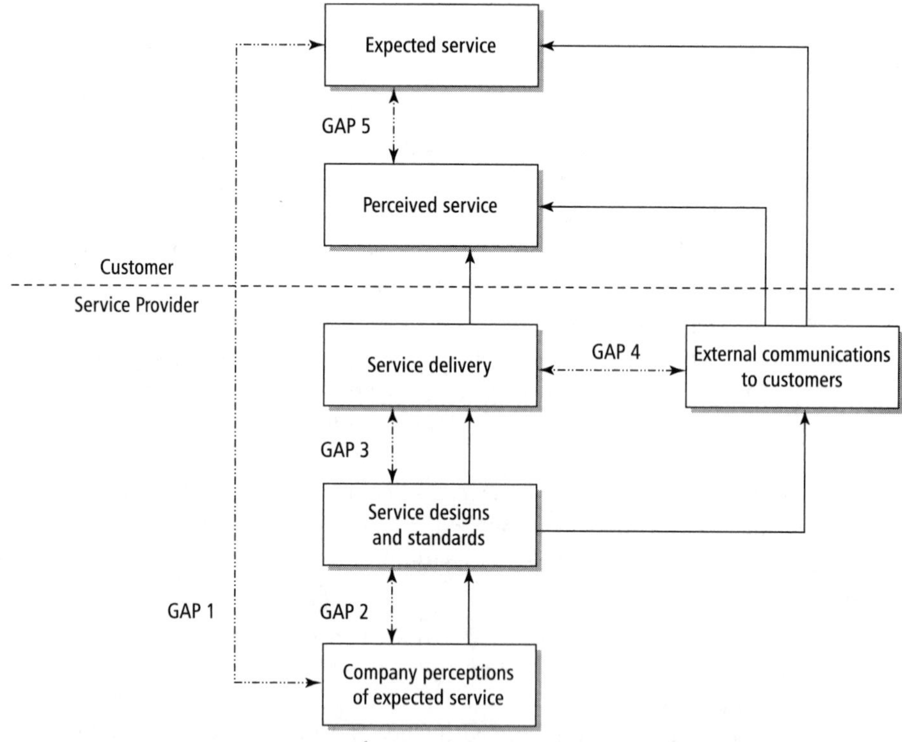

Figure 14.11 The gaps model of service quality (*Reprinted with permission from A. Parasuraman, V.A. Zeithaml & L.L. Berry,* A Conceptual Model of Service Quality and its Implication for Future Research, *in Journal of Marketing* **49**, *Fall 1985, pp. 41-50. Published by the American Marketing Association*)

availability constraints such as 99% availability, while the actual customer concern is with maximum downtime.

It is important for a maintenance organization to translate customer service expectations into clear service agreements. Preferably, the maintenance service commitments are specified in a contract – the **Service Level Agreement** – which specifies, amongst other things, the services themselves, the levels of service (i.e. how fast and how reliably will the service be delivered), what happens if the service provider does not reach the agreed upon service levels, when and how the customer will receive reports regarding the services actually delivered, when and how the service level agreement will be reviewed, and so on.

Gap 2 The service specification differs from the expected service as perceived by the service provider. This may arise if the (internal) service designs and standards do not match the service requirements as perceived by the service provider. For example, the customer expects a quick restart of the system, while the standard procedure of the maintenance organization is focused on analyzing the reason for the crash.

The maintenance activities as specified in the service level agreement have to be planned. This includes the planning of the activities themselves, the transfer of the results to the customer, the planning of releases, the estimation of resources needed, the scheduling of maintenance activities, and the identification of possible risks. Explicitly basing the planning of maintenance activities on the commitments as agreed with the customer helps to close this gap.

Gap 3 The actual service delivery differs from the specified services. This is often caused by deficiencies in human resource policies, failures to match demand and supply, and customers not fulfilling their role. For example, customers may bypass the helpdesk by phoning the maintainer of their system directly, thereby hindering a proper incident management process.

The service level agreement states which maintenance activities are to be carried out, and how fast, reliably, etc. this should be done. In order to be able to report on the performance of the maintenance organization in this respect, information about the actual maintenance activities must be gathered. This information can be used to monitor maintenance activities and take corrective actions if necessary.

For example, when the customer reports a bug, information about the bug itself (originator, type, etc.) is recorded, as well as the reporting time, the time when corrective action was started and ended, and the time when the bug was reported as fixed. If these data indicate that the average downtime of a system exceeds the level as specified in the service level agreement, the maintenance organization might assign more maintenance staff to this system, put maintenance staff on point-duty at the customer site, renegotiate the agreed upon service level, or take other action to realign agreement and reality.

By keeping a strict eye upon the performance of the maintenance organization and adjusting the maintenance planning or renegotiating the commitments with the customer when required, gap 3 is narrowed.

Gap 4 Communication about the service does not match the actual service delivery. This may be caused by ineffective management of customer expectations, promising too much, or ineffective horizontal communication. For example, a customer is not informed about the repair of a bug he reported.

An important instrument to help close this gap is event management. Event management concerns the management of events that cause or might cause the maintenance activities carried out to deviate from the levels as promised in the service level agreement. An event is either a change request, such as a user request for a new feature, or an incident. Incidents are software bugs and other hazards that the maintenance organization has promised to deal with, such as, say, a server being down.

The main purpose of event management is to manage all those events. To do so, an event management library system is employed, often in the form of a 'helpdesk system'. The event management library system provides for the storage, update, and retrieval of event records, and the sharing and transfer of event records between parties involved. This event management library system supports the communication with the customer about maintenance services delivered. It is also a highly valuable 'memory' for the maintainers: they may use the event library to search for similar incidents, to see why certain components were changed before, etc.[2]

Since the fifth gap is caused by the four other gaps, perceived service quality can be improved by closing those first four gaps, thus bringing the perceived quality in line with the expected quality. Since software maintenance organizations are essentially service providers, they need to consider the above issues. They need to manage their product – software maintenance – as a service in order to be able to deliver high quality.

[2]Note that the focus of the event management library system differs somewhat from that of configuration management as discussed in the next section. Configuration management emphasizes the *internal* use of information about change requests and the like. Our description of event management focuses on the *external* use of essentially the same information. In practice, the two processes may well be combined.

14.3.3 Control of Maintenance Tasks

Careful control of the product is necessary during software development. The vast amount of information has to be kept under control. Documentation must be kept consistent and up-to-date. An appropriate scheme for doing so is provided by the set of procedures that make up configuration control; see chapter 4. Configuration control pays particular attention to the handling of change requests. Since handling change requests is what maintenance is all about, configuration control is of vital importance during maintenance.

Effective maintenance depends on following a rigorous methodology, not only with respect to the implementation of changes agreed upon, but also with respect to the way change is controlled. Following IEEE Standard 1219, we suggest the following orderly, well-documented process for controlling changes during maintenance:

1. **Identify and classify change requests** Each change request (CR) is given a unique identification number and is classified into one of the maintenance categories (corrective, adaptive, perfective, preventive). The CR is analyzed to decide whether it will be accepted, rejected, or needs further evaluation. This analysis also results in a first cost estimate. The CR is finally prioritized and scheduled for implementation.

2. **Analysis of change requests** This step starts with an analysis of the CR to determine its impact on the system, the organization, and possible interfacing systems. Several alternative solutions to implement the CR may be devised, including their cost and schedule. The results of the analysis are documented in a report. Based on this report, a decision is made whether or not the CR will be implemented. The authority for this decision is usually assigned to the configuration control board; see also chapter 4.

3. **Implement the change** This involves the design, implementation and testing of the change. The output of this step is a new version of the system, fully tested, and well documented.

The above steps indicate a maintenance model in which each change request is carefully analyzed and, if (and only if) the request is approved, its implementation is carried out in a disciplined, orderly way, including a proper update of the documentation. This control scheme fits in well with the **iterative-enhancement** model of software maintenance; see figure 14.12. The essence of the iterative-enhancement model is that the set of documents is modified starting with the highest-level document affected by the changes, propagating the changes down through the full set of documents. For example, if a change request necessitates a design change, then the design is changed first. Only as a consequence of the design change will the code be adapted.

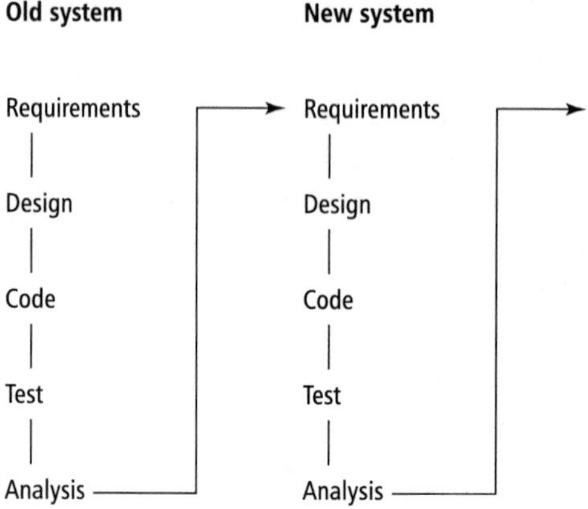

Figure 14.12 Iterative-enhancement model of software maintenance (*Source: V.R. Basili, Viewing maintenance as reuse-oriented software development,* IEEE Software **7**, *1 (1990) 19–25, ©1990 IEEE*)

Reality is often different. Figure 14.13 depicts the so-called **quick-fix** model of software maintenance. In the quick-fix model, you take the source code, make the necessary changes to the code and recompile the system to obtain a new version. The source-code documentation and other higher-level documents get updated after the code has been fixed, and usually only if time permits.

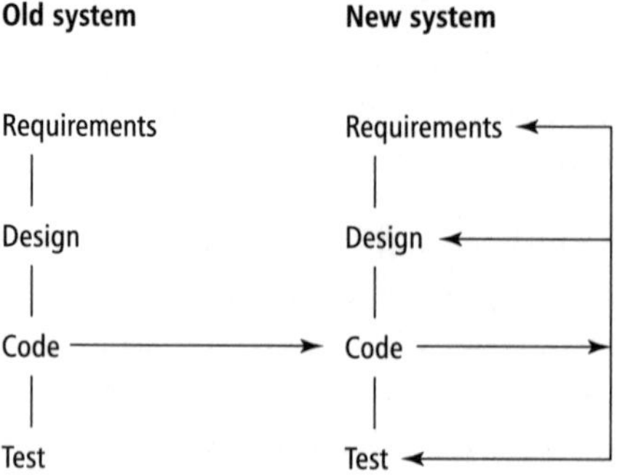

Figure 14.13 Quick-fix model of software maintenance (*Source: V.R. Basili, Viewing maintenance as reuse-oriented software development,* IEEE Software **7**, *1 (1990) 19–25, ©1990 IEEE*)

In the latter scheme, patches are made upon patches and the structure of the system degrades rather quickly. Because of the resulting increase in system complexity and inconsistency of documents, future maintenance becomes much more difficult. To be realistic, the quick-fix model cannot be completely circumvented. In an emergency situation there is but one thing that matters: getting the system up and running again as fast as possible. Where possible though, the quick-fix model should be avoided. If it is used at all, preventive maintenance activities should be scheduled to repair the structural damage done.

In a normal, non-emergency situation, change requests are often bundled into **releases**. The user then does not get a new version after each and every change has been realized, but after a certain number of change requests has been handled, or after a certain time frame. Three common ways of deciding on the contents and timing of the next release are:

- fixed staff and variable schedule. In this scheme, there is a fixed number of people available for the maintenance work. The next release date is fixed in advance. Often, the release dates are scheduled at fixed time intervals, say every six months. The next release will contain all changes that have been handled within the agreed time frame. So the next release is always on time. There also is some flexibility as to the contents of the next release, since the maintainers and the customer do not fix the contents in advance.

- variable staff and fixed schedule. Here, a release date is fixed in advance. The portfolio of change requests to be handled in this release is also negotiated and fixed in advance. Next, the number of people needed to implement the changes within the fixed time frame is decided. On the way, some renegotiation of both the contents and the schedule is possible. An advantage of this scheme is that change requests are assigned clear priorities and that communication with the customer about the contents of the next release is enforced.

- variable staff and variable schedule. As in the previous scheme, the portfolio of change requests to be handled in the next release is negotiated and fixed in advance. Then, the cost and schedule for this release are negotiated, and the number of maintainers required to achieve it is determined. This scheme requires more planning and oversight than the other two schemes. It is also likely to better accommodate the customer. As with ordinary development, schedule slippages and contents renegotiation are not uncommon in this scheme.

14.3.4 Quality Issues

Changing software impairs its structure. By a conscious application of software quality assurance procedures during maintenance, we may limit the negative effects. If we know the software quality factors that affect maintenance effort and cost, we may measure those factors and take preventive actions accordingly. In particular, such metrics can be used to guide decisions as to when to start a major overhaul of components or complete systems.

Quality control issues get quite some attention during software development. Software quality assurance however should broaden its scope to maintenance as well. The implementation of changes during maintenance requires the same level of quality assurance as development work. The ingredients of software quality assurance procedures, as discussed in chapter 6, apply equally well to software maintenance.

Software quality assurance can be backed up by measurements that quantify quality aspects. With respect to maintenance, we may focus on measures which specifically relate to maintenance effort, such as counting defects reported, change requests issued, effort spent on incorporating changes, complexity metrics, etc.

Relationships between such measures can then be sought. Observed trends can be used to initiate actions, such as:

- If maintenance efforts correlate well with complexity metrics like Henri and Kafura's Information Flow or McCabe's cyclomatic complexity (see chapter 11), then these complexity metrics may be used to trigger preventive maintenance. Various studies have indeed found such correlations.

- If certain modules require frequent changes or much effort to realize changes, then a re-design of such modules should be given serious consideration.

A particularly relevant issue during maintenance is to decide when to reengineer. At a certain point in time, maintaining an old system becomes next to impossible and a major reengineering effort is required. There are no hard figures on which to decide this, but certain system characteristics certainly indicate system degradation:

- Frequent system failures;

- Code over seven years old;

- Overly-complex program structure and logic flow;

- Code written for previous generation hardware;

- Running in emulation mode;

- Very large modules or subroutines;

- Excessive resource requirements;
- Hard-coded parameters that are subject to change;
- Difficulty in keeping maintenance personnel;
- Seriously deficient documentation;
- Missing or incomplete design specifications.

The greater the number of such characteristics present, the greater the potential for redesign.

Improvements in software maintenance requires insight into factors that determine maintenance cost and effort. Software metrics provide such insight. To measure is to know. By carefully collecting and interpreting maintenance data, we may discover the major cost drivers of software maintenance and initiate actions to improve both quality and productivity.

14.4 SUMMARY

Software maintenance encompasses all modifications to a software product after delivery. The following breakdown of maintenance activities is usually made:

Corrective maintenance concerns the correction of faults.

Adaptive maintenance deals with adapting software to changes in the environment.

Perfective maintenance mainly deals with accommodating new or changed user requirements.

Preventive maintenance concerns activities aimed at increasing a system's maintainability.

'Real' maintenance, the correction of faults, consumes approximately 25% of maintenance effort. By far the larger part of software maintenance concerns the evolution of software. This evolution is inescapable. Software models part of reality. Reality changes, and so does the software that models it.

Major causes of maintenance problems were discussed in section 14.1: the existence of a vast amount of unstructured code, insufficient knowledge about the system or application domain on the part of maintenance programmers, insufficient documentation, and the bad image of the software maintenance department.

Some of these problems are accidental and can be remedied by proper actions. Through a better organization and management of software maintenance, substantial quality and productivity improvements can be realized. These issues were discussed in section 14.3. Obviously, improved maintenance should start with improved development. Opportunities to improve the development process are a major topic in most chapters of this book.

A particularly relevant issue for software maintenance is that of reverse engineering, the process of reconstructing a lost blueprint. Before changes can be realized, the maintainer has to gain an understanding of the system. Since the majority of operational code is unstructured and undocumented, this is a major problem. Section 14.2 addresses reverse engineering, its limitations, and tools to support it.

The fundamental problem is that maintenance will remain a big issue. Because of the changes made to software, its structure degrades. Specific attention to preventive maintenance activities aimed at improving system structure are needed from time to time to fight system entropy.

Software maintenance used to be a rather neglected topic in the software engineering literature. Like programmers, researchers are more attracted to developing new, fancy methods and tools for software development. This situation is gradually changing. Major journals regularly feature articles on software maintenance, there is an annual IEEE Conference on Software Maintenance (since 1985), and the journal *Software Maintenance: Research and Practice* (launched 1989) is wholly devoted to it.

14.5 FURTHER READING

[Pig96] is a text book wholly devoted to software maintenance. [LS80] is a seminal booklet on software maintenance. It introduces the widely-known categories of maintenance tasks and provides data on their distribution. More recent data on the distribution of maintenance tasks are given in [NP90], [Dek92] and [SM98]. The practice of software maintenance is discussed in [Sin98] and [TG98].

The various types of reverse engineering are discussed in [CCI90]. The 100% equivalence issues in reverse engineering are discussed in [Ben98]. Reverse engineering tools are discussed in [WTMS94], [BMW94], [JW98] and [BG98]. Programming plans and beacons were originally proposed in [SE84] and [Bro83]. Recent research addressing the role of these concepts in program comprehension processes is described in [vMV95] and [vMVH97].

Possible organizations of maintenance activities as well as their major advantages and disadvantages are discussed in [SB90]. The service perspective on software maintenance is discussed in [NvV99]. The translation hereof into a Capability Maturity Model aimed at maintenance processes is described in [NvV98a].

The IEEE Process model for software maintenance is described in [IEE92]. The iterative-enhancement and quick-fix models of software maintenance are discussed in [Bas90]. Approaches to scheduling releases are the topic of [SO97].

The cost of software maintenance, and empirical relations between quality aspects and cost are the topic of [BDKZ93], [KS97a], [HC97] and [NvV97]. Indicators of system degradation are given in [MO83].

Exercises

1. Define the following terms: corrective maintenance, adaptive maintenance, perfective maintenance, and preventive maintenance.

2. Discuss the major causes of software maintenance problems.

3. What is reverse engineering?

4. What is the difference between design recovery and redocumentation?

5. Why does corrective maintenance have more service-like aspects than product-like aspects?

6. Discuss the iterative-enhancement and quick-fix models of software maintenance.

7. Discuss the major impediments to fully-automated design recovery.

8. Discuss advantages of software configuration control support during software maintenance.

9. Discuss the possible structure and role of an acceptance test by the maintenance organization prior to the release of a system.

10. ♡ An alternative classification of maintenance and development activities is as follows:

    - Functional maintenance = corrective maintenance + adaptive maintenance + non-functional perfective maintenance (i.e. improving quality) + replacement of a system by a functional equivalent.
    - Functional development = functional perfective maintenance (i.e. adding new features) + development of new systems.

    Could this classification provide us with a better picture of the *real* maintenance effort? See also [Kro94].

11. ♡ Assess opportunities of knowledge-based support for software maintenance (see [DBSB91] for a very interesting application of such ideas).

12. ♡ Give a primary classification of your maintenance organization as W-, A-, or L-Type (see figure 14.8). What are the major strengths and weaknesses of your particular organization?

13. ♡ Does your organization collect quantitative data on maintenance activities? If so, what type of data, and how are they used to guide and improve the maintenance process? If not, how is maintenance planned and controlled?

14. ♠ Study the technical documentation of a system whose development you have been involved in. Does the documentation capture the design rationale? In what ways does it support comprehension of the system? In hindsight, can you suggest ways to improve the documentation for the purpose of maintenance?

15. ♡ Discuss the impact of component reuse on maintainability.

16. ♡ Discuss the possible contribution of object-oriented software development to software maintenance.

17. ♡ Can you think of reasons why a 10% change in a program of 200 LOC would take more effort than a 20% change in a program of 100 LOC?

Part III

Supporting Technology

Contents

Chapters 15–19 deal with a number of additional important issues concerning large-scale software development.

Formal specification techniques constitute one way of dealing with requirements. Obviously, formal specifications are much more difficult to understand and develop than, say, natural-language specifications. In certain critical situations, though, it is of paramount importance to have very precise specifications. Chapter 15 touches upon the major techniques for doing so.

Software systems are used by humans. Cognitive issues are a major determinant of the effectiveness with which users go about their work. Why is one system more understandable than another? Why is system X more 'user-friendly' than system Y? In the past, the user interface was often only addressed after the system had been fully designed. However, the user interface concerns more than the size and placement of buttons and pull-down menus. Chapter 16 addresses issues about the human factors that are relevant to the development of interactive systems.

Chapter 17 addresses a topic that has become fashionable of late: software reusability. If we estimate the programmer population at three million people, and furthermore assume that each programmer writes 2000 lines of code per year, 6000 million lines of code are produced each year. There is bound to be a lot of redundancy in them. Reuse of software, or reuse of other artifacts that are produced in the course of a software development project, may lead to considerable productivity improvements and, consequently, cost savings. Software reuse bears on software architecture: reusable components are the prime candidates to be used as building blocks in a software architecture.

The testing phase of a software development process is aimed at finding faults in the software. One may argue though that faults are not all that interesting. Failures, i.e. manifestations of faults, are what really count. Chapter 18 is concerned with assessing and improving software reliability: the probability that a given piece of software will not fail within a certain period of time.

Chapter 19 is concerned with tools. In the past, CASE (Computer Aided Software Engineering) has been touted as the ultimate answer to the problems faced by software developers. A large number of software tools are available nowadays, and the topic has also received considerable attention in the research community. Chapter 19 identifies and discusses major trends in the development of CASE tools.

15 Formal Specification

LEARNING OBJECTIVES

- To appreciate the place of formal specification in the software engineer's toolbox
- To be aware of lessons learned from applying formal methods to real projects
- To understand the basics of model-oriented and algebraic specification methods

Although the formal methodists still have a way to go, the informalists have even farther to go – particularly for critical systems.
[Neu96]

It is often written that a (functional) specification tells us *what* should be done, not *how* it should be done, which also is the tack taken in this book. This is really an oversimplification, because the borderline between what and how cannot be sharply drawn. Some people speak about programs as 'specifications'. Also, systems exist in which the kind of specification we are discussing, may even be executed. These are so-called executable specifications.

It is probably better to view a specification as a (not necessarily executable) 'program' at a more abstract level. In a specification, we abstract from certain details that become concrete at lower levels. This is not fundamentally different from what happens when we program in a specific language. There, for instance, we abstract from the precise representation of data in memory. The difference is merely a difference in the level of abstraction.

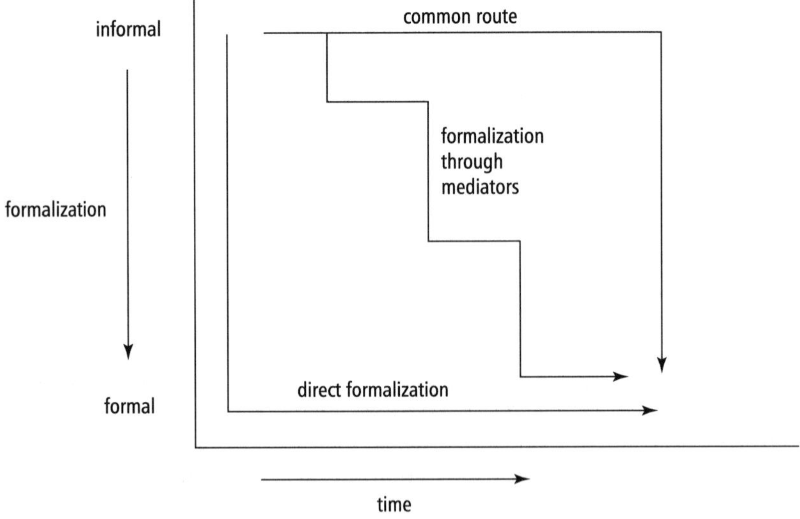

Figure 15.1 The formalization landscape

Usually, requirements are first expressed informally. During the subsequent stages, the requirements are refined, tuned, and made more specific by adding detail. The end product, the program, is formal, by definition.

There are various strategies by which formalization can be introduced into this transformation process. A still very common route is to postpone formalization until the very end. In this strategy, all the documentation, from the initial requirements up to detailed design specifications, use informal notations, such as natural language and various graphical techniques. At the other extreme, a formal specification may be derived directly from a precise natural language specification. As an alternative to this 'direct formalization process', one or more intermediate representations may help to move from the initial informal specification to the formal version thereof. SADT, JSD, and many other semiformal techniques may serve as mediators in such a strategy. The general flavor of these formalization strategies is depicted in figure 15.1.

As a consequence, the whole spectrum of specification techniques, from informal to formal, may enter the picture at different development phases. Given this wide spectrum, it will also come as no surprise that specifications may serve a number of different goals:

- Specifications may serve to clarify things. If we try to write precise specifications, we are almost inevitably forced to answer a great number of questions. The answers to these questions need not always be given in the specification itself. Sometimes, they continue to serve as a parameter to the specification. It does however prevent things from being overlooked.

- A well-documented specification may serve as a contract. Somewhat less formally, a specification plays a role in the communication between the parties involved.

- Specifications may serve as an aid during the design process. They constitute an essential element of the documentation of the design process. As such, design decisions, design alternatives, and the like, may be documented.

- Specifications may serve as a starting point for the actual implementation. During implementation we decide how the components specified will be realized.

- Specifications may serve as a starting point for verification and validation. Formal specifications can be subjected to all kinds of tests. In this way, errors may be detected and corrected early on.

- Specifications may serve as a starting point for maintenance activities. In particular, specifications should not be discarded once the system has become operational. Specifications should evolve with the system specified.

Each of the above uses is only feasible if the specifications are very precise. To that end, we had best use formal techniques. Formal descriptions are less amenable to ambiguity than informal descriptions. Moreover, ambiguities in a formal description can be detected through a formal analysis of that description. Such an analysis may be supported by tools. In that way, for instance, the consistency of a specification can be guaranteed.

Formal specifications may also be used as a starting point for correctness proofs. Certain properties of the specification itself can be proved. We may also try to prove the correctness of the final program with respect to its specification. We may do so automatically. As a third possibility, we may systematically try to derive the program from its specification. If each step in this derivation is correct, the program will evidently also be correct with respect to the original specification. And again, this derivation can be supported by automated tools.

We start off in section 15.1 with a short discussion of some well-known informal specification techniques and their shortcomings.

Sections 15.2–15.4 are devoted to formal specification techniques. Formal specification techniques can be broadly characterized as either **model-oriented** or **property-oriented**. Model-oriented techniques provide a direct way of describing the system's behavior. The system is specified in terms of mathematical structures like sets, sequences, tuples and maps. In contrast, the property-oriented techniques use indirect ways of specifying the system's behavior, by stating the properties (constraints) that the system is to satisfy.

The property-oriented techniques can be further broken down into two categories, which are referred to as the **algebraic** and **axiomatic** specification techniques. In the algebraic technique, a data type is viewed as an algebra and axioms state the properties of the data type's operations. The axiomatic technique has its origin in the early work on program verification. It uses (first-order predicate) logic in pre- and postconditions to specify operations.

Section 15.2 and 15.3 discuss the model-oriented and algebraic specification techniques, in particular, their role in the specification of abstract data types.

Section 15.4 discusses the use of pre- and postconditions. Pre- and postconditions may serve a variety of purposes. They can be used to prove the correctness of programs, to (axiomatically) specify the intended behavior of the program, and to (manually or automatically) guide the derivation of a program that satisfies the conditions.

Despite their advantages, the truth is that formal specification methods are not widely used. Over the years, there has been a lively, and sometimes heated, debate on the merits of formal methods. Proponents of formal methods have vigorously advocated their use. Some of them go as far as stating that formal methods are *the* answer to many of the problems that beset our trade. On the other hand, industry has been very reluctant to adopt them, for many reasons, both good and bad. In section 15.5 we will assess the arguments for and against formal methods, in an attempt to get a better perspective as to when and where to employ them.

15.1 INFORMAL SPECIFICATION TECHNIQUES

We often emphasize that specifications ought to be formal. In practice, they often are not. As with a requirements specification, specifications for subsystems, modules, and the like, are mostly expressed informally, using natural language, pictures with an unspecified structure, or both.

It seems as if this type of specification is even more dangerous than the initial informal requirements specification. A requirements specification is used by people having different backgrounds. They know this and may anticipate the possibility of misunderstanding each other. The type of specification we are discussing here is mainly used by programmers and analysts, people with the same background, using the same jargon. When using natural language, subtle differences in interpretation may arise. These differences may easily go unnoticed and lead to errors that are hard to detect. The seven sins of the analyst, discussed in chapter 9, strongly apply here as well. Parnas gives the following, non-fictitious, examples [Par77]:

- 'The first parameter should be the address of the new PSW.' The author may have meant the absolute (physical) address while the reader thought of it as the virtual address in the namespace of the calling routine.

- 'The value returned by the routine is the top of the stack.' Does this refer to the address of the top element or to its value?

- 'The date to be printed is three months after the input date.' What should be printed if the input date is November 30?

You may claim that these examples are not very honest, since these specifications are not sufficiently precise and complete. Indeed, they are neither precise nor complete. They are realistic, though. When using natural language, there are so many opportunities for the kind of subtle ambiguities given above that we strongly advise against using it when specifying software components.

These objections against the use of natural language as a descriptive tool may be partly circumvented if we restrict ourselves to a very constrained version of it – various forms of pseudocode being an example. A disadvantage of pseudocode is that it often strongly resembles some specific programming language. This increases the probability that implementation details creep into the specification.

The use of flowcharts (figure 15.2), Nassi-Shneiderman diagrams (figure 15.3), or similar drawing techniques, hardly provide us with a better alternative.[1] Some reasons for this are:

[1]Note that figures 15.2 and 15.3 do not correspond to the same program.

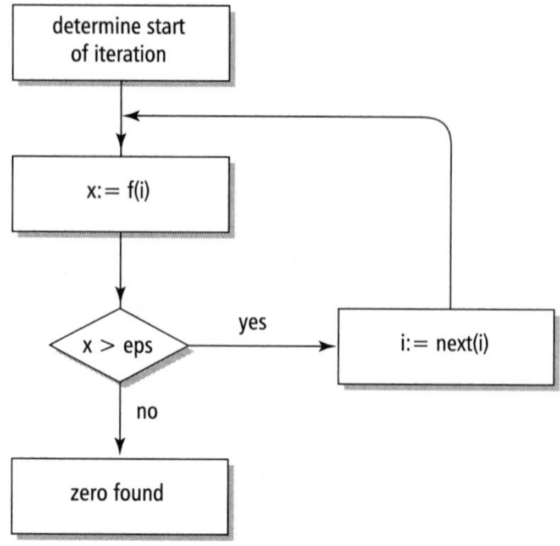

Figure 15.2 A flowchart

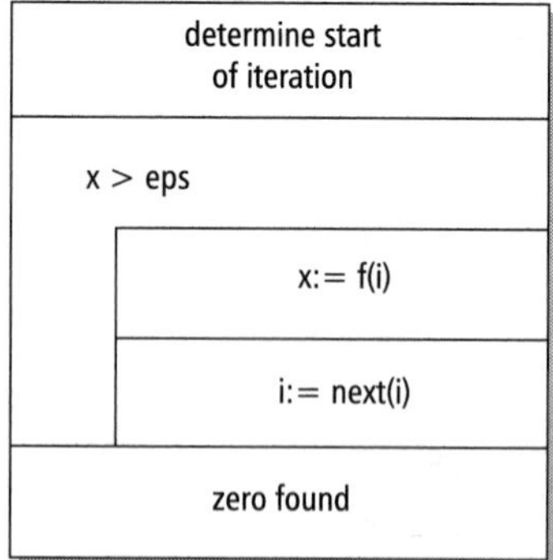

Figure 15.3 A Nassi-Shneiderman diagram

- The structure depicted by the drawings is a *control* structure. In this structure we may put components of widely different complexity or widely different levels of abstraction next to each other. This difference need not be obvious from the picture. A possible hierarchical structure is difficult to detect. Worse still, these drawing techniques hardly ever offer possibilities to depict the data structure organization.

- The resulting diagrams tend to be large. Even for individual routines, we often need more than one page which can mean that we have to leaf through many pages, thus losing an overview. Drawing this type of diagram takes a lot of time and there is a tendency not to update them as the software evolves. They thus become worthless as a means of documentation. This objection is obviously less the case if the picture is automatically generated from some other, usually formal, description.

- In these diagrams, we use natural language as well. The objections raised about the use of natural language in specifications hold equally well for pictures.

We may summarize this by saying that the various well-known drawing techniques fall short as a specification technique. You would be advised not to use them as such.

15.2 MODEL-ORIENTED SPECIFICATIONS

The specification techniques to be discussed in this section and the next both serve to formally specify the behavior of software components, in particular abstract data types. An abstract data type consists of a set of values of some type (also called **sort**) together with a set of functions that can be applied to these values.

In mathematics we may, for example, think of the positive integers with functions null (initialization), succ (successor), $+$, $\times$, ... In computer science we may think of examples such as:

- a stack, with functions Create, Top, Pop and Push;

- a binary tree, with functions Create, Insert, IsIn;

- a hierarchical table, with functions Create, IncrLevel, DecrLevel, Add, IsIn, Retrieve.

The set of values that concerns us here is the set of all stacks whose elements are of some given type, the set of all binary trees whose elements are of some given type, and the set of all hierarchical tables whose elements are of some given type, respectively.

The specification of an abstract data type is an implementation-independent description of all relevant properties of that data type. This specification concerns both the syntax of the functions (how they are written) and their semantics (what they mean). Only at the implementation phase need we decide on a certain representation of the values of the data type. After that, the functions are implemented using the representation chosen.

The two main specification techniques for abstract data types are algebraic specifications and model-oriented specifications. Figures 15.4 and 15.5 give an example of each. The main difference between the two techniques concerns the way in which the semantics of the functions is given. In an algebraic specification, the semantics is given *implicitly*, through relations between the functions. These relations are also called axioms, or rewrite rules. For example, the line Pop(Push(s, i)) = s in figure 15.4 denotes the well-known fact that popping the last element pushed onto a stack yields the old stack again. We will return to these issues in the next section.

```
type Intstack;
functions
    Create:                  → Intstack
    Push: Intstack × Int     → Intstack
    Pop: Intstack            → Intstack
    Top: Intstack            → Int
    Isempty: Intstack        → Boolean
axioms
    Isempty(Create) = true
    Isempty(Push(s, i)) = false
    Pop(Create) = Create
    Pop(Push(s, i)) = s
    Top(Create) = 0
    Top(Push(s, i)) = i
end Intstack;
```

Figure 15.4 Algebraic specification of a stack

In model-oriented specifications, some abstract object is chosen to represent the data type to be specified. The semantics of the various functions is then given *explicitly*, by specifying the effect of those functions on the abstract object. In figure 15.5, the abstract object is a sequence, denoted as $< \ldots x_i \ldots >$. We further use a number of operations on sequences, such as $\sim$ (concatenation) and length. Figure 15.5 uses the notation of the programming language Alphard. In Alphard, the postfix accent denotes the value of a variable prior to the call of a routine.

The most well-known model-oriented specification techniques are Z and VDM. There are many similarities between Z and VDM. Both use mathematical structures like sets, sequences and functions to model a system, and the notation of predicate logic to describe operations. One striking feature of Z is the way in which its building blocks, called **schemas**, are graphically laid out. A simple Z-schema to obtain the address of a person from a (name, address) mapping is given in figure 15.6. The top

```
let stack = < ... x_i ... > where x_i is int;
invariant 0 ≤ length(stack);
initially stack = nullseq;
function
    push(s: stack, x: int)
        pre 0 ≤ length(s)
        post s = s' ~ x,
    pop(s: stack)
        pre 0 < length(s)
        post s = leader(s'),
    top(s: stack) returns x: int
        pre 0 < length(s)
        post x = last(s'),
    isempty(s: stack) returns b: boolean
        post b = (s = nullseq)
```

Figure 15.5 Model-oriented specification of a stack

line contains the name of the operation. Next, some variables are declared. Both entry and entry' are partial functions with domain Name and range Address. Following Z conventions, a postfix accent denotes the value of the state after the operation. A name ending in ? denotes an input to the operation and a name ending in ! denotes an output. The bottom part of the schema contains the pre- and postconditions of the operation. The precondition states that name? is in the domain of entry, i.e. is of type Name. The postcondition states that addr! is the result of applying function entry to name?, i.e. it is the address that corresponds to that name. The postcondition further specifies that the table of (name, address) pairs has not changed.

The VDM version of this specification is given in figure 15.7. The input and output of a VDM operation are given in a Pascal-like notation. So, n is an input parameter of type Name and the result, addr, is of type Address. This example assumes a global state variable entry, a mapping from names to addresses. Global variables are indicated by the prefix **ext**. Since entry is a read-only variable, which is indicated by the prefix **rd**, the postcondition need not specify that its value has not changed. By definition, references to variables in the precondition, like n and entry, denote their value prior to the operation invocation. In the postcondition, the value of a variable *prior* to the execution of an operation is marked. The reference to addr in the postcondition thus denotes its value upon completion of the operation. VDM is dealt with in more detail in sections 15.2.1–15.2.3.

LookUp

$entry, entry' : Name \nrightarrow Address$
$name? : Name$
$addr! : Address$

$name? \in \mathrm{dom}(entry)$
$addr! = entry(name?)$
$entry' = entry$

Figure 15.6 An example Z schema

```
LookUp (n: Name) addr: Address
    ext rd entry
pre n ∈ dom entry
post addr = entry(n)
```

Figure 15.7 An example VDM specification

In model-oriented specifications new types are specified in terms of structures and relations that are assumed to be already known. The Alphard-specification in figure 15.5, for example, uses a sequence, an empty sequence, the length of a sequence, and so on. The new type is defined in terms of types which are, in a sense, more primitive. To start with, the system contains a fixed set of primitive types. In specifying new types, we may use this fixed set of primitive types as well as types specified earlier on. When specifying new types, the constructors provided by the system (such as the set- and sequence-constructors) are used.

This does however indicate a certain weakness in the model-oriented specification technique. If the type to be specified 'fits' the type constructors provided, then the specification looks fairly natural (as in figure 15.5). However, if the new type has some property which cannot easily be expressed in the abstract model, then the specification may soon become rather complex.

To illustrate this, let us look at part of the specification for a library (the example is discussed at length in section 15.2.2). The system is supposed to handle book reservations on a first-come, first-serve basis. Sequences have this property and are thus a prime candidate to model reservations. If the last copy of a book is removed from the library's catalog (because it is written off or known to be stolen), we have to remove all outstanding reservations for this book, the reason being that reservations can only be made for books that the library possesses. Specifying this removal function using sequences is not that easy. VDM does not have a built-in operation on sequences of the type 'remove all elements with a given property'. In the VDM-specification in figure 15.12, lines 116–123, this is solved by recursively removing each of these reservations until none remains. These lines are fairly complex relative to what they achieve.

The fact that we sometimes have to work around the base models in order to properly specify the new system is a disadvantage of the model-oriented specification technique. The drawback holds the more, since we may be inclined to take the kind of objects used in the specification as a starting point when implementing the data type.

15.2.1 Concepts of VDM

VDM stands for Vienna Development Method. It was developed in the early seventies at the IBM Research Laboratory in Vienna – hence its name. In the early days, VDM was used to formally specify the syntax and semantics of programming languages. Subsequent evolution of the technique has led to two VDM 'schools', a Danish one and an English one. The differences between these schools are marginal. Standardization efforts by the British Standards Institute try to amalgamate the two schools. We use the notation of [Jon90, JS90], which follows this consolidation.

A VDM specification consists of two parts:

- a collection of abstract variables that constitute the internal state of the system;
- a collection of operations to manipulate the state.

The abstract variables are defined in terms of predefined objects. VDM has a number of built-in models, such as the natural numbers (**N**), positive natural numbers (**N**$_1$), boolean values (**B**), real numbers (**R**), and characters (**char**). More complicated objects are built using **domain constructors**. VDM provides four such domain constructors:

- **Sets** A set is a finite, unordered collection of objects. Sets can be enumerated in different ways:
  - explicitly, for example $\{a, b, c\}$,
  - implicitly, for example $\{F(a) \mid a \in A \bullet P(a)\}$, or
  - inductively, for example ($\textbf{let } s = \{a, b, c\} \cup \{F(a) \mid a \in A \bullet P(a)\} \textbf{ in } E(s)$).

  A formula $S = \{F(a) \mid a \in A \bullet P(a)\}$ should be read as: S consists of the elements F(a) for which the condition $a \in A \bullet P(a)$ holds. The latter condition in turn stands for: the elements from the set A for which P(a) holds.

  The empty set is denoted by $\{\}$.

The definition (declaration) of a state-variable T which is a set of objects of type X is denoted as T = X-**set**.

Some of the built-in operations on sets are listed in figure 15.8.

Symbol	Name/meaning
$\in$	membership
$\notin$	nonmembership
$\subset$	proper subset
$\subseteq$	subset
$\cup$	union
$\cap$	intersection
$=$	equality
$\neq$	non-equality
card	cardinality, the number of elements in a set

Figure 15.8 Some operations on sets

- **Sequences** A sequence is a finite, ordered, collection of objects. The difference between a set and a sequence is that a sequence is ordered and may contain duplicate elements. Sequences can be enumerated in the same ways as sets, using square brackets ([ ]) rather than curly ones.

  VDM provides two ways to define sequences. X^* denotes a possibly empty sequence of elements of type X, and X^+ denotes a non-empty sequence of elements of type X.

  Some of the operations on sequences are given in figure 15.9.

Symbol	Name/meaning
$\frown$	concatenation of two sequences
hd	head element of a sequence
tl	tail
•(•)	application, i.e. s(i) yields the i-th element of the sequence s
len	length
ind	index set, i.e. for a sequence, s, **ind** s yields the set {1, 2, ..., **len** s}
elems	for a sequence s, **elems** s yields the set {s(1), s(2), ..., s(**len** s)}
†	sequence overide, to change the value of some sequence element. For example, s † {1 ↦ a} assigns a to the first element of s

Figure 15.9 Some operations on sequences

- **Maps** A map represents a mapping from *domain values* to *range values*. Maps look like partial functions. The relation between domain values and range values is explicit, however. We may view a map as a table of (domain, range) values, where a domain value is used as a key to obtain the corresponding range value. Maps may change dynamically, in the sense that new entries can be added and existing entries can be changed. Maps can be enumerated explicitly, implicitly, or inductively. The denotation of a map contains (domain, value) pairs, and is written as $\{a \mapsto x, b \mapsto y\}$. Here, a and b are domain values, whereas x and y are range values.

A map with domain T and range X is denoted as $T \xrightarrow{m} X$.

Figure 15.10 lists a number of operations on maps.

Symbol	Name/meaning
dom	domain, i.e. **dom** m yields the set whose elements are the domain values from the map m
rng	range, i.e. the set whose elements are the range values from the map
•(•)	application, i.e. given a map $M{:}D \xrightarrow{m} R$ that contains an element (d, r), M(d) yields r
†	map override. Given two maps M and N, the operation M † N yields a new map that contains all pairs from N plus those pairs from M whose domain value is not in **dom** N For example, $\{a \mapsto x, b \mapsto y\} \dagger \{a \mapsto t, c \mapsto z\}$ yields the map $\{a \mapsto t, b \mapsto y, c \mapsto z\}$.
∪	map union. The domains of both operands must be disjoint. So ∪ is the same as †, except that we know that ∪ is commutative, while † is not.
◁	map restriction. If s is a set and m is a map, s ◁ m is the map of pairs from m whose domain value is in the set s. So s ◁ m can be defined as: $\{d \mapsto m(d) \mid d \in (s \cap$ **dom** $m)\}$
⩤	map deletion. If s is a set and m is a map, s ⩤ m is the map of pairs from m whose domain value is *not* in the set s

Figure 15.10 Some operations on maps

- **Composite objects** A composite object describes a static aggregation of objects, like a record in Pascal. A composite object describes elements from the Cartesian product of its constituents.

  A composite object X with constituents A and B is written as X :: A B. (Note that the Cartesian product symbol × is not written in the type definition).

  If we have two domains X and Y that are both defined as the Cartesian product A × B, it is normally not possible to decide whether some element (a, b) belongs to X or Y. To make the distinction possible, VDM composite objects are *tagged*. In the context of X, Y :: A B, an element (a, b) of type X is different from an element (a, b) of type Y. We may conceive of these objects as (X, (a, b)) and (Y, (a, b)), respectively.

  The fields of a composite object may be labeled, as in

```
date::  day: {1, ... , 31}
        month: {1, ... , 12}
        year: N
```

These field names can be used as selector functions to obtain a projection from a composite object to one of its constituents. Some operations on composite objects are given in figure 15.11.

Symbol	Name/meaning
`mk-`	make. In the context of `T :: A B`, an element `(a, b)` of type `T` is constructed by `mk-T(a, b)`
μ	modify. To modify one field of an object, as in μ`(date, day`$\mapsto$`12)`
field name	selection/projection. If the fields of a composite object are labeled, then those field names can be used to decompose the object. If `X` is of type `date`, then `day(X)` yields the day field of `X`

Figure 15.11 Some operations on composite objects

We will illustrate the use of VDM in a non-trivial example. The example makes use of all four domain constructors and quite a few of the operations listed above. Since VDM has a rather rich notation, we will have to introduce quite some more as we go along.

15.2.2 A Sample VDM Specification

The example concerns a library system. In this library, clients can borrow and return books. Since the library may include more than one copy of a given book, we make a careful distinction between a book and a copy of a book. If a client wants to borrow a book all of whose copies are on loan, he can make a reservation. Reservations are taken up on a first-come, first-served basis. For simplicity's sake we assume that books have one author only. A client may ask for a list of all books by some given author. Finally, both clients and book copies can be added to and removed from the system. Some of the fine points are dealt with in the detailed discussion of the specification.

The full VDM specification for our library system is given in figure 15.12. The line numbers are not part of the specification proper, but are used in the annotations to the specification.

```
values
    maxBooks = 10 : N1
types
    Client:: name: Name
             address: Address
             id: Client_Id
    Name = char*
    Address = char*
    Client_Id = N1
    Book_Id = N1
    Book:: author: Author
           title: Title
    Author = char*
    Title = char*
    Reservation:: book: Book
                  client: Client

state Library of
    clients: Client-set
    books: Book_Id -m-> Book
    borrowed: Book_Id -m-> Client
    reserved: Reservation*

inv-Library (mk-Library (clients, books, borrowed, reserved)) △
    dom borrowed ⊆ dom books ∧
    rng borrowed ⊆ clients ∧
    ¬ (∃ i, j ∈ clients) • (id(i) = id(j) ∧ i ≠ j) ∧
    (∀ c ∈ clients) • BooksBorrowed(borrowed, c) ≤ maxBooks ∧
    (∀ r ∈ elems reserved) •
        (book(r) ∈ rng books) ∧ client(r) ∈ clients)

init-Library (mk-Library (clients, books, borrowed, reserved)) △
    clients = {} ∧
    books:= {} ∧
    borrowed:= {} ∧
    reserved:= []
end
operations
```

Continued Over

```
Borrow (c: Client, b: Book) bi: Book_Id
    ext rd books: Book_Id -m-> Book
        rd clients: Client-set
        wr borrowed: Book_Id -m-> Client
    pre (∃ copy ∈ dom books) •
            (books(copy) = b ∧ copy ∉ dom borrowed) ∧
        (c ∈ clients) ∧
        BooksBorrowed(borrowed, c) < maxBooks
    post let (copy ∈ dom books) •
        (books(copy) = b ∧ copy ∉ dom borrowed~) in
            borrowed = borrowed~ ∪ {copy} ↦ c ∧ bi = copy

Return (copy: Book_Id)
    ext wr borrowed: Book_Id -m-> Client
    pre copy ∈ dom borrowed
    post borrowed = {copy}  borrowed~

AddCopy (b: Book)
    ext wr books: Book_Id -m-> Book
    post let copy: Book_Id • copy ∉ dom books~ in
        books = books~ ∪ {copy ↦ b})

RemoveCopy (copy: Book_Id)
    ext rd borrowed: Book_Id -m-> Client
        wr books: Book_Id -m-> Book
        wr reserved: Reservation*
    pre (copy ∈ dom books) ∧ (copy ∉ dom borrowed)
    post books = {copy}  books~ ∧
        if books~(copy) ∈ rng books
        then true
        else reserved = RemoveBookRes (books~(copy), reserved~)

AddClient (c: Client)
    ext wr clients: Client-set
    pre c ∉ clients
    post clients = clients~ ∪ {c}

RemoveClient (c: Client)
    ext rd borrowed: Book_Id -m-> Client
```

Continued Over

```
            wr clients: Client-set
            rd reserved: Reservation*
        pre c ∈ clients ∧ BooksBorrowed(borrowed, c) = 0
        post (clients = clients↼ − {c}) ∧
             (reserved = RemoveClientRes (c, reserved↼))

    HandleReservation (i: N1)
        ext rd clients: Client-set
            rd books: Book_Id -m-> Book
            wr borrowed: Book_Id -m-> Client
            wr reserved: Reservation*
        pre i ≤ len reserved ∧
             ((∃ copy ∈ dom books) •
                 (books(copy) = book(reserved(i)) ∧
                     copy ∉ dom borrowed)) ∧
             BooksBorrowed(borrowed, client(reserved(i))) < maxBooks
        post reserved = reserved↼(1, . . . , i-1) ⌢
                 reserved↼(i+1, . . . , len reserved↼) ∧
             let (copy ∈ dom books) •
                 (books(copy) = book(reserved↼(i)) ∧
                 copy ∉ dom borrowed↼) in
             borrowed = borrowed↼ ∪ {copy ↦ client(reserved(i)) }

    AddReservation (b: Book, c: Client)
        ext rd clients: Client-set
            rd books: Book_Id -m-> Book
            wr reserved: Reservation*
        pre b ∈ books ∧ c ∈ clients
             post reserved = reserved↼ ⌢ mk-Reservation(b, c)

    ListBooks (a: Author) blist: Book-set
        ext rd books: Book_Id -m-> Book
        post (blist ⊆ rng books) ∧
             (∀ b ∈ blist) • (author(b) = a) ∧
             ¬ (∃ b ∈ rng books - blist) • (author(b) = a)

functions
    BooksBorrowed: (Book_Id -m-> Client) × Client → N
    BooksBorrowed (bor, c) △
```

Continued Over

```
105         card {b | b ∈ dom bor • bor(b) = c}
106     RemoveClientRes: Client × Reservation* → Reservation*

107     RemoveClientRes: (c, res) ≜
108         if card
109             {a | a ∈ elems res • a = mk-Reservation (–, c)} > 0
110         then let i ∈ ind res in
111             let res(i) = mk-Reservation (–, c) in
112                 RemoveClientRes(c, res(1, . . . , i-1) ⌒
113                     res(i+1, . . . , len res))
114         else res

115     RemoveBookRes: Book × Reservation* → Reservation*

116     RemoveBookRes: (b, res) ≜
117         if card
118             {a | a ∈ elems res • a = mk-Reservation (b, –)} > 0
119         then let i ∈ ind res in
120             let res(i) = mk-Reservation (b, –) in
121                 RemoveBookRes(c, res(1, . . . , i-1) ⌒
122                     res(i+1, . . . , len res))
123         else res
```

Figure 15.12 VDM specification of a library system *(Adapted from J. van Katwijk, Course Notes Software Engineering, University of Delft, 1991)*

The specification can be broken into three parts. Lines 1–16 contain definitions of constants and types that are used in the specification. Lines 17–34 give a definition of the state, its invariants, and the initial value of the state. Lines 35–123 contain the definitions of the various operations and functions.

The type definition part defines Client, Book and Reservation to be composite objects. By labeling the constituents of these objects, they can be selected. We will thus be able to select the address of a client or the author of a book. Client_Id and Book_Id range over the set of positive natural numbers. They serve to uniquely identify clients and (copies of) books, respectively. The other types do not play a role at the level of detail we are dealing with and are simply defined to be character sequences.

The state definition part (lines 17–21) defines the information that is to be kept by the system. It includes the clients of the library, its stock of books, a record of which books are borrowed by whom, and a record of outstanding reservations. The clients are kept in a set. Since the library may possess multiple copies of the same book we cannot specify the stock of books as a set. It is rather kept in a map. The elements from the domain of this map are by definition disjoint and serve to uniquely identify book copies. The range values then contain the familiar information that is kept about a book, such as its author and title. If the library has multiple copies of the same book, then different domain values will map onto the same range value. In a similar way, the information about which books are on loan is kept in a map from (unique) copy identifications to clients. Finally, the reservations are kept in a sequence of (book, client) pairs. The sequencing ensures that reservations can be handled on a first-come, first-served basis.

Lines 22–28 contain the global invariants that the state has to satisfy. By stating these global invariants once we need not repeat them in the specification of the individual operations. The global invariants can be thought of as global pre- and postconditions, which are conjoined to the pre- and postcondition of every operation and function.

The following global invariants are specified:

- line 23: Only copies of books that the library possesses can be borrowed.
- line 24: Only clients of the library can borrow books.
- line 25: Clients of the library are uniquely identifiable by their id.
- line 26: Clients can borrow up to Maxbooks (arbitrarily set at 10) books only. The function BooksBorrowed (defined in lines 103–105) determines the number of books borrowed by a given client c.
- lines 27–28: Reservations can only be made for books that the library possesses. Only clients can reserve books.

The initialization part (lines 29–34) is straightforward. All elements from the state are initially empty.

The specification of the various functions and operations starts at line 35. VDM functions are like mathematical functions: they are expressions that map domain values onto range values. BooksBorrowed is a simple example of a function. VDM operations manipulate the state. We could define these operations as functions too, but then the state variables must be passed as parameters. This often necessitates copying large data structures, such as the set of all books from the library, which is not needed if we use operations that access these global data structures directly.

For functions, it is customary to first state the signature of the function (as in line 103), and next indicate the names of the parameters (as in line 104). For operations, the definition of the signature and the naming of parameters is usually combined in a procedure-heading like notation, as in line 36. This difference in notation is historical and has no further significance.

The operations in our example are specified implicitly. *Implicit* specifications use pre- and postconditions to describe the effect of a function or operation. They require that the function or operation must satisfy the postcondition, given that the precondition is satisfied.

In contrast, *explicit* specifications contain algorithms that tell how the intended effect is obtained. As a simple example of the difference, consider the specification of a function to determine the larger one of two natural numbers. An implicit specification hereof might be the following:

```
max (i: N, j: N) r: N
    pre true
    post (r = i ∨ r = j) ∧ (i ≤ r ∧ j ≤ r)
```

An explicit specification of the same function could be:

```
max: N × N → N
max(i, j) △
    if i ≤ j then i else j
```

Note that explicit specifications may have preconditions as well. For both implicit and explicit specifications, nothing is assumed if the precondition is not satisfied, i.e. the function or operation is *partial*. If the precondition is true, the function or operation is *total*.

All operations in figure 15.12 are specified implicitly. The (total) functions RemoveClientRes and RemoveBookRes (lines 106–123) are specified explicitly. Usually, operations and functions at the higher levels of abstraction are specified implicitly.

Each operation has a heading that includes the parameters of the operation and their types. If the operation returns some value, the name used for that return value is given also, together with its type (as in line 36). After the keyword **ext**, there is then a list of constituents of the state that are accessible from the operation. This can be viewed as a list of global variables used by the operation. Constituents that are read-only are prefixed with **rd**; constituents (part of which) can be overwritten by the operation are prefixed with **wr**.

The precondition of operation Borrow states that there must be a copy of the requested book which is not yet borrowed by someone (lines 40–41), that the person who requests the book must be a client of the library (line 42), and that the number of books already borrowed by that client has not yet reached the maximum number allowed (line 43). The postcondition selects a copy of the book requested (line 44–45), updates the state by adding the pair (copy selected, client) to the map of books on loan, and returns the selected copy (line 46).

If an operation manipulates external variables from the state, we must be able to distinguish between the values of these variables before and after the operation is executed. In postconditions, the value of a variable prior to the execution of the operation is therefore marked with a backward-pointing hook (as in $\overleftarrow{\text{borrowed}}$). Line 46 should thus be read as: the new value of borrowed is the old value of borrowed plus the pair (copy, c). In the precondition we can only refer to the value of variables prior to the execution of the operation. In preconditions, these values are always written without the hook.

The specification of Borrow is an example of a non-deterministic, *loose specification*. The specification of an operation is loose if we can construct multiple, semantically different, implementations from it. In the postcondition of Borrow we select *a* copy of the book requested. The postcondition does not specify *which* copy to select if there is more than one. Once implemented, different invocations of this operation in the same state may lead to different results.

The precondition of AddCopy is true and has been left out. The postcondition states that the copy (with an id which does not yet exist) is added to the stock of books (lines 53–54).

The precondition of RemoveCopy states that the copy to be removed should be one from the stock of books and not be on loan (line 59). Note that the copy to be removed may be the last copy of a given book. In that case, possible outstanding reservations for that book are cancelled by simply removing them from the sequence reserved (line 63).

The precondition of RemoveClient checks that the client about to be removed has returned all his books (line 72). The postcondition ensures that possible outstanding reservations are cancelled (line 74).

The actual removal of outstanding reservations of a given client is handled by the total function RemoveClientRes (lines 106–114). The specification of this function is explicit, and looks very much like an algorithm. It recursively removes reservations of client c until no such reservation remains. The specification of RemoveClientRes is *loose*, since the order in which reservations are removed is not specified. Loose specifications of functions are *underspecified*. Though the order of removals is not specified, the final result will be the same, no matter which implementation is chosen. The specification of RemoveBookRes is very similar to that of RemoveClientRes.

The specification of RemoveClientRes illustrates another VDM-feature, *pattern matching*. RemoveClientRes starts with a check for the number of outstanding reservations for client c. This check in lines 108–109 looks for reservations whose second element is c. It does so through a search for a pattern ('don't care', c), which is written as (-, c).

HandleReservation takes care of a single reservation. Its precondition states that a copy of the book requested must be available (lines 81–83) and that the client in question has not yet borrowed the maximum allowed number of books (line 84). The postcondition tells us that the corresponding reservation has been removed (lines

85–86) and that the map of books on loan has been updated (lines 87–90). (Note that the present specification of HandleReservation does not exploit the sequencing aspect of book reservations. It may deal with a reservation i in the presence of an earlier reservation j (i.e. j < i) for the same book.)

The final operation is ListBooks (lines 97–101). The postcondition states that the resulting set blist is a subset of the set of available books (line 99), that all books from blist have author a (line 100), and that we have not left out any book whose author is a (line 101).

An intriguing question with respect to this example specification is: is it 'correct'? Does it specify the library system we had in mind? Some of the formulae may look terrifying to the uninitiated. They may seem less intelligible than plain English phrases expressing the very same idea.

15.2.3 Validation of a VDM Specification

A major advantage of formal methods over informal ones is that formal methods force you to reason methodically about each and every aspect of the design. VDM specifications, for example, give rise to so-called *proof obligations*. An important proof obligation concerns the satisfiability of functions and operations: for any function or operation, some result must exist for each valid input. Trying to prove *satisfiability* is a great help during the development of specifications.

In an earlier version of the library specification for example, line 43 was accidentally left out from the precondition of Borrow. As a result, clients could borrow 11 books. This conflicts with part of the state invariant. When trying to prove the satisfiability of Borrow, this error was quickly revealed. Informal methods do not offer this type of support. In implementations derived from such informal specifications, this type of error may go undetected for quite a while.

Obviously, the use of formal methods does not guarantee correctness. Specification and design involve the modeling of a Universe of Discourse. Whether this is done properly can never be proved by formal means. That is why we need both validation and verification.

VDM has more features than can be discussed in this brief space. Two of these deserve at least to be mentioned. VDM offers a mechanism to support the modularization of specifications. VDM specifications can be decomposed into modules that each consist of a state description and a collection of functions and operations. Such modules may import elements from other modules and export elements to other modules.

Next to a notation for specifications, VDM also offers a method to guide the development of software. Starting from a high-level specification, successive refinements result in a series of lower-level specifications. Each specification in this series must be proven correct with respect to the previous one. These proof obligations ensure that the final, executable, specification will be correct as well. VDM distinguishes two types of refinement step:

- **Data reification** In a data reification step, data types and domains are made more specific by adding implementation details. The term 'reify' is used to emphasize the transition from abstract to concrete data types.
- **Operation decomposition** In an operation decomposition step, implementation details are added to the operations and functions of the specification.

Normally, these refinement steps alternate. Some reification of a data type is chosen, after which operations and functions are made more specific, followed again by a data reification step, and so on.

15.3 ALGEBRAIC SPECIFICATIONS

Algebraic specifications constitute another very formal approach to the specification of abstract data types. The technique looks fairly simple if we restrict ourselves to small examples such as the specification of a stack or binary tree. Dangers lurk around the corner, however. A full treatment of this fairly mathematical topic is far beyond the scope of this book. If you are sufficiently well-versed in mathematics, you may consult [GTW78], for example. Without going too deeply into the mathematics involved, we will try to put across the essentials of the technique. We will largely do so by discussing a number of simple examples.

Let us start by looking at an algebraic specification for the natural numbers:

```
1  type Nat
2  functions
3      Null:                  → Nat
4      Succ: Nat              → Nat
5      Add: Nat * Nat         → Nat
6  axioms
7      Add(i, Null) = i
8      Add(i, Succ(j)) = Succ(Add(i, j))
```

The numbers at the start of the lines are used for reference purposes only; they are not part of the specification. Line 1 states that this is the specification of a data type called Nat. Lines 3–5 list the functions of this data type. The first function, Null, is a constant yielding some start element from the set Nat. The two other functions, Succ and Add, are obviously meant to denote the successor and plus functions, respectively. Lines

7–8 give the properties of the data type. i and j are variables. Their type, Nat, can be deduced from the parameter positions at which they are used. We will come back to this example in section 15.3.1.

An algebraic specification, such as the one given above for natural numbers, comprises two parts:

- a **signature**, in which the names of the data types involved (also called **sorts**) are listed with the names of the functions and their domain and range (lines 1–5 in this example).
- an **equation** part, in which we list the properties that the actual implementation of the data type should have (lines 6–8). This is done by giving a set of equations, also called **axioms**, or **rewrite rules**. In general, the equation part is allowed to contain conditional expressions. We will encounter examples of this in the following.

The signature can be viewed as a context-free grammar for the **terms** that can be constructed using those symbols. Some examples of such terms are given in figure 15.13. The first three terms given are **closed** terms, i.e. they contain only constants (such as Null) and other function symbols (such as Succ and Add). The last two terms are **open**, i.e. they contain variables. Formally, the set of terms of a given signature of a data type S is inductively defined as follows:

1. The constants and variables of type S are the *basic* terms of that type;
2. If $t_1, \ldots, t_n$ are terms of type $s_1, \ldots, s_n$, and f is a function of type $(s_1, \ldots, s_n) \rightarrow s$, then $f(t_1, \ldots, t_n)$ is a term of type s.

Null

Succ(Succ(Add(Succ(Null), Succ(Null))))

Add(Succ(Null), Succ(Succ(Null)))

i

Add(Succ(i), j)

Figure 15.13 Example terms resulting from signature Nat

Viewed in this way, the equation part can be considered as a set of *rewrite rules* for these terms. As an example, the third term from figure 15.13 can be rewritten as indicated in figure 15.14. For each step in the derivation, the part of the term being rewritten is underlined.

So, an algebraic specification is a completely *formal* system, in which the only thing we can do is manipulate sequences of symbols.

Add(Succ(Null), Succ(Succ(Null)))
(use axiom from line 8; substitute Succ(Null) for both i and j)

⇓

Succ(Add(Succ(Null), Succ(Null)))
(use axiom from line 8; substitute Succ(Null) for i and Null for j)

⇓

Succ(Succ(Add(Succ(Null), Null)))
(use axiom from line 7; substitute Succ(Null) for i)

⇓

Succ(Succ(Succ(Null)))

Figure 15.14 A rewriting example

In the end, we are interested in very down-to-earth things, such as natural numbers, stacks with elements of type integer, bags of marbles, and so on. In mathematics, these are called algebras. Algebras are very concrete. They consist of a set of objects and clearly-defined functions that map objects onto objects. An algebraic specification, in general, characterizes a *collection* of algebras.

So, besides the algebraic specification, we need a mechanism to couple the specification to one of the algebras it characterizes. We need to attach an *interpretation*, or *semantics*, to the specification. By means of this semantics, we make a choice from the class of possible algebras.

15.3.1 Initial and Final Semantics

There are two semantics that are often used in conjunction with algebraic specifications: **initial semantics** and **final semantics**. Informally speaking, initial semantics yields the algebra with the largest number of elements, while final semantics yields the algebra with the least number of elements. Obviously, the algebras have to obey the axioms in both cases.

Assigning an interpretation to an algebraic specification involves choosing some set of objects for each of the sorts occurring in the specification, as well as some function of the right type for each function symbol in the specification. In our example Nat we may choose the set of natural numbers $N = \{0, 1, 2, \dots\}$ and functions

$$Null_N = 0,$$
$$Succ_N(n) = n + 1$$

and

$$Add_N(n, m) = n + m$$

The axioms give us the well-known relations in that case:

$$n + 0 = n$$

and

$$n + (m + 1) = (n + m) + 1$$

However, this is not the only possible choice. If we take the trivial set T containing just one element, 0, and furthermore choose

$$Null_T = 0$$

$$Succ_T(0) = 0$$

$$Add_T(0, 0) = 0$$

then the axioms are also satisfied. So there is more than one 'solution'. An important question which arises when using algebraic specifications is: given such a specification, how do we determine whether it really specifies the data type we had in mind to start with?

In our example Nat, the initial semantics results in the algebra of natural numbers, the one intended from the start. The final semantics, however, results in the trivial algebra mentioned before. In many cases, the initial semantics yields the algebra sought for. We will consider an example where this is not the case, though.

We saw earlier that an algebraic specification defines terms which can be rewritten into other terms using the axioms from the specification. In this way, we obtain a number of equivalence classes. Each equivalence class contains all terms which can be transformed into one another, using the rewrite rules, in a finite number of steps. When looking for a correspondence between terms and objects in the real world, we are obviously only interested in closed terms, i.e. terms that do not contain variables. Figure 15.15 lists some equivalence classes for Nat, with example closed terms for each class. It is easy to see that each equivalence class can be characterized by a 'canonical' closed term of the form $\mathsf{Succ}^n(\mathsf{Null})$.

Obviously, all closed terms from one and the same equivalence class should denote the same real object. In the initial semantics, this is all that is required. In the initial semantics, two closed terms correspond to one and the same object *if and only if we can prove them to be equivalent using the axioms given*. This is also known as the 'no junk, no confusion' rule. The 'no junk' part of this rule expresses the requirement that the set of real objects should not be too large; there should be no objects that do not correspond to some equivalence class. For example, Nat does not specify the set of complex numbers. Conversely, the 'no confusion' part specifies that the set of real

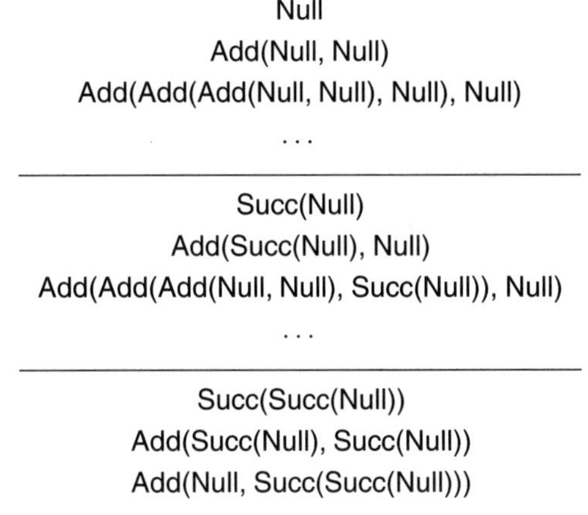

Figure 15.15 Example equivalence classes for Nat

objects should not be too small; different equivalence classes should not be mapped onto the same real object. So, the trivial algebra does not satisfy.

On the other hand, in the final semantics two terms denote the same object, *unless we can prove them to be not equal, using the axioms given*. The mechanism we use, in which conditional equations are allowed, does not allow us to give a formal definition of final semantics. It would also be beyond the scope of the present discussion.

The initial and final semantics are not the only two possibilities for assigning a meaning to an algebraic specification. They represent two extreme possibilities. There is a large spectrum of algebras in between.

We will try to further clarify the distinction between initial and final semantics through the following example. The data type Set, with parameter Item, corresponds to sets of elements of type Item. It could be algebraically specified as in figure 15.16.

In this specification we assume the presence of an equality operator Eq for objects of type Item. A set as specified here may contain multiple copies of one and the same element, so it is really a bag. In the initial semantics for this specification, the order in which the elements are inserted into the bag, is 'remembered'. If item1 and item2 denote different elements of type Item, we cannot prove from the above axioms that

```
Insert(Insert(s, item1), item2) = Insert(Insert(s, item2), item1)
```

for any value of s. In the initial semantics, therefore, closed terms of this type will end up in different equivalence classes, and the corresponding objects are therefore different as well. The final semantics would not register this. If we wish to specify

```
type Set[Item]
    functions
        Create:                    → Set
        Isempty: Set               → Boolean
        Insert: Set × Item         → Set
        Isin: Set × Item           → Boolean
    axioms
        Isempty(Create) = true
        Isempty(Insert(s, i)) = false
        Isin(Create, i) = false
        Isin(Insert(s, i), j) =
            if Eq(i, j) then true else Isin(s, j)
```

Figure 15.16 Algebraic specification of a data type Set

a 'real' set using initial semantics, the above commutativity rule should be added, together with an axiom to prevent multiple copies in the set:

Insert(Insert(s, i), i) = Insert(s, i)

We may summarize this as follows: in the initial semantics the order in which an object is built up, is remembered, unless the axioms specifically tell us not to do so. In the final semantics this order is forgotten, unless we provide for extra features to prevent it, such as a counter. In this sense, the final semantics is most 'economic', while the initial semantics is most 'conservative'.

15.3.2 Some Difficulties

We would like an algebraic specification of a data type to be *consistent* and *complete* with respect to the semantics used. All necessary axioms should be there and they should not contradict one another. Even for simple examples it is not always easy to show consistency and completeness. In general, both problems are undecidable.

This observation may give you the impression that algebraic specifications merely offer a nice mathematical framework and have no practical merit whatsoever. This is not true. Interesting results can be obtained for most actual specifications using computer-supported tools.

There are some serious problems, however, which make the practical use of algebraic specifications not a simple affair. We will discuss two such problems:

- hidden functions, and
- readability.

Suppose we want to write an algebraic specification of the natural numbers, with operations Null, Succ (the successor function as introduced earlier) and Square(x), yielding the square of x.

One can prove that the proper axioms for this can only be given if at least one extra function is introduced. If, for example, we add the function Add, introduced earlier, the axioms for Square may be phrased as follows:

```
Square(Null) = Null
Square(Succ(x)) = Succ(Add(Square(x), Add(x, x)))
```

Here, Add is a so-called **hidden function**. The function Add is not needed for the application itself, but is merely introduced to allow us to define the proper axioms for the other functions. If we want to algebraically specify some data type, there is always the possibility that the axioms cannot be expressed directly, but that we first need to invent some new functions. These new functions, with their own axioms, only serve the purpose of making the specification complete. As with the invariants used in program correctness proofs, there is no algorithm for finding those hidden functions.

There is a second, quite practical problem to cope with: the readability of algebraic specifications. One of the reasons why the, admittedly simple, specifications in this section are still quite understandable, is the fact that we have chosen simple examples and meaningful names. All of you know what we mean by the operator Square. All of you can understand its axioms. Probably, you could have come up with them yourself. If the names used do not ring a bell, it becomes much more difficult to grasp the meaning of an algebraic specification. As an example, you may try to deduce the data type specified in figure 15.17.

If the examples become more complex, and certainly when they are generated by some system, it will become hard to understand what they mean.

This problem is not so different from what we experience in ordinary programming. Small programs with well-chosen variable names don't give us any problems. Large programs tend to become incomprehensible.

15.3.3 How to Construct an Algebraic Specification

In the previous sections, we already came across some simple algebraic specifications. You probably had no difficulty in reading and understanding the axioms. The situation is different if you are asked to come up with a set of axioms for a given data type all by yourself. In this section, we will present some guidelines as to how to get at these axioms.

Suppose we have the following signature for a data type Intstack:

type Intstack;

type x
functions

e:	x	→ x
t:	x × y	→ x
c:		→ x
l:	x	→ y
s:	x	→ z

axioms

e(t(a, b)) = **if** s(a) **then** a **else** t(e(a), b)
s(t(a, b)) = false
l(t(a, b)) = **if** s(a) **then** b **else** l(a)
s(c) = true
e(c) = c
l(c) = 0

Figure 15.17 A somewhat obscure algebraic specification

functions

Create:	→ Intstack
Push: Intstack × Int	→ Intstack
Pop: Intstack	→ Intstack
Top: Intstack	→ Int
Size: Intstack	→ Int
Isempty: Intstack	→ Boolean

These functions all have their obvious meanings. For instance, Size yields the number of elements in the stack. We may categorize the functions into four classes:

- **Basic constructors** The set of basic constructors enables us to generate each possible element of the data type being defined. In our case, the functions Create and Push are the basic constructors. All possible values of type Intstack can be expressed in terms of those two functions.

- **Extra constructors** The remaining functions that yield a value of the data type being specified are the extra constructors. In our case, Pop is the only extra constructor.

- **Basic observers** Let S be the set of functions whose range is not the data type being specified. The set of basic observers S_1 is a subset of S such that each function from $S \setminus S_1$ can be expressed in terms of functions from S_1. In our case, Top and Size are the basic observers, since Isempty(s) is equivalent to Size(s) = 0.

- **Extra observers** All that remains, i.e. $S \setminus S_1$. In our case, Isempty.

In order to satisfy certain desirable properties, an algebraic specification should be *sufficiently complete*. This means that there is a set of operators F which suffices to generate all possible values of the data type that is being specified. For an algebraic specification of a data type X to be sufficiently complete, we have to prove the following two facts:

- Each closed term with range X which contains a function not in F, can be rewritten such that we obtain a term which only contains functions from F. This rewriting is to be done using the axioms of the specification. This generating set F is exactly the set of basic constructors introduced before. For the Intstack example this means that we should be able to rewrite a closed term containing Pop to some term which only contains Create and Push.

- Each closed term with a range other than X can be rewritten to a term which does not contain a function with range X. A term which has as its range a data type other than X, has an observer as its outermost function. For the Intstack example, therefore, this requirement means that each term starting with any of Top, Size or Isempty can be rewritten so that the resulting term does not contain Create, Push or Pop.

One procedure that leads to an algebraic specification which is sufficiently complete, is given below. In explaining its various steps, we refer back to the Intstack example. The procedure runs as follows:

1. Determine a set of basic constructors: Create and Push.

2. For each extra constructor, add as many axioms as there are basic constructors. A closed term Pop(s) is either of the form

   ```
   Pop(Create)
   ```

   or

   ```
   Pop(Push(s, i))
   ```

   For both cases, we need an axiom. (If we have an extra constructor whose domain contains the data type specified more than once, the situation becomes somewhat more complex. In principle, each combination of basic constructors in the domain has to be considered in that case. Section 15.3.4 contains some examples of this, such as the Merge operator for Slists.)

3. For each basic observer, we also have to give as many axioms as there are basic constructors, one for each possible head of one of the parameters of the data

type to be specified. In our case, this leads to the following left-hand sides of the axioms:

```
Top(Create)
Top(Push(s, i))
Size(Create)
Size(Push(s, i))
```

4. For each extra observer, we need an axiom which relates this observer to the basic observers. In the Intstack example, we thus have a left-hand side:

   ```
   Isempty(s)
   ```

5. The right-hand sides of these axioms have to be such that the earlier-mentioned proofs can be given. These proofs are usually done by induction on the length of the term in question. A complete set of axioms for the Intstack example could read as follows:

   ```
   Pop(Create) = Create
   Pop(Push(s, i)) = s
   Top(Create) = 0
   Top(Push(s, i)) = i
   Isempty(s) = (Size(s) = 0)
   Size(Create) = 0
   Size(Push(s, i)) = 1 + Size(s)
   ```

   Only the last axiom may need some clarification. By induction on the length of the argument of Size, i.e. the number of occurrences of Push and Create, it is easy to prove that it is possible to rewrite any term starting with Size into one which no longer contains any of the basic constructors.

The specifications given in the previous subsections all satisfied the requirements for being sufficiently complete. If a set of axioms is sufficiently complete, this does not necessarily mean that it also completely specifies the data type we are interested in. For instance, the above procedure does not yield a commutativity rule for sets as given in section 15.3.1.

In section 15.3.4, the guidelines for producing sufficiently complete algebraic specifications will be applied to a couple of other examples.

15.3.4 Some Example Algebraic Specifications

Let us consider the data type Set from figure 15.16, with functions Create, Isempty, Insert and Isin. The basic constructors are Create and Insert. Isin and Isempty are basic observers. Suppose we want to extend the data type with functions Union and Intersect. Both functions have their usual meaning from set theory. The signature of Set will be extended to include those two functions:

Union: Set $\times$ Set $\rightarrow$ Set
Intersect: Set $\times$ Set $\rightarrow$ Set

In order to obtain a sufficiently complete specification we have to add axioms with the following left-hand sides:

```
Union(Create, s)
Union(Insert(s₁, x), s₂)
Intersect(Create, s)
Intersect(Insert(s₁, x), s₂)
```

(Note that we need not separately consider the various possibilities for the second argument of Union and Intersect. Without considering the structure of the second argument, we may already remove these extra constructors from any term containing them. However, it is not erroneous to separately consider the various possible forms of the second argument. Doing so introduces some redundancy, since the rules will partly overlap. There also is a danger of introducing inconsistencies.)

The axioms could read as follows:

```
Union(Create, s) = s
Union(Insert(s₁, x), s₂) = Insert(Union(s₁, s₂), x)
Intersect(Create, s) = Create
Intersect(Insert(s₁, x), s₂) =
    if Isin(s₂, x) then Insert(Intersect(s₁, s₂), x)
                   else Intersect(s₁, s₂)
```

To clarify these axioms, we may observe the following. For the intersection of a set consisting of a first element x and tail s_1 with a set s_2, we distinguish two cases. If x is a member of s_2, it is also a member of the intersection. We may then proceed by taking the intersection of s_1 and s_2, and adding x to the result. If x is not a member of s_2, it is not a member of the intersection either. The result is then simply the intersection of s_1 and s_2.

The second axiom for Union is much simpler, since the existing axioms

```
Insert(Insert(s, i), j) = Insert(Insert(s, j), i)
```

and

```
Insert(Insert(s, i), i) = Insert(s, i)
```

will take care of the removal of possible duplicates in the union of the two sets.

The proof that a term of the form Union(s_1, s_2) or Intersect(s_1, s_2) can be rewritten to a term which only contains Create and Insert, follows easily by induction on the length of s_1.

Our second example concerns a sorted list Slist. Its signature is given in figure 15.18.

type Slist;
functions

Create:	→ Slist
Cons: Item × Slist	→ Slist
Isin: Item × Slist	→ Boolean
Isempty: Slist	→ Boolean
Add: Item × Slist	→ Slist
Delete: Item × Slist	→ Slist
Merge: Slist × Slist	→ Slist

Figure 15.18 Signature of Slist

Here, Cons is a function which cannot be directly called by the user. Cons and Create are the basic observers. Any non-empty sorted list can be written as Cons(x_n, Cons(x_{n-1}, ... , Cons(x_1, Create) ...), where $x_n \geq x_{n-1} \geq \ldots \geq x_1$. If the user wants to add an Item to a sorted list, he calls Add. Internally, i.e. hidden to the user, Add invokes Cons. The axioms for this specification may look as in figure 15.19.

An axiom Merge(Create, Create) = Create is not needed here, since it is induced by the other axioms for Merge. Also here, we must take care not to introduce inconsistencies. If the above scheme contains an axiom Merge(Create, s) = s', with s ≠ s', then a term Merge(Create, Create) could be rewritten to different terms, using different axioms.

Again, rewriting terms so that the result only contains basic constructors or no functions with range Slist at all, can be easily shown by induction. For a term of the form Merge(s_1, s_2), for instance, this can be done by induction on the sum of the number of occurrences of Create and Cons in s_1 and s_2.

Our final example concerns a binary search tree Tree, with the signature given in figure 15.20.

Again, Make(t_1, x, t_2) is a function not available to the user. The user will call Add to include an element in the search tree. Make is used internally. It is only used if both t_1 and t_2 are binary search trees, all elements from t_1 are less than x, and all elements from t_2 are greater than x. Create and Make are the basic constructors. A possible set of axioms is given in figure 15.21.

```
Isin(x, Create) = false
Isin(x, Cons(y, s)) = if x = y then true else Isin(x, s)
Isempty(Create) = true
Isempty(Cons(y, s)) = false
Add(x, Create) = Cons(x, Create)
Add(x, Cons(y, s)) = if x ≥ y then Cons(x, Cons(y, s))
        else Cons(y, Add(x, s))
Delete(x, Create) = Create
Delete(x, Cons(y, s)) =
    if x = y then s else Cons(y, Delete(x, s))
Merge(Create, s) = s
Merge(s, Create) = s
Merge(Cons(x, s1), Cons(y, s2)) =
    if x ≥ y then Cons(x, Merge(s1, Cons(y, s2)))
           else Cons(y, Merge(Cons(x, s1), s2))
```

Figure 15.19 Axioms for Slist

```
type Tree;
functions
    Create:                          → Tree
    Make: Tree × Item × Tree         → Tree
    Left: Tree                       → Tree
    Right: Tree                      → Tree
    GetItem: Tree                    → Item
    Isin: Item × Tree                → Boolean
    Isempty: Tree                    → Boolean
    Add: Item × Tree                 → Tree
    Delete: Item × Tree              → Tree
```

Figure 15.20 Signature of Tree

Here, we see that the axioms for Delete make use of extra (hidden) functions Leftmost and Minusleftmost. If we remove a root of some subtree, that node has to be replaced by some other node. If either of its children is the empty tree, it is easy. Otherwise, the smallest element of its right subtree replaces the root. (Alternatively, we could have chosen the largest element from the left subtree.)

Note that the axioms for Delete are algorithmic in character. They closely mimic the well-known algorithm for node deletion in a binary search tree, as it is

```
Left(Create) = Create
Left(Make(t1, x, t2)) = t1
Right(Create) = Create
Right(Make(t1, x, t2)) = t2
GetItem(Create) = NullItem
GetItem(Make(t1, x, t2)) = x
Isin(x, Create) = false
Isin(Make(t1, x, t2)) =
    if x < y then Isin(x, t1) else
    if x = y then true else Isin(x, t2)
Isempty(Create) = true
Isempty(Make(t1, x, t2)) = false
Add(x, Create) = Make(Create, x, Create)
Add(x, Make(t1, y, t2)) =
    if x < y then Make(Add(x, t1), y, t2) else
    if x = y then Make(t1, y, t2)
    else Make(t1, y, Add(x, t2))
Delete(x, Create) = Create
Delete(x, Make(t1, y, t2)) =
    if x < y then Make(Delete(x, t1), y, t2) else
    if x > y then Make(t1, y, Delete(x, t2)) else
    if Isempty(t1) then t2 else
    if Isempty(t2) then t1 else
        Make(t1, Leftmost(t2), Minusleftmost(t2))
Leftmost(Make(t1, x, t2)) =
    if Isempty(t1) then x else Leftmost(t1)
Minusleftmost(Make(t1, x, t2)) = if Isempty(t1) then t2
    else Make(Minusleftmost(t1), x, t2)
```

Figure 15.21 Axioms for Tree

found in standard texts on data structures. This phenomenon occurs fairly often if we try to specify dynamic data structures algebraically.

15.3.5 Large Specifications

A large specification that has no structure imposed on it, is unreadable, just as a large, unstructured program is unreadable. In chapter 11 we discuss the module concept in order to impose structure on a design. Many programming languages offer the module concept as a means of structuring software. In order to retain an overview of large specifications, one also looks for similar constructs. In a notation which supports the modular construction of algebraic specifications, the signature of a data type Set could start as follows:

```
type Set [Item];
    imports true, false from Boolean, Eq from Item;
    exports Create, Isempty, Insert, Isin;
```

Such a notation resembles that of modules in programming languages like Modula-2 and Ada. If an import clause states that module A imports module B, then this could be taken to mean that the signature and axioms of B are added to those of A. The export clause indicates which part of the signature is exported. Operations not exported remain hidden to the users of the module. If a specification has parameters, different instantiations of the specification are obtained by substituting suitable actual values for these parameters.

Research in this area is far from finished. The technical problems involved are similar to those of module constructs in programming languages. However, they are much harder to tackle, because of the strict formal framework in which they occur.

15.4 SPECIFICATION BY PRE- AND POSTCONDITIONS

If we want to formally prove that some program performs a given function, we start by searching for assertions that have to hold before and after execution of that program, respectively. Next, we prove that the program transforms one assertion – the precondition – into the other – the postcondition. The usual notation in this technique is

$$\{P\}S\{Q\}$$

Here, S denotes some program while P and Q denote the pre- and postconditions, respectively. This expression should be read as follows: if the execution of S is started in a state where P holds, then Q will hold afterwards, provided that S terminates. For a simple summation program, this might look as follows:

{sum = 0}
for i:= 1 **to** n **do** sum:= sum + a[i]
$\{\text{sum} = \sum_{j=1}^{n} \text{a[j]}\}$

Finding a correctness proof of a program after the program has been written is often a tedious affair. To prove the correctness of the above program, we have to find an assertion which is an invariant of the loop construct. For the summation example, this invariant is

$$\{\text{sum} = \sum_{j=1}^{i} \text{a[j]}\}$$

Unfortunately, there is no algorithm for finding these invariants.

For a larger program, the proof has to be split into a number of smaller steps. We then put an assertion between each pair of subsequent instructions and prove each transition separately. Again, these intermediate assertions may be hard to find.

Proving termination is usually done by induction. For instance, to prove the termination of a loop, we may look for a function f which is monotonically decreasing and has some lower bound, say 0. For the above example, f could be the function $n - i$.

As an alternative to this tedious process, we may let the proof go hand in hand with the construction of the program. At each step in the derivation, the set of pre- and postconditions obtained so far is viewed as a specification of the program to be constructed. In the above example, the two assertions may be viewed as a specification of a certain summation program.

Software development is then seen as a series of correctness-preserving transformations. The high-level initial specification is refined and transformed a number of times until an executable version is obtained. This approach to software development is known as the **transformational approach**. We may also conceive of tools that support the stepwise derivation of executable code from high-level specifications. Starting from a high-level formal specification, such a tool assists in finding successively more detailed specifications. Languages that allow expression of the whole spectrum of such specifications are called **wide-spectrum languages**.

Even if the actual construction of the program does not follow this procedure, pre- and postconditions are still a valuable way of specifying software components. The pre- and postconditions give the constraints that the implementation has to satisfy. This axiomatic specification technique is often used to specify the properties of the operations of an abstract data type.

As an example, figure 15.22 gives the pre- and postconditions of an operation to search for some element x in a list A. The precondition simply states that the value of n, the upper bound of array A, is at least 0. The postcondition states that the value returned is 0 if none of the elements of A equals x. The value returned is some positive number i if at least some element of A equals x. i then is the index of the first occurrence of x in A.

These pre- and postconditions give a formal characterization of the relation between the input and output of this procedure. For that reason, they are also known as input–output specifications. They constitute a precise description of what a user may expect when the operation is invoked. They also constitute a precise description of the implementor's task.

proc Search (A, n, x) **int**:
  pre $n \geq 0$
  post $(\text{result} = 0 \land \forall i \in 1, \ldots, n: A[i] \neq x) \lor$
    $(\text{result} = i \land 1 \leq i \leq n \land A[i] = x \land \forall j \in 1, \ldots, i\text{-}1: A[j] \neq x)$

Figure 15.22 Input--output specification of a search operation

15.5 THOU SHALT FORMALIZE

If the advantages of formal methods are so obvious, then why didn't the software engineering community at large embrace them long ago? In an attempt to shed light on the issues that have precluded widespread use of formal methods, [Hal90] articulated and dispelled the major arguments of their detractors by paraphrasing them in seven myths. [BH95b] extended this list with seven more myths (see figure 15.23).

1. Formal methods can guarantee that software is perfect
2. Formal methods are all about program proving
3. Formal methods are only useful for safety-critical systems
4. Formal methods require highly trained mathematicians
5. Formal methods increase the cost of developments
6. Formal methods are unacceptable to users
7. Formal methods are not used on real, large-scale software
8. Formal methods delay the development process
9. Formal methods lack tools
10. Formal methods replace traditional engineering design methods
11. Formal methods only apply to software
12. Formal methods are unnecessary
13. Formal methods are not supported
14. Formal methods people always use formal methods

Figure 15.23 Fourteen myths of formal methods ([Hal90] and [BH95b]. ©IEEE)

In a companion article ([BH95c]), these myths are rephrased as ten commandments of formal methods. These commandments can be viewed as the collective lessons drawn from a number of projects, both successful and otherwise, in which formal methods have been applied:[2]

[2]These commandments seem to have a much broader validity. If we replace 'formal methods' by 'object orientation', 'prototyping', or any fashionable software engineering topic, the same lessons can be drawn, by and large.

Thou shalt use an appropriate notation Each specification technique allows us to specify some class of concepts in a natural way. Concepts outside this class can only be specified in a more complex way and involve a lot of effort. Care should be taken to select a technique whose vocabulary fits the problem at hand. The (abstract) objects to be specified must still be recognizable in the specification. The 'cognitive distance' between the specification and the objects specified should not be too great. For example, model-oriented techniques like VDM and Z are ill-suited for specifying concurrency.

At a more pragmatic level, the baroque notations of many formal methods are also an impediment. Having to incorporate ever more weird glyphs into your documents may easily become a nightmare and certainly does not promote widespread use of formal methods.

Thou shalt formalize but not overformalize[3] With the current state of the art, it is not feasible to formally specify each and every aspect of a system. For example, visual aspects of user interfaces require extensive communication with users and are probably best described by example screens and natural language.

This, however, should not lead us to conclude that formal methods are totally unnecessary. Formal specifications force us to be very precise about matters and thereby help to prevent ambiguities, misunderstandings and lack of clarity. By carefully concentrating formalization efforts on error-prone or critical areas of the system, large benefits can be gained with a modest effort.

Thou shalt estimate costs Formal methods require extensive training and this had better be budgeted. Most existing cost-estimation models are based on historical data from past projects (see chapter 7). Extrapolation from the past is only valid insofar as the future resembles that past. Since there is little or no data on projects that have used formal methods, the experience base needed for accurate cost estimation for projects involving formal methods is still very small.

Thou shalt have a formal methods guru on call This is a lesson learned from the more successful formal methods projects. Most software engineers are not very familiar with the mathematics and logic involved in formal methods. Many have not been adequately trained in these fields. Professional guidance and tutoring is necessary, both to take away the initial fear of the water and to learn to use a screwdriver rather than a hammer on screws.

Thou shalt not abandon thy traditional development methods Most organizations have invested a lot in traditional methods for software development. In many respects, these traditional methods have been very successful. Rather than totally aban-

[3] So I cheated a bit in the title of this section.

doning them in favor of a new fad, you would be advised to integrate formal methods with existing methods to get the best of both.

Thou shalt document sufficiently A formal specification provides very rigorous documentation. However, formal specifications alone don't suffice. For communication with other parties, such as end users, an informal version of the formal specification, or an informal annotation of it, is a necessity. The various stakeholders must all 'understand' the specifications. They must be able to determine what is being specified and not be forced to rely on the 'experts', only to become disillusioned later on.

Thou shalt not compromise thy quality standards Formal methods do not *guarantee* correctness. They are just another powerful means to achieve higher-quality software. Additional procedures to keep the process up to standards, such as feedback to customers, document reviews, careful change-control procedures, and the like, remain indispensable.

Thou shalt not be dogmatic Formal methods are no silver bullet. They are just one of many tools. For example, the transition from informal requirements to formal specification can *never* be proven correct, so other methods are needed for their validation.

Thou shalt test, test, and test again Though formal methods increase confidence, bugs will still be found. Human fallibility can never be totally excluded. At each stage, whether it be a formal proof of correctness or the coding of a module, mistakes can and will be made. Formal specifications can *never* replace a thorough testing phase.

Thou shalt reuse When formally specifying software components, we strive for a high level of abstraction. Components thus specified have clearly defined interfaces and exhibit no implementation bias. These properties make them good candidates for reuse.

The history of formal methods is not unlike that of many other innovations in our field. The discussion has been much more passionate though, with formal methods zealots trying to persuade everyone to follow their lead on one side, and a jibbing industry on the other side. By trial and error, those of us who persevered and believed in formal methods have discovered the rules for using them, as expressed in these commandments. Definite successes have also helped in establishing a realistic perspective on formal methods.

15.6 SUMMARY

In this chapter we discussed a number of specification techniques. We argued that informal specification techniques may lead to all kinds of problems and are better not used. Fortunately, formal approaches to software specification provide a good alternative.

It used to be the case that formal approaches were dispatched by their detractors using arguments like the ones given in figure 15.23. However, formal specification methods are beginning to mature. Though industry is still reluctant to adopt these methods, it is also clear that real progress has been made. The primary purpose in using formal approaches often is not to prove the correctness of the system. Rather, the process of building a formal specification helps to get insight into the universe being modeled. It helps to unveil ambiguities and inconsistencies. It helps to get better specifications and, as a consequence, better systems.

In [FKV94], different strategies for incorporating formal methods in software development are identified and assessed. In the process dimension, the authors distinguish direct and transitional strategies. In a direct strategy, the formal specification is directly derived from the initial informal specification. In a transitional strategy, intermediate, semiformal representations are used as stepping stones. In the support dimension, a distinction is made between unassisted and computer-assisted strategies.

For small, well-structured problems with which the analyst is familiar, a direct, unassisted strategy is quite appropriate. Such strategies however do not scale up well to large, real-life problems. For large problems, intermediate representations as well as (heuristics-based) tool support become a necessity. Inadequate tool support is often noted as one of the impediments to formal methods.

We distinguished model-oriented and property-oriented specification techniques. Model-oriented techniques provide a direct means to specify the system's behavior. In model-oriented techniques, the system is specified in terms of mathematical structures like sets and sequences. Property-oriented techniques provide an indirect means and state the properties (constraints) that the system is to satisfy. Often, a mixture of several techniques is used.

The most well-known model-oriented specification formalisms are VDM and Z. There are many similarities between these formalisms. Both use mathematical structures like sets, sequences, and functions to model a system, and the notation of predicate logic to describe operations.

Algebraic specifications are the major type of property-oriented methods. In algebraic specifications, data types are viewed as algebras and axioms are used to state properties of the data type's operations.[4]

The use of pre- and postconditions is another example of a property-oriented technique. It is widely used to specify procedural abstractions. This type of input-output specification can also be used as a starting point for deriving software constructively from a statement of its pre- and postconditions.

15.7 FURTHER READING

A general introduction to formal methods is given in [Win90]. An excellent roundtable forum on the question 'What is hindering the use of formal methods in industry' is reported on in [Se96]. The use of formal specification methods is reflected in [HB95], [Hal96], [TrS98a], [CCPC$^+$99] and [CdV98]. These papers reflect state-of-the-art applications of formal approaches in real projects. The transfer of formal methods into practice is addressed in [JSS98].

There are good textbooks for model-oriented specification methods: [Spi92] and [Dil94] for Z; and [Jon90] and [WH93] for VDM. Case studies in using these methods for a variety of problems are collected in [Hay93] and [JS90], respectively. For a comparison of VDM and Z, see [Hay92].

The idea of specifying data types and their operations algebraically emerged in the 1970s [Zil74], [Gut75] and [GTWW75]. A good overview of this material can be found in [BT83] and [Wir90]. The more mathematically-oriented reader should look to [GTW78] or [EM85]. The procedure to obtain a sufficiently complete algebraic specification is given in [LG86]. Examples of formalisms for structured algebraic specifications are ASF [BHK89] and Larch [GH93].

Seminal articles on proving program correctness from a statement of its pre- and postconditions are [Flo67] and [Hoa69]. Well-known texts on the derivation of software from a statement of its pre-and postconditions are [Dij76] and [Gri81].

[4]For the reader who has not solved the puzzle in figure 15.17: the specification concerns a queue. Substitute Remove for e, Append for t, Create for c, First for l and IsEmpty for s. The types x, y and z stand for Queue, Integer and Boolean, respectively. a and b are variables of type Queue and Integer, respectively.

Exercises

1. What is the main difference between model-oriented and property-oriented formal specification methods?

2. What is the difference between a function and an operation in VDM?

3. When is the specification of a VDM function or operation called *loose*?

4. Describe the two main parts that make up an algebraic specification.

5. Discuss the difference between the initial semantics and final semantics of an algebraic specification.

6. When is an algebraic specification sufficiently complete?

7. What is the difference between a constructor and an observer in an algebraic specification?

8. Why is it necessary to still test your software if formal methods have been used throughout its development?

9. ♡ The following is the signature of a data type List:

Create:	→ List
Add: List × Course × Points × Score	→ List
PartyTime: List	→ Boolean
GradePoints: List	→ Integer

   The data type List is used to store data about student scores. Create is used to create an empty list. Add adds a new entry to the list. An entry consists of the course name, the grade points for that course (a cardinal number), and the student's score (a cardinal number between 0 and 100). If an entry is added whose course name equals that of an entry already in the list, then the new entry replaces the old one, provided the score of the new entry is larger than that of the old one. Only entries whose score exceeds 50 are incorporated in the list. GradePoints yields the sum of the grade points of all entries in the list. PartyTime yields true if and only if the total number of grade points exceeds 126.

   Give the axioms for the data type List, using initial semantics. You are free to use any operations needed for the auxiliary types Course, Points, Score, Integer and Boolean. You may also use if-then-else constructs in the right-hand-sides of axioms. You must also give axioms for hidden functions of the data type List.

10. ♡ Would the axioms for the data type List from exercise 9 be any different if final semantics were used instead of initial semantics?

11. ♡ The following signature is given for a data type String:

Create:	$\rightarrow$ String
Append: String $\times$ Char	$\rightarrow$ String
Delete: String $\times$ Integer	$\rightarrow$ String
Substring: String $\times$ String	$\rightarrow$ Boolean

Create creates an empty string. Append adds a character at the end of a string. The second parameter of Delete denotes the position of the character that is to be deleted. The character positions are numbered from 1 onwards. Delete is a void operation if the position given is out of bounds. Finally, Substring(s1, s2) yields true if and only if s2 is a substring of s1.

Give the axioms for the data type String, using initial semantics.

12. Prove the following equality, using the axioms derived in exercise 11:

Substring(Append(Append(Append(Append(Create, a), a), b), a),
    Append(Append(Create, a), a)) = true

13. ♡ Give a model-oriented specification for the string operations of exercise 11, assuming the sequence type and its usual operations are predefined.

14. ♡ Try to do the same if only the set type and associated operations are predefined.

15. ♠ Consider a sequence of numbers $A = (a_1, \ldots, a_n)$. A subsequence of length $n - l$ is obtained by deleting l (not necessarily adjacent) elements from A. A subsequence is called an upsequence if its values are in non-decreasing order.

State pre- and postconditions for a program to calculate the length of the longest subsequence of a given sequence A, and constructively develop the program from these pre- and postconditions. (After having done so, you may wish to study section 20.2 of [Gri81].)

16. ♠ The Knuth–Morris–Pratt (KMP) algorithm searches a string for the (first) occurrence of some other string. It has a running time proportional to the length of the string to be searched. (Unfortunately, this is of little help since the dumbest string-searching algorithm has the same running time in practice. Actual string-searching algorithms in application programs like text editors are more

complicated.) For a given string S and a substring p to be looked for, KMP is as follows:

```
j:= k:= 1;
while k <= n do
    while j > 0 and S[k] # p[j] do j:= F[j] end;
    if j = m
        then return "substring found at position k-m"
        else k:= k+1; j:= j+1
    end
end;
return "substring not found"
```

In this algorithm, m and n are positive integers denoting the length of p and S, respectively. F is an auxiliary array of length m. Prior to the execution of the above algorithm, F is determined as follows:

```
j:= 1; i:= 0; F[1]:= 0;
while j < m do
    while i > 0 and p[j] # p[i] do i:= F[i] end;
    i:= i + 1; j:= j + 1;
    if p[j] = p[i]
        then F[j]:= F[i]
        else F[j]:= i
    end
end;
```

State pre- and postconditions for the KMP-algorithm and prove its correctness. (Hint: F[j] is the largest index i < j such that p[1 ... i-1] = p[j - (i-1) ... j-1] and p[i] # p[j].)

Also prove that the running time of the KMP-algorithm is $O(n + m)$. (See also [Smi82].)

17. ♡ Add an operation ChangeAddr to the VDM-specification in figure 15.12 that updates the address field of a client, given the identification number of that client.

18. ♠ In the VDM-specification of the library system given in figure 15.12, a copy of a book is either borrowed by some client or it is available from the library. Change the specification such that a copy of a book may also be temporarily unavailable (it could, for instance, be in repair).

19. ♠ Write an essay on the virtues of formal specifications as opposed to natural language specifications.

16 User Interface Design[1]

LEARNING OBJECTIVES

- To be aware of different architectural styles for interactive systems
- To appreciate the role of different types of expertise in user interface design
- To understand that a user interface entails considerably more than what is represented on the screen
- To be aware of the role of various models in user interface design
- To recognize the differences between a user-centered approach to the design of interactive systems and other requirements engineering approaches

[1]This chapter has been written in cooperation with Gerrit C. van der Veer, Vrije Universiteit, Amsterdam.

> *Today, user needs are recognized to be important in designing interactive computer systems, but as recently as 1980, they received little emphasis.*
> [Gru91]

> *We can't worry about these user interface issues now. We haven't even gotten this thing to work yet!*
> [MAS91]

A system in which the interaction occurs at a level which is understandable to the user will be accepted faster than a system where it is not. A system which is available at irregular intervals, or gives incomprehensible error messages, is likely to meet resistance. A 1992 survey found that 48% of the code of applications was devoted to the user interface, and about 50% of the development time was devoted to implementing that part of the application [MR92]. Often, the user interface is one of the most critical factors as regards the success or failure of a computerized system. Yet, most software engineers know fairly little about this aspect of our trade.

Users judge the quality of a software system by the degree in which it helps them to accomplish their tasks and by the sheer joy they have in using it. This judgment is to a large extent determined by the quality of the user interface. Good user interfaces contribute to a system's quality in the following ways [BM94]:

- Increased efficiency. If the system fits the way its users work and if it has a good ergonomic design, users can perform their tasks efficiently. They do not lose time struggling with the functionality and its appearance on the screen.

- Improved productivity. A good interface does not distract the user, but rather allows him to concentrate on the task to be done.

- Reduced errors. Many so-called 'human errors' can be attributed to poor user interface quality. Avoiding inconsistencies, ambiguities, and the like reduces user errors.

- Reduced training. A poor user interface hampers learning. A well-designed user interface encourages its users to create proper models and reinforces learning, thus reducing training time.

- Improved acceptance. Users prefer systems whose interface is well-designed. Such systems make information easy to find and provide the information in a form which is easy to use.

In a technical sense, the user interface often comprises one or more layers in the architecture of a system. Section 16.1 discusses two well-known architectural styles that highlight the place and role of the user interface in interactive systems. A common denominator of these and other schemes is that they separate the functionality of the system from the interaction with the user. In a similar vein, many software engineering methods also separate the design of the functionality from the design of the user interface. The design of the user interface then reduces to a mere design of the screen layout, menu structure, size and color of buttons, format of help and error messages, etc. User interface design then becomes an activity that is only started *after* the requirements engineering phase has finished. It is often done by software engineers who have little specialized knowledge of user interface design.

Software engineers are inclined to model the user interface after the structure of the implementation mechanism, rather than the structure of the task domain. For instance, a structure-based editor may force you to input ↑ 10 2 in order to obtain 10^2, simply because the former is easier for the system to recognize. This resembles the interface to early pocket calculators, where the stack mechanism used internally shows itself in the user interface. Similarly, user documentation often follows implementation patterns and error messages are phrased in terms that reflect the implementation rather than the user tasks.

In this chapter we advocate a rather different approach. This approach may be summarized as 'The user interface *is* the system'. This broader view of the concept user interface and the disciplines that are relevant while developing user interfaces are discussed in section 16.2. Within the approach discussed, the design of the user interface replaces what we used to call requirements engineering. The approach is inspired by the observation that the usability of a system is not only determined by its perceptual appearance in the form of menus, buttons, etc. The user of an interactive system has to accomplish certain tasks. Within the task domain, e.g. sending electronic mail or preparing documents, these tasks have a certain structure. The human–computer interaction (HCI) then should have the same structure, as far as this can be accomplished. Discovering an adequate structuring of the task domain is considered part of user interface design. This discovery process and its translation into user interface representations requires specific expertise, expertise that most software engineers do not possess. Section 16.5 discusses this eclectic approach to user interface design. Its main activities – task analysis, interface specification, and evaluation – are discussed in sections 16.6–16.8.

In order to develop a better understanding of what is involved in designing user interfaces, it is necessary to take a closer look at the role of the user in operating a complex device such as a computer. Two types of model bear upon the interplay between a human and the computer: the user's mental model and the conceptual model.

Users create a model of the system they use. Based on education, knowledge of the system or application domain, knowledge of other systems, general world knowledge, and the like, the user constructs a model, a knowledge structure, of that system. This is called the mental model. During interaction with the system, this mental model is used to plan actions and predict and interpret system reactions. The mental model reflects the user's understanding of what the system contains, how it works, and why it works the way it does. The mental model is initially determined through metacommunication, such as training and documentation. It evolves over time as the user acquires a better understanding of the system. The user's mental model need not be, and often is not, accurate in technical terms. It may contain misunderstandings and omissions.

The conceptual model is the technically-accurate model of the computer system created by designers and teachers for their purposes. It is a consistent and complete representation of the system as far as user-relevant characteristics are involved. The conceptual model reflects itself in the system's reaction to user actions.

The central question in human–computer interaction is how to attune the user's mental model and the conceptual model as well as possible. When this is achieved to a higher degree, an interactive system becomes easier to learn and easier to use. Where the models conflict, the user gets confused, makes errors, and gets frustrated. A good design starts with a conceptual model derived from an analysis of the intended users and their tasks. The conceptual model should result in a system and training materials which are consistent with the conceptual model. This, in turn, should be designed such that it induces adequate mental models in the users.

Section 16.4 discusses various models that play a role in HCI. As well as the aforementioned mental and conceptual models, attention is given to a model of human information processing. When interacting with a system, be it a car or a library information system, the user processes information. Limitations and properties of human information processing have their effect on the interaction. Knowledge of how humans process information may help us to develop systems that users can better cope with.

There are many factors that impact human–computer interaction. In this chapter, we just scratch the surface. Important topics not discussed include the socio-economic context of human–computer interaction, input and output media and their ergonomics, and workplace ergonomics. Section 16.10 contains some pointers to relevant literature.

16.1 WHERE IS THE USER INTERFACE?

A computerized library system will include a component to search the library's database for certain titles. This component includes code to implement its function as well as code to handle the interaction with the user. In the old days, these pieces of code tended to be entangled, resulting in one large, monolithic piece of software.

In 1983, a workshop on user interface management systems took place at Seeheim in West Germany [Pfa85]. At this workshop, a model was proposed which separates the application proper from the user interface. This model has become known as the **Seeheim model**.

The Seeheim model describes the user interface as the outer layer of the system. This outer layer is an agent responsible for the actual interaction between the user and the application. It, in turn, consists of two layers supporting

- the presentation – perceptible aspects including screen design and keyboard layout;
- the dialog, i.e. the syntax of the interaction including metacommunication (help functions, error messages, and state information). If the machine is said to apply a model of its human partner in the dialog, e.g. by choosing the user's native language for command names, this model is also located in the dialog layer.

This conceptualization of the user interface does not include the application semantics, or 'functionality'. In the Seeheim model, the tasks the user can ask the machine to perform are located in another layer, the application interface.

The architecture of the Seeheim model is depicted in figure 16.1. It shows the separation of concerns into three parts. For efficiency reasons, an extra connection is drawn between the application and the display. In this way, large volumes of output data may skip the dialog layer.

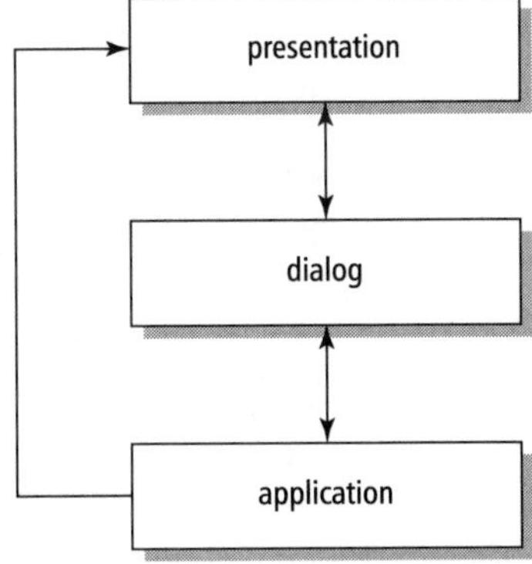

Figure 16.1 The Seeheim model

The Seeheim model provides some very relevant advantages. For example, we may provide the same outer layer to different applications. We may apply the same look and feel to a text editor, a spreadsheet, and so on, as in Microsoft products. In this way the user does not have to learn different dialog languages for different applications. Conversely, we may provide a single application to be implemented behind several different outer layers, so as to allow different companies to adopt the same application with their own corporate interface style.

In both these cases, it is assumed that the changes are likely to occur in the interface part of the system, while the application part remains largely unaffected. Alternatively, we may assume that the functionality of the system will change. We then look for an architecture in which parts of the system can be modified independently of each other. A first decomposition of an interactive system along these lines is depicted in figure 16.2. Each component in this decomposition handles part of the application, together with its presentation and dialog. In a next step, we may refine this architecture such that the input or output device of each component may be replaced. The result of this is shown in figure 16.3. This result is in fact the model–view–controller (MVC) paradigm used in Smalltalk. It is also the archetypical example of a design pattern; see section 10.3. The dialog and application together constitute the model part of a component. In MVC, the output and input are called view and controller, respectively.

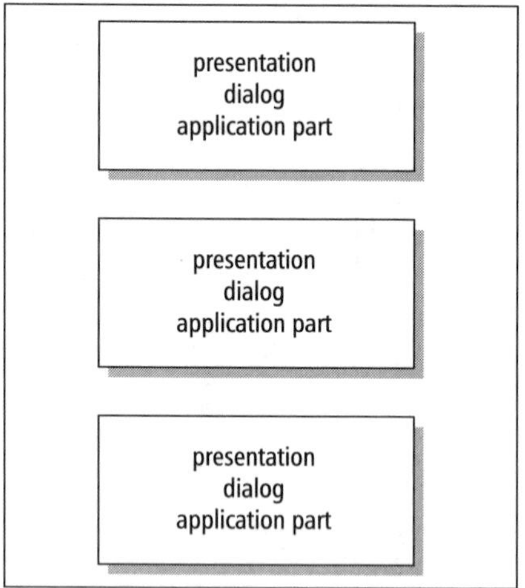

Figure 16.2 A part--whole decomposition of interactive systems

Both the Seeheim model and MVC decompose an interactive system according to quality arguments pertaining to flexibility. The primary concern in the Seeheim model is with changes in the user interface, while the primary concern of MVC is

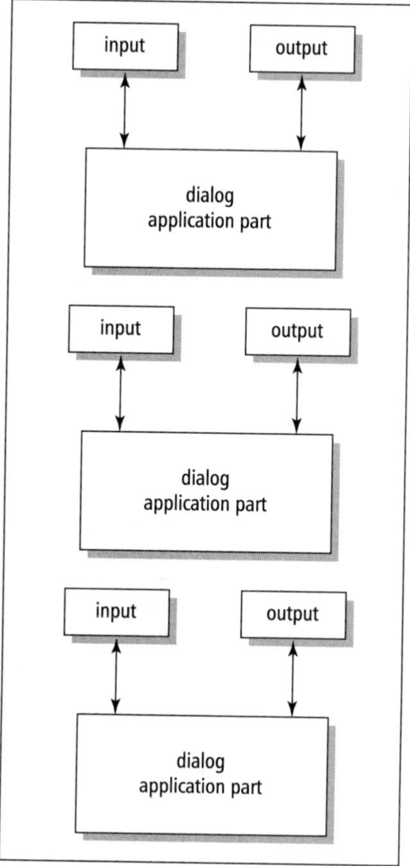

Figure 16.3 The Model--View--Controller paradigm for interactive systems

with changes in the functionality. This difference in emphasis is not surprising if we consider the environments in which these models were developed: the Seeheim model by a group of specialists in computer graphics and MVC in an exploratory Smalltalk software development environment. Both models have their advantages and disadvantages. The project at hand and its quality requirements should guide the design team in selecting an appropriate separation of concerns between the functionality proper and the part which handles communication with the user.

16.2 WHAT IS THE USER INTERFACE?

The concept 'user interface' has several meanings. It may denote the layout of the screen, 'windows', or a shell or layer in the architecture of a system or the application. Each of these meanings denotes a *designer's* point of view. Alternatively, the user interface can be defined from the point of view of the intended *user* of a system. In most cases, users do not make a distinction between layers in an architecture and they often do not even have a clear view of the difference between hardware and software. For most users an information system as a whole is a tool to perform certain tasks. To them, the user interface *is* the system.

In this chapter we use the term **user interface** to denote all aspects of an information system that are relevant to a user. This includes not only everything that a user can perceive or experience (as far as it has a meaning), but also aspects of internal structure and processes *as far as the user should be aware of them*. For example, car salesmen sometimes try to impress their customers and mention the horse-power of each and every car in their shop. Most customers probably do not know how to interpret those figures. They are not really interested in them either. A Rolls-Royce dealer knows this. His answer to a question about the horse-power of one of his cars would simply be: 'Enough'. The same holds for many aspects of the internal structure of an information system. On the other hand, the user of a suite of programs including a text editor, a spreadsheet and a graphics editor should know that a clipboard is a memory structure whose contents remain unchanged until overwritten.

We define the user interface in this broad sense as the **user virtual machine** (UVM). The UVM includes both hardware and software. It includes the workstation or device (gadget) with which the user is in physical contact as well as everything that is 'behind' it like a network and remote data collections. In this chapter, we take the whole UVM, including the application semantics, as the subject of (user interface) design.

In many cases, several groups of users have to be distinguished with respect to their tasks. As an example, consider an ATM. One type of user consists of people, bank clients, who put a card into the machine to perform some financial transaction. Other users are specially-trained people who maintain the machine and supply it with a stock of cash. Their role is in ATM maintenance. Lawyers constitute a third category of users of ATM machines. They have to argue in favor of (or against) a bank to show that a transaction has been fraudulent, using a log or another type of transaction trace that is maintained by the system. Each of these three user categories represents a different role in relation to the use of the ATM. For each of these roles, the system has a different meaning; each role has to be aware of different processes and internal structures. Consequently, each has a different interface. If we are going to design these interfaces, however, we have to design all of them, and, moreover, we have to design the relation between them. In other words, within the task domain of the ATM we have to design a *set* of related UVMs, with respect to the tasks that are part of the various roles.

We may look at the user interface from different viewpoints:

- how to design all that is relevant to the user (the design aspect)
- what does the user need to understand (the human side)

In practice these aspects will often have to be combined. The next section is concerned with the human side. Later sections focus on the design aspects of the user interface.

16.3 HUMAN FACTORS IN HUMAN–COMPUTER INTERACTION

Attention to the user interface is often located in the later phases of the software life cycle. The design approach we elaborate in this chapter, however, requires attention to the human user (or to the different user roles) from the very start of the design process. The various design activities are carried out in parallel and in interaction with each other, even though a large design team may allocate to specialists the tasks of analyzing, specifying, and evaluating user interface aspects. The design of the user interface consists of a complex of activities, all of which are intended to focus on the human side of the system.

The human side cannot be covered by a single discipline or a single technique. There are at least three relevant disciplines:

- the humanities,
- artistic design, and
- ergonomics.

16.3.1 Humanities

In this view we pay attention to people based on psychological approaches (how do humans perceive, learn, remember, think, and feel), and to organization and culture (how do people work together and how does the work situation affect the people's work). Relevant disciplines are cognitive psychology, anthropology, and ethnography. These disciplines provide a theoretical base and associated techniques for collecting information on people's work as well as techniques to assess newly designed tools and procedures. Designers of the virtual machine or user interface need some insight into the theories and experience with techniques from these disciplines. For example, in specifying what should be represented at a control panel, one may have to consider that less information makes it easier for the user to identify indications of process irregularity (the psychological phenomenon of attention and distraction). On the other hand, if less of the relevant information is displayed, the user may have to remember more, and psychology teaches us that human working memory has a very limited capacity.

16.3.2 Artistic design

Creative and performing artists in very different fields have developed knowledge on how to convey meaning to their public. Graphical artists know how shapes, colors, and spatial arrangements affect the viewer. Consequently, their expertise teaches interface designers how to draw the attention of users to important elements of the interface. For example, colors should be used sparingly in order not to devalue their possible meaning. Well-chosen use of colors helps to show important relations between elements on the screen and supports users searching for relevant structures in information. Design companies nowadays employ graphical artists to participate in the design of representational aspects of user interfaces.

Complex systems often need a representation of complex processes, where several flows of activity influence each other. Examples of this type of work situation are the team monitoring a complex chemical process and the cockpit crew flying an intercontinental passenger airplane. In such situations, users need to understand complex relations over time. The representation of the relevant processes and their relations over time is far from trivial. Representing in an understandable way what is going on and how the relations change over time is only part of the question. Frequently, such complex processes are safety critical, which means that the human supervisor needs to make the right decision very soon after some abnormal phenomenon occurs, so immediate detection of an event as well as immediate understanding of the total complex of states and process details is needed. Experts in theater direction turn out to have knowledge of just this type of situation. This type of interface may be compared with a theater show, where an optimal direction of the action helps to make the audience aware of the complex of intentions of the author and the cast [Lau90] and [Lau93]. Consequently, theater sciences are another source for designing interfaces to complex processes.

Another type of artistic expertise that turns out to be very relevant for interface design is cinematography. The art form of film design has resulted in systematic knowledge of the representation of dynamics and processes over time [MB95]. For example, there are special mechanisms to represent the suggestion of causality between processes and events. If it is possible to graphically represent the causing process with a directional movement, the resulting event or state should be shown in a location that is in the same direction. For example, in an electronic commerce system, buying an object may be represented by dragging that object to a shopping cart. If the direction of this movement is to the right of the screen, the resulting change in the balance should also be shown to the right.

In the same way there are 'laws' for representing continuity in time. In a movie, the representation of a continuing meeting between two partners can best be achieved by ensuring that the camera viewpoints do not cross the line that connects the location points of the two partners. As soon as this line is crossed, the audience will interpret this as a jump in time. This type of expertise helps the design of animated representations of processes and the like.

In general, artists are able to design attractive solutions, to develop a distinctive style for a line of products or for a company, and to relate the design to the professional status of the user. There are, however, tradeoffs to be made. For example, artistic design sometimes conflicts with ergonomics. When strolling through a consumer electronics shop you will find artistic variants of mobile phones, coffee machines, and audio systems where the designer seems to have paid a tribute to artistic shape and color, at the same time making the use less intuitive and even less easy from the point of view of fitting the relevant buttons to the size of the human hand. A similar fate may befall a user interface of an information system.

16.3.3 Ergonomics

Ergonomics is concerned with the relation between human characteristics and artifacts. Ergonomics develops methods and techniques to allow adaptation between humans and artifacts (whether physical tools, complex systems, organizations, or procedures). In classical ergonomics, the main concern is on anthropometrics (statistics of human measures, including muscle power and attributes of human perception). During the past 20 years, **cognitive ergonomics** developed as a field that focuses mainly on characteristics of human information processing in interaction with information systems. Cognitive ergonomics is increasingly considered to be the core view for managing user interface design. A cognitive ergonomist is frequently found to be the leader of the design team as far as the virtual machine is concerned.

For beginning users, the human–computer conversation is often very embarrassing. The real beginner is a novice in using a specific computer program. He will often be a novice in computer use in general. Sometimes he is also relatively new to the domain of the primary task (the office work for which he will use the PC or the monitoring of the chemical process for which the computer console is the front end). In such a situation, problems quickly reach a level at which an expert is asked for help and the user tends to blame the program or the system for his failure to use the new facility.

There seems to be a straightforward remedy for this dilemma: start by educating the user in the task domain, next teach him everything about the facility, and only thereafter allow him access to the computer. This, however, is only a theoretical possibility. Users will insist on using the computer from the outset, if they intend ever to use it, and introducing a task domain without giving actual experience with the system that is designed for the task is bad education. So the cure must be found in another direction. The designer of the system must start from a detailed 'model of the user' and a 'model of the task'. If he knows that the user is a novice both on the task domain and on the system, he will have to include options for learning both these areas at the same time.

In general, the system designer will try to apply cognitive ergonomic knowledge and adapt the interface to the intended task rather than vice versa. The system should be made transparent (unobtrusive) as far as anything but the intended task is concerned. This should facilitate the user's double task: to delegate tasks to the system and to learn how to interact with the system. However, in many cases this can not be accomplished completely in one direction and a solution has to be found by adapting the human user to the artifact, i.e. by teaching and training the user or by selecting users that are able to work with the artifacts. Adapting the user to the artifacts requires a strong motive, though. Constraints of available technology, economic aspects, and safety arguments may contribute to a decision in this direction. Instead of designing an 'intuitive' airplane cockpit that could allow an average adult to fly without more than a brief series of lessons, analogous to driving a car, most airlines prefer to thoroughly select and train their pilots.

Cognitive ergonomics is a relatively young discipline. It developed when information technology started to be applied by people whose expertise was not in the domains of computer science or computer programming. The first ideas in this field were elaborated more or less simultaneously in different parts of the world, and in communities that used different languages, which resulted in several schools with rather specific characteristics. Much of the early work in the US and Canada, for instance, is based on applying cognitive ergonomics to actual design problems. Also, success stories like the development of the Xerox Star were, after the fact, interpreted in terms of ergonomic design concepts [SIK$^+$82]. In [Car90] this is phrased as 'the theory is in the artifact'. Conversely, European work in the field of cognitive ergonomics has concentrated on the development of models: models of computer users, models of human–computer interaction, models of task structures, and so on. By now, these differences are fading away, but a lot of important sources still require some understanding of their cultural background.

16.4 THE ROLE OF MODELS IN HUMAN–COMPUTER INTERACTION

The concept of a *model* has an important place in the literature on human–computer interaction and cognitive ergonomics. Models represent relevant characteristics of a part of reality that we need to understand. At the same time, models are abstract: they represent only what is needed, thus helping us to find our way in complex situations. We need to be aware of differences between types of model, though, and of the inconsistent use of names for the various types of model. First, we discuss the difference between internal and external models in human–computer interaction:

- **Internal models** are models 'for execution'. Internal models use an agent (a human or a machine) who makes a decision based on the behavior of the model. If the agent is human, this model is termed a **mental model** in psychology. Humans apply these models whenever they have to interact with complex systems. We discuss mental models in section 16.4.2.

  If the agent is a machine, the internal model is a program or a knowledge system. For example, a user interface may retain a model of the user. In that case the literature mostly speaks of a **user model**: a model of the user that is used by the interface. The model could help the interface to react differently to different users or, alternatively, to adjust to the current user depending on the machine's understanding of that user's current goals or level of understanding. User models of this type may be designed to learn from user behavior and are commonly used in so-called intelligent user interfaces. A third type of internal model in machines is a model of the task domain, which enables the user and the system to collaborate in solving problems about the task. The latter type of internal model leads to systems that can reason, critique user solutions, provide diagnosis, or suggest user actions. User models are not discussed further in this book.

- **External models** are used for communication and, hence, are first of all represented in some type of formalism (which could also be a graphical representation like a Petri net or flow diagram). The formalism should be chosen in relation to what is being modeled, as well as to the goal of the communication. In designing user interfaces, there are several domains where external models are needed. Designers need to understand some relevant aspects of the user, especially human information processing. Cognitive psychology provides such type of knowledge, hence in section 16.4.1 we briefly discuss a recent variant of the model of human information processing, only mentioning those aspects that are relevant when designing for users of computers. Another type of model is used in the various types of design activity. These external models help designers to document their decisions, to backtrack when one design decision overrules another, and to communicate the result of one design phase to people responsible for another phase (e.g. to communicate a view of the task to a colleague responsible for usability evaluation). In section 16.4.3, we give some examples of external models used in various design activities. These models are the HCI-oriented counterparts of the requirements representation formats discussed in chapter 9.

Some types of model, such as task knowledge models, refer to aspects that are both internal and external. Task knowledge is originally to be found in the memory of human beings, in documents about the work domain, and in the actual situation of the work environment. These are internal models, applied while doing the work. Designers need to understand this knowledge and apply it as the base of their design, hence they need to perform task analysis and model the task knowledge. This is an external model for use in design. Task models and task modeling are treated in section 16.6.

16.4.1 A Model of Human Information Processing

The model of human information processing is an example of an external model. We only briefly mention some notions that need to be understood in analyzing human–computer interaction. We focus on human perception, memory, and the processing of information in relation to the input and output of the human in interaction with an outside system. Figure 16.4 depicts this model. In text books on psychology a figure like this is often adorned with formulae that allow calculation of the speed of processing, the effect of learning, etc.

In modern cognitive psychology, perception (the input of human information processing) is considered to proceed through a number of phases:

- Edge detection. During edge detection, the large amount of unstructured information that bombards our senses is automatically and quickly structured into a '2.5-D sketch' based on movement, color, and location.

- Gestalt formation. Gestalts, a small number of understandable structures (such as a triangle, a spoken sound, and a tactile shape), are formed, based on similarities detected in the sketch, on spatial relations and on simplicity.

- Combination. The gestalts are combined into groups of segments that seem to belong together: an object consisting of triangles, cubes and cylinders; a spoken utterance consisting of a series of sounds.

- Recognition. The group of segments is recognized: a picture of a horse; a spoken sentence.

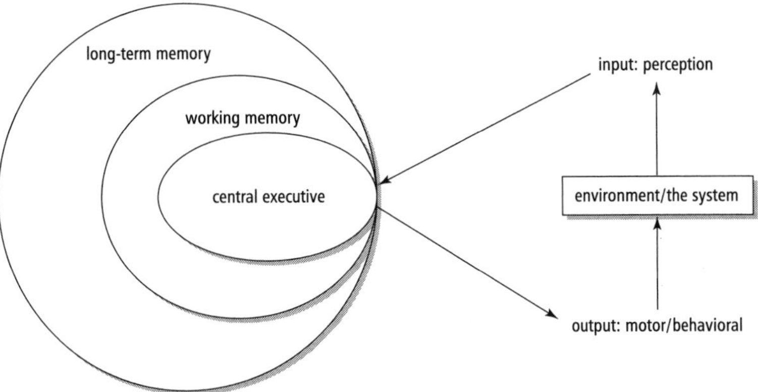

Figure 16.4 A model of human information processing

The processing in the later phases is done less and less automatically. People will be aware of the gestalt formation and combination when any problem arises, for example because of irregularity or exceptional situations like 'impossible' figures. Recognition leads to a conscious perception.

The whole series of phases takes a fraction of a second. It takes more time when a problem occurs because of an unexpected or distorted stimulus. It takes less time when the type of stimulus is familiar. So we may train our computer users to perceive important signals quickly and we may design our signals for easy and quick detection and discrimination. Psychologists and ergonomists know when a signal is easy to detect, what color combinations are slow to be detected, and what sounds are easy to discriminate.

The output of human beings is movement. People make gestures, manipulate tools, speak, or use a combination of these. For computer use, manipulation of keys, mouse or touch-screen, and speaking into microphones are common examples of output. According to modern psychology all those types of output are monitored by a central processing mechanism in the human. This central executive decides on the meaning of the output (say yes, move the mouse to a certain location, press the return key) but leaves the actual execution to motor processes that, in normal cases, are running 'unattended', i.e. the actual execution is not consciously controlled. Only in case of problems is attention needed. For example, if the location to be pointed to on the screen is in an awkward position, if a key is not functioning properly, or if the room is so noisy that the person cannot properly hear his own spoken command. So we should design for human movements and human measures. It pays off to ask an ergonomist about the most ergonomic design of buttons and dials.

The central executive unit of human information processing is modeled as an instance that performs productions of the form if condition then action, where the condition in most cases relates to some perceived input or to some knowledge available from memory. The action is a command to the motor system, with attributes derived from working memory. The central executive unit has a very limited capacity. First of all, only a very small number of processes can be performed simultaneously. Secondly, the knowledge that is needed in testing the condition as well as the knowledge that is processed on behalf of the motor output has to be available in working memory. Most of the time we may consider the limitations to result in the execution of one process at a time and, consequently, in causing competing processes to be scheduled for sequential execution based on perceived priority. For example, when a driver approaches a crossroads, the talk with his passenger will be temporarily interrupted and only resumed when the driving decisions have been made. The amount of available resources has to be taken into account when designing systems. For example, humans cannot cope with several error messages each of which requires an immediate decision, especially if each requires complex error diagnosis to be performed before reaction is feasible.

Working memory is another relevant concept in the model. Modern psychology presumes there is only one memory structure, **long-term memory**, that contains knowledge that is permanently stored. Any stimulus that reaches the central executive unit leads to the activation of an element in long term memory. The activated elements together form the current working memory. The capacity of the set of activated elements is very limited. The average capacity of the human information processor is 5–9 elements. If new elements are activated, other elements lose their activation status and, hence, are no longer immediately available to the central executive. In other words, they are not in working memory any more.

Long-term memory is highly structured. One important type of relation concerns semantic relations between concepts, such as part-of, member-of, and generalization–specialization. In fact, each piece of knowledge can be considered a concept defined by its relation to other elements. Such a piece of knowledge is often called a **chunk**. It is assumed that working memory has a capacity of 5–9 chunks. An expert in some task domain is someone who has available well-chosen chunks in that domain, so that he is able to expand any chunk into relevant relations, but only when needed for making decisions and deriving an answer to a problem. If not needed, an expert will not expand the chunk that has been triggered by the recognition phase of perception or by the production based on a stimulus. For example, the sequence of digits '85884' could occupy five entries in working memory. However, if it is recognized as your mother's telephone number, it is encoded as such and only occupies one entry. When the number has to be dialed, this single entry is expanded to a series of digits again. Entries in working memory can thus be viewed as labels denoting some unit of information, like a digit, your mother's telephone number, or the routine quicksort. In this way an expert can cope with a situation even with the restrictions of working memory capacity.

The structures in long-term memory are the basis for solving problems in a domain and for expertise. When working with a system, people develop the best knowledge structure for performing their tasks. If they are able to understand the system as much as they need (we defined this as the **virtual machine** in section 16.2), they may develop a coherent and useful structure in long-term memory. As far as this structure can be considered a model of the system, we consider it to be the **mental model** of the system.

16.4.2 Mental Models of Information Systems

Mental models are structures in long-term memory. They consist of elements and relations between those elements. They represent relevant knowledge structures analogous to physical, organizational, and procedural structures in the world. These mental models become 'instantiated' when activated by an actual need, e.g. when one needs to make a decision related to an element of this knowledge. The activated mental model is, to a certain extent, run or executed in order to predict how the structure in the world that is represented by the mental model would behave in relation to the current situation and in reaction to the possible actions of the person. In the terminology introduced before, mental models are internal models.

When working with complex systems, where part of the relevant structure and processes of the system cannot be perceived by a human being or cannot be completely monitored, a mental model is needed to behave optimally in relation to the system. Hence, people develop mental models of such situations and systems. If the system is a computer system, there are four functions of using the system that require the activation of a mental model:

- When planning the use of the technology, users will apply their knowledge (i.e. their mental model) to find out for what part of their task the system could be used and the conditions for its use. Users will determine what they need to do beforehand, when they would like to perform actions and take decisions during the use of the system, and when they would abort execution or reconsider use.

  Suppose I want to use our library information system to search for literature on mental models of computer systems. I may decide to search by author name. First, I must find one or a few candidate authors.

- During execution of a task with a system, there is a continuous need for fine-tuning of user actions towards system events. The mental model is applied for monitoring the collaboration and for reconsidering decisions taken during the planning stage.

If the result of my search action is not satisfactory, I may decide to look up alternative author names or switch to a keyword search. If the keywords used by the system are keywords listed in the titles of publications, there is quite a chance that relevant literature is not found by a search using the keywords mental model. I may then consider other keywords as well, such as human–computer interaction.

- If the system has performed some tasks for the user and produced output, there is the need to evaluate the results, to understand when to stop, and to understand the value of the results in relation to the intended task. The mental model of the system is needed to evaluate the system's actions and output, and to translate these to the goals and needs of the user.

  Some of the literature sources found may have titles that indicate a relation between mental models and learning, while others relate mental models to personality factors. I may decide to keep only those titles that relate mental models to HCI, since the others are probably not relevant.

- Modern computer systems are frequently not working in isolation and more processes may be going on than those initiated by current use. The user has to cope with unexpected system events, and needs to interpret the system's behavior in relation to the intended task as well as to the state of the system and the network of related systems. For this interpretation, users need an adequate mental model of the system and its relation to the current task.

  I may accept a slow response to my query knowing that the answer is quite long and network traffic during office hours is heavy.

Mental models as developed by users of a system are always just models. They abstract from aspects the user considers not relevant and they have to be usable for a human information processor with his restricted resources and capacities. Consequently, we observe some general restrictions in the qualities of human mental models of computer systems. [Nor83] has shown that mental models of systems of the complexity of a computer application have the following general characteristics:

- They are incomplete and users are generally aware of the fact that they do not really know all details of the system, even if relevant. They will know, if they are experts, where details can be found.

- They can only partly be 'run', because of the nature of human knowledge representation. I may know how to express a global replacement in my text editor (i.e., I know the start and end situation) without knowing how the intended effect is obtained.

- They are unstable. They change over time, both because of users using different systems and spoiling the knowledge of the previously applied system and because of new experiences, even if the user has been considered a guru on this system for the past ten years.
- They have vague boundaries. People tend to mix characteristics of their word processor with aspects of the operating system and, hence, are prone to occasionally make fatal errors based on well-prepared decisions.
- They are parsimonious. People like to maintain models that are not too complex, and try to stick to enough basic knowledge to be able to apply the model for the majority of their tasks. If something uncommon has to be done they accept having to do some extra operations, even if they know there should be a simpler solution for those exceptions.
- They have characteristics of superstition that help people feel comfortable in situations which they know they do not really understand. An example is the experienced user who changes back to his root directory before switching off his machine or before logging out. He knows perfectly well there is no real need for this, but he prefers to behave in a nice and systematic way and hopes the machine will behave nicely and systematically in return.

Designers of user interfaces should understand the types of mental structures users tend to develop. There are techniques to acquire information about an individual user's mental models, as well as about generic mental structures of groups of users. Psychological techniques can be applied and, in the design of new types of system, it is worthwhile to apply some expert help in assessing the knowledge structures that may be needed for the system, as well as those that may be expected to be developed by users. If the knowledge needed differs from the mental models developed in actual use, there is a problem and designers should ask for expert help before the design results in an implementation that does not accord with the users' models.

16.4.3 Conceptual Models in User Interface Design

A central part of user interface design is the stepwise refined specification of the system as far as it is relevant for the user. This includes the knowledge the user needs in order to operate the system, the definition of the dialog between user and system, and the functionality that the system provides to the user. All that is specified in the design process is obviously also explicitly modeled, in order to make sure implementation will not result in a system that differs from the one intended. In cognitive ergonomics all that is modeled about the system as far as relevant to its different sets of users is called the **conceptual model** of the system [Nor83].

Formal design modeling techniques have been developed in order to communicate in design teams, to document design decisions, to be able to backtrack on specifications, and to calculate the effects of design specifications. Some techniques model the user's knowledge (so-called competence models), others focus on the interaction process (so-called process models), and others do both. Reisner's Psychological BNF [Rei81] is an example of a competence model. In this model, the set of valid user dialogs is defined using a context-free grammar. Process models may model time aspects of interaction, as in the Keystroke model [CMN83] which gives performance predictions of low-level user actions. Task Action Grammar (TAG) [PG89] is an example of a combined model. It allows the calculation of indexes for learning (the time needed to acquire knowledge) and for ease of use (mental load, or the time needed for the user's part of executing a command).

Moran was one of the first to structure the conceptual model into components, somewhat akin to the Seeheim model [Mor81]. Even though at that time command dialogs were the only type of interactive user interface available to the general public, his **Command Language Grammar** (CLG) still provides a remarkably complete view of the types of design decision to be made during user interface design. Additionally, Moran was the first to state that a conceptual model can be looked upon from three different viewpoints:

- the psychological view considers the specification as the definition of all that a user should understand and know about the new system,
- the linguistic view describes the interaction between human and system in all aspects that are relevant for both participants in the dialog, and
- the design view specifies all that is needed to decide about the system from the point of view of the user interface design.

Moran distinguishes six levels in the conceptual model, structured in three components. Each level details concepts from a higher level, from the specific point of view of the current level. The formalism that Moran proposes (the actual grammar) would nowadays be replaced by more sophisticated notations, but the architectural concepts show the relevance of analyzing design decisions from different viewpoints and at the same time investigating the relationships between these viewpoints:

a. Conceptual component. This component concerns design decisions at the level of functionality: what will the system do for the users.

   a.1 Task level. At this level we describe the task domain in relation to the system: which tasks can be delegated to the machine, which tasks have to be done by the user in relation to this (preparation, decisions in between one machine task and the next, etc.). A representation at this level concerns tasks and task-related objects as seen from the eyes of the user, not detailing anything about the system, such as 'print a letter on office stationery' or 'store a copy'.

a.2 Semantic level. Semantics in the sense of CLG concern the system's functionality in relation to the tasks that can be delegated. At this level, task delegation is specified in relation to the system. The system objects are described with their attributes and relevant states, and the operations on these objects as a result of task delegation are specified. For example, there may be an object letter with an attribute print date and an operation to store a copy in another object called printed letters with attributes list of printed letters and date of last storage operation.

In terms of the Seeheim model, this level describes the application interface.

b. Communication component. In terms of the Seeheim model, Moran's communication component describes the dialog.

b.1 Syntax level. This level describes the dialog style, such as menus, form-filling, commands, or answering questions, by specifying the lexicographical structure of the user and system actions. For example, to store a letter, the user has to indicate the letter to be stored, then the storage location, then the storage command, and, finally, an end-of-command indication.

b.2 Keystroke level. The physical actions of the user and the system are specified at this level, such as clicking the mouse buttons, pointing, typing, dragging, blinking the cursor, and issuing beeping signals.

c. Material component. At this level, Moran refers to the domain of classical ergonomics, including perceptual aspects of the interface, as well as relevant aspects of the hardware. The presentation aspect of the Seeheim model is located at the spatial layout level.

c.1 Spatial layout level. The screen design, for example, the shape, color, and size of icons and characters on the screen, and the size of buttons, is specified at this level. This level is also intended to cover sound and tactile aspects of the interface (such as tactile mouse feedback) not covered by the hardware.

c.2 Apparatus level. At this level, Moran suggests we specify the shape of buttons and the power needed for pressing them, as well as other relevant hardware aspects.

Moran's CLG provides a fairly complete specification model for the user interface or UVM. The actual grammar representation is no longer relevant, but the layers and their relations are important, and the design models discussed in the next section cover most of them: task models relate to Moran's task level, the UVM specifications include the semantic level, the communication component, and parts of the spatial layout level.

16.5 THE DESIGN OF INTERACTIVE SYSTEMS

The concept *user interface* as used in this chapter denotes the complete UVM, the user's virtual machine. Traditional user interface design mainly concerns the situation of a single user and a monolithic system. In current applications, computers are mostly part of a network, and users are collaborating, or at least communicating, with others through networks. Consequently, the UVM should include all aspects of communication between users as far as this communication is routed through the system. It should also include aspects of distributed computing and networking as far as this is relevant for the user, such as access, structural, and time aspects of remote sources of data and computing. For example, when using a Web browser, it is relevant to understand mechanisms of caching and of refreshing or reloading a page, both in terms of the content that may have changed since the previous loading operation and in terms of the time needed for operations to complete.

These newer types of application bring another dimension of complexity into view. People are collaborating in various ways mediated by information technology. Collaboration via systems requires special aspects of functionality. It requires facilities for the integration of actions originating from different users on shared objects and environments, facilities to manage and coordinate the collaboration, and communication functionality. Such systems are often denoted as **groupware**. Modern user interface design techniques cater for both the situation of the classical single user system and groupware. We expect this distinction to disappear in the near future.

There are several classes of stakeholder in system development. These include at least (see also chapter 9):

- the clients, i.e. the people or organizations that pay for the design or acquisition of systems, and

- the users, i.e. the people or groups that apply the systems as part of their daily work, often referred to as the **end users**.

Throughout the process of design, these two classes of stakeholders have to be distinguished, since they may well have different goals for the system, different (and possibly even contradictory) knowledge about the task domain, and different views on what is an optimal or acceptable system. This does not mean that in certain situations these classes will not overlap. But even if this is the case, individual persons may well turn out to have contradictory views on the system they need. In many situations there will be additional classes of stakeholders to cater for, like people who are involved in maintaining the system, and people who need traces or logs of the system to monitor cases of failure or abuse, such as lawyers.

In relation to these different classes of stakeholders, designers are in a situation of potential political stress. Clients and users may have contradictory inputs into the specification of the system. Moreover, the financial and temporal constraints on the amount of effort to be invested in designing the different aspects of the system (like specifying functionality and user interface, implementation, and testing) tend to counteract the designers' ambitions to sufficiently take care of the users' needs.

Making a distinction between classes of stakeholders does not solve the problem of user diversity. In complex systems design, we are confronted with different end users playing different roles, as well as end-user groups that, as a group, have knowledge or a view on the task domain that need not be equivalent to the (average or aggregated) knowledge and views of the individuals.

16.5.1 Design as an Activity Structure

Viewing design as a structure of interrelated activities, we need a process model. The model we use will be familiar to readers of this book: it is a cyclical process with phases devoted to analysis, specification, and evaluation. Figure 16.5 depicts this process model.

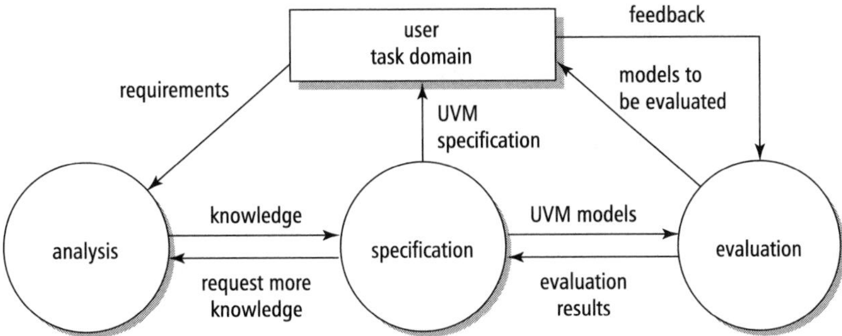

Figure 16.5 A process model for user interface design

Analysis Since the system to be developed will feature in a task situation, we start with task analysis. We further structure this activity into the development of two models, which we label task model 1 and task model 2. The first one models the current task situation. Task model 2 models the task domain of the future situation, where the system to be developed will be used, including changes in the organization of people and work procedures. The relationship between task models 1 and 2 reflects the change in the structure and organization of the task world as caused by the implementation of the system to be developed. As such, the difference is relevant both for the client and the user.

The development of task model 2 from task model 1 uses knowledge of current inadequacies and problems concerning the existing task situation, needs for change as articulated by the clients, and insight into current technological developments. Section 16.6 discusses task analysis.

Specification The specification of the system to be designed is based on task model 2. It has to be modeled in all details that are relevant to the users, including cooperation technology and user-relevant system structure and network characteristics. Differences between the specification of the new system (the user's virtual machine or UVM) and task model 2 must be considered explicitly and lead to design iteration. Specifying the UVM is elaborated in section 16.7.

Evaluation The specification of the new system incurs many design decisions that have to be considered in relation to the system's prospective use. For some design decisions, guidelines and standards might be used as checklists. In other situations, formal evaluation may be applied, using formal modeling tools that provide an indication of the complexity of use or learning effort required. For many design decisions, however, evaluation requires confronting the future user with relevant aspects of the intended system. Some kind of prototyping is a good way to confront the user with the solution proposed. A prototype allows experimentation with selected elements or aspects of the UVM. It enables imitation of (aspects of) the presentation interface, it enables the user to express himself in (fragments of) the interaction language, and it can be used to simulate aspects of the functionality, including organizational and structural characteristics of the intended task structure. We discuss some evaluation techniques in section 16.8.

Figure 16.5 is very similar to figure 9.1. This is not surprising. The design of an interactive system as discussed in this chapter is very akin to the requirements engineering activity discussed in chapter 9. The terminology is slightly different and reflects the user-centered stance taken in this chapter. For example, 'elicitation' sounds more passive than 'analysis'. 'Evaluation' entails more than 'validation'; it includes usability testing as well. Finally, we treat the user and the task domain as one entity from which requirements are elicited. In the approach advocated here, the user is observed *within* the task domain.

16.5.2 Design as Multi-Disciplinary Collaboration

The main problem with the design activities discussed in the previous section is that different methods may provide conflicting viewpoints and goals. A psychological focus on individual users and their capacities tends to lead to Taylorism, neglecting the reality of a multitude of goals and methods in any task domain. On the other hand, sociological and ethnographical approaches towards groupware design tend to omit analysis of individual knowledge and needs. Still, both extremes provide unique contributions.

In order to design for people, we have to take into account both sides of the coin: the individual users and clients of the system, and the structure and organization of the group for which the system is intended. We need to know the individuals' knowledge and views on the task, on applying the technology, and the relation between using technology and task-relevant user characteristics (expertise, knowledge, and skills). With respect to the group, we need to know its structure and dynamics, the phenomenon of 'group knowledge' and work practice and culture. These aspects are needed in order to acquire insight into both existing and projected task situations where (new) cooperation technology is introduced. Both types of insight are also needed in relation to design decisions, for functionality and for the user interface. Consequently, in prototyping and field-testing we need insight in acceptance and use of individuals, and in the effect of the new design on group processes and complex task dynamics.

For example, in a traditional bank setting, the client and the bank employee are on different sides of a counter. The bank employee is probably using a computer, but the client cannot see the screen, and does not know what the clerk is doing. In a service-oriented bank setting, the clerk and client may be looking at the screen *together*. They are together searching for a solution to the client's question. This overturns the existing culture of the bank and an ethnographer may be asked to observe what this new set up brings about.

The general framework for our approach to user interface design is depicted in figure 16.6. It is a refinement of figure 16.5, emphasizing the specialties involved in carrying out different activities. Task model 1 is based on knowledge of single users (psychological variables, task-related variables, knowledge and skills) and on complex phenomena in the task situation (roles, official and actual procedures, variation in strategies, and variation in the application of procedures). The integration of this insight in a model often does not provide a single (or a single best) decomposition of tasks and a unique structure of relationships between people, activities, and environments. The model often shows alternative ways to perform a certain task, role-specific and situation-specific methods and procedures, and a variety of alternative assignments of subtasks to people. For example, the joint problem-solving approach to the bank counter as sketched above cannot be applied to the drive-in counter of

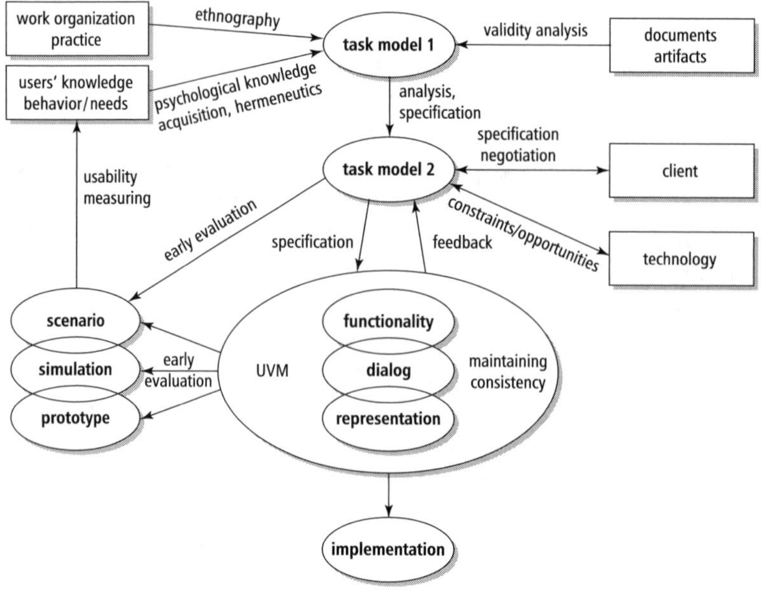

Figure 16.6 Structure of design team activities

the bank. The drive-in counter requires a different approach and a different user interface.

From this, and because of client requirements, compromises often have to be made in defining task model 2, the new task situation for which the technology has to be designed. This process includes the interpretation of problems in the current task situation, negotiation with the client regarding his conditions and the resources available for design (including both financial impacts and time constraints). Ultimately, decisions have to be made about complex aspects, such as re-arranging the balance of power and the possibilities for users in various roles to exercise control.

Again, when detailed design decisions are being considered, early evaluation needs to include analytical methods (formal evaluation and cognitive walkthrough techniques) in combination with usability testing where users in different roles are studied both in the sense of traditional individual measures and in the sense of ethnographic interaction analysis.

16.6 TASK ANALYSIS

Analyzing a complex system means analyzing the world in which the system functions, or the *context of use*, which comprises (according to standards like [ISO96]):

- the users;
- the tasks;
- the equipment (hardware, software, and materials);
- the social environment;
- the physical environment.

If we design systems for the context of use, we must take these different aspects of the task world into consideration. In traditional literature on task analysis from the HCI mainstream, the focus is mostly on users, tasks, and software. Design approaches for groupware and Computer Supported Collaborative Work (CSCW), on the other hand, often focus on analyzing the world first of all from the point of view of the (physical and social) environment. Recent approaches to task modeling include some aspects that belong to both categories, but it still looks like one has to, by and large, opt for one view or the other. Section 16.6.1 presents task analysis approaches from the classical HCI tradition and distinguishes different phases in task analysis. Section 16.6.2 presents an ethnographic point of view, as frequently applied to the design of CSCW systems, where phases in the analysis process are hardly considered.

[Jor96], though originally working from an ethnographic approach and focusing on groupware applications, provides a view on analyzing knowledge of the task world that is broad enough to cover most of the context of use as now defined by the above-mentioned ISO standard. We illustrate Jordan's view in section 16.6.3. The Groupware Task Analysis (GTA) framework of modeling task knowledge combines approaches from both HCI and CSCW design. GTA is described in section 16.6.4.

16.6.1 Task Analysis in HCI Design

Classical HCI features a variety of notions regarding task analysis. Task analysis can mean different activities:

- analyzing a current task situation,
- envisioning a task situation for which information technology is to be designed, or
- specifying the semantics of the information technology to be designed.

Many HCI task analysis methods combine more than one of these activities and relate them to actual design stages. Others do not bother about the distinction. For example, Goals, Operators, Methods, Selection rules (GOMS, see [CMN83]) can be applied for any or a combination of the above activities.

In many cases the design of a new system is triggered by an existing task situation. Either the current way of performing tasks is not considered optimal, or the availability of new technology is expected to allow an improvement over current methods. A systematic analysis of the current situation may help formulate requirements and allow later evaluation of the design. In all cases where a current version of the task situation exists, it pays off to model this. Task models of this type pretend to describe the situation as it can be found in real life, by asking or observing people who know the situation (see [Joh89]). Task model 1 is often considered to be generic, indicating the belief that different expert users have at their disposal basically the same task knowledge.

Many design methods in HCI that start with task modeling are structured in a number of phases. After describing a current situation (in task model 1), the method requires a re-design of the task structure in order to include technological solutions for problems and technological answers to requirements. [JJWS88] provides an example of a systematic approach where a second task model is explicitly defined in the course of design decisions. Task model 2 is in general formulated and structured in the same way as task model 1. However, it is not considered a *descriptive* model of users' knowledge, though in some cases it may be applied as a *prescriptive* model of the knowledge an expert user of the new technology should possess.

A third type of modeling activity focuses on the technology to be designed. This may be considered part of task model 2. However, some HCI approaches distinguish specific design activities which focus on the technology (e.g. see [Tau90]). This part of the design activity is focused on a detailed description of the system as far as it is of direct relevance to the end user, i.e. the UVM. We separate the design of the UVM from the design of the new task situation as a whole, mainly because the UVM models the detailed solution in terms of technology, whereas task model 2 focuses on the task structure and work organization. In actual design, iteration is needed between the specification of these two models. This should be an explicit activity, making the implications of each obvious in its consequences for the other. Specifying the UVM is treated in more detail in section 16.7.

HCI task models represent a restricted point of view. All HCI task modeling is rather narrowly focused, mainly considering individual people's tasks. Most HCI approaches are based on cognitive psychology. [Joh89] refers to knowledge structures in long-term memory. [Tau90] refers to 'knowledge of competent users'. HCI approaches focus on the knowledge of individuals who are knowledgeable or expert in the task domain, whether this domain already exists (task model 1) or still has to be re-structured by introducing new technology (task model 2 and the UVM).

As a consequence of their origin, HCI task models seldom provide an insight into complex organizational aspects, situational conditions for task performance, or complex relationships between tasks of individuals with different roles. Business processes and business goals (such as the service focus of a modern bank counter, which may be found in a business reengineering project) are seldom part of the knowledge of individual workers and, consequently, are seldom related to the goals and processes found in HCI task modeling.

16.6.2 Analysis Approaches for Collaborative Work

CSCW work stresses the importance of situational aspects, group phenomena and organizational structure and procedures [Sch96] and [Sha96a]. Shapiro even goes so far as to state that HCI has failed in the case of task analysis for cooperative work situations, since generic individual knowledge of the total complex task domain does not exist. The CSCW literature strongly advocates ethnographic methods.

Ethnographers study a task domain (or community of practice) by becoming a participant observer, if possible with the status of an apprentice. The ethnographer observes the world 'through the eyes of the aboriginal' and at the same time is aware of his status as an outside observer whose final goal is to understand and describe for a certain purpose and a certain audience (in the case of CSCW, a design project). Ethnographers start their observation purposely without a conceptual framework regarding characteristics of task knowledge, but, instead, may choose to focus on activities, environments, people, or objects. The choice of focus is itself based on prior ethnographic observations, which illustrates the bootstrapping character of knowledge elicitation in ethno-methodology. Methods of data collection nowadays start with video recordings of relevant phenomena (the relevance of which, again, can only be inferred from prior observation) followed by systematic transaction analysis, where inter-observer agreement serves to improve the reliability of interpretation. Knowledge of individual workers in the task domain may be collected as far as it seems to be relevant, but it is in no sense a priori considered the main source and is never considered indicative of generic task knowledge.

The ethnographic approach is unique in its attention to all relevant phenomena in the task domain that can not be verbalized explicitly by (all) experts (see [Nar95]). The approach attends to knowledge and intentions that are specific for some actors only, to conflicting goals, to cultural aspects that are not perceived by the actors in the culture, to temporal changes in beliefs, to situational factors that are triggers or conditions for strategies, and to non-physical objects like messages, stories, signatures and symbols, of which the actors may not be aware while interacting.

Ethno-methodology covers the methods of collecting information that might serve as a basis for developing task model 1 (and no more than this since ethnomethodology only covers information on the current state of a task domain). However, the methodology for the collection of data and its structuring into a complete task domain description is often rather special and difficult to follow in detail. The general impression is that CSCW design methods skip the explicit construction of task models 1 and 2 and, after collecting sufficient information on the community of practice, immediately embark on specifying the UVM, based on deep knowledge of the current task situation that is not formalized. This may cause two types of problem. Firstly, the relationship between specifications for design and analysis of the current task world might depend more on intuition than on systematic design decisions. Secondly, skipping the development of task model 2 may lead to conservatism with respect to organizational and structural aspects of the work for which a system is to be (re)designed.

16.6.3 Sources of Knowledge and Collection Methods

Collecting task knowledge for analyzing the current situation of a complex system has to start by identifying the relevant knowledge sources. In this respect, we refer to a framework derived from [Jor96], see figure 16.7. The two dimensions of this framework denote where the knowledge resides and how it can be communicated. For example, A stands for the explicit knowledge of an individual, while D stands for the implicit knowledge of a group.

		Sources of knowledge	
		individual	group
Levels of communicability	explicit	A	C
	implicit	B	D

Figure 16.7 Dimensions of knowledge for complex task domains

Jordan's framework has been applied in actual design processes for large industrial and government interactive systems. We may expand the two factors distinguished from dichotomies to continuous dimensions to obtain a two-dimensional framework for analyzing the relevant sources of knowledge in the context of use. This framework provides a map of knowledge sources that helps us to identify the different techniques that we might need in order to collect information and structure this information into a model of the task world.

To gather task knowledge in cell A, psychological methods may be used: interviews, questionnaires, think-aloud protocols, and (single-person oriented) observations. For knowledge indicated in cell B, observations of task behavior must be complemented by hermeneutic methods to interpret mental representations (see [vdV90]). For the knowledge referred to in cell C, the obvious methods concern the study of artifacts like documents and archives. In fact all these methods are to be found in classical HCI task analysis approaches and, for that matter, the requirements elicitation techniques discussed in chapter 9.

The knowledge indicated in cell D is unique in that it requires ethnographic methods like interaction analysis. Moreover, this knowledge may be in conflict with what can be learned from the other sources. First of all, explicit individual knowledge often turns out to be abstract with respect to observable behavior, and turns out to ignore the situation in which task behavior is exhibited. Secondly, explicit group knowledge such as expressed in official rules and time schedules is often in conflict with actual group behavior, and for good reasons. Official procedures do not always work in practice and the literal application of them is sometimes used as a political weapon in labor conflicts, or as a legal alternative to a strike. In all cases of discrepancy between sources of task knowledge, ethnographic methods will reveal unique and relevant additional information that has to be explicitly represented in task model 1.

The allocation of methods to knowledge sources should not be taken too strictly. The knowledge sources often cannot be located completely in single cells of Jordan's conceptual map. The main conclusion is that we need different methods in a complementary sense, as we need information from different knowledge sources.

16.6.4 An Integrated Approach to Task Analysis: GTA

Groupware Task Analysis (GTA) is an attempt to integrate the merits from the most important classical HCI approaches with the ethnographic methods applied for CSCW (see [vdVLB96]). GTA contains a collection of concepts and their relations (a conceptual framework) that allows analysis and representation of all relevant notions regarding human work and task situations as dealt with in the different theories.

The framework is intended to structure task models 1 and 2, and, hence, to guide the choice of techniques for information collection in the case of task model 1. Obviously, for task model 2 design decisions have to be made, based on problems and conflicts that are present in task model 1 and the requirement specification.

Task models for complex situations are composed of different aspects. Each describes the task world from a different viewpoint and each relates to the others. The three viewpoints are:

- **Agents** Agents often indicate people, either individually or in groups. Agents are considered in relation to the task world. Hence, we make a distinction between agents as actors and the roles they play. Moreover, we need the concept of organization of agents. Actors have to be described with relevant characteristics (e.g. for human actors, the language they speak, the amount of typing skill, or their experience with MS-Windows). Roles indicate classes of actors to whom certain subsets of tasks are allocated. By definition roles are generic for the task world. More than one actor may perform the same role, and a single actor may have several roles at the same time. Organization refers to the relation between actors and roles in respect to task allocation. Delegating and mandating responsibilities from one role to another is part of the organization.

  For example, an office may have agents such as 'a secretary', 'the typing pool', and 'the answering machine'. A possible role is 'answer a telephone call'. Sometimes it is not relevant to know which agent performs a certain role: it is not important who answers a telephone call, as long as it is answered.

- **Work** We consider both the structural and the dynamic aspects of work, so we take task as the basic concept. A task has a goal as an attribute. We make a distinction between tasks and actions. Tasks can be identified at various levels of complexity. The unit level of tasks needs special attention. We need to make a distinction between

  - the lowest task level that people want to consider in referring to their work, the **unit task**, and
  - the unit level of task delegation that is defined by the tool that is used in performing work, for example a single command in command-driven computer applications. The latter type of task we call a **basic task** (after [Tau90]).

  Unit tasks are often role-related. Unit tasks and basic tasks may be decomposed further into (user) actions and (system) events, but these cannot really be understood without a frame of reference created by the corresponding task, i.e. actions derive their meaning from the task. For instance, hitting a return key has a different meaning depending on whether it ends a command or confirms the specification of a numerical input value.

  The task structure is often at least partially hierarchical. On the other hand, performance on certain tasks may influence the procedures for other tasks (possibly with other roles involved). For example, the secretariat has to deliver the mail on time and may have to interrupt other tasks to be able to do so. Therefore we also need to understand task flow and data flow over time as well as the relationship between several concurrent flows.

- **Situation** Analyzing a task world from the viewpoint of the situation means detecting and describing the environment (physical, conceptual, and social) and the objects in the environment. Each thing that is relevant to the work in a certain situation is an object in the sense of task analysis. Objects may be physical things, or conceptual (non-material) things like messages, gestures, passwords, stories, or signatures. The task environment is the current situation for the performance of a certain task. It includes actors with roles as well as conditions for task performance The history of past relevant events in the task situation is part of the actual environment if this features in conditions for task execution.

16.7 SPECIFICATION OF THE USER INTERFACE DETAILS

Specifying details of the user interface means elaborating all aspects of the machine that are relevant for the user, hence the concept of a user virtual machine (UVM). When there are several types of user for the system we need to specify several separate UVMs, since each user role is defined by another subset of tasks. As suggested by the Seeheim model, we need to consider each of the representation, the dialog, and the application, all of these in relation to the type of user (the role) on which we are focusing. The application proper, i.e. the functionality of the system, is the first aspect. It defines what the user can do with the system (cf. Moran's semantic level). Techniques for specifying the functionality are dealt with in chapter 9.

The other activities in relation to the specification of the UVM concern the interaction between user and system, with its two aspects:

- the dialog (corresponding to the dialog layer in the Seeheim model, and the syntax and keystroke level in Moran's CLG), and

- the presentation interface (corresponding to the presentation layer in the Seeheim model, and Moran's spatial layout level).

The three components of the UVM lead to three specifications that are strongly related. The dialog and the presentation are two sides of the coin of user–system interaction, and both express, each in its own way, the semantics and functionality of the system.

16.7.1 Dialog

The dialog in modern user interfaces is frequently a combination of several dialog styles, such as command language, menu choice, answering of questions generated by the interface, fill-in-the-blanks forms, and direct manipulation of interface objects. For an overview of the various styles and options for using them in different situations depending on task and user characteristic, see [May92] and [Shn98]. Dialog styles may often be seen as implementations of different dialog metaphors:

- In a command language or natural language, the user and the interface 'speak' to each other. Legal dialogs obey a certain grammar. The user feels in control as long as he understands what is possible and remembers the right terminology. The user does not perform a task directly but is rather obliged to persuade the system to perform it.

- When the user has to choose from a menu, fill in labeled slots in a form on the screen, or answer questions from the interface, the interface provides a structure where the user is prompted to react by selecting an option. The user does not have to remember too many options. On the other hand, he may not feel totally in control of the dialog.

- In a direct manipulation type interface, the user moves in a 'space' and by acting in the space he shows the computer what he needs, whether the space is a two-dimensional screen where he may drag and drop icons, a 3-D virtual reality environment, or something in between ('augmented reality interfaces'). The direct manipulation style provides the user with a sense of direct engagement. It feels as if the user is in direct contact with the objects from the task domain.

It makes sense to relate the metaphor to the actual task domain. For example, a space can be specified as a desktop, or a virtual library, depending on whether the task domain concerns the management of documents or a search for objects.

In specifying the dialog further, the syntax of the interaction has to be specified in detail, including the sequence of user actions. For example, in the Macintosh interface, the user has to indicate the object first and then the operation. The reverse is true in the UNIX command language. Also, the lexicon has to be specified. This includes deciding on the verbal labels for objects and operations, the iconic representations, the gestures (such as a cross or a series of connected up and down strokes to indicate rubbing out on a drawing pad), and sounds. The lexicon includes both the symbols that the user can use in communicating with the machine and the symbols the machine will output to the user.

There are various modeling techniques for specifying the dialog. A promising dialog specification technique is User Action Notation (UAN, see [HH93]) which combines the specification of functionality with dialog details. UAN is relatively easy to use, especially since the actual formalism may to a large extent be tailored to the designer's needs without losing the benefits of a formal model. UAN provides a representation of the specification of the UVM with separate columns to specify user actions, interface actions, interface states, and connections to underlying system events. Each of these columns is filled in with the amount of detail the designer needs at a certain moment. Later on, any item may be refined. For example, the designer may specify a user action enter pincode and later on specify a detailed interaction enter pincode where he elaborates details of inputting each digit, erasing a wrong keystroke, and what the interface should show on the screen at each point in time.

16.7.2 Representation

This aspect of the UVM contains the details of the interface that determine the perceptible aspects. The lexicon indicated in the previous section includes all interface elements. Their representation concerns their shape, color, contrast, pitch, loudness, size, etc. Representation also concerns all aspects of screen design, like the size of windows, the speed of movement displayed, and the timbre of generated sounds. The representation aspect may need the assistance of artists or at least specialists who understand the laws of graphical representation, sound representation, and animation.

This part of design is the one for which no general formal representation models have been developed. Sketches, video clips, and verbal descriptions of what one intends to have represented are commonly used, and frequent communication between the designer and the implementor is needed. Artists may have very useful ideas but may propose very convincing solutions that could easily change the essence of the intended specification.

16.8 EVALUATION

Evaluation is needed whenever decisions are made in the course of the design process. This will be the case during both analysis and specification. Evaluating analysis decisions is mostly related to the phase where the future task world is envisioned. During the process of developing detail specifications of the UVM, many decisions have to be made that relate technical details to aspects of usability.

Evaluation does not solve problems, it merely points to them. A valid diagnosis often requires several complementary techniques as well as expertise. Evaluation is done by presenting design decisions such that questions can be answered. Sometimes the questions may be answered in an unbiased way by the designer himself (e.g. if indexes can be calculated in a straightforward way), but in many cases there is a need to include others in the evaluation process, either specialists in design or in humanities, or stakeholders in the design.

16.8.1 Evaluation of Analysis Decisions

During the early development of task model 2 there is not enough detail to develop a prototype. However, scenarios can be developed regarding the future task world, and it can be modeled with the help of formalisms. Both scenarios and formalisms offer opportunities to apply evaluation techniques:

- **Scenario-based evaluation** In general, scenarios will be developed concerning those parts of task model 2 that concern a change in comparison to the current situation. In this phase of the design it is worthwhile to represent not only the new use of technology, but also the situational aspects of this use and the organizational consequences. Developing a scenario means describing a process of using the intended system in an actual situation and organizational setting. The scenario may be described verbally, but a video representation is often used because that may show more relevant situational details, even though the technology may be represented in a way that reveals no details (for example, a laptop may be represented by a sheet of paper if the details of the screens have not yet been decided). In order to evaluate a scenario, a 'claims analysis' can be performed. Apart from the designer and the constructor of the scenario, (future) users, representatives of the client, and other relevant stakeholders may participate in the claims analysis. It often makes sense to choose not only representatives who have a positive attitude towards the intended change but also people who are afraid of the future developments or who have a pronounced opinion on the possible negative effects of future implementation. For each aspect of the task delegation to the new system that is an explicit change from the current system, the participants of the claims analysis try to identify

  - to what extent the change is providing a solution in the intended direction, and
  - what the positive and negative side effects of the change are.

  Another way to evaluate a scenario is to ask a group of stakeholders to act out the written scenario and videotape the performance, possibly collecting several takes where people change roles, and where the non-believers in particular get a chance to show where things may go wrong. Analyses of this type will show not only the possible success of the envisioned changes but also the potential problems. The latter in particular are the base for reconsidering decisions and for developing measures to counteract unwanted side-effects. The scenarios that are acted by stakeholders, in particular, often reveal possible changes in the design that may provide a breakthrough.

- **Formal evaluation techniques** Hierarchical Task Analysis (HTA) [KA92] describes the task domain as a hierarchical structure of tasks and subtasks with a complete representation of the procedural structures of the decomposition. Such a formalism allows specific questions to be answered. HTA formal evaluation may consider the length of a sequence of subtasks, given the relevant conditions. The same type of formalism allows an evaluation of possible modular procedures (similar subtrees that occur in different places and the aspects of consistency between their execution), which is indicative of the amount of learning involved for understanding the new task domain.

16.8.2 Evaluation of UVM Specifications

As soon as details of the UVM have been specified, other representations may be used for evaluation, even though it may still be worthwhile to analyze scenarios. At this stage in the design, scenarios are often elaborated and executed with the help of mock-up representations or simulations of the intended system, especially if hardware aspects in relation to the physical work conditions are expected to matter. The simulations concern the size, weight, and perceptible aspects of the intended UVM, even if the interactive aspects have not yet been specified. Many evaluation techniques from classical ergonomics may be applied as well [CC95].

Formal evaluation will certainly play an important role for the UVM. Many formalisms have been developed with certain usability aspects explicitly in mind. For example, TAG allows us to measure ease of learning and use by indexing the complexity of rules and the number of features to be considered during each command to the machine; UAN representations allow systematic reasoning about dialog specification details.

Detail specification of the UVM permits other evaluation techniques as well, in particular **heuristic evaluation** and **cognitive walkthrough**. In both cases it is useful to employ experts in user interface design who have not been part of the team that developed the specification. Experienced designers know the criteria applied in these techniques and will have considered them during their decisions. Only somebody for whom the design is new can have an unbiased view concerning these criteria. A last type of evaluation technique, **user testing and observation**, requires future users to be involved and a working prototype. Obviously, a prototype may also be the basis for heuristic evaluation and cognitive walkthrough.

Heuristic evaluation is based on some definition of usability. Usability is a complex of aspects like ease of use, ease of learning, ease of recall after a period of not using a system (known as re-learnability), affection, help, likeability, etc. Approaches toward heuristic evaluation provide checklists of characteristics of the user interface or UVM that describe the different usability aspects. Such a checklist may also be applied as a guideline for making design decisions. Checklists exist in different forms, and often include a technique to calculate usability indexes. Each item may be checked when applicable and, additionally, each item that is diagnosed as non-optimal may give rise to design changes. Example items from such a checklist are ([Shn98] and [Nie93]):

- **Use a simple and natural dialog** Humans can only pay attention to a few things at a time. Therefore, dialogs should not contain information that is irrelevant or rarely needed. Information should appear in a logical and natural order to ease comprehension.

- **Speak the user's language** A dialog is easier to understand if it uses concepts and phrases that are familiar to the user. The dialog should not be expressed in computer-oriented terms, but in terms from the task domain.

- **Minimize memory load** The user should not have to remember information from one part of the dialog to another. Long command sequences, menus with a large number of entries, and uncertainty about 'where we are' hamper interaction. There must be easy ways to find out what to do next, how to retrace steps, and get instructions for use.

- **Be consistent** Users should not have to wonder whether different words or actions mean the same thing. Metaphors should be chosen carefully, so as not to confuse the user.

- **Provide feedback** The system should keep the user informed of what is going on. If certain processes take a while, the user should not be left in the dark. A moving gadget informs the user that the system is doing something, a percentage-done indicator informs him about the progress towards the goal.

- **Provide clearly-marked exits** Users make mistakes, activate the wrong function, follow the wrong thread. There must be an easy way to leave such an unwanted state.

- **Provide shortcuts** Novice users may be presented with an extensive question–answer dialog. It gives them a safe feeling and helps them to learn the system. Experts are hindered by a tedious step-by-step dialog and the system should provide shortcuts to accommodate them.

- **Give good error messages** Error messages should be explained in plain language. They should not refer to the internals of the system. Error messages should precisely state the problem and, if possible, suggest a solution.

Items from such a checklist should be used with care, though. Design involves trade-offs between conflicting goals. Consider for example the two function-key layouts in figure 16.8. Interface designers might prefer the star as the best design. It is a symmetric design, consistent with directional indicators on a compass. Yet, studies have shown that the inverted 'T' is the most useful configuration. With the index finger on the cursor-left key and the ring finger on the cursor-right key, the middle finger can efficiently cover the cursor-up and cursor-down keys. Designers of computer games seem to have known this for quite a while.

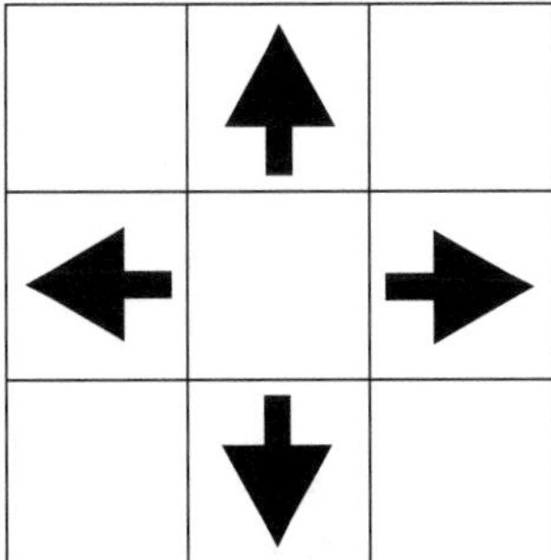

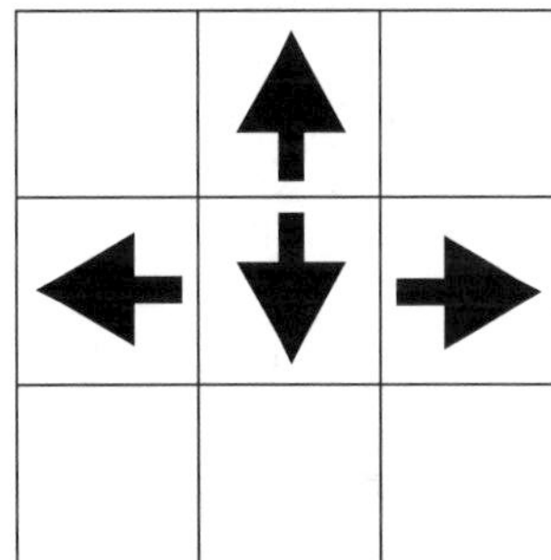

Figure 16.8 Two possible cursor key arrangements

Cognitive walkthroughs focus solely on the cognitive aspects of the dialog. The technique can be applied early in the specification phase and it helps to detect failures that would otherwise make the system incomprehensible for users. Like heuristic evaluation, it requires only a small number of expert colleagues who are confronted with the specification of the dialog and the content of the representation. Screen design need not have finished yet, but the content of the screen must be known. The technique requires a specification of scenarios of normal, faultless dialog examples. A scenario might for example read as follows: 'in checking in you have to put your credit card in the slot; the machine will ask you to enter your pin code; you type ... '. Based on a specification of this type, the start state is described to the evaluator, along with all information on the task as the user would know it, and the background of the user (education and systems experience). The evaluator is asked to answer a small set of questions about the next move. After these have been answered, the intended move is described with the resulting state of the interface, after which the evaluator is again asked the same set of questions.

An example of such a set of questions is:

- what should the user do now?

- based on what knowledge or information would the user do this?

- what would the user expect to be the next step of the system?

Techniques like this quickly expose any invalid expectations of user knowledge and understanding and any lack of relevant information at the interface. Additionally, they show inconsistencies in the interface information as well as inconsistencies in dialog conventions.

16.8.3 Evaluation of Prototypes

The proof of the pudding is in the eating. An evaluation should, at some point, be carried out with real users. As soon as a mock-up or simulation is available, users can be asked to perform tasks. We are then asking users to 'play a scenario' even if we do not mention this explicitly. As soon as details of the dialog have been established, a more interactive type of testing is possible.

Evaluation by the user is often based on a prototype implementation of the system. In early phases of detail design the prototype will often not represent the total UVM. A single aspect of the task to be delegated, one instance of the dialog and representation with hardly any real functionality available, may be enough to detect problems early on. Several types of user testing may be done. Users may be provided with tasks or allowed to explore. Observations during the interaction, complemented with subsequent discussions with the user, may reveal problems and misunderstandings. In addition, user performance may be measured, such as the time to complete a task or the frequency of errors. Users may be asked for their subjective understanding of the system, and standardized measurement techniques are commercially available, focusing on subjective learnability, ease of use, and mental load.

[ISO96] defines usability in terms of efficiency, effectiveness and satisfaction. Usability evaluation of prototypes (and systems) is usually based on more specific

ISO 9241	Schneiderman	Nielsen
Efficiency	Speed of performance	Efficiency
	Time to learn	Learnability
Effectiveness	Retention over time	Memorability
	Rate of errors by users	Errors/Safety
Satisfaction	Subjective satisfaction	Satisfaction

Figure 16.9 Usability characteristics according to ISO 9241, [Shn98] and [Nie93]

definitions of usability characteristics, such as those defined in [Shn98] and [Nie93]. Figure 16.9 gives an overview of these usability characteristics. They have an almost one-to-one correspondence with the user interface quality factors as listed in the introduction to this chapter. For each of the usability characteristics, a number of (indirect) metrics exist. These metrics are gathered by observing users at work and by asking subjective questions.

16.9 SUMMARY

The user interface of a system is important. About half of the code of an interactive system is devoted to the user interface. Consequently, about half of the time and effort is spent on that interface as well. The quality of the user interface is a critical success factor. Good user interfaces increase the efficiency and productivity of their users, reduce errors and training time, and improve user acceptance.

In a technical sense, the user interface of a system often consists of two components or layers:

- a presentation component that handles the perceptible aspects of the interface, including screen design and keyboard layout;
- a dialog component that handles the syntax of the interaction, including metacommunication such as help functions and error messages.

As a result of this limited view of what a user interface is, it is often designed rather independently of the system's functionality. The design of the user interface is then seen as a separate activity, not in the mainstream requirements engineering–design–implementation–testing phases. Chances are then that it does not get the attention it deserves.

In this chapter we take a different stance. In the approach we sketch, the design of the interface and the design of the functionality go hand in hand. A provocative heading could have been 'The user interface *is* the system'. There are two main reasons for taking this broader view of what a user interface is:

- The system, and hence its interface, should help the user perform certain tasks. The user interface should therefore reflect the structure of the task domain. The design of tasks and the design of the corresponding user interface influence each other and should be part of the same cyclical process. Like quality, the user interface is not a supplement.
- The dialog and representation alone do not provide sufficient information to the user. In order to be able to work with a system, the user sometimes needs to know 'what is going on behind the screen'.

When thinking about user interface design, it is important to make a distinction between the user's mental model, the user virtual machine, and the conceptual model.

The mental model is a model in human memory. It is the user's model of the system he uses. It is based on education, knowledge of other systems, knowledge of the application domain, general knowledge about the world, etc. The mental model is used during interaction with the system, to plan actions and interpret system reactions. The mental model is often incomplete and inconsistent.

The user virtual machine (UVM) includes everything the user should know about the system in order to use it. It includes aspects ranging from the physical outlook of the computer and connected devices to the style of interaction and the form and content of the information exchange.

The conceptual model is the explicit model of the system created by designers and teachers. It is a consistent and complete representation of the system as far as relevant for the users. The conceptual model shows itself in the interface. If there is only one class of users, the user virtual machine and the conceptual model are the same. If there is more than one class of users (such as ATM clients, ATM maintainers, and lawyers), there is one UVM for each class, and the conceptual model is the union of those UVMs.

The central issue in human–computer interaction is to attune the user's mental model and the conceptual model as closely as possible. When this is achieved, the system becomes easier to learn and easier to use. When the models conflict, the user gets confused and starts making errors. Good design starts with the derivation of a conceptual model from an analysis of users and their tasks. This conceptual model is then built into the system (the UVM) in such a way that it induces adequate mental models in the users.

The design of a user interface involves different disciplines. Psychologists know how humans perceive, learn, remember, think and feel, how people work together, and how the work situation affects work. Cognitive psychology, anthropology and ethnography provide techniques for collecting information on how people work. Artists know how to design attractive things that function effectively. Cognitive ergonomics is concerned with the characteristics of human information processing in interaction with information systems. Design teams for interactive systems may thus contain quite a variety of expertise alongside software engineering.

16.10 FURTHER READING

There is a growing collection of books on user interface design. [NL95] and [DFAB98] cover most aspects of design, and are, at the same time introductory, i.e. they do not require too much background on the subject. [MC96] considers the design process from the point of view of management and provides techniques to monitor the design space and design decisions.

The classical HCI approaches to task analysis are best exemplified in [JJ91]. Additional insight into methods of task knowledge elicitation may be found in [Seb88]. General task analysis representation techniques are discussed in detail in [KA92]. [JH95] gives a detailed account of ethnographic methods and techniques from the background of CSCW and groupware design.

For an overview of modeling techniques and examples see [HvdVvV91]. Task Action Grammar (TAG) is discussed in [PG89], User Action Notation (UAN) in [HH93] and Groupware Task Analysis (GTA) in [vdVLB96].

A classical collection of user interface guidelines can be found in [SM86]. Two volumes that consider dialog styles in detail are [Shn98] and [May92]. A view on details of representation and dialog design from an artistic point of view is presented in [Lau93]. Representation aspects, as well as the hardware aspects, are discussed in detail in [CC95].

[NM94], [JTWM96] and [Lin94] provide collections of evaluation techniques for various stages in design. [Car95] discusses scenario evaluation techniques, as well as the application of scenarios to other design phases.

Exercises

1. Define the following terms: mental model, conceptual model, and user virtual machine.

2. Discuss the differences between the Seeheim model and MVC (Model–View–Controller).

3. Describe the role of cognitive ergonomics in user interface design.

4. Sketch a model of human information processing.

5. What is the difference between working memory and long-term memory?

6. In which ways is the user's mental model activated while using a computer system?

7. Describe the constituents of Command Language Grammar (CLG).

8. Discuss the differences between single-user systems and groupware with respect to task analysis.

9. Discuss the following user interface evaluation methods:

  - scenario-based evaluation;
  - heuristic evaluation;
  - cognitive walkthrough.

10. ♡ Study the desktop metaphor as it is commonly used in user interfaces for PCs and workstations. Can you spot places where the metaphor breaks down or may even lead you astray?

11. ♡ Try to answer the following questions from the manual of your favorite word processor:

    - how do I swap two paragraphs?
    - how do I include the text of some other document at a given position?
    - how do I let the page numbering start at 0 rather than 1?
    - how do I align a picture at the top or bottom of the page?

    Assess whether the user documentation is organized by the functionality offered or whether it addresses typical tasks faced by its users.

12. ♠ Discuss the requirements for online help facilities for a word processor.

13. ♡ Augment the waterfall model such that user interface issues are dealt with at appropriate phases.

14. ♠ Discuss the pros and cons of the following approaches to user interface development:

    - discussing manually constructed usage scenarios with prospective users;
    - prototyping screen displays and iteratively enhancing them;
    - developing the user interface after the functional parts of the system are completed and accepted by the users;
    - formally describing and analyzing the user interface prior to or concurrent with system design.

17 Software Reusability

LEARNING OBJECTIVES

- To appreciate various dimensions along which approaches to reuse may be classified
- To be aware of a number of composition-based and generation-based reuse techniques
- To see how reuse can be incorporated into the software life cycle
- To recognize the relation between reuse and various other software engineering concepts and techniques
- To understand the major factors that impede successful reuse

> *Meanwhile Daedalus, tired of Crete and of his long absence from home, was filled with longing for his own country, but he was shut in by the sea. Then he said: 'The king may block my way by land or across the ocean, but the sky, surely, is open, and that is how we shall go. Minos may possess all the rest, but he does not possess the air.' With these words, he set his mind to sciences never explored before, and altered the laws of nature. He laid down a row of feathers, beginning with tiny ones, and gradually increasing their length, so that the edge seemed to slope upwards. In the same way, the pipe which shepherds used to play is built up from reeds, each slightly longer than the last. Then he fastened the feathers together in the middle with thread, and at the bottom with wax; when he had arranged them in this way, he bent them round into a gentle curve, to look like real birds' wings.*
> Ovid: Metamorphoses, VIII, 183–194.

Daedalus deserves a place in the mythology of software engineering. In King Minos' days, software did not exist; and yet the problems and notions which we still find in today's software engineering existed. One example is the construction of complex systems. Daedalus certainly has a track record in that field. He successfully managed a project that can stand a comparison with today's software development projects: the construction of the Labyrinth at Knossos.

After a while, Daedalus wanted to leave Crete, as narrated above in Ovid's words. King Minos, however, did not want to let him go. We know how the story continues: Daedalus flies with his son Icarus from Crete. Despite his father's warnings, Icarus flies higher and higher. He gets too close to the sun and the wax on his wings melts. Icarus falls into the sea and drowns. Daedalus safely reaches the mainland of Italy.

Daedalus' construction is interesting from the point of view of reuse. The fact that it concerns hardware rather than software is not important here. What concerns us in the present framework, is the application of certain principles in the construction:

- **reuse of components**: Daedalus used real feathers;
- **reuse of design**: he imitated real wings;
- **glue to connect the various components**: at that time, people used wax to glue things together. The quality of the glue has a great impact on the reliability of the end product.

Through a justified and determined application of these principles, a successful and ambitious project (Daedalus' flight to Italy) was realized. An effort to storm heaven with an insufficient technology turned into a disaster (Icarus' fall into the sea).

We make a small jump in history, to the end of the 1970s. The software crisis has been rampant for many years. The demand for new applications far surpasses the ability of the collective workforce in our field. This gap between demand and supply is still growing. Software reuse is one of the paths being explored in order to achieve a significant increase in software productivity.

Why code well-known computations over and over again? Cannot reliability and productivity be drastically increased by using existing high-quality software components?

It sounds too good to be true. But it isn't that simple. The use of existing software components requires standardization of naming and interfaces. The idea of gluing components together is not directly transferable to software.

Is software reuse a myth or can it really be achieved? In the following sections, we will give an overview of the developments, opportunities and expectations of software reusability. A tentative conclusion is that we should not expect miracles. By patiently developing a sound reuse technology, a lot of progress is possible. There is no philosopher's stone. There are, however, a great number of different developments that may reinforce and supplement one another.

The modern view does not restrict the notion of software reuse to component reuse. Design information can be reused also, as can other forms of knowledge gathered during software construction.

Software reuse is closely related to software architecture. A software architecture provides a context for the development of reusable building blocks. Conversely, a software architecture provides a skeleton into which building blocks can be incorporated. Attention to architectural issues is one of the prime software reuse success factors. A new style of software development, emphasizing component reuse within an architectural framework, is emerging. It is known as **Component-Based Software Engineering** (CBSE). Developments in interface technology such as provided by middleware interface description languages provide additional leverage for CBSE.

Closely coupled to software reuse is software flexibility. Software is continuously adapted to changed circumstances. In developing the next release of a system, we would like to reuse as much as possible from the present release. This is sometimes considered to be software reuse. Flexibility aspects have been extensively discussed in previous chapters, notably chapters 6 and 10, albeit not explicitly in the context of reusability.

Various aspects of software reuse are discussed in sections 17.1 to 17.4. Section 17.1 discusses the main dimensions along which reuse approaches can be distinguished. Section 17.2 elaborates upon one of these dimensions, the type of product to be reused. Section 17.3 discusses another of these dimensions, viz. the various process models incorporating reuse. Specific tools and techniques to support reuse are the topic of section 17.4. Section 17.5 addresses the perspectives of software reuse. In particular, a domain-oriented, evolutionary approach is advocated. Finally, non-technical aspects of software reuse are addressed in section 17.6.

17.1 REUSE DIMENSIONS

Software reuse has many dimensions or facets. The main dimensions along which approaches to software reuse can be distinguished are listed in figure 17.1. We will discuss each of these dimensions in turn, by highlighting essential characteristics of extreme orientations along the axes. Most reuse systems, however, will exhibit a mixture of these characteristics. For example, a typical reuse system may use a combination of a compositional and a generative approach.

Dimension	Description
substance	components, concepts, procedures
scope	horizontal or vertical
approach	planned, systematic or ad hoc, opportunistic
technique	compositional or generative
usage	black-box, as-is or white-box, modified
product	code, object, design (architecture), text,...

Figure 17.1 Reuse dimensions

The first dimension along which approaches to reuse may differ concerns the substance, the essence of the things that are reused. Most often, the things being reused are components. A component can be any piece of program text: a procedure, a module, an object-oriented class, etc. Components can be generic (data structures like binary trees or lists, widgets for graphical user interfaces, sorting routines) or domain-specific. A point of recurring concern when reusing components is their quality, in particular their reliability. Instead of encapsulating a chunk of knowledge as a component in some programming language, we may also describe it at a more abstract level, for example as a generic algorithm, or a concept. Finally, rather than reusing product elements, we may also reuse process elements, such as procedures on how to carry out an inspection or how to prototype. To be able to do so, these process elements have to be formally captured, for example in a process model.

The scope of software reuse can be horizontal or vertical. In horizontal reuse, components are generic. They can be used across a variety of domains. A library of mathematical subroutines or GUI widgets is a typical example of horizontal reuse. In vertical reuse, components within a particular application domain are sought for. This often involves a thorough domain analysis to make sure that the components do reflect the essential concepts of the domain. The choice of a particular domain incurs a challenging trade-off: if the domain is narrow, components can be made to fit precisely and the pay-off is high when these components are reused. On the other hand, the chance that these components can be reused outside this narrow domain is fairly small. The reverse holds for large domains.

Software reuse may be undertaken in a planned, systematic way or it may be done in an ad hoc, opportunistic fashion. Planned reuse involves substantial changes in the way software is developed. Extra effort is needed to develop, test, and document reusable software. Specific process steps must be introduced to investigate opportunities to reuse existing components. The economics of software development change, since costs and benefits relate to more than just the present project. Planned reuse requires a considerable investment upfront. For a while, extra effort is needed to develop reusable components. Only at a later stage can the benefits be reaped. With the opportunistic approach, individuals reuse components when and if they happen to know of their existence, and when and if these components happen to fit. In this approach, components are not developed with reuse in mind. Populating a library with a large enough number of reusable components is often a problem when using the opportunistic approach. In the process-model perspective, the planned and opportunistic approaches to reuse are known as software development *for* reuse and software development *with* reuse, respectively.

In a composition-based technology, reuse is achieved by (partly) composing a new system from existing components. The building blocks used are passive fragments that are copied from an existing base. Retrieval of suitable components is a major issue here. In a generation-based technology, it is much more difficult to identify the components that are being reused. Rather, the knowledge reused (usually domain-specific) is to be found in a program that generates some other program. In a generation-based technology, reusable patterns are an active element used to generate the target system. Prime examples of these two technologies are subroutine libraries and application generators, respectively.

In a black-box reuse approach, elements are reused as-is: they are not modified to fit the application in which they are going to be incorporated. Often, the person reusing the component does not know the internals of the element. Commercial, off-the-shelf (COTS) components are a prime example of this approach. Quality and the legal aspects of such components are critical issues. In a white-box approach, elements can be modified before they are incorporated. White-box reuse is most often done in combination with an opportunistic approach.

Finally, we may categorize reuse approaches according to the type of product that is reused: source code, design, architecture, object, text, and so on. Most often, some form of source code is the reuse product. There is a strong trend to capture reusable design knowledge in the form of design patterns and software architectures; see chapter 10. Text is a quite different kind of reusable product, for instance in the form of pieces of documentation. The 'user manual' of a modern airplane, for example, easily runs to thousands of pages. Quite likely, each airplane is unique in some aspects and so is its documentation. By developing reusable pieces of documentation, the user manual can be constructed by assembling it from a huge number of documentation fragments.

17.2 REUSE OF INTERMEDIATE PRODUCTS

Libraries with ready-to-use pieces of code, such as those for numerical or statistical computations, have been with us for a long time and their use is widespread. This form of software reuse is not necessarily suited for other domains. In other domains we may be better off reusing 'skeleton' components, i.e. components in which some details have not been filled in yet. In an environment in which the same type of software is developed over and over again, these skeletons may be molded in a reusable design. A similar technique is to reuse the architecture of a software system, as is found in the construction of compilers, for example. These are all examples of composition-based reuse techniques.

By incorporating domain knowledge in *supporting* software, we arrive at the area of transformation systems, application generators and fourth-generation languages. These are examples of generation-based reuse techniques.

17.2.1 Libraries of Software Components

No one in his right mind will think of writing a routine to compute a cosine. If it is not built into the language already, there is bound to be a library routine `cos`. By investigating the question of why the reuse of mathematical functions is so easy, we come across a number of stumbling blocks that hamper the reuse of software components in other domains:

- **a well-developed field, with a standardized terminology**: 'cosine' means the same to all of us;
- **a small interface**: we need exactly one number to compute a cosine;
- **a standardized data format**: a real number may be represented in fixed point, floating point, or double precision, and that's about all.

Reuse of subroutines works best in an application domain that is well disclosed, one whose notions are clear and where the data to be used is in some standardized format.

The modern history of software reuse starts with McIlroy, who envisaged a bright future for a software component technology at the NATO software engineering conference back in 1968. In his view, it should be possible to assemble larger components and systems from a vast number of ready-to-use building blocks, much like hardware systems are assembled using standard components.

It hasn't come to that, yet. In order for large-scale reuse of software components to become feasible, we first have to solve the following problems:

- **Searching** We have to search for the right component in a database of available components, which is only possible if we have proper methods available to describe components. If you don't know how to specify what you are looking for, there is little chance you will find it.

- **Understanding** To decide whether some component is usable, we need a precise and sufficiently complete understanding of what the component does.

- **Adaptation** The component selected may not exactly fit the problem at hand. Tinkering with the code is not satisfactory and is, in any case, only justified if it is thoroughly understood.

- **Composition** A system is wired from many components. How do we glue the components together? We will return to this topic in section 17.4.1.

To ease the searching process, hardware components are usually classified in a multi-level hierarchy. Since the naming conventions in that field have been standardized, people are able to traverse the hierarchy. At the lowest level, alternative descriptions of components are given, such as a natural language description, logic schema, and timing information, which describe different aspects of the components. These alternative descriptions further improve the user's understanding of these components.

Several efforts have been made to classify software components in a hierarchical fashion as well. One such effort is described in [Boo87]. In his taxonomy, a component is first described by the abstraction it embodies. Part of this taxonomy is depicted in figure 17.2. Secondly, components are described by their time and space behavior, for instance, whether or not objects are static in size or handle their own memory management.

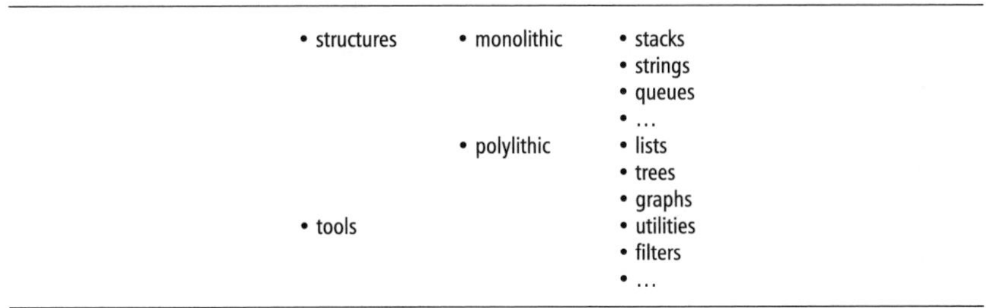

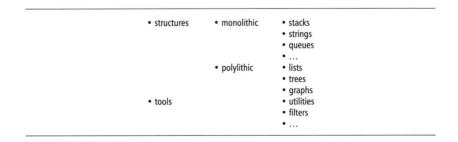

Figure 17.2 Part of a taxonomy of reusable software components

The retrieval problem for software components is very similar to that for textual sources in an ordinary library. Quite a number of classification, or indexing, techniques have been developed for the latter type of problem. Figure 17.3 identifies the main indexing techniques.

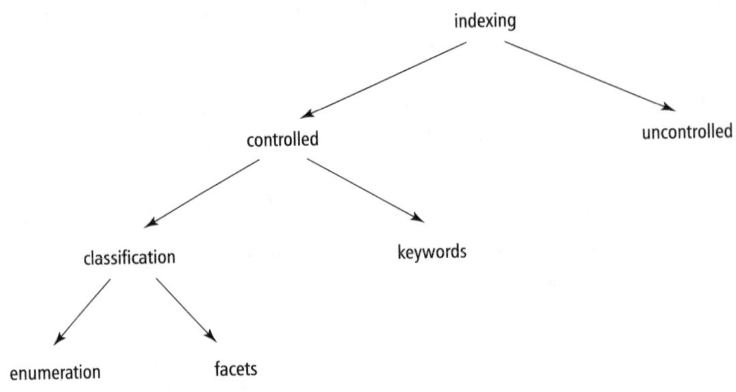

Figure 17.3 Main indexing techniques

An indexing scheme is either controlled or uncontrolled. In a controlled indexing scheme, classifiers are chosen from a finite set of terms. This set of terms may be predefined and immutable. It may also change over time, though only in a controlled way. With controlled indexing, a list of synonyms is often provided to make both searching and indexing more flexible. In an uncontrolled indexing scheme, there is no restriction on the number of terms. Uncontrolled indexing is mostly done by extracting terms from the entity to be indexed. For example, the terms that occur most frequently can be taken as index terms. An advantage of uncontrolled indexing is that it can be done automatically. A disadvantage is that semantic knowledge gets lost.

In controlled indexing, one option is simply to use a list of keywords. This list is not ordered and there are no relations between the keywords. An advantage of this scheme is that it is easy to extend the set of index terms. In a classification scheme, on the other hand, the set of index terms is structured in some way. One way of doing so is through some enumerated hierarchical structure, as in figures 17.2 and 17.3. The power of a hierarchical scheme is its structure. This same structure, however, is also a weakness.

An enumerated scheme offers one specific view on the structure of a domain. Figure 17.2 offers one such view on the domain of generic data structures. Figure 17.4 offers an alternative view on that same domain. In the latter scheme, the structural relationships between elements of a compound data structure have been used to set up the taxonomy. For example, there is a 1–1 relationship between elements of a linear structure such as a list or queue. The taxonomies in figures 17.2 and 17.4 both seem to be reasonable. Each of them can be used effectively, provided the user knows *how* the hierarchy is organized.

This phenomenon holds for component hierarchies in general. If you don't know how the hierarchy is organized, there is little chance that you will be able to find the component you were looking for.

structures	0-0	sets
	1-1	stacks
		queues
		lists
		...
	1-n	trees
	n-m	graphs

Figure 17.4 An alternative component hierarchy

Strictly enumerative schemes use a predefined hierarchy and force you to search for a node that best fits the component to be classified. Though cross-references to other nodes can be included, the resulting network soon becomes fairly complicated. Faceted classification has certain advantages over the enumerative classification used in the examples of figures 17.2 and 17.4. A faceted classification scheme uses a number of different characteristics, or *facets*, to describe each component. For example, components in a UNIX environment could be classified according to the action they embody, the object they manipulate, the data structure used, and the system they are part of. Classifying a component is then a matter of choosing an n-tuple which best fits that component.

The essence of an indexing technique is to capture the relevant information of the entities to be classified. This requires knowledge of the kind of questions users will pose, as well as knowledge of the users' search behavior. This is difficult, which makes the development of an indexing language a far from trivial undertaking. Librarians know this. Software engineers responsible for a library of reusable components should know this too. Any user of the Internet will have experienced that finding something that exactly fits your needs is a very difficult task.

The examples contained in figures 17.2 and 17.4 are somewhat misleading, in that the components found at the leaf nodes of the hierarchy embody abstractions that are known all too well. In other domains, there will be less mutual understanding as regards primitive concepts and their naming. Therefore, setting up a usable taxonomy, i.e. defining an indexing language, is likely to be much more difficult in other domains.

Once a set of candidate components has been found, we need to evaluate these components for their suitability in the current reuse situation. The main types of information useful for such an evaluation are:

- Information about the quality of the component, for example by giving a rating for each ISO 9126 quality characteristic (see chapter 6). Valuable quality information is also provided by comments about the reuse history of the component: successful experiences,[1] critical notes about circumstances in which reuse was found to be less successful, etc.

- Administrative information, such as the name and address of the developer, the component's modification history, and information on the price of reuse.

- Documentation about what the component does and details about the internals of the component (if it may be adapted).

- Information about the interface to the component (most often types of parameters).

- Information to help the testing of the component in the current reuse situation, such as a set of test cases with the associated expected results.

One further observation that can be made about the reuse of components regards their granularity. The larger a component is, the larger the pay-off will be once it is reused. On the other hand, the reusability of a component decreases as its size grows, because larger components tend to put larger constraints on their environment. This is analogous to Fisher's fundamental theorem of biology: the more an organism is adapted to some given environment, the less suited it is for some other environment.

Some actual experiences suggest that practical, useful component libraries will not contain a huge number of components. For example, [PD91a] reports that the asset collection of GTE went from 190 in 1988 to 128 in 1990. [Pou99] asserts that the best libraries range from 30 components to, in rare cases, as many as 250 components. For that reason, the classification and retrieval of components is often not the main impediment for a successful reuse program. Rather, filling the library with the *right* components is the real issue. This aspect will be taken up again in section 17.5.

[1] Be careful though. The software that caused the Ariane 5 disaster was reused from the Ariane 4 and *never* caused any problems there [Lio96]; see also section 1.4.1. This phenomenon may be termed the antidecomposition property of software reuse: if a component has been successfully used in some environment, this does not imply that it can be successfully reused in some other environment.

17.2.2 Templates

In the preceding section, we silently assumed library components to be ready-to-use pieces of code. The applicability of a component can be increased by leaving certain details unspecified. **Templates** or **skeletons** are 'unfinished' components. By *instantiating* them, i.e. by filling in the holes, a (re)usable component results.

An example of a possible template is a procedure that implements the quicksort algorithm. Details like the bounds of the array to be sorted, the type of the array elements and the relational operator used to compare array elements, are not important for the essence of the algorithm.

As more and more details are left open, a template can be applied more generally. However, there is a price to be paid. The cost of obtaining a complete application is likely to increase proportionally with the number of holes to be filled in.

Templates need not be constrained to just subroutines. It is realistic to think of a template that can be instantiated into a full program for a very specific application domain. Such templates are called application generators and are the topic of section 17.2.6.

17.2.3 Design Reuse

It seems plausible that design reuse pays off in an environment where the same type of program is developed over and over again. In many a business environment, applications are incorrectly considered to be unique. As a consequence, they are designed and coded from scratch each time the need for yet another application arises. Lanergan and Grasso state that there are but a few different basic operations in business Cobol programs, like sorting, updating and reporting [LG84]. Based on an analysis of a vast number of existing programs at Raytheon Company, MA, they designed seven 'logic structures'. A logic structure is an unfinished Cobol program. Some data declarations are empty, i.e. have a 01-level only. Some paragraphs have no code yet.

After some experimentation it was decided that all new programs to be developed at Raytheon were to use one of these predefined logic structures. The biggest advantage of using logic structures, according to Lanergan and Grasso, shows up during maintenance. It seems as if all software is written by the same team. If a programmer adapts a program written by someone else, there are likely to be few surprises, since the structure and much of the code will already be familiar.

At Raytheon, there was a library of Cobol components alongside the logical structures. Standard components are certain data types (file descriptors or record descriptors) and a great number of routines. After a start-up phase, the combination of standard designs and standard components resulted in a productivity increase of 50%.

This type of design reuse is nowadays known as an **(application) framework**. Application frameworks often contain both a collection of generally useful components (such as those for handling addresses and dates) and one or more collections of domain-specific components from which applications can be configured.

17.2.4 Reuse of Architecture

For each problem, we must look for an architecture which best fits that problem. An inappropriate architecture can never be the basis for a good system. The situation becomes rather different if a problem recurs over and over again in different variants. If a useful standard architecture exists for a particular type of problem, it can be applied in all future variants.

A prime area within computer science where a software architecture is routinely reused is in building compilers. Most compilers are built out of the same components: a lexical analyzer, a parser, a symbol table, a code generator, and a few others. There exist certain well-defined types of parser, such as LL(1) or LALR(1) parsers. There is a large body of theory about how compilers function and this theory is known to the people building compilers. In this way, a generally-accepted standard architecture for compilers has evolved. Obviously, it has never been proved that this is the only, or best, way to build compilers. But it constitutes a sound and well-known method of attacking problems in a notoriously difficult domain.

Large-scale reuse of architecture is still seldom found in other areas. The main reason is that a similar body of shared, crystallized, knowledge just does not exist yet for most domains. We may, however, observe that this situation is changing rapidly. In many fields, people are explicitly building such a body of knowledge and molding it into the form of a software architecture. It may be called a domain-specific software architecture (DSSA), a product line architecture (in which case the architecture provides the basis for a family of similar systems), or an application framework (if the emphasis is on the rapid generation of an application from existing building blocks); see also chapter 10.

17.2.5 Transformation Systems

We already mentioned the transformational nature of the software development process. A requirements specification describes the system to be realized in some notation, be it a natural language, a formal language, or a pictorial language. Through a number of intermediate stages this description is transformed into the final product, encoded in some programming language.

Two types of transformation recur in this process:

- **refinements**: by adding details and implementation decisions, the product's description is refined;
- **linguistic transformations**: during some steps, the product's description in one language is translated into an equivalent description in some other language.

Obviously, both types of transformation can be carried out manually; they often are. We may, however, also consider the possibility of having a computer assist us in realizing those transformations – precisely the aim of a transformation system.

The easiest starting point for this is provided by the class of linguistic transformations. A construct like

```
IfExists i in 1..N SuchThat A[i] = x
then ...
```

leaves no doubt as to its meaning. Unfortunately, this construct does not exist in most high-level programming languages that are in use today. At some point, the IfExists-construct will have to be replaced by a semantically-equivalent code sequence in an existing language.

The IfExists-construct is fairly low-level. It is immediately obvious that the formalism is already fairly close to, say, Pascal. An important point is that it is indeed a *formalism*. Translations between formal languages are far easier to achieve than a translation to or (especially) from a natural language. A design completely written in Dutch or English is hardly palatable to a transformation system. The use of transformation systems incurs a further formalization of higher-level product descriptions.

In a so-called **wide-spectrum language**, the solution to a problem can be expressed at different levels of abstraction. Correctness-preserving transformations from one level to the next are guided by transformation rules, while all intermediate results stay within the realm of the same, formal language.

An interesting question is whether we can formalize *all* levels and build an intelligent compiler which translates a design into executable code without human intervention. This is indeed possible if we restrict ourselves to a very narrow application domain. In order to be able to *meaningfully* rewrite a design, a sufficient amount of application domain knowledge somehow has to be built into the system. Such systems are called **application generators**; see section 17.2.6.

A transformation system for a broad application domain will in general need human guidance in making refinements. For example, if some high-level description talks about *sets* of objects, this may be refined into a representation using binary trees or hash tables or some other form. In general, the programmer will decide which data structure best fits the application, since the transformation system lacks the knowledge to do so properly.

17.2.6 Application Generators and Fourth-Generation Languages

Application generators write programs. An application generator has a fair amount of application-domain knowledge. Usually, the application domain is quite narrow. In order to obtain a program one obviously needs a specification of that program. Once the specification is available, the program is generated automatically.

The principle being used is the same as that behind a generic package or template: the actual program to be generated is already built into the application generator. Instantiation of an actual program is done by filling in a number of details. The difference is that the size of the code delivered is much bigger with an application generator than with a template. Also, the details are generally provided at a higher level of abstraction, in terms of concepts and notions drawn from the application domain.

An application generator can be employed in each domain with a structure such that complicated operations within that domain can be largely automated. One example is the production of graphical summaries from a database. So-called compiler–compilers are another typical example of application generators: given a grammar (i.e. the details) of some programming language, a parser for that language is produced.

Fourth-generation languages or **very high level languages** (VHLLs) are often mentioned in one and the same breath with application generators. Fourth-generation languages offer programming constructs at a much higher level than third-generation programming languages.

Expressions from a given application domain can be directly phrased in the corresponding fourth-generation language. Consequently, the fourth-generation language must have knowledge of that application domain. This generally means that fourth-generation languages are only suited for one specific, limited, domain.

There is no fundamental difference between fourth-generation languages and application generators. When one wants to stress the generative capabilities of a system, the term application generator is mostly applied. The term fourth-generation language highlights the high-level programming constructs being offered. For many such systems, the terms are used interchangeably.

Application generators and fourth-generation languages potentially offer a number of cost savings, since implementation details need not be bothered with: less code is written, the software is more comprehensible, there are fewer errors, and the software is easier to maintain. In practice, this theory often does not come up to expectations. For one thing, the user may want something which is not offered by the system. In that case, a piece of handwritten code must be added to the software being generated automatically. By doing this, one of the main advantages of using fourth-generation languages, viz. easily comprehensible programs at a high level of abstraction, is lost.

17.3 REUSE AND THE SOFTWARE LIFE CYCLE

Reuse affects the way we develop software. We may distinguish two main process models incorporating reuse:

- software development **with** reuse, and
- software development **for** reuse.

Both these approaches to reuse may be combined with any of the software life cycle models discussed earlier. Also, combinations of the with and for reuse models are possible.

The software-development-with-reuse model may be termed a *passive* approach to reuse. It presupposes a repository with a number of reusable assets. At some point during the development process, this repository is searched for reusable assets. If these are found, they are evaluated for their suitability in the situation at hand and, if the evaluation yields a positive answer, the reusable assets are incorporated. The process does not actively seek to extend the repository. As a side effect of the present project, we may add elements to the repository, but no extra effort is spent while doing so. For instance, we will not put in extra effort to test the component more thoroughly, to document it more elaborately, or to develop a more general interface to it. From a reuse perspective, the software development with reuse approach is an opportunistic approach.

A pure software-development-with-reuse model is routinely applied in, e.g. circumstances where we need some mathematical routine. If our project requires some numerical interpolation routine, we will search a mathematical library. We may find some routine which uses Gaussian interpolation, fits our needs, and decide to incorporate it. Most likely, the project will not result in a new interpolation routine to be included in the library.

Development with reuse is most often applied at the component level. It has its main impact, therefore, during the architectural design stage when the global decomposition into components is decided upon. We search the repository for suitable candidates, evaluate them, and possibly include them in our architecture. This is a cyclical process, since we may decide to adjust the architecture because of characteristics of the components found. The resulting process model is depicted in figure 17.5. The model includes some further communication links between later phases of the software development life cycle and the repository. These reflect less far-reaching adaptations to the process model. For example, the repository may contain test cases that can be retrieved and used when testing the system, or we may be able to add our own test results to the repository.

The software-development-for-reuse process model constitutes an *active* approach to reuse. Rather than merely searching an existing base, we *develop* reusable

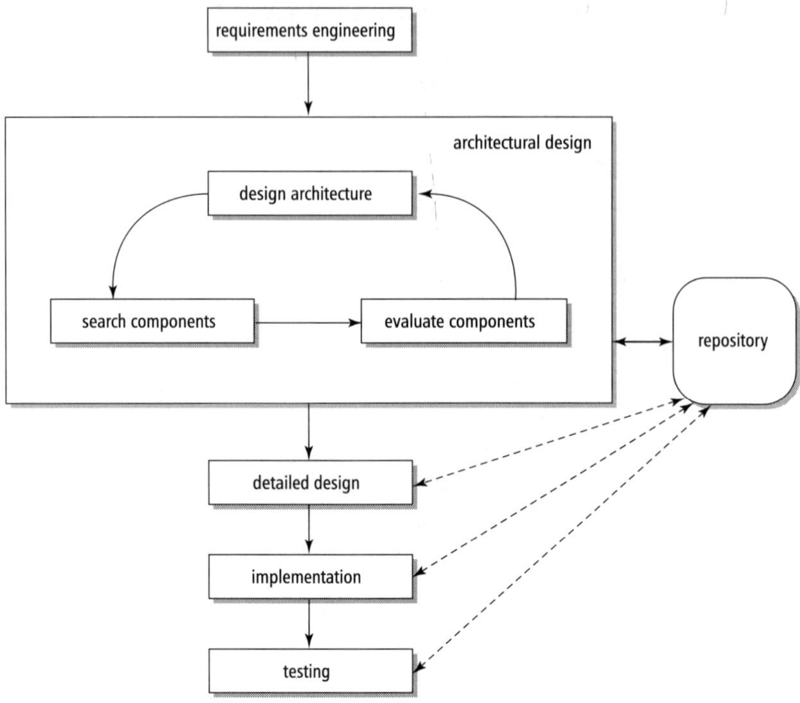

Figure 17.5 Software-development-with-reuse process model

assets. The software-development-for-reuse approach is thus a planned approach to reuse. Again, this approach most often involves reusable components, and we will illustrate the approach by considering that situation. During architectural design, extra effort is now spent to make components more general, more reusable. These components are then incorporated into the repository, together with any information that might be of help at a later stage, when searching for or retrieving components. Software-development-for-reuse thus incurs extra costs to the present project. These extra costs are only paid back when a subsequent project indeed reuses these components.

Software-development-for-reuse process models may differ with respect to the point in time at which components are made reusable and incorporated in the repository. In one extreme form, reusable components are extracted from the system after it has been developed. This may be termed the a posteriori approach. In an a priori software-development-for-reuse approach, reusable components are developed *before*

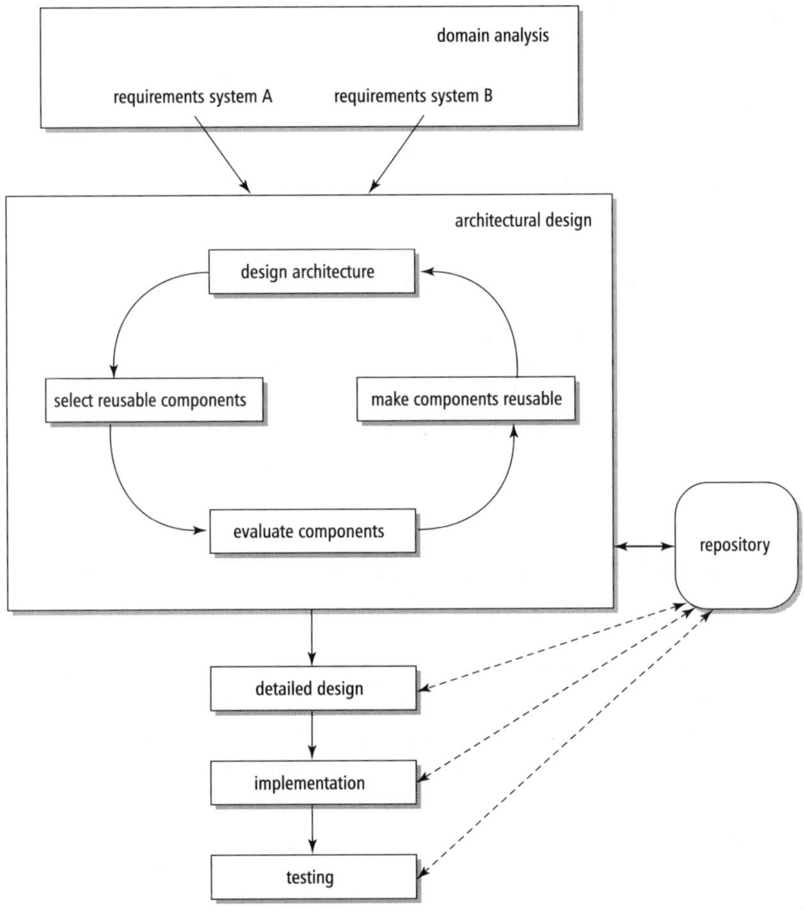

Figure 17.6 Software-development-for-reuse process model

the system in which they are to be used. The latter approach has become known as the **software factory** approach.

If the architecture is developed for one specific problem, chances are that peculiarities of that situation creep into the architecture. As a result, components identified might fit the present situation very well, but they need not fit a similar future situation. The extra effort spent to make these components reusable then might not pay off. To prevent this, development for reuse generally involves a different requirements engineering process as well. Rather than only considering the present situation, the requirements for a family of similar systems are taken into account. So, instead of devising an architecture for the library of our own department, we may decide to develop an architecture which fits the other departments of our university as well. We may even decide to develop an architecture for scientific libraries in general. This more general requirements engineering process is known as domain engineering. The resulting architecture is also termed a product-line architecture; see also chapter 10. The resulting process model is depicted in figure 17.6.

17.4 REUSE TOOLS AND TECHNIQUES

In this section we consider a number of concepts, methods and techniques that may have a positive impact on software reuse. In doing so, we will reconsider the approaches discussed in the previous section, thus establishing a relation between the reusable software assets discussed in the previous section and the notions to be discussed here.

17.4.1 From Module Interconnection Language to Architecture Description Language

The relation between different modules of a system can be formally expressed in a **Module Interconnection Language** (MIL). A MIL is an important tool when designing and maintaining large systems consisting of many different modules. A MIL-description is a formal description of the global structure of a software system. It can be used to verify the integrity of the system automatically. It can also be used to check whether the various modules conform to the agreed interfaces.

Figure 17.7 contains a small fragment of (hypothetical) MIL-code to illustrate the general flavor. The example concerns the structure of the KWIC-index program using abstract data types (see section 10.1.2). For each component, it specifies what the component provides to its environment and what it requires from its environment. The overall result is a complete uses-structure of the system. For each component, one or more implementations are also indicated. The composition given at the end of the description selects a number of building blocks defined previously.

MILs originated as a consequence of the separation between programming-in-the-small and programming-in-the-large. The essential ideas behind the development of MILs are:

- **A separate language for system design** A MIL is not a programming language. Rather, it describes desirable properties of modules that are to become part of the system being considered.

```
system kwic
    provide kwic_system

    module control_mod
        provide procedure control
        require input_procs, output_procs
        implementation CONTROL
    end control_mod

    module input_mod
        provide package input_procs is
            ...
        end input_procs
        require store_procs
        implementation INPUT1 .. Java
        implementation INPUT2 .. Pascal
    end input_mod

    module store_mod
        provide package store_procs is
            procedure InitStore
            procedure PutCharacter(r, w, c, d)
            procedure CloseStore
            procedure Lines
            procedure Words(r)
            procedure Characters(r, w)
            procedure Character(r, w, c)
        end store_procs
        implementation STORE1 .. Java
        implementation STORE2 .. Pascal
    end store_mod

    ...

    COMPOSITION
    KWIC_SYSTEM_1 = [CONTROL, INPUT2, STORE2, SHIFT2, SORT2, OUTPUT2]
end kwic
```

Figure 17.7 Partial MIL description of a KWIC-index system

```
system kwic
    interface is type filter
        player input is StreamIn
        player output is StreamIn
    end interface
    implementation is
        uses Inp instance component Input
        uses Sto instance component Store
        uses Shi instance component Shift
        uses Sor instance component Sort
        uses Out instance component Output

        uses P instance connector ProcedureCall
        uses Q instance connector ProcedureCall

        connect input to Inp.in
        connect output to Out.out

        connect Inp.out to P.caller
        connect Store.Putchar to P.definer
        connect Out.in to Q.caller
        connect Sor.Ith to Q.definer
        ...
    end implementation
end kwic

component Store
    interface is type ADT
        player InitStore is RoutineDef signature ( → void)
        player PutCharacter is RoutineDef signature (int × int × int × char → void)
        player CloseStore is RoutineDef signature ( → void)
        player Lines is RoutineDef signature ( → int)
        player Words is RoutineDef signature (int → int)
        player Characters is RoutineDef signature (int × int → int)
        player Character is RoutineDef signature (int × int × int → char)
    end interface
    implementation is
        variant STORE2
end Store
```

Figure 17.8 Partial ADL description of a KWIC-index system

- **Static type-checking between different modules** This automatically guarantees that different modules obey the interface. An interface can only be changed after the corresponding change has been realized in the design.

- **Design and binding of modules in one description** In the early days of programming-in-the-large the various modules of a system were assembled by hand. Using a MIL, it is done automatically.

- **Version control** Keeping track of the different versions of (parts of) a system during development and maintenance requires a disciplined approach.

A number of different MILs have been developed. The basic concepts, however, are the same:

- **resources**: everything that can have a name in a programming language (constants, types, variables, and procedures) and can be made available by a module for use in another module;

- **modules**: make resources available or use them;

- **systems**: groups of modules which together perform a well-defined task. To the outside world, a system can be viewed as one single module.

The coupling between modules can be modeled as a graph: the nodes of the graph denote modules while the (directed) edges denote the uses-relation. Depending on the sophistication of the MIL, this graph can be a tree, an acyclic directed graph, or a directed graph without any restrictions.

To describe the architecture of a system, we need more than is generally provided by a MIL. MILs emphasize components and uses-relations between components. In particular, MILs neither treat connectors as first-class citizens nor describe the architectural configuration (topology) of the system. MILs have evolved into Architecture Description Languages (ADLs) that express the latter aspects also.

Figure 17.8 contains part of a (hypothetical) ADL-description of the KWIC-index program using abstract data types. It defines Store as a component with an abstract data type interface. It also lists the various routines, with their signatures, that make up this interface. The main program, kwic, is a component too. Its interface is defined to be of type filter; both its input and output are streams of characters. The implementation part of kwic is a formalization of the architectural description depicted in figure 10.2. It lists all components and connectors as instances of certain types of component or connector. Furthermore, all connections are made explicit, so that the topology of the system is completely specified. For example, a procedure call connector has two ends: a defining end and a calling end. The defining end of P in figure 17.8 is connected to the routine Putchar of module Store, while its calling end is connected to the output routine of module Input.

MILs and ADLs generally show the same limitations: they only engage themselves in the *syntax* of interfaces. Whether the resources passed on are meaningful or not cannot be assessed.

With respect to the previous section we may note that MILs and ADLs fit in well with transformation systems (section 17.2.5) and other forms of reuse where design plays an essential role (see sections 17.2.3 and 17.2.4).

17.4.2 Middleware

In the object-oriented paradigm, it is often stated that two objects, a client and a server, have agreed upon some contract, whereby the client object is allowed to request certain services from the server object. A natural next step is to isolate the contents of this contract, or interface, from both client and server. This is essentially what happens in CORBA,[2] the Common Object Request Broker Architecture. CORBA has been developed by the Object Management Group (OMG), a multivendor effort to standardize object-oriented distributed computing. JavaBeans and Microsoft's COM are similar solutions to the problem of connecting components with a very long wire.

CORBA interfaces are expressed in IDL, the Interface Definition Language. Figure 17.9 contains part of such an interface definition for the KWIC index program using abstract data types. IDL is a strongly typed language; it is not case-sensitive; and its syntax resembles that of C++.[3] The interface construct collects operations that form a natural group. Typically, the operations of one abstract data type constitute such a group. For each operation, the result type is given, followed by the operation names, and finally the parameters. A result type **void** indicates that no value is returned. Parameters are prefixed by either **in**, **out**, or **inout**, denoting an input, output, or input–output parameter.

Note the similarity between the texts of figures 17.7, 17.8 and 17.9. Each of these figures expresses interfaces of components, though with a slightly different syntax and for slightly different purposes.

The purpose of an interface expressed in IDL is to be independent of platform, operating system, language, and network protocol. CORBA tools, in particular the so-called Object Request Brokers (ORBs), handle the actual communication between objects that provide services and objects that request them. CORBA thus provides us with a layer which promotes reuse across platforms, operating systems, and programming languages.

[2]CORBA, ORB, Object Request Broker, OMG-IDL, CORBAservices and CORBAfacilities are trademarks of the Object Management Group.

[3]Reserved words are printed in bold in figure 17.9 for legibility.

```
module KWIC{
    interface Store
        {void InitStore;
         void PutCharacter (in int l, in int w, in int c, in char d);
         void CloseStore;
         int Lines;
         int Words (in int l);
         int Characters (in int l, in int w);
         char Character (in int l, in int w, in int c);
        }
    interface Input ...
    interface Shift ...
    interface Sort ...
     ...
}
```

Figure 17.9 Partial IDL description of a KWIC-index system

Plain CORBA connects only objects. The Object Management Architecture (OMA) integrates CORBA with component reuse. It thus serves as a framework for component-based software development. The general structure of OMA is depicted in figure 17.10. The CORBAservices level provides basic functionality for objects, e.g. for naming objects, moving them around, and copying them. CORBAfacilities provide basic functionality to applications. Typical examples are groups of services to handle user interfaces, or for a particular application domain, such as financial systems.

17.4.3 Object-Oriented Programming

Object-oriented programming is one of the buzzwords of our trade. What is the potential of object-oriented languages as regards software reuse? [Cox84] and [Mey87] both argue that reuse is primarily a technical problem that can be solved by using the proper, i.e. object-oriented, techniques. Many others also see managerial, organizational and psychological problems that hinder the fast promulgation of a large-scale reuse technology.

It goes without saying that module libraries become much more usable if they contain object-oriented modules. If the module looked for is not present, it is not necessary to adapt an almost fitting module by tinkering with the code – always a dangerous affair. Desirable features can be inherited from a suitable class already present

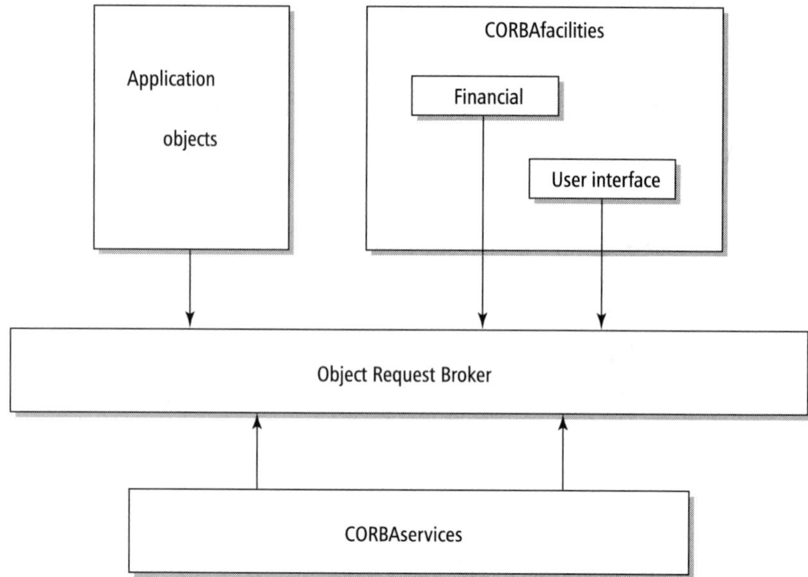

Figure 17.10 Object Management Architecture (*Source: J. Siegel,* CORBA Fundamentals, *1995 ©John Wiley & Sons. Reprinted by permission of John Wiley & Sons Inc.*)

in the library, and the extra bells and whistles can be added to a newly-defined subclass.

Conversely, the inheritance and polymorphism features of object-oriented languages by themselves provide opportunities for constructing reusable parts. They promote the emergence of abstract classes that may serve as a starting point from which more specific components are derived.

The object-oriented paradigm has a particular affinity with software reuse. Object orientation combined with reuse may substantially improve productivity. Some caution is required, though. The shift to object orientation does not automatically result in higher productivity caused by large-scale reuse. Object orientation and reuse are better viewed as separate issues. In particular, object orientation does not remove other barriers to reuse. It is merely an enabler, albeit a powerful one.

17.4.4 Software Development Environments

A software development environment is a set of facilities offered to a developer or a team of developers. If such an environment is to support the type of software development discussed in section 17.3, it has to include facilities to interact with the repository. Specific tools may support the search for components, their evaluation, or their incorporation in the repository.

The software development environment is of only limited use if the reuse assets offered are just (passively) present. A more optimal use of the environment can be made if it has *knowledge* of the information that can be reused and actively uses this knowledge. Not accidentally, the AI contribution to reuse will be discussed here. If the environment *knows* the intention of the developer, if it knows how and where to find that information, we are far better off. An interesting project in this area is the Programmer's Apprentice.

The Programmer's Apprentice (PA) has been developed at the MIT Artificial Intelligence Laboratory [RW88]. As its name suggests, the PA acts as an apprentice to the programmer using it. The PA serves as an active agent in the development process rather than as a passive tool. The PA fills in the coding details, helps with the documentation, debugging and changing of programs, while the programmer does the real hard work. In order to be able to do its job properly, the PA must *understand* what is going on. There must be a body of shared knowledge between the programmer and the PA. A central focus in the PA project is to develop a knowledge representation for programs and program fragments (**clichés**). This type of knowledge is codified and stored in **plans**. Plans constitute the representation underlying the whole system.

The Programmer's Apprentice idea is very elegant. It is used as a starting point to explore opportunities to provide knowledgeable assistance at the design and requirements analysis stages through a Design Apprentice [WT91] and Requirements Apprentice [RW91]. Both employ a cliché library, a repository of codified fragments of reusable knowledge. Through its very nature, a Programmer's Apprentice is best suited to an environment where explicit knowledge from a limited domain is available.

This resembles the application generators from section 17.2.6. Application generators also manage to achieve high productivity gains by limiting their domain of application. It is feasible that a new generation of application generators can be developed using an AI-approach like the one used in the Programmer's Apprentice. Such application generators could be more dynamic, more flexible, and easier to handle than their limited, rigid, predecessors.

Software development environments may in principle concern themselves with all types of reuse discussed in section 17.2. The practical value of a database of reusable modules increases if the environment automatically checks the interface consistencies. A transformation system will always be embedded in some kind of programming environment. The added value of a software development environment over a set of separate tools is that the various constituents are integrated, which potentially results in a more directed and uniform support for reuse.

17.5 PERSPECTIVES OF SOFTWARE REUSE

Useful abstractions are discovered, not invented.
[JF88]

In any reuse technology, the building blocks being reused, whether in the form of subroutines, templates, transformations, or problem solutions known to the designers, correspond to crystallized pieces of knowledge, which can be used in circumstances other than the ones for which they were envisaged originally.

A central question in all reuse technologies discussed above is how to exploit some given set of reusable building blocks. This is most paramount in various projects in the area of component libraries, where the main goal is to provide ways of retrieving a useable component for the task at hand.

Alternatively, we may look at software reusability from an entirely different angle: what building blocks do we need in order to be able to use them in different applications?

Reuse is not the same as reusability. Reuse of software is only profitable if the software is indeed reusable. The second approach addresses the question of how to identify a useful, i.e. reusable, collection of components in an organized way.

Such a collection of reusable components is tied to a certain application domain. Examples are a mathematical subroutine library, Lanergan's collection of 'logic structures', and the primitives of a fourth-generation language. The latter two aim at providing useful primitives for business-type applications.

When trying to identify a reusable set of components, the main question is to decide *which* components are needed. A reusable component is to be valued, not for the trivial reason that it offers relief from implementing the functionality yourself, but for offering a piece of the *right* domain knowledge, the very functionality you need, gained through much experience and an obsessive desire to find the right abstractions.

Components should reflect the primitive notions of the application domain. In order to be able to identify a proper set of primitives for a given domain, considerable experience with software development for that domain is needed. While this experience is being built up, the proper set of primitives will slowly evolve.

Actual implementation of those primitives is of secondary importance. A collection of primitives for a given domain defines an *interface* that can be used when developing different programs in that domain. The ideas, concepts and structures that play an important role in the application domain have to be present in the interface. Reuse of that interface is more important than reuse of its implementation. The interface structures the software. It offers a focal point in designing software for that application area.

In [SvV88], such a collection of primitives is called a Domain-Oriented Virtual Machine (DOVM). A domain is a 'sphere or field of activity or influence'. A domain is defined by consensus and its essence is the shared understanding of some community. It is characterized by a collection of common notions that show a certain coherence, while the same notions do not exist or do not show that coherence outside the domain. Domains can be taken more or less broadly. Example domains are, for instance:

– accounting software,

– accounting software for multinationals,

– accounting software for multinationals, developed by Soft Ltd.

All accounting software will incorporate such notions as 'ledger' and 'balance'. Accounting software for multinationals will have some notions in common that do not exist in accounting systems for the grocery store or milkman, such as provisions for cross-border cash flow. Representation of notions in software developed by Soft Ltd. will differ from those of other firms because of the use of different methodologies or conventions.

The essential point is that certain notions play an important role in the domain in question. Those notions also play a role in the software for that domain. If we want to attain reuse within a given domain, these domain-specific notions are important. These notions have certain *semantics* which are fixed within the domain, and are known to people working in that domain. These semantically primitive notions should be our main foci in trying to achieve reusability.

For most domains, it is not immediately clear which primitives are the right ones. It is very much a matter of trial and error. By and by, the proper set of primitives show themselves. As a domain develops, we may distinguish various stages:

- At the start, there is no clear set of notions and all software is written from scratch. Experience slowly builds up, while we learn from previous mistakes.

- At the second stage, similar problems are being recognized and solved in a similar way. The first semantic primitives will be recognized. By trial and error, we find out which primitives are useful and which are not.

- At the third stage, the domain is ripe for reuse. A reasonable amount of software has been developed, the set of concepts has stabilized, there are standard solutions for standard problems.

- Finally, the domain has been fully explored. Software development for the domain can largely be automated. We do not program in the domain anymore.

Instead, we use a standard interface formed by the semantic primitives of the domain.

Most reuse occurs at the last stage, by which time it is not recognized as such. A long time ago, computers were programmed in assembly language. In high-level languages, we 'just write down what we want' and the compiler makes this into a 'real' program. This is generally not seen as reuse anymore. A similar phenomenon occurs in the transition from a third-generation language to a fourth-generation language.

From the reusability point of view, the above classification is one of a normal, natural, evolution of a domain. The various stages are categorized by reuse at qualitatively different levels:

- at the first stage, there is no reuse;
- at the second stage, reuse is ad hoc;
- at the third stage, reuse is structured. Existing components are reused in an organized way when new software is being developed;
- at the fourth stage, reuse is institutionalized and automated. Human effort is restricted to the upper levels of abstraction.

Within a given domain, an informal language is used. In this informal domain language, the same thing can be phrased in quite different ways, using concepts that are not sharply defined. Yet, informal language is understandable, because the concepts refer to a universe of discourse that both speaker and listener share.

Concepts in a formal language do not refer to experience or everyday knowledge. They merely have a meaning in some formal system. A virtual machine is such a formal system and its language is a formal language.

To formalize a domain is to construct a formal (domain) language that mimics an existing informal language. We then have to choose from the different semantic primitives that exist informally. Sometimes also, it is convenient to add new primitives, primitives that fit neatly within the formalized domain.

As an example of the latter, consider the domain of computerized typesetting. Part of formatting a document concerns assembling words into lines and lines into paragraphs. The sequence of words making up a paragraph must be broken into lines such that the result is typographically pleasing.

Knuth describes this problem in terms of 'boxes', 'glue' and 'penalties' [KP81]. Words are contained in boxes, which have a certain width. White space between words is phrased in terms of glue, which may shrink or stretch. A nominal amount of white space between adjacent words is preferred and a penalty of 0 is associated with this nominal spacing. Putting words closer together (shrinking the glue), or wider apart (stretching the glue), incurs a non-negative penalty. The more this glue is stretched or shrunk, the higher the penalty. The penalty associated with formatting a complete paragraph in some given way then is the sum of the penalties associated with the inter-word spacing within that formatted paragraph. The problem may now be rephrased as: break the line into paragraphs such that the total penalty is minimal. (Note that penalties may also be associated with other typographically less-desirable properties, such as hyphenation.)

The notions 'box', 'glue', and 'penalty' give a neat formalization to certain aspects of typography. They also lead to an efficient solution for the above problem, using a dynamic programming technique.

In practice, formalizing is not a one-shot activity. Rather, it is an iterative process. The formalized version does not exactly describe the informal language. It fixes one possible interpretation. If we study its semantics, it may have some undesirable aspects. In due course, an acceptable compromise is reached between those who use the language (in higher domains) and those who implement it (in lower domains). Once the formal domain language is fixed, it also affects the informal domain language. People working within the domain start to use the primitives of the formal language.

It is now clear that it is in general not wise to go directly from stage one (no reuse) to stage three (structured reuse). Formalization has much in common with standardization. It has a solidifying effect on the semantic primitives of the domain. Our notion of these primitives changes, because we do not any longer consider them as coming from the intuitive universe of discourse, but as being based on the underlying formalism. A crucial question, namely whether we formalized the *right* semantic primitives, then becomes harder to answer.

Stage two (ad hoc reuse) is crucial. In this stage, we get insight into the application domain and discover *useful* semantic primitives. This experience, both in working with the primitives and in implementing them, is of vital importance for the formalization of the domain in the right way.

The above discussion suggests an evolutionary approach to reuse. To start with, potentially reusable building blocks can be extracted from existing software products. While gaining experience with the reuse of these building blocks, better insight is obtained and better abstractions of concepts and mechanisms from the application domain are discovered. The library of reusable building blocks will thus evolve and stabilize over time.

This evolutionary process can be structured and guided through **domain analysis**, a process in which information used in developing software for a particular domain is identified, captured, structured, and organized for further reuse. Domain analysts and domain experts may use a variety of sources when modeling a domain, including expert knowledge, existing implementations and documentation. They extract and abstract the relevant information and encapsulate them in reusable building blocks.

Domain analysis often results not only in a collection of reusable building blocks. It also yields a reusable architecture for that domain: the domain-specific software architecture, product-line architecture, or application framework mentioned in section 17.2.4. To increase the reusability of these building blocks across different operating systems, networks, and the like, they are put on top of some middleware platform. The CORBAservices are an example of this. The San Francisco framework uses the same philosophy [BJNR98].

17.6 NON-TECHNICAL ASPECTS OF SOFTWARE REUSE

> *The problem is not lack of technology but unwillingness to address the most important issues influencing software reuse: managerial, economic, legal, cultural, and social.*
> [PD91b]

> *Myth #1: Software reuse is a technical problem.*
> [Tra88]

Up until now, we have only discussed technical aspects of software reuse. Software engineering is not only concerned with technical aspects but with people and other environmental aspects as well.

By being embedded within a society, the field of software engineering will also be influenced by that society. Software reuse in the US is likely to be different from software reuse in Japan or Europe. Because of cultural differences and different economic structures, it is not a priori clear that, say, the Toshiba approach to reuse can be copied by Europeans, with the same results.

Though our discussion so far has concerned the technical aspects of software reuse, it is not complete without a few words on non-technical issues. These non-technical issues are intimately intertwined with the more technical ones. Various practitioners in the field of software reuse have argued that the technology needed for software reuse is available, but that the main problems inhibiting a prosperous reuse industry are non-technical in nature.

Successful reuse programs share the following characteristics:

- Unconditional and extensive management support. A reuse program requires changes in the way software is developed. Management commitment is essential for making such changes work. In particular, building a base of reusable assets requires an initial investment which may not pay off for some time.

- Establishment of an organizational support structure. The organization must provide the initiative for the reuse program, funding, and policies. A separate body is needed to assess potential candidates for inclusion in the reuse library. A librarian is needed to maintain the library.

- Incremental program implementation. A first catalog with potential reusable assets can be built at a relatively low cost. Positive experiences with such an initial library will raise awareness and provide the necessary incentives (and funding) to expand the library, devise a classification scheme, etc.

- Significant success, both financial and organizational. Raytheon for example reports a 50% increase in productivity over a period of several years.

- Compulsory or highly incentivized. Programmers suffer from the 'not invented here' syndrome. By creating an environment that values both the creation of reusable software and the reuse of software, an atmosphere is established in which reuse may become a success.

- Domain analysis was conducted either consciously or unconsciously. Domain analysis identifies the concepts and mechanisms underlying some well-understood domain. This way, the *really* useful concepts are captured in reusable resources.

- Explicit attention to architectural issues, such as a common architecture across a product line.

Some of the non-technical aspects are discussed in the subsections below.

17.6.1 Economics

Reuse is a long term investment
[Tra90]

Reuse does not come for free. In a traditional development environment, products are tailored to the situation at hand. Similar situations are likely to require slightly different products or product components. For a software component to become reusable, it has to be generalized from the situation at hand, thoroughly documented and tested, incorporated in a library and classification scheme, and maintained as a separate entity. This requires an initial investment, which only starts to pay off after a certain period of time. One of the real dangers for a software reuse program is that it gets trapped in a devil's loop of the kind depicted in figure 17.11.

The major factors that determine the cost of a reusable building block are:

- the initial development cost of that component,

- the direct and indirect costs of including the component in a library, and

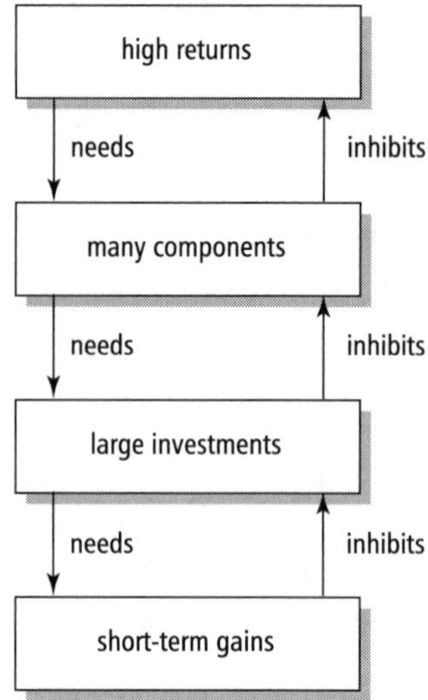

Figure 17.11 Software reuse devil's loop

- the cost of (possibly) adapting the component and incorporating it into the system under development.

It is obvious that the development of a reusable component is more costly than the development of a nonreusable component with the same functionality. Estimates of this extra cost vary from 50% to at least 100% (see also section 7.3.6 on the COCOMO 2 cost estimation model). It depends on the usage frequency of the component whether its development eventually pays off.

More immediate returns on investment can be obtained if the reuse program starts small, with an initial library whose members are extracted from existing products. Expansion of the program can then be justified on the basis of positive early experiences. But even then, non-project-specific funds must be allocated to the reuse program.

The economic consequences of software reuse go beyond cost savings in production and maintenance. The nature of the software development process itself changes. Software becomes a *capital* good. High initial costs are coupled with returns over a longer time period. The production of software thus becomes a *capital-intensive* process [Weg84]. The production of non-reusable software, on the other hand, is a *labor-intensive* process. Many man-months are spent, but the profits are reaped as soon as the project is finished.

Whereas labor-intensive software production tends to concentrate on finishing the project at hand on time and within budget, capital-intensive software production takes into account long-term business concerns such as the collective workers' knowledge and the collection of reusable assets. The software factory paradigm discussed in section 3.7 as well as the various approaches emphasizing the architecture of a software system fit this view of the software development organization.

17.6.2 Management

Myth #9: Software reuse will just happen.
[Tra88]

Getting software reuse off the ground cannot depend on spontaneity. Rather, software production ought to be organized so that reuse is promoted. In chapter 3, we noted that the traditional waterfall model tends to impede software reuse. In the waterfall model, emphasis is placed on measuring and controlling project progress. The product quality with respect to reusability is hard to measure. There is no real incentive to pursue reusability, since the primary (and often the only) goal is to finish the current project within time and budget. There is no motivation to make the next project look good. Consequently, software reusability tends to have a low priority.

If reuse is not a clear objective of our software development process, it is bound to remain accidental. Programmers tinker with code they have written before if and when they happen to notice similarities between successive problems. This unplanned approach to reuse is also known as **code scavenging** or **code salvaging**. This is distinct from the process of reusing software that was *designed* to be reused. In the life cycle perspective, this difference shows up as the difference between software-development-with-reuse and software-development-for-reuse.

In software-development-for-reuse, software reuse has been incorporated in the software development process. In this process model, reusable assets are actively sought. The concepts and mechanisms underlying some domain are identified and captured in reusable resources. The focus of software management then shifts from the delivery of individual products to maintaining and nurturing a rich collection of reusable artifacts. Some of the successful reuse programs, such as those reported in [PD91b], have followed this approach.

The library of reusable assets itself needs to be managed. An organizational infrastructure must be created which makes the library accessible (through documentation and classification schemes), assesses candidates for inclusion in the library, maintains and updates the library, etc. A separate organizational role, the librarian, may be created for this purpose. Its tasks resemble that of a database administrator.

One type of reuse only mentioned in passing, is *reuse of good people*. Expert designers are worth their weight in gold. Every average programmer is capable of writing a complicated, large program. In order to obtain a better, smaller, more elegant, radically new solution for that same problem, we need a person who has bright ideas from time to time.

A major problem in our field is that managers are rated higher than programmers or designers. If you are really good, you will sooner or later, but usually sooner, rise in the hierarchy and become part of the management. According to Brooks, there is only one way to counteract this phenomenon [Bro87]. To ensure that bright people remain system designers, we need a dual ranking scheme, one in which good designers have the same job prospects as good managers. Once again: the software process must be reconsidered as one of growing both people and the base of reusable assets [Cur89].

17.6.3 Psychology of Programmers

> *Reusing other people's code would prove that I don't care about my work. I would no more reuse code than Hemingway would reuse other authors' paragraphs.*
> [Cox90]

Software reuse means that programmers have to adapt, incorporate, or rejuvenate software written by other programmers. There are two important psychological aspects to this process:

- Are programmers willing to do so?
- Are they capable of doing so?

The first aspect is often mentioned as a major stumbling-block to establishing a positive attitude towards software reuse. [BB91] phrases this problem of image as follows: 'Anyone who has ever gone to an auto salvage yard to pick up a spare part for his old car "knows" what reuse is.'

Many authors suggest a solution to this problem that is both simple and effective: change the programming culture. The experiences at Raytheon, Toshiba and other places suggest that it is indeed possible, given the right incentives and, more importantly, a management attitude that pays attention to longer-term goals and developers' expectations about the nature of their work.

Research into the comprehensibility of software, such as reported in [SE84], shows that programmers use certain standard schemes in standard situations. Experienced programmers tend to get confused when a known problem has been tackled using (to them) non-standard solutions. As a consequence, the reusability of components is likely to be increased if the components embody abstractions the programmers are familiar with. Domain analysis addresses the same issues by trying to identify the notions that are shared by experts in a particular domain.

In the studies of Lanergan and Grasso, discussed in section 17.2.3, it appeared that one side-effect of the use of standard designs and standard components is the increased comprehensibility of the resulting software. Once all programmers got used to the Raytheon house style, it seemed as if all programs were written by one and the same team. Any team could understand and adapt a program written by some other team. This effect is stronger if we are able to explicitly name these larger constructs, as is done with design patterns and architectural styles.

17.7 SUMMARY

Reuse projects vary considerably in a number of dimensions:

- The thing to be reused may be a concrete component such as a piece of code or a software architecture, a more abstract concept, or even a process element such as a procedure to handle change requests.

- The scope of reuse may be horizontal or vertical. In horizontal reuse, components are generic. In vertical reuse, they are domain-specific.

- The approach to reuse may be planned or opportunistic. In planned reuse, software is *designed* to be reused. In opportunistic reuse, software is reused haphazardly, if and when we happen to know of its existence, if and when it happens to fit the current situation. Planned reuse is software development *for* reuse, opportunistic reuse is software development *with* reuse.

- Reuse may be compositional or generative. A composition-based technology aims at incorporating existing components into software to be newly developed. In a generation-based technology, the knowledge reused is to be found in some program that generates some other program.

- Reuse may be black-box or white-box. In black-box reuse, elements are reused as-is. In white-box reuse, they may be adapted to fit the situation at hand.

Classification schemes for reusable elements resemble those for textual sources in an ordinary library. They vary from a simple Key Word In Context approach to fully automated keyword retrieval from existing documentation, and may even involve elaborate knowledge of the application domain. With respect to retrieval, systems may employ an extensive thesaurus to relate similar terms or offer browsing facilities to inspect 'similar' components.

Software reusability is an objective, rather than a field. It emerged as an issue within software engineering, not because of its appeal as a scientific issue per se, but driven by the expected gain in software development productivity.

The history of software reuse starts in 1968. At the first software engineering conference, McIlroy already envisaged a bright future for a software component technology, somewhat similar to that for hardware components. The first conference specifically devoted to software reuse was held in 1983 [ITT83]. Since then, the topic has received increased attention. Over the years, a shift in research focus can be observed from domain-independent technical issues, such as classification techniques and component libraries, to domain-specific content issues, such as architectural frameworks and domain analysis.

A central question in all reuse technologies discussed is how to exploit some set of reusable building blocks. As argued in section 17.5, an equally important question is which building blocks are needed to start with. Answering the latter question requires a much deeper understanding of the software design process than we currently have.

Successful reuse programs share a number of characteristics:

- Unconditional and extensive management support,
- An organizational support structure,
- Incremental program implementation,
- Significant success, both financial and organizational,
- Compulsory or highly incentivized,
- Domain analysis conducted either consciously or unconsciously,
- Explicit attention to architectural issues.

Reuse is not a magic word with which the productivity of the software development process can be substantially increased at one blow. But we do have a sufficient number of departure-points for further improvements to get a remunerative reuse technology off the ground. Foremost amongst these are the attention to non-technical issues involved in software reuse and an evolutionary approach in conjunction with a conscientious effort to model limited application domains.

17.8 FURTHER READING

The modern history of software reuse starts at the first NATO software engineering conference [McI68]. The first conference specifically devoted to software reuse was held in 1983 [ITT83]. [BP89] and [Fre87] are well-known collections of articles on software reuse. [Kar95] is a good textbook on the subject. It is the result of an Esprit project called REBOOT. Amongst other things, it describes the software-development-with-reuse and software-development-for-reuse process models. [Rei97] is another good textbook on software reuse. [Kru92] is a survey article. [MMM95] is another survey article, emphasizing research issues, and with lots of further pointers to the literature. Component-based software engineering (CBSE) is addressed in [Sof98]. [Wey98] discusses the testing of reusable components.

The various reuse dimensions are discussed in [PD93]. A survey of methods for classifying reusable software components is given in [FG90]. The application of faceted classification to software reuse is described in [PD91a].

[PDN86] gives an overview of Module Interconnection Languages. [MT97] gives an overview of major types of Architecture Description Languages. CORBA is described in [Sie95]. [Szy98] is a textbook about component software; it contains chapters on CORBA, COM and JavaBeans. [CAC97a] contains a collection of articles on object-oriented application frameworks.

The non-technical nature of software reuse is discussed in [Tra88] and [Faf94]. Software reuse success factors are discussed in [PD91b] and [RS98]. Models to quantify reuse levels, reuse maturity, reuse costs and benefits are discussed in [FT96]. The Raytheon approach to software reuse is described in [LG84]. The Toshiba software factory is described in [Mat87]. Experiences with successful reuse programs are collected in [SPDM93], [Sof94b] and [JSS95b].

Exercises

1. What is the difference between composition-based reuse and generation-based reuse?

2. What is a faceted classification scheme?

3. What is the difference between horizontal and vertical reuse?

4. Describe the software-development-with-reuse process model. Where does it differ from the software-development-for-reuse process model?

5. Discuss the main differences between Module Interconnection Languages (MILs) and Architecture Description Languages (ADLs). How do these differences relate to software reuse?

6. How does CORBA promote reuse?

7. To what extent do you consider a domain-independent library of reusable software components a realistic option?

8. ♠ For a domain with which you are familiar, identify a set of potentially reusable software components and devise a classification scheme for them.

Consider both a hierarchical and a faceted classification scheme and assess their merits with respect to ease of classification and search, and extensibility.

9. ♠ For the same domain, assess its maturity level and that of the components identified. Can you relate the maturity level of components to their perceived reusability?

10. ♡ Devise a managerial setting and a software development process model for a component-based software factory.

11. ♠ Assess one or more of the following domains and determine the extent and kind of reuse that has been achieved:

    - window management systems;
    - (2D) computer graphics;
    - user-interface development systems;
    - office automation;
    - salary administration;
    - hypertext systems.

12. ♡ For the domains studied in the previous exercise, is there any relation between the reuse level achieved and (de facto or de jure) standardization within the domain? Can you discern any influence of standardization on reuse, or vice versa?

13. ♠ Discuss possible merits of knowledge-based approaches to software reusability.

14. ♡ From your own past in software development, make an inventory of:

    - components developed by yourself which you reused more than once, and
    - components developed by others and reused by you.

    To what extent does the Not-Invented-Here syndrome apply to your situation? Is reuse in your situation accidental or deliberate? Were the components designed for reuse or was it, rather, a form of code scavenging?

15. ♡ Suppose you developed a routine to determine the inverse of a matrix. The routine is to be incorporated in a library of reusable components. Which aspects of this routine should be documented in order that others may determine the suitability of the routine for their application?

16. ♡ In developing Abstract Data Types (ADTs) we try to strictly separate (and hide) implementation concerns from the users of those ADTs. To what extent could these implementation concerns be relevant to the person reusing them?

18 Software Reliability

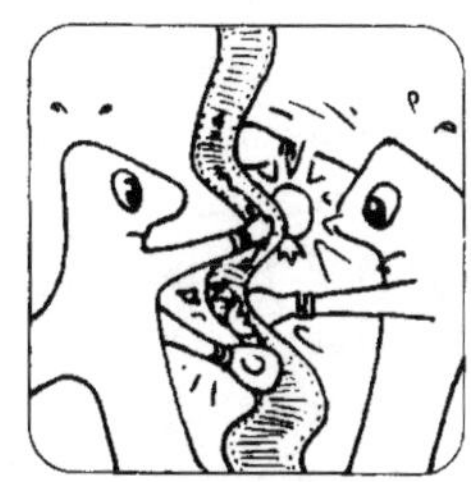

LEARNING OBJECTIVES

- To appreciate fault tolerance as one approach to increasing the reliability of software
- To be aware of some mathematical models to estimate the reliability of software

Creating reliable software is one of the central objectives of the field of software engineering. Unreliable software can be a nuisance to its users. Unreliable software may incur (large) financial losses to its users. It may even cause deaths. The column 'Risks to the public in computer systems' in the *ACM Software Engineering Notes* gives many examples of (near) accidents caused by faulty software.

In a narrow sense, we may consider reliability aspects of programming languages and programming language constructs. For instance, the use of goto statements is often discouraged. Gotos result in complex and error-prone software. The intended effect can often be obtained through alternative constructs, such as exceptions or an exit statement. Another example is type-checking. Type-checking in languages like Pascal detects both clerical typing errors and more subtle mistakes. As a third example, automatic garbage collection frees the programmer from the housekeeping tasks concerned with storage management.

A second aspect of reliability shows up when we consider the input domain of a software component. Most often, the valid input to a component is somehow constrained. We may expect the system to issue a proper error message or otherwise notify the caller of a component for those cases in which these constraints are not met.

The set of correct inputs to some software component is sometimes called its **standard domain**, while the set of incorrect inputs is referred to as the **exception domain**. Some subset of the exception domain is caught by the software: the **expected exception domain**. The part not caught makes the component unreliable. Errors in this category may have quite unexpected effects.

For example, suppose we implement a module that manipulates stacks of a certain maximum length. This maximum length is given as a parameter to the routine Create. The routines Pop, Push and Top properly test for the stack being empty or full. These cases belong to the expected exception domain. However, the routine Create does not test whether its actual parameter has a positive value. If the value of the actual parameter is negative, this is an unexpected exception.

In an ideal situation, the domain of unexpected exceptions is empty. We have then taken precautions against all possible interface faults in routine invocations. This can be obtained by assuming a precondition true for all routines of a program.

In any case, we must try to keep the domain of unexpected exceptions as small as possible. Prudence is the mother of wisdom. Even if we know that a component is only invoked from within a certain context, it is better to ensure the proper functioning of that component irrespective of its context. This will increase the program's reliability. This technique is called **robust programming** or **defensive programming**.

In general, we assume that our programs work perfectly. That is, if a sorting routine is being called, we expect the resulting file to be sorted; if a binary tree is built, we expect the resulting data structure to be a binary tree; if we write certain information to a disk, we expect the disk to contain that information and we expect to be able to retrieve that information at a later stage.

But what if this is not true? The sorting component may contain a fault, the system's memory allocation facilities may run havoc, disk tracks may become unreadable.

There are various techniques to detect and correct this type of hazard. When storing data we may add some redundant information and use this redundancy later to check the correctness of the data stored. Simple forms of this are the addition of a parity bit or a checksum. In section 18.1, we will give a more elaborate example of the use of redundant information to increase the reliability of a piece of software.

For all kinds of physical products, reliability requirements are set. Cars, bridges, radios, etc., are not 100% reliable. They do function properly most of the time, though. By setting thresholds like 'the probability that component A will not fail within 5000 hours of operational use is greater than 0.999', and through extensive testing and a proper statistical analysis of the test data, the validity of such reliability claims can be assessed.

We may apply the same statistical notion of reliability to software, and try to answer such questions as: what is the probability that a given software system will not fail during the next hour of operational use? Answering such questions hinges on the use of a valid model of failure behavior for software, and the availability of data on past failures of the system. Some of these statistical software reliability models are discussed in section 18.2.

18.1 AN EXAMPLE: FAULT-TOLERANT DISKS

Information written to a disk does get lost once in a while. How then should we design and implement a system in which the probability that information gets lost irrevocably is less than some threshold α?

This example is taken from [Cri85]. In the solution given there, the information is written to *two* disks. The redundancy thus obtained can be used when reading information from the disk: if one disk fails, we try the second one. The corresponding routines safewrite and saferead are given in figure 18.1.

The system under discussion can handle two types of adverse event:

- The contents of one or more blocks from a disk may become unreadable. The frequency with which this happens is supposed to be known from some hardware analysis procedure. As usual, an exponential distribution is assumed for the frequency with which such failures occur.

- The processor on which the system runs crashes. If this happens during a write operation, we assume that the block in question becomes unreadable. The content of the disk is not affected if the crash occurs somewhere else in the program. This process is also assumed to follow an exponential distribution, with known parameters.

By combining these two types of adverse event, something will go wrong with frequency s. If this occurs, we would like to quickly bring both disks in line again. This is achieved by regularly calling the routine recover (see figure 18.1). Recover compares the information on the disks and, if necessary, takes corrective action.

```
proc safewrite(a: address, b: block);
    begin write(disk1, a, b); write(disk2, a, b) end;

proc saferead(a: address, b: block);
    begin
        if ¬ read(disk1, a, b) then read(disk2, a, b)
    end;

proc recover;
var s1, s2: boolean; x, y: block; a: address;
    begin
        for a from 0 to max do
        begin s1:= read(disk1, a, x);
            s2:= read(disk2, a, y);
            if ¬ s1 then write(disk1, a, y);
            if (¬ s2) or (x ≠ y) then write(disk2, a, x)
        end
    end;
```

Figure 18.1 Read, write and recovery routines for fault-tolerant disks. (*Source: F. Cristian, A rigorous approach to fault-tolerant programming,* IEEE Transactions on Software Engineering, *©1985 IEEE*)

The routine recover treats the two disks asymmetrically. For, if we are able to read a certain block from both disks and their contents differ, then the processor must have crashed between the two write actions of safewrite. In that case, the first disk was written last, so we still have to adjust the contents of the second disk accordingly.

It is the intention that recover is called with a frequency such that the probability of more than one failure in between two successive calls is less than the given threshold α. Note that the routine recover as given is also capable of handling multiple failures, provided they affect mutually disjoint sets of blocks.

Each of the disks can be in one of two states:

ok – each block is readable and has the right contents, and

ko – at least one block is unreadable or has incorrect contents.

We may view each disk as a random variable d_i $(i = 1, 2)$. Each of these random variables is in one of the states {ok, ko}. The stochastic process (d_1, d_2) thus has four possible states.

Transitions $(x, \text{ok}) \rightarrow (x, \text{ko})$ or $(\text{ok}, y) \rightarrow (\text{ko}, y)$ occur if one or more blocks of the disk in question have the wrong contents written to them. As noted before, the frequency of this is assumed to be s.

Transitions in the opposite direction occur when recover is called. If the frequency of calling recover is $1/2\delta$, then the time between the occurrence of a fault and the start of the next corrective action is δ hours, on average. If the corrective action itself takes ρ hours on average, then the frequency of the transition (ko, ok) → (ok, ok) or (ok, ko) → (ok, ok) equals $r = 1/(\delta + \rho)$.

If the system inadvertently reaches the state (ko, ko), the routine recover will still work correctly if the faults concern different blocks. If not, we will have to fall back onto a different procedure, such as manual repair. Obviously, our goal is to prevent this situation occurring – which is why we built the model to start with. However, this situation cannot be ruled out altogether. If this latter procedure takes ω hours on the average, then the frequency of the transition (ko, ko) → (ok, ok) equals $R = 1/(\delta + \omega)$.

The various possible states and transitions are depicted graphically in figure 18.2. It easily follows that the system in equilibrium satisfies the following equations:

$$
\begin{aligned}
2s\, p_{\text{ok,ok}} &= r\, p_{\text{ok,ko}} + r\, p_{\text{ko,ok}} + R\, p_{\text{ko,ko}} \\
s\, p_{\text{ok,ko}} + r\, p_{\text{ok,ko}} &= s\, p_{\text{ok,ok}} \\
s\, p_{\text{ko,ok}} + r\, p_{\text{ko,ok}} &= s\, p_{\text{ok,ok}} \\
s\, p_{\text{ok,ko}} + s\, p_{\text{ko,ok}} &= R\, p_{\text{ko,ko}}
\end{aligned}
$$

We may safely assume the process to be symmetric – there is no a priori reason to think that one disk is better than the other – so:

$$p_{\text{ok,ko}} = p_{\text{ko,ok}}$$

The various probabilities add up to 1, so:

$$p_{\text{ok,ok}} + p_{\text{ok,ko}} + p_{\text{ko,ok}} + p_{\text{ko,ko}} = 1$$

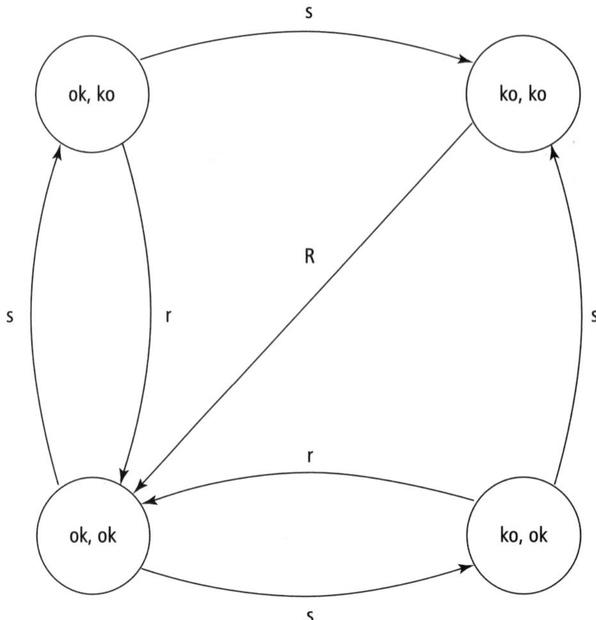

Figure 18.2 Possible states and their transitions (*Source: F. Cristian, A rigorous approach to fault-tolerant programming,* IEEE Transactions on Software Engineering, *©1985 IEEE*)

Finally, the probability that the system reaches state (ko, ko) is given through the threshold α:

$$p_{\mathrm{ko,ko}} \leq \alpha$$

If values for α, ρ, ω and s are given, the value of r (i.e. the frequency with which recover has to be called) can be determined by solving the above set of equations.

In certain applications, such as databases containing financial data, this type of analysis and the resulting algorithms are often applied. We term these systems **fault-tolerant**.

The routine saferead employs a fault tolerance technique that resembles **recovery blocks**. Another main technique that has evolved for software fault tolerance is **N-version programming**. Both these techniques are based on design diversity. Different versions of the software are developed independently and it is hoped that these versions are (at least partly) independent in their failure behavior. This is not necessarily true though. In one analysis of faults in N-version programming for example it was found that programmers do make identical errors.

When using recovery blocks, versions of components are executed serially. An acceptance test is used to check their outcomes. An alternative version is executed only if the current version fails the acceptance test. In that case, the state of the system as it was just prior to the execution of the component has to be recovered before an alternative can be tried. In N-version programming, the different versions are executed in parallel and the results are voted on.

18.2 ESTIMATING SOFTWARE RELIABILITY

In much of this book the reader will find references to the fact that most software does not function perfectly. Faults are found in almost every run-of-the-mill software system: the software is not 100% reliable. In this section we concentrate on quantitative, statistical, notions of software reliability.

One benefit of such information is that it can be put to use in planning our maintenance effort. Another reason for collecting reliability information could be contractual obligations regarding a required reliability level. Software for telephone switching systems, for instance, requires such quantitative knowledge of the system's expected availability. We need to know what the probability is of wrong connections being due to faults in the software.

A second application of reliability data is found in testing. A major problem with testing is deciding when to stop. One possibility is to base this decision on reaching a certain reliability level. If the required reliability level is not reached, we need an estimate of the time it will take to reach that level.

In order to be able to answer this type of question, a number of **software reliability models** have been developed which strongly resemble the well-known hardware reliability models. These are statistical models where the starting point is a certain probability distribution for expected failures. The precise distribution is not known a priori. We must measure the points in time at which the first n failures occur and look for a probability distribution that fits those data. We can then make predictions using the probability distribution just obtained.

In this section we will concentrate on two models which are not too complicated and yet yield fairly good results: the **basic execution time model** and the **logarithmic Poisson execution time model**.

The goal of many test techniques discussed in chapter 13 is to find as many faults as possible. What we in fact observe are *manifestations* of faults, i.e. failures. The system fails if the output does not meet the specification. Faults in a program are static in nature, failures are dynamic. A program can fail only when it is executed. From the user's point of view, failures are much more important than faults. For example, a fault in a piece of software that is never, or hardly ever, used is, in general, less important than a fault which manifests itself frequently. Also, one and the same fault may show up in different ways and a failure may be caused by more than one fault.

In the following discussion on reliability, we will not be concerned with the expected number of faults in a program. Rather, the emphasis will be on the expected number of failures. The notion of time plays an essential role. For the moment, we will define reliability as: the probability that the program will not fail during a certain period of time.

The notion of time deserves further attention. Ultimately, we are interested in statements regarding calendar time. For example, we might want to know the probability that a given system will not fail in a one-week time period, or we might be interested in the number of weeks of system testing still needed to reach a certain reliability level.

Both models discussed below use the notion of execution time. Execution time is the time spent by the machine actually executing the software. Reliability models based on execution time yield better results than those based on calendar time. In many cases, an a posteriori translation of execution time to calendar time is possible. To emphasize this distinction, execution time will be denoted by τ and calendar time by t.

The failure behavior of a program depends on many factors: quality of the designers, complexity of the system, development techniques used, etc. Most of these cannot adequately be dealt with as variables in a reliability model and therefore are assumed to be fixed. Reliability, when discussed in this section, will therefore always concern one specific project.

Some factors affecting failure behavior can be dealt with, though. As noticed before, the models discussed are based on the notion of execution time. This is simple to measure if we run one application on a stand-alone computer. Translation between machines that differ in speed can be taken care of relatively easily. Even if the machine is used in multiprogramming mode, translation from the time measured to proper execution time may be possible. This is the case, for instance, if time is relatively uniformly distributed over the applications being executed.

The input to a program is also variable. Since we estimate the model's parameters on the basis of failures observed, the predictions made will only hold insofar as future input resembles the input which led to the observed failure behavior. The future has to resemble the past. In order to get reliable predictions, the tests must be representative of the later operational use of the system. If we are able to allocate the possible inputs to different equivalence classes, simple readjustments are possible here too.

We may summarize this discussion by including the environment in the definition of our notion of software reliability. Reliability then is defined as the probability that a system will not fail during a certain period of time in a certain environment.

Finally, software systems are not static entities. Software is often implemented and tested incrementally. Reliability of an evolving system is difficult to express. In the ensuing discussion, we therefore assume that our systems are stable over time.

We may characterize the failure behavior of software in different ways. For example, we may consider the expected time to the next failure, the expected time interval between successive failures, or the expected number of failures in a certain time interval. In all cases, we are concerned with random variables, since we do not know exactly when the software will fail. There are at least two reasons for this uncertainty. Firstly, we do not know where the programmer made errors. Secondly, the relation between a certain input and the order in which the corresponding set of instructions is being executed is not usually known. We may therefore model subsequent failures as a stochastic process. Such a stochastic process is characterized by, amongst other things, the form and probability distribution of the random variables.

When the software fails, we try to locate and repair the fault that caused this failure. In particular, this situation arises during the test phase of the software life cycle. Since we assume a stable situation, the application of reliability models is particularly appropriate during system testing, when the individual modules have been integrated into one system. This system-test situation in particular will be discussed below.

In this situation, the failure behavior will not follow a constant pattern but will change over time, since faults detected are subsequently repaired. A stochastic process whose probability distribution changes over time is called *non-homogeneous*. The variation in time between successive failures can be described in terms of a function $\mu(\tau)$ which denotes the average number of failures until time τ . Alternatively, we may consider the failure intensity function $\lambda(\tau)$, the average number of failures per unit of time at time τ. $\lambda(\tau)$ then is the derivative of $\mu(\tau)$. If the reliability of a program increases through fault correction, the failure intensity will decrease.

The relationship between $\lambda(\tau)$, $\mu(\tau)$ and τ is graphically depicted in figure 18.3. The models to be discussed below, the basic execution time model (BM) and the logarithmic Poisson execution time model (LPM), differ in the form of the failure intensity function $\lambda(\tau)$.

Both BM and LPM assume that failures occur according to a non-homogeneous Poisson process. Poisson processes are often used to describe the stochastic behavior of real-world events. Examples of Poisson processes are: the number of telephone calls expected in a given period of time, or the expected number of car accidents in a given period of time. In our case, the processes are non-homogeneous, since the failure intensity changes as a function of time, assuming a (partly) successful effort to repair the underlying errors.

In BM, the decrease in failure intensity, as a function of the number of failures observed, is constant. The contribution to the decrease in failure intensity thus is the same for each failure observed. In terms of the mean number of failures observed (μ), we obtain

$$\lambda(\mu) = \lambda_0(1 - \mu/\nu_0)$$

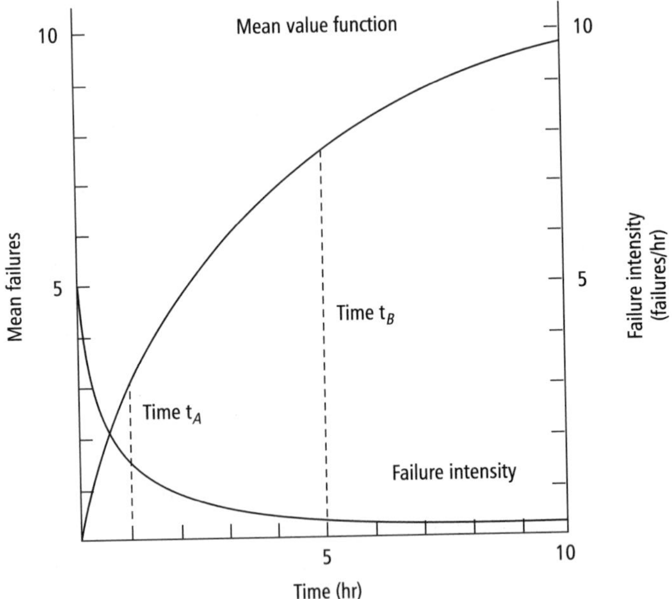

Figure 18.3 Failure intensity $\lambda(\tau)$ and mean failures $\mu(\tau)$ as functions of τ *(Source: J.D. Musa, A. Iannino and K. Okumoto,* Software Reilability, *Copyright McGraw-Hill Book Company, 1987. Reproduced by permission of McGraw-Hill, Inc.)*

Here, λ_0 denotes the initial failure intensity, i.e. the failure intensity at time 0. ν_0 denotes the number of failures observed if the program is executed for an infinite time period. Note that, since λ is the derivative of μ, and both are functions of τ, λ in fact only depends on τ. We will return to this later.

In LPM, the first failure contributes more to the decrease in failure intensity than any subsequent failures. More precisely, the failure intensity is exponential in the number of failures observed. We then get:

$$\lambda(\mu) = \lambda_0 \exp^{-\theta\mu}$$

In this model, θ denotes the decrease in failure intensity. For both models, the relation between λ and μ is depicted in figure 18.4. (Note that the two curves intersect in this picture. This need not necessarily be the case. It depends on the actual values of the model parameters.)

Both models have two parameters: λ_0 and ν_0 for BM, and λ_0 and θ for LPM. These parameters have yet to be determined, for instance from the observed failure behavior during a certain period of time.

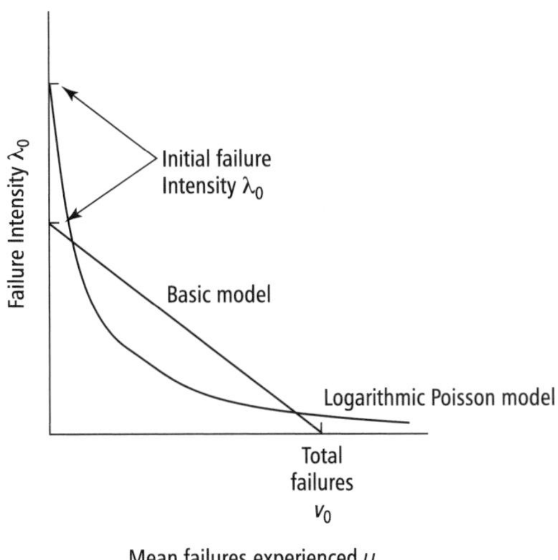

Figure 18.4 Failure intensity λ as a function of μ (*Source: J.D. Musa, A. Iannino and K. Okumoto,* Software Reilability, *Copyright McGraw-Hill Book Company, 1987. Reproduced by permission of McGraw-Hill, Inc.*)

We can explain the shape of these functions as follows: given a certain input, the program in question will execute a certain sequence of instructions. A completely different input may result in a completely different sequence of instructions to be executed. We may partition all possible inputs into a number of classes such that input from any one class results in the execution of the same sequence of instructions. Some example classes could be a certain type of command in an operating system or a certain type of transaction in a database system.

The user will select input from the various possible classes according to some probability distribution. We define the **operational profile** as the set of possible input classes together with the probabilities that input from those classes is selected.

The basic execution time model implies a uniform operational profile. If all input classes are selected equally often, the various faults have an equal probability of manifesting themselves. Correction of any of those faults then contributes the same amount to the decrease in failure intensity. It has been found that BM still models the situation fairly well in the case of a fairly non-uniform operational profile.

With a strong non-uniform operational profile the failure intensity curve will have a convex shape, as in LPM. Some input classes will then be selected relatively often. As a consequence, certain faults will show up earlier and be corrected sooner. These corrections will have a larger impact on the decrease in failure intensity.

In both models, λ and μ are functions of τ (execution time). Furthermore, failure intensity λ is the derivative of mean failures μ. For BM, we may therefore write

$$\lambda(\mu) = \lambda_0(1 - \mu/\nu_0)$$

as

$$\frac{\mathrm{d}\mu(\tau)}{\mathrm{d}\tau} = \lambda_0(1 - \mu(\tau)/\nu_0)$$

Solving this differential equation yields

$$\mu(\tau) = \nu_0(1 - \exp^{-\lambda_0\tau/\nu_0})$$

and

$$\lambda(\tau) = \lambda_0 \exp^{-\lambda_0\tau/\nu_0}$$

In a similar way, we obtain for LPM:

$$\mu(\tau) = \ln(\lambda_0\theta\tau + 1)/\theta$$

and

$$\lambda(\tau) = \lambda_0/(\lambda_0\theta\tau + 1)$$

For LPM, the expected number of failures in infinite time is infinite. Obviously, the number of failures observed during testing is finite.

Both models allow that fault correction is not perfect. In BM the effectiveness of fault correction is constant, though not necessarily 100%. This again shows up in the linearity of the failure intensity function. In LPM, the effectiveness of fault correction decreases with time. Possible reasons could be that it becomes increasingly more difficult to locate the faults, for example because the software becomes less structured, or the personnel less motivated.

If the software has become operational and faults are not being corrected any more, the failure intensity will remain constant. Both models then reduce to a homogeneous Poisson process with failure intensity λ as the parameter. The number of failures expected in a certain time period will then follow a Poisson-distribution. The probability of exactly n failures being observed in a time period of length τ is then given by

$$P_n(\tau) = (\lambda\tau)^n \times \exp^{-\lambda\tau} /n!$$

The probability of 0 failures in a time frame of length τ then is $P_0(\tau) = \exp(-\lambda\tau)$. This is precisely what we earlier denoted by the term software reliability.

Given a choice of one of the models BM or LPM, we are next faced with the question of how to estimate the model's parameters. We may do so by measuring the points in time at which the first N failures occur. This gives us points $T_1, \ldots, T_n$. These points can be translated into pairs $(\tau, \mu(\tau))$. We may then determine the model's parameters so that the resulting curve fits the set of measuring points. Techniques like Maximum Likelihood or Least Squares are suited for this.

Once these parameters have been determined, predictions can be made. For example, suppose the measured data result in a present failure intensity λ_P and the required failure intensity is λ_F. If we denote the additional test time required to reach failure intensity λ_F by $\Delta\tau$, then we obtain for BM:

$$\Delta\tau = (\nu_0/\lambda_0)\ln(\lambda_P/\lambda_F)$$

And for LPM we get

$$\Delta\tau = (1/\theta)(1/\lambda_F - 1/\lambda_P)$$

Obviously, we may also start from the equations for μ. We then obtain estimates for the number of failures that have yet to be observed before the required failure intensity level is reached.

For BM, this extrapolation is graphically depicted in figure 18.5. Since estimating the model's parameters is a statistical process, we do not actually obtain one solution. Rather, we get reliability intervals. Such a reliability interval denotes the interval which will contain a parameter with a certain probability. For example, λ_0 may be in the interval [80,100] with probability 0.75. So the curve in figure 18.5 is actually a band. The narrower this band is, the more accurately the parameters have been estimated for the same reliability of the interval. In general the estimates will be more accurate if they are based on more data.

In the above discussion, we used the notion of execution time. That calendar time is a less useful notion on which to base our model can be seen as follows: suppose the points in time at which the first N failures occurred were expressed in terms of calendar time. Suppose also that we try to correct a fault as soon as it manifests itself. If the manpower available for fault correction is limited, and this manpower is capable of solving a fixed number of problems per day, the failure intensity will be constant if it is based on calendar time. We then do not observe any progress.

Quite a few reliability models have been proposed in the literature. The major differences concern the total number of failures (finite or infinite) that can be experienced in infinite time and the distribution of the failures experienced at a given point in time (Poisson, binomial, etc.).

An important question then arises as to which model to choose. By studying a number of failure data sets, it has been observed that no one model is consistently

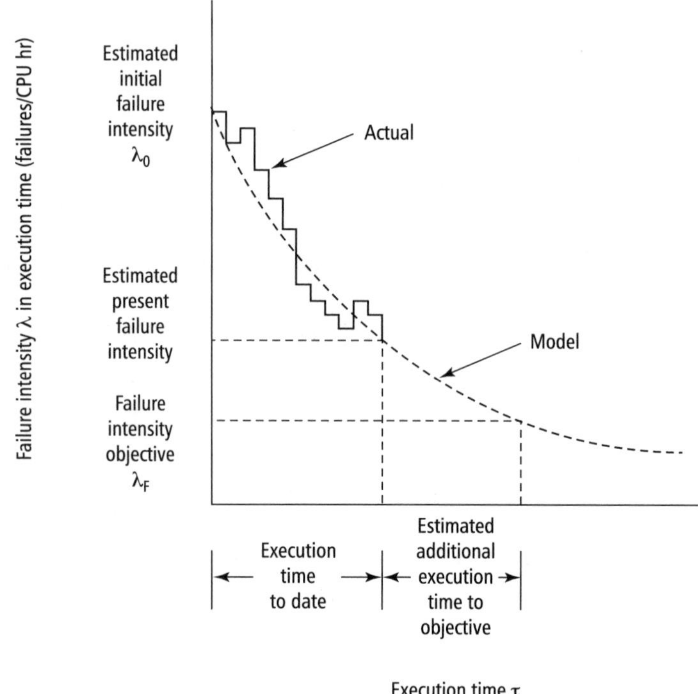

Figure 18.5 A conceptual view of the parameter-estimating process (*Source: J.D. Musa, A. Iannino and K. Okumoto,* Software Reilability, *Copyright McGraw-Hill Book Company, 1987. Reproduced by permission of McGraw-Hill, Inc.*)

the best. We therefore have to look for the model that gives the best prediction on a project-by-project basis. Since we do not know in advance which model will perform best, it is wise to adopt an eclectic approach, and use a number of different models simultaneously.

18.3 SUMMARY

This chapter focused on software reliability, a topic of increasing importance, not least because of the many accidents and near-accidents that are caused by software failures.

The reliability of software may be increased in various ways. First, we may study programming languages in order to identify error-prone constructs. The reliability of software will be increased by using only safe constructs. Secondly, reliability may be increased through robust programming, in which software components as far as possible test for faulty input. Finally, we may increase the reliability through **fault-tolerant programming**. In fault-tolerant programming, we make use of a number of functionally-equivalent software components that have been developed independently. These components may then be executed in parallel after which their output is voted on. This is known as **N-version programming**. Alternatively, one version may be executed and, if its output is not acceptable, another version is tried. In the latter case, the status of the system just prior to the execution of the component must be recovered. Hence, this scheme is known as **recovery blocks**.

The second part of this chapter was devoted to a discussion of how to quantitatively estimate the reliability of a piece of software. The currently-available software reliability models are limited in their immediate practical value. In particular, no model consistently performs best. Much research and experimentation is needed to further refine and validate these models.

18.4 FURTHER READING

An in-depth treatment of fault-tolerance is given in [Lyu95b]. Whether fault-tolerance actually increases reliability is a controversial issue; see for instance [But93] or [Hat97].

The basic execution time model and the logarithmic Poisson execution time model are extensively discussed, and compared with a number of other models, in [MIO87]. [Lyu95a] is a very comprehensive source on software reliability.

Research on software reliability and fault-tolerance is reported on in various special journal issues: [Com96b], [Com97], [TrS93].

Exercises

1. What is fault-tolerant programming?

2. What is the main difference between recovery blocks and N-version programming?

3. What is the major difference between the basic execution time model and the logarithmic Poisson execution time model of software reliability?

4. Give a definition of software reliability. Give a rationale for the various parts of this definition.

5. Discuss arguments for and against the use of N-version programming to increase software reliability.

6. Why is it important to consider the operational profile of a system while assessing its reliability?

7. Can you think of reasons why reliability models based on execution time yield better results than those based on calendar time?

8. Can software reliability be determined objectively?

9. ♡ Discuss the possible contribution of

   - strongly-typed programming languages,
   - *goto*-less programming,
   - abstract data types,
   - object-oriented programming languages, and
   - procedures having precondition **true**

   to the construction of reliable software.

10. ♡ Discuss the following claim: 'Reliability assessment is more important than testing.' Can you think of reasons why both are needed?

11. ♡ Give an intuitive account of the role of pre- and postconditions in software development (consider the contract-theory proposed by [Mey88]).

19
Software Tools

LEARNING OBJECTIVES

- To be able to distinguish various dimensions along which tools can be classified
- To be aware of the major trends in (collections of) software tools
- To appreciate the role of tools in the software development process

The demand for software grows faster than the increase in software development productivity and available manpower. The result is an ever-increasing shortage of personnel; we are less and less able to satisfy the quest for software. To turn the tide, we must look for techniques that result in significant productivity gains.

One of the most obvious routes to pursue is automation itself. We may use the computer as a tool in the production of software. In the past, all sorts of things were automated, save software development itself. Programmers knew better than that.

We have long been accustomed to employ the computer as a tool for the implementation of software. To this end, programmers have a vast array of tools at their disposal, such as compilers, linkers and loaders. Also during testing, tools like test drivers and test harnesses have been used for a long time. The development of tools to support earlier phases of the software life cycle is much more recent. One example of the latter is software to aid the drawing and validation of UML diagrams.

The use of software tools may have a positive effect on both the productivity of the people involved and the quality of the product being developed. Tools may support checking conformance to standards. Tools may help to quantify the degree of testing. Tools may support progress tracking. And so on. This is what tool vendors want us to believe. Actual studies of tool adoption and usage, however, show mixed results. The study reported on in [NN89], for example, concludes that, in the perception of software engineers, productivity is improved with the use of automated tools. Several years later, [TKS95] explored the attitudes of IT professionals about tools prevalent in the development environment. Their subjects were not convinced that tools improve the design development process.[1]

The application of tools in the software development process is referred to as **Computer Aided Software Engineering (CASE)**. Apart from the traditional implementation and test tools, CASE has a relatively short history. The first tools to support design activities appeared in the early 1980s. Today, the number of CASE products is overwhelming.

As the number of available CASE products proliferates, it becomes expedient to classify them. One way of doing so is according to the breadth of support they offer. Figure 19.1 gives a classification of CASE products along this dimension. Some products support a specific task in the software development process. Others support the entire software process. The former are called **tools**, the latter **environments**. In between these two extremes it is useful to identify CASE products that support a limited set of activities, such as those which comprise the analysis and design stages. Such a coherent set of tools with a limited scope is referred to as a **workbench**.

[1] The difference may (partly) be caused by a different focus. The first study concerned productivity, the second emphasized design quality.

CASE product	supports
Tool	One task
Workbench	Limited set of activities
Environment	Entire software process
Toolkit	
Language-centered environment	
Integrated environment	
Process-centered environment	

Figure 19.1 Classification of CASE products

Environments can be further classified according to the mechanism that ties together the individual tools that make up the environment. In a **toolkit**, tools are generally not well integrated. The support offered is independent of a specific programming language or development paradigm. A toolkit merely offers a set of useful building blocks. A **language-centered environment** contains tools specifically suited for the support of software development in a specific programming language. Such an environment may be hand-crafted or generated from a grammatical description of the language. In the latter case, the environment tends to focus on the manipulation of program structures.

The essence of **integrated** and **process-centered environments** is the sharing of information between the tools that make up the environment. Integrated environments focus on the resulting product. The heart of an integrated environment is a data repository, containing a wealth of information on the product to be developed, from requirements up to running code. Process-centered environments focus on sharing a description of the software development process.

Obviously, classifying actual CASE products according to this framework is not always easy. For example, many environments that span the complete life cycle evolved from workbenches that supported either front-end activities (analysis and global design) or back-end activities (implementation and test). These environments tend to contain tools specifically geared at supporting tasks from the corresponding part of the life cycle, augmented by a more general support for the other phases (such as for editing, text processing, or database access).

The framework of figure 19.1 classifies CASE products according to the parts of the life cycle they support. Figure 19.2 lists a number of dimensions along which CASE products can be classified. Using all of these dimensions to classify a CASE product yields a faceted classification scheme, which provides more information and is more flexible than the one-dimensional framework of figure 19.1.

No development method is suited for all classes of problems. Likewise, there is no CASE product for all problem classes. Specific properties of a given class of

Dimension	Typical values
Breadth of support	Tool, workbench, or environment
Class of problem	Embedded, business, real-time,...
Size of system	Small, medium, or large
User scale	Individual, family, city, or state
Process scale	Product, people, or product-and-people
Process support	None, fixed, or variable
Execution paradigm	State machine, Petri net, production rules, procedures,...

Figure 19.2 Faceted classification structure for CASE products

problems will impact the tools for that class. An important property of embedded systems is that the software is often developed on some host machine which is different from the ultimate target machine. Specific tools will be required for the development of such systems, for instance tools that allow us to test the software on the host machine.

For many business applications, the human–computer interaction plays a prominent role, while the requirements analysis of such systems tends to be problematic. A development environment for such systems had better contain tools that support those aspects (analyst workbench, prototyping facilities, and facilities to generate screen layouts).

As a final example, when developing real-time software, it would be preferable to have tools that allow us to analyze system performance at an early stage.

A second dimension relates the set of tools to the size of the system to be developed. In practice, it shows that tool usage increases with problem size. For a small project, we may confine ourselves to a simple configuration control system, simple test tools, and a shared database system to store documents. In a medium-sized project, more advanced support could be used, such as a structured database with objects like design documentation, test plans, or code components. Certain relations between objects, such as A uses B, or A implements B, could be maintained. For a medium-sized project, the toolset would also include tools to support management tasks, for example to create CPM or PERT charts. For a large project, we may require that the tools be mutually compatible. The toolset for a large project will generally also impose more constraints on their users.

The user scale refers to the number of users the product supports. Not surprisingly, the user-scale dimension is closely related to the system size dimension. Larger systems require larger development teams, don't they? Using a sociological paradigm, possible values along the user-scale dimension are called individual, family, city and state. Some products support the individual developer. These products are dominated by issues of software construction. The emphasis is on tools that support software construction: editors, debuggers, compilers, etc. CASE products that offer configuration management and system build facilities can be classified as belonging to the family model of software development environments. In the family model, a great deal of freedom is left to the individual developer, while a number of rules are agreed upon to regulate critical interactions between developers.

This model is not appropriate any more if projects get really big. Larger populations require more complicated rules and restrictions on individual freedom. Within my family, a few simple rules suffice (Jasper and Marieke take turns in washing dishes), and adjustments and local deviations are easily established (Jasper has a party today and asks Marieke to take over). Within a large company, policies have to be more strictly obeyed and cooperation between individuals is enforced (like in a city). Likewise, toolsets to support the development of large systems should enforce the proper cooperation between individual developers.

A state may be viewed as a collection of cities. A company may be viewed as a collection of projects. In the state model, the main concern is with commonality and standardization, to allow developers to switch between projects, to be able to reuse code, designs, test plans, etc.

The process scale specifies whether the CASE product supports code production activities, people activities, or both. CASE products focusing on code production concentrate on support for the evolution of software. They contain tools to write, compile, test, debug, and configure code. These are all activities done by a computer. Other CASE products concentrate on personnel interactions, such as the scheduling of review meetings. Still others do both. Values along this axis may be termed product, people, and product-and-people.

CASE products may or may not support the development *process*. If the development process is supported, some tools do so on the basis of a predefined model of the process. Others allow the user to define his own process model. If the CASE product supports the development process, it may employ various internal means to guide the execution (or enactment) of the development process, such as state machines, Petri nets, production rules, or procedures.

The various approaches to collections of software tools are addressed in sections 19.1 to 19.4, using the simple classification scheme of figure 19.1. Toolkits are discussed in section 19.1. UNIX is a prime example from this category. Section 19.2 discusses language-centered environments. This encompasses both environments created manually around some given programming language, and environments generated from a grammatical description of the program structures being manipulated. In both cases, the support offered mostly concerns the individual programmer. Section 19.3 and 19.4 discuss integrated and process-centered environments, respectively. Since most workbenches may be viewed as trimmed-down integrated environments, workbenches are discussed in section 19.3 as well.

The discussion below is fairly global in nature. We will skim over details of individual tools. Our aim is to sketch discernible trends in this area and to have a critical look at the possible role of tools in the software development process.

19.1 TOOLKITS

With a toolkit, developers are supported by a rather loosely-coupled collection of tools, each of which serves a specific, well-defined, task. The analogy with a carpenter is obvious. His toolkit contains hammers, screwdrivers, a saw, and the like. These tools each serve a specific task. However, they are not 'integrated' in the way a drill and its attachments are.

The prime example of a toolkit environment is UNIX. UNIX may be viewed as a general support environment, not aimed at one specific programming language, development method, or process model. UNIX offers a number of very convenient, yet very simple, building blocks with which more complicated things can be realized [KM81]:

- The file system is a tree. The leaves of this tree are the files, while inner nodes correspond to directories. A specific file can be addressed absolutely or relative to the current directory. The addressing is through a pathname, analogous to the selection of record fields in Pascal. Directories are files too, though the user cannot change their contents.

- Files have a very simple structure. A file is but a sequence of characters (bytes). So there are no physical or logical records, there is no distinction between random access files and sequential access files, and there are no file types.

  An I/O device is a file too; if it is opened, it automatically activates a program which handles the traffic with that device. In this way, a user may write programs without knowing (or, indeed, without having to know) where the input comes from or where the output goes to.

- All system programs (and most user programs) assume that input comes from the user's terminal, while the output is again written to that terminal. The user can easily redirect both input and output. Through a call of the form

  ```
  prog <in >out
  ```

  input is read from file in, while output is written to file out. The program itself need not be changed.

- UNIX offers its users a very large set of small, useful, programs. To name but a few: wc counts the number of lines, words and characters in files, lpr prints files, grep does pattern matching.
- UNIX programs can easily be combined to form larger programs. If the output of one program is to serve as input to another program, they can be connected through a *pipe*, denoted by '|':

  ```
  ls | pr
  ```

  makes a list of all file names and subsequently prints that list. There is no need for an auxiliary file to store intermediate results.

In this way, users are led to try to reach their goals by gluing existing components together, rather than writing a program from scratch. For example, a UNIX guru could solve the KWIC-index problem from chapter 10 in the following way:

```
ptx -i /dev/null <input |
sed -e 's/.xx "" "\([^"]*\)" "\([^"]*\)".*$/\2 \1' |
lpr
```

To some of you, the above program may require some clarification:

- ptx generates a permuted index of the input. It is often used in conjunction with one of the available text processing programs. The parameter '-i' is followed by the name of a file that contains words to be ignored in the permutation. The file /dev/null is a standard empty file. So in this case all words count in the permutation. For an input line

  ```
  This is an example.
  ```

  the above call to ptx would generate the following output:

  ```
  .xx "" "This is " "an example." ""
  .xx "" "This is an " "example." ""
  .xx "" "This " "is an example." ""
  .xx "" "" "This is an example." ""
  ```

  Note that ptx also takes care of sorting. Sorting is done lexicographically on the third string of each line.
- sed is a stream editor. The above cryptic command makes sure that the second and third substring on each line are output in reverse order, while the rest of

the line is deleted (the command assumes that the symbol '"' itself does not occur in the original input).

- Finally, lpr prints the resulting file.

Quite a few users of UNIX will not immediately think of the above solution. Neither did I. Another disadvantage of UNIX is that there is little consistency in interfaces and the choice of command names. For different programs, the '-k' option, say, may well mean something rather different. To stop a dialogue, you may try kill, stop, quit, end, leave, and a few others. If you get tired, CTRL-c is likely to work too.

The average UNIX user knows only a fairly limited subset of the available commands and tools [Fis86]. It is quite likely that, after a while, a workable set of commands will be known and used, and then the learning process stops. Inevitably, the facilities offered under UNIX are far from optimally used.

In UNIX, the different tools have minimal knowledge of the objects they manipulate. Various integrated and process-centered environments have been built on top of UNIX. They make use of the attractive features of UNIX, but try to overcome its disadvantages by imposing more structure.

Besides tools that support the individual programmer, UNIX also offers support for programming-in-the-large, through configuration management and system build facilities like SCCS and Make. These will be discussed in section 19.3.2.

19.2 LANGUAGE-CENTERED ENVIRONMENTS

Nowadays, most software is developed interactively, changes are made interactively, and programs are tested and executed interactively. Much research in the area of language-centered environments is aimed at developing a collection of useful, user-friendly, effective tools for this type of activity. Since most of these environments focus on supporting programming tasks, this type of environment is often called a **programming environment**. To emphasize their graphic capabilities to manipulate program constructs, they are sometimes called **visual programming environments**.

Conventional operating systems are not well suited for these activities, for the following reasons:

- Most operating systems in use today have evolved from earlier, non-interactive, operating systems: the man–machine interface often strikes the user as unnatural and impractical; the user dialog is rigid in form and, sometimes, the 80-column punched card format is still evident.

- Most operating systems support a large variety of programming languages. Part of the facilities offered, such as the text editor and file system, are the same for all languages. As a consequence, these facilities are either too dumb or too complicated for most tasks. For example, a text editor may well perform simple syntactic checks (more about this later on). The file system is usually very complex; peculiarities of all kinds of programming languages as well as different I/O devices come forward.

- When using an operating system to develop software, you have to master a number of different languages: the programming language itself, the editor's language, the system's command language, the debugger's language, etc. Each of these languages has its own syntax and semantics.

In short, many operating systems have become overly complex and the solution to this problem commonly comes in one of two forms:

- try to make a better operating system (the toolkit approach of UNIX could be classified as such).
- try to make the operating system 'invisible' by building a collection of tools on top of the operating system. This collection can be based on and built around a specific programming language. The principle then is that, to the software developer, the programming environment replaces the operating system.

Environments that are built around a specific programming language exploit the fact that a program entails more than a mere sequence of characters. Programs have a clear structure. This structure can be used to make the editing process more effective, to handle debugging in a structured way, and the like. Knowledge of properties of the objects to be manipulated can be built into the tools and subsequently used by these tools. Well-known early examples of language-centered environments are Interlisp and the Smalltalk-80 environment.

In such an environment, it is often not easily possible to make a clear separation between the language and its environment. The Smalltalk environment is a case in point. Smalltalk-80 is an object-oriented programming language. The Smalltalk environment is aimed at supporting a single user. This user creates object classes (modules) with the corresponding messages (procedures). The new object classes are added to the environment the user is working in. To start with, the environment already contains a number of useful classes. Working this way tends to be exploratory in nature. The user builds himself an evolving system. The state of the machine can be saved at the end of a working session and restored at the start of the next session. The user is thus provided with a persistent virtual memory which is not shared with other users.

One tool often available in such an environment is a browser. Browsers offer introspective capabilities to their users. They allow us to traverse and inspect the set of program objects in a systematic way. Such tools know about the semantics of the objects to be manipulated. As a consequence, they provide powerful support for tasks like program comprehension or debugging.

In general, a standard editor can only handle text, i.e. unstructured sequences of characters. A special editor for language X could have built-in knowledge of that language. The Cornell Program Synthesizer [TR81] is an early example of such an editor. If the user of the Cornell Program Synthesizer wants to create an if-statement, he indicates so by typing a one- or two-character code. As a result, the following template appears:

```
IF (<condition>)
    THEN <statement>
    ELSE <statement>
```

The user is next asked to fill in the holes ('placeholders'). In this way, the user is supported in keying in a program text. Trivial mistakes, like the omission of parentheses around the condition, cannot be made.

Quite often, systems like the one described above offer additional support as well. For example, the system may easily take care of program indentation. Programs can also be analyzed incrementally, so that the user is immediately informed about, say, an undeclared variable. In the Cornell Program Synthesizer, an incomplete program can even be executed. For example, if the ELSE-part of some IF-statement is left open, the program could be executed up to that ELSE-part. Only if the ELSE-branch has to be executed does program execution stop. The system then brings you back into edit mode, in order to enable you to fill in the missing code, and then execution of the program can be resumed. In systems such as this, where incremental software development is supported, users may sometimes guide program execution. They may for instance inspect the values of all variables after each instruction or procedure call and interactively assign them new values.

The above list can be extended with numerous other bells and whistles. The net result is an interactive system with a great many possibilities. Language-centered environments provide capabilities for the direct manipulation of program structures, multiple views of programs, incremental checking of static semantics, and program debugging [PT91]. Obviously, having such a system available changes the working procedures of the programmer. The compile-load-execute cycle of program development is replaced by an incremental program construction paradigm.

Language-centered environments mostly run on workstations or PCs with good graphical capabilities. They support the individual programmer during the implementation and test phases. They offer little or no support for group activities such as configuration control and sharing information between group members. If the latter type of support is provided, it usually requires abandoning the exploratory programming paradigm offered by the environment.

19.3 INTEGRATED ENVIRONMENTS AND WORKBENCHES

This section is devoted to CASE products that support (parts of) the software development process. Depending on the scope of the set of tools available, such an environment is called an Analyst WorkBench (AWB), a Programmer WorkBench (PWB), a Management WorkBench (MWB), or an Integrated Project Support Environment (IPSE); see also figure 19.3. The acronym CASE (Computer-Aided Software Engineering) is often used to indicate any type of tool support in the software development process. The qualified terms Upper-CASE and Lower-CASE refer to tool support during the analysis–design and implementation–test phases, respectively.

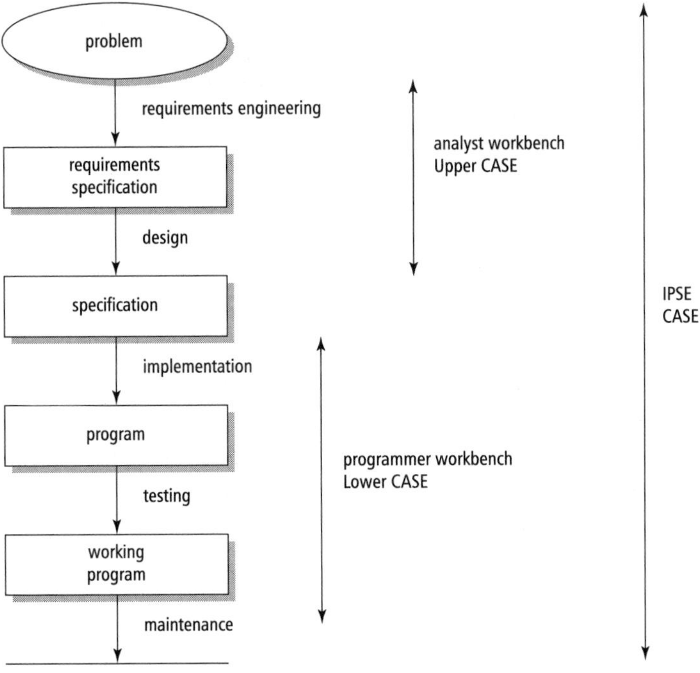

Figure 19.3 Scope of tool sets

In the ideal case, the choice of a specific set of tools will be made as follows. First, a certain approach to the software development process is selected. Next, techniques are selected that support the various phases in that development process. As a last step, tools are selected that support those techniques. Some steps in the development process may not be supported by well-defined techniques. Some techniques may not be supported by tools. Thus, a typical development environment will have a pyramid shape as in figure 19.4.

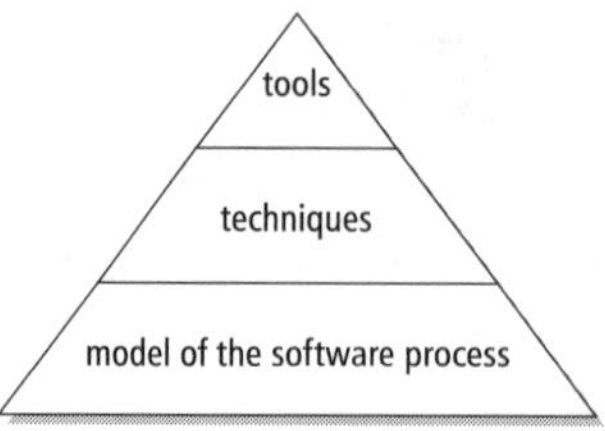

Figure 19.4 Support in a typical development environment

In practice, we often find the reverse conical form: a barely-developed model of the development process, few well-defined techniques, and a lot of tools. In this way, the benefits of the tools will be limited at best. To paraphrase the situation: for many a CASE, there is a lot of Computer-Aided, and precious little Software Engineering.

The different tool sets identified above are discussed in the subsections to follow.

19.3.1 Analyst WorkBenches

Analyst workbenches serve to support the activities in the early phases of software development: requirements engineering and (global) design. In these phases, analysis and design data is gathered. Often, a graphical image of the system is made, for instance in the form of a set of data flow diagrams. From a practical point of view, important problems concern the drawing and redrawing of those diagrams and guarding the consistency and completeness of the data gathered. AWB tools specifically address these points.

The kernel of an AWB is a database in which the information gathered is stored. The structure of the database can be rather free, or it can be derived from the techniques supported. The AWB will also contain tools to support the following types of activity:

- Drawing, changing and manipulation of pictures. This may vary from simple drawing programs that have no knowledge of the pictures' semantics, to programs that have an elaborate knowledge of the semantics of the drawing technique in question. As far as the latter is concerned, we may think of automatic generation of pointers to subpictures, the automatic reconfiguration of pictures to circumvent intersecting lines, and the like. If the drawing technique has been sufficiently formalized, the user support can be comparable to that offered by a syntax-directed editor for programming languages.

- Analysis of data produced, as regards consistency and completeness. The possibilities of doing this are strongly dependent upon the degree to which the drawing technique itself imposes strict rules. There is a choice as to when this checking takes place. If the user is immediately notified when an error is made, there is little chance for errors to cascade. On the other hand, the freedom to 'play' during the exploratory development stages is also limited. If checking is done at a later stage, the user may continue on the wrong track for quite a while before detection, and it then becomes more difficult to identify the proper error messages.

- Generating reports and documentation. It is important to be able to adapt the precise form of reports and documentation to the requirements of the user. For instance, internal standards of some organization may enforce certain report formats. It should be possible to configure the tools to adhere to these standards.

Further tools of an AWB may support, amongst others, prototyping, the generation of user interfaces, or the generation of executable code. [PKK98] found that users perceive two types of (Upper-CASE) tool: those that are good at supporting analysis and design tasks and those that are good at code generation and prototyping. Apparently, the tools tend to emphasize one of these uses.

Given the number and variety of Upper-CASE tools on the market and the rapid progress in the capabilities of these tools, the selection process can be a bewildering task. Choosing an Upper-CASE tool requires a thorough analysis of the needs of the software development organization that is about to procure such a tool. [Zuc89] and [BS89] give useful guidelines for this selection and evaluation process.

19.3.2 Programmer Workbenches

A programmer workbench consists of a set of tools to support the implementation and test phases of software development. The term originated in the UNIX world [DHM78]. The support offered by UNIX mainly concerns these types of activity. Many programming environments constructed around a certain programming language also support these phases in particular. In a PWB, we find tools to support, amongst others:

- editing and analysis of programs;

- debugging;
- generation of test data;
- simulation;
- test coverage determination.

The tools that support teamwork on large projects deserve our special attention. In a typical environment, a group of programmers will be working on the same system. The system will have many components, developed, tested, and changed by different people. During the evolution of the system, different versions of components will result. Automatic support for the control of such a set of components, both technically and organizationally, is a sheer necessity.

One of the early systems for configuration control is the Source Code Control System (SCCS), originally developed for IBM OS and best known from UNIX. SCCS enables the user to keep track of modifications in files (which may contain such diverse things as program code, documentation, or test sets). The system enables the user to generate any version of the system. New versions can be generated without old versions being lost. Important aspects of SCCS are:

- no separate copies of versions are kept: only the modifications (so-called deltas) to previous versions are stored;
- access to files is protected: only authorized users can make changes;
- each file is identified by author, version number, and date and time of modification;
- the system asks the user for information on the reason for a change, which change is made, where, and by whom.

Figure 19.5 illustrates the main operations provided by SCCS. Within SCCS, all information is kept in so-called **s-files**. The operation create creates the s-file for the first time. If the original file is named prog, then the SCCS file is named s.prog. The operation get yields a read-only copy of the file requested. This read-only copy can be used for compiling, printing, and the like. It is *not* intended to be edited. The operation edit retrieves a copy to be edited. SCCS takes care of protection in the sense that only one person can be editing a file at one time. Finally, the delta operation stores the revised version of the file edited.

Versions of SCCS files are numbered, 1.1, 1.2, 1.3, 2.1, etc. The number to the left of the period is the major version number (release number). The number to the right of the period is the minor version number. The first version is numbered 1.1. By default, get and edit retrieve the latest version of a file, while delta results in an

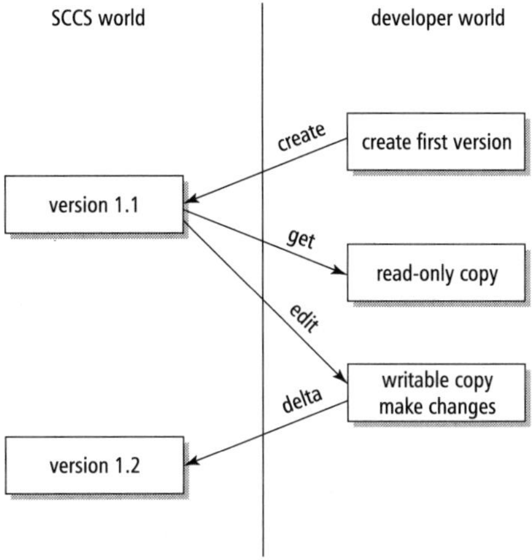

Figure 19.5 Main operations of SCCS

increase of the minor version number. If an older version is required or the major version number is to be increased, this must be specified explicitly.

The above scheme results in a linear sequence of versions. SCCS also provides the possibility of creating branches (**forks**), as illustrated in figure 19.6. For example, starting from version 1.2 we may create versions 1.3, 1.4, etc to represent normal development of a system component, and versions 1.2.1.1, 1.2.1.2, etc to represent bug fixes in version 1.2. In SCCS, the merging of development paths must be done manually.

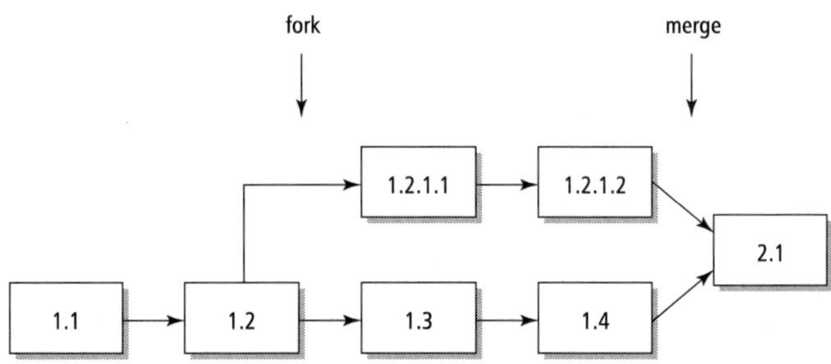

Figure 19.6 Forking and merging of development paths

When different versions of the same system are maintained in this way, the need to automate the construction of new executable versions arises. Make is a tool that does this [Fel78]. Make uses a description of the various components of a system and their mutual dependencies. When generating a new executable system, Make inspects the date and time of the latest changes to components and only recompiles components when needed (i.e. components that have been changed since the last compilation). A tool like Make not only saves machine time, but also ensures that the most recent version of each component is used.

The basic functionality of configuration control systems has not really changed since the development of SCCS in the early 1970s. Additional features offered in present-day systems are mainly directed at increasing the flexibility and usability of such systems:

- The ability to symbolically tag file versions. If the repair of some bug requires changes in a number of modules, each of these revised modules may be given the same tag, say bug27. In a subsequent build of the system, this tag bug27 may then be used to reference file versions in which this bug has been taken care of. This frees the user from the need to remember that the bug concerns version 1.12 of module A, 1.3.1.7 of module B, etc.

- The ability to automatically merge branches. This is by no means a fool-proof operation and should be used with care. The possibility of merging branches hinges on the availability of appropriate merge tools. If changes are made in disjoint parts of a file, merge tools can generally merge these changes fully automatically.

- Flexible support for multiple developers working on the same system. In SCCS, only one person can be editing a file at a time. This rather restrictive scheme is known as **reserved checkout**. It may unnecessarily restrict the work in a team. For example, one developer may check out a file he is not going to work on until next week. However, the fact that he did so prevents other developers from working on that file during this week. In another model, known as **unreserved checkout**, each developer has a working copy of a file. After a while, one developer writes back his updated copy of that file, and other developers will be notified if they want to do the same. These other developers will then, one by one, have to merge their changes with the already updated copy.

- Support for communication within a development team. For example, if one developer checks out a file someone else is already working on, he may be given a notification of this, so that the developers can start a dialog and coordinate their activities. The latter type of support connects the pure archival function of configuration control systems with the communication and coordination functions of workflow management systems.

Language-centered environments as discussed in section 19.2 support the individual developer. These environments are dominated by issues of software construction. The emphasis is on tools that support software construction: editors, debuggers, compilers, etc. Toolsets that offer configuration management and system build facilities like those offered by SCCS and Make can be classified as belonging to the family model of software development environments: a great deal of freedom is left to the individual developers, while a number of rules are agreed upon to regulate critical interactions between developers.

Most programmer workbenches offer this family type of support. For example, Make assumes that files whose names end in .c are C source files. Members of the development family follow this rule and may even have agreed upon further naming conventions. The development environment however has no way of enforcing those rules. It is up to management to make sure that the rules are followed.

19.3.3 Management Workbenches

A management workbench contains tools that assist the manager during planning and control of a software development project. Example tools in an MWB include:

Configuration control Besides the control of software components as discussed in the previous section, we may also think of the control of other project-specific information, like design and analysis data, or documentation. An essential aspect of this type of configuration control concerns the control of change requests. Changes are proposed, assessed, approved or rejected, given a priority and cost estimate, planned, and executed. The corresponding procedures are described in a configuration control plan. The administration and workflow of those change requests may well be supported through a tool. See also chapter 4.

Work assignment Given a number of components, their mutual dependencies, and resources needed (both people and hardware), tools can be used to determine critical paths in the network of tasks, and work packages may be assigned accordingly. This is a central feature of process-centered environments; see section 19.4.

Cost estimation Various quantitative cost-estimation models have been developed. These models yield cost estimates, based on project characteristics. Tools have been developed that assist in gathering quantitative project data, calibrating cost-estimation models based on these data, and making cost estimates for new projects.

Reliability For reliability models, like the ones discussed in chapter 18, tools have been developed that give estimates of the present reliability, test time needed, and the like, based on project data.

19.3.4 Integrated Project Support Environments

An Integrated Project Support Environment is meant to support all phases of the software life cycle. Thus, such an environment has to contain the various tools as discussed in the previous sections. Environments that span the complete life cycle usually emphasize the support of either front-end activities (analysis and global design – Upper-CASE) or back-end activities (implementation and testing – Lower-CASE). They then contain tools specifically geared at supporting tasks from the corresponding part of the life cycle, augmented by a more general support for the other phases (such as for editing, text processing, or database access).

When developing an IPSE, we may strive for either a strong or a weak integration of its tools. A strong integration, as realized in the language-centered environments discussed in section 19.2, has both advantages (like better control capabilities) and disadvantages. One disadvantage is that such an IPSE tends to be less flexible. If the tools are not integrated, as in UNIX, there is more flexibility. On the other hand, a more stringent management control is then needed.

We may also look for intermediate forms. For example, all objects may be stored in the UNIX file system, controlled by SCCS, and the relationships between objects may be represented using a relational database system.

The heart of an integrated environment is the data repository, containing the information shared between the tools that make up the environment. The constraints imposed on the structure of this repository mirror the degree to which the tools are integrated. A stricter integration of tools allows for a stricter definition of the structure of the data they share, and vice versa.

Support environments are built on top of an (existing) operating system. Current operating systems do not offer a suitable platform on which to base an integrated environment directly. For example, the UNIX file system does not allow us to type files or indicate relationships between objects stored in different files. Moreover, environments based on existing operating systems are not portable.

Much research within the field of (integrated) environments has been done on defining an infrastructure for such environments. Portable, integrated tool sets are to be built on top of such an infrastructure and should not directly refer to the underlying operating system.

A major example hereof is the ESPRIT project that resulted in the Portable Common Tool Environment (PCTE). PCTE is a public tool interface intended to serve as a platform for environment builders. PCTE's objectives include i) the definition of a 'complete' interface, sufficient for all of the needs of tool writers, ii) support for tools written in a variety of languages, and iii) a well-defined migration path for existing tools [BMT88].

The PCTE interface offers four general classes of service:

- Basic mechanisms for the execution, composition and communication of tools. This includes functions for starting and stopping processes, functions that handle the I/O between a file system and a process, message-passing functions to handle data traffic between processes, and the like.

- Distribution mechanisms. PCTE is designed to be implemented on a distributed hardware platform which is made transparent by this set of features.

- User-interface facilities to enable uniform interfaces across tools.

- Object-management facilities. The Object Management System (OMS) provides functions to manipulate the various objects within the development environment.

The major novel aspect of PCTE is the Object Management System. The OMS generalizes the notion of a file system. The OMS lets you store information on objects and relationships between objects in an entity–relationship style. Object types in OMS are organized into a hierarchy and they inherit the attributes and links defined for their ancestor types.

The root of the hierarchy is Object. Predefined subtypes of Object include, amongst others, File and Pipe. Objects of type File have contents, an unstructured sequence of bytes as found in the file systems of most operating systems. An OMS object is further characterized by:

- a set of attributes that describe characteristics of the object;

- a set of links that associates the object with other objects.

For example, an element representing a module may have attributes like 'id' and 'status'. It may be linked to an element that constitutes the subsystem of which the module is a component, and to an element that represents the person responsible for the module. In this way we are able to create an explicit model of both the development environment and the application to be developed.

There exist several 'versions' of PCTE. The ESPRIT project mentioned earlier resulted in PCTE1.5. A number of improvements were incorporated in PCTE+. Standardization efforts by both the European Computer Manufacturers Association (ECMA) and ISO have led to ECMA-PCTE and ISO-PCTE. Several implementations of PCTE have been developed and several environments have been built on top of PCTE. Efforts similar to PCTE+ within the Ada community have led to the definition of the Common APSE Interface Set (CAIS) [MOPT88]. Both PCTE+ and CAIS are aimed at providing public tool interface definitions for the development of high-security applications.

19.4 PROCESS-CENTERED ENVIRONMENTS

In a process-centered software engineering environment (PSEE), a description of the software development process is shared by the tools that make up the environment. Not surprisingly, developments in process-centered environments are closely tied to developments in process modeling, and vice versa. For example, the kinds of description used in process modeling (state transition diagrams, Petri nets, and the like) are also the formalisms used in PSEEs. Process modeling is discussed in section 3.8.

Like an integrated environment, a process-centered environment may cover the complete life cycle. Like an IPSE, a PSEE tends to be geared towards supporting tasks from a specific part of the software development life cycle. Since back-end activities (implementation and testing) are somewhat easier to structure and formalize, work in process modeling and PSEEs has, consequently concentrated on modeling and supporting back-end activities.

Figure 19.7 gives a model of the process of conducting a code review. The notation is that of Petri nets. In section 3.8, this same figure was used to explain the role of different formalisms in process modeling. Here, we will use it to discuss its role in a process-centered software engineering environment.

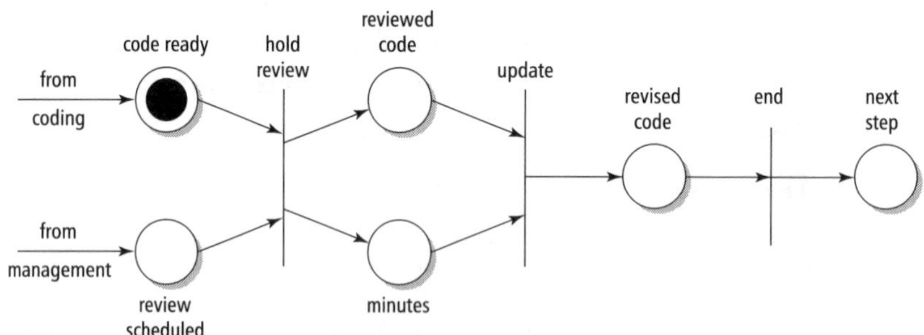

Figure 19.7 Petri net view of the review process

If the developer indicates that some piece of code is ready for review, the environment is notified and comes into a state as indicated in figure 19.7. Parallel to the coding activity, management schedules a review meeting. Once this is done, the place[2] labeled review scheduled is marked. The support environment then 'knows' that the review can be held and may offer support for doing so. In this way, the environment guides the developers and other participants through the steps of the review process, alerts them when certain actions are required, maintains status information

[2]See section 3.8 for the terminology of Petri nets.

of code products and other pieces of information, etc. Thus, PSEEs provide support for software development by automating routine tasks, invoking appropriate development tools, and enforcing rules and practices.

Formal models of a software process are rigid. In practice, this rigidity is a hindrance, since there will always be exceptions. For example, the minutes of a review meeting might get lost, management may decide to skip a certain review meeting, a review meeting may have to be rescheduled because some participant became ill, etc. The Petri model of figure 19.7 can not cope with these situations. A number of them can be accommodated by making the model more complex. But the model will never cover all situations. There is thus a need to be able to intervene. Some PSEEs, for example, offer means to update process models on the fly. A fully satisfactory solution has not been found yet, and the rigidity of formal models is likely to continue to conflict with the requirements of flexibility in process support.

This holds the more where it supports the early stages of software development. A designer or requirements engineer is not helped by an environment that dictates the detailed order of process steps to be taken. Broadly speaking, we may distinguish two types of activity: the unstructured, creative, and cooperative activities that characterize the early stages of software development; and the repetitive and structured activities that characterize the later stages. A similar dichotomy may be observed in PSEEs. PSEEs focusing on the early stages have much in common with groupware and Computer Supported Cooperative Work (CSCW) systems. These PSEEs support coordination of activities, such as access to and sharing of information, and cooperation activities, such as communication between people and scheduling meetings. PSEEs focusing on the later stages have much in common with workflow management and configuration control systems. Present-day configuration control systems not only offer the basic versioning and access capabilities known from systems like SCCS (see section 19.3.2) but they also offer ways to define and enact software configuration tasks and policies. Some even claim that configuration management tools are the 'real' PSEEs [CFJ98].

19.5 SUMMARY

Developments in the area of (integrated) collections of tools move very fast. For many a facet of the software development process, good tools are available. The proper integration and mutual tuning of tools is less well-developed. In this chapter, we have discussed the major developments as regards computer-aided software engineering (CASE). We have done so using a simple, one-dimensional classification of CASE products, which expresses the parts of the life cycle they support:

- a **tool** supports one specific task;

- a **workbench** supports a limited set of activities, such as those which comprise the implementation and testing stages;

- an **environment** supports the entire process.

We have further classified environments according to the mechanism that ties together the tools that make up the environment:

- In a **toolkit**, the tools are generally not so well integrated. A toolkit merely offers a set of useful building blocks. UNIX is a prime example of this.

- A **language-centered environment** contains tools specifically aimed at supporting software development in a specific programming language.

- An **integrated environment** contains tools that share information about the resulting product. This information is stored in a data repository, and the tools read and write this repository.

- A **process-centered environment** contains tools that share a description of the software-development process.

Though environments are supposed to cover the entire life cycle, they tend to emphasize certain parts of the process. They then contain tools specifically geared at supporting tasks from that part of the process, augmented by a more general, and often limited, support for the other parts. For example, language-centered environments tend to focus on the implementation and testing stages.

One of the major impediments to the widespread use of tools is their rigidity. Software tools are driven by formal models of what can and can not be done. A tool for requirements engineering is likely to enforce certain rules of well-formedness on the diagrams it handles. A tool to support the testing process is likely to prescribe a certain order of process steps. The requirements engineer, though, may well want to play with ill-formed diagrams for a while. Likewise, the tester may want to deviate from the pre-established order of steps if circumstances require this. The tension between the demands for flexibility of tool users and those for formality of tool builders is one of the major challenging research themes in this area.

An interesting open question is whether tools really help. Studies of tool adoption and usage show mixed results. Some conclude that tools offer real improvements, while others conclude that users have not found tools to be helpful. There are definitely certain impediments to tool adoption. Tools cost money, sometimes a lot of money. There also is a learning curve for tool users. And, while many tools may be good at a given specific task, their scope and mutual integration do merit improvement. Finally, there is quite a gulf between the state of the art as reported in this chapter and the state of the practice.

For many an organizational problem, automation seems to be the panacea. Likewise, the use of tools is often seen as a panacea for our problems in software engineering: CASE as prosthesis. Tools, though, remain mere tools. Within the software development process, other factors play a role as well. If the tools do not fit the procedures used within your organization, they are likely to have a far from optimal effect. Also, tools cannot make up for an ineffective development method or badly-qualified personnel. Good people deliver good products and mediocre people deliver mediocre products, irrespective of the tools they use.

19.6 FURTHER READING

An early taxonomy of CASE products is given in [DEFH87]. [Fug93] extended this framework with a category 'process-centered environments'. The latter classification is used in this chapter. Additional dimensions for classifying CASE products are given in [Lot93]. The sociological paradigm (individual, family, etc.) for the user scale stems from [PK91].

[BSS84] is a collection of seminal articles on programming environments, including the UNIX toolkit approach and early language-centered environments like Interlisp. The Source Code Control System (SCCS) is described in [Roc75]. The state of the art in configuration management is reflected in [Tic94]. A good overview of PCTE is provided by [LM93]. Further information can be found at the PCTE homepage: http://gille.loria.fr:7000/pcte/

In the 1980s, tool research focused on creating integrated environments. [TS90] is an annotated bibliography of articles on software engineering environments from that period. Present-day research in the area of tools focuses on PSEEs. The state of the art in this area is reflected in [FW96], [ACF97], and proceedings like [Gru98]. The case for more flexibility in software engineering environments is made in [Jan94], [CdNFG96] and [JH98].

Tool integration issues are addressed in [SB95]. Tools assessment is the topic of [Sof96b]. Studies of tool adoption and usage can be found in [NN89], [TKS95], [Iiv96] and [PKK98].

Exercises

1. What does the acronym CASE stand for?

2. Define the following terms:

   - tool,

   - workbench,
   - environment.

3. What are the main distinguishing features of:

   - a toolkit,
   - a language-centered environment,
   - an integrated environment, and
   - a process-centered environment.

4. What is the difference between Upper-CASE and Lower-CASE?

5. What is the basic functionality of a tool for configuration management?

6. What is PCTE?

7. Discuss the fundamental tension between formality and informality in tools.

8. Why is the user scale an important issue when considering the adoption of tools?

9. ♡ Defend the statement that configuration management tools are the only 'real' process-centered environments (see [CFJ98]).

10. ♠ For the development environment you are currently working in, prepare a list of:

    - utilities you use on a regular basis;
    - utilities you use infrequently or vaguely know about.

    Next compare these lists with the manuals describing the environment. What percentage of the environment's functionality do you really need?

11. ♠ Select and evaluate some commercial Upper-CASE tool using the criteria given in [Zuc89] or [BS89].

12. ♡ Discuss the possible role of automatic support for configuration control in the management of artifacts other than source code modules.

13. ♡ One of the claims of CASE-tool providers is that CASE will dramatically improve productivity. At the same time though, customers seem to be disappointed with CASE and take a cautionary stand. Can you think of reasons for this discrepancy?

14. ♡ Why is tool integration such an important issue?

Appendix A
ISO 9001: Quality Systems

ISO 9001 lists the following ingredients for a quality system:[1]

1. **Management responsibility** It is the management's responsibility to formulate the quality policy, to provide for an adequate organization of the quality system and to conduct reviews of the quality system. First, the supplier's management has to define and document its policy and objectives for, and commitment to, quality. The organization of the quality system includes a specification of the responsibility, authority and interrelation of all personnel involved, as well as the identification of verification requirements, the provision of resources and the assignment of trained personnel. Finally, the quality system adopted has to be reviewed on a regular basis to ensure its continuing suitability.

[1]Reproduced by permission of ISO.

2. **Quality system** The product's conformity to requirements is to be ensured through a quality system. This is done through a set of procedures and instructions, to be prepared and implemented by the supplier.

3. **Contract review** Procedures have to be established for contract reviews. Contract reviews address the following issues:

   - requirements must be adequately defined and documented;
   - requirements differing from those in the tender must be resolved;
   - the supplier should be capable of meeting the contractual requirements.

4. **Design control** Procedures must be established to control and verify that the design meets its requirements. This includes procedures for planning design activities, identification and documentation of design input and output requirements, design verification and design changes.

5. **Document and data control** All documents and data that relate to this standard must be controlled. Changes to documents must be recorded and approved.

6. **Purchasing** The supplier must ensure that purchased products conform to the requirements. Amongst other things, this includes an assessment of subcontractors.

7. **Control of customer-supplied product** Products supplied by the customer must also be verified.

8. **Product identification and traceability** The supplier must have procedures to identify products. For traceability purposes, products must have a unique identification.

9. **Process control** The production and installation processes that affect product quality must be identified and carried out under controlled procedures.

10. **Inspection and testing** Incoming products must be inspected or verified before they are used. The product itself must be tested as required by the quality plan or other documented procedures.

11. **Control of inspection, measuring and test equipment** This equipment must be controlled and maintained. Test software must be checked to prove that it is capable of verifying the acceptability of the product.

12. **Inspection and test status** The inspection and test status of the product must be identified. Records should identify the inspection authority responsible for the release of the conforming product.

13. **Control of nonconforming product** Procedures must be established to ensure that a product which does not conform to the specifications is not inadvertently used or installed.

14. **Corrective and preventive action** The supplier should establish procedures for:

    - investigating the cause of nonconforming product and the corrective actions needed to prevent recurrence;
    - analyzing quality records, customer complaints, and the like, to detect and eliminate potential causes of nonconforming products;
    - initiating preventive actions to deal with problems to a level corresponding to the risks encountered;
    - applying controls to ensure that corrective actions are taken and that they are effective;
    - implementing and recording changes in procedures resulting from corrective actions.

15. **Handling, storage, packaging, preservation and delivery** Procedures for handling, storage, packaging, preservation and delivery of the product must be established and documented.

16. **Control of quality records** Procedures for identification, collection, indexing, filing, storage, maintenance and disposal of quality records must be established.

17. **Internal quality audits** A comprehensive system of planned and documented internal quality audits must be carried out to verify whether quality activities comply with planned arrangements and to determine the effectiveness of the quality system.

18. **Training** Procedures must be established for identifying the training needs and provide for the training of all personnel performing activities affecting quality.

19. **Servicing** Where servicing is specified in a contract, procedures must be established to ensure that it meets the requirements.

20. **Statistical techniques** Where appropriate, procedures must be established for identifying appropriate statistical techniques.

Appendix B
IEEE Standard 730: Software Quality Assurance Plans

IEEE standard 730 specifies the following constituents for a software quality assurance plan:[1]

1. **Purpose** What is the purpose of this quality assurance plan? For which products is it intended?

2. **Reference documents** Which other documents are referred to in this plan?

3. **Management** What are the tasks and responsibilities of the project's management and how is this management organized. The key parts of the project's organization and the responsibilities of the key roles are dealt with as well. One has carefully to delineate dependencies between people involved in development and those in charge of quality assurance. The tasks of the quality

[1]Reproduced by permission of IEEE.

assurance team should be indicated, together with the order in which these tasks will be executed.

4. **Documentation** One has to indicate which documents will be produced in the course of the project, and in which way the quality of these documents will be assessed. This documentation encompasses at least the following: requirements specification, a description of the design, test plan, test report, user documentation and configuration management. One has to specify the format and content of each of these documents.

5. **Standards, practices, conventions and metrics** Which standards for coding, documentation, etc., will be used? One should also indicate how compliance with these items is assured.

6. **Reviews and audits** Under this heading is indicated how the technical and organizational assessment will take place. Technical assessment concerns the way in which verification and validation activities will be carried out in the various phases. Organizational assessment concerns the execution of the quality assurance plan.

7. **Test** How will the software be tested? Part of this information will have been covered in section 4 of this document already.

8. **Problem reporting and corrective action** Which procedures are being followed for reporting, tracking and resolving problems, and who is responsible for the implementation of this.

9. **Tools, techniques and methodologies** Which tools, techniques and methodologies are used to determine whether or not the quality criteria are being met. Possible tools include debuggers, structure analyzers and test drivers. Possible techniques include formal verification, inspections and walkthroughs. Many of these have been elaborated upon in the chapter on testing.

10. **Code control** How are the different versions of the product stored and maintained. Once a baseline has been established, careful procedures for changing and protection of the associated documents is needed. If a configuration control plan is used, this is probably handled in that document.

11. **Media control** The physical protection against unauthorized access and damage is described here.

12. **Supplier control** Software written or delivered by others should also meet the quality criteria set for this project. How is the quality of this third-party software assessed?

13. **Records collection, maintenance, and retention** In which way is quality assurance documented, protected, maintained and preserved?

14. **Training** Which training activities are needed to implement the software quality assurance plan?

15. **Risk management** How are risks handled during software quality assurance?

Appendix C
IEEE Standard 830: Software Requirements Specifications

The various components of IEEE Standard 830 should provide the following information:[1]

1. **Introduction** This section contains an overview of the complete document.

    1.1 **Purpose** What is the purpose of this document and for whom is it written?

    1.2 **Scope** An identification of the product to be developed, what does it do (and what does it not do), why is the product being developed (including a precise description of its benefits, goals and objectives)?

    1.3 **Definitions, acronyms and abbreviations** This subsection contains definitions of all the terms, acronyms and abbreviations used in the document.

[1]Reproduced by permission of IEEE.

Special attention should be paid to the clarification of terms and concepts from the domain of application.

1.4 **References** References to all documents that are referred to in the remainder of the requirements specification.

1.5 **Overview** This subsection contains an outline of the remainder of the document.

2. **Overall description** This section contains a description of matters that concern the overall product and its requirements. It provides a perspective for understanding the specific requirements from section 3 of this document.

2.1 **Product perspective** Does it concern an independent product or is it part of a larger product? In the latter case, the other components should be identified, and the interfaces with those components should be described. This section also contains an identification of the hardware to be used.

2.2 **Product functions** An overview of the functions of the system to be delivered. This should be confined to an overview. A detailed discussion of the functions is given in section 3 of the requirements specification.

2.3 **User characteristics** An indication of general user characteristics, in as far as these are relevant for the requirements specification. Experience, training and technical expertise of future users may influence specific requirements of the system to be developed.

2.4 **Constraints** An indication of any other constraints that apply. These may concern government regulations, hardware constraints, security regulations, and so on. Again, we are concerned with the rationale at this point. A further elaboration follows in section 3 of this document.

2.5 **Assumptions and dependencies** This does not concern constraints on the system to be developed, but things which may influence the requirements specification if they change. As an example, we may think of the availability of certain supporting software, such as a given operating system or a numeric library. If that operating system or library turns out not to be available, the requirements specification will have to be adapted accordingly.

2.6 **Requirements subsets** Requirements which may be delayed until future versions of the system are listed here.

3. **Specific requirements** This section contains all the details which are relevant for the design phase to follow. The ordering given here is just one way to present the specific requirements in a logical way. Specific requirements should be such that one may objectively determine whether they are fulfilled or not.

3.1 **External interface requirements**

3.1.1 **User interfaces** A description of the characteristics of the user interfaces, such as screen layout, function keys, help functions. In order to support testing, verifiable requirements regarding learning time for the system functions should be included either here or in some subsection of 3.5 (Attributes).

3.1.2 **Hardware interfaces** A description of the logical characteristics of hardware interfaces, such as interface protocols, or screen-oriented versus line-oriented terminal control.

3.1.3 **Software interfaces** A description of software needed, such as a certain operating system or subroutine package. Interfaces to other application software is also discussed here.

3.1.4 **Communications interfaces** An example is a communication protocol for LANs.

3.2 **Functional requirements** In this subsection, a description is given of how the transformation of inputs to outputs is achieved. The description is given for each class of functions, and sometimes for each individual function. The structure of this section may be improved by grouping the functions into categories, e.g. according to the class of users they support. To a certain extent, the contents of this section can be seen as a solution to the user. This component of the requirement specification is the main starting point for the design phase.

3.2.1 **Functional requirement 1**

3.2.1.1 **Introduction** A description of the purpose of this function and the approaches and techniques used. The introduction should include information to clarify the intent of the function.

3.2.1.2 **Inputs** A precise description of the function's inputs (source, quantities, range of acceptable values, and the like).

3.2.1.3 **Processing** A definition of the operations that must be performed, such as checking for acceptable values, reaction to abnormal situations, or a description of algorithms to be used. As an example of the latter, one may think of the use of some mathematical model for strength computations within a CAD program.

3.2.1.4 **Outputs** A precise description of the outputs (destination, quantities, error messages, and the like).

3.3 **Performance requirements** Performance requirements encompass both static and dynamic requirements. Static requirements concern, amongst other things, the number of terminals to be connected and the number of users that can be handled concurrently. Dynamic requirements concern the operational performance of the system: how frequently will certain functions be called for and how fast should the system's reaction be. It is important that these requirements be stated in measurable terms.

3.4 **Design constraints** Design constraints may result from such things as the prescribed use of certain standards or hardware.

3.4.1 **Standards compliance** Which existing standards or regulations must be followed, and what requirements result from these. For example, certain report formats or audit procedures may be prescribed.

3.4.2 **Hardware limitations** A description of the characteristics of the hardware environment, in as far as they lead to software requirements. An example of this might be the amount of memory available.

3.5 **Software system attributes** In this section, particular attention is paid to quality aspects. These requirements must be measurable and verifiable. They must be stated in objective terms (see also chapter 6). The subsections below by no means comprise a complete list of such attributes.

3.5.1 **Availability** Factors that guarantee a certain level of availability, such as restart procedures. In this subsection we may also enlist requirements regarding fault tolerance (with respect to both hardware failures and software failures).

3.5.2 **Security** Requirements regarding unauthorized access and other forms of misuse. Certain cryptographic techniques may be prescribed, and we may put constraints on the communication between different parts of the system.

3.5.3 **Maintainability** Requirements to guarantee a certain level of maintainability of the system, such as a maximum allowable coupling between components.

3.6 **Other requirements** A description of requirements that are specific to certain software, and which have not been discussed yet.

Appendix D
IEEE Standard 1012: Software Verification and Validation Plans

The various constituents of IEEE 1012, the Software Verification and Validation (V&V) Plan, contain the following information:[1]

1. **Purpose** The purpose and scope of this plan. This includes the project for which the plan is written, the product items covered, and the goals of the V&V effort.

2. **Referenced documents** Documents referenced by this plan are identified, as well as documents that supplement or implement this plan. Examples of such related documents are the Quality Assurance Plan and Unit Test Plan.

3. **Definitions** The acronyms and notations used are explained. A definition of all terms is given, or a reference to a document which defines these terms.

[1]Reproduced by permission of IEEE.

4. **Verification and validation overview**

   4.1 **Organization** This section describes the organization of the test effort. It describes the relationships with other efforts, such as development, project management, and quality assurance. It defines the lines of communication within the V&V effort, the authority to resolve issues, and the authority to approve test products. For example, different test tasks, such as unit testing and integration testing, may be handled by different groups. Results from one such task must be communicated to the relevant parties. A discrepancy between, say, some test results and the requirements specification may be due to a fault in either the software or the requirements specification. It must be clear where the authority lies which resolves such issues.

   4.2 **Master schedule** This section describes the project's life cycle, its milestones and completion dates. This information can be copied from the project plan. It gives a summary of verification and validation tasks, and describes how the results of these tasks provide feedback to the development process. The description used here assumes a waterfall-like mode of operation. A different process model may necessitate adaptations in subsequent sections of this document. V&V efforts are highly iterative. Faults detected result in documents or products being updated after which that V&V task is repeated. Enhancements or other changes to products under development result in iterations as well.

   4.3 **Resources summary** This section summarizes the resources needed for verification and validation (personnel, tools, special requirements such as access rights, etc.). The planning of these resources should be done with care; projects tend to get under pressure, and V&V efforts tend to get the worst of it.

   4.4 **Responsibilities** In this section, the organizational elements responsible for performing V&V tasks are identified. Since these responsibilities are also given for each of the development phases, a summary may suffice here.

   4.5 **Tools, techniques and methodologies** The specific tools, techniques and methodologies for V&V tasks are identified. Each of these may require acquisition, training, or support, and the plan should include information on these aspects as well.

5. **Life-cycle verification and validation** This section contains the detailed verification and validation plan. In each of its subsections, the following topics must be addressed:

- *Verification and validation tasks* The identification of tasks for this phase. The contribution of these tasks to the overall goals of verification and validation should be stated. For each phase, Standard 1012 gives minimum tasks required for critical systems as well as a number of optional V&V tasks. Many of these tasks have been discussed in section 13.2. The required documentation for these tasks is indicated as well. Note that specific documents, for example those covering test designs, may be contributed to by tasks in different life-cycle phases.
- *Methods and criteria* The methods and procedures for performing each task are identified, together with the criteria used to evaluate the results. For example, the design evaluation task could be done using a review process, which involves certain rules for setting up meetings and procedures to follow up the results of such meetings.
- *Inputs and outputs* A specification of the input and output for each task. The input of a design evaluation for example is some design document. The output of this task includes documents like anomaly reports that provide feedback to both management and the development process.
- *Schedule* The schedule for V&V tasks, in particular the milestones for initiating and completing tasks, are listed under this entry.
- *Resources* The resources for performing tasks (personnel, training, tools, computer usage, etc). A summary of resource requirements is given in section 4.3 of this plan.
- *Risks and assumptions* The risks and assumptions may relate to the schedule, resources, or approach. For example, we might have assumed that unit testing will start on a certain date and that certain qualified personnel will then be available. The V&V plan should specify a contingency plan in case such assumptions prove not to hold.
- *Roles and responsibilities* The organizational elements or individuals responsible for performing tasks must be identified. For each task, a specific responsibility should be assigned.

5.1 **Management of V&V** The management of V&V spans all phases of the development life cycle. Since software development tends to be iterative, and changes or enhancements necessitate iterations, V&V activities also have to be performed again.

5.2 **Requirements phase V&V** During the requirements phase, the requirements themselves are evaluated. Furthermore, plans for system and acceptance testing are generated at this stage.

5.3 **Design phase V&V** During the design phase, the design itself is tested. More detailed plans for unit and integration testing are developed.

5.4 **Implementation phase V&V** At this stage, the source code is evaluated. Test cases and test procedures for the various forms of testing are developed. In Standard 1012, this phase includes unit testing.

5.5 **Test phase V&V** The test phase encompasses integration, system and acceptance testing.

5.6 **Installation and checkout phase V&V** If the software is to be installed on a different configuration, that configuration package must be tested. This phase also includes making a summary of V&V activities and results.

5.7 **Operation and maintenance V&V** Modifications, enhancements and other changes must be treated as development activities and therefore require performing certain V&V tasks again, along the lines prescribed in this plan. Part of the activities that go under this heading (such as the handling of change requests) may also be covered by the Configuration Management Plan.

6. **Software verification and validation reporting** This section describes how the results of verification and validation activities are documented and reported. Examples of V&V reports include: task reports that document results and status of V&V tasks, phase summary reports to be delivered at the end of each phase, reports that describe anomalies detected, and a final report that gives a summary of the complete V&V effort.

7. **Verification and validation administrative procedures**

7.1 **Anomaly reporting and resolution** Methods for reporting and resolving anomalies detected are given under this heading.

7.2 **Task iteration policy** This section describes criteria used to determine the extent to which V&V tasks must be performed again when their input changes. For example, depending on the type of change or the criticality of a system component, updating a design document may require certain V&V tasks to be performed again.

7.3 **Deviation policy** Specific procedures are needed for possible deviations from this plan. The possible effect of such deviations on system quality must be indicated. This section also identifies the authority for approving such deviations.

7.4 **Control procedures** Like anything else, V&V efforts must be controlled. This section may refer back to plans for configuration control and quality assurance.

7.5 **Standards, practices and conventions** Standards, practices and conventions that apply to the V&V effort are identified in this section.

Bibliography

[AAG95] G.D. Abowd, R. Allen, and D. Garlan. Formalizing Style to Understand Descriptions of Software Architecture. *ACM Transactions on Software Engineering and Methodology*, 4(4):319–364, 1995.

[Abb90] R.J. Abbott. Resourceful Systems for Fault Tolerance, Reliability, and Safety. *ACM Computing Surveys*, 22(1):35–68, 1990.

[ABC+97] G. Abowd, L. Bass, P. Clements, R. Kazman, L. Northrop, and A. Zaremski. Recommended Best Industrial Practice for Software Architecture Evaluation. Technical Report CMU/SEI-96-TR-025, Software Engineering Institute, 1997.

[ACF97] V. Ambriola, R. Conradi, and A. Fuggetta. Assessing Process-Centered Software Engineering Environments. *ACM Transactions on Software Engineering and Methodology*, 6(3):283–328, 1997.

[AE92] W.W. Agresti and W.M. Evanco. Projecting Software Defects From Analyzing Ada Designs. *IEEE Transactions on Software Engineering*, 18(11):988–997, 1992.

[AG83] A.J. Albrecht and J.E. Gaffney. Software Function, Source Lines of Code, and Development Effort Prediction: A Software Science Validation. *IEEE Transactions on Software Engineering*, 9(6):639–648, 1983.

[AHM86] T.K. Abdel-Hamid and S.E. Madnick. Impact of Schedule Estimation on Software Project Behavior. *IEEE Software*, 3(4):70–75, 1986.

[AHSR93] T.K. Abdel-Hamid, K. Sengupta, and D. Ronan. Software Project Control: An Experimental Investigation of Judgment with Fallible Information. *IEEE Transactions on Software Engineering*, 19(6):603–612, 1993.

[AIS77] C. Alexander, S. Ishikawa, and M. Silverstein. *A Pattern Language*. Oxford University Press, 1977.

[Alb79] A.J. Albrecht. Measuring Applications Development Productivity. In *Proceedings Application Development Symposium*, pages 83–92. SHARE/GUIDE, 1979.

[Ale79] C. Alexander. *The Timeless Way of Building*. Oxford University Press, 1979.

[AR92] A. Abran and P.N. Robillard. Function Points: A Study of Their Measurement Processes and Scale Transformations. *Journal of Systems and Software*, 25(2):171–184, 1992.

[AR96] A. Abran and P.N. Robillard. Function Points Analysis: An Empirical Study of Its Measurement Processes. *TrSE*, 22(12):895–910, 1996.

[Bab82] R.L. Baber. *Software Reflected*. North-Holland Publishing Company, 1982.

[Bab86] W.A. Babich. *Software Configuration Management*. Addison-Wesley, 1986.

[Bag99] D.J. Bagert. Taking the Lead in Licensing Software Engineers. *Communications of the ACM*, 42(4):27–29, 1999.

[Bak72] F.T. Baker. Chief Programmer Team Management of Production Programming. *IBM Systems Journal*, 11(1):56–73, 1972.

[Bas90] V.R. Basili. Viewing Maintenance as Reuse-Oriented Software Development. *IEEE Software*, 7(1):19–25, 1990.

[BB91] B.H. Barnes and T.B. Bollinger. Making Reuse Cost-Effective. *IEEE Software*, 8(1):13–24, 1991.

[BBK+78] B.W. Boehm, J.R. Brown, H. Kaspar, M. Lipow, G.J. MacLeod, and M.J. Merrit. *Characteristics of Software Quality*. Number 1 in TRW Series of Software Technology. North-Holland, 1978.

[BBM96] V.R. Basili, L.C. Briand, and W.L. Melo. A Validation of Object-Oriented Design Metrics as Quality Indicators. *IEEE Transactions on Software Engineering*, 22(10):751–761, 1996.

[BC89] K. Beck and W. Cunningham. A Laboratory For Teaching Object-Oriented Thinking. In *OOPSLA '89 Proceedings, ACM SIGPLAN Notices 24(10)*, pages 1–6, 1989.

[BCH+95] B.W. Boehm, B. Clark, E. Horowitz, C. Westland, R. Madachy, and R. Selby. Cost Models for Future Software Life Cycle Processes: COCOMO 2.0. *Annals of Software Engineering*, 1:57–94, 1995.

[BCK+94] C. Billings, J. Clifton, B. Kolkhorst, E. Lee, and W.B. Wingert. Journey to a Mature Software Process. *IBM Systems Journal*, 33(1):46–61, 1994.

[BCK98] L. Bass, P. Clements, and R. Kazman. *Software Architecture in Practice*. Addison-Wesley, 1998.

[BCN92] C. Batini, S. Ceri, and S.B. Navathe. *Conceptual Database Design: An Entity–Relationship Approach*. Benjamin Cummings, 1992.

[BD91] E.H. Bersoff and A.M. Davis. Impacts of Life Cycle Models on Software Configuration Management. *Communications of the ACM*, 34(8):104–118, 1991.

[BDKZ93] R.D. Banker, S.M. Datar, C.F. Kemerer, and D. Zweig. Software Complexity and Maintenance Costs. *Communications of the ACM*, 36(11):81–94, 1993.

[Be95] S. Bandinelli *et al.* Modeling and Improving an Industrial Software Process. *IEEE Transactions on Software Engineering*, 21(5):440–454, 1995.

[Bei90] B. Beizer. *Software Testing Techniques*. Van Nostrand Reinhold, second edition, 1990.

[Bei95] B. Beizer. *Black Box Testing*. John Wiley & Sons, 1995.

[Ben83] H.D. Benington. Production of Large Computer Programs. In *Proceedings ONR Symposium (1956), reprinted in Annals of the History of Computing 5(4)*, pages 350–361, 1983.

[Ben98] K.H. Bennett. Do Program Transformations Help Reverse Engineering? In *Proceedings International Conference on Software Maintenance (ICSM'98)*, pages 247–254. IEEE, 1998.

[BG81] G.D. Bergland and R.D. Gordon. *Tutorial: Software Design Strategies*. IEEE, EZ389, 1981.

[BG98] B. Bellay and H. Gall. An Evaluation of Reverse Engineering Tool Capabilities. *Journal of Software Maintenance: Research and Practice*, 10:305–331, 1998.

[BH95a] H.R. Beyer and K. Holtzblatt. Apprenticing with the Customer. *Communications of the ACM*, 38(5):45–52, 1995.

[BH95b] J.P. Bowen and M.G. Hinchey. Seven More Myths of Formal Methods. *IEEE Software*, 12(4):34–41, 1995.

[BH95c] J.P. Bowen and M.G. Hinchey. Ten Commandments of Formal Methods. *IEEE Computer*, 28(4):56–63, 1995.

[BHK89] J.A. Bergstra, J. Heering, and P. Klint. *Algebraic Specification*. Addison-Wesley, 1989.

[BHS80] E.H. Bersoff, V.D. Henderson, and S.G. Siegel. *Software Configuration Management*. Prentice-Hall, 1980.

[Big89] T.J. Biggerstaff. Design Recovery for Maintenance and Reuse. *IEEE Computer*, 22(7):36–50, 1989.

[BJ66] C. Böhm and G. Jacopini. Flow Diagrams, Turing Machines, and Languages With Only Two Formation Rules. *Communications of the ACM*, 9(5):366–371, 1966.

[BJ82] D. Björner and C.B. Jones. *Formal Specification and Software Development*. Prentice-Hall, 1982.

[BJNR98] K. Bohrer, V. Johnson, A. Nilsson, and B. Rudin. Business Process Components for Distributed Object Applications. *Communications of the ACM*, 41(6):43–48, 1998.

[BKK91] R. Banker, R. Kauffman, and R. Kumar. An Emperical Test of Object-Based Output Measurement Metrics in a Computer Aided Software Engineering (CASE) Environment. *Journal of Management Information Systems*, 8(3):127–150, 1991.

[Blu94] B.I. Blum. A Taxonomy of Software Development Methods. *Communications of the ACM*, 37(11):82–94, 1994.

[BM94] G. Bias and D. Mayhew, editors. *Cost-Justifying Usability*. Academic Press, 1994.

[BM95] M. Ben-Menachem. *Software Configuration Management Guidebook.* McGraw-Hill, 1995.

[BMP86] H.J. Barnard, R.F. Metz, and A.L. Price. A Recommended Practice for Describing Software Designs: IEEE Standards Project 1016. *IEEE Transactions on Software Engineering*, 12(2):258–263, 1986.

[BMR+96] F. Buschmann, R. Meunier, H. Rohnert, P. Sommerlad, and M. Stal. *A System of Patterns.* John Wiley & Sons, 1996.

[BMT88] G. Boudier, R. Minot, and I. Thomas. An Overview of PCTE. In SIGSOFT88 [SIG88], pages 248–257.

[BMW94] J.J. Biggerstaff, B.G. Mitbander, and D.E Webster. Program Understanding and the Concept Assignment Problem. *Communications of the ACM*, 37(5):72–83, 1994.

[Boe75] B.W. Boehm. Some Experience with Automated Aids to the Design of Large-Scale Reliable Software. In *Proceedings International Conference on Reliable Software, ACM SIGPLAN Notices 10(6)*, pages 105–113. ACM, 1975.

[Boe76] B.W. Boehm. Software Engineering. *IEEE Transactions on Computers*, C-25(12):1226–1241, 1976.

[Boe81] B.W. Boehm. *Software Engineering Economics.* Prentice-Hall, 1981.

[Boe83] B.W. Boehm. The Economics of Software Maintenance. In *Proceedings Software Maintenance Workshop*, pages 9–37. IEEE, 83CH1982-8, 1983.

[Boe84a] B.W. Boehm. Software Life Cycle Factors. In C.R. Vick and C.V. Ramamoorthy, editors, *Handbook of Software Engineering*, pages 494–518. Van Nostrand Reinhold, 1984.

[Boe84b] B.W. Boehm. Verifying and Validating Software Requirements and Design Specifications. *IEEE Software*, 1(1):75–88, 1984.

[Boe87a] B.W. Boehm. Improving Software Productivity. *IEEE Computer*, 20(9):43–57, 1987.

[Boe87b] B.W. Boehm. Industrial Software Metrics Top 10 List. *IEEE Software*, 4(5):84–85, 1987.

[Boe88] B.W. Boehm. A Spiral Model of Software Development and Enhancement. *IEEE Computer*, 21(5):61–72, 1988.

[Boe89] B. Boehm. *Software Risk Management*. IEEE, 1989.

[Boe97] B.W. Boehm. COCOMO II Model Definition Manual. Technical report, University of Southern California, 1997.

[Boo87] G. Booch. *Software Components with Ada: Structures, Tools, and Subsystems*. Benjamin Cummings, 1987.

[Boo94] G. Booch. *Object-Oriented Analysis and Design with Applications*. Benjamin-Cummings, second edition, 1994.

[BP88] B.W. Boehm and P.N. Papaccio. Understanding and Controlling Software Costs. *IEEE Transactions on Software Engineering*, 14(10):1462–1477, 1988.

[BP89] T.J. Biggerstaff and A.J. Perlis, editors. *Software Reusability, Volume I: Concepts and Models, Volume II: Applications and Experience*. Addison-Wesley, 1989.

[BR69] J.N. Buxton and B. Randell, editors. *Software Engineering Techniques, Report on a Conference*. NATO Scientific Affairs Division, Rome, 1969.

[BRJ98] G. Booch, J. Rumbaugh, and I. Jacobson. *The Unified Modeling Language User Guide*. Addison-Wesley, 1998.

[Bro83] R. Brooks. Towards a Theory of the Comprehension of Computer Programs. *International Journal of Man-Machine Studies*, 18:543–554, 1983.

[Bro87] F.P. Brooks, Jr. No Silver Bullet: Essence and Accidents of Software Engineering. *IEEE Computer*, 20(4):10–20, 1987.

[Bro95] F.P. Brooks. *The Mythical Man-Month*. Addison-Wesley, second edition, 1995.

[BS87] V.R. Basili and R.W. Selby. Comparing the Effectiveness of Software Testing Strategies. *IEEE Transactions on Software Engineering*, 13(12):1278–1296, 1987.

[BS89] G. Baram and G. Steinberg. Selection Criteria for Analysis and Design CASE Tools. *ACM Software Engineering Notes*, 14(6):73–80, 1989.

[BS93] M.J. Bickerton and J. Siddiqi. The Classification of Requirements Engineering Methods. In *Proceedings 1st International Symposium on Requirements Engineering (RE93)*, pages 182–186, San Diego, 1993. IEEE.

[BSS84] D. Barstow, H. Shrobe, and E. Sandewall, editors. *Interactive Programming Environments*. McGraw-Hill, 1984.

[BT83] A.T. Berztiss and S. Thatte. Specification and Implementation of Abstract Data Types. In M.C. Yovits, editor, *Advances in Computers*, volume 22, pages 295–353. Academic Press, 1983.

[Bud93] D. Budgen. *Software Design*. Addison-Wesley, 1993.

[Bus85] E. Bush. The Automatic Restructuring of COBOL. In *Proceedings Conference on Software Maintenance*, pages 35–41. IEEE, 1985.

[But93] R.W. Butler. The Infeasibility of Quantifying the Reliability of Life-Critical Real-Time Software. *IEEE Transactions on Software Engineering*, 19(1):3–12, 1993.

[BYAR94] G. Bounds, L. Yorks, M. Adams, and G. Ranney. *Beyond Total Quality Management*. McGraw-Hill, 1994.

[CAB+94] D. Coleman, P. Arnold, S. Bodoff, C. Dollin, H. Gilchrist, F. Hayes, and P. Jeremaes. *Object-Oriented Development: The FUSION Method*. Prentice-Hall, 1994.

[CAC93a] Special Issue on Participatory Design. *Communications of the ACM*, 36(6), 1993.

[CAC93b] Special Issue on Project Organization and Management. *Communications of the ACM*, 36(10), 1993.

[CAC94] Special Issue on Object-Oriented Software Testing. *Communications of the ACM*, 37(9), 1994.

[CAC95] Special Issue on Object-Oriented Experiences. *Communications of the ACM*, 38(10), 1995.

[CAC96] Special Issue on Software Patterns. *Communications of the ACM*, 39(10), 1996.

[CAC97a] Special Issue on Object-Oriented Application Frameworks. *Communications of the ACM*, 40(10), 1997.

[CAC97b] Special Issue The Quality Approach: Is It Delivering. *Communications of the ACM*, 40(6), 1997.

[Cam89] J.R. Cameron. *JSP & JSD, The Jackson Approach to Software Development*. IEEE, 1989.

[Car90] J.M. Carroll. *The Nurnberg Funnell*. MIT Press, 1990.

[Car95] J.M. Carroll. *Scenario-Based Design*. John Wiley & Sons, 1995.

[CB88] J. Conklin and M.L. Begeman. gIBIS: A Hypertext Tool for Exploratory Policy Discussion. *ACM Transactions on Office Information Systems*, 6(4):303–331, 1988.

[CC95] E.N. Corlett and T.S. Clark. *The Ergonomics of Workspaces and Machines*. Taylor & Francis Ltd., London, 1995.

[CCI90] E.J. Chikofsky and J.H. Cross II. Reverse Engineering and Design Recovery: A Taxonomy. *IEEE Software*, 7(1):13–18, 1990.

[CCPC+99] E. Ciapessoni, A. Coen-Porisini, E. Crivelli, D. Mandrioli, P. Mirandola, and A. Morzenti. From Formal Methods to Formally Based Methods: An Industrial Experience. *ACM Transactions on Software Engineering and Methodology*, 8(1):79–113, 1999.

[CDM86] P.A. Currit, M. Dyer, and H.D. Mills. Certifying the Reliability of Software. *IEEE Transactions on Software Engineering*, 12(1):3–11, 1986.

[CdNFG96] G. Cugola, E. di Nitto, A. Fuggetta, and C. Ghezzi. A framework for Formalizing Inconsistencies and Deviations in Human-Centered Systems. *ACM Transactions on Software Engineering and Methodology*, 5(3):191–230, 1996.

[CDS86] S.D. Conte, H.E. Dunsmore, and V.Y. Shen. *Software Engineering Metrics and Models*. Benjamin Cummings, 1986.

[CdV98] J. Crow and B. di Vito. Formalizing Space Shuttle Software Requirements: Four Case Studies. *ACM Transactions on Software Engineering and Methodology*, 7(3):296–332, 1998.

[CFJ98] R. Conradi, A. Fuggetta, and M.L. Jaccheri. Six Theses on Software Process Research. In V. Gruhn, editor, *Software Process Technology, 6th European workshop, EWSPT'98*. Springer Verlag, LNCS 1487, 1998.

[Cha87] N. Chapin. The Job of Software Maintenance. In *Proceedings Conference on Software Maintenance*, pages 4–12. IEEE, 1987.

[Che76] P.P. Chen. The Entity–Relationship Model: Toward a Unifying View of Data. *ACM Transactions on Data Base Systems*, 1(1):9–36, 1976.

[Chi90] E.J. Chikofsky. CASE & Reengineering: From Archeology to Software Perestroika. In *Proceedings 12th International Conference on Software Engineering (ICSE12)*, page 122. IEEE, 1990.

[CK94] S.R. Chidamber and C.F. Kemerer. A Metrics Suite for Object Oriented Design. *IEEE Transactions on Software Engineering*, 20(6):476–493, 1994.

[CKI88] B. Curtis, H. Krasner, and N. Iscoe. A Field Study of the Software Design Process for Large Systems. *Communications of the ACM*, 31(11):1268–1287, 1988.

[CKSI87] B. Curtis, H. Krasner, V. Shen, and N. Iscoe. On Building Software Process Models Under the Lamppost. In *Proceedings 9th International Conference on Software Engineering (ICSE9)*, pages 96–103, 1987.

[CLS88] S.S. Cha, N.G. Leveson, and T.J. Shimeall. Safety Verification in MURPHY using Fault-Tree Analysis. In *Proceedings 10th International Conference on Software Engineering (ICSE10)*, pages 377–386. IEEE, 1988.

[CMN83] S.K. Card, T.P. Moran, and A. Newell. *The Psychology of Human–Computer Interaction*. Erlbaum, 1983.

[Coc96] A. Cockburn. The Interaction of Social Issues and Software Architecture. *Communications of the ACM*, 39(10):40–46, 1996.

[Col96] D. Coleman. Fusion with Use Cases: Extending Fusion for Requirements Modelling. Technical report, available through URL http://www.hpl.hp.com/fusion/index.html, 1996.

[Com94] Special issue on Software Metrics. *IEEE Computer*, 27(9), 1994.

[Com96a] Special issue on Managing Object-Oriented Software Development. *IEEE Computer*, 29(9), 1996.

[Com96b] Special issue on System Testing and Reliability. *IEEE Computer*, 29(11), 1996.

[Com97] Special issue on Fault Tolerance. *IEEE Computer*, 30(4), 1997.

[Con87] J. Conklin. Hypertext: An Introduction and Survey. *IEEE Computer*, 20(9):17–41, 1987.

[Con93] L.L. Constantine. Work Organization: Paradigms for Project Management and Organization. *Communications of the ACM*, 36(10):34–43, 1993.

[Con97] R. Conradi, editor. *Proceedings Workshop on Software Configuration Management (SCM7)*. Springer Verlag, LNCSL1235, 1997.

[Cor89] T.A. Corby. Program Understanding: Challenge for the 1990s. *IBM Systems Journal*, 28(2):294–306, 1989.

[Cor97] D.D. Corkill. Countdown to Success: Dynamic Objects, GBB, and RADARSET-1. *Communications of the ACM*, 40(5):48–58, 1997.

[Cox84] B.J. Cox. Message/Object Programming, an Evolutionary Change in Programming Technology. *IEEE Software*, 1(1):50–61, 1984.

[Cox90] B.J. Cox. Planning the Software Industrial Revolution. *IEEE Software*, 7(6):25–33, 1990.

[CPRZ89] L.A. Clarke, A. Podgurski, D.J. Richardson, and S.J. Zeil. A Formal Evaluation of Data Flow Path Selection Criteria. *IEEE Transactions on Software Engineering*, 15(11):1318–1332, 1989.

[Cri85] F. Cristian. A Rigorous Approach to Fault-Tolerant Programming. *IEEE Transactions on Software Engineering*, 11(1):23–31, 1985.

[CS90] P. Checkland and J. Scholes. *Soft Systems Methodology in Action*. John Wiley & Sons, 1990.

[CS95a] N.I. Churcher and M.J. Shepperd. Comments on 'A Metrics Suite for Object Oriented Design'. *IEEE Transactions on Software Engineering*, 21(3):263–265, 1995.

[CS95b] J.O. Coplien and D. Schmidt, editors. *Pattern Languages of Program Design*. Addison-Wesley, 1995.

[CSKB+89] B. Curtis, S.B. Sheppard, E. Kruesi-Bailey, J. Bailey, and D.A. Boehm-Davis. Experimental Evaluation of Software Documentation Formats. *Journal of Systems and Software*, 9(2):167–207, 1989.

[CSM79] B. Curtis, S. Sheppard, and P. Milliman. Third Time Charm: Stronger Prediction of Programmer Performance by Software Complexity Metrics. In *Proceedings 4th International Conference on Software Engineering (ICSE4)*, pages 356–360. IEEE, 1979.

[Cur89] B. Curtis. Three Problems Overcome with Behavioral Models of the Software Development Process. In *Proceedings 11th International Conference on Software Engineering (ICSE11)*, pages 398–399. IEEE, 1989.

[Cus89] M.A. Cusumano. The Software Factory: A Historical Interpretation. *IEEE Software*, 6(2):23–30, 1989.

[CW89] J.S. Collofello and S.N. Woodfield. Evaluating the Effectiveness of Reliability-Assurance Techniques. *Journal of Systems and Software*, 9(3):191–195, 1989.

[CWG93] E. Carmel, R.D. Whitaker, and J.F. George. PD and Joint Application Design: A Transatlantic Comparison. *Communications of the ACM*, 36(6):40–48, 1993.

[CY91] P. Coad and E. Yourdon. *Object-Oriented Analysis*. Yourdon Press, second edition, 1991.

[Das94] M.K. Daskalantonakis. Achieving Higher SEI Levels. *IEEE Software*, 11(4):17–24, 1994.

[Dav82] G.B. Davis. Strategies for Information Requirements Determination. *IBM Systems Journal*, 21(1):4–30, 1982.

[Dav93a] T.H. Davenport. *Process Innovation: Reengineering Work through Information Technology*. Harvard Business School Press, Cambridge, MA, 1993.

[Dav93b] A.M. Davis. *Software Requirements: Objects, Functions and State*. Prentice-Hall, second edition, 1993.

[Dav95] A.M. Davis. Object-Oriented Requirements to Object-Oriented Design: An Easy Transition? *Journal of Systems and Software*, 30(1 & 2):151–159, 1995.

[DBSB91] P. Devanbu, R.J. Brachman, P.G. Selfridge, and B.W. Ballard. LASSIE: A Knowledge-Based Software Information System. *Communications of the ACM*, 34(5):34–49, 1991.

[DCC92] E. Downs, P. Clare, and I. Coe. *SSADM: Structured Systems Analysis and Design Method*. Prentice-Hall, second edition, 1992.

[DEFH87] S.A. Dart, R.J. Ellison, P.H. Feiller, and A.N. Habermann. Software Development Environments. *IEEE Computer*, 20(11):18–28, 1987.

[Dek92] S.M. Dekleva. Delphi Study of Software Maintenance Problems. In *Proceedings International Conference on Software Maintenance (ICSM'92)*, pages 10–17. IEEE, 1992.

[DeM79] T. DeMarco. *Structured Analysis and System Specification*. Prentice-Hall, 1979.

[DeM82] T. DeMarco. *Controlling Software Projects.* Yourdon Press, 1982.

[DFAB98] A. Dix, J. Finlay, G. Abowd, and R. Beale. *Human-Computer Interaction.* Prentice-Hall, 1998.

[DG90] N. Delisle and D. Garlan. Applying Formal Specification to Industrial Problems: A Specification of an Oscilloscope. *IEEE Software*, 7(5):29–37, 1990.

[DHM78] T.A. Dolotta, R.C. Haight, and J.R. Mashey. UNIX Time-Sharing System: The Programmer's Workbench. *The Bell System Technical Journal*, 57(6):2177–2200, 1978.

[Dij76] E.W. Dijkstra. *A Discipline of Programming.* Prentice-Hall, 1976.

[Dil94] A. Diller. *Z: An Introduction to Formal Methods.* John Wiley & Sons, 1994.

[DK76] F. DeRemer and H.H. Kron. Programming-in-the-large Versus Programming-in-the-small. *IEEE Transactions on Software Engineering*, 2(2):80–86, 1976.

[DL87] T. DeMarco and T. Lister. *Peopleware.* Dorset House, 1987.

[DL89] T. DeMarco and T. Lister. Software Development: State of the Art vs. State of the Practice. In *Proceedings 11th International Conference on Software Engineering (ICSE11)*, pages 271–275. IEEE, 1989.

[dLM95] F. Van der Linden and J. Müller. Creating Architectures with Building Blocks. *IEEE Software*, 12(6):51–60, 1995.

[DLP79] R.A. DeMillo, R.J. Lipton, and A.J. Perlis. Social Processes and the Proofs of Theorems and Programs. *Communications of the ACM*, 22(5):271–280, 1979.

[Don99] P. Donohoe, editor. *Software Architecture, Proceedings of the First Working IFIP Conference on Software Architecture.* Kluwer Academic Publishers, 1999.

[DS97] M. Diaz and J. Sligo. How Software Process Improvement Helped Motorola. *IEEE Software*, 14(5):75–81, 1997.

[EEBS96] K. El Emam, L. Briand, and R. Smith. Assessor Agreement in Rating SPICE Processes. *Software Process – Improvement and Practice*, 2(4):291–306, 1996.

[EEDM97] K. El Emam, J. Drouin, and W. Melo. *SPICE: The Theory and Practice of Software Process Improvement and Capability Determination*. IEEE, 1997.

[EEM95a] K. El Emam and N.H. Madhavji. A Field Study of Requirements Engineering Practices in Information Systems Development. In *Proceedings 2nd International Symposium on Requirements Engineering (RE95)*, pages 68–80. IEEE, York, England, 1995.

[EEM95b] K. El Emam and N.H. Madhavji. The Reliability of Measuring Organizational Maturity. *Software Process – Improvement and Practice*, 1(1):3–25, 1995.

[Els76] J.L. Elshoff. Measuring Commercial PL-1 Programs Using Halstead's Criteria. *ACM SIGPLAN Notices*, 11(5):38–76, 1976.

[EM85] H. Ehrig and B. Mahr. *Fundamentals of Algebraic Specifications, Vol. 1, Equations and Initial Semantics*. Springer Verlag, 1985.

[EN95] S. Easterbrook and B. Nuseibeh. Managing Inconsistencies in an Evolving Specification. In *Proceedings 2nd International Symposium on Requirements Engineering (RE95)*, pages 48–55. IEEE, York, England, 1995.

[Eps97] R.G. Epstein. *The Case of the Killer Robot*. John Wiley & Sons, 1997.

[Faf94] D. Fafchamps. Organizational Factors and Reuse. *IEEE Software*, 11(5):31–41, 1994.

[Fag76] M.E. Fagan. Design and Code Inspections to Reduce Errors in Program Development. *IBM Systems Journal*, 15(3):182–211, 1976.

[Fag86] M.E. Fagan. Advances in Inspections. *IEEE Transactions on Software Engineering*, 12(7):744–751, 1986.

[Fai92] R.E. Fairley. Recent Advances in Software Estimation Techniques. In *Proceedings 14th International Conference on Software Engineering (ICSE14)*, pages 382–391. IEEE Computer Society, 1992.

[Fay97] M.E. Fayad. Software Development Process: A Necessary Evil. *Communications of the ACM*, 40(9):101–103, 1997.

[Fel78] S.I. Feldman. Make: A Program for Maintaining Computer Programs. Technical report, AT&T, 1978.

[Fet88] J. H. Fetzer. Program Verification: The Very Idea. *Communications of the ACM*, 31(9):1048–1063, 1988. See also ref: *Communications of the ACM* 32(3):374–381 (1989) and 32(4):506–512 (1989).

[FG90] W.B. Frakes and P.B. Gandel. Representing Reusable Software. *Information and Software Technology*, 32(10):653–664, 1990.

[FH79] R.K. Fjelstad and W.T. Hamlen. Application Program Maintenance Study: Report to our Respondents. In *Proceedings of GUIDE 48*, 1979.

[Fis86] G. Fischer. From Interactive to Intelligent Systems. In J.K. Skwirzynski, editor, *Software System Design Methods*, volume 22 of *NATO ASI Series F: Computer and Systems Sciences*, pages 185–212. Springer Verlag, 1986.

[FKV94] M.D. Fraser, K. Kumar, and V.K. Vaishnavi. Strategies for Incorporating Formal Specifications in Software Development. *Communications of the ACM*, 37(10):74–86, 1994.

[FL78] A. Fitzsimmons and T. Love. A Review and Evaluation of Software Science. *ACM Computing Surveys*, 10(1):3–18, 1978.

[FL97] M.E. Fayad and M. Laitinen. Process Assessment Considered Wasteful. *Communications of the ACM*, 40(11):125–128, 1997.

[Flo67] R.W. Floyd. Assigning Meaning to Programs. In J.T. Schwartz, editor, *Mathematical Aspects of Computer Science*, pages 19–31. American Mathematical Society, 1967.

[Flo96] S. Flowers. *Software Failure: Management Failure.* John Wiley & Sons, 1996.

[FMR+89] C. Floyd, W.-M. Mehl, F.-M. Reisin, G. Schmidt, and G. Wolf. Out of Scandinavia: Alternative Approaches to Software Design and System Development. *Human-Computer Interaction*, 4:253–350, 1989.

[FO99] B. Fitzgerald and T. O'Kane. A Longitudinal Study of Software Process Improvement. *IEEE Software*, 16(3):37–51, 1999.

[FP96] N.E. Fenton and S. Lawrence Pfleeger. *Software Metrics: A Rigorous & Practical Approach.* Thomson Computer Press, second edition, 1996.

[Fre87] P. Freeman, editor. *Tutorial: Software Reusability*. IEEE, EZ750, 1987.

[FS97] M. Fowler and K. Scott. *UML Distilled*. Addison-Wesley, 1997.

[FT96] W. Frakes and C. Terry. Software Reuse: Metrics and Models. *ACM Computing Surveys*, 28(5):415–435, 1996.

[Fug93] A. Fuggetta. A Classification of CASE Technology. *IEEE Computer*, 26(12):25–38, 1993.

[FW83] P. Freeman and A.I. Wasserman, editors. *Tutorial: Software Design Techniques*. IEEE EZ514, 1983.

[FW93a] P.G. Frankl and S.N. Weiss. An Experimental Comparison of the Effectiveness of Branch Testing and Data Flow Testing. *IEEE Transactions on Software Engineering*, 19(8):774–787, 1993.

[FW93b] P.G. Frankl and E.J. Weyuker. A Formal Analysis of the Fault-Detection Ability of Testing Methods. *IEEE Transactions on Software Engineering*, 19(3):202–213, 1993.

[FW93c] P.G. Frankl and E.J. Weyuker. Provable Improvements on Branch Testing. *IEEE Transactions on Software Engineering*, 19(10):962–975, 1993.

[FW96] A. Fuggetta and A. Wolf, editors. *Software Process – Improvement and Practice*. John Wiley & Sons, 1996.

[FWH97] P.G. Frankl, S.N. Weiss, and C. Hu. All-Uses vs Mutation Testing: An Experimental Comparison of Effectiveness. *Journal of Systems and Software*, 38(3):235–253, 1997.

[Gar84] D.A. Garvin. What does 'Product Quality' really mean? *Sloan Management Review*, Fall 1984.

[GB94] V.S. Gordon and J.M. Bieman. Rapid Prototyping: Lessons Learned. *IEEE Software*, 12(1):85–95, 1994.

[GC87] R.B. Grady and D.L. Caswell. *Software Metrics: Establishing a Company-Wide Program*. Prentice-Hall, 1987.

[GC88] R. Guindon and B. Curtis. Control of Cognitive Processes during Design: What Tools Would Support Software Designers? In *Proceedings CHI'88*, pages 263–268. ACM, 1988.

[GG75] J.B. Goodenough and S.L. Gerhart. Toward a Theory of Test Data Selection. *IEEE Transactions on Software Engineering*, 1(2):156–173, 1975.

[GG93] T. Gilb and D. Graham. *Software Inspection*. Addison Wesley, 1993.

[GH88] D. Gelperin and B. Hetzel. The Growth of Software Testing. *Communications of the ACM*, 31(6):687–695, 1988.

[GH93] J.V. Guttag and J.J. Horning. *Larch: Languages and Tools for Formal Specification*. Springer Verlag, 1993.

[GH96] D. Garmus and D. Herron. *Measuring the Software Process: A Practical Guide to Functional Measurements*. Prentice-Hall, 1996.

[GHJV95] E. Gamma, R. Helm, R. Johnson, and J. Vlissides. *Design Patterns: Elements of Reusable Object-Oriented Software*. Addison-Wesley, 1995.

[Gib89] N.E. Gibbs. The SEI Education Program: The Challenge of Teaching Future Software Engineers. *Communications of the ACM*, 32(5):594–605, 1989.

[Gib91] N.E. Gibbs. Software Engineering and Computer Science: The Impending Split? *Education & Computing*, 7(1-2):111–117, 1991.

[Gil86] T. Gilb. Estimating Software Attributes: Some Unconventional Points of View. *ACM Software Engineering Notes*, 11(1):49–59, 1986.

[Gil88] T. Gilb. *Principles of Software Engineering Management*. Addison-Wesley, 1988.

[GKN92] D. Garlan, G.E. Kaiser, and D. Notkin. Using Tool Abstraction to Compose Systems. *IEEE Computer*, 25(6):30–38, 1992.

[GL93] J.A. Goguen and C. Linde. Techniques for Requirements Elicitation. In *Proceedings 1st International Symposium on Requirements Engineering (RE93)*, pages 152–164, San Diego, 1993. IEEE.

[GMR97] D. Gotterbarn, K. Miller, and S. Rogerson. Software Engineering Code of Ethics. *Communications of the ACM*, 40(11):110–118, 1997.

[Gog86] J. Goguen. An Introduction to OBJ: A Language for Writing and Testing Formal Algebraic Program Specifications. In N. Gehani and A.D. McGettrick, editors, *Software Specification Techniques*, pages 391–419. Addison-Wesley, 1986.

[Gri81] D. Gries. *The Science of Programming*. Springer Verlag, 1981.

[Gru91] J. Grudin. Interactive Systems: Bridging the Gaps Between Developers and Users. *IEEE Computer*, 24(4):59–69, 1991.

[Gru98] V. Gruhn, editor. *Software Process Technology, 6th European workshop, EWSPT'98*. Springer Verlag, LNCS 1487, 1998.

[GS79] C. Gane and T. Sarson. *Structured Analysis and Systems Analysis: Tools and Techniques*. Prentice-Hall, 1979.

[GS89] V.R. Gibson and J.A. Senn. System Structure and Software Maintenance Performance. *Communications of the ACM*, 32(3):347–358, 1989.

[GTW78] J.A. Goguen, J.W. Thatcher, and E.G. Wagner. An Initial Algebra Approach to the Specification, Correctness, and Implementation of Abstract Data Types. In R.T. Yeh, editor, *Current Trends in Programming Methodology*, volume 4, pages 80–149. Prentice-Hall, 1978.

[GTWW75] J.A. Goguen, J.W. Thatcher, E.G. Wagner, and J.B. Wright. Abstract Data Types as Initial Algebras and Correctness of Data Representations. In *Proceedings Conference on Computer Graphics, Pattern Recognition and Data Structures*, pages 89–93, 1975.

[Gun68] R. Gunning. *The Technique of Clear Writing*. McGraw-Hill, 1968.

[Gut75] J.V. Guttag. *Specification and Application to Programming of Abstract Data Types*. PhD thesis, University of Toronto, 1975.

[GvS94] R.B. Grady and T. van Slack. Key Lessons in Achieving Widespread Inspection Use. *IEEE Software*, 11(4):46–57, 1994.

[Hal77] M.H. Halstead. *Elements of Software Science*. North-Holland Publishing Company, 1977.

[Hal90] A. Hall. Seven Myths of Formal Methods. *IEEE Software*, 7(5):11–20, 1990.

[Hal96] A. Hall. Using Formal Methods to Develop an ATC Information System. *IEEE Software*, 13(2):66–76, 1996.

[Har88] D. Harel. On Visual Formalisms. *Communications of the ACM*, 31(5):514–530, 1988.

[Hat97] L. Hatton. N-Version Design vs. One Good Version. *IEEE Software*, 14(6):71–76, 1997.

[Hay92] I.J. Hayes. VDM and Z: A Comparative Case Study. *Formal Aspects of Computing*, 4(1):76–99, 1992.

[Hay93] I. Hayes, editor. *Specification Case Studies*. Prentice-Hall, second edition, 1993.

[HB95] M.G. Hinchey and J.P. Bowen, editors. *Applications of Formal Methods*. Prentice-Hall, 1995.

[HC72] H.Koontz and C.O'Donnell. *Principles of Management: An Analysis of Managerial Functions*. McGraw-Hill, 1972.

[HC97] J.E. Henry and J.P. Cain. Comparison of Perfective and Corrective Software Maintenance. *Journal of Software Maintenance: Research and Practice*, 9:281–297, 1997.

[HCN98] R. Harrison, S.J. Counsell, and R.V. Nithi. An Investigation into the Applicability and Validity of Object-Oriented Design Metrics. *Empirical Software Engineering*, 3(3):147–154, 1998.

[Hee89] F.J. Heemstra. *How Much Does Software Cost*. PhD thesis, Technical University of Eindhoven, The Netherlands, 1989. In Dutch.

[HF97] T. Hall and N. Fenton. Implementing Effective Software Metrics Programs. *IEEE Software*, 14(2):55–65, 1997.

[HH93] D. Hix and H.R. Hartson. *Developing User Interfaces: Ensuring Usability Through Product and Process*. John Wiley & Sons, 1993.

[HK81] S. Henri and D. Kafura. Software Structure Metrics Based on Information Flow. *IEEE Transactions on Software Engineering*, 7(5):510–518, 1981.

[HK89] R. Hirschheim and H.K. Klein. Four Paradigms of Information Systems Development. *Communications of the ACM*, 32(10):1199–1216, 1989.

[HKK89] W.S. Humphrey, D.H. Kitson, and T.C. Kasse. The State of Software Engineering Practice: A Preliminary Report. In *Proceedings 11th International Conference on Software Engineering (ICSE11)*, pages 277–288. IEEE, 1989.

[HLN+90] D. Harel, H. Lachover, A. Naamad, A. Pnueli, M. Politi, R. Sherman, A. Shtull-Trauring, and M. Trakhtenbrot. STATEMATE: A Working Environment for the Development of Complex Reactive Systems. *IEEE Transactions on Software Engineering*, 16(4):403–414, 1990.

[HM96] M. Hitz and B. Montazeri. Chidamber and Kemerer's Metrics Suite: A Measurement Theory Perspective. *IEEE Transactions on Software Engineering*, 22(4):267–271, 1996.

[HO96] W.W. Ho and R.A. Olsson. A Layered Model for Building Debugging and Monitoring Tools. *Journal of Systems and Software*, 34(3):211–222, 1996.

[Hoa69] C.A.R. Hoare. The Axiomatic Basis of Computer Programming. *Communications of the ACM*, 12(10):576–583, 1969.

[Hos61] W.A. Hosier. Pitfalls and Safeguards in Real-Time Digital Systems With Emphasis on Programming. *IRE Transactions on Engineering Management*, pages 99–115, 1961.

[HOT97] M.J. Harrold, A.J. Offutt, and K. Tewary. An Approach to Fault Modeling and Fault Seeding Using the Program Dependence Graph. *Journal of Systems and Software*, 36(3):273–295, 1997.

[How82] W.E. Howden. Validation of Scientific Programs. *ACM Computing Surveys*, 14(2):193–227, 1982.

[How85] W.E. Howden. The Theory and Practice of Functional Testing. *IEEE Software*, 2(5):6–17, 1985.

[HRPL+95] B. Hayes-Roth, K. Pfleger, P. Lalanda, P. Morignot, and M. Balabanovic. A Domain Specific Software Architecture for Adaptive Intelligent Systems. *IEEE Transactions on Software Engineering*, 21(4):288–301, 1995.

[HS92] B. Henderson Sellers. Modularization and McCabe's Cyclomatic Complexity. *Communications of the ACM*, 35(12):17–19, 1992.

[HS93] G.M. Hødalsvik and G. Sindre. On the purpose of Object-Oriented Analysis. In *OOPSLA'93 Proceedings, ACM SIGPLAN Notices 28 (10)*, pages 240–255, 1993.

[HS95] J.M. Hops and J.S. Sherif. Development and Application of Composite Complexity Models and a Relative Complexity Metric in a Software Maintenance Environment. *Journal of Systems and Software*, 31(2):157–169, 1995.

[HSG+94] P. Hsia, J. Samuel, J. Gao, D. Kung, Y. Toyoshima, and C. Chen. Formal Approach to Scenario Analysis. *IEEE Software*, 11(2):33–41, 1994.

[HT90] D. Hamlet and R. Taylor. Partition Testing Does Not Inspire Confidence. *IEEE Transactions on Software Engineering*, 16(12):1402–1411, 1990.

[Hum88] W.S. Humphrey. Characterizing the Software Process: A Maturity Framework. *IEEE Software*, 5(2):73–79, 1988.

[Hum89] W.S. Humphrey. *Managing the Software Process*. SEI Series in Software Engineering. Addison-Wesley, 1989.

[Hum95] W.S. Humphrey. *A Discipline for Software Engineering*. Addison-Wesley, 1995.

[Hum96] W.S. Humphrey. Using a Defined and Measured Personal Software Process. *IEEE Software*, 13(3):77–88, 1996.

[Hum97a] W.S. Humphrey. *Introduction to the Personal Software Process*. Addison-Wesley, 1997.

[Hum97b] W.S. Humphrey. *Managing Technical People*. Addison-Wesley, 1997.

[HvdVvV91] G. de Haan, G.C. van der Veer, and J.C. van Vliet. Formal Modelling Techniques in Human-Computer Interaction. *Acta Psychologica*, 78:27–67, 1991.

[HZG+97] J. Herbsleb, D. Zubrow, D. Goldenson, W. Hayes, and M. Paulk. Software Quality and the Capability Maturity Model. *Communications of the ACM*, 40(6):30–40, 1997.

[IEE83] *IEEE Standard for Software Test Documentation*. IEEE Std 829, 1983.

[IEE86a] *IEEE Standard for Software Verification and Validation Plans*. IEEE Std 1012, 1986.

[IEE86b] *IEEE Standard on Software Quality Assurance Planning*. IEEE Std 983, 1986.

[IEE89] *IEEE Standard for Software Quality Assurance Plans*. IEEE Std 730, 1989.

[IEE90a] *IEEE Standard Glossary of Software Engineering Terminology*. IEEE Std 610.12, 1990.

[IEE90b] *IEEE Standard for Software Configuration Management Plans*. IEEE Std 828, 1990. Revision of IEEE Std 828-1983.

[IEE92] *IEEE Standard for Software Maintenance*. IEEE Std 1219, 1992.

[IEE93] *IEEE Recommended Practice for Software Requirements Specifications*. IEEE Std 830, 1993.

[Iiv96] J. Iivari. Why are CASE tools not used? *Communications of the ACM*, 39(10):94–103, 1996.

[Ish85] K. Ishikawa. *What Is Total Quality Control? The Japanese Way*. Prentice-Hall, 1985.

[ISO96] ISO DIS 9241-11, Ergonomic Requirements for Office Work with Visual Display Terminals (VDTs): – Part 11: Guidance on Usability. Technical report, ISO, 1996.

[ISO97] *ISO/IEC 9126: Software Quality Characteristics and Metrics – Part 1: Quality Characteristics and Sub-characteristics, Part 2: External Metrics.* ISO, 1997.

[ITT83] *Proceedings Workshop on Reusability in Programming.* ITT, 1983.

[Jac75] M.A. Jackson. *Principles of Program Design.* Academic Press, 1975.

[Jac83] M.A. Jackson. *System Development.* Prentice-Hall, 1983.

[Jan94] D.J. Jankowski. The Feasibility of CASE Structured Analysis Methodology Support. *ACM Software Engineering Notes*, 19(2):72–82, 1994.

[JBR99] I. Jacobson, G. Booch, and J. Rumbaugh. *The Unified Software Development Process.* Addison-Wesley, 1999.

[JCJO92] I. Jacobson, M. Christerson, P. Johnsson, and G. Övergaard. *Object-Oriented Software Engineering: A Use Case Driven Approach.* Addison-Wesley, 1992.

[JF88] R.E. Johnson and B. Foote. Designing Reusable Classes. *Journal of Object Oriented Programming*, 1(1):22–35, 1988.

[JH95] B. Jordan and A. Henderson. Interaction Analysis: Foundations and Practice. *The Journal of the Learning Sciences*, 4(1):39–103, 1995.

[JH98] S. Jarzabek and R. Huang. The Case for User-Centered CASE Tools. *Communications of the ACM*, 41(8):93–98, 1998.

[JJ91] H. Johnson and P. Johnson. Task Knowledge Structures: Psychological Basis and Integration into System Design. *Acta Psychologica*, 78:3–26, 1991.

[JJWS88] P. Johnson, H. Johnson, R. Waddington, and A. Shouls. Task-Related Knowledge Structures: Analysis, Modeling and Application. In D.M. Jones and R. Winder, editors, *People and Computers IV*, pages 35–62. University Press, Cambridge, 1988.

[JM97] J.-M. Jézéquel and M. Meyer. Design by Contract: The Lessons of Ariane. *IEEE Computer*, 30(1):129–130, 1997.

[Joh89] P. Johnson. Supporting System Design by Analyzing Current Task Knowledge. In D. Diaper, editor, *Task Analysis for Human-Computer Interaction.* Ellis Horwood, Chichester, 1989.

[Jon86] C. Jones. *Programming Productivity.* McGraw-Hill, 1986.

[Jon89] C. Jones. Software Enhancement Modelling. *Journal of Software Maintenance: Research and Practice*, 1(2):91–100, 1989.

[Jon90] C.B. Jones. *Systematic Software Development Using VDM*. Prentice-Hall, 1990.

[Jon99] C. Jones. The Euro, Y2K, and the US Software Labor Shortage. *IEEE Software*, 16(3):55–61, 1999.

[Jor96] B. Jordan. Ethnographic Workplace Studies and CSCW. In D. Shapiro, M.J. Tauber, and R. Traunmueller, editors, *The Design of Computer Supported Cooperative Work and Groupware Systems*, pages 17–42. North-Holland, Amsterdam, 1996.

[JS90] C.B. Jones and R.C. Shaw. *Case Studies in Systematic Software Development*. Prentice-Hall, 1990.

[JSS95a] Special issue on Software Metrics. *Journal of Systems and Software*, 31(2), 1995.

[JSS95b] Special Issue on Software Reuse. *Journal of Systems and Software*, 30(3), 1995.

[JSS98] Special issue on Formal Methods Technology Transfer. *Journal of Systems and Software*, 40(3), 1998.

[JTWM96] P.W. Jordan, B. Thomas, B.A. Weerdmeester, and I.L. McClelland. *Usability Evaluation in Industry*. Taylor & Francis, London, 1996.

[JW98] S. Jarzabek and G. Wang. Model-based Design of Reverse Engineering Tools. *Journal of Software Maintenance: Research and Practice*, 10:353–380, 1998.

[KA85] J.C. Knight and P.E. Ammann. An Experimental Evaluation of Simple Methods for Seeding Program Errors. In *Proceedings 8th International Conference on Software Engineering (ICSE8)*, pages 337–342. IEEE, 1985.

[KA92] B. Kirwan and L.K. Ainsworth. *A Guide to Task Analysis*. Taylor & Francis, London, 1992.

[Kar95] E.-A. Karlsson, editor. *Software Reuse: A Holistic Approach*. John Wiley & Sons, 1995.

[KC93] G.M. Karam and R.S. Casselman. A Cataloging Framework for Software Development Methods. *IEEE Computer*, 26(2):34–47, 1993.

[KC95] M. Keil and E. Carmel. Customer-Developer Links in Software Development. *Communications of the ACM*, 38(5):33–44, 1995.

[Kee91] P. Keen. *Shaping the Future: Business Design through Information Technology*. Harvard Business School Press, Cambridge, MA, 1991.

[Kem93] C.F. Kemerer. Reliability of Function Points Measurement. *Communications of the ACM*, 36(2):85–97, 1993.

[Kin88] D. King. *Creating Effective Software: Computer Program Design Using the Jackson Methodology*. Yourdon Press, 1988.

[Kin89] R. King. My Cat is Object-Oriented. In W. Kim and F. Lochovsky, editors, *Object-Oriented Concepts, Databases and Applications*, pages 23–30. Addison-Wesley, 1989.

[KKB+98] R. Kazman, M. Klein, M. Barbacci, T. Longstaff, H. Lipson, and J. Carriere. The Architecture Tradeoff Analysis Method. In *Proceedings 4th International Conference on Engineering of Complex Computer Systems*, 1998.

[KL95] E. Kamsties and C.M. Lott. An Emperical Evaluation of Three Defect-Detection Techniques. In W. Schäfer and P. Botella, editors, *Software Engineering – ESEC '95, LNCS 989*, pages 362–383. Springer Verlag, 1995.

[KM81] B.W. Kernighan and J.R. Mashey. The UNIX Programming Environment. *IEEE Computer*, 14(4):12–24, 1981.

[KM93] J.C. Knight and E.A. Myers. An Improved Inspection Technique. *Communications of the ACM*, 36(11):50–61, 1993.

[KM99] B. Keepence and M. Mannion. Using Patterns to Model Variability in Product Families. *IEEE Software*, 16(4):102–108, 1999.

[KP81] D.E. Knuth and M.F. Plass. Breaking Paragraphs Into Lines. *Software, Practice & Experience*, 11:1119–1184, 1981.

[KP88] G.E. Krasner and S.T. Pope. A cookbook for using the Model–View–Controller user interface paradigm in Smalltalk-80. *Journal of Object Oriented Programming*, 1(3):26–49, 1988.

[KP92] C.F. Kemerer and B.S. Porter. Improving the Reliability of Function Point Measurement: An Empirical Study. *IEEE Transactions on Software Engineering*, 18(11):1011–1024, 1992.

[KP96] B. Kitchenham and S.L. Pfleeger. Software Quality: The Elusive Target. *IEEE Software*, 13(1):12–21, 1996.

[KPF95] B. Kitchenham, S.L. Pfleeger, and N.E. Fenton. Towards a Framework for Software Measurement Validation. *IEEE Transactions on Software Engineering*, 21(12):929–943, 1995.

[Kro94] J. Krogstie. On the Distinction between Functional Development and Functional Maintenance. *Journal of Software Maintenance: Research and Practice*, 7:383–403, 1994.

[Kru92] C.W. Krueger. Software Reuse. *ACM Computing Surveys*, 24(2):131–183, 1992.

[Kru95] P.B. Kruchten. The 4 + 1 View Model of Architecture. *IEEE Software*, 12(6):42–50, 1995.

[Kru96] D. Kruglinski. *Inside Visual C++*. Microsoft Press, 1996.

[KS95] R.E. Kraut and L.A. Streeter. Coordination in Software Development. *Communications of the ACM*, 38(3):69–81, 1995.

[KS97a] C.F. Kemerer and S.A. Slaughter. Determinants of Software Maintenance Profiles: An Empirical Investigation. *Journal of Software Maintenance: Research and Practice*, 9:235–251, 1997.

[KS97b] G. Kotonya and I. Sommerville. *Requirements Engineering, Processes and Techniques*. John Wiley & Sons, 1997.

[KSK+94] P. Kuvaja, J. Simila, L. Krzanik, A. Bicego, G. Koch, and S. Saukonen. *Software Process Assessment and Improvement: the BOOTSTRAP aproach*. Blackwell Publishers, Oxford, UK, 1994.

[KT84] B.A. Kitchenham and N.R. Taylor. Software Cost Models. *ICL Technical Journal*, pages 73–102, 1984.

[KT85] B.A. Kitchenham and N.R. Taylor. Software Project Development Cost Estimation. *Journal of Systems and Software*, 5:267–278, 1985.

[Lau90] B. Laurel, editor. *The Art of Human-Computer Interface Design*. Addison-Wesley, 1990.

[Lau93] B. Laurel. *Computers as Theatre*. Addison-Wesley, 1993.

[Law81] M.J. Lawrence. Programming Methodology, Organizational Environment, and Programming Productivity. *Journal of Systems and Software*, 2:257–269, 1981.

[LB85] M.M. Lehman and L.A. Belady, editors. *Program Evolution*. Number 27 in APIC Studies in Data Processing. Academic Press, 1985.

[Lea94] D. Lea. Christopher Alexander: An Introduction for Object-Oriented Designers. *ACM Software Engineering Notes*, 19(1):39–46, 1994.

[Leh74] M.M. Lehman. *Programs, Cities and Students: Limits to Growth?* Number 9 in Inaugural Lecture Series. Imperial College, London, 1974.

[Leh80] M.M. Lehman. Programs, Life Cycles, and Laws of Software Evolution. *Proceedings of the IEEE*, 68(9):1060–1076, 1980.

[Leh87] M.M. Lehman. Process Models, Process Programs, Programming Support. In *Proceedings 9th International Conference on Software Engineering (ICSE9)*, pages 14–16. IEEE, 1987.

[Lev86] N.G. Leveson. Software Safety: What, Why, and How. *ACM Computing Surveys*, 18(2):125–164, 1986.

[Lev91] N.G. Leveson. Software Safety Issues in Embedded Computer Systems. *Communications of the ACM*, 34(2):34–46, 1991.

[Lev92] N.G. Leveson. High-Pressure Steam Engines and Computer Software. In *Proceedings 14th International Conference on Software Engineering (ICSE14)*, pages 2–14. IEEE, 1992.

[Lew98] S.M. Lewandowski. Frameworks for Component-Based Client/Server Computing. *ACM Computing Surveys*, 30(1):3–27, 1998.

[LG84] R.G. Lanergan and C.A. Grasso. Software Engineering with Reusable Designs and Code. *IEEE Transactions on Software Engineering*, 10(5):498–501, 1984.

[LG86] B. Liskov and J. Guttag. *Abstraction and Specification in Program Development*. MIT Press, 1986.

[LH93] W. Li and S. Henry. Object-Oriented Metrics that Predict Maintainability. *Journal of Systems and Software*, 23(2):111–122, 1993.

[Lin94] G. Lindgaard. *Usability Testing and System Evaluation*. Chapman & Hall, London, 1994.

[Lio96] J.L. Lions. Ariane 5 Flight 501 Failure, Report by the Inquiry Board. Technical report, http://www.cnes.fr/actualites/news/rapport_501.html, 1996.

[LK95] P. Loucopoulos and V. Karakostas. *Systems Requirements Engineering*. McGraw-Hill, 1995.

[LM93] F. Long and E. Morris. An Overview of PCTE: A Basis for a Portable Common Tool Environment. Technical Report CMU/SEI-93-TR-1, Software Engineering Institute, Pittsburgh, 1993.

[LMPR92] M. Lubars, G. Meredith, C. Potts, and C. Richter. Object-Oriented Analysis for Evolving Systems. In *Proceedings 14th International Conference on Software Engineering (ICSE14)*, pages 173–185. IEEE, 1992.

[LMW79] R.C. Linger, H.D. Mills, and B.I. Witt. *Structured Programming, Theory and Practice*. Addison-Wesley, 1979.

[Lok96] C.J. Lokan. Early Size Prediction for C and Pascal Programs. *Journal of Systems and Software*, 32(1):65–72, 1996.

[Lot93] C.M. Lott. Process and Measurement Support in SEEs. *ACM Software Engineering Notes*, 18(4):83–93, 1993.

[LPR93] M. Lubars, C. Potts, and C. Richter. A Review of the State of the Practice in Requirements Modeling. In *Proceedings 1st International Symposium on Requirements Engineering (RE93)*, pages 2–14. IEEE, San Diego, 1993.

[LS80] B.P. Lientz and E.B. Swanson. *Software Maintenance Management*. Addison-Wesley, 1980.

[LSJ97] L.P.W. Land, C. Sauer, and R. Jeffery. Validating the Defect Detection Performance Advantage of Group Designs for Software Reviews: Report of a Laboratory Experiment Using Program Code. In M. Jazayeri and H. Schauer, editors, *Software Engineering – ESEC/FSE '97, LNCS 1301*, pages 294–309. Springer Verlag, 1997.

[LT93] N.G. Leveson and C.S. Turner. An Investigation of the Therac-25 Accidents. *IEEE Computer*, 26(7):18–41, 1993.

[Lyo81] M.J. Lyons. Salvaging Your Software Asset (Tools Based Maintenance). In *AFIPS Conference Proceedings*, volume 50, pages 337–341, 1981.

[Lyu95a] M.R. Lyu, editor. *Handbook of Software Reliability Engineering*. McGraw-Hill, 1995.

[Lyu95b] M.R. Lyu, editor. *Software Fault Tolerance*. John Wiley & Sons, 1995.

[Mar91] J. Martin. *Rapid Application Development*. MacMillan, 1991.

[MAS91] R.M. Mulligan, M.W. Altom, and D.K. Simkin. User Interface Design in the Trenches: Some Tips on Shooting from the Hip. In *Proceedings CHI'91*, pages 232–236. ACM, 1991.

[Mat87] Y. Matsumoto. A Software Factory: An Overall Approach to Software Production. In Freeman [Fre87], pages 155–178.

[May92] D.J. Mayhew. *Principles and Guidelines in Software User Interface Design*. Prentice-Hall, 1992.

[MB87] A. Macro and J. Buxton. *The Craft of Software Engineering*. Addison-Wesley, 1987.

[MB95] J. May and P. Barnard. Cinematography and Interface Design. In K. Nordby *et al.*, editor, *Human-Computer Interaction: Proceedings Interact'95*, pages 26–31. Chapman and Hall, 1995.

[MC96] T.P. Moran and J.M. Carroll. *Design Rationale: Concepts, Techniques and Use*. Lawrence Erlbaum Ass., New Jersey, 1996.

[McC68] R.M. McClure. Production-Management Aspects. In Naur and Randell [NR68], page 72.

[McC76] T.J. McCabe. A Complexity Measure. *IEEE Transactions on Software Engineering*, 2(4):308–320, 1976.

[McI68] M.D. McIlroy. Mass-Produced Software Components. In Naur and Randell [NR68], pages 88–98.

[MDL87] H.D. Mills, M. Dyer, and R. Linger. Cleanroom Software Engineering. *IEEE Software*, 4(5):19–25, 1987.

[Met87] P.W. Metzger. *Managing Programming People*. Prentice-Hall, 1987.

[Mey85] B. Meyer. On Formalism in Specifications. *IEEE Software*, 2(1):6–26, 1985.

[Mey87] B. Meyer. Reusability, the Case for Object-Oriented Design. *IEEE Software*, 4(2):50–64, 1987.

[Mey88] B. Meyer. *Object-Oriented Software Construction*. Prentice-Hall, 1988.

[Mey92] B. Meyer. Design by Contract. *IEEE Computer*, 25(10):40–51, 1992.

[Mey96] B. Meyer. Reality: A cousin twice removed. *IEEE Computer*, 29(7):96–97, 1996.

[MFS90] B.P. Miller, L. Fredrikson, and B. So. An Experimental Study of the Reliability of UNIX Facilities. *Communications of the ACM*, 33(12):32–44, 1990.

[Min83] H. Mintzberg. *Structures in Fives: Designing Effective Organizations*. Prentice-Hall, 1983.

[MIO87] J.D. Musa, A. Iannino, and K. Okumoto. *Software Reliability: Measurement, Prediction, Application*. McGraw-Hill, 1987.

[MJ81] D.D. McCracken and M.A. Jackson. A Minority Dissenting Position. In W.W. Cotterman *et al.*, editor, *Systems Analysis and Design: A foundation for the 1980s*, pages 551–553. North Holland, 1981.

[MLC96] R. Malan, R. Letsinger, and D. Coleman, editors. *Object-Oriented Development at Work: Fusion in the Real World*. Prentice-Hall, 1996.

[MM88] D.A. Marca and B.C.L. McGowan. *SADT: Structured Analysis and Design Technique*. McGraw-Hill, 1988.

[MMM95] H. Mili, F. Mili, and A. Mili. Reusing Software: Issues and Research Directions. *IEEE Transactions on Software Engineering*, 21(6):528–562, 1995.

[MO83] R.J. Martin and W.M. Osborne. *Guidance on Software Maintenance*. National Bureau of Standards, Washington, 1983. NBS Special Publication 500-106.

[Moh81] S.N. Mohanty. Software Cost Estimation: Present and Future. *Software, Practice & Experience*, 11(7):103–121, 1981.

[MOPT88] R. Munck, P. Obendorf, E. Ploedereder, and R. Thall. An Overview of DOD-STD-1838A (proposed), the Common APSE Interface Set, Revision A. In SIGSOFT88 [SIG88], pages 235–247.

[Mor81] T.P. Moran. The Command Language Grammar: A Representation of the User Interface of Interactive Computer Systems. *International Journal of Man-Machine Studies*, 15(1):3–50, 1981.

[Moy96] T. Moynihan. An Experimental Comparison of Object-Orientation and Functional-Decomposition as Paradigms for Communicating System Functionality to Users. *Journal of Systems and Software*, 33(2):163–170, 1996.

[MP96] R. Motschnig-Pitrik. Analyzing the Notions of Attribute, Aggregate, Part and Member in Data/Knowledge Modeling. *Journal of Systems and Software*, 33(2):113–122, 1996.

[MR92] B.A. Myers and M.B. Rosson. Survey on User Interface Programming. In *Human Factors in Computing Systems, Proceedings SIGCHI'92*, pages 195–202. ACM, 1992.

[MRW77] J.A. McCall, P.K. Richards, and G.F. Walters. Factors in Software Quality. Technical Report RADC-TR-77-369, US Department of Commerce, 1977.

[MSG96] R.R. Macala, L.D. Stuckey, Jr., and D.C. Gross. Managing Domain-Specific, Product-Line Development. *IEEE Software*, 13(3):57–68, 1996.

[MT97] N. Medvidovic and R.N. Taylor. A Framework for Classifying and Comparing Architecture Description Languages. In M. Jazayeri and H. Schauer, editors, *Proceedings 6th European Software Engineering Conference, LNCS 1301*, pages 60–76. Springer Verlag, 1997.

[MTG92] R.A. Mata-Toledo and D.A. Gustafson. A Factor Analysis of Software Complexity Measures. *Journal of Systems and Software*, 17(3):267–273, 1992.

[Mum83] E. Mumford. *Designing Human Systems: the ETHICS Method*. Manchester Business School, Manchester, 1983.

[Mye79] G.J. Myers. *The Art of Software Testing*. John Wiley & Sons, 1979.

[Mye86] W. Myers. Can Software for the SDI ever be Error-Free? *IEEE Computer*, 19(10):61–67, 1986.

[Mye88] W. Myers. Shuttle Code Achieves Very Low Error Rate. *IEEE Software*, 5(5):93–95, 1988.

[Nar95] B. Nardi, editor. *Context and Consciousness: Activity Theory and Human Computer Interaction*. MIT Press, Cambridge MA, 1995.

[Nel66] E.A. Nelson. *Management Handbook for the Estimation of Computer Programming Costs*. Systems Development Corp. AD-A648750, 1966.

[Neu95] P.G. Neumann. *Computer-Related Risks*. Addison-Wesley, 1995.

[Neu96] P.G. Neumann. Using Formal Methods to Reduce Risks. *Communications of the ACM*, 39(7):114, 1996.

[Nie93] J. Nielsen. *Usability Engineering*. Academic Press, 1993.

[NKF94] B. Nuseibeh, J. Kramer, and A. Finkelstein. A Framework for Expressing the Relationship Between Multiple Views in Requirements Specification. *IEEE Transactions on Software Engineering*, 20(10):760–773, 1994.

[NL95] W. M. Newman and M. G. Lamming. *Interactive System Design*. Addison Wesley, 1995.

[NM94] J. Nielsen and R.L. Mack. *Usability Inspection Methods*. John Wiley & Sons, 1994.

[NN89] R.J. Norman and J.F. Nunamaker, Jr. CASE Productivity Perceptions of Software Engineering Professionals. *Communications of the ACM*, 32(9):1102–1108, 1989.

[Nor70] P.V. Norden. Useful Tools for Project Management. In M.K. Starr, editor, *Management of Production*, pages 71–101. Penguin Books, 1970.

[Nor83] D.A. Norman. Some Observations on Mental Models. In D. Gentner and A.L. Stevens, editors, *Mental Models*, pages 7–14. Erlbaum, 1983.

[NP90] J.T. Nosek and P. Palvia. Software Maintenance Management: Changes in the Last Decade. *Journal of Software Maintenance: Research and Practice*, 2(3):157–174, 1990.

[NR68] P. Naur and B. Randell, editors. *Software Engineering, Report on a Conference*. NATO Scientific Affairs Division, Garmisch, 1968.

[NvV97] F. Niessink and H. van Vliet. Predicting Maintenance Effort with Function Points. In *Proceedings International Conference on Software Maintenance (ICSM'97)*, pages 32–39. IEEE, 1997.

[NvV98a] F. Niessink and H. van Vliet. Towards Mature IT Services. *Software Process – Improvement and Practice*, 4(2):55–71, 1998.

[NvV98b] F. Niessink and H. van Vliet. Towards Mature Measurement Programs. In P. Nesi and F. Lehner, editors, *Proceedings 2nd Euromicro Conference on Software Maintenance and Reengineering*, pages 82–88. IEEE, 1998.

[NvV99] F. Niessink and H. van Vliet. Software Maintenance from a Service Perspective. Technical report, Vrije Universiteit, 1999.

[OHK93] A.J. Offutt, M.J. Harrold, and P. Kolte. A Software Metric System for Module Coupling. *Journal of Systems and Software*, 20(3):295–308, 1993.

[OHM+88] T.W. Olle, J. Hagelstein, I.G. MacDonald, C. Rolland, H.G. Sol, F.J. van Assche, and A.A. Verrijn-Stuart. *Information Systems Methodologies: a Framework for Understanding*. Addison-Wesley, 1988.

[OL94] A.J. Offutt and S.D. Lee. An Emperical Evaluation of Weak Mutation. *IEEE Transactions on Software Engineering*, 20(5):337–344, 1994.

[Ost87] L. Osterweil. Software Processes Are Software Too. In *Proceedings 9th International Conference on Software Engineering (ICSE9)*, pages 2–13. IEEE, 1987.

[Oul96] M.A. Ould. CMM and ISO 9001. *Software Process – Improvement and Practice*, 2(4):281–289, 1996.

[Oz94] E. Oz. When Professional Standards are Lax: The CONFIRM Failure and its Lessons. *Communications of the ACM*, 37(10):29–36, 1994.

[Par72] D.L. Parnas. On the Criteria to be Used in Decomposing Systems Into Modules. *Communications of the ACM*, 15(12):1053–1058, 1972.

[Par77] D.L. Parnas. The Use of Precise Specifications in the Development of Software. In *Proceedings IFIP77*, pages 861–867. North-Holland Publishing Company, 1977.

[Par78] D.L. Parnas. Designing Software for Ease of Extension and Contraction. In *Proceedings 3rd International Conference on Software Engineering (ICSE3)*, pages 264–277. IEEE, 1978.

[Par85] D.L. Parnas. Software Aspects of Strategic Defense Systems. *ACM Software Engineering Notes*, 10(5):15–23, 1985.

[Par87] D.L. Parnas. SDI 'Red Herrings' Miss the Boat. *IEEE Computer*, 20(2):6–7, 1987.

[Pau95] M.C. Paulk. The Evolution of the SEI's Capability Maturity Model for Software. *Software Process – Improvement and Practice*, 1(Pilot Issue):3–15, 1995.

[PC87] D.L. Parnas and P.C. Clements. A Rational Design Process: How and Why to Fake it. *IEEE Transactions on Software Engineering*, 12(2):251–257, 1987.

[PCB92] S. Patel, W. Chu, and R. Baxter. A Measure for Composite Module Cohesion. In *Proceedings 14th International Conference on Software Engineering (ICSE14)*, pages 38–48. IEEE, Melbourne, 1992.

[PD91a] R. Prieto-Diaz. Implementing Faceted Classification for Software Reuse. *Communications of the ACM*, 34(5):88–97, 1991.

[PD91b] R. Prieto-Diaz. Making Software Reuse Work: An Implementation Model. *ACM Software Engineering Notes*, 16(3):61–68, 1991.

[PD93] R. Prieto-Diaz. Status Report: Software Reusability. *IEEE Software*, 10(3):61–66, 1993.

[PDN86] R. Prieto-Diaz and J.M. Neighbors. Module Interconnection Languages. *Journal of Systems and Software*, 6:307–334, 1986.

[Pet81] J.L. Peterson. *Petri Net Theory and the Modelling of Systems*. Prentice-Hall, 1981.

[Pet94] H. Petroski. *Design Paradigms: Case Histories of Error and Judgment in Engineering*. Cambridge University Press, 1994.

[Pfa85] G.E. Pfaff, editor. *User Interface Management Systems*. Springer Verlag, 1985.

[Pfl95] S.L. Pfleeger. Maturity, Models and Goals: How to Build a Metrics Plan. *Journal of Systems and Software*, 31(2):143–155, 1995.

[PG89] S.J. Payne and T.R.G. Green. Task-Action Grammar: The model and its Developments. In D. Diaper, editor, *Task Analysis for Human-Computer Interaction*, pages 75–105. Ellis Horwood, Chichester, 1989.

[Pig96] T.M. Pigoski. *Practical Software Maintenance*. John Wiley & Sons, 1996.

[Pit93] M. Pittman. Lessons Learned in Managing Object-Oriented Development. *IEEE Software*, 10(1):43–53, 1993.

[PJ97] A.A. Porter and P.M. Johnson. Assessing Software Review Meetings: Results of a Comparative Analysis of Two Experimental Studies. *IEEE Transactions on Software Engineering*, 23(3):129–145, 1997.

[PK89] P.E. Pintelas and V. Kallistros. An Overview of Some Software Design Languages. *Journal of Systems and Software*, 10(2):125–138, 1989.

[PK91] D.E. Perry and G.E. Kaiser. Models of Software Development Environments. *IEEE Transactions on Software Engineering*, 17(3):283–295, 1991.

[PKK98] G. Post, A. Kagan, and R.T. Keim. A Comparative Evaluation of CASE Tools. *Journal of Systems and Software*, 44(2):87–96, 1998.

[Poh93] K. Pohl. The Three Dimensions of Requirements Engineering. In C. Rolland, F. Bodart, and C. Cauvet, editors, *Proceedings Fifth International Conference on Advanced Information Systems Engineering (CAiSE'93)*, pages 275–292. Springer Verlag, 1993.

[Pos87] R.M. Poston. Preventing Most-Probable Errors in Requirements. *IEEE Software*, 4(5):81–83, 1987.

[Pos95] R.M. Poston. Testing Tools Combine Best of Old and New. *IEEE Software*, 12(2):122–127, 1995.

[Pot93] C. Potts. Software-Engineering Research Revisited. *IEEE Software*, 10(5):19–28, 1993.

[Pou99] J.S. Poulin. Reuse: Been There, Done That. *Communications of the ACM*, 42(5):98–100, 1999.

[PSMV98] A. Porter, H. Siy, A. Mockus, and L. Votta. Understanding the Sources of Variation in Software Inspections. *ACM Transactions on Software Engineering and Methodology*, 7(1):41–79, 1998.

[PSTV97] A.A. Porter, H.P. Siy, C.A. Toman, and L.G. Votta. An Experiment to Assess the Cost-Benefits of Code Inspections in Large Scale Software Developments. *IEEE Transactions on Software Engineering*, 23(6):329–346, 1997.

[PT91] P. Pintelas and S. Tragoudas. A Comparative Study of Five Language Independent Programming Environments. *Journal of Systems and Software*, 14(1):3–15, 1991.

[PTA94] C. Potts, K. Takahashi, and A.I. Antón. Inquiry-Based Requirements Analysis. *IEEE Software*, 11(2):21–32, 1994.

[Put78] L.H. Putnam. A General Empirical Solution to the Macro Software Sizing and Estimating Problem. *IEEE Transactions on Software Engineering*, 4(4):345–361, 1978.

[PVB95] A.A. Porter, L.G. Votta, Jr., and V.R. Basili. Comparing Detection Methods for Software Requirements Inspections: A Replicated Experiment. *IEEE Transactions on Software Engineering*, 21(6):563–575, 1995.

[PW87a] D.L. Parnas and D.M. Weiss. Active Design Reviews: Principles and Practices. *Journal of Systems and Software*, 7(4):259–265, 1987.

[PW87b] L. Power and Z. Weiss, editors. *Addendum to the Proceedings of OOPSLA87*. ACM, 1987.

[PW92] D.E. Perry and A.L. Wolf. Foundations for the Study of Software Architecture. *ACM Software Engineering Notes*, 17(4):40–52, 1992.

[PWB93] D. Page, P. Williams, and D. Boyd. *Report of the Inquiry into the London Ambulance Service*. South West Thames Regional Health Authority, 1993.

[PWCe94] M.C. Paulk, C.V. Weber, B. Curtis, and M.B. Chrissis *et al*. *The Capability Maturity Model: Guidelines for Improving the Software Process*. Addison-Wesley, 1994.

[PZ95] A.S. Parrish and S.H. Zweben. On the Relationships Among the All-Uses, All-DU-Paths, and All-Edges Testing Criteria. *IEEE Transactions on Software Engineering*, 21(12):1006–1009, 1995.

[RAC90] J.A. Redmond and R. Ah-Chuen. Software Metrics: A User's Perspective. *Journal of Systems and Software*, 13(2):97–110, 1990.

[RAvG96] J. Rooijmans, H. Aerts, and M. van Genuchten. Software Quality in Consumer Electronic Products. *IEEE Software*, 13(1):55–64, 1996.

[RBP+91] J. Rumbaugh, M. Blaha, W. Premerlani, F. Eddy, and W. Lorensen. *Object-Oriented Modeling and Design*. Prentice-Hall, 1991.

[Red70] W.J. Reddin. *Managerial Effectiveness*. McGraw-Hill, 1970.

[Rei81] P. Reisner. Formal Grammar and Human Factors Design of an Interactive Graphics System. *IEEE Transactions on Software Engineering*, 7(2):229–240, 1981.

[Rei90] S.P. Reiss. Connecting Tools Using Message Passing in the Field Environment. *IEEE Software*, 7(4):57-66, July 1990.

[Rei97] D.J. Reifer. *Practical Software Reuse: Strategies for Introducing Reuse Concepts in Your Organization*. John Wiley & Sons, 1997.

[Ren82] T. Rentsch. Object-Oriented Programming. *ACM SIGPLAN Notices*, 17(9):51–57, 1982.

[Ret91] M. Rettig. Nobody Reads Documentation. *Communications of the ACM*, 34(7):19–24, 1991.

[RH96] G. Rothermel and M.J. Harrold. Analyzing Regression Test Selection Techniques. *IEEE Transactions on Software Engineering*, 22(8):529-551, 1996.

[RJB98] J. Rumbaugh, I. Jacobson, and G. Booch. *The Unified Modeling Language Reference Manual*. Addison-Wesley, 1998.

[Roc75] M.J. Rochkind. The Source Code Control System. *IEEE Transactions on Software Engineering*, 1(4):364–370, 1975.

[Ros77] D.T. Ross. Structured Analysis (SA): A Language for Communicating Ideas. *IEEE Transactions on Software Engineering*, 3(1):16–34, 1977.

[Rou95] T.P. Rout. SPICE: A Framework for Software Process Assessment. *Software Process – Improvement and Practice*, 1(Pilot Issue):57–66, 1995.

[Roy70] W.W. Royce. Managing the Development of Large Software Systems: Concepts and Techniques. In *Proceedings IEEE WESCON*, pages 1–9. IEEE, 1970.

[RR85] S.T. Redwine and W.E. Riddle. Software Technology Maturation. In *Proceedings 8th International Conference on Software Engineering (ICSE8)*, pages 189–200. IEEE, 1985.

[RS77] D.T. Ross and K.E. Schoman, Jr. Structured Analysis for Requirements Definition. *IEEE Transactions on Software Engineering*, 3(1):6–15, 1977.

[RS98] D.C. Rine and R.M. Sonnemann. Investments in Reusable Software. A Study of Software Reuse Investment Success Factors. *Journal of Systems and Software*, 41(1):17–32, 1998.

[Rub83] H.A. Rubin. Interactive Macro-Estimation of Software Life Cycle Parameters via Personal Computer: A Technique for Improving Customer/Developer Communication. In *Proceedingss of the Symposium on Application and Assessment of Automated Tools for Software Development*, pages 44–49. IEEE CH1936-4, 1983.

[Rub85] H.A. Rubin. A Comparison of Cost Estimation Tools (Panel Discussion). In *Proceedings 8th International Conference on Software Engineering (ICSE8)*, pages 174–180. IEEE, 1985.

[Rum95a] J. Rumbaugh. OMT: The dynamic model. *Journal of Object Oriented Programming*, 7(9):6–12, 1995.

[Rum95b] J. Rumbaugh. OMT: The functional model. *Journal of Object Oriented Programming*, 8(1):21–27, 1995.

[Rum95c] J. Rumbaugh. OMT: The object model. *Journal of Object Oriented Programming*, 7(8):21–27, 1995.

[Rum97] J. Rumbaugh. Modeling through the Years. *Journal of Object Oriented Programming*, 10(4):16–19, 1997.

[RW88] C. Rich and R.C. Waters. The Programmer's Apprentice: A Research Overview. *IEEE Computer*, 21(11):10–25, 1988.

[RW91] H.B. Reubenstein and R.C. Waters. The Requirements Apprentice: Automated Assistance for Requirements Acquisition. *IEEE Transactions on Software Engineering*, 17(3):226–240, 1991.

[SB90] E.B. Swanson and C.M. Beath. Departmentalization in Software Development and Maintenance. *Communications of the ACM*, 33(6):658–667, 1990.

[SB91] R.W. Selby and V.R. Basili. Analyzing Error-Prone System Structure. *IEEE Transactions on Software Engineering*, 17(2):141–152, 1991.

[SB95] D. Sharon and R. Bell. Tools That Bind: Creating Integrated Environments. *IEEE Software*, 12(2):76–85, 1995.

[SBA97] T. Stålhane, P.C. Borgersen, and K. Arnesen. In Search of the Customer's Quality View. *Journal of Systems and Software*, 38(1):85–94, 1997.

[SBB87] R.W. Selby, V.R. Basili, and F.T. Baker. Cleanroom Software Development. *IEEE Transactions on Software Engineering*, 13(9):1027–1037, 1987.

[SBR95] L.B. Strader, M.A. Beims, and J.A. Rodgers. The Motivation and Development of the Space Shuttle Onboard Software (OBS) Process Automation. *Software Process – Improvement and Practice*, 1(2):107–114, 1995.

[SBRS94] I. Sommerville, R. Bentley, T. Rodden, and P. Sawyer. Cooperative System Design. *The Computer Journal*, 37(5):357–366, 1994.

[SC96] M. Shaw and P. Clements. A Field Guide to Boxology: Preliminary Classification of Architectural Styles for Software Systems. Technical report, Carnegie Mellon University/Software Engineering Institute, 1996.

[Sch96] T. Schael. Information Systems in Public Administration: from Transaction Processing to Computer Supported Cooperative Work. In D. Shapiro, M.J. Tauber, and R. Traunmueller, editors, *The Design of Computer Supported Cooperative Work and Groupware Systems*. North-Holland, Amsterdam, 1996.

[SDK+95] M. Shaw, R. DeLine, D.V. Klein, T.L. Ross, D.M. Young, and G. Zelesnik. Abstractions for Software Architecture and Tools to Support Them. *IEEE Transactions on Software Engineering*, 21(4):314–335, 1995.

[SE84] E. Soloway and K. Ehrlich. Empirical Studies of Programming Knowledge. *IEEE Transactions on Software Engineering*, 10(5):595–609, 1984.

[Se96] H. Saiedian *et al.* An Invitation to Formal Methods. *IEEE Computer*, 29(4):16–32, 1996.

[Seb88] S. Sebillotte. Hierarchical Planning as a Method for Task-Analysis: The Example of Office Task Analysis. *Behaviour and Information Technology*, 7(3):275–293, 1988.

[Sel93] R.W. Selby. Interconnectivity Analysis Techniques for Error Localization in Large Systems. *Journal of Systems and Software*, 20(3):267–272, 1993.

[SG86] A. Spector and D. Gifford. A Computer Science Perspective of Bridge Design. *Communications of the ACM*, 29(4):267–283, 1986.

[SG96] M. Shaw and D. Garlan. *Software Architecture: Perspectives on an Emerging Discipline*. Prentice-Hall, 1996.

[Sha96a] D. Shapiro. Ferrets in a Sack? Ethnographic Studies and Task Analysis in CSCW. In D. Shapiro, M.J. Tauber, and R. Traunmueller, editors, *The Design of Computer Supported Cooperative Work and Groupware Systems*. North-Holland, Amsterdam, 1996.

[Sha96b] M. Shaw. Some Patterns for Software Architectures. In *Proceedings Second Workshop on Pattern Languages for Programming*. Addison-Wesley, 1996.

[She90] M. Shepperd. Design Metrics: An Empirical Analysis. *Software Engineering Journal*, 5(1):3–10, 1990.

[Shn98] B. Shneiderman. *Designing the User Interface*. Addison-Wesley, 1998.

[SHO90] S. Sutton, D. Heimbigner, and L. Osterweil. Language Constructs for Managing Change in Process-centered Environments. In *SIGSOFT'90, Proceedings of the Fourth Symposium on Software Development Environments*. ACM, 1990.

[SI93] M. Shepperd and D.C. Ince. A Critique of Three Metrics. *Journal of Systems and Software*, 26(3):197–210, 1993.

[Sie95] J. Siegel. *CORBA Fundamentals and Programming*. John Wiley & Sons, 1995.

[SIG88] *Proceedings of the ACM SigSoft/SIGPLAN Software Engineering Symposium on Practical Software Development Environments*, ACM SigSoft Software Engineering Notes 13(5), 1988.

[SIK+82] D.C. Smith, C. Irby, R. Kimball, W. Verplank, and E. Harslem. Designing the Star User Interface. *Byte*, 7(4):242–282, 1982.

[Sim96] P. Simmons. Quality Outcomes: Determining Business Value. *IEEE Software*, 13(1):25–32, 1996.

[Sin98] J. Singer. Practices of Software Maintenance. In *Proceedings International Conference on Software Maintenance (ICSM'98)*, pages 139–145. IEEE, 1998.

[SK97] J. Simonsen and F. Kensing. Using Ethnography in Contextual Design. *Communications of the ACM*, 40(7):82–88, 1997.

[SM86] S.L. Smith and J.N. Mosier. Design Guidelines for User-System Interface Software. Technical report, MITRE Corporation, 1986.

[SM92] S. Shlaer and S. Mellor. *Object Lifecycles: Modeling the World in States*. Prentice-Hall, 1992.

[SM98] M.J.C. Sousa and H.M. Mozeira. A Survey on the Software Maintenance Process. In *Proceedings International Conference on Software Maintenance (ICSM'98)*, pages 265–274. IEEE, 1998.

[SMC74] W.P. Stevens, G.J. Myers, and L.L. Constantine. Structured Design. *IBM Systems Journal*, 13(2):115–139, 1974.

[Smi82] G. De V. Smit. A Comparison of Three String Matching Algorithms. *Software, Practice & Experience*, 12(1):57–66, 1982.

[SNH95] D. Soni, R.L. Nord, and C. Hofmeister. Software Architecture in Industial Applications. In *Proceedings 17th International Conference on Software Engineering (ICSE17)*, pages 196–207. IEEE, 1995.

[SO92] X. Song and L.J. Osterweil. Toward Objective, Systematic Design-Method Comparisons. *IEEE Software*, 9(3):43–53, 1992.

[SO97] G.E. Stark and P.W. Oman. Software Maintenance Management Strategies: Observations from the Field. *Journal of Software Maintenance: Research and Practice*, 9:365–378, 1997.

[Sof94a] Special issue on Process Improvement. *IEEE Software*, 11(4), 1994.

[Sof94b] Special Issue on Systematic Reuse. *IEEE Software*, 11(5), 1994.

[Sof96a] Special Issue on Managing Large Software Projects. *IEEE Software*, 13(4), 1996.

[Sof96b] Special Issue on Software Tools Assessment. *IEEE Software*, 13(5), 1996.

[Sof97a] Special issue on Managing Risk. *IEEE Software*, 14(3), 1997.

[Sof97b] Special issue on Measurement. *IEEE Software*, 14(2), 1997.

[Sof97c] Special Issue on The State of SE Education and Training. *IEEE Software*, 14(6), 1997.

[Sof98] Special Issue on Component-Based Software Engineering. *IEEE Software*, 15(5), 1998.

[Sof99] Special Issue on Critical Success Factors. *IEEE Software*, 16(3), 1999.

[Sol86] E. Soloway. Learning to Program = Learning to Construct Mechanisms and Explanations. *Communications of the ACM*, 29(9):850–858, 1986.

[Som96] I. Sommerville, editor. *Proceedings Workshop on Software Configuration Management (SCM6)*. Springer, LNCS1167, 1996.

[SPDM93] W. Schaeffer, R. Prieto-Diaz, and R. Matsumoto, editors. *Software Reusability*. Ellis Horwood, 1993.

[Spi92] J.M. Spivey. *The Z Notation: A Reference Manual*. Prentice-Hall, second edition, 1992.

[SS97] M. Shepperd and C. Schofield. Estimating Software Project Effort Using Analogies. *IEEE Transactions on Software Engineering*, 23(11):736–743, 1997.

[SS98] J.S. Sherif and P. Sanderson. Metrics for Object-Oriented Software Projects. *Journal of Systems and Software*, 44(2):147–154, 1998.

[SSK96] M. Shepperd, C. Schofield, and B. Kitchenham. Effort Estimation Using Analogy. In *Proceedings 18th International Conference on Software Engineering (ICSE18)*, pages 170–178. IEEE Computer Society, 1996.

[Str67] J.M. Stroud. The Fine Structure of Psychological Time. *Annals NY Academy of Sciences*, 138:623–631, 1967.

[Sut88] A. Sutcliffe. *Jackson System Development*. Prentice-Hall, 1988.

[SvV88] K. Sikkel and J.C. van Vliet. Growing Pains of Software Reuse. In *Proceedings Software Engineering in the Nineties*. SERC, Utrecht, 1988.

[Sym88] C.R. Symons. Function Point Analysis: Difficulties and Improvements. *IEEE Transactions on Software Engineering*, 14(1):2–11, 1988.

[Szy98] C. Szyperski. *Component Software, Beyond Object-Oriented Programming*. Addison-Wesley, 1998.

[Tai93] A. Taivalsaari. On the Notion of Object. *Journal of Systems and Software*, 21(1):3–16, 1993.

[Tau90] M.J. Tauber. ETAG: Extended Task Action Grammar — a Language for the Description of the User's Task Language. In D. Diaper *et al.*, editor, *Proceedings INTERACT '90*. Elsevier, Amsterdam, 1990.

[TBS92] C.J. Trammell, L.H. Binder, and C.E. Snyder. The Automated Production Control Documentation System: A Case Study in Cleanroom Software Engineering. *ACM Transactions on Software Engineering and Methodology*, 1(1):81–94, 1992.

[TC93] D. Tapscott and A. Caston. *Paradigm Shift: The New Promise of Information Technology*. McGraw-Hill, 1993.

[TG98] W.-G. Tan and G.G. Gable. Attitudes of Maintenance Personnel Towards Maintenance Work: A Comparative Analysis. *Journal of Software Maintenance: Research and Practice*, 10:59–74, 1998.

[Tic94] W.F. Tichy, editor. *Configuration Management*. John Wiley & Sons, 1994.

[TKS95] D.B. Tesch, G. Klein, and M.G. Sobol. Information Systems Professionals' Attitudes: Development Tools and Concepts. *Journal of Systems and Software*, 28(1):39–48, 1995.

[TPW81] R.H. Thayer, A.B. Pyster, and R.C. Wood. Major Issues in Software Engineering Management. *IEEE Transactions on Software Engineering*, 7(4):333–342, 1981.

[TR81] T. Teitelbaum and T. Reps. The Cornell Program Synthesizer: A Syntax-Directed Programming Environment. *Communications of the ACM*, 24(9):563–573, 1981.

[Tra88] W. Tracz. Software Reuse Myths. *ACM Software Engineering Notes*, 13(1):17–21, 1988.

[Tra90] W. Tracz. Where Does Reuse Start? *ACM Software Engineering Notes*, 15(2):42–46, 1990.

[Tri88] L.L. Tripp. A Survey of Graphical Notations for Program Design – An Update. *ACM Software Engineering Notes*, 13(4):39–44, 1988.

[TrS93] Special issue on Software Reliability. *IEEE Transactions on Software Engineering*, 19(11), 1993.

[TrS98a] Special issue on Formal Methods in Software Practice. *IEEE Transactions on Software Engineering*, 24(1), 1998.

[TrS98b] Special Issue on Scenario Management. *IEEE Transactions on Software Engineering*, 24(12), 1998.

[TS90] V.-P. Tahvanainen and K. Smolander. An annotated CASE Bibliography. *ACM Software Engineering Notes*, 15(1):79–92, 1990.

[TvSKS83] A.S. Tanenbaum, H. van Staveren, E.G. Keizer, and J.W. Stevenson. A Practical Toolkit for Making Portable Compilers. *Communications of the ACM*, 26(9):654–662, 1983.

[VC94] I. Vessey and S.A. Conger. Requirements Specification: Learning Object, Process, and Data Methodologies. *Communications of the ACM*, 37(5):102–113, 1994.

[VC97] J.M. Verner and N. Cerpa. Prototyping: Does Your View of its Advantages Depend on Your Job. *Journal of Systems and Software*, 36(1):3–16, 1997.

[VCK96] J.M. Vlissides, J.O. Coplien, and N.L. Kerth, editors. *Pattern Languages of Program Design 2*. Addison-Wesley, 1996.

[vdV90] G.C. van der Veer. *Human-Computer Interaction: Learning, Individual Differences, and Design Recommendations*. PhD Dissertation, Vrije Universiteit, Amsterdam, 1990.

[vdVLB96] G.C. van der Veer, B.F. Lenting, and B.A.J. Bergevoet. GTA: Groupware Task Analysis — Modeling Complexity. *Acta Psychologica*, 91:297–322, 1996.

[vG91] M. van Genuchten. *Towards a Software Factory*. PhD thesis, Technical University of Eindhoven, The Netherlands, 1991.

[vLDL98] A. van Lamsweerde, R. Darimont, and E. Letier. Managing Conflicts in Goal-Driven Requirements Engineering. *IEEE Transactions on Software Engineering*, 24(11):908–926, 1998.

[vMV95] A. von Mayrhauser and A.M. Vans. Program Comprehension During Software Maintenance and Evolution. *IEEE Computer*, 28(8):44–55, 1995.

[vMVH97] A. von Mayrhauser, A.M. Vans, and A.E. Howe. Program Understanding Behaviour during Enhancement of Large-scale Software. *Journal of Software Maintenance: Research and Practice*, 9:299–327, 1997.

[vSvV93] V. van Swede and J.C. van Vliet. A Flexible Framework for Information Systems Modelling. *Information and Software Technology*, 35(9):530–548, 1993.

[Wan84] A.S. Wang. *The Estimation of Software Size and Effort: An Approach Based on the Evolution of Software Metrics*. PhD thesis, Dept. of Computer Science, Purdue University, 1984.

[War74] J.-D. Warnier. *Logical Construction of Programs*. Stenfert Kroese, 1974.

[WCS94] D.P. Wood, M.G. Christel, and S.M. Stevens. A Multimedia Approach to Requirements Capture and Modeling. In *Proceedings 1st International Conference on Requirements Engineering*, pages 53–56. IEEE, 1994.

[Web88] D.E. Webster. Mapping the Design Information Representation Terrain. *IEEE Computer*, 21(9):8–24, 1988.

[Web96] D.W. Weber. Change Sets Versus Change Packages. In I. Sommerville, editor, *Proceedings Workshop on Software Configuration Management (SCM6)*, pages 25–35. Springer, LNCS1167, 1996.

[Weg84] P. Wegner. Capital-Intensive Software Technology. *IEEE Software*, 1(3):7–45, 1984.

[Weg92] P. Wegner. Dimensions of Object-Oriented Modeling. *IEEE Computer*, 25(10):12–21, 1992.

[Wei71] G.M. Weinberg. *The Psychology of Computer Programming*. Van Nostrand Reinhold, 1971.

[Wel93] E.F. Weller. Lessons from Three Years of Inspection Data. *IEEE Software*, 10(5):38–45, 1993.

[Wen86] I. Wendel. Software Tools of the Pleistocene. *Software Maintenance News*, 4(10):20, 1986.

[Wey88] E.J. Weyuker. The Evaluation of Program-Based Software Test Data Adequacy Criteria. *Communications of the ACM*, 31(6):668–675, 1988.

[Wey90] E.J. Weyuker. The Cost of Data Flow Testing: An Empirical Study. *IEEE Transactions on Software Engineering*, 16(2):121–128, 1990.

[Wey93] E.J. Weyuker. More Experience with Data Flow Testing. *IEEE Transactions on Software Engineering*, 19(9):912–919, 1993.

[Wey98] E.J. Weyuker. Testing Component-Based Software: A Cautionary Tale. *IEEE Software*, 15(5):54–59, 1998.

[WF77] C.E. Walston and C.P. Felix. A Method of Programming Measurement and Estimation. *IBM Systems Journal*, 16(1):54–73, 1977.

[WH93] M. Woodman and B. Heal. *Introduction to VDM*. McGraw-Hill, 1993.

[Wie96] R.J. Wieringa. *Requirements Engineering: Frameworks for Understanding*. John Wiley & Sons, 1996.

[Wie97] R. Wieringa. Advanced Object-Oriented Requirement Specification Methods. Technical report, International Symposium on Requirements Engineering, Annapolis, 1997.

[Win88] J.M. Wing. A Study of 12 Specifications of the Library Problem. *IEEE Software*, 5(4):66–76, 1988.

[Win90] J.M. Wing. A Specifier's Introduction to Formal Methods. *IEEE Computer*, 23(9):8–24, 1990.

[Wir90] M. Wirsing. Algebraic Specification. In J. van Leeuwen, editor, *Handbook of Theoretical Computer Science, volume B*, pages 675–789. Elsevier Science Publishers, 1990.

[WM85] P. Ward and S. Mellor. *Structured Analysis for Real-Time Systems*. Prentice-Hall, 1985.

[Wol74] R.W. Wolverton. The Cost of Developing Large-Scale Software. *IEEE Transactions on Computers*, pages 615–636, 1974.

[WPJH98] K. Weidenhaupt, K. Pohl, M. Jarke, and P. Haumer. Scenarios in System Development: Current Practice. *IEEE Software*, 15(2):34–45, 1998.

[WR94] H. Wohlwend and S. Rosenbaum. Schlumberger's Software Improvement Program. *IEEE Transactions on Software Engineering*, 20(11):833–839, 1994.

[WRBM97] M. Wood, M. Roper, A. Brooks, and J. Miller. Comparing and Combining Software Defect Detection Techniques. In M. Jazayeri and H. Schauer, editors, *Proceedings 6th European Software Engineering Conference, LNCS 1301*, pages 262–277. Springer Verlag, 1997.

[WT91] R.C. Waters and Y.M. Tan. Toward a Design Apprentice: Supporting Reuse and Evolution in Software Design. *ACM Software Engineering Notes*, 16(2):33–44, 1991.

[WTMS94] K. Wong, S.R. Tilley, H.A. Müller, and M.-A.D. Storey. Structural Redocumentation: A Case Study. *IEEE Software*, 12(1):46–54, 1994.

[YC75] E. Yourdon and L.L. Constantine. *Structured Design*. Yourdon Press, 1975.

[Zac87] J.A. Zachman. A Framework for Information Systems Architecture. *IBM Systems Journal*, 26(3):276–292, 1987.

[Zel88] M.V. Zelkowitz. Resource Utilization During Software Development. *Journal of Systems and Software*, 8(4):331–336, 1988.

[ZHM97] H. Zhu, P.A.V. Hall, and J.H.R. May. Software Unit Test Coverage and Adequacy. *ACM Computing Surveys*, 29(4):366–427, 1997.

[Zhu96] H. Zhu. A Formal Analysis of the Subsume Relation Between Software Test Adequacy Criteria. *IEEE Transactions on Software Engineering*, 22(4):248–255, 1996.

[Zil74] S.N. Zilles. Algebraic Specification of Data Types. Technical report, Project MAC Progress Report 11, MIT, Cambridge, MA, 1974.

[ZS92] J.A. Zachman and J.F. Sowa. Extending and Formalizing the Framework for Information Systems Architecture. *IBM Systems Journal*, 31(3), 1992.

[Zuc89] L. Zucconi. Selecting a CASE Tool. *ACM Software Engineering Notes*, 14(2):42–44, 1989.

[Zus90] H. Zuse. *Software Complexity: Measures and Methods*. De Gruyter, 1990.

Index